HISTORICAL DICTIONARIES OF ANCIENT CIVILIZATIONS AND HISTORICAL ERAS
Series Editor: Jon Woronoff

Historical Dictionary of Modern China (1800–1949)

James Z. Gao

*Historical Dictionaries of Ancient
Civilizations and Historical Eras, No. 25*

The Scarecrow Press, Inc.
Lanham, Maryland • Toronto • Plymouth, UK
2009

SCARECROW PRESS, INC.

Published in the United States of America
by Scarecrow Press, Inc.
A wholly owned subsidiary of
The Rowman & Littlefield Publishing Group, Inc.
4501 Forbes Boulevard, Suite 200, Lanham, Maryland 20706
www.scarecrowpress.com

Estover Road
Plymouth PL6 7PY
United Kingdom

British Library Cataloguing in Publication Information Available

Library of Congress Cataloging-in-Publication Data

Gao, James Zheng
    Historical dictionary of modern China (1800–1949) / James Z. Gao.
        p. cm. — (Historical dictionaries of Ancient Civilizations and Historical
Eras ; no. 25)
    Includes bibliographical references.
    ISBN 978-0-8108-4930-3 (hardback : alk. paper)
    ISBN 978-0-8108-6308-8 (e-book)
    1. China—History—19th century—Dictionaries. 2. China—History—20th
century—Dictionaries. I. Title. DS755.G368 2009
951'.0303—dc22   2008053695

∞™ The paper used in this publication meets the minimum requirements of
American National Standard for Information Sciences—Permanence of Paper for
Printed Library Materials, ANSI/NISO Z39.48-1992. Manufactured in the United
States of America.

In memory of my parents

Contents

Editor's Foreword

Over its very long history, China has usually been a calm and predictable place. But one period stands out for its radical, dramatic, and often bloody change—with different forces pulling in different directions, so evenly balanced that until the very end no one could foresee the outcome. What occurred during the century-and-a-half "modern China" period is not only unprecedented; it was also largely unexpected and is still not fully understood. At the beginning of this period, the long and heavy Manchu rule finally collapsed—mostly under its own weight, but it was also undermined by new political, social, and cultural forces. The country also fell apart, with provinces breaking away from central control and within them cities and districts pulling in different directions, while some came under the control of warlords fighting against one another. Meanwhile, all the certainties of Confucianism were questioned by countless other philosophies and learning, both indigenous and Western. And all of this occurred in the midst of foreign imperialist conquest and encroachment as well as World War II. It was during this period that China, the largest, most populous country in the world, finally awoke from a long slumber and flexed its increasing strength.

This *Historical Dictionary of Modern China (1800–1949)* presents a chronology that charts events from year to year. The introduction then establishes the background and describes major trends and prominent forces. But the core is the dictionary, with nearly 700 entries on assorted political parties and organizations that emerged and contended, crucial events, major issues, essential places, and above all the incredible cast of characters—including emperors and warlords, generals and rebels, party politicians and businessmen, intellectuals and teachers, and writers and artists. The bibliography then provides resources for further investigation.

This compendium was written by James Z. Gao, who was born and grew up in China and studied at Peking University, where he received a master's degree in political science in 1983. He then attended Yale University, where he received a master's and a PhD in history. He was also an assistant professor at both Peking University and Newport News University before becoming an associate professor of history at the University of Maryland at College Park. Gao has written extensively on modern China, including numerous articles and two books, *Meeting Technology's Advance* and *The Communist Takeover of Hangzhou*, and is presently working on a third book, this one regarding the Shanghai rice market. His academic background has certainly been excellent preparation for this far-ranging work.

Jon Woronoff
Series Editor

Preface

Since the 1990s, in response to the dramatic political and economic changes in China and the world, Chinese studies have developed a new paradigm. Current scholars, drawing on newly available records, including a large mass of governmental and family archives, have been examining various subsets of Chinese society and the daily lives of ordinary people. Modernization narratives have replaced the previous revolutionary paradigm, revealing new facts and offering new interpretations of 19th- and 20th-century China. Consequently, we now have more knowledge and a better understanding of Chinese history. The *Historical Dictionary of Modern China (1800–1949)* reflects the changing scholarship in the field. Instead of focusing merely on the political elites of China, it presents an array of entries on significant people, women, ethnic minorities, new historical concepts, cultural and educational institutions, and economic activities. The chronology records not only political and military events but also other experiences of the Chinese people. It is my belief that the information as such is much needed for people who are interested in China's 150-year drive toward modernization and who read the new literature of Chinese studies.

In writing this dictionary, I would like to acknowledge several people. First of all, I would like to thank Dr. Victor Cunrui Xiong, who suggested and persuaded me to do this project. My graduate students Robert Peterson, Hongxia Liu, and William Howes helped me collect materials and proofread most entries. My friend Dr. Yelong Han has checked part of the spellings of Chinese names and places. Special thanks go to my wife, Laura Liu, for her essential technical assistance and all kinds of support. My parents, as intelligent and honest people, experienced part of the human drama of modern China. I devote this book to them in memory of their lives, which were short and suffering but full of love. Finally, I much appreciate the series editor, Jon Woronoff. For health reasons, I postponed submission of the manuscript several times, but his patience and remarkable editing work makes the completion of this volume possible.

Reader's Notes

Chinese and Japanese personal names are given in their original order, with surname coming first and then the given name. The *pinyin* system for romanizing Chinese is now the official transliteration system of the People's Republic of China; it has been adopted by the United Nations and other world agencies and is most commonly used in scholarship and journalism, largely supplanting the older Wade-Giles system. The dictionary uses the pinyin system of transliterating Chinese names, with some exceptions for place and personal names that are long familiar in the West, such as Sun Yat-sen and Chiang Kai-shek. In addition, a few institutions have made statements for keeping their old English translation, such as Peking University, and the dictionary follows this practice. Nonetheless, some places have changed their names over the years, the most notable being Beijing/Peking during the Qing dynasty, Beiping between 1928 and 1949, and Beijing again after September 1949; the dictionary uses the name that was in effect at the time. Chinese, Japanese, and Russian dates have been transcribed in accordance with the Gregorian calendar. Cross-references within the entry are indicated in **bold**, and other related entries are given in *See also* references at the end of entries.

Acronyms and Abbreviations

ACFL	All-China Federation of Labor
BIS	Bureau of Investigation and Statistics
CCP	Chinese Communist Party
CDL	China Democratic League
CER	Chinese Eastern Railway
CERC	Chinese Eastern Railway Corporation
CIA	Central Intelligence Agency
CIFRC	China International Famine Relief Commission
CMSNC	Chinese Merchant Steamship Navigation Company
CNA	Central News Agency
CNRRA	Chinese National Relief and Rehabilitation Administration
CPPCC	Chinese People's Political Consultative Conference
CPWDP	Chinese Peasants' and Workers' Democratic Party
CY	Communist Youth League
CZGP	China Zhi Gong Party
ETR	Eastern Turkestan Republic
GMD	Guomindang (Chinese Nationalist Party)
HSBC	Hong Kong and Shanghai Banking Corp.
IMTFE	International Military Tribunal for the Far East
KMT	Kuomintang (Wade-Giles spelling of Guomindang)
MFN	Most Favored Nation
NRA	National Revolutionary Army
NRC	National Resource Committee
OCCL	Operation Committee for the Chinese Liberation
PLA	People's Liberation Army
POC	Provisional Operation Committee
PRC	People's Republic of China
RCCK	Revolutionary Committee of the Chinese Kuomintang
ROC	Republic of China

SDCK	Society for the Diffusion of Christian and General Knowledge
SMR	South Manchuria Railway
SMRC	South Manchuria Railway Company
TDSL	Taiwan Democratic Self-Government League
UNRRA	United Nations Relief and Rehabilitation Administration

Maps

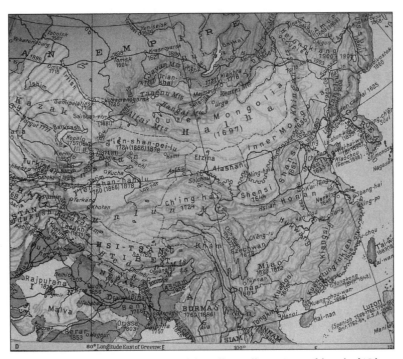

Map of Qing China, www.c-ref.de/gallery/albums/maps/historical/Qing-Empire1.jpg

Map of modern China. Source: Central Intelligence Agency (CIA) and State Department of the United States, www.reliefweb.int/mapc/asi_east/cnt/chn/chncia.html

Chronology

1799   **7 February:** Death of Emperor Qianlong. Emperor Jiaqing assumes power. **February:** Hoshen is ordered to commit suicide, his family holdings are confiscated.

1800   China's population reaches 300 million. Under the Canton system, private trade in Canton rises by 44 percent since 1780.

1802   Establishment of Nguyen dynasty in Annam by pro-Confucian emperor Gia-long.

1804   The White Lotus Rebellion is suppressed.

1816   **February:** Lord Amherst leads a mission to China.

1820   **25 July:** Death of Emperor Jiaqing. Emperor Daoguang ascends the throne. China still enjoys surplus in foreign trade. China's importation of opium increases. There are 1 million opium addicts in China.

1833   **December:** Lord William John Napier is appointed chief superintendent of the British trade in China. Lord Napier leads a mission to China.

1836   **May:** Xu Naiqi memorializes the emperor, suggesting that the court legalize the opium trade. **September:** Emperor Daoguang orders abolition of the opium trade.

1838   The Qing court debates the legalization of the opium trade again. **December:** Lin Zexu is appointed imperial commissioner to put down the opium trade.

1838–1839 Opium imports to China reach 40,000 chests.

1839   **10 May:** Lin Zexu arrives in Canton. Chinese opium dealers are arrested and opium houses are destroyed. Charles Elliot orders the

British traders to surrender their stocks of opium. **4 June:** Lin Zexu destroys tons of opium in Humen, Guangdong.

1840 **January:** The Indian government issues a declaration of war against China on behalf of the British Crown. **August:** The British Expedition troops reach Tianjin and the court sues for peace.

1841 **January:** Imperial commissioner Qishan signs the Qunbi Convention with Elliot, but the emperor refuses to ratify it. The war continues. **27 May:** Canton Convention. **29 May:** Villagers attack the British troops at Sanyuanli.

1842 **18 March:** Lin Zexu exiled to Kuldya. **29 August:** Treaty of Nanjing, ceding Hong Kong to Great Britain.

1843 **June:** Hong Xiuquan is exposed to Christian readings. **18 October:** Supplementary Treaty of the Bogue.

1844 Publication of Wei Yuan's *Illustrated Treatise on the Maritime Kingdoms* (*Haiguo Tuzhi*). **3 July:** Sino-American Treaty of Wangxia. Li-Fournier Agreement between China and France on the issue of Vietnam.

1845 **June:** Sino-French Treaty.

1850 **9 March:** Death of Emperor Daoguang. Emperor Xianfeng ascends the throne. **September:** Taiping Rebellion begins. Henry Sherman founds *North China Herald* in Shanghai.

1851 **1 January:** Taipings win a major victory at Guiping, Guangxi Province. **11 January:** Hong Xiuquan declares himself Heavenly King. **26 August:** Sino-Russian Treaty of Kuldya, opening Xinjiang to Russian trade.

1852 **November:** Outbreak of the Nian Rebellion.

1853 **29 March:** Taipings take Nanjing and make it the capital of the Taiping Kingdom. **8 September:** The Small Sword Society revolts in Shanghai. The Maritime Customs Committee (later Imperial Maritime Customs Service) is established.

1854 **17 June:** The Triads revolt in Guangdong. **23 June:** Three foreign inspectors are appointed to collect Shanghai customs. **November:** Talks on treaty revision in Tianjin, and the court refuses to accept foreign proposals.

1855 **May:** Final destruction of the Taiping northern expedition. **August:** Yellow River changes its course, causing 7 million refugees.

1856 **September:** Power struggle and massacres among Taiping leaders. **October:** Shi Dakai's troops are forced to flee. The Arrow War breaks out.

1857 **July:** Muslim rebels under Ma Hualong rise in Yunnan. **29 December:** Canton taken by British and French troops.

1858 **May:** The court refuses the British, French, Russian, and American demands. Dagu falls to foreign forces. Treaty of Aigun, ceding the north bank of the Amur to Russia. **June:** Treaty of Tianjin signed with the British, French, Russians, and Americans.

1860 **September:** Prince Gong is ordered to negotiate with Great Britain and France. The emperor flees. **October:** To reaffirm and upgrade the treaty of Tianjin, the British and French storm Beijing and burn the Old Summer Palace. **November:** In the convention with the Russians, China cedes all territory east of the Usuli River.

1861 **11 March:** Establishment of the Zongli Yamen. **22 August:** Death of Emperor Xianfeng. Tongzhi ascends the throne. **5 September:** The Taipings defeated in the decisive battle in Anqing. **November:** Dowager Empress Cixi becomes the co-regent. **December:** Zeng Guofan sets up an arsenal in Anhui. Publication of the Chinese edition of *North China Daily News*.

1862 **10 February:** Li Xiucheng is defeated by Frederick Townsend Ward's "Ever Victorious Army." The court decides to make large orders of foreign arms. **1 March:** The leader of the Southern Muslim rebels, Ma Hualong, surrenders and is executed. The northwestern Muslims revolt after two weeks. **3 June:** Li Hongzhang defeats the Taipings with foreign help in Shanghai. **11 July:** *Tongwenguan* (foreign languages school) opens and departments of mathematics and astronomy are added in later years. **December:** Sino-French treaty imposed on Annam.

1863 **January:** British officers are allowed to serve in Qing military forces. Robert Hart is appointed general inspector of the Imperial Maritime Customs Service. **13 June:** Shi Dakai surrenders and is executed two months later. **4 December:** Li Hongzhang executes the leaders of the surrendered Taipings in Suzhou.

1864   **2 June:** Li Hongzhang memorializes the emperor asking for investigation of Western machinery. Xinjiang Muslim rebellion. **19 July:** Fall of Nanjing; the Taiping Kingdom collapses.

1865   **27 January:** William A. P. Martin's translation of *Elements of International Law* presented to the emperor. **April:** Establishment of the Hong Kong and Shanghai Banking Corporation. **September:** Establishment of the Jiangnan Arsenal and Canton Textile Mill. **18 December:** Oil lamps are installed for street lighting on Nanjing Road in Shanghai.

1866   **25 September:** Zuo Zongtang is sent to Shaanxi and Gansu to suppress the Muslim rebellion. **26 November:** New appointment of Li Hongzhang, commanding the *Xiang* and *Huai* armies.

1867   **May:** Establishment of the Jinlin Arsenal in Nanjing. **21 November:** Burlingame Mission leaves.

1868   **5 January:** East Nian Rebellion is extinguished in Jiangsu Province. **18 January:** Fuzhou dockyard begins operation. Jiangnan Arsenal begins production. **16 August:** West Nian Rebellion is extinguished in Shandong Province.

1870   **21 June:** Tianjin Massacre. **8 November:** Yakub Beg takes Turfan.

1871   *Shenbao* is founded in Shanghai. **12 May:** First Chinese students leave for the United States. **3 June:** Undersea cable from Shanghai to London completed. **4 July:** Russian troops occupy Yili. **14 December:** Yunnan Muslim rebellion is suppressed.

1873   **23 February:** Emperor Tongzi assumes power from the regents. **14 June:** Establishment of the China Merchant Steamship Navigation Company. **4 November:** Zuo Zongtang puts down the Muslim rebellion in Gansu.

1874   Young J. Allen founds *Globe Magazine* in Shanghai. **15 March:** Franco-Vietnamese Treaty of Saigon, establishing French sovereignty over Cochin China.

1875   **12 January:** Death of Emperor Tongzhi at the age of 18; Emperor Guangxu, aged five, ascends the throne, and Cixi serves as the co-regent again. **28 August:** China's first ambassador, Guo Songtao, is sent to Great Britain.

1876 **1 July:** The first Chinese railroad, the Shanghai–Wuson line, is constructed (and soon dismantled). **13 September:** Shenfu Convention.

1879 **4 April:** Japan annexes the Liuqiu (Ryukyu). **2 October:** Chong Hou signs the Treaty of Livadia with Russia, ceding considerable territory to Russia.

1880 **19 February:** China renounces the Treaty of Livadia. **5 September:** Lanzhou woolen mill starts production.

1881 **12 February:** Treaty of St. Petersburg replaces the Treaty of Livadia. **14 February:** Establishment of the Kaiping Coal Mines. The first commercial railway, the Tangshan–Xugezhuang line, is completed, serving coal mines and their outlets to the sea.

1882 **22 March:** Kuldya is handed back to China. **May:** U.S. Congress approves the Chinese Exclusion Act, suspending immigration by Chinese laborers, which lasts for over 60 years. **20 December:** China and France agree on the independence of Annam.

1883 **19 May:** The Black Flags defeat the French. **October–November:** Debate on policy toward French actions in Indo-China.

1884 **May:** Li Hongzhang tries to sign a treaty with France, but fighting continues. **July:** Taiwan becomes a full province; Liu Mingchuan is appointed first governor.

1885 **9 June:** Sino-French Treaty. **October:** John Fryer founds the Shanghai Polytechnic Institute.

1886 **1 January:** Burma becomes part of British India but continues to send tribute to China.

1887 **11 June:** Zhang Zidong founds the Western-style Guangya Academy. Kang Youwei writes *The Book of Universal Commonwealth* (*Datong Shu*).

1888 **March:** The British destroy Tibetan positions at Lingtu. **September:** British troops occupy Xigang Province. **17 December:** Li Hongzhang creates the Beiyang fleet.

1889 **4 March:** Emperor Guangxu assumes power. **April:** Zhang Zhidong proposes railway from Beijing to Hankou. Rice riots in Fujian.

1890   **4 December:** Establishment of the Hangyang Iron and Steel Works. Zhang Zhidong moves the Guangzhou Arsenal to Wuhan, renamed as the Hangyang Arsenal.

1891   Publication of Kang Youwei's *The Forged Classics of Xin.* **April:** Several conflicts between Chinese and Christian missionaries occur in Yangzhou (1 April), Wuhu (3 April), Danyang (25 April), Yichang (28 April), and Wuxue (29 April).

1894   **March:** The Tonghak Rebellion in Korea; Chinese troops are sent to Korea at the request of the Korean king. **June:** A Japanese army is sent to Seoul. **1 August:** Outbreak of the Sino-Japanese War. **17 September:** The Beiyang fleet is destroyed by the Japanese navy. **24 November:** Sun Yat-sen founds the Revive China Society in Honolulu.

1895   **17 April:** Treaty of Shimonoseki. Triple intervention. **2 June:** Japan occupies Taiwan. **26 October:** Sun Yat-sen's first abortive uprising in Guangzhou. Alicia Archibald Little founds the Natural-Foot Society in Shanghai.

1896   **2 June:** The secret Sino-Russian treaty of alliance. **5 June:** First railway concession is offered to France. **15 June:** Big Sword Society attacks Chinese Christians. **October:** Sun Yat-sen is kidnapped in London. Qing court sets up the General Railway Company. **12 November:** Qing court decides to set up a Western-style bank.

1897   **12 June:** France begins to build a railway from Annam to Yunan and obtains mining rights en route. **14 November:** Germany occupies Jiaozhou Bay, Shandong. Publication of Yan Fu's translation of T. H. Huxley's *Evolution and Ethics.* Publication of Kang Youwei's *A Study of Confucius on Institutional Reform.* French concession in Shanghai begins to use electricity for street lighting. The first Society for Women Studies is established in Shanghai.

1898   Imperial University of the Capital is founded. Li Yun founds *Nüxue Bao* in Shanghai. **24 January:** Kang Youwei discusses the reform with the Zongli Yamen. **27 March:** China leases Lushun and Dalian to Russia. **April:** France secures the lease of Guangzhou Bay. **3 June:** The court approves a 99-year lease of Kowloon to Great Britain. **11 June:** The Hundred Day Reform is initiated. **21 September:** The reform aborts; Emperor Guangxu is put under house arrest. Cixi resumes the regency. Kang Youwei flees. **28 September:** Tan Sitong and five other leading reformers are executed.

1899 **1 June:** Russia obtains the right to build a railway north of Beijing. Germany is to build one from Jinan to Tianjin. **6 September:** The Open Door Policy note is sent to the Treaty Powers by the United States. The Boxers begin to attack churches and Christian converts.

1900 **13 June:** Boxers enter Beijing. Siege of foreign legations. **19 June:** The court declares war on the eight powers. Von Ketteler, the German minister, is killed. **3 July:** A second Open Door note proposes the territorial integrity of China. **16 July:** Incident of the Amur River; Russia invades Manchuria. **14 August:** The Allies enter Beijing. Cixi flees. **22 October:** Sun Yat-sen's second abortive uprising in Huizhou, Guangdong Province.

1901 **January:** The Xinzheng Reform is initiated. **21 April:** Dowager Cixi ordered to form a new government. Suppression of the Boxers. **7 September:** Boxer Protocol.

1902 The court urges abolition of footbinding and legalization of intermarriage between Chinese and Manchus.

1903 **May:** Publication of Zou Rong's *The Revolutionary Army.* **June:** The Qing court bans the *Subao* and arrests Zhang Binglin and Zou Rong. **1 July:** British expedition troops reach Lhasa.

1904 **8 February:** The Russo-Japanese War breaks out in China. **15 May:** Tibet declares war on Great Britain. **3 August:** British troops occupy Lhasa. **23 October:** Huang Xing leads an uprising in Hunan.

1905 **3 June:** Zuo Rong dies in jail. **June:** Merchants in four cities boycott American goods to protest American discrimination against Chinese laborers. **July:** Chinese Eastern Railway is completed. **30 July:** Sun Yat-sen forms the Chinese United League (*Tongmenghui*) in Tokyo. The Qing court sends a mission abroad to study foreign constitutions. Abolition of the Civil Service Examination system. **5 September:** Treaty of Portsmouth.

1906 Yuan Shikai founds the Beiyang Military Academy in Tianjin. **April:** Jing–Han Railway is completed. **September:** The Qing court announces a constitutional reform. **6 November:** The Six Boards are replaced by 11 modern ministries. **December:** Two republican uprisings in Jiangxi and Hunan are suppressed.

1907   February–November: Six republican uprisings in Guangdong and one in Anhui are launched but fail to topple the Qing regime in south China. **15 July:** Tongmenghui uprisings in Anhui and Zhejiang are suppressed; Qiu Jin is executed. **20 September:** The court orders the establishment of provincial assemblies.

1908   13 January: The Tianjin–Pukou Railway is to be constructed with the Deutsche Asiatische Bank's loan. **6 March:** A mass boycott of Japanese goods is staged. Contract with Great Britain for a loan to build the Shanghai–Hangzhou–Ningbo Railway. **14–15 November:** Death of Emperor Guangxu and Dowager Cixi. **2 December:** Accession of Puyi (Emperor Xuantong, the last emperor).

1909   1 January: China regains control of the Beijing–Hankou Railway from Belgium. Provincial assemblies meet. **December:** Qing troops are dispatched to Tibet.

1910   12 February: An uprising in Guangzhou is put down. **23 May:** Formation of an international consortium to handle loans to China. **4 July:** A secret treaty between Russia and Japan divides their spheres of interests in Manchuria. **18 December:** The Qing court refuses to establish a responsible cabinet government.

1911   30 January: Nationalist rising in Guangzhou is suppressed, with 86 revolutionaries killed. **9 May:** Edict on nationalization of China's railways. **17 June:** The Railway Protection League is set up in Sichuan. **September:** Jin–Pu Railway is completed. **10 October:** Wuchang Uprising takes place; Qing dynasty collapses. **25 December:** Sun Yat-sen returns from abroad.

1912   1 January: Official proclamation of the Republic. Provincial President Sun Yat-sen recognizes all Chinese treaties with the Powers, promising to protect foreign interests. **12 February:** The emperor abdicates. **13 February:** Yuan Shikai declares support for the Republic; Sun resigns in favor of Yuan. **13 March:** Tang Shaoyi becomes the first prime minister. **2 April:** The senate decides to make Beijing the capital. **5 May:** British troops move into Tibet. **10 August:** A general election is held. **27 August:** The National Library of Peking is opened to the public. **3 November:** Russia recognizes the independence of Mongolia; China protests.

1913 **20 March:** Song Jiaoren is assassinated. **April:** Yuan Shikai negotiates the "reorganization loan" from the Five Power Consortium. **July–September:** The Second Revolution. **10 October:** Yuan is formally inaugurated as president. **4 November:** Yuan orders the dissolution of the Nationalist Party. **26 November:** Yuan orders the replacement of the National Assembly by his Political Council.

1914 **1 May:** Yuan Shikai promulgates the Constitutional Compact. **3 July:** Simla Convention establishes autonomy for Tibet but China refuses to ratify it. **28 July:** Outbreak of World War I. **29 December:** Yuan issues the Presidential Election Law.

1915 Gingling College for Women is founded. **January:** The Twenty-one Demands proposed by Japan. **9 May:** The National Humiliation Day when Yuan Shikai accepts the Twenty-one Demands. **August:** The Peace-Planning Society is organized. **15 September:** Chen Duxiu creates the journal *New Youth* in Shanghai. **13 December:** Yuan restores the monarchy and declares that his new reign will start next year. **25 December:** Yunnan declares independence. Cai E organizes the National Protection Army. **27 December:** Guizhou declares independence.

1916 **1 January:** Yuan Shikai's reign, Glorious Constitution (*Hongxian*), starts. **22 March:** Yuan is forced to abandon monarchy and the "Glorious Constitution." **March–May:** More provinces declare independence. **6 June:** Death of Yuan Shikai; Vice President Li Yuanhong succeeds as president.

1917 **January:** Hu Shih advocates literary reform in *New Youth* magazine. **1 July:** Abortive coup by Zhang Xun to restore Puyi to the throne. **10 September:** Sun Yat-sen establishes a military government at Guangzhou, serving as generalissimo. **7 November:** The Bolshevik Revolution in Russia. **10 November:** War between the northern and southern warlords begins.

1918 **April:** Publication of Lu Xun's *A Madman's Diary.* **May:** The local military leaders begin to control the Guangdong military government and Sun Yat-sen leaves Guangzhou. **August:** Chinese troops are involved in the Allied intervention in Siberia. **15 October:** Publication of Li Dazhao's *Victory of Bolshevism.*

1919 **April:** Publication of a translation of *The Communist Manifesto.* **May:** Li Dazhao publishes "My Marxist Views" in *New Youth.* **4 May:**

The May Fourth Movement, a popular protest against the resolution of the Paris Conference on the Shandong issue. The New Culture Movement gains momentum. **4 May–11 June:** John Dewey lectures in China. **28 June:** Chinese delegation refuses to sign the Treaty of Versailles. **10 October:** Sun Yat-sen's *Gemingdang* (Revolutionary Party) becomes the Guomindang (Nationalist Party, GMD). **December:** The Society for the Study of Socialism is founded at Peking University.

1920 **March:** Ministry of Education adopts *baihuawen* (vernacular Chinese) as the language of textbooks. **May:** Under the influence of Grigori Naumovich Voitinsky of the Comintern, Chen Duxiu and others secretly plan to form the Chinese Communist Party (CCP). **14 July:** War between the Anhui and Zhili cliques. The Fengtian clique assists the Zhili.

1921 **5 May:** Sun Yat-sen is named extraordinary president. **1 July:** First Congress of the CCP. Chen Duxiu is elected general secretary of the CCP. **6 July:** The China Labor Union secretariat is set up in Shanghai. **October:** Publication of Liang Shuming's *The Cultures of East and West and Their Philosophies*. The Washington Conference opens. **December:** Sun Yat-sen lectures on Three Principles of People. Publication of Lu Xun's *The True Story of Ah-Q*.

1922 **13 January:** The Hong Kong seamen's strike begins. **3 February:** Sun Yat-sen initiates the Northern Expedition. **26 February:** General strike in Hong Kong. **28 April:** The First Zhili-Fengtian War begins. **May:** Peng Bai leads a peasant movement in Haifeng and Lufeng, Guangdong Province. **16 June:** Chen Jiongming attacks Guangzhou and Sun Yat-sen takes refuge on a gunboat. **July:** The Second Congress of the CCP concludes with the resolution on the united front with the Nationalist Party (GMD). **22 August:** Sun Yat-sen reorganizes the GMD and allows Communists to join it. **13 September:** Li Lisan and Liu Shaoqi lead the Anyuan Miners Strike.

1923 **26 January:** The Sun-Joffe Manifesto. **3 June:** The Third Congress of the CCP reasserts the united front with the GMD. **6 October:** Michael Markovich Borodin of the Comintern arrives to serve as Sun Yat-sen's adviser.

1924 **3 May:** Sun Yat-sen appoints Chiang Kai-shek as commandant of the Whampoa Military Academy and commander in chief of the

Nationalist forces. **1 September:** The Second Zhili-Fengtian War begins. **21 November:** Duan Qirui convenes the Aftermath Conference. **31 December:** Sun Yat-sen arrives in Beijing for the Aftermath Conference.

1925 **12 March:** Death of Sun Yat-sen. **30 May:** The May Thirtieth Incident with nine Chinese killed. **20 August:** Assassination of Liao Zhongkai, leader of the left wing of the GMD. **23 November:** The Western Hill Group is formed.

1926 **January:** The Hunan Peasant Movement begins. **20 January:** The Zhongshan incident. **1 July:** Chiang orders the Northern Expedition to begin.

1927 **January:** The GMD headquarters moves the capital to Wuhan. **March:** Publication of Mao Zedong's *Report on the Peasant Movement in Hunan.* **22 March:** Shanghai falls to the GMD. **12 April:** Chiang Kai-shek attacks and eliminates the Communist-led workers' pickets in Shanghai. **1 August:** The CCP forms its first military force and launches an unsuccessful uprising in Nanchang. **7 August:** An emergency conference of the CCP Politburo at Hankou makes radical changes in leadership and strategy. **8 September:** Mao Zedong leads the Autumn Harvest Uprising and retreats to Jinggangshan. **11–13 December:** The Canton Commune.

1928 **28 February:** The Haifeng and Lufeng Soviets are suppressed. **28 April:** Li Dazhao is executed in Beijing. **June–July:** The Sixth Congress of the CCP is held in Moscow. **10 October:** The Nationalist government is formed under the New Organic Law; Chiang Kai-shek is elected chairman of the government in Nanjing. Beijing is renamed Beiping.

1929 **10 February:** Mao Zedong establishes a base of the Jiangxi Soviet. **30 April:** Chiang Kai-shek defeats the Guangxi warlords. **June:** The Nationalist government unifies China's weights and measures to the metric system.

1930 **February–November:** Following the Lisan Route, the Communist military campaigns end in disaster. **October:** Chiang Kai-shek defeats warlords Feng Yuxiang, Yan Xishan, and Li Zongren. **5 November:** Chiang launches the first Encirclement and Suppression Campaign against the Communists. **18 November:** Mao Zedong's wife, Yang Kaihui, is executed by the GMD. **8 December:** Futian Incident. **27 December:** First Encirclement Campaign is defeated.

1931 **16–30 May:** Second Encirclement Campaign. **18 September:** The Manchuria Incident. China's nonresistance policy. **29 December:** Japan occupies the whole of Manchuria.

1932 **28 January:** Japan attacks Shanghai and meets strong resistance by the 19th Route Army. **9 March:** Establishment of Manchukuo with Puyi as "the chief executive." **18 June:** Fourth Encirclement Campaign begins.

1933 **January:** The Central Committee of the CCP moves from Shanghai to the Jiangxi Soviet. The Twenty-eight Bolsheviks control power and Mao Zedong loses influence in the party and the Red Army. **March:** Fourth Encirclement Campaign is defeated. **29 April:** Japan invades north China. **31 May:** Tangu Truce is signed. **2 June:** The land reform campaign begins in the Red Army–controlled areas. **6 October:** Fifth Encirclement Campaign begins. Inner Mongolia declares autonomy.

1934 **19 February:** Chiang Kai-shek initiates the New Life Movement. **1 March:** Puyi is crowned in Manchukuo by the Japanese. **April:** Yue–Han Railway is completed. **16 October:** Chiang Kai-shek's Fifth Encirclement and Suppression Campaign ejects the Red Army from the Jiangxi Soviet and forces it on the Long March.

1935 **6–8 January:** Zunyi Conference. Mao Zedong becomes the de facto top leader of the CCP. **30 June:** The Ho-Umezu Agreement is signed. **26 October:** Mao and the Central Red Army arrive in Shanbei; the Long March ends. **9 December:** The Communists lead the December Ninth Movement in Beijing against Japanese aggression.

1936 **19 October:** Death of Lu Xun. **December:** Communists move to Yan'an. **12 December:** The Xi'an Incident: Zhang Xueliang forces Chiang Kai-shek to stop the civil war.

1937 **7 July:** The Marco Polo Bridge Incident triggers the War of Resistance against Japan. **25 September:** Lin Biao defeats the Japanese at Pingxingguan. **20 November:** Nationalist capital moves to Chongqing. **December:** Rape of Nanjing. The Southwestern Union University is established in Kunming.

1938 **April:** Nationalist military victory at Taierzhuang. **7 June:** Nationalists breach the Yellow River dikes to stem the Japanese advance. **18 December:** Wang Jingwei launches the Peace Movement. In the course of the year, the Japanese occupy most Chinese cities and provinces.

1939 **May:** The Communist New Fourth Army forms a guerrilla base south of the Yangtze River. **3 September:** Outbreak of World War II. **December:** The Burma Road opens.

1940 **March:** Wang Jingwei sets up the Japanese puppet government in Nanjing. **20 August:** The Eighth Route Army launches the Hundred Regiments Offensive.

1941 **4 January:** New Fourth Army Incident. **May:** The "Rectification Movement" in Yan'an. **20 August:** The New Fourth Army is re-formed in north Jiangsu. **7 December:** The Japanese attack Pearl Harbor and the Pacific War breaks out. The Flying Tigers begin to fight the Japanese.

1942 **February:** The Japanese begin mopping-up campaigns against the Communist guerrilla bases but soon fail. **2 June:** Lend-lease signed. **November:** Joseph Warren Stillwell assumes command as chief-of-staff of the China theater.

1943 **11 January:** Great Britain and the United States sign treaties with China, abrogating extraterritoriality, the concessions, and the Boxer Protocol. **10 March:** Publication of Chiang Kai-shek's *China's Destiny*. **1 December:** Chiang Kai-shek attends the Cairo Conference. The Cairo Declaration requires that Japan return the occupied Manchuria, Taiwan, and the Pescadores to China.

1944 **15 June:** First U.S. air raid on Japan from a base in Chengdu, China. **1–23 July:** China participates in the Bretton Woods Conference. **September:** Establishment of the China Democratic League. **7 November:** Patrick Hurley flies to Yan'an.

1945 **4–11 February:** Yalta Conference. Russia promises to fight the Japanese in Manchuria. **23 April:** Mao Zedong emerges supreme at the CCP Seventh Congress. **6 and 8 August:** Dropping of the atomic bombs on Hiroshima and Nagasaki. **14 August:** Japan surrenders unconditionally. **28 August:** Mao Zedong flies to Chongqing for peace negotiations with Chiang Kai-shek. China recovers Taiwan. **27 November:** George Marshall arrives in China.

1946   **January:** Chiang Kai-shek begins to airlift troops to Manchuria. The Communists enter Changchun and Mukden with Russian help. **1 May:** The Communist military forces are renamed the People's Liberation Army (PLA). **4 May:** The land reform is initiated in the CCP-controlled north China. **12 July:** Full-scale civil war begins.

1947   **28 January:** George Catlett Marshal announces that American mediation attempts have failed to prevent the war between the GMD and CCP. **28 February:** The February Twenty-Eighth Incident in Taiwan. **19 March:** The GMD captures Yan'an; early nationalist military victories. **4 April–13 May:** The PLA launches major offensives in Shanxi, Shandong, and Manchuria. **May–June:** "Anti-hunger, anti-persecution" demonstrations in big cities. Soaring inflation feeds urban protest. **24 August:** Albert Wedermeyer is sent on fact-finding mission to China; he calls for radical reforms of the government. **10 October:** The CCP issues the Outline of Land Law. **30 December:** The gold yuan is seriously devaluated; the new exchange rate is 290,000 yuan to £1.

1948   **March:** The PLA storms the city of Luoyang; Mao adopts a new urban policy. **August:** The PLA launches a counteroffensive in north China. **September:** The GMD's financial reform fails and the new gold yuan note collapses. **12 September:** The PLA launches the final attack in Manchuria. **2 November:** The Battle of Liao-Sheng ends with CCP's conquest of Manchuria. **6 November:** The Battle of Huai-Hai begins. **December:** Lin Biao leads the Fourth Field Army to take Beijing and Tianjin.

1949   **10 January:** The Battle of Huai-Hai concludes with Chiang Kai-shek's leading forces destroyed. **21 January:** Chiang Kai-shek resigns; he is succeeded by Li Zongren as acting president. **23 January:** The PLA "peacefully liberates" Beiping, ending the Battle of Ping–Jin. **21 April:** Mao Zedong orders the PLA to cross the Yangtze River to take the whole of China. **23 April:** The PLA storms Nanjing. **1 July:** Publication of Mao Zedong's *On the People's Democratic Dictatorship*. **21 September:** The Chinese People's Political Consultative Conference opens. **September:** The Common Program is adopted. Mao Zedong is elected chairman of the People's Republic of China, and Zhou Enlai is appointed prime minister. **1 October:** The People's Republic of China is proclaimed. **December:** Chiang Kai-shek, most of his government, and a large number of GMD supporters and military flee to Taiwan.

REFERENCES

Gao, James Z. *Meeting Technology's Advance: Social Change in China and Zimbabwe in the Railway Age.* Westport, CT: Greenwood, 1997.

Gray, Jack. *Rebellions and Revolutions: China from 1800 to 2000.* New York: Oxford University Press, 2002.

Hsu, Immanuel C.Y. *The Rise of Modern China.* 6th ed. New York: Oxford University Press, 2000.

Spence, Jonathan D. *The Search for Modern China.* 2nd ed. New York: W. W. Norton, 2001.

Introduction

By 1800, the Qing dynasty had completed its territorial expansion and institutional consolidation. Manchu rulers had also achieved significant accomplishments of cultural integration with the Han Chinese, keeping China a Confucian society, in which people were governed by Confucian moral codes and bureaucrats were chosen for their intellectual merits and virtue. The Chinese had long cherished a self-confident sense of greatness, while the philosophes of the European Enlightenment considered China an ideal state. These optimistic views, however, were eclipsed in the early 19th century when the country began to face problems of overpopulation, economic stagnation, rampant corruption, and drug addiction. Various reforms were initiated by the government or gentry-scholars in an attempt to bring Manchu China back to its previous prosperity. After failing in these efforts, the Chinese perceived that their country was hopelessly impoverished and mismanaged. This erosion of confidence was reinforced by devastating domestic rebellions and foreign imperialist intrusions. The government's failure to overcome the inertia of enduring tradition and its failure to orient the country toward the application of science and democracy led to the collapse of the Manchu monarchy and the birth of the Republic of China in 1911.

The Republic of China brought about a brief interlude of rising hope and expectations, but the first democracy soon proved unsuccessful. The country dissolved into regionally based warlordism, marked by chaos, riots, and revolts. During this period, China witnessed further cultural shifts: intellectual criticism of Confucianism and other traditions, the embrace of Western liberal and radical ideologies, feminist movements, and educational campaigns for the labor class. All these paved the way for the formation of two revolutionary forces: the Nationalist Party or Guomindang (GMD), and the Chinese Communist Party (CCP). The leitmotif of 20th-century China remained independence, democracy, and economic development. The GMD and CCP cooperated in the struggles for China's reunification and opposition to Japan, but they finally split and fought one another over ideological differences. The civil war between the GMD and CCP concluded with the founding of the People's Republic of China in 1949 and the division of the country into the Communist Mainland and Nationalist Taiwan. This division lasts to the present day.

LAND AND PEOPLE

Situated in Eastern Asia on the west side of the Pacific Ocean, China possessed its largest territory during the Qing dynasty. In 1644, after the Manchus conquered China and established the capital of the Qing dynasty in Beijing, they brought the huge land of Manchuria into China. The first three emperors of the dynasty launched imperial expeditions in almost all directions. They defeated the Mongols and Turks in the northwest, building a new province known as Xinjiang (New Territory) there, and the sphere of influence of the Qing court reached 13 million square kilometers. The Manchus recaptured Taiwan, more strongly controlled Tibet, quelled the rebellions in southern China, and developed tributary relations, making a dozen Asian countries its vassal states. Starting in the middle of the 19th century, however, China began to suffer territorial loss. In 1842, China ceded Hong Kong to Great Britain in the Treaty of Nanjing. Then, impaired by other unequal treaties, it lost huge territories east of the Usuli River and west of the Yili Valley to czarist Russia. In 1895 Japan seized Taiwan, and the Mongolian Communist regime declared the independence of Outer Mongolia during World War II. By 1949, China had an area of 9.6 million square kilometers, remaining the third-largest country in the world next to Russia and Canada, or fully one-fifteenth of the world's land mass.

China's topography gives this country two characteristics of Chinese civilization and society. First, for centuries, the high mountains and deserts in the west and northwest were almost impassable, and seaborne traffic between China and other countries remained difficult and dangerous. This topography insulated China from other major civilizations until the advent of modern technology, but it also served, for thousands of years, as a unifying factor incorporating the mainland into one country. Second, mountains and rivers fragment China into several "macroregions," each embracing parts of several provinces, that developed their own communication networks, periodic markets, and self-sufficient societies. The biggest differentiation was between north and south. The land in north China is dry, arid, with irregular rainfall and soil erosion, suitable only for dry crops such as wheat, millet, and maize; the land in south China is of rich alluvium, with abundant rainfall and suitable for paddy rice and myriad fruits. The people in the north are tough and stern while those in the south are softer and quick-witted. Due to the huge size of China, it is necessary to take into account its regional diversity in terms of levels of development, local organizations, and subcultures. The Chinese speak thousands of different dialects, each used to carry its own tradition and way of life, and only the unified written characters bind the nation together.

China is a multination state, consisting of 56 ethnic groups. Most Chinese call themselves Han; these make up 92 to 95 percent of the total population. The areas in which they live compose 40 percent of the country's territory but 90 percent of the total arable land. Most non-Han Chinese live in areas that compose 30 percent of the territory but only 10 percent of arable land. The remaining 30 percent of Chinese land is in the alpine-cold region of Qinghai–Tibet, which contains only 1 percent of the arable land resource.

China's last empire was founded by the Manchus, who used to live in China's northeast frontier and made up less than 1 percent of the country's population. Although they identified with Confucianism and Han culture, the Manchus were regarded as "foreigners" by the Han Chinese for a long time after they conquered China proper. The ethnic issue became a major problem again after 1900, when China was frustrated by defeats at the hands of Western powers and failures of institutional reforms. The Han people blamed the Qing court's impotency and corruption and called for the expulsion of the "foreign regime" from China. This anti-Manchu nationalism served Dr. Sun Yat-sen as an effective weapon for mass mobilization. Nonetheless, after the victory of his revolution in 1912, Sun began to advocate harmonious coexistence of the five major Chinese nationalities (Han, Manchu, Hui, Mongol, and Tibetan) in the Republic of China. Similar policy shifts were also carried out by the Communists, who first encouraged a "self-determination" of Chinese ethnic minorities to get rid of the central control of the GMD and then emphasized a "national solidarity" of the People's Republic of China after 1949.

THE QUEST FOR MODERN CHINA

From 1800 through 1949, Chinese history is a process of searching for a new definition of modern China. When the Qianlong emperor died in 1799, the golden age of imperial China was gone. The legacy he left to his descendants was a huge empire with an empty treasury and seeds of decline. China began to suffer from decline, humiliation, turmoil, and ravages, and it also resorted to various resources, domestic and foreign, material and spiritual, to solve its pressing needs. The 150-year history can be divided into three phases, each comprising about 50 years: decline and crises (1800–1850), rebellions and reforms (1851–1900), and wars and revolutions (1900–1949).

The First Phase (1800–1850)

This period experienced an increasing number of social explosions. In 1800, less than one year after the Jiajing emperor ascended to the throne, he began to investigate his father's favorite, Heshen, whose personal treasury held the equivalent of two years of state revenue. Heshen was executed and his family holdings confiscated, but corruption was spreading like a cancer on the body of the state. Corruption caused low morale among the Manchu troops, who continued to fight the White Lotus Rebellion. Military expenses accounted for more than one-third of government revenue every year, and the rebellion was not suppressed until 1804. To make the situation worse, more revolts occurred throughout the country, including the uprising led by Lin Qing near Beijing, Muslim rebellions in northwest China and Yunnan Province, and revolts of the Triads in many southern provinces.

One of the major reasons for the social unrest was the economic crises of the empire. China was an agrarian society. The major agricultural products were grains and vegetables, which provided the Chinese more than 90 percent of their food requirements. During the Qing dynasty, the Chinese population rose from 143 million in 1741 to 430 million in 1850, a nearly threefold increase. In about the same period, the cultivated land increased by only 35 percent, which led to a sharp decrease in per capita cultivation. Without substantial technological innovation in agricultural production, the yield of a small acreage of land could not sustain the lives of many peasants. The government did not have enough funds to maintain irrigation systems or improve waterway transportation; this made it difficult to develop agricultural production and domestic commerce. In addition, banditry and revolts were inspired by periodic famine and exorbitant taxes.

In the early 19th century, China's foreign trade was small in volume but important for the country's revenue. The Chinese exported tea, silk, rhubarb, and other articles, earning silver from the Western traders, but they showed little interest in purchasing foreign goods. The imbalance of foreign trade in China's favor did not change until the mid-1820s. In addition to the regular commerce tax, the 13 Chinese foreign trade companies in Canton contributed, over a 60-year period down to 1883, about 4 million teals of silver for the government's military campaigns, river conservancy, and other public works. Nonetheless, the Qing court missed the opportunity to expand foreign trade and continued its isolationist policy. European countries sent several delegations to Beijing, including the McCartney Mission in 1793, the Amherst Mission in 1816, and the Napier Mission in 1833, to demand free trade, diplomatic representation, and missionary access, but they were all to no avail. China continued to restrict Westerners to trading only at Canton and to living on an island in the Pearl River. They were not allowed to have permanent residences or to communicate directly with Chinese officials.

Chinese intellectuals were aware of the domestic turbulence and the changing world situation, but they were too weak to alter the inert bureaucracy. Another catalytic agent was needed. This agent was opium exported by the British to China in the 19th century. The Qing court regarded the opium traffic as both an economic and moral issue and decided to ban it absolutely, while the British valued the substantial contribution of opium revenues to the balance of trade with China and responded with military force.

The British defeated China and in 1842 imposed the Treaty of Nanjing, which ended China's isolationism and fundamentally changed its relations with foreigners. According to the Treaty of Nanjing, China would pay Great Britain a war indemnity of 21 million taels, cede the island of Hong Kong to Great Britain, and open five port cities to foreign trade. British gunboats were permitted to anchor at the Chinese ports, and foreign concessions were established in Shanghai and other cities along the Yangtze River. Following this model, other Western powers asked China for more privileges, including extraterritoriality and most favored nation status.

Although it signed treaties or conventions with the European powers, the Qing government did not want to implement its treaty obligations. Sometimes the Qing court used a strategy known as *yimin zhiyi* (use the people to control the barbarians), encouraging ordinary people to break the treaties or attack foreigners. Consequently, conflicts and clashes between China and foreign countries intensified; this led to more wars, more defeats, and more unequal treaties.

China's opening after the Opium War resulted in the influx of Western-manufactured goods, undermining local handicraft industries and locally self-sufficient economies. The war revealed the military weakness of Manchu China and also brought intellectual changes. Some scholars, such as Wei Yuan, realized China's backwardness and advocated learning about the West. Ironically, foreign intrusion provided a spiritual weapon for Chinese revolution. The largest peasant rebellion in Chinese history, the Taiping Uprising, was inspired by the Christian belief in the equality of every soul in the eyes of God.

The Second Phase (1851–1900)

The Taiping rebels revolted in September 1850 and established their kingdom in Nanjing three years later. The new regime controlled half of China, and its war with the Manchus lasted for 14 years, taking a heavy toll of human lives. In 1855, the Yellow River in the north shifted its course from Jiangsu Province to northern Shandong Peninsula. The flood broke dikes in Henan, destroyed thousands of villages in four provinces, and brought suffering to more than 7 million people in Shandong. This was a disaster that repeated about every hundred years, but the destruction would take 30 years to fix. The Qing court was not able to control the flood, and its relief granaries were empty when the famine occurred. Since Confucianism believes that an emperor rules China benevolently by the Mandate of Heaven, the disaster indicated that the legitimacy of the Manchu regime was in jeopardy. In addition, the Taiping rebels were echoed by the Nian rebels in Shandong and the Muslims in northwest China. Some European observers, including Karl Marx, predicted that the Manchu regime would soon fall apart.

However, the Qing dynasty managed to survive these challenges. The Confucian scholars placed their loyalty to traditional cultural values above all other concerns and thus supported the government's fight against the foreign religion–motivated Taiping rebels. A new type of army, such as the Hunan Army led by Zeng Guofan and the Anhui Army led by Li Hongzhang, was built up based on the gentry's militia. These armies were locally recruited, depended on local resources, were organized with a Confucian sense of loyalty, and were equipped with Western weaponry. The Taiping rebels proclaimed land reform and other revolutionary programs, but these were never really implemented. Instead, no better than any of the emperors, the rebel leaders let corruption and power struggles crumble their movement in 1864. The victory of the Hunan and Anhui armies over the Taiping rebels provided a stimulus to the dying dynasty. As the central government became weak and impotent, the growth of local power and autonomy enabled the dynasty to outlive the internal and external crises.

In 1861, when the Tongzhi emperor ascended the throne, he was only five years old. The power of state was firmly in the grasp of his mother, the Empress Dowager Cixi. Cixi sat behind a silk screen while administering state affairs (*chulian tingzheng*) and thus remained the real ruler of China for 48 years until her death in 1908. The Tongzhi Restoration, a reform in the emperor's name, was initiated in 1861 to seek the dynasty's "second blossoming." The major institutional change of the restoration was the establishment of the Zongli Yamen (Office for General Management) to deal with foreign affairs. The head of the Zongli Yamen, Prince Gong, was China's major negotiator, and he tried to modernize China's diplomacy. At his suggestion, the Qing court accepted foreign legations in Beijing and sent Chinese diplomats abroad. The Zongli Yamen sponsored a foreign-language school to train diplomats and promoted translation and publication of Western works.

A more important reform than the Zongli Yamen was the Self-Strengthening Movement, initiated by provincial leaders. The self-strengthening efforts attempted to build a strong national economy and military might, resulting in the establishment of the first Chinese industries, modern military forces, and communication and transportation facilities. The first group of arsenals, dockyards, machine factories, steam navigation companies, coal mines, textile mills, and ironworks was established. Progress was also made in terms of communication and transportation. Previously in south China, local transportation was facilitated by the river-lake-canal system, while in the north transportation was by cart and on the backs of humans or animals. Since a British company constructed the first railway in China, south–north communication quickly improved. The farming population began to be drawn to the treaty ports and new industrial centers. These developments can be fairly referred to as sprouts of capitalism.

However, the sprouts never matured into modern industrialism. The new enterprises established during the Self-Strengthening Movement were poorly managed and suffered from a shortage of capital for further development. Due to their poor quality, the products of the new Chinese enterprises could hardly compete with foreign-manufactured goods. Even Chinese silk lost most of its global market to Japan, whose silk was cheaper and of a better quality. Also, the operation and management of the Chinese railways were controlled by foreign companies. China did not achieve a breakthrough in industrialization. The failure of the Self-Strengthening Movement was proved when China was defeated by Japan in 1894–1895.

Despite any modest accomplishments, the Self-Strengthening Movement finally ended with China's defeat by Japan in 1895. The military failure was irrefutable proof that reforms focusing on technological innovation and industrialization but not touching traditional institutions could not help China much. More comprehensive reforms modeled after those of the Japanese emperor Meiji were launched by radical intellectuals, such as Kang Youwei and Liang Qichao, who gained support from the young emperor, Guangxu. Several drastic changes were proposed, including establishment of a constitutional monarchy, a congress, a new system of schools, and a new mechanism for the recruitment of government officials. These reforms encountered strong resistance from conservatives and Manchu nobles. They also provoked a power struggle between the Dowager Cixi and the Guangxu Emperor. Cixi detained the emperor, ordered the arrest and execution of the reform leaders, and suppressed the Hundred Days' Reform.

Although radical reform suffered a setback, subtle but profound cultural and social changes took place in China. Oil and electric lamps, department stores, modern advertisements, newspapers, women's organizations, nighttime entertainments, and night schools emerged in Shanghai and other port cities, exposing Chinese people to a new urban life and new ideas. Confucian education declined and new Western-style schools mushroomed throughout the country. The rural gentry sent their children to the United States, Japan, or Chinese port cities to study Western science and humanities, and the young urban intellectuals, male and female, became pioneers of changing China.

In the last two years of the 19th century, reactionary Manchu nobles gained increasing influence in formulating domestic and foreign policies. They instigated xenophobic sentiments among the Chinese peasants, who blamed foreigners for all of China's problems. In 1898, a Chinese secret society known as the Boxers began to attack foreign Christian churches, schools, hospitals, and Chinese converts. The Boxers were patronized by the Dowager Cixi, who declared war on eight foreign powers to support the Boxers' besieging of foreign legations in 1900. The conflict led to the military invasion of China by eight foreign nations and resulted in the harsh Boxer Protocol with its massive indemnity. The Dowager Cixi soon joined the Eight-Power Alliance to suppress and ban the Boxers forever.

The Third Phase (1900–1949)

The controversy of Cixi's policy toward the Boxers indicated that the Qing court was not only impotent but also unreliable. In the early 20th century, many Chinese tried to "save China" through industrialization, education, or constitutional reforms, but all their efforts ended in failure. Then they turned their sights to radical revolution.

Early revolutionary organizations included the Revive China Society led by Sun Yat-sen, the China Revival Society by Huang Xing, and the Recovery Society by Cai Yuanpei. These societies were merged into the United League (Tongmenghui) in Japan in 1905, defining their revolutionary objectives as "expelling the Manchus, restoring China for the Chinese, establishing a republic, and equalizing land holdings." The United League gained strong support from Overseas Chinese and their secret organization—Hongmeng. Between 1900 and 1911, Sun Yat-sen, Huang Xing, and other Tongmenghui leaders organized 10 uprisings in China; all were bloodily suppressed by the Qing government.

On 10 October 1911, a group of New Army soldiers and low-ranking officers finally led a successful uprising in the city of Wuchang, and 15 provinces supported the revolution by proclaiming their independence from the Qing dynasty. Sun Yat-sen and other leaders returned to China and established the Republic of China. Despite the collapse of the Qing dynasty, its Beiyang Army under General Yuan Shikai still controlled northern China. Sun negotiated with Yuan and reached a compromise: Yuan promised to support the republic and force the emperor to abdicate, and in return, Sun resigned the presidency and persuaded the provisional assembly to elect Yuan as president. However, Yuan quickly betrayed the revolution. He tried to restore the monarchy and made himself an emperor.

Yuan's plan provoked strong protests from revolutionaries and most provincial leaders. Yuan died in a desperate situation in 1916, leaving the power of state to his subordinates, various local warlords. Warlordism caused chaos, unrest, and civil wars in China. On 4 May 1919, college students in Beijing held a demonstration against the decision to hand over Shandong to Japan made by the Versailles Peace Conference after World War I. The workers and merchants in Shanghai and other cities held general strikes to support the students. The May Fourth Movement promoted the New Culture Movement, in which Confucianism and Chinese traditions were sharply criticized, vernacular writing was encouraged, modern science and democracy were embraced by the Chinese people, and various radical Western ideologies, including Marxism, received increasing attention for their possibilities of solving China's problems.

On 1 July 1921, a group of Marxist intellectuals held a conference in Shanghai to found the Chinese Communist Party (CCP). The Communist International organization (Comintern) sent its representatives to China to guide the CCP's operation. The Comintern's representatives also met Sun Yat-sen and helped him reorganize the Nationalist Party (GMD) and form a GMD-CCP United Front against warlordism. The two parties fought together in the successful Northern Expedition, which destroyed the warlords and reunified China. Nonetheless, the GMD-CCP alliance was short lived. In spring 1927, the GMD leader Chiang Kai-shek began to purge the CCP members from the army and government, ban Communist organizations, and arrest and execute its leaders in Shanghai. The CCP had to evacuate the cities and it withdrew to the countryside.

The central Communist rural base was established by Mao Zedong and Zhu De in the Jinggangshan area, where they developed guerrilla warfare and established the Jiangxi Soviet. Mao's policy and strategy was not approved by the Comintern, which sent the Russian-trained leaders Wang Ming and Bo Gu to replace him. In 1934, Chiang Kai-shek organized the Encirclement and Suppression Campaign against the Jiangxi Soviet. Under the command of Bo Gu and Comintern adviser Otto Braun, the Red Army was defeated and the Jiangxi Soviet was destroyed. The Communists had to begin the Long March, a retreat to northwest China. Along the way of the retreat, the Red Army continued to suffer military defeats until Bo Gu and Braun were replaced by Mao Zedong in January 1935. In November, Mao finally led 8,000 survivors to complete the journey of 6,000 miles and arrive at their destination in northwest China, where he rebuilt a new Communist base with Yan'an as its headquarters.

The best achievements of Chinese economic development were during the Nanjing Government period (1928–1937). Its record revealed some good accomplishments in the fields of finance, communication, and industrial development. The national government completed the unification of currencies, weights, and measures. It also substituted the silver dollar for the tael and introduced the fabi, a new paper currency to stabilize the country's finance. Four national banks were established, and for the first time in China's history, foreign exchanges were controlled by government banks. China's railway network was formed during this period, and postal service and telecommunication were much improved and expanded. Over a period of 10 years, China spent CH$500 million importing industrial equipment, and progress was realized in cotton weaving, flour production, matches, cement, and chemical manufacturing. Nanjing worked out an ambitious plan for national reconstruction, but most projects were interrupted by the Second Sino-Japanese War.

In 1931, when the Japanese invaded Manchuria, Chiang Kai-shek was busy fighting the Communists. He adopted the "non-resistance" policy, ordering the Chinese troops in Manchuria led by Zhang Xueliang to evacuate. The next year, the Japanese installed the last Qing emperor, Puyi, in the puppet government of Manchukuo. Zhang Xueliang was dispatched to northwest China to fight the Red Army. In an attempt to force Chiang to change the anti-CCP policy and declare war on Japan, Zhang staged a coup to kidnap Chiang in Xi'an on 12 December 1936. This was the notorious Xi'an Incident, which inspired the Second United Front between the CCP and GMD in the resistance movement against Japan. The Communist Red Army was incorporated into the National Army under the united command of Chiang Kai-shek.

After the Japanese stormed Nanjing, Chiang moved his capital to Chongqing and withdrew his troops to southwest China, where he continued conventional warfare against the Japanese. On the other hand, the CCP waged guerrilla warfare, penetrating the Japanese rear areas, establishing guerrilla bases, and attacking Japanese military targets. Beginning in 1941, the Japanese adopted the "three alls" policy (kill all, burn all, and loot all) in north China to wipe out the guerrilla fighters. At the same time, it intensified the bombing of Chongqing to force Chiang to surrender. The United States provided China with vital economic and military support, including dispatching General Joseph Stilwell to command the China-India-Burma theater and organizing the American Volunteer Group of Pilots (better known as the Flying Tigers) to fight the Japanese air force.

During the Second Sino-Japanese War, the CCP used peasant nationalism for war mobilization, launched moderate social reforms such as "reduction of rent and interest rates," organized democratic governments, and developed self-sufficient economies in its rural base areas, thus expanding its military power and political influence. Even during the period of the United Front, the Communist Party and the Nationalist Party were involved in military clashes. Due to American mediation, a peace agreement was signed by Mao Zedong and Chiang Kai-shek on 10 October 1945, but deep-rooted distrust and political divergences quickly led to the outbreak of the Chinese civil war.

At the beginning of the war, the GMD took the initiative. From July to December 1946, the Nationalists captured 165 cities and 174,000 square kilometers of territory from the Communists. Mao Zedong had to give up Yan'an and resume his guerrilla warfare fighting in one village after another. Mid-1947 was a turning point when the CCP mobilized a majority of Chinese peasants to join its troops and organized a counteroffensive. The Communist military forces destroyed the GMD's leading troops in three decisive battles: the Battle of Liao-Shen (September 1948–November 1948), the Battle of Ping-Jing (December 1948–January 1949), and the Battle of Huihai (November 1948–January 1949).

The GMD's military defeat was followed by political and economic blunders. Chiang never recognized the importance of cooperating with the Chinese "Third Force," mainly Western-style liberals. Instead, he arrested and assassinated key figures of the democratic parties. In waging war against the Japanese aggression, the GMD government incurred a foreign debt of CH$1,494 billion. In an attempt to bridge the gap between revenue and expenses the Nationalist government increased note issues, which rocketed from CH$1.9 billion at the outset of the war in 1937 to CH $1,031.9 billion in1945, and to CH$24,558,999 billion by the end of 1948. In the postwar years, as the Nationalist government's financial reforms ended in failure, rampant inflation and the rapid rise in retail prices were beyond control. A standard sack of rice (171 lbs) sold for CH$12 in 1937 and for CH$63 million in August 1948. The government could not curb rampant inflation or stop speculation and hoarding. In April 1949, the price of grain was 785,400,000 times more than in 1937.

The economic crises touched off massive anti-hunger, anti-persecution, and anti–civil war demonstrations in various cities. Although the GMD still controlled the areas south of the Yangtze River in 1949, it had no means to stem the Communist advance. Chiang was forced to step down, and Li Zhongren became the acting president. Li asked for peace talks, but he had no bargaining chips for negotiations. In May 1949, the Communists crossed the Yangtze River and stormed Nanjing, the capital of the Republic of China. Chiang Kai-shek and 300,000 troops loyal to the GMD fled to Taiwan. On 1 October 1949, Mao Zedong proclaimed the formal establishment of the People's Republic of China.

UNDERSTANDING MODERN CHINA

The date 1800 is taken as a point of departure for modern China, when the Qing dynasty began the decline from its apogee of wealth and power. In the meantime, some "modern elements" were developing for substantial changes. To understand the history of modern China, it is necessary to pay special attention to one of the major modern elements, a cultural change, which challenged Confucian orthodoxy and undermined the traditional society.

The heart of Confucian orthodoxy was the civil service examination system, which was designed to recruit the best scholars to serve the imperial bureaucracy. Those who passed a three-tiered examination would obtain a *jinshi* degree and an appointment in the government. These exams set the standard of scholarship and parameters of political correctness. The convergence in government of educated men from all walks of life and all parts of the country created a major avenue of social mobility and was a source of national unity. However, during the late Qing dynasty the exam system lost its fairness. Honest scholars could pass the exams only with difficulty, while rich men could easily buy the degrees and government positions. As chances for poor students appeared slim, social distinctions grew apparent and class conflict was intensified. More often than not, some unsuccessful examinees, such as Hong Xiuquan, became leaders of various riots.

From the standpoint of scholarship, the civil service exam also lost its significance. The exams tested students' literacy excellence and their memory of Confucian narratives, which were irrelevant to current problems and urgent needs. Intelligent students began to seek new knowledge and new skills. An illuminating example was the *kaozheng* scholars, whose academic inquiries moved beyond Confucian studies to new realms of mathematics, geography, astronomy, hydraulics, and cartography. In the 19th century, most children of the gentry class went to new Western-style schools or traveled abroad to study. They were not trained in an orthodox way of thought and action but became radical urban intellectuals. They would not return to their home villages to serve their families and local communities. Rather, they worked in the cities as teachers, journalists, doctors, engineers, managers, and other urban professionals. On one hand, having lost these young elite in the rural areas, the gentry class was significantly weakened; on the other hand, the new urban intellectuals became a pool of pioneer reformers and revolutionaries.

One remarkable feature of the reforms and revolutions in 19th- and 20th-century China was their expansion of mass participation. New intellectuals criticized filial piety and other Confucian ethics, proclaiming them as the root of despotism, backwardness, and degeneration. Their slogan "Down with Confucianism" was especially appealing to the younger generation, who were determined to destroy Chinese traditionalism. Criticism of the patriarchal family structure not only made women's issues a major social concern but also, for the first time in history, engaged a considerable number of Chinese women in social movements. In an attempt to secure understanding of modern science and democracy, the New Culture Movement in the early 20th century advocated vernacular writing and promoted popular education; these steps took the written culture across class lines, made communication more accessible to the broad masses, introduced new thought, and instilled social consciousness in the public. From an economic or military perspective, it is fair to say that the accomplishments of the Self-Strengthening Movement were limited. Nonetheless, the movement empowered new social groups, including merchants, new army men, intelligent professionals, and urban laborers. The advance of industrial technology and modern communication facilities spread news of China's defeats, national humiliation, and public grievance, reinforcing a sense of misery and crisis. It was the new science and culture that awakened the Chinese and changed China.

Nineteenth-century history indicated that China began to change before the impact of Western intrusion was fully felt, but real revolutions were propelled by various forms of Western thought. Social Darwinism, humanitarianism, anarchism, and Marxism—all came from Europe or Japan. The Chinese selectively adapted the Western ideologies to serve the goal of national salvation. They were often frustrated by the fact that despite great efforts at learning Western science and imitating Western institutions, China was defeated and abused by Western powers. This gave rise to Chinese nationalism in wars against Western imperialism and Japanese aggression. The Chinese iconoclasts had a strong nationalist sentiment and commitment to saving China. For this reason, when Marxism condemned both Western capitalism and Chinese despotism, its radical programs and Utopian ideals appeared to be most appealing to the Chinese people.

In the 20th century, the Chinese revolutionaries and the advocates of modernity were wrestling with the similar issue of cultural clashes between the old and new and between foreign and Chinese. Mao Zedong's work was to sinicize Marxism, serving the Chinese Revolution, while the reformers' attempt was to embrace Western modernism but also preserve the distinctive Chinese identity. They wished to avoid both total Westernization as well as betrayal of the iconoclasm of the New Culture Movement. Nonetheless, Confucian tradition was resilient; it continued to dominate some aspects of social life and influenced ideas and policies of revolutionary leaders. For example, there is a Confucian ideal that honorable government officials are the people's *fumuguan* (parent officials), who care about the people and do good things for them but also dominate and control them as a father would. Every Chinese leader, from Manchu bureaucrats to the GMD officials and the CCP cadres, despite important differences in their political rhetoric, shared a belief in this standard. Each claimed himself as the custodian of the people with a "mandate of heaven" to rule China. In the 20th century, the Chinese were exposed to Western concepts of democracy. However, neither Sun Yat-sen's constitutional democracy nor Mao Zedong's democratic centralism did away with the Confucian influence of being a fatherlike ruler. It was apparent that the Chinese adopted, distorted, and transformed the Western idea of democracy in their efforts at creating a new China.

This new China was created in two parallel processes. One was the rural revolution led by the Chinese Communist Party, involving land reform, guerrilla warfare, and Communist state building. The other was urban development following the pattern of the Self-Strengthening Movement, to enhance industrial productivity, intensify international ties, and improve modern communication facilities. Although the last process was often interrupted by wars and social unrest, leaving many projects incomplete, some progress was still made. The city became the site not only of banks and factories but also of schools, presses, cinemas, and associations. The city, especially the treaty ports such as Shanghai, took the lead in modernizing China. Liberal intellectuals set the "modern" city against the "backward" countryside, while in Mao Zedong's discourse, the rural–urban tension was expressed as conflict between the "revolutionary" countryside and the "counterrevolution-ary" city.

In fact, the urban–rural relationship should be seen in less dichoto-mous terms. The city was the origin of the Communist movement, and the urban financial crises and social resistance contributed the vital blow to the ultimate collapse of the GMD government. During the Second Sino-Japanese War, urban culture continued to radiate to rural areas through the movement of a large number of young students and intellectuals from the Japanese-controlled cities to Mao's rural bases. Because he highly valued the revolutionary potential and traditional virtue of Chinese peasants, Mao Zedong required the urban intellectu-als to learn from peasants and integrate with the rural masses so as to establish a new cultural orthodoxy for the People's Republic. The Com-munist system was inaugurated in 1949, setting the new direction of de-velopment along Soviet lines. However, Chinese history demonstrated a remarkable continuity. In later years, China shifted from the Russian model to self-reliance and then to the open-door policy, returning to the "consensual agenda" of the economic reform and cultural transforma-tion, which had started in the late 19th and early 20th centuries. The Chinese Revolution interrupted but also paved a way for the country's modernization.

The Dictionary

– A –

AB LEAGUE (ANTI-BOLSHEVIK LEAGUE). Known also as AB Tuan. This was an anti-Communist organization established at the end of 1926 by the rightists of the **Nationalist Party** in Nanchang, Jiangxi Province. It existed for a short time and was disbanded in early April 1927. In 1930, the southwestern base of the Communists launched a campaign to check and wipe out members of the AB League in the **Red Army** and local governments. **Mao Zedong** appointed Li Shaoju and Gu Bo to lead the campaign. These two tortured and murdered officers and soldiers, which led to the revolt of the 20th Army of the Red Army. To quell the rebellion, Mao then sent **Peng Dehuai** and **Lin Biao**, who disarmed the 20th Army and arrested and executed all 700 commanders of the troops at platoon level or above. Afterward, the massive arrests and executions continued. It is estimated that about 70,000 innocent people were accused of being members of the AB League and were slaughtered.

AFTERMATH SOLUTION MEETING (1924). A temporary legislature established by Duan Qirui. In the 1920s, China witnessed a South-North confrontation. **Sun Yat-sen** established a military government in Guangzhou, challenging the **Beijing government** headed by the **Anhui Clique** warlord, Duan Qirui. On 21 November 1924, Duan called the Aftermath Solution Meeting to discuss how to organize a new national assembly and to reform the government's military and fiscal systems. It was required that the participants include military leaders, provincial leaders, distinguished scholars, and celebrities. The meeting opened on 1 February 1925 and was attended by 86 delegates. By its close on 21 April, the meeting had passed several resolutions, including "Regulations of the Military Aftermath

1

Solution Meeting," "Regulations of the Fiscal Aftermath Solution Meeting," and "Regulations of the National Assembly." Sun Yat-sen and the Guangzhou government refused to recognize the legitimacy of the meeting and criticized its resolutions. In the following months, the Beijing government managed to hold the military and fiscal meetings, but the national assembly was aborted with the resignation of Duan Qirui.

AGREEMENT OF PRINCE QING. Memorandum on tobacco tax by Prince Qing. By the end of the 19th century, the Anglo-American Tobacco Company had monopolized the Chinese tobacco market. The Qing government collected import tax on its cigarettes as on other foreign commodities. According to the tax rate, the company had to pay a 5 percent tax on the cigarettes they sold in Chinese markets. The company complained and asked for a reduction. On 26 December 1904, Prince Qing sent the memorandum to the British minister, accepting the company's demand that it would pay only 0.45 tael silver per hundred *jin* of cigarettes. This adjusted tax rate was as low as 0.3–0.7 percent.

AH Q SPIRIT. Ah Q is a character in **Lu Xun**'s short story "The True Story of Ah Q," published in 1921. In Ah Q, Lu Xun created an image of the typical Chinese peasant who had the following characteristics: first, Ah Q had a sense of inflated self-importance and derision toward whatever he did not know; second, he bullied the weak and feared the strong; third, he indulged in sexual fantasies; fourth, he was shameless and speculative, and deceived himself as well as others; and finally, Ah Q was the epitome of servility. Being at the bottom of society, Ah Q was insulted, abused, and finally framed and sentenced to death, but he always engaged in self-deception by declaring he was a "victor." Although he was a pathetic loser, Ah Q never faced the truth and had no intention of doing something to change his life. Lu Xun argued that Ah Q's tragedy was not in his poverty but in his apathy, self-deception, and distorted soul. Lu sharply criticized the Ah Q spirit, arguing that it was a common weakness of Chinese people and it made China backward.

AI QING (1910–1996). The pen name of Jiang Haicheng, a prominent poet of modern China. Born into a landlord family in Jinhua, Zhejiang

Province, Ai was bought up by his babysitter, a poor rural woman, to whom Ai devoted his famous poem, "Dayanhe, My Babysitter." The sad tone of his writing about the toil and hardships of a rural woman as his babysitter and family servant touched thousands of young readers. The poem made him a rising star in Chinese poetry circles. Ai began to study at the village school at the age of five, and after graduating from middle school, he entered the National Xihu School of Arts in 1928. The next year, encouraged by the president of the school, Li Fengmian, Ai traveled to France to join the work-study program. There he studied the impressionist arts, including works by Pierre-Auguste Renoir and Vincent van Gogh. He also read a great deal of European literature, especially the fiction of Russian realistic writers.

In January 1932, Ai returned to China and engaged in the revolutionary culture movement, immediately becoming a famous poet in Shanghai. In July 1932, he was arrested by the Nationalist government, but he did not put down his pen. As soon as he was released in 1935, he published nine volumes of poetry. His creative writing reached its peak during the **Second Sino-Japanese War**. He went to **Yan'an**, joined the **Chinese Communist Party**, and began to write for workers, peasants, and soldiers who bravely fought the Japanese invaders. He also served as the chief editor of *Shikan* (Journal of Poetry). In September 1945, Ai was appointed associate dean of the School of Arts at North China Union University, and he offered students courses on creative writing and literary theory. After 1949, he continued to write poems and held some administrative positions. Ai was persecuted during the Antirightist Campaign in 1957 and the Cultural Revolution in 1966–1976 and was exiled to farms in Manchuria and Xinjiang. Ai regained his freedom and right to write in 1976.

AIGUN, TREATY OF (1858). The Russo-Chinese treaty signed on 28 May 1858 by the Russian representative Nikolay Muravyov and the Qing representative Yishan in the town of Aigun, China. Since 1847, the Russians had made advances into the Amur region. They constructed fortified posts and came into conflict with Chinese residents in the lower reaches of the river. The Qing government tried to solve the problem by negotiation, which resulted in the Treaty of Aigun. The treaty granted Russia the left bank of the **Amur River** (about

600,000 sq. km of land), which was a Chinese territory according to the Russo-Chinese **Treaty of Nerchinsk** of 1689. According to the Treaty of Aigun, the **Manchu** residents north of the Amur River would be allowed to remain, China would continue to administer the 64 villages east of the Amur River, and the three rivers, Amur, Sungari, and Ussuri, were to be open exclusively to Chinese and Russian ships. Because the Treaty of Aigun completely ignored the boundaries established by the Treaty of Nerchinsk, the **Xianfeng Emperor** refused to ratify the treaty and dismissed Yishan. During the **Arrow War**, Russia offered to mediate between China and the Anglo-French Allies and asked for a new treaty as a reward for its service to China. The new treaty, the Convention of Beijing of 1860, finally confirmed the provisions of the Treaty of Aigun.

ALCOCK CONVENTION (1869). Treaty between China and Great Britain. As the Western powers agreed on a policy of cooperation, Britain and China began to negotiate for treaty revision in an atmosphere of peace for the first time since the **Opium War**s. The negotiation was carried out by **Prince Gong** and the British minister Rutherford Alcock, who was instructed to sign the treaty by the British foreign secretary. The positive result of the negotiation was the Alcock Convention of 1869, which allowed China to establish a consulate in Hong Kong to increase the import duty on opium from 30 to 50 taels per picul and export duty on silk from 10 to 20 taels. The convention also limited the unilateral **most favored nation** clause of the original treaty. British merchants strongly opposed the terms of the convention and forced the British government to not ratify it. This was seen as a betrayal by the Chinese and provoked a new tide of antiforeign sentiment throughout China during the 1870s.

ALL-CHINA FEDERATION OF LABOR (ACFL). Chinese trade union run by the Communist Party. Its predecessor was the National General Labor Union, founded on 11 August 1921 in Shanghai. **Zhang Guotao** was the first secretary-general and **Mao Zedong** was the director of the Hunan branch. On 1 May 1925, the ACFL was formally established in Guangzhou, replacing the National General Labor Union. The ACFL was repressed in 1927 by **Chiang Kai-shek**, many trade unionists were executed, and government-sponsored "yellow" unions were installed. By 1949, with the Communist takeover of the whole of mainland China, the ACFL had been reestablished as the nation's sole trade union center.

ALLEN, YOUNG JOHN (1836–1907). American Methodist missionary sent by the American Southern Methodist Episcopal Mission to China. Allen was best known in China by his local name, Lin Lezhi. He was born in Burke County, Georgia, to a mother who died 12 days after his birth. Allen's father had died only two months previously. Allen was brought up by his aunt Nancy Wiley Hutchins and did not learn about his parents until the age of 15. Allen converted in 1853 and graduated with honors from Emory College in 1858. In the same year, Allen married Mary Houston, a graduate of Wesleyan College. On 18 December 1859, Young and Mary Allen and their infant daughter, Mellie, sailed from New York and arrived in Shanghai on 13 July 1860. From 1861 to 1866, while he was cut off from his church at home by the American Civil War, Allen had to work as a coal and rice broker, cotton buyer, teacher, and editor. In 1868, he established *Church News*, later renamed **Globe Magazine**. Allen made the magazine influential by introducing Western learning and advocating Chinese reform. In 1882, he founded the Anglo-Chinese College and served as its president from 1885 to 1895. Allen was also instrumental in founding the McTyeire Home and School, which opened in 1892 with most students coming from rich and influential families in Shanghai.

Due to ill health, Allen resigned from the Anglo-Chinese College, but he continued writing. Allen published about 250 volumes of original and translated works, including *Women in All Lands*. His analyses of the reasons for China's defeat by Japan in 1905 produced wide repercussions among the Chinese intellectuals and government officials. The leader of the **Hundred Days' Reform**, **Kang Youwei**, said that he owed his conversion to reform chiefly due to the writings of two missionaries, the Rev. **Timothy Richard** and the Rev. Dr. Young J. Allen. Liang Shiqiu said that Allen's works and the *Globe Magazine* had changed his whole life.

AMO DOCTRINE. Known as the "Monroe Doctrine of Asia" and issued in 1934 by Eiji Amo, head of the information department of the Japanese Foreign Ministry, the Amo Doctrine stated that Japan was to be the sole leader in the security of East Asia, with a strong commitment to defeating communism and Western colonialism. It rejected the **Open Door Policy** and required European countries to adopt a "hands-off" policy in China. Amo advocated an ultranationalist ideology. He called on Western powers not to render assistance to China and warned that any action supporting Chinese unification would undermine Japanese authority over China and surely encounter Japanese opposition. After World War II, Eiji Amo was arrested as a Class A war criminal. However, he was never tried and was released in 1947.

AMUR RIVER. Known as the Heilong River (meaning Black Dragon) in China, it is the world's ninth-longest river. The name Black Dragon, referring to the dark color of the water, was regarded as sacred by the **Manchu**s, who lived in the river valley and adjacent areas. In the 19th century, Russian expansion reached the area of the Amur River. There have been territorial conflicts regarding control over the river basin since then. Czarist Russia signed several treaties with the Qing government and seized the territory north and east of the Amur River. Recently, China and Russia have recognized that the river forms the border between the Russian Far East and northeastern China.

ANARCHISM. *See* CHINESE ANARCHISM.

ANFU PARLIAMENT. After the leader of the **Anhui Clique**, Duan Qirui, became premier of the **Beijing government** in 1917, he formed the Anfu Club to rally the support of his civilian followers. In August 1918, he put forward the slogan "reconstruct the republic" and called a new parliament. The election was manipulated by the Anfu Club, and the overwhelming majority of the elected congressmen were its members. The parliament was thus called the Anfu Parliament. In 1920, the Anhui Clique was defeated by the **Zhili Clique** in a war. Duan was forced to resign in July and the Anfu Parliament was dissolved the next month.

ANHUI ARMY (*HUAIJUN*). Local military force of the Qing government built up by **Li Hongzhang**. In 1853, Li was ordered to organize local militias to fight the Taiping rebels. In 1858, he began to work with **Zeng Guofan** in the **Hunan Army**. Using Zeng's Hunan Army as a model, which was loyal only to Zeng, Li established his personal

Anhui Army. Li recruited officers and soldiers in his home province, equipped them with Western weapons, and trained them in a Western way. Nonetheless, Chinese officers commanded the troops in battle. Li even bought British warships to build the Anhui Navy. His army rapidly increased from 6,000 to 70,000 in two years. Collaborating with the **Ever Victorious Army**, the Anhui Army defeated the Taiping rebels in the province of Jiangsu. Li's troops stormed Suzhou in 1863 and Changzhou and Nanjing in 1864. Afterward, they moved to North China and suppressed the **Nian Rebellion**. The Anhui Army gradually replaced the Hunan Army to become the leading military force of the Qing regime, a predecessor of the **Beiyang Army** and Beiyang Navy. In 1884, the Anhui Army was defeated by the French in Guangxi. Moreover, in the **First Sino-Japanese War**, Li Hongzhang's **Beiyang Fleet** was destroyed by the Japanese. The influence of the Anhui Army began to decline. However, when **Yuan Shikai** was ordered to rebuild the army for the Qing regime, many of the commanders of the **New Army**, including Yuan Shikai himself, were previous subordinates of Li Hongzhang. In later years, they constituted the **Anhui Clique** of warlords in the Republic of China.

ANHUI CLIQUE. One of the cliques of the **Beiyang warlords**. It was named after Anhui Province, where its founder, General Duan Qirui, was born. Duan was once the premier and minister of army of the Republic of China and controlled the central government and congress in Beijing. In 1917, the Anhui Clique expanded its troops, took out foreign loans, and attempted to unify China by military force. In 1920, the Anhui Clique was defeated by the **Zhili Clique** and lost control over central power. In 1924, various political forces, including the Zhili, Fengtian, and Anhui cliques, made a compromise in their power struggle and elected Duan as acting executive. However, in the same year, the last troops of the Anhui Clique commanded by Lu Yongxiang were crushed in the battle of Zhejiang-Jiangsu, marking the collapse of the Anhui Clique.

ANNAM (VIETNAMESE: AN NAM). Name that the Chinese gave to the core area of today's Vietnam. It surrounds the city of Hanoi and runs from the Gulf of Tonkin to the mountains surrounding the plains of the Red River. Historically, it referred to a larger area, including part of the Chinese province of Guangxi. Annam was an independent country and later in the 15th century became China's tributary state. In 1803, the Chinese Jiajing Emperor changed its formal name to Viet Nam, but Annam continued to be used in many documents. After the **Sino-French War**, the French seized it and Viet Nam became a French colony, part of the Federation of French Indochina from 1887 until its collapse in 1954.

ANTI-FOOTBINDING MOVEMENT. During the 19th century, anti-footbinding was propagated by the **Taiping** rebels as one of their objectives of bringing about gender equality. In the following years, both Chinese reformers and Western missionaries vigorously advocated the ending of footbinding. Between 1875 and 1878, *Globe Magazine,* edited by **Young Allen**, published a series of articles to criticize the practice. In 1895, the first Natural Foot Society (*tianzuhui*) was founded in Shanghai with Mrs. Archibald **Little** as its first president. Later, **Kang Youwei** also organized an anti-footbinding society in Guangdong; the **Guangxu Emperor** supported Kang's initiative and ordered all other provinces to follow suit. Unfortunately, these early efforts failed with the abortive **Hundred Days' Reform**. Nonetheless, the **Dowager Cixi** finally ordered the government to persuade people to stop this practice in 1902. A few days after the Wuchang Uprising in 1911, the new military government of Hubei Province issued a note encouraging women to release their feet. On 13 March 1912, the provisional president of the Republic of China, **Sun Yat-sen**, issued an order to prohibit **footbinding**; this order became a law of the Republic of China in 1932. During the **New Culture Movement**, the Anti-footbinding Movement gained momentum. Feminists attacked footbinding because it caused women much suffering, while social Darwinists argued that it weakened the Chinese nation. Revolutionaries tried to combine the Anti-footbinding Movement with their own political programs. The footbinding practice waned in the early 20th century and gradually disappeared in mainland China in the 1950s.

ANTI-HUNGER, ANTI-OPPRESSION, AND ANTI–CIVIL WAR MOVEMENT. Student demonstrations in Nationalist-controlled cities in May and June 1947. These began as spontaneous protests against political persecution and the Chinese civil war and demanded the government supply sufficient food to the people. The first demonstration took place on 4 May in Shanghai. After the movement was banned by police, urban students staged a general strike. On 9 May, more than 20,000 workers held a demonstration in support of the students and asked for an increase in salary. On 15 May about 3,000 students went to the Ministry of Education in Nanjing to present a peaceful petition. The next day, the students of **Peking University** took the same action and put forward a clear slogan for the protestors: "Anti-hunger and anti–civil war." This terrified the government and martial law was declared. On 20 May, the largest demonstration took place in Nanjing when 6,000 students from 16 universities in Beiping, Shanghai, Nanjing, and Hangzhou gathered in the capital and held a rally in the front of the **National Assembly** building. The Nationalist government sent policemen and troops to disperse them. In the conflict, hundreds of students were wounded and 20 were arrested. This was followed by student demonstrations in Tianjin and 60 other cities. The **Chinese Communist Party** then became involved and helped the students and protesters further organize against the Nationalist government.

ANTI-JAPANESE MILITARY AND POLITICAL UNIVERSITY (KANGDA). Kangda grew out of the Anti-Japanese Red Army University, which was established on 1 June 1936 in Bao'an, Shaanxi Province. Soon after it moved to **Yan'an** in 1937, the school changed its name to Kangda. **Mao Zedong** served as the chairman of the university's education committee, and **Lin Biao** was appointed the commandant of Kangda. The Communist Kangda equaled the Nationalist **Whampoa Military Academy** in terms of producing senior army officers for their troops. The mission of the Kangda was to educate, train, and inspire the officers of the Red Army so that they were committed to Mao Zedong's requirements of "correct political orientation, plain, hard-working style, flexible strategy, and tactics." The motto of Kangda was "unity, alertness, earnestness, and liveliness." During the **Second Sino-Japanese War**, Kangda set up 12 branches in various rural bases, producing thousands of Communist military commanders and political commissars of high and middle rankings.

ANTI-MANCHU NATIONALISM. This was a political tool used by **Sun Yat-sen** in staging the **Republican Revolution**. In 1905, the Sun-led **Tongmenghui** took an oath "to expel the **Manchu**, and restore China for the Chinese, establish a republic, and equalize the land." Also, in Sun's **Three People's Principles** (nationalism, democracy, and the people's livelihood), nationalism was interpreted as anti-Manchu nationalism. Anti-Manchu nationalism regarded the Manchus as foreigners and the Qing dynasty as a foreign regime. Sun's rhetoric was focused on the central argument that the corruption and incapability of the Manchu government was the source of China's backwardness and humiliation. Anti-Manchu nationalism was a powerful revolutionary slogan and tactic aiming at the overthrow of the Manchu monarchy. After the Qing dynasty collapsed, Sun replaced anti-Manchu nationalism with a policy emphasizing harmonic coexistence between Manchu, Han, and other Chinese ethnic groups. His new interpretation of nationalism was referred to as "anti-Western imperialism."

ANYUAN MINE STRIKE (1922). An early worker strike organized by the **Chinese Communist Party** (CCP). The Anyuan Mines were a big enterprise in Hunan Province employing more than 10,000 workers. There were also a considerable number of unemployed workers living in that area, making it an important site for the labor movement. As soon as the CCP was established in 1921, **Li Lisan**, **Liu Shaoqi**, and **Mao Zedong** went to the Anyuan Mines to investigate how to initiate a labor movement there. In May 1922, they established the Worker's Club. In September, the mine manager refused to increase workers' salaries and tried to disband the Worker's Club. Li Lisan led a general strike and successfully forced the mine's managers to accept the demands of the workers by signing the 13 Article Agreement on 18 September 1922. The Worker's Club existed until 1925, and afterward many of the workers of the Anyuan Mines joined the **Northern Expedition**. In **Ye Ting**'s Independent Regiment, two-thirds of the soldiers were from the mines. The labor movement in Anyuan produced some important Communist cadres, such as Yang Dezhi and Xiao Jiguan.

APRIL TWELFTH INCIDENT (1927). A clash between the **Communist Party** (CCP) and the **Nationalist Party** (GMD). It was referred to as the April Twelfth Massacre by the CCP and the Party Purge by the GMD. In 1923, **Sun Yat-sen** announced his policy of alliance with the Communists. A large number of CCP members joined the GMD and held important positions in the Nationalist army and government. More often than not, there were minor conflicts between the CCP and GMD members. After the **Northern Expedition** succeeded, **Chiang Kai-shek** believed the CCP's influence had waxed within the GMD and would soon be beyond control. He decided to purge the Communists from the party and the government. After Chiang led the **National Revolutionary Army** to storm the city of Shanghai, he encouraged the **Green Gang** leaders, Huang Jinrong and **Du Yuesheng**, to organize right-wing worker organizations to confront the CCP-led Shanghai General Trade Union. On the morning of 12 April 1927, Chiang used the excuse of "pacification of workers' conflict" to disarm the worker pickets; this caused the deaths of more than 300 workers. That afternoon the workers launched a strike and regained the office of the General Trade Union. The next morning the workers held a demonstration. Chiang gave the order to open fire on the worker-demonstrators, killing more than 100 men. Chiang then ordered the disbanding of the Shanghai General Trade Union, Shanghai Provisional Government, and Communist organizations. It was reported that about 300 were killed, 500 were arrested, and 5,000 went missing during the following massive arrest and execution campaign. Prominent CCP leaders, including Chen Yannian and Zhao Shiyan, were arrested and executed. The White Terror also raged in other cities. The Communists had to retreat from cities to rural areas and rebuild their strength. The April Twelfth Incident marked the split between the GMD and CCP and the beginning of the first 10-year civil war. *See also* UNITED FRONT, FIRST (1924–1927).

ARROW WAR (SECOND OPIUM WAR, 1856–1860). The war between China and the Anglo-French alliance triggered by opium traffic, thus called the Second Opium War. On 8 October 1856, Qing officials in Guangzhou checked the *Arrow*, a Chinese-owned ship registered in Hong Kong, and arrested 12 Chinese sailors who were suspected of being involved in opium smuggling. The British consul, Harry Parkes, argued that because it was British registered, the ship was protected by British **extraterritoriality**. The viceroy of Liangguang, Ye Mingchen, first refused to release the suspects but then compromised. On 22 October, Ye delivered the sailors to the British consulate but refused to apologize. The next day, British gunboats shelled the city. Ye put up strong resistance and aroused Chinese people in Canton to burn the foreign factories. Based on Parkes's report of the Arrow Incident, the British government decided to seek redress from China and dispatched a marine force led by Lord Elgin. France joined the British action because the Chinese had murdered a French missionary, Father August Chapdelaine, in Guangxi Province. After coordination with each other, the British and French formed allied forces that stormed Canton in December 1857. Viceroy Ye was captured and the governor of Guangdong, Bogui, surrendered. In May 1858, the alliance moved north to demand a treaty from the Qing court. As the alliance's warships approached the **Dagu Forts**, the imperial commissioner, Tang Yanxiang, escaped.

On 20 May, the alliance captured the Dagu Forts, stormed Tianjin, and threatened Beijing. The Qing court asked for peace and signed the Treaty of **Tianjin** with Great Britain on 26 June and with France on 27 June 1858. However, the **Xianfeng Emperor** refused to ratify the treaty until the foreigners withdrew the demand for diplomatic representation in Beijing. The alliance insisted on the treaty terms and had a navy force escort their envoys to the capital. When this group of Europeans tried to move inland at Tianjin, the Qing general **Sengge Rinchen** stopped them, informing them that no armed forces would be allowed to accompany the envoys to Beijing. War broke out again. After 24 hours of fighting, the British lost four gunboats and had another two severely damaged. But the reinforced allied forces sailed from Hong Kong, including 11,000 British and 6,700 French troops, 41 warships, and 143 transports. Sengge Rinchen's troops were defeated and he escaped. As the allied forces advanced toward Beijing, the Qing court suggested a negotiation during which the Qing officials kidnapped the British envoy and journalists as hostages. The hostages were tortured at the jail of the Qing Board of Punishment and some were murdered. This prompted Lord Elgin to order his soldiers to loot and burn the Old Summer Palace (**Yuan Ming Yuan**) as soon as they captured Beijing. The emperor and his entourage fled to Rehe, while **Prince Gong** stayed and cleaned up the mess. Prince Gong resumed the negotiation and signed the Convention of Beijing with the alliance on 24 October 1860, which ratified the Treaty of Tianjin and brought the Arrow War to an end. *See also* OPIUM WAR.

ARTICLES OF FAVORABLE TREATMENTS. Special terms offered by the government of the Republic of China to the abdicated

Qing emperor. On 12 February 1912, the **Xuantong Emperor** announced his acceptance of the Favorable Treatment of the Manchu Royal Family. These favorable terms promised that the Republican government would treat the deposed Qing Emperor with the same courtesy as a foreign sovereign; subsidize him and the royal family with 4 million taels annually; allow the deposed emperor to tentatively live in the Forbidden City and then move to the Summer Palace with the usual number of guards and attendants; protect the shrine, tombs, and temples of the royal family; and protect the private property of the royal family.

AUGUST SEVENTH CONFERENCE (1927). An urgent meeting of the Politburo of the **Chinese Communist Party** (CCP) held on 7 August 1927 in Hankou. The participants included 22 members and alternate members of the CCP Central Committee as well as the **Comintern**'s representatives, Neinz Neumann and Bessd Lominadze, from Russia. In the meeting, CCP general secretary **Chen Duxiu** and his policy of cooperation with the **Nationalist Party** (GMD) were discredited. Although Chen's policy was basically made in light of Moscow's instructions, he was criticized by the Comintern representative and other participants as a right opportunist and was deemed responsible for the failure of the CCP-GMD alliance and the Chinese Revolution. The meeting was presided over by the Comintern's representative, Bessd Lominadze, who decided to launch a series of insurrections against **Chiang Kai-shek**. The meeting also elected a new politburo headed by **Qu Qiubai** to implement the new policy.

AUTUMN HARVEST UPRISING. A peasant uprising led by **Mao Zedong** in Hunan in September 1927. After **Chiang Kai-shek** launched a coup in Shanghai and purged Communists from the **National Revolutionary Army** in April 1927, the **Chinese Communist Party** (CCP) was eager to build up its own military forces and thus launched a series of uprisings; the Autumn Harvest Uprising was one of them. The 5,000 participants included the Guards Regiment of the National Government in Wuhan and worker pickets of the Anyuan Coal Mines, but most of them were the peasant militia from the counties of Liuyan and Pingjiang. They were organized into a division and ordered by the CCP Central Committee to make a long-range raid on the city of Changsha. Due to poor weaponry and limited combat experience, the insurrectionary army was quickly defeated by the **Nationalist Party** on the way to Changhsha. The uprising ended in failure. Mao decided to give up the attack of Changsha and transferred the troops to the Jiangxi-Hunan border area of Jingguangshan. On 29 September, about 1,000 survivors arrived at the village of Sanwan, Jiangxi Province, where their division was reduced to a regiment. In the course of this reorganization, Mao Zedong put forward two famous principles to ensure the CCP's control over military forces: "The party commands the gun," and "Establishing party branches at the company level."

– B –

BA JIN (PA CHIN, 1904–2005). The pen name of Li Yaotang, one of the most prominent and widely read Chinese writers of the 20th century. Born in Chengdu, Sichuan Province, into a scholar-official family, Li studied at the Chengdu Foreign Language School and several high schools in Shanghai and Nanjing. In his early years, he was exposed to the ideology of Peter Alexeyevich Kropotkin and claimed to be an anarchist. In 1927, Li traveled to France for advanced studies, where he created the pen name Ba Jin to publish his first novel, *Miewang* (*Destruction*). As soon as the novel was reprinted in Shanghai, he came to fame in China. After this burst of popularity, he became the most prolific Chinese writer of the 1930s and 1940s. He wrote numerous novels and short stories, the most noted being *Family*, which illuminated the collapse of the traditional family structure and clashes between the younger generation and old Confucian morality. He spoke out for love and a new humanity, which had a tremendous appeal for young readers of that time. After 1949, his career as a noteworthy writer was blighted. His previous reputation and low-key style helped him survive many political campaigns, and he was elected the chair of the All-China's Writers Association.

BAI CHONGXI (1893–1966). Prominent military commander, one of leaders of the **Guangxi Clique**, and general of the first class of the Nationalist (GMD) army. Born in Guilin, Guangxi Province, into a Chinese Muslim family of Hui nationality, Bai graduated from **Baoding Military Academy** in 1918. After graduation, he joined the Guangxi army and rose from company commander to battalion commander to chief of staff of the Guangxi army. In 1921, Bai went to see his schoolmate Huang Shaohong and joined Huang in supporting **Sun Yat-sen**'s revolution. Sun appointed Huang as commander and Bai as chief of staff in the expedition against local warlords. Cooperating with another general, **Li Zongren**, Huang and Bai defeated Lu Rongting, Sheng Hongying, and other Guangxi warlords in 1924, making Li, Bai, and Huang the leaders of the new Guangxi Clique. During the **Northern Expedition** (1926–1928), Bai was the chief of staff of the **National Revolutionary Army** and commander in chief to the Eastern Route Army, moving and fighting in several provinces. His troops destroyed the **warlord** Sun Chuanfang's leading force of 10,000 troops in the east suburbs of Nanchang, winning him a great reputation. Bai stormed the cities of Nanchang, Hangzhou, and Shanghai. He also commanded the forward units that first entered Beijing, and he was credited with being the senior commander on site at the completion of the Northern Expedition. For his battlefield exploits during the Northern Expedition, he was known as one of the greatest strategists in Chinese history.

As garrison commander of Shanghai, Bai supported **Chiang Kai-shek**'s campaign of purging the Communists from the National Revolutionary Army. On 4 April 1927, with the support of the **Green Gang**, Bai's troops destroyed the headquarters of the trade unions, disarmed the worker pickets, and arrested and executed Communists in Shanghai. In 1929, Bai engaged in war between his Guangxi Clique and Chiang Kai-shek. He was defeated and fled to Vietnam. From 1930 to 1936, with **Li Zongren**, Bai was involved in the program of the reconstruction of Guangxi, making the province a model area in terms of economic development and administrative efficiency. During the **Second Sino-Japanese War**, Bai was made deputy chief of staff of the Nationalist army, responsible for military operations and training. Bai assisted Li in organizing the Battle of Tai'erzhuang in Shandong Province, which checked the Japanese advance for several months. Bai also retook South Guangxi from the Japanese. He commanded the Battle of Wuhan and defeated the Japanese troops twice at Kunlun Pass in Guangxi. Bai's strategy for the Chinese resistance movement was well reflected in his suggestion for a "combination of conventional war with guerrilla operations, accumulate small victories to reach the final victory, and exchange land for time." He believed in China's triumph after a protracted war against Japan.

In May 1946, Bai was appointed minister of national defense and assisted Chiang in waging civil war to destroy the Communists. He went to Manchuria and proposed a plan of destroying the Communist troops there. However, this plan was not accepted by Chiang. When the GMD troops lost all decisive battles in Manchuria and North China, Chiang resigned and Bai's fellow Guangxi general, Li Zongren, became the acting president of the Republic of China. Bai opposed Li's plan for peace negotiations with the Chinese Communist Party. He tried to build a solid defense line along the Yangtze River so as to keep half of China for the GMD government. However, the defense line was quickly broken by the **People's Liberation Army**. Bai's last military campaign took place in Hunan and Guangxi, as the Communist forces led by **Lin Biao** and Lu Bocheng outflanked his Guangxi troops on both wings. As his troops were crushed by the Communist forces, Bai fled to Taiwan. Bai did not hold any significant position in Taiwan and died a mysterious death on 1 December 1966 in Taipei.

BAI SHANGDI HUI. *See* GOD WORSHIPPING SOCIETY.

***BAIHUAWEN* (VERNACULAR CHINESE).** *Baihuawen* are texts written using the spoken Chinese language. Traditionally, government documents and formal literature were written in classical Chinese. Since the 17th century, some fiction that was written in vernacular Chinese emerged and became popular among businessmen and educated urban people. In January 1917, **Hu Shih** published the article "A Tentative Suggestion on Literary Improvement" in *New Youth*, advocating abolishing the use of classical Chinese and replacing it with baihuawen. The next year, the chief editor of *New Youth*, **Chen Duxiu**, decided that his magazine would publish articles only in the vernacular language. The leading writers in vernacular Chinese included **Li Dazhao**, Qian Xuantong, **Lu Xun**, **Fu Sinian**, and **Guo Moruo**. Along with the vernacular writing, Chinese scholars and educators adopted Western punctuation and Arabic numerals, which never appeared in traditional Chinese literature. After the **May Fourth Movement** in 1919, more than 400 newspapers and magazines were published in vernacular Chinese. Despite opposition by some conservative scholars, the **Beijing government** ordered that all textbooks be in the vernacular in 1920. Because Lu Xun's short stories and Guo Moruo's poems were masterpieces of baihuawen and very influential among the younger readers, the domination of classical Chinese writing came to an end.

BANK OF CHINA. Bank founded in 1905 as Daqing Hubu Yinhang (Grand Qing Bank of the Board of Revenue). The bank's headquarters were in Beijing, but its major operation was at the Shanghai branch. It was renamed Daqing Yinhang (Bank of Grand Qing) in 1908. After the founding of the Republic of China, **Sun Yat-sen** renamed it the Bank of China. On 26 October 1928, it became a bank focusing on international remittance business, and its headquarters moved from Beijing to Shanghai. In the next year, it opened a branch in London. In 1949, the general administration office of the Bank of China followed the Nationalists in retreat to Taipei, where it was renamed the International Commercial Bank of China, while the other departments of the Bank of China remained in mainland China and continued business to the present day.

BANK OF COMMUNICATION. Bank founded in Beijing in 1907 and controlled by the **Communication Clique**, headed by Liang Shiyi. The bank was authorized to issue paper currency for the Qing government, and because of its close relations between the Communication Clique and the **Beiyang warlords**, it became a major financial source for the **Yuan Shikai** government. In 1928, the **Executive Yuan** of the Republic of China issued a "Regulations of Bank of Communication," making its business focus on investment in agriculture, mining, and industry. Its headquarters moved from Beijing to Shanghai. The Bank of Communication, except for its Hong Kong branch, was merged into the People's Construction Bank of China in the 1950s and no longer existed in mainland China until its reorganization in 1987 after China's "open-up" economic reforms.

BANNER REORGANIZATION OFFICE (*BIANTONG QIZHI CHU*). An institution established during the constitutional reform of the Qing regime. In August 1908, the Qing government issued the "Imperial Outline for a Constitution," which allowed intermarriage between **Manchu** and **Han** Chinese and encouraged the Manchu to become involved in agricultural production and other businesses. On 17 December, the Banner Reorganization Office was established.

The main goals of the office were to "provide for the Eight Banners' livelihood" and to "eliminate Manchu–Han differences" by no later than 1915. The office announced that the distribution of stipends to bannermen would continue indefinitely, but the new policy would change the tradition that Manchu should not be involved in farming and commerce. The office was to help the Manchu soldiers find jobs so as to promote "self-strength and self-reliance." The Banner Reorganization Office was replaced by the Office to Manage Eight Banners' Livelihood (*chouban baqi shengji chu*) in 1912. *See* also BANNER SYSTEM.

BANNER SYSTEM. Created by Nurhaci in 1615, this system was the principal institution of the **Manchu**s, which unified the Manchu people and defined Manchu identity. Nurhaci organized all the Jurchen tribes in Manchuria into eight groups, called the Eight Banners. Each of the groups was identified by the color (yellow, white, red, or blue) of its flag, which was either plain or bordered with a red or white fringe. The Eight Banners were ranked in descending order of social importance: bordered yellow, plain yellow, plain white, plain red, bordered white, bordered red, plain blue, and bordered blue. The first three, known as the Upper Three Banners, were under the direct command of the emperor, while the Lower Five Banners were commanded by Manchu princes. All Manchu people, including women and children, belonged to one of the banners. Membership was hereditary, but women changed their banner affiliation by marriage. The banner system was organized along military lines, for hunting and farming in peacetime and fighting in wartime. Each banner was divided into battalions, then subdivided into companies. The company was the primary social organization for the banner people and was headed by a captain whose major functions included military command, population registration, and taking care of the members' livelihood and welfare. The Manchu also incorporated other people, who submitted to their rule, into the banner system. The Mongol Banners and the Chinese Banners were established in 1635 and 1642, respectively. The Manchu banners, however, remained the more numerous and prestigious. In 1644, the Manchus conquered China and the Eight Banners were dispatched to station at various garrisons throughout the country. *See also* BANNER REORGANIZATION OFFICE.

BANNERMEN. Another name of the Manchus. As early as 1615, the Manchu leader Nurhaci established the Eight **Banner system**, which organized all the Jurchen tribes in Manchuria into eight groups, called the Eight Banners. Members of the Eight Banners were called *bannermen*. After they conquered China, the banner soldiers became more professional and bureaucratized. The male bannermen were required to be warriors, but they and their families were not allowed to farm land or do business. The state offered them land, but bannermen could only hire **Han** Chinese peasants to cultivate it for them. If they lost land, the government would provide them with food. The bannermen, even when not on active duty, could get stipends from the Qing government. Under all circumstances, bannermen were fed by the state. In addition, they enjoyed some legal privileges, including being tried by separate courts, reducing penalties, and others. *See also* BANNER REORGANIZATION OFFICE.

BAO DAI (1913–1997). A Vietnamese ruler of the Nguyen dynasty. Bao was crowned in 1926 at the age of 12 and served as king of **Annam** until June 1945, when he proclaimed the unification of Vietnam and himself as emperor of Vietnam. Two months later, he abdicated and handed power over to Ho Chi Minh. Afterward, he left Vietnam and lived in Hong Kong. In 1949, the French persuaded him to return, making him the "head of state" of South Vietnam, while Ho Chi Minh founded the Democratic Republic of Vietnam in the north. In 1955, a referendum was held and 98 percent of people voted to remove him. Bao Dai abdicated again and left for Paris.

BAODING MILITARY ACADEMY. One of four leading military academies in early modern China. It was first founded in 1903 in Baoding, Hebei Province, by **Yuan Shikai** and then rebuilt in June 1912 by the **Beijing government** of the Republic of China. The academy offered two-year training programs. It admitted nine terms of cadets, producing 6,574 military officers, of which 1,600 became generals. Many military leaders of early 20th-century China, including warlords and Nationalist and Communist generals, such as **Wu Peifu**, Sun Zhuanfan, **Chiang Kai-shek**, **Bai Chongxi**, and **Ye Ting**, studied or graduated from this academy. It served as a model for other military schools in the Republican period. Some of its graduates later became the instructors at the **Whampoa Military Academy**. The Baoding Military Academy was closed in August 1923.

***BAOJIA* SYSTEM.** A Chinese population registration system begun in the 11th century. It was built on a neighborhood basis to ensure law enforcement and civil control. Each bao consisted of 10 jias, while a jia consisted of 10 households. The leaders of the baos and jias were responsible for local order, taxation, security, and civil projects. Bao and jia were the basic social organizations in imperial China. In the Republican period, this system was further developed by **Chiang Kai-shek** in his **Encirclement and Suppression Campaigns** against the Communists. It was first pursued in the areas around the Communist bases and then carried out throughout the country. In 1936, Chiang Kai-shek pointed out that the baojia system had four functions: administration, education, economy, and military. He also argued that the purpose of the baojia system was to militarize the Chinese grassroots organizations. In 1939, the Nationalist government issued a law, Regulations on Organizations at the County Level or Below, which stipulated that a jia should typically consist of 10 households, no more than 15 and no fewer than six. These regulations also emphasized the mutual obligation of the baojia family members so that if one person committed a crime, all 10 families of the jia would be punished. The baojia system was abolished in 1949 after the Communists took over China.

BAOYI. "Slave" or "domestic slave" in the **Manchu** language. *Baoyi* were deprived of personal freedom and compelled to perform labor or services. Most baoyi were **Han** Chinese captured in wars before the Manchus conquered China. Some baoyi were sold to Manchu nobles by their parents, or by themselves, as a means of surviving extreme conditions. Nonetheless, the Manchu slavery system allowed baoyi to engage in different work for their masters or for the Manchu state. Some baoyi serving in the army or in the government might be promoted to high positions and own properties, but their relations to the previous masters would never change.

BAZAAR. "Marketplace" in Uighur. The earliest bazaars were established by the Russian merchants in Kashga (Kashi) and Khotan (Hetian) in 1775. After Urumqi became the capital of Xinjiang Province, more Chinese/Uighur bazaars were opened in that city. The primary trade between the Chinese and Russians was tea, silk, rhubarb, local wool, and hides in exchange for Russian spun thread, woven cloth, manufactured products, kitchen implements and tools, and kerosene. In 1762, the Qing government began to collect commercial taxes on the Russian–Chinese trade in Xinjiang. Most Russian merchants in 18th- and 19th-century bazaars were actually Uzbeks and Tatars, who were subsequently joined by Americans, Germans, and White Russians in the Republican era.

BEIJING, CONVENTION OF (1860). The Convention of Beijing consisted of three treaties China signed in 1860 with Great Britain, France, and Russia as a result of the **Arrow War**. The Sino-British treaty was signed on 24 October by **Prince Gong** and Lord Elgin; it clarified the Sino-British Treaty of **Tianjin** and added the following articles: (1) open Tianjin to foreign trade, (2) allow the British to recruit and export Chinese laborers, (3) cede a part of the Kowloon Peninsula to Britain, and (4) increase the war indemnity to 8 million taels silver. The treaty between China and France signed by Prince Gong and Baron Gros on 25 October included the same articles on Tianjin, Chinese labor, and the war indemnity. The treaty also stipulated that China would return all properties of the French churches confiscated by the Chinese government and offer French missionaries the right to buy or rent land in China. Russia claimed that it contributed to the treaty settlement between China and the Anglo-French alliance and pressured Prince Gong to sign a treaty with **Nikolai Ignatiev** on 14 November on the following terms: (1) ratify the Treaty of **Aigun**, (2) settle an eastern border along the Ussuri River to the limits of Korea and determine principles for demarcation of the western border, and (3) open Kashgar and Urga to Russian trade and consulates. Through the treaty, the Russians gained some 300,000 to 400,000 sq. mi. of territory from China. Because of the **most favored nation** treatment, Britain, France, and Russia also shared the benefits of all three treaties.

BEIJING GOVERNMENT (PEKING GOVERNMENT, 1912–1928). The central government of the Republic of China situated in Beijing. In 1912, after the South-North negotiation, **Sun Yat-sen** resigned in Nanjing. **Yuan Shikai** was elected president of the Republic of China, and he moved the capital to Beijing in March 1912. **Tang Shaoyi** was made the first premier of the government and won recognition by major foreign states. The Beijing government was the first democratic government in China, though it was a weak and inefficient one. It was often controlled by various **Beiyang warlords** and was therefore referred to as the "Beiyang government." In its 16 years, the presidency changed hands 15 times. Because Yuan quickly betrayed the republic and attempted to restore a monarchy, Sun established a military government in Guangzhou and staged the anti-Yuan **Second Revolution**. In 1926, Sun's successor, **Chiang Kai-shek**, launched the **Northern Expedition**, which defeated warlord military forces and established the new government of the Republic of China in Nanjing. The Beijing government formally ended with the recognition of the Nanjing government by the last northeastern warlord, **Zhang Xueliang**, in 1928.

BEIJING WOMEN'S NEWS (BEIJING NÜBAO). One of the earliest women's newspapers in modern China. It was founded on 20 August 1905 by Zhang Zhanyun and his daughter. Published in the vernacular language, it targeted lower-class women as its main readers. Zhang stated that the mission of the *Beijing Women's News* was to "promote women's learning and virtue." Besides reporting on major events, it created a special column on household management and discussed women's issues, such as self-education, professions, child education, economic self-sufficiency, and Western-style hygienic concerns. It also opened a section for a series of romantic novels. The editors offered free delivery of the papers to subscribers.

BEIPING PEACE NEGOTIATION (1949). By the end of 1948, the **People's Liberation Army** (PLA) had won a decisive victory in the civil war between the **Chinese Communist Party** (CCP) and the **Nationalist Party** (GMD). **Chiang Kai-shek** had to resign, and **Li Zongren** succeeded him as acting president of the Republic of China (ROC). In early 1949, the CCP destroyed the GMD's leading military forces and occupied North China, while the provinces south of the Yangtze River were still in the hands of the GMD government. Li asked for peace and sent a delegation headed by General **Zhang Zhizhong** to Beijing for negotiations. The negotiation started on 1 April 1949 in Beijing. After two weeks' talk, the CCP delegation headed by **Zhou Enlai** handed its draft agreement to the Nanjing delegation, demanding punishment of the GMD leaders as war prisoners, abolition of the constitution of the ROC, abolition of the legal system of the ROC, reorganization of the GMD's military forces, confiscation of all properties of bureaucratic capitalism, **land reform**, abolition of all unequal treaties with foreign countries, and convening of the **Chinese People's Political Consultative Conference**, excluding all reactionary elements, to establish a democratic coalition government and take over the power of the Nanjing Nationalist government and all its local governments.

The GMD's main purpose for the negotiations was to make peace and maintain the status quo in which the CCP controlled the north of the Yangtze River and the GMD governed the south. However, the CCP was determined to take over the whole of China and overthrow the Nationalist government. Zhou Enlai insisted that the CCP would not compromise on the eight terms, and he asked the GMD government to reply before 20 April. The Nanjing government felt that the terms were not acceptable, and on the night of 20 April, President Li Zongren sent a telegraph to the GMD delegation asking them to persuade the CCP to consider a new agreement. It was too late for Zhang to forward the request to the CCP, as the PLA had already recommenced its military campaign. The PLA crossed the Yangtze River in the early morning of 21 April 1949 and stormed the ROC's capital of Nanjing on 23 April. After the Beiping Peace Negotiation broke down and the Nanjing government fell apart, Zhang Zhizhong and other members of the GMD delegation decided to stay in Beiping.

BEIYANG ARMY. A Western-style military force of the Qing dynasty, founded in the late 19th century. In 1895, after China's defeat by Japan, the **Guangxu Emperor** ordered **Yuan Shikai** to train a brigade-sized army at Xiaozhan, near Tianjin. Since Yuan was **Li Hongzhang**'s previous subordinate, most troops Yuan trained at Xiaozhan originated from Li's Huai Army. The emperor attempted to build up the new military force, which was called the **New Army**. This army followed the organizational system of Western armies, was equipped with Western weaponry, and was placed under Yuan's personal control. Like a personal army, the soldiers and officers of the Beiyang Army were loyal not to the emperor or the central government but only to its commander, Yuan Shikai. Because of this, when Yuan was appointed minister of Beiyang affairs in 1901, the army was referred to as the Beiyang Army. Yuan recruited soldiers in North China and built the **Baoding Military Academy** to train its officers. Many of the officers of the Beiyang Army later became leading figures in modern China, including three presidents of the Republic of China, one premier, and many warlords.

BEIYANG FLEET. One of the modernized Chinese naval forces during the late Qing dynasty. Its development was prompted by the Japanese attack against Taiwan in 1874. In that year, the Qing court decided to allocate 4 million taels per year to build up a naval force consisting of four fleets. The Beiyang Fleet was in charge of the coastal defense of Beijing and North China, the Nanyang Fleet protected the south of Shandong Province, and the Liangguang Fleet defended the provinces of Guangdong and Guangxi. The Beiyang Fleet was created by Li Hongzhang, the governor of Zhili, who began purchasing warships from Germany and Great Britain in 1875. In 1881, two naval bases were constructed in Lushun (Port Arthur) and Weihaiwei, and four years later the Naval Yamen (Ministry of Navy) was formally constituted. The Beiyang Fleet had 78 warships with a total tonnage of 83,900 tons, which was believed to be the "best navy in Asia" and "the 6th best in the world" during the late 1880s. However, it was defeated by the Japanese fleet in 1894 and was finally annihilated in Weihaiwei in 1895.

BEIYANG WARLORDS. In 1895, **Yuan Shikai** began to train a new army at Xiaozhan, near Tianjin. This army was called the **Beiyang Army** and was loyal to Yuan Shikai. After Yuan's death, the powerful officers of this army were divided into three cliques: the **Anhui Clique** headed by Duan Qirui, the **Zhili Clique** headed by Feng Guozhang, and the **Fengtian Clique** headed by **Zhang Zuolin**. They were the major Beiyang warlords in modern China. Moreover, people usually referred to all warlords north of the Yangtze River as "Beiyang warlords," including the Feng Clique headed by **Feng Yuxiang** and the Jin Clique headed by **Yan Xishan**. These warlords were supported by different foreign countries, either by Great Britain, Japan, or Russia/Soviet Union. The warlords not only turned the regions under their control into independent kingdoms but also fought for control over the whole of China. Therefore, the different cliques often engaged in military conflicts.

The most disastrous wars included that between the Zhili and the Anhui cliques in 1920, in which the Zhili Clique defeated its rival and took control of the **Beijing government**. Another war erupted between the Zhili Clique and the Fengtian Clique between 1922 and 1924; this led to the domination of the Fengtian Clique in Beijing. Seeing that these wars brought endless suffering to the Chinese people and destroyed the Chinese economy, **Sun Yat-sen** was determined to eliminate **warlordism**. After Sun's death, the **Nationalist Party** took up his unfinished task and launched the **Northern Expedition** in 1927. In the next year, the **National Revolutionary Army** destroyed the leading forces of the Zhili Clique and drove the Fengtian Clique out of China proper. The other local warlords were either eliminated in the following campaigns or forced to proclaim their acceptance of the leadership of the Nationalist government in Nanjing.

BETHUNE, HENRY NORMAN (1890–1939). Canadian doctor and national hero in China. Born in Gravenhurst, Ontario, Bethune was the son of a Presbyterian minister. His grandfather, Dr. Norman Bethune Sr., was a noted Canadian physician who in the 1850s cofounded Trinity College Medical School, which was later absorbed by the University of Toronto. The young Bethune enrolled at the University of Toronto in September 1909 and completed an accelerated medical degree in December 1916. His first private medical practice was in Detroit, Michigan, where he contracted tuberculosis from working with the poor. Bethune joined the Communist Party of Canada in 1935 and went to Spain (1936–1937) to help in the struggle for democracy against totalitarian fascism. In Spain, he created mobile medical units, models for the later development of the U.S. Mobile Army Surgical Hospital (MASH), and developed the first practical method for transporting blood in a battlefield.

Bethune went to China (1938–1939) to help the Communists fight against Japanese imperialism. In China, he worked with carpenters and blacksmiths to forge new surgical tools and established a training school for doctors, nurses, and orderlies. He improved on a number of surgical instruments. His most famous instrument was the Bethune Rib Shears. Bethune died on 12 November 1939 of blood poisoning from a cut he received while performing surgery for a solder of the Communist **Eighth Route Army**. Bethune finally received international recognition when **Mao Zedong** published his essay titled "In Memory of Norman Bethune," in which Mao argues that Bethune is "noble-minded and pure, a man of moral integrity and above vulgar interests, a man who is of value to the people." Bethune is one of the few Westerners to whom Communist China has dedicated statues. He is buried in the Revolutionary Martyrs' Cemetery in Shijiazhuang, Hebei Province. In this city, Bethune Military Medical College, Bethune Specialized Medical College, and Bethune International Peace Hospital were established to commemorate him. Following the 1973 visit to China by Canadian prime minister Pierre Trudeau, the government of Canada purchased the Ontario home in which Bethune was born. In 1976, the restored building was opened to the public as Bethune Memorial House.

BIG FOUR. The four major Allied powers in World War II: the United States, Great Britain, the Soviet Union, and China. In 1943, U.S. secretary of war Henry Stimson spoke highly of "the brilliant resistance to aggression which the Chinese have made and are making." Based on this, U.S. president Franklin D. Roosevelt and Secretary of State Cordell Hull persuaded British foreign minister Anthony Eden and Soviet foreign minister Vyacheslav Molotov to accept China as one of the cosigners of the Moscow Declaration of 1 November 1943. This document indicated that China was one of the Big Four who pledged to prosecute the war until the final victory.

BIG SWORD SOCIETY. One of the secret societies of peasants in the late Qing period, most popular in the provinces of Shandong, Henan, Anhui, and Jiangsu. Big swords used to be their weapons and later became the logo of the society. While most of its members were peasants, some craftsmen, peddlers, and poor intellectuals also joined. They believed in mystical rituals that would make them immune to bullets. In 1896, led by Liu Shirui and Cao Deli, the society revolted in Shandong Province. They killed two German missionaries, attacked other missionaries and Chinese Christians, and burned Christian churches. Their slogan was "Overthrow the Qing and eliminate the foreigner." The Big Sword Society was regarded as the pioneer of the **Boxer Rebellion**. The Qing government suppressed the rebellion and tried to wipe out its influence, but the Big Sword Society survived up to the 1930s. The society did not have a clear political program and was often used by local strongmen. However, the society and its members also contributed to several revolutionary movements. For example, the Big Sword Society offered major support to **Nationalist Party** leader **Song Jiaoren**, engaged in a military campaign against the Fengtian warlord **Zhang Zuolin**, and joined the Anti-Japanese Volunteer Armies in Manchuria, resisting the Japanese invasion in the 1930s.

BING XIN (1900–1999). The pen name of Xie Wanyin, prominent writer of children's literature. Born in Fuzhou, Fujian Province, into the family of a naval officer, Bing grew up in a small coastal town, Yantai, Shandong Province, where her father served as principal of a naval school. Bing returned to Fuzhou after the **Republican Revolution** and in 1912 was enrolled at the middle school attached to the Fuzhou Women's Normal School. One year later, her father was offered a position in the Republican government and took the family to Beijing. Dreaming of becoming a good doctor, Bing went to the Preparatory School for Beijing Women's Medical Union College. However, the **New Culture Movement** changed her career. She began to write in the vernacular language and publish essays, novels, and poems in various journals. In 1923, Bing traveled to the United States and studied at Wesleyan University. In the meantime, she published her essay series "To Juvenile Readers." The essays were so appealing to Chinese children that they made her a rising star in the literary world. In the United States, Bing met Wu Wenchao, a Chinese student of sociology at Dartmouth College, and she married him. After she obtained her master's degree in literature in 1926, Bing returned to China and began to teach literature at **Yenching University**, Peking Women's College, and Tsinghua University.

During the **Second Sino-Japanese War**, Bing and her husband moved to southwest China and continued their teaching careers. In 1940, she was elected a member of the National Senate and published more influential essays, including "To Juvenile Readers (II)" and "On Women." At the end of the war, Bing traveled to Japan and taught at Japanese universities. In 1949, she returned to China. When she was 70 years old, the Cultural Revolution began and Bing was sent to the countryside to do physical work. However, her attitude toward life remained optimistic. She published "To Juvenile Readers (III)" after the Cultural Revolution. On 28 February 1999, Bing died in the Beijing Hospital at the age of 99.

BLACK FLAG ARMY. A local military force in the province of Guangxi. The name came from its use of black flags with seven stars. Most of its troops were remnants of the **Taiping** rebels and largely of ethnic Zhuang background. Because of the offensive of the Qing army, the Black Flag Army retreated to Vietnam in 1867. However, under their leader Liu Yongfu (a **Hakka**, his Vietnamese name was Luu Vinh Phuc), the Black Flag Army joined the Qing troops to participate in the **Sino-French War**. Liu's troops defeated a battalion of the French Foreign Legion at Tuyen Quang. Although the Annamite court bestowed official rank on Liu Yongfu, he returned to China after the war. From April to June 1868, the Qing court issued nine decrees to call the Black Flag Army back to China. After the return of the 3,000 troops in October, the court offered Liu a low position and cut the army down to 300. In July 1894, the Black Flag Army was reorganized and dispatched to Taiwan to join the **First Sino-Japanese War**. Although China lost the war and signed the **Treaty of Shimonoseki** ceding Taiwan to Japan, the Black Flag Army resisted the Japanese takeover, and most of its soldiers and officers died in subsequent fighting.

BLUE SHIRTS (SOCIETY FOR DILIGENT PRACTICE). An organization within the **Nationalist Party** (GMD). The formal name was *li xing she* (Society for Diligent Practice). In its early days, one of its leaders, Liu Jianquan, required all its members to wear blue shirts. Founded by a group of GMD members with ethics and ideals in the early 1930s, it was modeled on the Italian Blackshirts and German Brownshirts, believing in the application of fascism in China. The early members of the Blue Shirts were alumni of the **Whampoa Military Academy**, and its leaders included He Zhonghan, Liu Jianquan, Hu Zhongnan, and Kang Ze. They believed that the GMD had become too weak and degenerate and had disappointed the broad masses of the people. They called for a **second revolution** to recreate the image and soul of the GMD. The Blue Shirts proposed a series of programs, including quelling local warlord remnants and strengthening the central government, rebuilding military forces to resist Japanese aggression, banning opium smoking, uprooting corruption, and reviving rural areas. The society also required its members to have minimum salaries and to be honest, assiduous, and devoted. The society's programs were appreciated by **Chiang Kai-shek**, who defined the mission of the Blue Shirts and encouraged people to join it. The Blue Shirts existed for only a short period of time and were disbanded after China declared war on Germany and Italy in the 1940s.

BLUE SKY, WHITE SUN. The party flag and emblem of the **Chinese Nationalist Party (Guomindang)**. It is also the naval jack of the Navy of the Republic of China. The flag was originally designed by Lu Hao-tung, a martyr of the **Republican Revolution**, for the uprising launched by the **Revive China Society** in 1895. It was to be raised if the revolutionaries captured the city of Guangzhou. In 1905, **Sun Yat-sen** added a red field to the design and suggested its adoption as the national flag of China. Due to the objection of **Huang Xing** and other **Tongmenghui** leaders, the suggestion was not accepted. Instead, when the Republic of China was founded, it adopted the "five-colored" flag, implying harmonic coexistence of five major ethnic groups in China: **Han, Manchu,** Hui, Mongol, and Tibetan. It was not until 1927, when **Chiang Kai-shek** reunified China, that the "Blue Sky, White Sun, and a Wholly Red Earth" became the national flag of the Republic of China.

BO GU (QIN BANGXIAN, 1907–1946). An early leader of the **Chinese Communist Party** (CCP) and one of the **Twenty-eight Bolsheviks**. Born in Wuxi, Jiangsu Province, Bo Gu studied at the Suzhou Industrial School in his early years. Actively involved in the local student movement against imperialism and warlords, Bo Gu was elected chairman of the Suzhou Student Association. In 1925, Bo Gu entered the Communist-sponsored Shanghai University, where he joined the CCP. In 1926, Bo Gu was sent to Moscow to receive further training at Sun Yat-sen University. With **Wang Ming, Zhang Wentian,** Wang Jiaxiang, **Yang Shangkun,** and others, he formed a radical Communist group known as the Twenty-eight Bolsheviks. This group of Chinese Communist students won the full trust of the **Comintern** and thus became the leading faction in the CCP Politburo. When he returned to China, Bo Gu was 25 years old, but between 1931 and 1935 he was the de facto leader of the CCP.

During Chiang Kai-shek's fifth **Encirclement and Suppression Campaign,** Bo Gu, **Zhou Enlai,** and **Otto Braun,** the military adviser from the Comintern, formed a three-man team to command the **Red Army.** Due to the incompetency of this three-man team, the Red

Army was defeated by Chiang's troops and forced to evacuate from the **Jiangxi Soviet**. Because his leadership continued to cause heavy casualties in the Red Army, Bo Gu was replaced by **Mao Zedong** in January 1935. Bo Gu was appointed minister of the Organization Department of CCP in 1937, and then served as director of the CCP's formal newspaper, *Jie fang Daily,* and Xinhua News Agency. In the 7th National Congress of the CCP in 1945, Bo Gu was listed as the last member of the Central Committee. At the end of the **Second Sino-Japanese War**, Bo Gu was a member of the CCP delegation sent to **Chongqing** for negotiations with the **Chinese Nationalist Party**. On the way back to **Yan'an**, the delegates' plane crashed in Shanxi and Bo Gu was killed with all the other passengers.

BOGUE, CONVENTION OF (1846). The full name of this treaty was the Convention between Great Britain and China Relative to the Admission of Foreigners into the City of Canton and to the Evacuation of the Stand of Chushan by the British Forces. It was signed on 4 April 1846 by Qiying, the Chinese imperial commissioner, and governor of Hong Kong John Francis Davis at Fort Humen, Guangdong Province. Qiying felt pressure from both sides. On one hand, the British demanded to enter Canton; on the other, the gentry and the people of Canton resolutely opposed the opening of the city. Agreements in the treaty included the following: the British would return Zhoushan to China, and the Qing government promised the nonalienation of Zhoushan Island to any other power. The British would postpone their entry into the city, but China promised to let the British enter the city of Canton soon and would ensure the security of those who did so.

BOGUE, TREATY OF (HUMEN TREATY, 1843). The formal name of this treaty was the Supplement Treaty at Bogue. It was signed on 8 October 1843 by Qiying, the Chinese imperial commissioner, and Sir Henry Pottinger at Fort Humen, Gaungdong Province. The treaty conferred on Great Britain unilateral most favored nation status, which meant that China would grant it whatever privileges might be conceded to other powers later. The treaty also stipulated a fixed tariff of 4 to 13 percent for import duty and 1.5 to 19.75 percent for export duty. Another important article was on **extraterritoriality**, which offered British citizens an exemption from Chinese law.

BOXER PROTOCOL • 31

BORODIN, MIKHAIL MARKOVICH (1884–1951). The representative of the **Comintern** in China between 1923 and 1927. Borodin joined the Bolshevik Party in 1903 and was subsequently arrested by the czarist government. He then immigrated to the United States and in 1907 joined the American Socialist Party in Chicago. After the Bolshevik Revolution, Borodin returned to Russia and worked for the Committee of Foreign Affairs. From 1919 to 1921, he served as the Comintern's special agent in Mexico and the United States. In 1923, the Comintern assigned him to China as the preeminent adviser to **Sun Yat-sen**. Borodin worked out a concrete plan to reorganize the GMD, attended the First National Conference of the GMD, and drafted the conference resolution. He helped Sun found the **Whampoa Military Academy** and enabled Sun to gain Soviet support in terms of funds, armaments, and personnel. Borodin persuaded the CCP to cooperate with the GMD and accept **Chiang Kai-shek**'s leadership.

When Chiang began to expel the Communists and attacked a peasant movement led by the Communists, Borodin compromised his principles. It was not until the open split between the CCP and the GMD that Borodin began to criticize Chiang, but he still felt that the left-wing GMD leaders, such as **Wang Jingwei**, would support him. Borodin became disillusioned with the GMD when the government issued an order to arrest him. He then fled to Russia, where he served briefly as the acting head of the Soviet government's news agency and chief editor of the English journal *Moscow News*. Borodin had to bear the responsibility for the Comintern's failure in China and had no chance of regaining power. In February 1949, Borodin was accused of being an American spy and was sent to a labor camp in Siberia. He died two years later.

BOXER PROTOCOL (INTERNATIONAL PROTOCOL, 1901). Treaty signed by the Qing government with the eight nations that took part in the war with China in 1900, caused by the **Boxer Rebellion**. The eight nations, including Great Britain, France, Germany, Italy, Belgium, Russia, the United States, and Japan, engaged in the suppression of the Boxers and required compensation from the Qing government. On 24 December 1900, the eight powers came to an agreement on a joint note of 12 demands. The Chinese representatives, **Li Hongzhang** and Prince Qing, accepted their terms and signed the

Boxer Protocol on 7 September 1901. Consequently, the Qing government promised (1) to ban the Boxers forever, (2) to punish and execute the leading supporters of the Boxers, (3) to allow the eight powers to establish a permanent legation guard, (4) to destroy the Daku Forts and other forts in the area extending from Beijing to the sea, (5) to allow the stationing of foreign troops in key points between Beijing and the sea, (6) to suspend the Chinese importation of arms for two years, (7) to suspend the **civil service examination** for five years, and (8) to pay the eight powers an indemnity of 450 million taels. This was an overwhelming burden for China since its total annual income was only 200 million taels. The payment had to be completed in 39 years at 4 percent annual interest. The Chinese maritime customs, *lijin* (a sort of domestic transportation tax), and a salt tax served as security. When the indemnity was eventually paid off by the end of 1940, it would total about 1 billion taels. The indemnity drastically crippled China's economy, and the treaty severely infringed on China's sovereignty.

BOXER REBELLION (1899–1901). Violent antiforeign and anti-Christian movement. The rebellion was a Chinese response to domestic crises and foreign intrusion. Today, controversy still exists about the nature and significance of the movement. The Boxers were a semireligious and semimartial secret society in Shandong Province. They believed that they could use charms, incantations, and rituals to invoke supernatural powers, making themselves immune to swords and bullets. Because of their anti-**Manchu** and antigovernment inclinations, the Qing government had banned the activities of the Boxers. As Germany took Shandong as its concession, however, the conflicts between foreign churches and Chinese peasants on the issues of land and lawsuits came to the fore. When the Boxers turned their attention to the missionaries and their Chinese converts, the Qing government saw a possibility to use the Boxers.

In October 1898, the Boxers in the county of Guanxian, headed by Yan Shuqin, burned a church and revolted. In the meantime, the Boxers dropped their anti-Manchu slogan and replaced it with "Revive the Qing and destroy the foreigner." The governor of Shandong, Zhang Rumei, suggested that the Qing court offer amnesty and enlistment to the Boxers. The leading supporters of the Boxers included Prince Tuan, Prince Chuan, and Grand Secretary Kangyi. Having just pulled down the **Hundred Days' Reform**, the **Dowager Cixi** was frustrated with foreign influence and readily embraced the suggestion. Inspired by the Qing court, the Boxers attacked missionaries; destroyed churches, missionary schools, and hospitals; and harried and even killed Chinese converts and those who possessed foreign objects. Finally, the Boxers entered Beijing, and with old-style swords and lances as their weaponry, laid siege to the foreign legations in June 1900.

When the German envoy, Klemens Freiherr von Ketteler, was killed en route to the **Zongli Yamen** on 20 June, the Western powers demanded redress. The next day, the Dowager Cixi declared war on eight foreign countries, namely, Great Britain, France, Germany, Belgium, Italy, Russia, Japan, and the United States. In response to this, the **Eight-Nation Alliance** was formed, and on 4 August 1900, its expeditionary column of about 20,000 troops launched a counterattack. They quickly crushed the Boxers and began looting Chinese property in Beijing. The Dowager Cixi fled to Xi'an, and **Li Hongzhang** was called to Beijing to negotiate with the foreign powers. As a result, the treaty known as the **Boxer Protocol** was signed in September 1901. The Qing court ordered suppression of the Boxers and punished the leading Boxer supporters. It also agreed to pay the eight powers an indemnity of 450 million taels.

BRAUN, OTTO (1900–1974). Military adviser of the **Comintern** to the **Chinese Communist Party** (CCP), known to most Chinese as Li De. Born in Munich, Germany, Braun grew up in an orphanage. He joined the German Communist Party in 1918. He was arrested twice (1921 and 1926) and rescued by the Communists, and then fled to Moscow. After training at the Soviet Military Academy, Braun was dispatched to China as the military adviser to the Chinese Red Army. With **Bo Gu** and **Zhou Enlai**, Braun formed the three-man group in charge of the CCP's military affairs. He repudiated **Mao Zedong**'s **guerrilla warfare** and maintained a strategy of conventional warfare with **Chiang Kai-shek**'s troops. Due to Braun's incompetent command, the Red Army was defeated in the **Jiangxi Soviet** and suffered great casualities during the **Long March**. In January 1935, Braun was dismissed from office and Mao Zedong became the de facto leader of the CCP. Later during the Long March, Braun supported Mao in his struggle with **Zhang Guotao** and followed the Central Red Army to **Yan'an**.

In 1939, Braun was called back to the Soviet Union. He asked to bring his second wife, Li Lilian, with him, but this request was not approved. Braun worked in a labor camp as a political instructor in Siberia between 1941 and 1945. After the death of Joseph Stalin in 1953, Braun was allowed to return to Germany, where he worked as a researcher and translator at the German Institute for Marxist Studies. In 1973, he published his memoirs of his experience in Yan'an. Braun died on 15 August 1974 in Berlin.

BRITISH EAST INDIA COMPANY. Generally known as the East India Company, it was founded by royal charter on 31 December 1600. The company was organized for the London businessmen who banded together to make money importing spices from South Asia. The company encouraged British merchants in India to do business with China by granting charters to private ships, whose business made up 30 percent of the total British trade in China between 1764 and 1800. In addition, the company's policy allowed the crews to carry a certain amount of goods to do private business to compensate their small salaries. This private trade accounted for about 15 percent of the total British trade with China. The British bought tea, silk, chinaware, rhubarb, lacquered ware, and cassia from China and tried to sell woolens, lead, tin, iron, copper, furs, linen, and various knickknacks in Canton. However, the Chinese showed less interest in buying British commodities, and the East India Company suffered a 25.1 million–tael deficit from 1755 to 1795.

The balance of trade did not reverse in British favor until the company begun to export opium from India to China. In the late 18th century, the company established a monopoly over the opium cultivation from seedling to sale of the finished product. Because the opium trade was illegal in China, the East India Company officially disengaged from trafficking opium but offered licenses to private ships to sail to China for distribution. Opium production provided over 5 percent of the company's revenue in India in 1826, and the proportion increased to 12 percent in 1850. The company monopoly over the lucrative China trade came under severe attack by other British merchants. During its heyday, the British East India Company not only occupied the Asian market but was also the de facto ruler of India. After the 1857 Indian Mutiny, the British Colonial Office took over the company's power, and it went out of existence in 1873.

BUCK, PEARL S. (1892–1973). Famous American writer who is most known for her novels set in China. Born into a missionary family in Hillsboro, West Virginia, Buck went to China with her family when she was three months old. Growing up in China with Chinese as her native language, Buck learned English as a second language from her mother and a private tutor. In 1910, Buck left China and went to Randolph-Macon Woman's College to study psychology; she also obtained a master's in art from Cornell University. Buck married John Lossing Buck, who was an agricultural economist working at Jingling University in Nanjing. Buck joined her husband there to teach English. With the publication of *East Wind, West Wind*, Pearl Buck began her literary career. *The Good Earth*, the story of a Chinese farmer's experience of turmoil during the revolution, won Buck the Pulitzer Prize for the Novel in 1932. She continued to write about China and won the William Dean Howells Medal in 1935. Buck wrote over 100 works, including the famous biographies of her parents, *The Exile* and *Fighting Angel*, and the nonfiction book *China as I See It*. In 1938, she became the first American woman to win the Nobel Prize for Literature. Buck divorced and then got remarried to Richard J. Walsh, president of the John Day Publishing Company. With Walsh, she adopted six children. In 1949, protesting the American adoption services that refused Asian and mixed-race children, Buck established the Welcome House, Inc., the first international and interracial adoption agency. She also established the Pearl S. Buck Foundation in 1964 to support child sponsorship programs in Asia. Pearl Buck died on 6 March 1973 in Danby, Vermont.

BURHAN SHAHIDI (1894–1989). Prominent leader of Uighur nationality and statesman of modern China. Born in Aksu, Xinjiang, Burhan was recognized for his talent with languages. He could fluently speak Chinese, Russian, German, and his native Uighur. In 1912, Burhan traveled to Germany and enrolled in the Department of Political Science and Economics at the University of Berlin. After graduation, he returned to Xinjiang via Moscow. Burhan worked in the Chinese warlord governments in Xinjiang, serving as an interpreter and junior government officer. He also successfully managed a cross-border trading business with Russians. In 1937, the warlord governor **Sheng Shicai** accused him of being a "Trotskyite element" and jailed Burhan for seven years. In 1944, after the collapse of Sheng

Shicai's government, Burhan was released and appointed a deputy commissioner of civil affairs and commander of the Peace Preservation Corps in Xinjiang. He took part in the Soviet-supported **Three Districts Revolution** in west Xinjiang and served as vice-chairman of its revolutionary government. **Zhang Zhizhong**, the chief leader of the Nationalist government in Northwest China and chairman of the Northwest China Administrative Committee, saw Burhan as a "patriotic person who had a good sense of the motherland [China]," and recommended that Burhan be appointed governor of Xinjiang. In 1949, Burhan established close relations with the Soviet Union and the **Chinese Communist Party** (CCP) and then worked with **Tao Zhiyue** to launch an uprising, which made the Communist takeover of Xinjiang a "peaceful liberation." In 1949, Burhan joined the CCP and continued as governor of Xinjiang. He was also appointed vice chairman of the Committee for Ethnic Affairs of the Chinese Congress and vice-chairman of the **Chinese People's Political Consultative Conference**.

BURLINGAME, ANSON (1820–1870). American lawyer, statesman, and diplomat. Burlingame was the only foreigner who served as Chinese ambassador to the United States and Europe. Born in New Berlin, New York, Burlingame graduated from Harvard Law School in 1846 and married Jane Cornelia Livermore in the next year. He was elected a member of the Massachusetts constitutional convention in 1853, a state senator from 1853 to 1854, and a U.S. representative from 1855 to 1861. A famous abolitionist, Burlingame was also a founding member of the Republican Party. On 14 June 1861, President Abraham Lincoln sent him to China, and Burlingame arrived in Beijing on 20 July 1862 as part of the first group of foreign ministers in China. During his service in Beijing, Burlingame proposed a "cooperative policy," advocating the recognition of Chinese territorial sovereignty and declaring that the United States did not seek any concessions in China.

When Burlingame completed his six-year service on 16 November 1867, **Prince Gong** suggested appointing him as Chinese envoy extraordinary and minister plenipotentiary to head a Chinese diplomatic mission to the United States and Europe. The **Guangxu Emperor** approved this suggestion. After the mission arrived in the United States in March 1868, Burlingame signed with the American government the first equal international treaty for China in the 19th century—the Supplemental **Reed Treaty** of 1868, later known as the Burlingame Treaty. Burlingame's visit to London was also successful: Queen Victoria met him on 20 October and the British foreign minister presented a formal note to express his agreement with Burlingame's policy toward China. On 2 January 1869, his mission arrived in Paris. Burlingame stayed in France for half a year to seek a favorable treaty for China, but he could not make any progress. During the next year, the mission went to Berlin and had the German premier make a diplomatic statement in favor of China. On 1 February 1870, Burlingame went to Russia. In meeting the czar, Burlingame was frustrated by the Russians, who refused to broach the issue of the country's territorial conflicts with China. While in Russia, Burlingame contracted pneumonia and died suddenly at Saint Petersburg on 23 February 1870. The Guangxu Emperor granted him a first-rank official title and a 10,000-tael pension. Two towns, in California and Kansas, are named after Anson Burlingame. *See also* COOPERATIVE POLICY.

BUTTERFIELD & SWIRE. A major British company in Shanghai. In 1861, a Liverpool import-export merchant, John Swire, began to trade with China through agents Augustine Heard & Co. In 1866, in partnership with R. S. Butterfield, Butterfield & Swire was established in Shanghai. Although the alliance was dissolved after two years, the company kept the name and thrived for another century. Swire also gave the company a Chinese name, "Taikoo" (Great and Ancient), which has been more widely known in Asia. Soon the company shifted its major business from import-export to navigation, becoming a major competitor of China Merchants Steam Navigation Company. It had only four ships in the beginning but quickly increased this to 87 by 1933. Butterfield & Swire closed its China offices in 1953, four years after the establishment of the People's Republic of China. Its Butterfield & Swire branch in Hong Kong was renamed John Swire & Sons (H.K.) Ltd. in 1974.

BUTTERFLIES FICTION (*YUANYANG HUDIE PAI*). A genre of fiction that flourished in the early Republican period. This type of novel and short story was first popular in Shanghai and then became popular all over the country. The theme of this fiction was always love and death, but the stories covered various social settings and people: imperial palaces, court rooms, family compounds, gangsters, prostitutes, bandits, detectives, students, and revolutionaries. The most famous work was *Jade-Pear Spirit*, the best-selling novel by Xu Zhenya (published in 1912). This extremely passionate love story portrays a protagonist who chooses to die for the 1911 Revolution; the book gave meaning to a work of "idle amusement" and won the acclaim of a great number of urban readers. The commercial success of butterfly fiction was ascribed to its operation as mere play, entertainment, and a weekend pastime. The writers of this fiction were referred to as the "Mandarin Duck and Butterfly School." After 1949, as the Communists' policies advocated that literature serve politics, no more works of butterfly fiction were published in mainland China.

– C –

CAI E (1882–1916). Military leader in modern China and the initiator of the **Republic Protection Campaign**. Born into the family of a poor peasant in Shaoyang, Hunan Province, Cai enrolled in the Changsha Modern School, where he studied with **Liang Qichao** and **Tan Sitong** and accepted their reformist ideas. In 1899, Cai traveled to Japan to study business and then enrolled at the Japanese Imperial Military Academy in Tokyo. In 1904, he returned to China and was appointed brigade commander in Yunnan, where he began to train the Chinese imperial army using Western methods. He also served as a military instructor for the **New Armies** in Hunan and Guangxi. Cai did not join the **Tongmenghui**, but he established close ties with revolutionaries and promised his support to anti-Manchu uprisings. On 30 October 1911, with Li Genyuan, a local leader of the Tongmenghui, Cai led the uprising of the New Army in Kunming and established the provincial military government, in which he served as the chief commander of the insurrectionary army and governor of Yunnan. In 1913, **Yuan Shikai** failed to woo Cai to join his monarchist movement and decided to detain him in Beijing, but Cai managed to flee to Kunming. When Yuan proclaimed himself emperor, Cai made Yunnan the first province to declare its independence. Many other provinces followed suit. Cai launched the anti-Yuan campaign to "eliminate the country's thief, defend the republic, uphold democracy, and develop the spirit of popular sovereignty." His Republic Protection Army defeated Yuan's troops in Sichuan; this forced Yuan to abandon monarchism. After Yuan's death, Cai was made military governor of Yunnan. In August 1916, he went to Japan for medical treatment but died there three months later in Fukuoka at the age of 34.

CAI TINGKAI (1892–1968). Chinese general. Born in Luoding, Guangdong Province, Cai graduated from **Baoding Military Academy**. He served in the Guangdong Army during the **Northern Expedition**. In 1927, Cai took part in the **Nanchang Mutiny** but soon led his troops to break with the Communists. Cai became famous for commanding the **Nineteenth Route Army** in the defense of Shanghai during the Shanghai War of 1932. Despite inferior military equipment and heavy casualties, his Nineteenth Route Army put up such fierce resistance that the Japanese were unable to take the city. After the cease-fire in Shanghai, Cai and his Nineteenth Route Army were dispatched to Fujian to fight the **Chinese Communist Party** (CCP). In November 1933, with **Li Jishen** and Jiang Guangnai, Cai revolted and established the Fujian People's Government against the Japanese and **Chiang Kaishek**. Although Cai successfully reformed his army and enhanced its combat capacity, he did not gain enough local support or cooperation from the Communists. On 21 January 1934, the Nineteenth Route Army was defeated by Chiang, and Cai was forced into exile. During the **Second Sino-Japanese War**, Cai returned to China and was made commander of the 26th Army Group in the Battle of South Guangxi. In 1947, he defected to the CCP, leading his military to join the **People's Liberation Army**. After 1949, he served as a member of the National Defense Committee of the People's Republic of China.

CAI YUANPEI (1868–1940). Prominent educator of modern China. Born in Shanying, Zhejiang Province, Cai obtained the *jinshi* degree and was appointed to the **Hanlin Academy**. In 1898, he gave up this government position and devoted himself to promoting education in China. He became involved in the administrations of various institutions, such as the Shaoxing Chinese-Western School and the Aiguo School for Girls in Shanghai. In 1904, he established the *guangfuhui* (**Recovery Society**), which was merged into the **Tongmenghui** the next year. In 1907, he traveled to Germany and studied philosophy, psychology, and art history at the University of Leipzig. Cai was appointed the minister of education of the Republic of China in 1912 but soon resigned and went to Europe again. From 1917 through 1927, he was the chancellor of **Peking University**, where he encouraged the introduction of new ideas, recruited scholars of various political and academic perspectives, and advocated research and academic freedom, making Peking University a birthplace of the **New Culture Movement**.

Cai sharply criticized the Chinese traditional education philosophy, supported vernacular literature, and spoke out for women's rights. To promote education reforms, he addressed the equal importance of five dimensions of education: "Virtue, Wisdom, Health, Collectivity, and Beauty." He created a credit system for students at Peking University and suggested that professors run the university. He also opened night schools attached to the university for workers and the poor. In 1927, he cofounded the National College of Music in Shanghai, and he established the National School of Art in Hangzhou the next year. He refused all government appointments and held only the position of the first president of the Academia Sinica. Cai published extensively on education, ethics, aesthetics, and ethnic studies. He married three times, his first two wives dying early of sickness. From these three marriages, he had five sons and two daughters. Cai died in Hong Kong at the age of 72.

CAIRO CONFERENCE. An international conference attended by the Chinese leader **Chiang Kai-shek**, American president Franklin D. Roosevelt, and British prime minister Winston Churchill on 25–26 November 1943. The conference announced the Allied position against Japan in World War II and made decisions regarding the postwar global order in Asia. On 27 November 1943, the three leaders signed the Cairo Declaration, which was released in the Cairo Communiqué via radio on 1 December. This document pledged the continuation of the war against Japan until Japan's unconditional surrender, forswore territorial ambitions, and promised to strip Japan of all territory acquired since 1895. The Cairo Declaration made the clear assertion that "all the territories Japan has stolen from the Chinese, such as Manchuria, Formosa, and the Pescadores, shall be restored to the Republic of China."

CALLIGRAPHY. The art of writing Chinese characters with an ink brush, which gives form to characters in an expressive, harmonious, and skillful manner. It was a basic skill for Confucian students to learn, and for centuries the Chinese literati were expected to master the art of calligraphy. The main categories of Chinese-character calligraphy include seal script, clerical script (official script), regular script (block script), running script (semicursive script), and grass script (cursive script). Calligraphy should be included in all Chinese paintings and artistic works.

CANTON COMMUNE (1927). The revolutionary committee established by the **Chinese Communist Party** during the **Guangzhou Mutiny** in December 1927. The commune was quickly suppressed by the troops of the **Nationalist Party**.

CANTON SYSTEM. The regulations governing foreign trade with Qing China. The main codes were the following: (1) Canton was the only port open to foreign commerce; (2) foreign trade must be conducted through the *hong* merchants, and foreigners could communicate with Chinese officials only through the *co-hong*; (3) foreign traders must not remain in Canton after the trading season, and no foreign women were allowed to be brought into the foreign factories; (4) all foreign pilots and compradors must register with the Chinese authorities in Macao, and foreign ships may anchor at Huangpu but nowhere else; and (5) foreigners must not directly communicate with Chinese people or merchants without supervision, and foreigners could neither buy Chinese books nor learn Chinese. This system was formulated by the Qing court degree in 1757 and lasted until the end of the **Opium War** in 1842.

CAO KUN (1862–1938). Born into a poor family in Tianjin, Cao began his military career by joining Yuan Shikai's Beiyang Army. He was admired by Yuan and promoted to general rather quickly. After the death of Feng Guozhang, Cao began to lead the **Zhili Clique**. In 1918, he allied with the leader of the **Anhui Clique**, Duan Qirui, who controlled the National Assembly and manipulated the election. For Cao's military cooperation, Duan promised him the vice presidency. However, most members of the National Assembly did not participate in the election, and Cao did not get the position. Believing that he was betrayed by Duan, Cao mobilized the Zhili Clique's troops to attack Duan's Anhui Army. In 1920, he defeated Duan, forced two presents—**Xu Shichang** and **Li Yuanhong**—to resign, and called another presidential election. Finally, he made himself president of the Republic of China (in Beijing) from 10 October 1923 to 2 November 1924. Shamefully, Cao openly bribed assembly members in the election, paying each 5,000 silver dollars to vote for him for president. This scandal ruined the reputation of the Beiyang government and National Assembly. It also split the Zhili Clique. During a war against **Zhang Zuolin** in October 1924, his subordinate, General **Feng Yuxiang**, launched a coup in Beijing. He put Cao under house arrest and forced him to resign. Cao was released two years later and moved to Tianjin, where he died in his home in May 1938.

CAO YU (1910–1996). Pen name of Wan Jiabo, a renowned Chinese playwright. Born into a wealthy family in Qianjiang, Hubei Province, Cao was brought to Tianjin when he was an infant, where his father worked for a time as secretary to President **Li Yuanhong**. Cao studied at Nankai High School and became interested in Western drama (*huajiu*). He took an active part in students' performances, including playing the female role of Nora in Henrik Ibsen's *A Doll's House*. He enrolled in Nankai University's Department of Political Science but transferred the next year to Tsinghua University, majoring in Western languages and literature. Cao published his first play, *Thunderstorm*, at the age of 24. It was considered a milestone in China's modern theatrical ascendancy and made Cao a rising star in Chinese theatrical circles. Two years later, he published *Sunrise*, which was also a great success. His third play, *The Wilderness*, was influenced by Eugene O'Neill's expressionist works, telling a story of love, murder, and revenge. It evoked criticism from writers who believed in Socialist realism.

Nonetheless, in 1980, when Cao was 70 years old, the Chinese audience rediscovered the aesthetic value of this play and again staged it in Chinese theaters. During the **Second Sino-Japanese War**, Cao followed the Nationalist government to **Chongqing**, where he published another famous work, *Peking Men*. He also taught at the city's School of Dramatic Art. During this period, he completed a translation of William Shakespeare's *Romeo and Juliet*. At the end of the war, Cao traveled to the United States and lived there for a year. In 1946, after his return to China, Cao wrote the screenplay for *Day of the Radiant Sun* and directed the movie that was made. After the founding of the

People's Republic of China, Cao was appointed director of Beijing People's Theater, but he produced no more important work.

CC CLIQUE. A right-wing faction of the **Nationalist Party** (GMD) led by the brothers **Chen Guofu** and **Chen Lifu**. In February 1928, **Chiang Kai-shek** appointed Chen Lifu acting director of the GMD Central Organization Department, and authorized the Chen brothers to set up the Central Statistics Bureau, a secret intelligence agency of the GMD and the power base of the CC Clique. The Chen brothers supported Chiang as an absolute leader of China and held an uncompromising stance against communism. The Central Statistics Bureau and Military Statistics Bureau were two major security apparatuses established to consolidate Chiang Kai-shek's personal domination over the GMD and China. In 1931, 15 percent of the 72 members of the Central Executive Committee were members of the CC Clique and, in 1935, when the committee expanded, 50 of 180 newly elected committee members were Chen's people. By the outbreak of the **Second Sino-Japanese War**, the clique had reached its peak of power with 10,000 members. Chen Guofu was referred to as the party's godfather. The CC Clique also controlled the National Farmers Bank of China and penetrated educational and cultural spheres. In 1949, when the Chen brothers retreated to Taiwan and their political enemies within the GMD blamed the CC Clique for the GMD's failure, Chiang Kai-shek began to whittle down their influence. Chen Guofu was dismissed from office and Chen Lifu was forced to retire.

CENTRAL ARMY. When the **National Revolutionary Army** (NRA) was established in 1926, its First Army was composed of divisions trained at the **Whampoa Military Academy** and commanded directly by **Chiang Kai-shek**. These troops were regarded as Chiang's *dixi* (direct descendants) and were loyal to Chiang Kai-shek personally. After Chiang established the central government in Nanjing and unified China, people began to refer to his dixi as the Central Army. In the meantime, other divisions of the NRA, originally regional or provincial armies commanded by non-Whampoa commanders, were called *zaipai jun* (miscellaneous units). The provincial troops usually retained considerable independence from the central government, but they were not as well equipped as the Central Army and received fewer supplies from Chiang's central government.

CENTRAL BANK OF CHINA. A state bank founded in Shanghai, its primary capital was ¥20 million and increased to ¥1 billion in 1934. The first president was T. V. Soong, followed by **H. H. Kung**. The National Government granted the Central Bank the privileges of issuing paper currency, minting money, managing the national treasury, and issuing state bonds. Due to the Fiscal Reform of 1935, the **Bank of China**, **Bank of Communication**, and Bank of Peasants were also authorized to issue paper currency. Nonetheless, power was centralized in the hands of the Central Bank again in 1942. This bank also had a monopoly on China's foreign exchange. On the eve of the founding of the People's Republic of China, **Chiang Kai-shek** ordered the bank to ship all its gold and foreign currency to Taiwan. In 1949, the immovable properties of the Central Bank in mainland China were confiscated.

CHAMBER OF COMMERCE OF SHANGHAI (GENERAL CHAMBER OF COMMERCE OF SHANGHAI). In September 1905, the Qing government established the Ministry of Commerce, which issued "Brief Regulations of the Chamber of Commerce." The regulations "encouraged but did not enforce the establishment of local chambers of commerce." On 5 June 1904, the Chamber of Commerce of Shanghai was established using these regulations. Besides coordinating the business operations of its members, the chamber led boycotts against foreign goods and built up a militia to participate in the Shanghai Uprising during the 1911 Revolution. After the founding of the Republic of China, a group of merchants in Shanghai refused to recognize the chamber because it was sponsored by the Qing government, and they established the Shanghai Association of Commerce. After some negotiation, the two organizations merged into the General Chamber of Commerce of Shanghai in February 1912 and elected Zhou Jingzheng as president. In May 1927, it was reorganized by the order of the new municipal government in Shanghai.

CHANG, EILEEN. *See* ZHANG AILING.

CHANGMAO. The nickname for the **Taiping rebels**, literally meaning "long hair." This was because the Tiaping rebels typically wore a uniform of red jackets with blue trousers and grew their hair long. The rebels also distinguished themselves by recruiting women to serve in their army and government. The name *changmao* also implied a negative meaning for their belief in Christianity and betrayal of **Confucianism**. The Qing officials and rural gentry created the image of the Changmao as bloodthirsty ghosts to terrify the peasants and urban populace.

CHEFOO CONVENTION (YANTAI CONVENTION, 1876). Treaty between the Qing and British governments. In 1874, British colonel Browne went to China's southern border to investigate routes between Burma and China. The British embassy dispatched interpreter Augustus Raymond Margary to join Browne. Upon his arrival at the border area, however, Margary was killed by local Chinese villagers. The Qing Court ordered Minister of Beiyang Affairs **Li Hongzhang** to negotiate with the British ambassador, **Sir Thomas Wade**, to solve this problem. Consequently, they signed a treaty on 21 August 1876 in Yantai (Chefoo), Shandong Province. The convention consisted of 16 articles. The main points included (1) to pay indemnity of 200,000 taels to Margary's family, (2) to offer the British the right to investigate cases involving the lives and property of British people, (3) to open more ports to British goods, and (4) not to levy *lijin* (surcharges) on British goods at the ports. In addition, China would send an official mission to London and make an apology. The Qing government sent **Guo Songtao** to London as the head of the mission. Guo eventually became the first Chinese ambassador to a Western country.

For several reasons, the British government did not ratify this convention. First, other powers criticized its unilateral action. Second, the British merchants demanded a complete abolition of *lijin*. Third, the colonial government in India opposed the increased tax on opium by Chinese customs. In 1885, the negotiations were resumed in London. On 18 July, both governments signed the Supplement to the Chefoo Convention. Several new articles were added to the original convention, stipulating that each box (50 kg) of British opium exported to China would pay customs 110 taels silver, and no other tax or lijin would be levied on the way to Chinese interior provinces. Now both the Chefoo Convention and the Supplement to the Chefoo Convention were ratified by the British government.

CHEN BAOZHEN (1831–1900). Chinese statesman and reformer in the Qing dynasty. Born in Xiushui, Jiangxi Province, Chen obtained the *jinshi* degree in 1851. He took an active part in the **Self-Strengthening Movement**, associating with **Zeng Guofan**. In 1895, he was appointed governor of Hunan Province, where he invited the reformist scholars **Tan Sitong** and **Liang Qichao** to come and initiate local reforms, including building new schools, constructing the Guangzhou-Wuhan Railway, and opening local mines. He supported the reformists in publishing the *Xiangxuebao* (Journal for Hunan Studies) and ordered all city and county governments to subscribe to and read this newspaper. He sympathized with the **Hundred Days' Reform** and thus offended his superiors. Because of this, he was dismissed from office in 1898 and died in Nanjing two years later.

CHEN BODA (1940–1989). Communist theorist, political secretary to **Mao Zedong**, and major document writer of the **Chinese Communist Party** (CCP). Born into a peasant family in Hui'an, Fujian Province, Chen received his education first at the Chi-Mei Normal School and then Shanghai Labor University. He participated in the **Northern Expedition** and joined the CCP in 1927. After the CCP's split, the **Nationalist Party** began to purge Communists from the army, so Chen traveled to Russia and studied at **Moscow Sun Yat-sen University**, where he was excluded from the **Twenty-eight Bolsheviks**. For this reason, when he returned to China in 1929, he was not assigned to any important position but began to teach at Chinese University in Beiping. Chen traveled to **Yan'an** in the summer of 1937, lecturing at the CCP Central Party School and Academy of Marxism-Leninism, and worked at the Propaganda Department, the Military Committee of the Central Committee, and the Political Research Division of the CCP Central Committee.

A few months after his arrival, Chen edited the first collection of Mao's works and began to draft the party's documents and Mao's personal speeches. The following year, he published *The Arch Usurper of State Power—Yuan Shikai* (1945), *Four Big Families in China* (1946), *The Public Enemy Chiang Kai-shek* (1948), and numerous articles. Mao appreciated Chen's Marxist perspective and his writing style. In 1945, Chen was elected an alternate member of the CCP Central Committee and became a full member in 1946. After 1949, he continued to work with Mao Zedong. His two articles, "On Mao Zedong Thought: The Integration of Marxism-Leninism with the Chinese Revolution" and "Mao Zedong on the Chinese Revolution" made him the authority on Maoist theory in the CCP. In 1966, he was appointed head of the leading group of the Cultural Revolution. Nonetheless, he lost Mao's trust and was dismissed from office in 1971. After the death of Mao Zedong, Chen was arrested by **Deng Xiaoping**. He was accused of promoting the excesses of the Cultural Revolution and sentenced to an 18-year imprisonment.

CHEN DUXIU (1879–1942). Leading figure in the **New Culture Movement** and a cofounder of the **Chinese Communist Party** (CCP). Born in Anqing, Anhui Province, into the family of a gentry-scholar, Chen received a thorough Confucian education and obtained the *xiucai* degree at the age of 17. From 1902 to 1907, he traveled three times to Japan and studied Japanese language and military science, where he was exposed to Western radicalism and organized anti-**Manchu** associations. Chen took an active part in the **Republican Revolution** and the **Second Revolution** against **Yuan Shikai**'s monarchism. In 1915, Chen founded the most influential monthly periodical of its time, *New Youth*, in Shanghai. The magazine introduced Western science and democracy, published essays and novels in vernacular Chinese, and initiated the anti-**Confucianism** campaign. Chen taught Chinese literature at Peking University and served as the dean of its School of Arts. He first was an iconoclast who sharply criticized Chinese traditionalism and called on the Chinese young generation to be independent instead of servile, progressive instead of conservative, aggressive instead of retrogressive, cosmopolitan instead of isolationist, utilitarian instead of impractical, and scientific instead of visionary. In the 1920s, Chen appeared to be a Marxist and advocated for entirely changing China through a radical revolution.

In 1921, the CCP was established with the support of the **Comintern** and Chen was elected its general secretary. Under his leadership, the CCP cooperated with the **Nationalist Party** (GMD) in launching the military campaign against **warlordism**. In 1927, the CCP–GMD alliance broke down and **Chiang Kai-shek** began to purge the Communists. Chen was charged with having carried out the policy of **rightist opportunism** and dismissed from the CCP's leadership. However, he insisted that the **Comintern** should be responsible for the failure of the Chinese Communist movement and criticized Joseph Stalin's policies toward Chinese revolution. For this reason, he was branded as a Trotskyist and expelled from the CCP in 1929.

Chen upheld the orthodox Marxist view on the role of the proletariat in the Chinese Revolution and opposed **Mao Zedong**'s analyses of Chinese social classes and his emphasis on the peasant movement. Chen supported the **Shanghai War of 1932** and denounced Chiang Kai-shek's nonresistance policy. From 1932 to 1937, he was imprisoned by the GMD; this imprisonment ruined his health. After he was released, Chen refused reconciliation with the CCP leaders and turned down the offer of a living subsidy by the GMD government. He retired from public life and lived in poverty. On 27 May 1942, Chen died of a heart attack at the age of 62. *See also* AUGUST SEVENTH CONFERENCE; UNITED FRONT, FIRST.

CHEN GONGBO (1892–1946). Head of the **Legislative Yuan** of the Japanese puppet government in Nanjing during the Chinese War against the Japanese Aggression (1938–1945). Chen was born into a noble family in Nanhai, Guangdong Province. As a student at **Peking University**, Chen took an active part in the **May Fourth Movement** of 1919 and was exposed to Marxism and other radical ideologies. Having graduated from the Department of Philosophy in 1920, he returned to Guangzhou, where he created the newspaper *Qunbao* (Mass Daily) and began to propagandize Marxism and socialism. Attending the First Congress of the **Chinese Communist Party** in Shanghai in 1921, he became a founding member of the party. However, two years later, he was expelled because of his support for the Guangdong warlord, **Chen Jiongming**. He then traveled to the United States to study economics at Columbia University, where he obtained his master's degree. In the United States, he made the public statement that communism does not apply to China.

Returning to Guangzhou in 1925, Chen joined the **Chinese Nationalist Party** (GMD) and was appointed head of the Department of Peasants. In 1928, he worked together with **Wang Jingwei** to launch an anti–**Chiang Kai-shek** coup, formed the Society for Reorganizing the GMD, and edited the journal *Revolutionary Review.* After the reconciliation between Wang Jingwei and Chiang Kai-shek in 1931, Chen was appointed minister of entrepreneurs. In 1938, he and Wang Jingwei staged the "peace movement" and cooperated with the Japanese military. When the Nanjing Nationalist government was established under Japanese sponsorship, Chen became the number two leader next to Wang. As head of the Legislative Yuan, he acted as the president of Wang's government when Wang was out of the country visiting Japan. He was also mayor of the Special City of Shanghai during the war. At the end of the **Second Sino-Japanese War**, he fled to Japan but was soon extradited back for trial. Chen was sentenced to death as a traitor and executed by a firing squad at Suzhou, Jiangsu Province, in 1946.

CHEN GUOFU (1892–1951). Director of the Organizational Department of the **Nationalist Party** (GMD). Born in Wuxing, Zhejiang Province, Chen Guofu was the elder brother of **Chen Lifu**. Influenced by his uncle, **Chen Qimei**, Guofu joined **Sun Yat-sen's Tongmenghui**. He was admitted to Zhejiang Army School in 1907 and joined the revolutionary army in Wuhan and participated in the anti–**Yuan Shikai** campaign led by Chen Qimei. In 1918, he was **Chiang Kai-shek's** business partner in Shanghai. Chen was in charge of military purchasing for the **Whampoa Military Academy** in 1924, and he served as director of the GMD Organizational Department and was elected a member of the GMD Central Executive Committee. Together with his brother Chen Lifu, he founded the **CC Clique** and established the Central Statistics Bureau, a major security apparatus of the GMD. The CC Clique was one of the most influential factions of the GMD, and its members held many key positions in the party. For this reason, Chen was called the "Godfather of the GMD." He also held other important positions in the party and government, including governor of Jiangsu, vice president of the Supervision Yuan, president of Central Financial Committee, president of the Agricultural Bank of China, and others. After the Japanese surrendered, he was in charge of the confiscation of "enemy properties" and made many companies, banks, and cultural enterprises of the Japanese or their Chinese collaborators "party properties" of the GMD. In 1949, he went to Taiwan and died there two years later.

CHEN JIONGMING (1878–1933). Republican revolutionary and warlord of Guangdong. Born in Haifeng, Guangdong Province, Chen graduated from the Guangdong School of Political Science and Law, which was established to train students to be judges and lawyers for the Qing government. After graduation, Chen was appointed a provincial legislator. However, he joined the **Tongmenghui** in 1909 in Shanghai and devoted himself to the overthrow of the Qing regime.

He participated in the abortive Uprising of Yellow Flowers Mound in Guangzhou and became commander in chief of the Guangdong Army. After the Revolution of 1911, he successively served as military governor of Guangdong (1911–1912, 1913, 1920–1923), governor of Guangdong (1920–1922), and military governor of Guangxi (1921–1922). He advocated federalism, making Guangdong a "model province" of political stability and economic prosperity. He encouraged rich people to open private schools but saw it as a government responsibility to promote free public education. He invited the Communist leader, Professor **Chen Duxiu**, to be the provincial director of education. He banned opium smoking and gambling in Guangdong.

In 1917, Chen supported **Sun Yat-sen**'s **Constitutional Protection Movement** and was appointed by Sun as minister of the army and concurrent minister of civil affairs in 1921. However, he and Sun split on the issues of the **Northern Expedition** and unification of China. Chen strongly insisted on full autonomy for Guangdong and opposed any form of central government. In 1922, he revolted in Guangzhou and fired shells at Sun's residence. When Sun's supporters, including Chiang Kai-shek, organized a counterattack, Chen's troops were defeated. Chen led the remnants to resist Sun Yat-sen's leadership until they were destroyed by **Chiang Kai-shek**'s Eastern Expedition in 1925. In October, he traveled to San Francisco, where he founded the **China Zhi Gong Party** and was elected its first president; however, Chen could no longer play any important role in Chinese politics.

CHEN LIFU (1900–2001). Politician of the Republic of China. Born in Wuxing, Zhejiang Province, Chen Lifu was the younger brother of **Chen Guofu**, nephew of **Chen Qimei**. He graduated from the Mining Department of Beiyang University in 1922 and then traveled to the United States to study. He obtained his master's degree in mine engineering from the University of Pittsburgh. After his return to China in 1925, Chen served as the personal secretary of Chiang Kai-shek and was in charge of the GMD's personnel affairs. He was a cofounder of the **CC Clique** and the Central Statistics Bureau. After 1949, when the influence of the CC Clique began to wane, Chen Lifu left for the United States to run a small business. In 1969, he returned to Taiwan and focused on cultural activities, serving as president of the Society of Confucian Studies. He died of a heart attack in the city of Taizhong at the age of 102.

CHEN QIMEI (CHEN YINGSHI, 1878–1916). Revolutionary activist. Born to a merchant family in Wuxing, Zhejiang Province, Chen began to work at a pawnshop as an apprentice at the age of 14. In 1906, he traveled to Japan to study and joined **Sun Yat-sen**'s early revolutionary party, the **Tongmenghui**. Two years later, he returned to China and began to go back and forth between Beijing and Shanghai to coordinate activities of different revolutionary groups. He also created *Zhongguo gongbao* (Public Newspaper of China). In the same year, he joined the **Green Gang** in Shanghai and gained the support of the largest secret society in China. It was Chen who brought his countryman, **Chiang Kai-shek**, into the Tongmenghui and introduced him to Sun Yat-sen. In 1911, Chen was one of the leaders in the Republican uprising in Shanghai and, after the overthrow of the municipal government, he became military governor of the city. Upon the failure of the **Second Revolution** against **Yuan Shikai** in 1913, he fled to Japan. When the Chinese Revolutionary Party was founded in Tokyo in 1914, he was elected director of general affairs. Chen continued to organize anti–Yuan Shikai operations in the provinces of Jiangsu and Zhejiang. He was finally assassinated by Yuan Shikai at his home in Shanghai on 18 May 1916. Chen Qimei's two nephews, **Chen Lifu** and **Chen Guofu**, later became the leaders of the powerful **CC Clique** in the Nationalist Party.

CHEN SHAOYU *See* WANG MING.

CHEN TIANHUA (1875–1905). Revolutionary writer. Born in Xinhua, Hunan Province, into the family of a poor teacher in a rural school, Chen worked as a peddler when he was young. In 1903, he went to Japan to study on a government scholarship. There, he was deeply involved in revolutionary activities and wrote his best-known books, *Manhuitou* (Soul-Searching) and *Jingshizhong* (Alarm Bells). He returned to China to establish an anti-Qing revolutionary group in Changsha but was twice forced to flee to Japan. He and Song Jiangren worked together and created the official newspaper for the **Tongmenghui**. In the early 20th century, Japan became a playground for young Chinese revolutionaries—most of them students with a Qing government scholarship—who were regarded as a threat by the Japanese government. In November 1905, the Japanese government issued a law titled "Ban the Qing Government's Overseas Students in Japan." In protest of this law, Chen jumped into Tokyo Bay and drowned himself in December 1905.

CHEN XUJING (1903–1967). Prominent scholar. Born in Wenchang, Guangdong Province, Chen graduated from Fudan University in 1925 and then traveled to the United States to study. He obtained his PhD in sociology from the University of Illinois in 1928. In the same year, Chen returned to China and taught at Lingnan University, Nankai University, and Southwestern Union University. On 15 November 1934, Chen published an article in the *Guangzhou Republic Daily* titled "The Solution to Chinese Culture," in which he reiterated Hu Shih's argument that China lagged behind the West not only in science and technology but also in politics, literature, arts, morality, research methodology, and physical stature. The only solution for China was total Westernization. His article provoked a heated debate on Chinese culture and China's Westernization. Chen served as president or vice president at several universities. His major field was comparative study between Chinese and foreign cultures. After 1949, he focused mainly on the study of Chinese frontier history. During the Cultural Revolution, Chen was accused of being an American spy and died of a heart attack.

CHEN YUCHENG (1836–1862). A leader of the **Taiping Rebellion** in its later years. Born into a peasant family in Ten County, Guangxi Province, he joined the Taiping at the age of 15. He rose quickly through the ranks as a brave soldier and talented tactician. In 1858, the Taiping leadership was shaken up, and he was granted the title Prince Ying. In the later years of the rebellion, he commanded at several decisive battles, breaking through the Qing army's encirclement, but was finally defeated and captured by the enemy. He was executed in Henan Province at the age of 26.

CHENG QIAN (1882–1968). Full general of first class of the **Nationalist Party** army. Born in Liling, Hunan Province, Cheng graduated from the Hunan Military Academy in 1903. In 1904, he traveled to Japan and studied at the Imperial Military Academy, where he joined the **Tongmenghui** in 1905. After graduating in 1908, Cheng returned to Sichuan to train the **Chinese New Army**. During the Wuchang Uprising, Cheng commanded the artillery to help the revolutionaries defend the city. In 1916, he was elected commander in chief of the Hunan Public Protection Army in the anti–**Yuan Shikai** campaign. He also took part in the Eastern Expedition against Chen Jiongming in 1925 and was promoted to army commander a year later. He co-operated with the Communists in the **Northern Expedition** and led his Sixth Army to storm the cities of Nanchang and Jiujiang. He was then made commander in chief of the Right Route Army and led his troops to take Nanjing.

In 1927, Chen was dismissed from office on suspicion of having anti-Chiang sentiments. In addition, because of a conflict with the **Guangxi Clique**, Chen was placed under house arrest by **Li Zongren** from 1928 to 1931. After the **Manchuria Incident**, Cheng was re-leased and appointed chief of staff in 1935. He commanded troops to fight the Japanese along the Beijing-Hankou Railways. As military commander and governor of Hunan, Cheng fought Li Bocheng's Second Field Army in central China. On 4 August 1949, he started an uprising and crossed over to the Chinese Communist Party. After 1949, Cheng held several important government positions, including governor of Hunan, vice-chairman of the National Defense Commit-tee, and vice president of the Chinese Congress.

CHENNAULT, ANNA CHAN (CHEN XIANGMEI, 1925–). Journal-ist and political activist in both China and the United States. She was born in Beijing to a very distinguished family. Her grandfather served the Republic of China as the envoy to Cuba and as the ambassador to Japan, while her cousin later became vice president of the People's Congress of the People's Republic of China. Her father, Chen Yingye, obtained a doctor of law from Oxford and a PhD from Columbia, and her mother, Liao Xiangci, was educated in Europe. Anna received the best possible education and showed her talent in literature when she was only a little girl. Anna grew up during the Second Sino-Japanese War and followed her family from place to place. However, when she was admitted by an American university, she refused to go, saying that she would not leave her motherland while it suffered. In 1944, Anna was employed by the Central News Agency (CNA) and became the first female correspondent of the CNA. Anna wrote news reports and also published essays and novels.

In 1946, she was sent to interview General **Claire Lee Chennault**. Although Claire was 31 years her elder, he was her hero and she fell in love with him. Anna and Claire got married the next year. In 1949, Anna followed Claire's civilian navigation company in withdrawing to Taiwan and then in returning to the United States. She published several books, including *Chennualt and the Flying Tigers: Way of a Fighter*, *A Thousand Springs*, *The Education of Anna*, and *Letters from the USA*. She also helped her husband finish his memoir. After Claire's death in 1958, Anna brought up two young children and took an active part in American politics. She held various important positions in the Republican Party and worked for eight American presidents as a member of their advisory committee, starting with the Kennedy administration. Anna contributed a good deal to the improvement of U.S.–China relations.

CHENNAULT, CLAIRE LEE (1893–1958). Lieutenant general of the United States Air Force and founder of the **Flying Tigers** in China. Born in Commerce, Texas, Chennault attended Louisiana State University between 1909 and 1910 and graduated from Louisiana State Normal College. On 25 December 1911, he and Nell Thompson were married. The marriage lasted for 30 years and produced eight children. Chennault learned to fly in the army during World War I. From 1919 to 1936, he successfully served with the border patrol, the Hawaiian Pursuit Squadron (until 1926), and the U.S. Pursuit Development Board and Air Corp Exhibition Group. In 1937, Chennault was forced to retire from the Army Air Corps due to disagreements with his superiors and problems with his hearing. He was soon hired by **Chiang Kai-shek** as an adviser for the Chinese air force. Soon after, American president Franklin D. Roosevelt signed a "secret executive order" authorizing pilots on active duty to resign from the U.S. military, enabling Chennault to recruit pilots who volunteered to fly and fight for the Republic of China air force.

These volunteers formed the 1st American Volunteer Group, better known as the Flying Tigers, which consisted of three fighter squadrons that trained in Burma and first saw combat on 20 December 1941, 12 days after Pearl Harbor. In seven months, they destroyed almost 300 aircraft and lost only 14 pilots on combat missions, thereby dominating the skies over southwest China, northern Burma, and the Assam Valley of India. In China, Chennault met **Anna Chan (Chen Xiangmei)**, a young Chinese reporter for the Central News Agency, and married her on 2 December 1947. Chennault flew home when news of the Japanese surrender reached him via the plane radio. He soon returned to China and founded the Civil Air Transport to deliver seeds, medicine, food, farm equipment, and banknotes from Guangzhou and Shanghai into the interior of China. Chennault was promoted to lieutenant general one day before his death. He died of lung cancer on 27 July 1958 and was buried at Arlington National Cemetery.

CHIANG CHING-KUO (JIANG JINGGUO, 1910–1988). Prominent political leader of modern China. Born in Fenghua, Zhejiang Province, Chiang was the eldest son of **Chiang Kai-shek**. His mother was Mao Fumei, Chiang Kai-shek's first wife. Chiang Ching-kuo received his early education in Shanghai, where he was involved in the **May Thirtieth Movement**, showing his concern for workers and anti-imperialist sentiment. In October 1925, he traveled to Moscow to study at Sun Yat-sen University. Many of his classmates, such as **Deng Xiaoping**, were Communists, and Chiang joined the Russian Communist Party. Chiang Ching-kuo graduated in 1927, when his father purged the Communists from the **Nationalist Party** (GMD) and expelled the Soviet advisers. Although Chiang publicly criticized his father's actions, he was detained by Joseph Stalin as a hostage in Russia. Chiang was sent to the Urals and worked at the Ural Heavy Machinery Plant, where he met and married a Belarusian girl, Faina Ipatevan Vakhreva, later renamed Chiang Fang-liang, who bore him three sons and one daughter. On 25 March 1937, after living in Russia for 12 years, Chiang was allowed to return to China with his family. This was the time when Stalin and the **Comintern** began to support the **Chinese Communist Party** (CCP)-GMD United Front against Japan. The next year, Chiang joined the GMD and worked in Jiangxi Province. For his excellent service as an honest and upright administrator, he was referred to as "Chiang Clear Sky" by the local people.

After 1944, he was the major leader of the **Three People's Principles Youth League**, focusing on training young officers for the GMD. During his stay in Jiangxi, he had a romance with a girl, Zhang Ruoya, who bore him twin sons. In 1948, Chiang was sent to Shanghai as a liaison administrator to curb hyperinflation and stabilize the city's economy. He was determined to push financial reform and crack down on corruption, which conflicted with the interests of

GMD's noble families, including Chiang's relatives. His stepmother **Soong May-ling** asked Chiang Kai-shek to recall Ching-kuo, causing the GMD to lose its last chance to regain urban popularity, which contributed to the final collapse of Chiang's regime in mainland China. After 1949, Chiang moved to Taiwan. He served successfully as a member of the GMD Central Executive Committee, deputy minister and minister of defense, chairman of the Central Committee of Finance and Economics, and president of the **Executive Yuan**, and was elected president of the Republic of China to succeed President Yan Chia-kan in 1978. In his later years, Chiang ended martial law and allowed family visits to the mainland, which embarked on democratic reform and an improvement of cross-strait relations. On 13 January 1988, Chiang died of heart failure in Taipei at the age of 78.

CHIANG KAI-SHEK (JIANG JIESHI, 1887–1975). Political leader of China, head of the Nationalist government in mainland China (1928–1949) and later in Taiwan (1949–1975). Born in Fenghua, Zhejiang Province, into the family of a salt merchant, he began his military education at the Baoding Military Academy in 1907. Chiang then traveled to Japan and studied at Rikugun Shikan Gakko (the Imperial Japanese Army Academy) in 1908, where his countryman **Chen Qimei** brought him into the **Tongmenghui**. After graduating, Chiang served in the Imperial Japanese Army for two years. He returned to China to participate in the 1911 Revolution, serving in the revolutionary forces as an artillery officer. He was involved in the **Second Revolution** against **Yuan Shikai**. After its failure, he fled to Japan and the **foreign concessions** in Shanghai, where he established close ties with the **Green Gang**.

In 1917, when **Sun Yat-sen** moved to Guangzhou, Chiang followed him. Sun was impressed by Chiang's "Operation Plan of the Revolutionary Army against the Northern Troops" and appointed him in charge of military and party affairs in Shanghai. In 1919, when Sun Yat-sen established the **Chinese Nationalist Party** (GMD), Chiang became a founding member. In June 1923, Guangdong governor **Chen Jiongming** bombarded Sun's residence. Chiang's warship rushed to rescue Sun Yat-sen from Shanghai, helping Sun regain control over Guangzhou. In 1924, Sun Yat-sen decided to accept Russian support and cooperate with the Communists in the struggle against the northern **warlords**, allowing the Chinese Communists to join the

GMD. Chiang was sent to Moscow, as head of the Chinese delegation, to spend three months studying Soviet political and military systems. When the **Whampoa Military Academy** was established with Soviet help in 1924, Chiang was appointed commandant of the academy, working with Soviet agent **Mikhail Borodin** as its adviser and Chinese Communist **Zhou Enlai** as the director of its Political Department.

In July 1926, Chiang became commander in chief of the **National Revolutionary Army** and launched the **Northern Expedition** against the warlords. After his troops took Shanghai and Nanjing, he decided to break with the leftists. He began to purge the Communists from the GMD and staged a coup on 12 April 1927, arresting and executing Communist activists in Shanghai. After defeating the warlords (in North China) and his rivals and incorporating Manchuria, Chiang reunified China and established the National Government in Nanjing in April 1927. Chiang was named generalissimo of all Chinese military forces and chairman of the Nationalist government.

Chiang had had several marriages before he met the American-educated **Soong May-ling**. Besides a family-arranged wife, Mao Fumei, he had taken two concubines, Yao Yecheng in 1912 and Chen Jiru in 1921. However, after he met Soon May-ling in Shanghai, he fell in love with her and divorced or cut direct connections with his previous wife and concubines. Chiang married May-ling on 1 December 1927, making himself Sun Yat-sen's brother-in-law. He also shortly converted to his wife's religion, Christianity.

Despite domestic unrest and foreign threat, China's economy made remarkable progress in the period of the Nanjing government (1928–1937). Chiang initiated the **New Life Movement**, advocating Confucian moral values and healthy living. He launched military campaigns to wipe out the Communists. In his fifth **Encirclement and Suppression Campaign**, he defeated the **Red Army**, forcing the Communists to give up their **Jiangxi Soviet** and escape to Northwest China. However, he was unable to eliminate all the Communists. Through a bitter journey, known as the **Long March**, the survivors of the Red Army arrived in **Yan'an** and built up a new Communist base. In 1931, the Japanese invaded Manchuria and Chiang ordered the Chinese troops under **Zhang Xueliang**'s command to retreat. Chiang's stated policy was "First internal pacification, then external resistance"; this policy provoked sharp criticism from various circles.

In December 1936, Chiang flew to Xi'an to supervise the assault on Red Army forces. On 12 December, Chang Xueliang and several other Nationalist generals kidnapped Chiang Kai-shek, forcing him to form a Second **United Front** with the Communists against Japan. The **Xi'an Incident** was peacefully settled and civil war between the GMD and the **Chinese Communist Party** (CCP) halted. Chiang was propelled into the pinnacle of his political career as the supreme leader of China during the **Second Sino-Japanese War**. In July 1937, he made the famous speech "China's Last Moment," calling all Chinese to put up strong resistance against the Japanese invaders. Chiang organized the defensive battles in Shanghai and Nanjing, causing great casaulities of both Chinese and Japanese troops. Finally, the cities were overrun and the National Government had to move to **Chongqing**, Sichuan Province. Chiang could not organize a counterattack, but he succeeded in stretching Japanese supply lines and bogging down Japanese soldiers in the vast Chinese territory. After the Japanese bombed Pearl Harbor, China and the United States became allies. During the war, Chiang and his wife Soong May-ling obtained great support from the American government and people. Chiang was recognized as one of the **Big Four** Allied leaders along with Franklin Roosevelt, Winston Churchill, and Joseph Stalin.

More often than not, however, the GMD and CCP engaged in various clashes during the War against Japanese Aggression, and their relations became further conflicting when Japan surrendered in 1945. Although Chiang and Mao met in Chongqing and signed a peace agreemnt on 10 October 1945, the Chinese civil war soon broke out. Chiang felt confident that he could overcome the Communist forces in half a year. With American help, he was able to reclaim the coastal cities, while the Communists retreated to the rural areas and waited to strike the final blow on Chiang's troops in isolated cities. Chiang's government was deteriorating from corruption and inflation while the Communists were strengthened by mobilized peasants. Chiang's troops were numerically superior, but their morale was low. Due to defeats by the Communists in a number of major battles, Chiang resigned the presidency on 21 January 1949, and Vice President Li Zongren took over as acting president. Li asked for peace, but his negotiations with **Mao Zedong** failed. Li flew to the United States under a medical excuse and Chiang commanded the Nationalists' last resistance. In the early morning of 10 December 1949, as the

Communist troops prepared to storm the city of Chengdu, Chiang Kai-shek and his son **Chiang Ching-kuo** fled in the aircraft *May-ling* to Taiwan. They never returned to the Chinese mainland. Chiang Kai-shek died in Taiwan on 5 April 1975.

CHINA ASSOCIATION FOR PROMOTING DEMOCRACY. One of the eight legally recognized non-Communist parties in Communist China. It consisted mainly of junior and senior intellectuals in the fields of culture, education, and publishing. It was founded on 30 December 1945 by a group of famous scholars in Shanghai, including Ma Xulun, Zhou Jianren, and Xu Guangping. The association was devoted to the spirit of democracy and it promoted the democratic process in China. In June 1946, the association initiated a mass rally to protest the Chinese civil war. Its leaders, Ma Xulun and Lei Jiequn, also joined the students in Nanjing to petition for the end of the civil war. They were attacked by the **Nationalist Party** agents at the Nanjing railway station and seriously injured. In 1949, the China Association for Promoting Democracy joined the **Chinese People's Political Consultative Conference**, and some of its leaders held honorable positions in the central government of the People's Republic of China.

CHINA DEMOCRATIC LEAGUE (CDL). One of the eight legally recognized non-Communist parties in Communist China. The league was made up mainly of junior and senior intellectuals in the fields of culture, education, science, and technology. Founded on 19 March 1941 in **Chongqing** as the China Democratic Parties League with Huang Yanpei as its chairman, the China Democratic League attempted to unite different Chinese political forces to fight against Japanese aggression. The participants included the China Youth Party, the Democratic Social Party, the **Chinese Peasants' and Workers' Democratic Party**, the Chinese Professional Educators Society, the Association for Rural Development, and other noted intellectuals. Huang Yanpei was elected president. Six months later, **Zhang Lan** succeeded Huang. On 10 October 1941, its formal publication, *Guangming ribao* (Light daily) was published, announcing its goals of democracy, peace, independence, and a unified China. It also advocated cooperation with the **Chinese Communist Party** (CCP). In September 1944, the CDL held a national assembly to support the

CCP's suggestion for a coalition government. The CDL was banned in 1947 by the **Nationalist Party**. Although its headquarters were closed, the CDL continued operations. In 1949, the CDL joined the **Chinese People's Political Consultative Conference**. Zhang Lan was elected vice president of the People's Republic of China, and other CDL leaders were also appointed to various positions in the central government.

CHINA INTERNATIONAL FAMINE RELIEF COMMISSION (CIFRC). In 1910, the flooding of the Yangtze and Huai rivers destroyed villages in 20 counties and created more than 3 million refugees, 700,000 of whom starved to death. The American educator John Calvin Ferguson suggested that Chinese and foreign communities work together to organize the CIFRC to do fund-raising for the refugees. On 12 December 1910, the commission was formally established and elected eight Chinese and eight Westerners to the board of trustees. Ferguson and Shen Zhongli served as the cochairs. As soon as the CIFRC was established, it appealed to the Chinese government, local communities, merchants, and the British, American, French, German, and Japanese governments to donate money for this program. By 21 September 1911, the commission had received 1.53 million taels of silver. The commission developed three programs to help refugees: provide direct food supply, provide jobs as a form of relief, and help restore farming as a form of relief. These programs proved to be one of the few efficient efforts for famine relief in modern China.

CHINA LOBBY. A special interest group acting on behalf of the Republic of China. It was a collection of two groups of people. One included rich **Nationalist Party** officials, headed by **T. V. Soong** and **H. H. Kung**; the other was composed of powerful American rightist entrepreneurs and politicians who tried to influence the American people and government in opposition to the Chinese Communists. The Americans associated with the China Lobby included Henry R. Luce, Alfred Kohlberg, Frederick C. McKee, Republican representative Walter H. Judd of Minnesota, and Republican senators William F. Knowland of California and Joseph R. McCarthy of Wisconsin. The China Lobby began its activities in the summer of 1940 as T. V. Soong traveled to Washington, D.C. During the **Second**

Sino-Japanese War, the China Lobby helped convince the American Congress to pass several resolutions, offering billions of dollars in support of China's war against the Japanese. This support included hard cash, military material, and personnel. During the Cold War period, the China Lobby campaigned to prevent U.S. recognition of the People's Republic of China and to bar it from the United Nations.

CHINA MERCHANT STEAMSHIP NAVIGATION CO. (CM-SNC). Transportation company founded in 1872 in China, during the **Self-Strengthening Movement**. **Li Hongzhang** obtained permission from the emperor and did successful fund-raising among merchants to found the first government-supervised merchant undertakings in Shanghai. In the beginning, the CMSNC had only six ships, but it developed rapidly due to assistance from the government in the form of subsidies and the exclusive right to ship tributary grain to Beijing. The CMSNC engaged not only in the coastal trade but also in inland waters trasportation, especially on the Yangtze River, thus becoming a strong rival of the American and British steamship companies. In 1877, the American **Russell & Co.** closed its navigation business in China and sold all its steamships to the CMSNC, bringing its number of ships to 27, aggregating 60,000 tons. The company also owned warehouses, shipyards, and other properties with branches in six other Chinese cities and in Japan, the Philippines, and Singapore. The total capital suppassed 4.2 million taels, making it the largest navigation company in China. In 1877, 1883, and 1889, it signed agreements with **Jardine, Matheson & Co.**, and **Butterfield & Swire** on their navigation lines and the fixed prices. But in later years, because of the increasing involvement of the Qing bureaucrats and haphazrd management, the company deteriorated and was finally sold off in 1902.

CHINA REVIVAL SOCIETY (*HUAXINGHUI*). One of the secret revolutionary organizations during the Qing era. It was founded on 15 February 1904 in the city of Changsha. The China Revival Society had more than a hundred primary members who elected **Huang Xing** their president and **Song Jiaoren** and Liu Kuaiyi vice presidents. In an attempt to not draw public attention, the China Revival Society was registered as a commercial company. It did not work out a concrete revolutionary program, but all its activities were dedicated to the overthrow of the **Manchu** regime. It was planning to stage an uprising in October, but the plan was leaked. Huang and other leaders were forced to flee to Japan. In 1905, the China Revival Society merged with **Sun Yat-sen**'s **Revive China Society** (*xingzhonghui*) and **Cai Yuanpei**'s **Recovery Society** (*guangfuhui*) and thus became the *tongmenghui* (the United League).

CHINA ZHI GONG PARTY (CZGP). One of the eight legally recognized non-Communist parties in Communist China. Founded in October 1925 in San Francisco, the China Zhi Gong Party's first president was the military leader of Guangdong, Chen Joingming. The CZGP derived from the *hongmen*'s Zhi Gong Hall based in the United States, which was one of the major supporters of **Sun Yat-sen**'s 1911 Revolution. Before 1949, all its members were overseas Chinese. After the founding of the People's Republic of China, its headquarters moved to mainland China and its representatives attended the **Chinese People's Political Consultative Conference**, becoming one of the eight legally recognized non-Communist parties in Communist China. The party recruited its members among returned overseas Chinese, their relatives, and noted scholars who had overseas connections. The CZGP accepted **Chinese Communist Party** (CCP) leadership and sponsorship and followed the CCP's direction, and the CCP offered its leaders some positions in the government.

CHINESE ANARCHISM. Anarchism is a European political ideology, advocating an absolutely free society with no government or other authorities. Its influence in China can be traced back to the late 19th-century **anti-Manchu** movement. Chinese radical intellectuals defined anarchism as an "act that used violent means to destroy the organization of society." Inspired by the heroic self-sacrifice of the Russian anti-czarist anarchist groups, such as the People's Will and the Black Hand, these intellectuals organized the Chinese Assassination Corps and used assassination as a tool to strike the Manchu regime. The anarchist programs gained momentum among Chinese students in Paris and Tokyo in 1906. The **Paris group** was enamored of Western science and civilization, while the Tokyo group often linked their thoughts with Chinese traditional culture.

The Paris group advocated anarcho-syndicalism, drawing on the works of Mikhail Bakunin and Peter Kropotkin, while the Tokyo group advocated a peasant-based society of mutual aid based on a fusion of Taoism, Buddhism, and the agricultual romanticism of Leo Tolstoy. Nonetheless, both condemned the Confucian hierarchical society and both participated in the Chinese Nationalist movement, although they theoretically repudiated nationalism and the nation-state. Some anarchists, such as Jing Meijiu and Zhang Ji, compromised to gain power in the Nationalist government, believing it to be the first step toward their long-term goals of the abolition of capitalism, the state, and coercive authority. The Paris group argued that anarchists should be involved not in terrorist activities but in education. In 1912, most of its members returned to China and established the anarchist party, Promoting Virtue Society, whose leadership included Li Shezheng and **Wang Jingwei**. The anarchists engaged in the **New Culture Movement** and played a significant role in the **May Fourth Movement** in 1919. Like the Nationalists, the anarchists had their main base in the city of Guangzhou, where they formed a class struggle–oriented organization and were involved in the anti-Manchu revolution. In the 1910s, anarchism was not only an abstract philosophy of Western-educated intellectuals but also took root among workers, peasants, and other oppressed groups. However, the anarchist movement began to lose ground in 1921, after the **Chinese Communist Party** (CCP) was established. The immediate changes that bolshevism and the CCP promised seemed to be more appealing to workers and peasants than the long-term goals of anarchism. Also, the lack of coordination among the different anarchist organizations contributed to their decline.

CHINESE COMMUNIST PARTY (CCP). The **Chinese Communist Party** was founded in 1921 with help of the **Comintern**. It is a revolutionary organization based on the ideology of Karl Marx and Vladimir Lenin. In its early years, it was a branch of the Comintern, and the decisions of the Chinese Communist Revolution were made thousands of miles away in Moscow. The CCP did not totally rid itself of Russian influence until the 1940s. On 1 July 1921, 13 representatives of Marxist study groups from different provinces came to Shanghai and founded the CCP with **Chen Duxiu** as chairman of the party. In 1924, as **Sun Yat-sen** designed a new policy of collaborating with the Soviet Union and the Communists, the CCP members were encouraged to join the **Nationalist Party** (GMD) and the **Northern Expedition** against **warlordism**.

In 1927, the CCP and GMD split. The CCP launched several uprisings in an attempt to retake its urban bases. With the failure of all these insurrections, however, the CCP was forced to move to rural areas, where **Mao Zedong**'s guerrilla tactics won him recognition. According to Mao's principle that "the party commands the gun" and "the party had to build a branch in each company," the CCP took strict control of its military force from the very beginning. The CCP also established a Communist government, known as the **Jiangxi Soviet**, in the rural base. As the CCP central leaders, mostly the Russian-trained "Chinese Bolsheviks," moved to the Jiangxi Soviet, they kicked Mao out of the leading positions in the party and army. Under the commandership of **Bo Gu** and the Comintern's adviser **Otto Braun**, the **Red Army** was defeated by **Chiang Kai-shek** in his fifth **Encirclement and Suppression Campaign**. The CCP had to make a military retreat from southeast to northwest China in October 1934. In this legendary 6,000-mile trek, known as the **Long March**, the party's Politburo was shaken up and Mao Zedong became recognized as the de facto highest leader. Although the CCP troops had taken heavy casualties on the journey, Mao led the remnants finally to arrive at **Yan'an** in October 1935, where they built a new revolutionary base.

During the **Second Sino-Japanese War (1937–1945)**, the CCP reconciled with the GMD, and its Red Army was reorganized into the **Eighth Route Army** and the **New Fourth Army** under Chiang Kai-shek's leadership. During the war, the CCP employed Nationalist propaganda to recruit various groups of people, initiated social reforms to mobilize peasants to join its army, and used guerrilla tactics to fight the Japanese. All this led to the growth of the party's military force and political influence. It was also during this period that the CCP launched the **Rectification Movement**, squelching dissent over Mao Zedong's policies, formally establishing his position as the supreme leader of the party, and solidifying his sinicized Marxism-Leninism, known as **Mao Zedong Thought**, as party doctrine. After Japan surrendered in 1945, the CCP and GMD soon restarted their military conflicts. The civil war lasted for three years and concluded with the collapse of the Nationalist regime in mainland China. In October 1949, Mao Zedong proclaimed the founding of the People's Republic of China (PRC). The relationship between the CCP and the new republic was identical to Stalin's model that the party (CCP) controls the state (PRC).

CHINESE COMMUNIST PARTY, SEVENTH CONGRESS. Held from 23 April through 11 June 1945 and attended by 775 delegates representing 1.21 million party members.The congress passed a new party constitution, which referred to **Mao Zedong Thought** as the guiding line of all party work. It elected a new CCP Central Committee, consisting of 44 full members and 33 alternate members. The following meeting of the CCP Central Committee elected the Politburo of 13 members with **Mao Zedong** as chairman of the CCP Central Committee and Politburo. Mao Zedong Thought was fully recognized as Chinese Marxist orthodoxy, and Mao's position as supreme leader was formally established at the CCP Seventh Congress.

CHINESE EASTERN RAILWAY (CER). Railroad constructed by the Russians in China's Manchuria as a single-track line extending the Trans-Siberian Railway from the Sino-Russian border via Harbin across Manchuria to Vladivostok. In 1896, the Qing government sent **Li Hongzhang** as an emissary to Russia to negotiate with Count Witte for the **Sino-Russian secret alliance**. Li accepted the Russian demand for a **railway concession**, granting a private Russian company, the Chinese Eastern Railway Corporation (CERC), the permission to construct and manage the railway line. China would also cede a strip of land along the railway line, within which the Russians had the right to build residence houses, schools, hospitals, and other public facilities; Russia also had complete authority over the belt land, including stationing troops as "railway guards." Construction of the CER started in July 1897 and was completed in 1902. The CERC also extended southward from Harbin to Port Arthur, known as the **South Manchuria Railway** (SMR).

After the Russo-Japanese War in 1905, the Japanese took over the South Manchuria Railway and established the South Manchuria Railway Company to prepare for further encroachment into Manchuria. In 1935, the Soviet Union sold its rights in the CER to the Japanese puppet regime, Manchukuo. In the last year of the **Second Sino-Japanese War**, the Soviet Union sent troops to Manchuria, destroyed the Japanese Kuantung Army, and regained its control of the CER and SMR. After the founding of the People's Republic of China, **Mao Zedong** refused Joseph Stalin's demand for joint control of the CER and its southern branch, and the Soviet Union handed over the two railways to China in 1952.

CHINESE EDUCATIONAL MISSION (1872–1881). In 1872, the Qing government approved the suggestion by **Yung Wing** to send Chinese children to the United States to study Western science and engineering. This program, known as the Chinese Educational Mission, included four groups of 120 young Chinese students aged 12 to 14 who would study in the United States for 15 years. In 1872, the first group of Chinese boys arrived in New England. They lived in American families, studied and graduated from high school at Hartford, Connecticut, and then enrolled in American colleges. This mission was eventually disbanded in 1881, and most children were called back to China. However, some of the students managed to study in and graduate from American colleges. These graduates included **Zhan Tianyou**, the father of China's railway construction; **Tang Shaoyi**, the first premier of the Republic of China; and many others who returned to China and made significant contributions to China's modernization.

CHINESE FEMINISM. In traditional China, women's role and status were defined as inferior. **Confucianism** honored patriarchal domination, advocating three bonds of obedience for women: to fathers at home, to husbands in marriage, and to sons after being widowed. Feminism was a social movement during later Qing and Republican periods inspired by Western influence. It denounced **footbinding**, the cult of chastity and virginity, rules against the remarriage of widows, and family violence against women. The British feminist writer Mrs. Archibald **Little** founded the first Natural Foot Society in Shanghai; later, Chinese women took the lead in the antifootbinding campaign. Consequently, the century-long practice was banned by both the imperial and Republican governments. An equally important accomplishment was the women's pursuit of education. In the 20th century, as the traditional notion that "untalented women are virtuous" was criticized, most schools and colleges were opened to female students, and girls' schools mushroomed throughout the country. In the meantime, female journalists, such as **Lu Bicheng** and Wu Pingmei, founded women's newspapers and journals to discuss women's issues and advocate women's emancipation. The early feminist **Qiu Jin**, who had studied in Japan, returned to China for the overthrow of the **Manchu** regime. She opened a girls' school and founded a women's journal to discuss both women's emancipation and republican revolution.

Compared to their male comrades, the feminists had more tasks on their revolutionary agenda, including ending gender discrimination at home and in the society at large. Nonetheless, after the 1920s, feminism as a social movement was set aside in favor of the more urgent issues of revolution and War against Japanese Aggression. A few women played leading roles in the social movements, including **Xiang Jingyu** on the side of the Communists and the **Soong sisters** on the side of the Nationalists. Both the Nationalists and Communists were committed to women's liberation and used the women's issue as a powerful tool to mobilize all sectors of society for their revolutions. In 1930, the Nationalist government issued the Civil Code, offering women the right to inherit property as well as enjoy equal rights in the workplace. Its **New Life Movement**, however, returned to Confucian notions, encouraging women to pursue virtue rather than learning, family responsibility rather than a professional career. In this regard, the Communists did not do much better. As the feminist writer **Ding Ling** revealed, the Communists promoted women's participation in politics, war, and production, but did not reduce women's traditional roles at home; still less did they realize real gender equality in **Yan'an**. In 1949, after the People's Republic of China was established, the Communists launched the family reform campaign, indicating that Chinese feminism was still an unfinished revolution. *See also BEIJING WOMEN'S NEWS; CHINESE WOMEN'S JOURNAL*; MENG BUYU; SHI PINGMEI; ZHENG YUXIU.

CHINESE NATIONAL RELIEF AND REHABILITATION ADMINISTRATION (CNRRA). An organization established by the Nationalist government to distribute relief aid from 1945 to 1947. Under an agreement with the United Nations Relief and Rehabilitation Administration (UNRRA), it was authorized to take possession of relief supplies and distribute them. The Republic of China was one of four members of the Central Committee of the UNRRA. In 1945, the UNRRA worked with the CNRRA and proposed 10 programs of food, clothing, shelter, health, transportation, agriculture, industry, flood areas, welfare services, and displaced persons. They soon realized that all these were permanent efforts dependent on the reconstruction of the Chinese economy, and that only a few projects could actually be carried out. It was reported that much of the aid of the UNRRA was misappropriated.

CHINESE NATIONALIST PARTY (GUOMINDANG, GMD, OR KUOMINTANG, KMT). The Nationalist Party (GMD) grew out of the **Tongmenghui** (United League) organized on 20 August 1905 by **Sun Yat-sen, Huang Xing**, and **Song Jiaoren** in Tokyo. To be a majority party in the parliament after the founding of the Republic of China, the Tongmenghui needed to recruit more members. The Nationalist Party was therefore established by merging four other small parties in 1912. The GMD constitution consisted of five objectives: (1) to maintain the political unification of China, (2) to develop local autonomy, (3) to enhance ethnic similarity, (4) to promote social welfare, and (5) to maintain international peace. Sun Yat-sen was elected premier (the highest leader of the party) and Song Jiaoren was in charge of daily business. In the parliament election of 1913, the GMD won 132 seats of 174 in the Senate and 269 of 596 in the House of Representatives. In light of the provisional **Constitution of the Republic of China**, the GMD, as the majority party in the parliament, would organize the government, which was the last thing that President **Yuan Shikai** wanted to see. Eventually, Song was assassinated by Yuan Shikai's people and the parliament was dismissed.

Nevertheless, when Sun Yat-sen initiated the **Second Revolution** to attack Yuan Shikai, not all GMD members joined him; this led to the failure of the campaign. Disappointed with the GMD, Sun decided to transform it into a more disciplined and more devoted Revolutionary Party. He also required all the members of the new party to swear an oath of loyalty to him. Haung Xing and some other GMD leaders disagreed with Sun. They refused to join the new Revolutionary Party, keeping the name GMD to continue the anti–Yuan Shikai campaigns. In 1919, Sun Yat-sen resumed the name GMD, proclaimed that it was the GMD's sole purpose to practice the **Three People's Principles**, and launched the **Constitutional Protection Movement**. The failure of this movement in 1921 was a blow to the GMD. In the next year, Sun decided to reorganize the GMD again. It took two years of consulting and coordinating with other political forces for Sun Yat-sen to make a new policy of collaboration, this time with Soviet Russia and the Communists. The GMD and the **Chinese Communist Party** (CCP) worked together and launched the **Northern Expedition** against the **warlords**. The victory of the expedition established **Chiang Kai-shek** as Sun's successor and supreme leader of China.

In 1927, recognizing the increasing threat of the Communists to the GMD's leadership, Chiang began to purge them from the army and the government. The split between the GMD and the CCP evolved into a civil war. The GMD government launched five **Encirclement and Suppression Campaigns** against the Communists, which forced them to withdraw from their bases in southeast China to northwest areas in a massive retreat, known as the **Long March**. Despite its anti-Communist rhetoric, the GMD actually followed the Russian model to build a one-party state with one ideology (Three Principles of the People) and one leader (Chiang Kai-shek). After the Japanese invaded North China, the GMD reconciled with the CCP, forming an anti-Japanese **United Front**. Between 1937 and 1945, the GMD led China to defeat Japan, and it made China one of the **Big Four** nations on the international stage. The war, however, significantly weakened the ruling party and gave the Communists a chance to vastly expand their military force. In the following years, civil war, economic crises, political corruption, and military failures all contributed to the eventual downfall of the GMD government in mainland China. In December 1949, the GMD government fled to Taiwan.

CHINESE PEASANTS' AND WORKERS' DEMOCRATIC PARTY (CPWDP). One of the eight legally recognized non-Communist parties in Communist China. Founded in August 1930 by **Deng Yanda** in Shanghai. In May 1927, Deng came to believe that **Chiang Kai-shek** and **Wang Jingwei** had betrayed **Sun Yat-sen**'s policy of alliance with the Communists, and he began to prepare for the establishment of a new political party. On 9 August 1930, Deng presided over the First National Convention of the Carders **Nationalist Party** (GMD), proclaiming the formal establishment of the Provisional Operation Committee (POC) of the GMD. Deng was assassinated the next year by GMD agents, convincing the POC to cut off its relations with the GMD. The Second National Convention of the POC was held on 10 November 1935 in Hong Kong, where it announced its alliance with the **Chinese Communist Party** (CCP) to promote the national resistance movement against Japanese aggression. Furthermore, the party was renamed the Operation Committee for the Chinese Liberation (OCCL). In February 1947, the Fourth National Convention decided to rename the OCCL the Chinese Peasants' and Workers' Democratic

Party. The CPWDP joined the **Chinese People's Political Consultative Conference** in 1949. The party mainly consisted of junior and senior intellectuals in the field of public health and medicine. Its president, Zhang Naiqi, was appointed minister of communication of the People's Republic of China but was purged from the government in 1957.

CHINESE PEOPLE'S POLITICAL CONSULTATIVE CONFERENCE (CPPCC, 1949). Known also as the "new" Political Consultative Conference, as distinguished from the "old" Political Consultative Conference organized by the **Nationalist Party** (GMD) in 1946. At the end of the civil war, the **Chinese Communist Party** (CCP) called the Chinese People's Political Consultative Conference in 21–30 September 1949 in Beiping (present-day Beijing). A total of 640 delegates representing the CCP, the **People's Liberation Army**, local Communist governments, other political parties, and overseas Chinese attended the conference. The conference declared itself to be functioning as a national congress and the **Common Program** approved by the conference as the de facto constitution. It announced that the new republic would be a state of the people's democratic dictatorship as defined by **Mao Zedong** in *New Democracy*, in which he emphasized the absolute leadership of the CCP and indicated no power sharing with any other political parties. The conference approved the general principle in making China's domestic and foreign policies and passed several important resolutions regarding the establishment of the People's Republic of China. It determined the name and capital of the new republic, the national flag, and the national anthem. It elected Mao Zedong chairman of the Central Government and other Communist leaders, **Zhu De**, **Liu Shaoqi**, and **Gao Gang**, as vice-chairmen. **Sun Yat-sen**'s wife, **Song Qingling**; the previous leader of the GMD's **Guangxi Clique**, **Li Jishen**; and the chairman of the **China Democratic League**, **Zhang Lan**, were also elected vice-chairs of the Central Government. It was decided to create a standing committee of the CPPCC, consisting of 180 members with Mao Zedong as its chairman. From 1949 to 1954, the CPPCC functioned as the de facto legislature of the PRC. In September 1954, when the Chinese National People's Congress was established and the new constitution promulgated, the CPPCC lost its importance in Chinese politics.

CHINESE QUINTESSENCE. Scholarship into the study of Chinese philology, literature, historical figures, and political and cultural systems. Chinese quintessence became a hot topic of academic inquiry as the result of the establishment of the Chinese Culture Preservation Society in February 1905 by Zhang Binglun, Ma Xulun, and other prominent scholars. They advocated studying Chinese culture in the **anti-Manchu** movement and emphasized upholding Chinese cultural essence in learning Western science. They supported **Sun Yat-sen**'s **Three People's Principles** and tried to find some ground for democratic reforms in Chinese traditional culture. The school was influential before the 1911 Revolution. Nonetheless, the **New Culture Movement** attacked this scholarship for its lack of critical attitude toward China's historical legacy and for having less concern for current affairs.

CHINESE WOMEN'S JOURNAL (ZHONGGUO NÜBAO). Created on 14 January 1907 by **Qiu Jin** in Shanghai. Qiu stated that the mission of the journal was "to expose the darkness of society and danger of women and to help our sisters to move forward to a brighter world." Each issue of the journal was 60 pages in length, covering news, reports, translations, novels, and literary critiques. Qiu Jin was the chief editor and one of the major contributors. The other contributors were Republicans and early feminists. The journal published a story based on Qiu's autobiography, which was adapted for a performance of local storytelling. The bitter journey of a female revolutionary made many young readers burst into tears and evoked nationwide repercussions. The journal printed two issues but was banned before the third issue came out, as Qiu was arrested and executed.

CHONGQING (CHUNGKING). The temporary capital of the Republic of China during the **Second Sino-Japanese War**. Chongqing is located in Sichuan Province on the bank of the Yangtze River. In 1937, after Shanghai fell and the Japanese troops approached Nanjing, the Nationalist government issued a public notice on 20 November titled "Movement of the Nationalist Government to Chongqing." The National Government officially opened on 1 December, and it formally made Chongqing the wartime capital on 6 September 1940.

THE CHRISTIAN OCCUPATION OF CHINA. A report of Christian missionary works in China in the 20th century, published in 1922.

This report was a result of a three-year investigation by the Special Investigation Committee under the China Continuation Committee. This committee was established in autumn 1918, and it embarked on this project the following spring. All Christian missionary bodies in China were involved, and more than 150 people contributed to writing and compiling it. The report was edited by Milton Theobald Stauffer, an American missionary, and both Chinese and English versions came out in 1922. The report attempted to further the progress of missionary work in China on the basis of serious research. However, the scope of its investigation was far beyond that of missionary activities and covered all of China's administrative zones, boundaries, cities, population, geography, ethnic groups, language and dialects, natural resources, economic conditions, inland and sea transportation routes, communication, education system, medicine, and others. All this information made the report a most valued encyclopedia of Chinese society. However, the title of the report, *The Christian Occupation of China*, was criticized by some Chinese and Western scholars, who suggested alternative phrases such as "Christianity Settles Down in China" or "Rooting the Christian Church in Chinese Soil."

CHUANBI, CONVENTION OF (CONVENTION OF CHUEN- PEH, 1841). Soon after the **Opium War** broke out in 1840, the **Daoguang Emperor** asked for peace. He appointed **Qishan**, the governor of Guangdong Province, to be imperial commissioner to negotiate with the British. The Convention of Chuenpeh was a treaty signed by Qishan and Captain **Charles Elliot** in Chuenpeh, Guangdong Province, in January 1841. In light of the agreed terms, the Qing Empire would cede Hong Kong Island and pay an indemnity of 6 million taels to Great Britain. The city of Guangzhou would be opened to foreign traders as a commercial port. In return, the British troops would withdraw from the Chinese territory they occupied. However, the Convention of Chuenpeh was not ratified by the emperor, who denied that he had authorized Qishan to sign any treaty with the British. Qishan was dismissed, and Hong Kong was not formally ceded to Great Britain until the **Treaty of Nanjing** was signed in 1842.

CHULIAN TINGZHENG. Phrase meaning "sitting behind a silk screen and administering state affairs." After the **Xianfeng Emperor** died in 1861, his son, the **Tongzhi Emperor**, was crowned at the age of four. Tongzhi's mother, the **Dowager Cixi**, seized power through a coup and became one of his regents. Because Tongzhi was too young to administer state affairs, the Dowager Cixi sat behind a silk screen in the court, reviewed ministerial reports, asked questions, and made decisions on the emperor's behalf. Although the **Manchu** system did not allow women to get involved in politics, sitting behind a silk screen symbolized a woman's absence from the court. This practice did not stop until Tongzhi turned 16. Two years later, however, Tongzhi died and the Dowager Cixi handpicked another young boy to be the **Guangxu Emperor** so that she could resume *chulian tingzheng*. Also, after the abortive **Hundred Days' Reform** in 1889, Cixi put the Guangxu Emperor into detention and ruled the dynasty by chulian tingzheng for another 10 years. In so doing, the Dowager Cixi was able to rule China for 48 years.

CIVIL SERVICE EXAMINATIONS (*KEJU*). An examination system for recruitment of government officials. It created the mechanism by which Confucian students, regardless of their wealth or social status, could become government officials. It was divided into three levels. The first was held at the county level each year, and those who passed the exam would obtain the *xiucai* degree; the second was administered at the provincial level every three years to obtain the *juren* degree; and the last one was administered in the capital every three years, and those who were successful would be granted the *jinshi* degree and a position in the government. Usually, after the evaluation of the tests by ministers, the emperor would personally interview the first group of jinshi degree holders and then decide their final ranks. The exams tested the candidates' understanding and interpretation of Confucian classics by requiring a written essay in a fixed format. Exams lasted between 24 and 72 hours and were taken in isolated examination rooms. To guarantee fairness of the exams, the names of candidates were sealed and the evaluators could see only the order numbers. It was not uncommon in Chinese history for individuals to move from a low social status to political prominence through success in the imperial examination. However, since the process of studying for the exams was costly and time consuming, most successful candidates came from wealthy gentry families. The chances for poor students tended to be even smaller in the late Qing, when exam frauds were prevalent and offices were simply sold. In 1905, as part of the Qing constitutional reform, the civil service examinations were abolished to promote the new scholarship and new schooling system, but this also destroyed the traditional channel of social mobility, contributing to the collapse of the Qing Empire.

CIXI, EMPRESS DOWAGER (EMPRESS, 1835–1908). The de facto ruler of **Manchu** China from 1861 to 1908. Also known in China as the West Dowager Empress, named after her residence in the western palace of the Forbidden City. Born into the family of a low-ranking Manchu official of the Yehenara clan, Cixi was selected to be a concubine of the **Xianfeng Emperor** in 1851. Because of her beauty and talent, she quickly became the emperor's favorite. In 1856, Cixi bore to the emperor a son, Zaichun, who was the only male heir of Xianfeng. When the boy became the **Tongzhi Emperor** after Xianfeng's death, his mother, Cixi, was elevated to the position of Empress Dowager.

In 1860, British and French troops stormed Beijing, and the royal family fled to Rehe, where the Xianfeng Emperor died of sickness and depression. Before his death, the Xianfeng Emperor named eight of his most prestigious ministers, headed by Sushun, as the "Eight Regent Ministers" to direct and support the young emperor, who was only five years old. However, Cixi had been helping Xianfeng with state affairs when he was sick and thus became a manipulator of court politics. The appointment of the regents was meant to deprive Cixi of power. Consequently, Cixi used her alliance with **Prince Gong** and Prince Chun to stage the **Xinyou Coup** of 1861, in which she arrested Sushun and the other regents, charged them with treason, and had them executed. Cixi pronounced that she would aid her son in dealing with state affairs. With the young emperor sitting in court to meet the ministers, Cixi began to "listen to politics behind the curtains" and make decisions for her son. Thus she became the real ruler of the Qing dynasty.

To reward Prince Gong, Cixi bestowed on him the great power to head the **Grand Council** and the **Zongli Yamen**; this position enabled Prince Gong to promote an institutional reform in the emperor's name, the **Tongzhi Restoration**. Nonetheless, Cixi avoided giving Prince Gong too much power and kept the last say in decision making at the time of internal chaos and foreign intrusion. She supported

Zeng Guofan, **Zuo Zongtang**, and **Li Hongzhang** in organizing the **Hunan Army**, the **Anhui Army**, and other local military forces to suppress the **Taiping Rebellion**, and endorsed them in launching the **Self-Strengthening Movement** for China's industrialization and military modernization. In this sense, she endorsed certain programs of learning Western science and technology. Cixi also began to promote officials of **Han** ethnicity to key government positions in the Manchu-dominated court. In 1875, Tongzhi died without an heir and Cixi handpicked her nephew Zaitian, a four-year-old boy, to be the **Guangxu Emperor**. Technically, Guangxu gained the right to rule from Cixi at the age of 16. But even after he began to deal with the state routines at age 19, he was required to have every decision approved by the Empress Dowager.

Cixi did not like the emperor's support of radical reform toward a democratic monarchy advocated by **Kang Youwei** and **Liang Qichao**. In September 1898, she ordered General Ronglu and **Yuan Shikai** to stage another coup, which detained the Guangxu Emperor and arrested and executed major reform leaders. On foreign affairs, Cixi basically agreed with Li Hongzhang that China was unable to fight with Western powers, and she approved several unequal treaties with the foreigners, including the most humiliating **Treaty of Shimonoseki**. On the other hand, she was aware of the increasing threat of foreign intrusion and tried to use the people to contain Western influence. The typical example was her support of the **Boxer Rebellion** in 1899–1900, during which she declared war on eight foreign powers. The war ended with China's defeat and the **Boxer Protocol**, offering the foreigners war reparations of £67 million and the right to a foreign military presence in China. Cixi blamed the Boxers and ordered the suppression of the "rebellion." The way in which she first used the Boxers and then sold them out indicated that her regime was not only weak but also untrustworthy.

In her late years, Cixi felt it necessary to make a substantial reform. The **Xinzheng Reform** included the drafting of a constitution, the organizing of a congress, the abolition of Confucian exams, and the banning of footbinding. However, it was too late to revive the dying dynasty. The Chinese people began to see revolution as the only solution. Knowing that she and Guangxu were seriously ill, Cixi chose the two-year-old baby Puyi to be the next emperor. On 15 November 1908, Cixi died at the age of 73 and Puyi was crowned as the **Xuantong Emperor**. This was only three years before the final collapse of the Qing dynasty. *See also CHULIAN TINGZHENG.*

CLASS STRUGGLE. The core of Chinese Communist ideology, it stemmed from the Marxist-Leninist interpretation of human history and **Mao Zedong**'s theory on the Chinese Revolution. Mao differentiated the Chinese people into seven classes: (1) workers, (2) poor peasants and middle peasants, (3) landlords, (4) rich peasants, (5) bureaucratic bourgeoisie, (6) national bourgeoisie, and (7) petty bourgeoisie. According to Mao, the workers were the leading class; poor peasants were the main force of the revolution; landlords, rich peasants, and bureaucratic bourgeoisie were the enemies of the revolution; and other social classes might be friends or allies of the **Chinese Communist Party** (CCP). Mao used the theory of class struggle to mobilize people more successfully in the war and in the **land reform** movements. More often than not, Mao adjusted or intensified the class struggle in accordance with changes in the national political situation. During the **Second Sino-Japanese War**, the CCP formed an alliance with all social classes and individuals who were willing to fight Japan. However, this was only a tentative compromise because from the Maoist perspective, class struggle was the driving force for social progress and a perpetual factor of the Chinese Revolution. Even after the CCP came to power, the proletariat still had to continue to fight the bourgeoisie, including those inside the Communist Party and government. This theory explains one of the reasons for the Cultural Revolution. In most cases, class struggle degenerated into factional power struggles. The political campaigns of class struggle staged after 1949 victimized numerous innocents and hindered China's economic development.

COMINTERN (COMMUNIST INTERNATIONAL, 1919–1943). Also known as the Third International. An international Communist organization founded in March 1919 by Russian Bolshevik leader Vladimir Lenin. Its mission was to use "all available means, including armed force, for the overthrow of the international bourgeoisie and for the creation of an international Soviet republic." The Comintern sent representatives **Grigori Voitinsky** and **Hendricus Maring** to China to help the Chinese radical intellectuals establish the **Chinese Communist Party** (CCP); dispatched special agent Adolf

Joff to meet and convince **Sun Yat-sen** of the policy of alliance with the Soviet Union and the Chinese Communists; and assigned military advisers to China, including **Mikhail Borodin**, who worked at the Whampoa Academy, and **Otto Braun** for the **Red Army**. The Comintern made the CCP one of its branches in the Far East; the CCP had to follow the instructions of the Comintern and get material support from Moscow. The loyal CCP members of the Comintern were the **Twenty-eight Bolsheviks** who were trained in Russia and held leading positions in the CCP Politburo. Because the Comintern's guidance and the leadership of the Twenty-eight Bolsheviks led to several failures and setbacks in the Chinese Revolution, their leadership was challenged and replaced by **Mao Zedong** during the **Long March**. Mao's sinicized Marxism finally gained the dominant position in the CCP, and the Comintern lost its influence over the CCP after the **Rectification Movement** in **Yan'an**. On 15 May 1943, the president of the executive committee of the Third International announced the disbanding of the Comintern.

COMMERCIAL PRESS (*SHANGWU YINSHU GUAN*). The first modern publishing house in China. The Commercial Press was founded on 11 February 1897 by four young Chinese who had previously worked for the American Presbyterian Mission Press. In its early years, the Commercial Press focused on printing business account books. Five years after it was started, the press established a division of editing and translation and invited the famous liberal scholars **Cai Yuanpei** and Zhang Yuanji to be its directors. It was first under Cai and then under Zhang that the press hired more scholars and worked out a comprehensive development plan. The press imported Japanese printing equipment. In 1903, it published China's first textbooks for elementary, middle, and high schools. In the following years, its publication expanded to include popular magazines, such as *Student Journal* and *Juvenile Journal*, and dictionaries, which were regarded as authoritative reference books in China. With its precious collection of rare books and comprehensive reference books, the press built up the East Library and opened it to the public in 1909. The total capital volume of the press had increased to ¥1.5 million and had 750 employees by 1914. On 29 January 1932, Japanese bombing destroyed the press and its library. The press was partly rebuilt shortly thereafter and moved to the interior provinces during the **Second Sino-Japanese War**. Having returned to Shanghai in 1945, the press resumed full business. After 1949, the Commercial Press in mainland China began to focus on the publication of translated Western academic books. The Taiwan branch of the Commercial Press was established in 1948 and has had no relations with the headquarters on the mainland since 1949.

COMMON PROGRAM. A provisional constitution of the People's Republic of China (PRC) between 1949 and 1954. These first five years of the PRC were referred to as China's "transition period" from a democratic revolution to a Socialist revolution. The full title of the provisional constitution is the Common Program of the **Chinese People's Political Consultative Conference**. It was drafted under the leadership of the **Chinese Communist Party** (CCP), presented by **Zhou Enlai** at the Chinese People's Political Consultative Conference, and approved by the conference on 29 September 1949. The Common Program laid down the broad goals of the new republic consistent with **Mao Zedong**'s doctrine of new democracy. It stipulated that the PRC was a "people's democratic dictatorship founded on the worker-peasant alliance." It also emphasized unifying China's various classes and nationalities. The Common Program consisted of an introduction and 60 articles divided into seven chapters. It elaborated the nature of the republic, its government structure, military system, and basic policies concerning economy, culture, education, ethnic groups, and foreign affairs. The Common Program automatically ceased when the first Socialist constitution of the PRC was promulgated in 1954. *See also* NEW DEMOCRACY.

COMMUNICATION CLIQUE. A clique of politicians during the early republic. The old Communication Clique was headed by Liang Shiyi, and most of its members were government technocrats engaged in the construction of railways or the development of navigation business, telegraph and postal services, and modern banking systems. The Communication Clique closely allied with **Yuan Shikai** and had extensive connections with foreign countries that were involved in Chinese railway projects and that had obtained **railway concessions**. Since railways were the major sources of revenue of governments and **warlords**, the Communication Clique had powerful political leverage. Although power changed hands frequently in the **Beijing government**, the Communication Clique always had its person in the cabinet. Liang Shiyi was Yuan's secretary-general and controlled the **Bank of Communication**, the Bank of Salt Industry, several mines, and a navigation company; thus, he was regarded as the "second president" and the "god of future" of the central government. In 1916, Yuan died and Liang escaped from Beijing. The old Communication Clique lost political representation, but most financial institutions remained in the hands of its members.

The new Communication Clique was a group of pro-Japanese officials who helped premier Duan Qirui gain foreign loans and thus regain its influence. Its leader, the general manager of the Bank of Communication, Cao Rulin, was appointed minister of finance and minister of foreign affairs of the Beijing government. This clique suggested that China accept the decision of the **Paris Peace Conference** to hand over Shandong to Japan. Cao and two other major members of the clique, Lu Zhongyu and Zhang Zhongxiang, subsequently became targets of public attack. Under the pressure of the student demonstrations and an anti-Japanese boycott during the **May Fourth Movement** of 1919, the Beijing government dismissed these three from office. In the early years, the Communication Clique had support from the railway technicians and workers. However, since the **Chinese Communist Party** and the **Nationalist Party** engaged in labor organizations in the 1920s, the Communication Clique lost its previous power base.

COMMUNIST GROUPS. After the **May Fourth Movement**, radical urban intellectuals showed great interest in the study of Marxism and the Russian Bolshevik Revolution. The first group for Marxist studies was established in Shanghai by **Chen Duxiu**, and its leading members included Li Da, Li Hanjun, and 12 others. Inspired by the Shanghai group, five more Communist groups were organized in China from August 1920 to July 1921, including the Beijing group headed by **Li Dazhao**, the Hunan group headed by He Shuheng and **Mao Zedong**, the Hubei group headed by Dong Biwu, and the Shandong group headed by Wang Jinmei. There were also two Communist groups outside China: the **Paris group** headed by Zhang Songnian and **Zhou Enlai**, and the Tokyo group headed by **Shi Cuntong** and **Zhou Fohai**. These groups for Marxist studies were not academic societies but revolutionary organizations. In July 1921, the six Communist groups, totaling 55 members, sent 12 representatives to Shanghai. Under the direction of the **Comintern**, they held a conference and formed the Chinese Communist Party.

COMMUNIST PARTY. *See* CHINESE COMMUNIST PARTY.

COMMUNIST UNIVERSITY OF THE TOILERS OF THE EAST. Also known as the Far East University. Founded on 21 April 1921 in Moscow by the **Comintern**, it was devoted to the training of Communist cadres for the ethnic minorities in the far eastern areas of the Soviet Union and revolutionaries from East Asian countries. According to their origins, the students were organized into classes of China, Japan, Korea, Mongolia, and Soviet far east regions. The curriculum included basic theories of Marxism and Leninism, methods of mass mobilization, law and administration, and tactics of proletarian revolution. Many early leaders of the **Chinese Communist Party**, such as **Liu Shaoqi**, Ren Bishi, **Ye Jianying**, **Ye Ting**, and **Xie Xuehong**, studied at this university. In 1928, about 100 students of the China class were transferred to the **Moscow Sun Yat-sen University**. In the 1930s, the first president of the university, Karl Radek, was purged by Joseph Stalin and the university was closed. *See also* RETURNED BOLSHEVIKS.

COMMUNIST YOUTH LEAGUE OF CHINA (CY). An organization run by the Communist Party for Chinese youth between the ages of 14 and 28. The league is organized on the party pattern and its leaders at various levels are appointed by the **Chinese Communist Party** (CCP). Before the formal establishment of the CCP, a group of young students and intellectuals founded the Socialist Youth League in Shanghai in August 1920. It did not become a nationwide organization until May 1922, when its first National Representative Conference was held under the CCP leadership in Guangzhou. Three years later, it was renamed the Communist Youth League and it developed its membership along with the CCP. During the War against Japanese Aggression, the CY stopped its activities but joined other organizations in the anti-Japanese **United Front**. On New Year's Day 1949, the Central Committee of the CCP decided to reorganize the CY, changing its name to Chinese New Democracy Youth League. It was regarded as a reserve force of the CCP, but the Youth League members who wanted to join the CCP had to go through regular procedures of application and admission. The name Communist Youth League of China was resumed in May 1957 in light of the resolution of its Third National Representative Conference.

CONFEDERATION OF PROVINCIAL ASSEMBLIES. A political system suggested by various groups of people in the early years of the Republic of China. In July 1920, the **warlord** of Hunan, **Tan Yankai**, sent an open telegram rejecting the central government in Beijing and calling for a popular elected provincial government to rule the province. This proposal was supported by warlords in Sichuan, Yunnan, Zhejiang, Guangdong, Fengtian, and other provinces. In the meantime, some scholars, such as **Cai Yuanpei**, **Zhang Binglin**, and **Hu Shih**, cited the example of the American federation system to support the idea of the Confederation of Provincial Assemblies. **Sun Yat-sen** insisted on China's unification and firmly opposed this plan. In 1922, Sun established the headquarters of the **National Revolutionary Army** in Guangzhou to prepare for the military unification of China. His plan conflicted with that of the local military leader, **Chen Jiongming**, who sought local autonomy for Guangdong. On 16 June, Chen attacked Sun's residence and Sun fled to Shanghai escorted by **Chiang Kai-shek**. In 1926, Chiang carried on Sun's mission and launched the **Northern Expedition** against **warlordism**. The idea of the Confederation of Provincial Assemblies fizzled out after Chiang finally unified China.

CONFUCIANISM (*RUXUE* OR *RUJIAO*). Chinese ethical and philosophical system, originating from the teachings of Confucius (551–479 BC), which continues to have a profound influence on modern Chinese society. Confucianism also is an important influence in Korea, Japan, and Vietnam. Confucius has been referred to as a sage by the Chinese. He lived during the Warring States Period, when China was divided into dozens of small kingdoms contending for supremacy. Confucius traveled from place to place trying to persuade local kings to accept his political ideas and ruling philosophy. Having failed in this mission, he opened the first private school in China to teach students.

The primary source for his thoughts is the book *Analects of Confucius*, which is a collection of his speeches and lectures edited by his disciples. Confucianism includes the following values. First, *ren* (love or benevolence). Ren is a ruling philosophy, arguing the need "to lead the subjects with excellence and put them in their place through roles and ritual practice, developing a sense of shame, then order themselves harmoniously." Ren also means humaneness toward others, a principal way to develop solid social relations. Second, *li* (ritual). Li does not merely imply propriety and etiquette but rather sets up certain ceremonial performances and a comprehensive system of moral norms regulating people's everyday life. Third, *xiao* (**filial piety**) means respecting and obeying one's parents. Xiao is required as the highest virtue, the very foundation for a hierarchical society, in which absolute obedience of ruler by ruled, of elder by younger, of parents by children, and of men by women is required. Fourth, *zhong* (loyalty). Zhong is referred to as a high human virtue. Loyalty to ruler comes first, then extends to one's duties and obligation to family, friends, and spouse. Many Chinese regard *xin* (honesty and trustworthness) and *yi* (righteousness) as two important Confucian principles. These concepts are often used by certain Chinese to develop a sense of brotherhood and hold community members together.

Confucianism was made the orthodox ideology of the state by the **Han** emperor Wudi (141–86 BC), who emphasized governance by virtue. In the following centuries, Confucianism remained a mainstream of Chinese philosophy and borrowed Taoist and Buddhist ideas to renew its vigor. The famous scholars Zhu Xi (AD 1130–1200) and Wang Yangming (AD 1472–1528) made substantial contributions to Confucianism. The school they created is referred to as "neo-Confucianism," which emphasizes innate knowledge and self-cultivation. After the **Manchu** conquered China in 1644, China remained a Confucian society. The state's power hardly reached every corner of the country, and the majority of Chinese communities were governed by Confucian moral codes. Confucianism created the concept of meritocracy in China; this led to the establishment of the **civil service examination** system. This system served as the major avenue for social mobility, enabling those who passed the exam to become government officers, thus upgrading their social status.

In the 20th century, Confucianism was reevaluated by radical thinkers such as **Chen Duxiu**. During the **New Culture Movement**, Confucianism was denounced as a source of despotism, backwardness, and degeneration. That criticism struck a sympathetic chord among the educated youth. Nonetheless, Confucianism continued to dominate some aspects of social life and even influenced the ideas and policies of revolutionary leaders. In recent years, some scholars have argued that the economic miracles in Japan, Korea, and other East Asian countries suggest possible contributions of Confucianism to the modernization of these countries.

Confucianism is not considered a religion by the Chinese since it has no church, God, or organized priesthood. Confucian scholars can freely believe in Buddhism, Taoism, Islam, Christianity, or other religions. On the other hand, Confucianism is a belief system that includes moral codes, norms, and guides for daily life; it consists of comprehensive cosmological views, and it has developed worship rituals, including ancestor worship, sacrifice to ancestral spirits, and an abstract celestial deity. In that sense, Confucianism qualifies as a religion. *See also* MANDATE OF HEAVEN.

CONSTITUTION OF THE REPUBLIC OF CHINA. The basic governing document for the Republic of China. It was drafted in accordance with the constitutional theory of **Sun Yat-sen** and his **Three People's Principles**. It was formally adopted by the **National Assembly** on 25 December 1946, promulgated by the National Government on 1 January 1947, and put into effect on 25 December 1947. The constitution originally established a republic with a national assembly and five branches of government: **Executive Yuan**, **Legislative Yuan**, **Judicial Yuan**, Examination Yuan, and **Control Yuan**. In 1949, when the Communists took over China, the constitution and other laws made by the republican government were abolished on the mainland, but the constitution continues to be in effect in Taiwan.

CONSTITUTIONAL PROTECTION MOVEMENT. A series of campaigns led by **Sun Yat-sen** from 1917 to 1922 to protect the provisional **constitution of the Republic of China**. After the death of **Yuan Shikai**, the Zhili **warlord** Feng Guozhang and the Anhui warlord Duan Qirui began to manipulate the **Beijing government**. In June 1917, Sun Yat-sen called all congressmen to leave Beijing for the south to organize a new parliament. About 100 congressmen arrived in Guangzhou, where they held an extraordinary session of the parliament on 25 August. The session decided to form a military government to protect the provisional constitution of the republic. On 1 September, Sun was elected as grand marshal to exercise the republic's power. The Beijing government launched a military expedition against Sun, but its troops were defeated in Hunan in November, and Duan Qirui was forced to resign. In the next year, Beijing resumed its military operation but still could not make any progress. The war ended with the South-North peace negotiations.

However, the political situation changed dramatically in Guangzhou. In May 1918, the military government in Guangzhou was reorganized and Sun Yat-sen lost control of it. He resigned and left for Shanghai, which brought the first campaign of the Constitutional Protection Movement to an end. In November 1920, Sun returned to Guangzhou and embarked on a second campaign by reestablishing the military government. In April 1921, another extraordinary session of the parliament was helds, it proclaimed the establishment of central government of the Republic of China in the south and elected Sun president (known as **Extraordinary President**). Sun insisted on unifying China by military force. This plan came into conflict with the military leader of Guangdong, **Chen Jiongming**, who preferred an independent Guangdong. On 16 June, Chen ordered the shelling of the presidential residence, and Sun had to flee for Shanghai. The second campaign concluded in failure.

CONSTITUTIONAL REFORM. *See* XINZHENG REFORM.

CONSULTATIVE ASSEMBLY (*ZIZHENG YUAN*). An institution established by the Qing court in its constitutional reform (**Xinzheng Reform**). After 1900, the Qing government began to consider institutional reforms and sent government officials abroad to study Western government systems. Imitating the Western congress, the Qing court published the charter of the Consultative Assembly in 1908 and formally established the institution two years later in Beijing. The assembly had 100 members, with two presidents and two to four vice presidents. Half its membership was elected by the different provinces, and the other half was appointed by the emperor. The duty of the assembly was to review and approve state budgets, taxation, and public bonds; make state laws; and impeach derelict government officials. In the following years, its charter was revised three times, but the assembly did not do any substantial work, contrary to what its charter promised. The Consultative Assembly was dismissed when the Qing government collapsed in 1912.

CONTROL YUAN (*JIANCHA YUAN*). One of the five branches of the government of the Republic of China, designed by **Sun Yat-sen**. It grew out of the Chinese traditional Censorates and Sun's understanding of the balance of power in Western government systems. It consisted of 19 to 29 members whose major duties were to supervise government operations, audit the budget, and impeach derelict government officials.

COOPERATIVE POLICY. The policy of some Western powers toward China in the 1860s. As **Prince Gong** initiated diplomatic reform and established a new office for foreign affairs, the **Zongli Yamen**, foreign countries saw the possiblity of cooperation with the Qing court to protect their treaty rights. The American minister, **Anson Burlingame**, put forward the idea of a Cooperative Policy, which was championed by the British minister, Frederick Bruce. The policy advocated cooperation among Western powers, cooperation with the Chinese government, recognition of China's legitimate interests, and enforcement of the foreign countries' treaty rights.

COUNCIL OF ADVISOR PRINCES. The early policymaking institution of the Qing dynasty, founded in 1637 before the **Manchu** conquest of China. It consisted of eight imperial princes who were also the major military commanders of the Manchu eight banner troops. In 1643, the Sunzhi Emperor appointed one **Han** official to the council. The council would make final decisions on crucial state affairs, including the deposal of an emperor. This was an example of the Manchus' tradition of military democracy. As royal influence increased, the power of the council gradually waned and it was finally abolished in 1717.

COUNTRY TRADE. Trade between Qing China and India controlled by the **British East India Company** in the late 18th and early 19th centuries. The early trading commodities included spices and birds' nests, and in later years, the opium trade was emphasized.

CREATION SOCIETY (*CHUANGZAOSHE*). One of the most influential literary associations in modern China. Founded in July 1921 by a group of students studying in Japan, its major members included **Guo Moruo**, **Yu Dafu**, Tian Han, and Cheng Fangwu. In the fall of 1921, the Creation Society published a series of literature in the vernacular language, including the famous poem *Goddess* by **Guo Moruo** and the novel *Degradation* by **Yu Dafu**. This marked the beginning of the modern literary revolution. In addition, Guo's translation of Goethe's *Sorrows of Young Werther* also gained enormous popularity. In May 1923, the society began to publish *Creation Weekly* and to edit a literary supplement for the *New Post of China*. The Creation Society followed the romantic tradition and claimed to believe in "art for art's sake," disagreeing with the theory of the social functions of literature. The society's arguments that art was valuable *as* art and that artistic pursuits were their own justification were criticized by some "revolutionary writers" in 1928. In fact, most members of the society did not live in an ivory tower of art but took an active part in the Chinese Revolution. Their works showed a great concern for social transformation, making contributions to the shift from "literary revolution" to "revolutionary literature." In later years, the society joined leftist writers in criticizing the **Crescent Moon Society**.

CRESCENT MOON SOCIETY (*XINYUESHE*). One of the most influential literary associations during the **New Culture Movement**. Founded in 1923 by a group of liberal intellectuals, the Crescent Moon Society first took the shape of a dinner party and later became a club. The name Crescent Moon, chosen by the romantic poet **Xu Zhimo**, was taken from Rabindranath Tagore's poetry collection *Crescent Moon*. The main participants of the society included **Liang Qichao**, **Hu Shih**, Xu Zhimo, Ding Xilin, and **Lin Huiyin**. In October 1925, Xu Zhimo began to edit the literature supplement for *Morning Bell* (*Zhenbao*); he also created other literary magazines, with the members of the Crescent Moon club serving as their major contributors. In 1928, as Hu Shih and Xu Zhimo founded *Crescent Moon Monthly,* the society became more active and more writers joined it, among them Liang Shiqiu, Pan Guandan, Zhu Anping, and Wen Yiduo. In June 1933, the *Crescent Moon Monthly* was taken over by the **Commercial Press** and the society stopped operation.

The works of the society members were deeply influenced by English romantic poetry. It was a collective effort of the Crescent Moon Society to break away from the shackles of the traditional poetic mode and to develop a new writing style. Writing in the vernacular language, society members emphasized free expression and formal beauty, making a great contribution to modern Chinese poetry. The society presented itself as a group of friends interested in literature without any political program or bylaws. The political perspectives of the members varied, yet most of them shared an anti-**warlord** and antidictatorship inclination. They also opposed so-called proletarian literature, denying that the mission of literature was to serve the **class struggle**. They were, therefore, criticized by **Lu Xun** and other left-wing writers. *See also* CREATION SOCIETY.

CURRENCY OF THE JIANGXI SOVIET. In 1927, the Communists began to build their rural revolutionary bases. Some of the bases established local governments and banks, which issued paper money for local circulation. On 1 February 1932, the National Bank of the Chinese Soviet Republic was established in Ruijin, Jiangxi Province, with **Mao Zedong** as president and Mao's wife, He Zizhen, as head of the money-printing house. To unify the currency in the Communist-controlled areas, the bank issued three kinds of currency: paper bills, copper coins, and silver dollars. The paper bills had the characters for "Chinese Soviet Republic" and the portrait of Vladimir Lenin printed on them. The quality of the paper was poor. The paper bills could be used only in the Communist-controlled areas and did not circulate for long. The copper coins had the same characters engraved on them and circulated to a greater extent, but they were replaced by silver dollars shortly thereafter. The silver dollars were the predominant currency in the **Jiangxi Soviet**. Unlike the paper bills and copper coins, the silver dollars had no Communist symbols engraved on them; instead, they copied other silver dollars, such as the Mexican peso and **Yuan Shikai** dollars, enabling them to be circulated not only in the Soviet areas but also in Nationalist-controlled regions. The bank stopped issuing currency when the Communist **Red Army** started the **Long March** in October 1934.

– D –

DAGU FORTS (TAKU FORTS). Located 60 km southeast of the city of Tianjin, the Dagu Forts were built between 1522 and 1527 by the Ming government. They were consolidated and expanded in 1848 by the Qing Army to include five big forts and 20 small forts that were equipped with French artillery. The Dagu Forts consisted, in total, of 17 fortifications with 60 built-in cannons, making them a strategic point in protecting the gateway to Beijing. However, because of poor leadership and the low morale of the troops, the forts were stormed twice by the British and French armies during the two **Opium Wars**. After the **Eight-Nation Alliance** forces stormed Beijing and the **Boxer Protocol** was signed in 1901, most of the fortifications were dismantled.

DAI LI (1896–1946). A leader of the **Nationalist Party** (GMD) intelligence agency. Born in Jiangshan, Zhejiang Province, Dai was raised by his mother because his father died when he was four. When Dai studied at the Zhejiang Normal School, he enlisted in the student battalion of the 1st Division, Zhejiang Province. He deserted from the army and went to Shanghai, where he met Dai Jitao and **Chiang Kai-shek**. Dai then enrolled in the sixth class of the **Whampoa Military Academy** and became an aide-de-camp after graduation. He began his intelligence work in 1928 and won Chiang's trust and admiration. In 1932, Chiang established the **Blue Shirts Society**, a fascist organization headed by Dai. Six years later, a sophisticated intellegence institution, the Bureau of Investigation and Statistics (BIS), was set up with Dai as its acting director. In cooperation with the United States during World War II, the BIS learned and used new methods of espionage in the resistance movement and anti-Communist campaigns. Dai's agents penetrated the Chinese Communist and Japanese puppet organizations. Dai consciously avoided public appearances in order to remain a mysterious figure. He used fascist measures to attack Chiang's political enemies and persecuted many innocent people. His methods included secret arrests, torture, and assassination, making him the most feared person in China. Dai died in a plane crash on 17 March 1946 at Dai Mountain near Nanjing.

DAI ZHEN (DAI DONGYUAN, 1724–1777). One of the leading philosophers of the Qing dynasty. As the representative of new scholarship of the Kaozheng school (*kaozheng* meaning "evidential research"), his major contribution was his prominent critique of the Confucian orthodoxy of the Song and Ming dynasties, known as neo-Confucianism. Dai criticized neo-Confucianism's treatment of human desires as obstacles to moral deliberation and action. He argued that human desire was an integrative part of human experience and an origin of sympathetic concern for others. He criticized neo-Confucianism's overemphasis on the importance of introspective self-examination, and he argued that truth could be found only through investigation of the external world. Dai had broad academic interests and explored many new subjects of research. He published beyond philosophy and history, making contributions to astronomy, mathematics, and hydraulic engineering.

Dai was born to a poor family and received no real formal education. His success as a noble scholar was ascribed to his diligent self-study. In addition, Dai was a good teacher, having numerous students who followed his approach to academic inquiries. Dai failed to pass the **civil service exam** at the highest level. In 1773, however, the **Qianlong Emperor** found his scholarship to be excellent and appointed him to the distinguished board of compilers of the Siku Quanshu (Imperial Manuscript Library). His works are included in the *Complete Works of Dai Dongyuan*.

DALAI LAMA. The supreme spiritual leader of Tibetan Buddhism. He is considered one of innumerable incarnations of Avalokite vara, the bodhisattva of compassion. In 1578, the title "Dalai" was first bestowed by the Mongolian ruler Altan Khan on Sonam Gyatso, the most eminent lama of his time. In honor of leaders of previous generations, Sonam Gyatso was called the third Dalai Lama. In the 17th century, the fifth Dalai Lama, Lozang Gyatso, united Tibet and went to Beijing to meet the Shunzhi Emperor of the Qing dynasty, who gave him a gold seal with the title of Dalai Lama in four languages—Manchu, Chinese, Mongolian, and Tibetan—as the symbol of authority over Tibet. Since then, dalai lamas have executed ruling power in Tibet with the recognition of Chinese central governments. Within 170 years, five dalai lamas were murdered, and the current **14th Dalai Lama**, Tenzin Gyatso, fled to India in 1959. The Dalai Lama is succeeded by each of the spiritual leader's incarnations. Upon the death of a dalai lama, the search for his reincarnated child immediately begins. This process is usually confidential and takes a few years. Correct indentification of items owned by the previous Dalai Lama is considered the sign of reincarnation. Sometimes there is more than one candidate; when this happens, the children being considered are brought to Lhasa for final identification and recognition by the central government. After the reincarnated child is confirmed, a monastic training begins for the next Dalai Lama.

DALAI LAMA XIV (1935–). The current Dalai Lama, Tenzin Gyatso, is the supreme spiritual leader of Tibetan Buddhism. He was born into a farming family as Lhamo Thondup, in Huangzhong, Qinghai Province. At the age of three, he was identified as the reincarnated child of the 13th Dalai Lama. Therefore, he was renamed Jetsun Jamphel Ngawang Lobsang Yeshe Tenzin Gyatso (Holy lord, gentle glory, compassionate, defender of the faith, ocean of wisdom). In the West, he is referred to as "His Holiness the Dalai Lama." On 5 February 1940, the Chinese Nationalist government approved his succession, and he held the inauguration ceremony in Lhasa. Dalai Lama XIV underwent systematic monastic studies with distinguished tutors, passed the final exam with honor, and obtained the Lhaampa degree (a doctorate in Buddhist philosophy). In 1950, he was enthroned as the head of the Tibetan government. As the Communist troops approached the border between Tibet and Xikang in 1951, he sent a delegation to Beijing and signed the Seventeen Point Agreement for the Peaceful Liberation of Tibet, which allowed the Communist troops to enter Tibet while leaving its social system unchanged. In the military conflict with the Communists in 1959, the Dalai Lama fled Tibet and set up the Tibetan government in exile in Dharamsala, India. Recently he proposed a "Middle Way," an approach to a peaceful solution of the Tibetan issue, stating that he is not in favor of Tibetan independence but pursues democratic autonomy. This is denounced by the Chinese government as another version of the independence movement. The Dalai Lama has published extensively and received numerous awards, of which the most notable was the Nobel Peace Prize in 1989.

DAOGUANG EMPEROR (REIGNED 1821–1851). The seventh emperor of the Manchu Qing dynasty and the sixth Qing emperor to rule over China. Born in 1782, Daoguang was the second son of the **Jiaqing Emperor** and Lady Hitara of the Hitara clan, who was known posthumously as Empress Xiaoshu Rui. He was the emperor who was forced to cede Hong Kong to Great Britain, making himself the first emperor of the Qing dynasty who lost a portion of its sovereign territories. Daoguang was given the name *Mianning*, which changed to *Minning* when he became emperor. He was the second son of **the Jiaqing Emperor**. His mother was Jiaqing's principal wife. When Daoguang ascended the throne, he posthumously made his mother Empress Xiaoshu Rui. Daoguang was an intelligent but indecisive man.

During his reign, China's major problem was opium. Daoguang issued many edicts against opium and sent **Lin Zexu** to Guangdong as special commissioner to halt the opium trade; this touched off the First **Opium War**. When other provincial officials blamed Lin for provoking the British into military operations, Daoguang dismissed Lin from office and banished him to Xinjiang. He vacillated between war and a peace settlement and had no measures to win either the war or negotiation. As a result, he had to approve the **Treaty of Nanjing**, including the term of the cession of **Hong Kong**. Historians believe that the decline of the Qing dynasty began with the Jiaqing and Daoguan Emperors.

DASHENG COTTON MILLS. One of the first mechanized textile mills in China. The founder was Zhang Qian, a prominent scholar in the Qing dynasty, who believed in saving China by developing its industry. In 1895, Zhang planned to pool a private investment of 600,000 taels to build the mills in Nantong, Jiangsu Province, but he obtained less than 40,000 taels. Fortunately, he persuaded **Liu Kunyi** to buy 250,000 taels worth of shares at a fixed interest rate, helping the mills to quickly go into operation. Due to the low cost of local female labor, the mills proved to be profitable, especially during the period of 1917–1921. They had 40,800 spindles, making up 11.9 percent of the total spindles in the whole of China. However, because the equipment was not regularly renovated, the management remained inefficient, no new capital was invested, and the mills stagnated and could not compete with European and Japanese textile manufacturers in the market. After 1922, the mills began to decline and finally went bankrupt in 1935.

DATONG SHU (THE BOOK OF UNIVERSAL COMMONWEALTH). Book written by the reform scholar **Kang Youwei**. Kang had the idea of the universal commonwealth as early as 1884. He began to write in 1885 and finally finished the work in 1902 after the failure of his radical reforms and exile to India. The book consists of 30 volumes divided into 10 parts. In it, Kang argues that mankind progresses from the primitive Age of Disorder to the Age of Approaching Peace and eventually reaches the Age of Universal Peace. In the process, he writes, human nature will improve and the human institutions should evolve. In his view, the contemporary age was still in the stage of partial peace, not "universal commonwealth" (*datong*). According to his vision, the ideal world would have no nations, no families, no clans, and no autocracy. There would be public kindergartens, schools, homes for the elderly, hospitals, public dormitories, and dining halls. There would be cohabitation of men and women for the duration of one year, after which everyone would change mates. There would be a fair division of labor and rewards for public contributions. Kang writes in the book that in his ideal world everyone works and everyone gets access to education. Kang was proud of himself for discovering this truth and believed that he was capable of applying this utopian socialism to China by radical reform. However, no one except **Liang Qichao** and a few of his students read the complete manuscript of *Datong shu* when Kang was alive. In 1913 and 1919, two parts of the manuscript were published, but it was not until 1927, seven years after Kang's death, that his student Qian Anding gave the complete copy of the manuscript to the China Press for publication.

DECEMBER NINTH MOVEMENT. A student demonstration in Beijing led by the **Chinese Communist Party** (CCP) on 9 December 1935. The demonstration was touched off by a crisis in North China. After the **Tanggu Truce** and He-Umozu Agreement, the Japanese had gained considerable control over the provinces of Hebei and Chahar. They were now planning for the "Self-Government of Five Provinces of North China," so as to colonize the whole of North China. Despite the **Nationalist Party**'s policy of appeasement, thousands of students rallied in Beiping (today's Beijing) to protest the Japanese aggression. They established the Union of Students of Colleges and High Schools in Beijing with Guo Mingqiu, an 18-year-old female student at Peking First Women High School as the president. Behind Guo were Lin Feng, **Huang Jing**, and other leaders of the CCP secret organization in the city. The group first tried to submit a government petition. Since **He Yingqin**, director of the Beijing office of the **Executive Yuan**, refused to accept it, the group decided to hold a mass demonstration. Their demands included opposition to self-government in northern China; opposition to any secret deals with Japan and the immediate publication of the diplomatic policies combating the current crisis; security of the freedom of speech, press, and assembly; an end to the civil war and the preparation for a self-defense war against external threats; prohibition of arbitrary arrests of the people; and immediate release of the arrested students. The number of marching students subsequently increased to about 6,000. Police and military forces turned water hoses on the demonstrators in the freezing weather and clubbed or arrested students. When the students from **Peking University** and Tsinghua University were locked out of the city, they stood outside the city wall in the bitter cold and wept while telling the surrounding residents about the Japanese atrocities in Manchuria. At the end of the day, these fearless students forced the Hebei-Chahar Political Committee to adjourn its planned opening. The December Ninth Movement struck a national chord. In the following weeks, protests took place in the Nationalist capital of Nanjing and many other cities. The movement won wide support from women, workers, businessmen, peasants, and even the police themselves.

DEMOCRATIC CENTRALISM. A principle of organization and decision making for the **Chinese Communist Party** (CCP). The concept of democratic centralism was first created by the Russian Bolshevik leader Vladimir Lenin and further developed by **Mao Zedong** to describe the dialectical unity of democracy and centralism. On one hand, it encourages the widespread participation of people in decision making; on the other, it emphasizes the "iron discipline" of the revolutionary party and requires absolute obedience to superior leaders. In theory, democratic centralism embraces two opposite extremes. One is "bureaucratic centralism," which leads to dictatorship; another is "anarchism and spontaneity," which ruin the solidarity and fighting capacity of the revolutionary party. Democratic centralism allows free and substantial debate on policy issues before formal decisions are made. After the decisions are reached, individuals must be subordinate to the organization, the minority subordinate to the majority, and all organizations subordinate to the central party. In practice, democratic centralism has been used by CCP leaders to establish their personal rule.

DENG XIAOPING (1904–1997). A leader of the **Chinese Communist Party** (CCP) and the People's Republic of China. Born Deng Xian-shen in Guang'an, Sichuan Province, Deng went to **Chongqing** at the age of 15 to study at the preparatory school for a work-study program in France. Eighteen months later, he became one of the first 85 Chinese students leaving for France. First in Marseille, then Paris, Deng entered some language programs to improve his French and worked in various factories. He barely earned enough to survive, let alone pay tuition for a formal school. At the Renault factory in a Paris suburb, Deng worked as a bench worker and mastered this skill that helped him survive the Cultural Revolution when he was dismissed from office. Deng joined the European branch of the Chinese Communist League in 1922 and became a formal member of the CCP two years later. He joined the editorial board of the Communist journal *Chiguang* (Red Light) and was in charge of mimeographing the journal, which earned him the nickname "Doctor of Mimeography." On 7 January 1926, the CCP dispatched Deng to Moscow to study at Sun Yat-sen University for eight months. On 16 September 1926, Deng returned to China with the **Nationalist Party** (GMD) general **Feng Yuxiang** and worked as political commissar of the Seventh Division of Feng's army.

After the CCP-GMD split in 1927, Deng was called back to Wuhan and worked at the CCP Central Committee, where he changed his name to Deng Xiaoping. Deng was then sent to Shanghai to work with the party's new general secretary, **Xiang Zhongfa**. In the winter of 1929, Deng married his first wife, another Communist named Zhang Xiyuan. This marriage lasted only 18 months as Zhang died from puerperal fever. On 11 December 1929, Deng led the uprising in Baise, Guangxi Province, and established two revolutionary bases that existed for about one year. After August 1931, Deng worked in the **Jiangxi Soviet** and developed good relations with **Mao Zedong**. It was for this reason that when Mao was expelled from the party leadership in 1933, Deng was also dismissed from office, leading to his second wife's divorcing him. During the **Long March**, Deng was in charge of the Red Army's publication *Hongxing* (Red Star) and attended the **Zunyi Conference**. Because of his loyalty to Mao, Deng was appointed deputy director of the Political Department of the Red Army and began to play an important role in the CCP.

During the **Second Sino-Japanese War**, Deng was appointed political commissar of the 129th Division, working with the division commander Liu Bocheng. This troop, known as the Liu-Deng Army, was one of the leading military forces and developed into the Second Field Army during the civil war. Liu and Deng built the Jin-Ji-Lu-Yu base in the border area of four provinces and launched **land reform**s and other social programs. In September 1939, Deng married the daughter of a rich merchant from Yunnan Province, Zuo Lin, who bore him three daughters and two sons. In 1942, Deng returned to **Yan'an**. He strongly supported Mao Zedong's **Rectification Movement** and was promoted to secretary of the CCP North China Bureau. During the civil war, Deng and Liu commanded several decisive battles and stormed the GMD's capital, Nanjing. After 1949, Deng held a number of important posts, including first secretary of the CCP Southwest China Bureau, minister of finance, vice-premier, and general secretary of the CCP Central Committee. As one of the hard-liners, Deng played a key role in staging various political campaigns, including the Antirightist Campaign in 1957. During the Cultural Revolution of 1966–1976, Deng became a target. This taught him to understand the CCP's mistakes in previous political campaigns. Deng never held the office of head of party or state, but he was the de facto leader in post-Mao China. Deng initiated China's economic reforms.

DENG YANDA (1895–1931). A left-wing leader of the **Nationalist Party**. Born in Huiyang, Guangdong Province, Deng graduated from the **Baoding Military Academy** in 1919. When the Huangpu Military Academy was established in 1924, he was appointed provost. During the **Northern Expedition** in 1927, he was the director of the Political Department in the General Headquarters of the **National Revolutionary Army**. He was also a member of the Central Executive Committee, the Central Political Council, and the Presidium of the Central Military Committee of the Chinese Nationalist Party. He had close relations with the Communists. When the alliance between the Nationalist Party and the Communist Party broke down, he fled to Russia, where he and Song Qinling issued the "Manifesto to the Chinese and World Revolutionary People." In 1930, he returned to Shanghai and organized the Provisional Committee of the Chinese Nationalist Party (the predecessor of the **Chinese Peasants' and Workers' Democratic Party**). He was elected general secretary of the party, engaging in anti–**Chiang Kai-shek** campaigns. In August 1931, he was arrested in Shanghai and secretly executed three months later in Nanjing.

DENG YINGCHAO (1904–1992). Early member of the **Chinese Communist Party** (CCP) and wife of **Zhou Enlai**. Born in Nanning, Guangxi Province, Deng studied at the Nankai Middle School in Tianjing, where she met Zhou Enlai; both engaged in student movements there. With Zhou, Deng participated in the **May Fourth Movement** and organized the *juewushe* (a student society). Deng joined the **Communist Youth League** in 1924 and the CCP in 1925. She married Zhou and was appointed director of the women's department of the CCP Guangdong Provincial Committee. Deng held several less important positions within the CCP, and her major work was to assist Zhou in various capacities. After Zhou's death in 1976, Deng was made a member of the CCP Politburo, vice president of the Chinese congress, and president of the **Chinese People's Political Consultative Conference**. She died on 11 July 1992 in Beijing at the age of 88.

DENG ZHONGXIA (1894–1933). An early leader of the **Chinese Communist Party** (CCP). Born into a landlord family in Yizhang, Hunan Province, Deng first studied with a private tutor and was then enrolled at the Hunan Normal School, where he met and made friends with **Mao Zedong**. Believing that the only way to become a prominent statesman was to study Chinese traditional literature, he enrolled in the Department of Chinese Literature of **Peking University** in 1917. However, his belief was altered by his professor, the CCP cofounder **Li Dazhao**. Deng accepted Marxism and took an active part in the **May Fourth Movement**. He helped Li organize the **Communist group** in Beijing and opened a night school for railway workers, thus becoming a leader of the Chinese labor movement. In 1922, Deng was elected alternate member of the CCP executive committee and party secretary of the All-China Federation of Workers. He led several strikes of coal workers and railway men. He also initiated a campaign for making Chinese labor laws. In 1925, Deng was sent to Hong Kong, where he was one of the leaders of the **Solidarity Strikes**. Deng was the person who presented the first comprehensive report on the Chinese labor movement at the **Comintern**'s conference. Deng was elected alternate member of the CCP Politburo and joined the leadership in the **Guangzhou Mutiny**. In 1925, Deng went to Moscow to attend the CCP Sixth Congress; two years later he returned to China and served as political commissar of the Second Army Corps of the Red Army.

For the failure of a military operation, he was replaced by the ultraleftist leader Xia Xi. Deng was ordered to leave for Shanghai but was not given any new assignments. In 1935, Deng was arrested in Shanghai and executed on 21 September at Yuhuatai, Nanjing.

DEWEY, JOHN (1859–1952). An American philosopher, psychologist, and educational reformer. Dewey was one of the founders of the philosophical school of Pragmatism and is also recognized as the father of functional psychology. A number of China's famous scholars, including **Hu Shih**, **Tao Xingzhi**, and **Jiang Menglin** were Dewey's students. These scholars introduced Dewey's philosophy to China and advocated pragmatic evolutionary change. At the invitation of five Chinese academic institutions, Dewey went to China in April 1919. He spent two years in China, visiting Beijing, Shanghai, and 11 provinces. His most influential lectures were delivered at **Peking University**. Dewey left China on 11 July 1921. His lectures inspired some substantial changes in the Chinese school system. Dewey's philosophy was repudiated by the Chinese Communists, who did not recognize its significance until economic reform was initiated in the post-Mao era.

DING LING (1904–1986). Pen name of one of the most influential female writers of modern China, Jiang Bingzhi. Born into a declining noble family in Linli, Hunan Province, Ding Ling lost her father at the age of four, and she was deeply influenced by her mother, who received a Western education and advocated women's emancipation. A strong woman, Ding Ling's mother ran a women's night school, where Ding Ling grew up and received her early education. In 1919, Ding Ling was enrolled at a local women's school and took an active part in the **May Fourth Movement**. Three years later, she traveled to Shanghai and studied at a women's school run by Communist leaders **Chen Duxiu** and Li Da. Ding Ling then enrolled at **Shanghai University** and went to Beijing and audited courses at **Peking University**, where she was exposed to radical ideologies, among which she liked anarchism the most. In 1925, she married Communist writer Hu Yeping and then published her first short story in 1927. Ding Ling became well known for her work *Miss Sophie's Diary,* which put a "self-liberated woman" back into a mundane world, alone, sick, poor, and with confused romantic and sexual feelings. "Revolution plus love" was a theme and formula of her writing during this period.

Ding Ling joined the **League of Left-Wing Writers** in 1930 and the **Chinese Communist Party** (CCP) in 1932. Ding Ling's husband was executed by the **Nationalist Party** (GMD) in 1931; two years later, Ding Ling was kidnapped and secretly jailed in Nanjing. A group of famous writers and cultural celebrities finally rescued her in 1936, and the CCP took her to **Yan'an**. Ding Ling was appointed editor in chief of the literature supplement of the *Liberation Daily* and also led a performance troupe touring the North China front line. Her short piece "Reflections on 8 March" criticized the gender discrimination in Yan'an and invited sharp criticism. Ding Ling was forced to make a self-confession. Nevertheless, she continued to write for the revolution. Her novel *The Sun Shines over the Sanggan River* was the first book on the Communist **land reform** and rural revolution and won the Stalin Literature Award. After 1949, Ding Ling served as vice-chairman of the China Writers Association and editor in chief of the *People's Literature*. In 1957, she was purged by the CCP in the Anti-rightist Campaign. She and her husband, Chen Ming, were exiled to the Great Northern Wilderness. Ding Ling was rehabilitated and returned to Beijing in 1979.

DING WENJIANG (1887–1936). Prominent geologist and social activist. Born into a wealth gentry family in Taixing, Jiangsu Province, Ding, after receiving a traditional education at home, traveled to Japan at the age of 15. Two years later, he went to England to study zoology and geology at the University of Glasgow. After graduating in 1911, he returned to China and began to teach at Shanghai Nanyang Public School, which later became the University of Communication. Ding was influenced by both classical Chinese education and Western "scientism." His dedication to public service originated from his Confucian ethical training, while his scientific rationalism and his persistence in pursuing truth stemmed from his study of Western science. In 1913, he was appointed head of the Division of Geology of the Ministry of Industry and Commerce, and he conducted a geological survey of Shanxi and Yunnan. In 1921, he was made general manager of the Beipiao Coal Mining Company. He initiated the establishment of the Chinese Association of Geologists and served as vice president and editor in chief of *Annals of Paleontology*. He saw China as a country in need of modernization, and science as the only means by which to modernize it.

In 1923, he published an article, "Metaphysics and Science," which engaged in a heated debate on science and the philosophy of life. Ding pointed out that "the omnipotence, generality and connective power of Science do not lie in the raw material of science but in its method." He attempted to make "**Mr. Science**" an integral part of China's everyday life by his teaching and writing. In 1925, he was made director general of Greater Shanghai under the southern **warlord** Sun Chuanfang. Ding worked under Sun Chuanfang but did not support the concept of **warlordism**; he only wanted an opportunity to effect localized change. His brief service for Sun was criticized as a betrayal to the **New Culture Movement**. He reimmersed himself in geology and continued his mission of rational modernization through science. The **Manchuria Incident** in 1931 shocked Ding. With **Hu Shih**, he created the *Independent Review* in an attempt to discuss politics from the perspective of a nonpartisan intellectual. He published an article titled "If I Were **Zhang Xueliang**," proposing an operational strategy for General Zhang. He also wrote an article titled "If I Were **Chiang Kai-shek**," calling for national solidarity and cooperation with the **Nationalist Party** to fight the Japanese. Ding served as professor of geology at **Peking University** and director of the Institute of Geological Studies, and was appointed secretary-general of Academia Sinica. On 5 January 1936, Ding went to Hunan to prospect a coal mine and was killed by carbon monoxide poisoning.

DIXIE MISSION. The nickname of the U.S. Army Observation Group to **Yan'an**, a mission begun in July 1944. This was the first time a group of American military officers was allowed to enter the Communist capital during the **Second Sino-Japanese War**. The group consisted of 18 military and foreign-service officers, including Colonel David Barrett and **John Stewart Service**. The trip was successful for the Americans, who endeavored to be "informed by the people." They made an observation of the Communist-controlled area and had long interviews with the Communist leaders **Mao Zedong** and **Zhu De**. The Dixie Mission highly evaluated the potential contribution of the Communists to the war effort and looked forward to the assistance of the Communist troops in the Anti-Japanese War, hoping that the Communist and Nationalists would patch up their differences. The group gained a strong impression that the Communists would not be wiped out, and even predicted the real possiblity of the ultimate triumph of Mao's revolutionaries. The mission saw Yan'an as the "most modern place" and the Communists as "the real democrats in China." Although the U.S. State Department refuted John Service's view on the **Chinese Communist Party**, the report of the Dixie Mission did influence American policy toward the Chinese Communists during the war. The mission gave Yan'an a sort of international recognition.

DONG CHUNCAI (1905–1990). Educator, prominent writer of science books, and government official of the People's Republic of China. Born in Daye, Hubei Province, Dong graduated from Pudong High School in Shanghai and then studied at Nanfang University, National University, and Guanghua University. In 1928, he transferred to **Tao Xingzhi**'s Rural Teacher School in Nanjing and also served as an assistant to the school leaders. Seeing his potential, Principal Tao asked Dong to build a biology lab and write short pieces on biology for teaching material. This aroused Dong's interest in writing popular science books. Beginning in 1930, he wrote and translated a number of works for young readers who were interested in science and the natural world. In 1937, Dong went to **Yan'an** to work for the Education Bureau of the Shan-Gan-Ning regional government and joined the **Chinese Communist Party** the next spring. After 1940, Dong was in charge of editing textbooks for elementary schools and continued to write on science for *Jiefang Daily*. Dong was a rare expert in education within the Communist Party and the only government official who was devoted to writing popular science for children. During the Chinese civil war, he worked in Manchuria and served successively as chairman of the Textbook Editing Committee and vice-chairman of the Education Department of the Northeast Government. Beginning in 1952, Dong served as deputy minister of education in the central government and presided over the work of drafting the education regulations for elementary and high schools. On 22 May 1990, Dong died of a heart attack in Beijing at the age of 85.

DONG ZHUJUN (1900–1997). Female entrepreneur of modern China. Born in Shanghai into a very poor family, Dong was sold to a brothel as a geisha at the age of 13. Fortunately, Dong met Xia Zhishi, a revolutionary in exile, who helped her escape from the brothel and took her to Japan. When Xia and Gong got married, he was 27 and she 15. In Japan, Xia continued his revolutionary activities while Dong studied Japanese and home management with private tutors. In 1916, they returned to Xia's home province in China, where Xia was made deputy governor of Sichuan. A couple of years later, however, Xia was dismissed from office and then became infatuated with opium smoking and **mahjong** games. Dong bore four daughters but no sons to him. For this reason, her in-laws did not like her. Xia also began to treat Dong badly and did not allow his daughters to go to school.

Dong decided to leave Xia and take their four daughters to the schools in Shanghai. With the help of friends, she opened various businesses, including a rickshaw firm, a small textile mill, a sock factory, and a restaurant. More often than not, she had to sell or pawn her clothes and jewels to pay her daughters' tuition and her debts. Running the business, she had all kinds of painful experiences: being cheated by partners, blackmailed by mobs, and arrested by corrupt police. Dong had a gift for public relations and kept good connections with different people, including social celebrities, **Green Gang** leaders, revolutionaries, and Japanese. Although she managed to keep her factories operating, the warfare in Shanghai eventually destroyed her textile mills. She fled to the Philippines and did not return to Shanghai until the end of the war in 1945. The major businesses left for her were only the Sichuan restaurant and the Jinjiang hotel. After 1949, the municipal government looked for a safe and comfortable place to host visiting Communist leaders, such as **Mao Zedong** and **Zhou Enlai**. Dong agreed to hand over the management of her hotel, one of the largest hotels in Shanghai, to the Communist government. Dong became a member of the **Chinese People's Political Consultative Conference**. She was persecuted during the Cultural Revolution but was rehabilitated in 1979. On 6 December 1997, Dong died in Beijing at the age of 97.

DOUBLE TEN HOLIDAY. National Day of the Republic of China. It commemorates the successful anti-Qing uprising on 10 October 1911 in the city of Wuchang that led to the collapse of the Manchu monarchy. This event is recognized as the beginning of the Xinhai Revolution (**Republican Revolution** of 1911). This day continues to be celebrated as National Day in Taiwan, but it is celebrated as the victory of the Republican Revolution in mainland China.

DOWAGER CIXI. *See* CIXI, EMPRESS DOWAGER.

DU YUESHENG (1887–1951). A leader of the largest gangster organization in Shanghai, the **Green Gang**. Born in the suburbs of Shanghai, Du was initially an apprentice at a small fruit store, where he became involved in the opium trade and began his career by joining the gangsters. Du also worked as an informer for the police department and won the trust of Huang Jinrong, who was the chief detective in the French concession and also a leader of the Green Gang. With Huang's help, Du built up his own power base, controlling gambling dens, opium trafficking, and prostitution and protection rackets. Du also opened some legal businesses, including a private bank to expand his influence. Du never hesitated to spend money in buying off government officials and social celebrities.

In the conflict between the **Nationalist Party** (GMD) and the **Chinese Communist Party** (CCP) in 1927, Du attacked the Communist worker pickets for **Chiang Kai-shek**. In the early years of the Nanjing government, Chiang greatly depended on Du's cooperation in maintaining social order in Shanghai. In 1929, Du was appointed a member of the Municipal Committee of the **International Settlement in Shanghai**. This was the highest position a Chinese could get in the **foreign concession**. In 1931, Du organized his gangster organization *Hengshe* with disciples throughout southeast China. During the **Second Sino-Japanese War**, Du took an active part in the Chinese resistance movement by organizing his disciples to wage guerrilla war near Shanghai, smuggling war supplies from Shanghai to GMD-controlled areas, and donating money and equipment to both the GMD and CCP forces.

After the Japanese surrendered, Du's reputation reached its peak, but his relations with Chiang Kai-shek soured as Chiang began to worry about Du's expanding power; Chiang wanted to "civilize" Shanghai by cleaning out the gangster influence. In December 1946, Du was elected president of the Municipal Senate in Shanghai. However, after the Nationalist government refused to support him, Du resigned. In the GMD anticorruption campaign of 1948, Du's son and other relatives became targets and were jailed. In the last days of the civil war, Du tried to make a deal with the Communists, but he finally decided to flee to Hong Kong on 1 May 1949, where he died two years later.

DU YUMING (1904–1981). Noted military commander and lieutenant general of the **Nationalist Party** (GMD) army. Born into a landlord family in Mizhi, Shanxi Province, Du had a strong interest in the military that started in childhood. His father was a member of the **Tongmenghui** and participated in the expedition against **Yuan Shikai**. Du graduated from Yulin Middle School in 1923 and got married soon after graduation. His wife, Cao Xiuqing, was a daughter of a noted local merchant and was two years older than him. In 1924, Du enrolled at the **Whampoa Military Academy** and joined the GMD soon after the semester started. He participated in the **Northern Expedition** and was promoted to deputy division commander in 1932. Du was in charge of building China's first armored force, serving as commander of the armored regiment first and later being promoted to army commander. After Wuhan and Guangzhou fell into the hands of the Japanese troops, Southwest China became the main battlefield of the **Second Sino-Japanese War**. Du was ordered to lead the first armored army to attack Nanning. On 31 December, Du's army stormed the Kunlun Pass and destroyed the leading troops of the Japanese Fifth Division Corps. In 1941, Du was sent to the Burma theater. He returned to China in August 1942 and was promoted commander in chief of the Fifth Group Army.

During the civil war, Du's troops were defeated by **Lin Biao** in the Lao-Shen Campaign, but he managed to escape with a few troops from the port of Yingkou. In the following Huai-Hai Campaign, he was appointed commander in chief of the GMD troops in Xuzhou, where the GMD troops were totally destroyed and Du himself was captured by the **People's Liberation Army** on 1 October 1949. Du was listed as a war criminal and jailed until he received a special pardon on 4 December 1959. Du's wife bore him three daughters and three sons. His eldest son-in-law is Yang Zhenning, a winner of the Nobel Prize in Physics.

– E –

ECONOMIC MACROREGIONS. A theory dividing 19th-century Chin into nine economically self-sufficient macroregions. These macroregions embraced parts of several provinces. They were southern Manchuria, Shanxi, Peking-western Shandong, the coast around Nanjing, the upriver area around Hankou, deep up the Yangtze River in Sichuan, the east coast of Fujian, China's south centered around

Canton, and the remote provinces of Yunnan and Guizhou. Each of the economic macroregions had major cities at its core with a high population density, heightened economic activity, and sophisticated transportation networks for conveyance of food and merchandise. Each core was surrounded by a periphery, most of which were less populated and developed rural areas. The separate, self-sufficient macroregions provided leeway for the survival of bandits, **warlords**, and revolutionary guerrillas. This theory is associated with William Skinner's model of the periodic market system in rural China.

EIGHTH ROUTE ARMY. A Communist military force in northern China during the **Second Sino-Japanese War**. In 1937, as a result of negotiation between the **Nationalist Party** (GMD) and the **Chinese Communist Party** (CCP) regarding the **United Front** against Japanese aggression, the Communist Red Army in North China was reorganized as the Eighth Route Army with **Zhu De** as commander and **Peng Dehuai** as deputy commander. The Eighth Route Army, with the strength of 30,000 men, consisted of three divisions: the 115th Division under **Lin Biao** and **Nie Rongzhen**, the 120th under He Long and Guang Xiangying, and the 129th under **Liu Bocheng** and **Deng Xiaoping**. In September 1937, the 115th Division under command of Lin Biao ambushed the Japanese 21st Brigade and annihilated about 1,000 Japanese troops. Despite the heavy casualties of the 115th Division, the Chinese responded to the first victorious battle in the resistance war with great enthusiasm. In 1940, Peng Dehuai organized a coordinated offensive by 105 regiments to attack Japanese troops along the railway lines that separated the Communist base areas. They destroyed about 600 miles of railways and several Japanese garrisons. Despite some military accomplishments, the offensive was criticized by **Mao Zedong** because it violated Mao's **guerrilla warfare** strategy. Following Mao's instruction, the Eighth Route Army infiltrated behind the Japanese line and built up new bases from which to promote its revolutionary programs and expand its forces. The army grew from 30,000 troops in July 1937 to 600,000 men in 1945. In March 1947, the Eighth Route Army merged with the **New Fourth Army** and became the **People's Liberation Army** in the civil war against the GMD.

EIGHT-NATION ALLIANCE (1900). Military force of the eight allied powers (Austria-Hungary, France, Germany, Italy, Japan, Russia, the United Kingdom, and the United States) with German field marshal Count von Waldersee as commander in chief during the **Boxer Rebellion**. The troops entered Beijing to put down the Boxers in 1900 and forced China to sign the **Boxer Protocol** of 1901. Today, Chinese remember the Eight-Nation Alliance for the fire its soldiers set in the Yuan Ming Yuan (Old Summer Palace), in which the palace buildings and priceless artifacts were destroyed.

ELEMENTS OF INTERNATIONAL LAW. A work by Henry Wheaton, translated into Chinese in 1864 by an American missionary, **William Alexander Parsons Martin**. Martin saw it as a requisite book for the Chinese because it was required reading for the British civil service exam. The book consists of four volumes and 12 chapters providing a comprehensive introduction to international law and diplomatic practice. As the first international law handbook and a practitioners' guide for diplomats, it exposed the Chinese to some fresh but important concepts and principles of international relations, such as sovereignty, national interests and rights, international treaties, and obligation. The book also taught Chinese diplomats about basic methods for solving international disputes and conflicts. To translate the Western work into Chinese, Martin and his assistants had to create many new Chinese legal terms for the reader, some of which are still used in China today.

ELLIOT, CHARLES (1801–1875). British knight, admiral, and drug trafficker. In 1815, Elliot joined the Royal Navy and was sent to China in 1834 as secretary to the trade commissioner. Two years later, he became the British trade superintendent and plenipotentiary in the city of Guangzhou. Elliot was in charge of English trade with China, which mainly involved opium. In 1839, Commissioner **Lin Zexu** was sent to Guangzhou to stop the illegal opium trade. Lin confined 350 British traders for six weeks. Under pressure, Elliot persuaded the British merchants to surrender their chests of opium. Lin failed to pay the promised compensation for the loss, and Elliot then went to London to ask the British government to take steps to protect the interest of British merchants. His demand was approved by Parliament and an expeditionary force was dispatched to Guangzhou. After the **Opium War** broke out in 1840, Elliot negotiated with Chinese plenipotentiary Qi-shan and signed the Convention of Chuenpee (**Chuanbi**) in January 1841. However, the Qing court refused to ratify the treaty. The British government was also displeased with the terms of the convention, arguing that the indemnity was too small to cover the value of the surrendered opium. Therefore, Henry Pottinger came to replace Elliot. Having left China, Elliot served in North America and was promoted to admiral in September 1865. He died in Witteycombe, England.

***EMILY* CASE.** The *Emily* was an American merchant ship. In 1821, it went to Canton for business. A crewman named Terranova dropped an earthenware pitcher onto the head of a Chinese woman whose rowboat had approached the *Emily* to sell fruits. The woman fell overboard and drowned. The Qing government asked the *Emily* to surrender Terranova. The captain first refused and then compromised. With a quick trial, Terranova was found guilty and executed the next day. The hurried judgment of the Qing court was obviously motivated by a xenophobic sentiment. It not only violated international law but also did not follow regular Chinese legal procedures in reviewing cases of accidental homicide.

EMPEROR PROTECTION SOCIETY. An organization of reformers advocating a constitutional monarchy in China. The Emperor Protection Society was established in 1906 by **Kang Youwei** and **Liang Qichao** in Japan. After the failure of the **Hundred Days' Reform**, Kang and Liang were exiled to Japan. The monarchist reformers vehemently attacked the ideas of revolution and republicanism. They argued that China's problem was people's ignorance and that French or American ideologies could not save China. They emphasized that a monarchy was the best political institution for China. At the turn of the 20th century, monarchism had a large number of supporters among the overseas Chinese. Before the 1911 **Republican Revolution**, **Sun Yat-sen** and other revolutionaries engaged in a heated debate with Kang and Liang, and the influence of the Emperor Protection Society subsequently began to wane.

EMPIRE OF CHINA. *See* GLORIOUS CONSTITUTION (*HONGXIAN*).

ENCIRCLEMENT AND SUPPRESSION CAMPAIGNS (1930–1934). Five military campaigns launched by the Nationalist government in an attempt to encircle and destroy the **Chinese Communist Party** (CCP). After the first four failed, the Nationalists finally forced the Communists to give up their **Jiangxi Soviet** and undertake a transfer from southeast to northwest China; this transfer was known as the **Long March**.

In October 1930, the Nationalists organized 100,000 troops with Lu Diping, governor of Jiangxi and the commander of the 9th Route Army, as the commander in chief, and Zhang Huizan as frontline commander in chief. They adopted a strategy of "simultaneous advance" from different directions in an attempt to envelop and annihilate the Communist Red Army. In the beginning, the Communists disagreed on how to defend their Jiangxi Soviet, but they eventually accepted **Mao Zedong**'s tactic of "luring the enemy deep" and allowed the Nationalist troops to enter the base area. As the general political commissar of the **Red Army**, Mao led the leading force to cross the Gan River, leaving small troops in this base area to harass the enemy via **guerrilla warfare**. On the east bank of the Gan River, the Red Army successfully organized a counterattack, crushing the Nationalist troops and capturing its commander, Zhang Huizan.

The second Encirclement and Suppression Campaign started in April 1931. **Chiang Kai-shek** appointed **He Yingqin** chief commander of the troops. The Nationalist armies were double the size of the Red Army, but factionalism crippled their coordination. He adopted a better strategy of "proceeding steadily step by step," while the Red Army continued the same guerrilla warfare tactics and repelled Chiang's second campaign.

On 1 July 1931, Chiang Kai-shek personally led 300,000 troops to stage the third campaign. Most of the officers were graduates of the **Whampoa Military Academy**, and they were eager for a quick victory. However, they could not trace the leading force of the Red Army, and still less organize a decisive battle. With flexible guerrilla tactics, the Communists penetrated and cut up the enemy forces. Two of Chiang's isolated regiments were destroyed. On 18 September, the Japanese began their military operation to occupy Manchuria, and Chiang had to return to Nanjing, which brought the third campaign to an end. Although the military pressure on the Communists relaxed, the inner-party struggle between Mao and other CCP leaders tended to be fierce.

When the fourth campaign began in 1932, Mao Zedong had been expelled from his leading position; the Red Army followed the orders of the CCP Central Military Committee to launch an offensive against the oncoming enemy's force and suffered a big loss. Then the Red Army resumed Mao's strategy and regained the initiative.

In October 1933, Chiang initiated the fifth Encirclement and Suppression Campaign, mobilizing 500,000 troops and taking counsel from German advisers. This time Chiang adopted a strategy "strategically offensive but tactically defensive" so that his troops moved gingerly and constructed fortresses and pillboxes to block the Red Army's supplies and communication. Chiang also emphasized that this campaign was "70 percent political and 30 percent military." Accordingly, his campaign was also to promote the rural economy and to maintain social order by strengthening the *baojia* **system**. The command of the Red Army now was in the hands of **Otto Braun**, a German officer and representative of the **Comintern**, and **Bo Gu**, a Russian-trained Communist leader. They refused Mao's test-proved guerrilla warfare and organized conventional positional warfare. They decided not to give up "an inch of the Soviet land," making the Red Army suffer incalculable losses. By October 1934, the Communist troops were almost crushed. The Communists had no choice but to withdraw and embark on the Long March.

EVER VICTORIOUS ARMY. A mercenary army of the Qing government created to suppress the **Taiping Rebellion**. It was sponsored by the Chinese government but trained and commanded by foreign officers. In 1860, the American officer Frederick Townsend Ward founded this army of 100 men and introduced new military structures, discipline, and weaponry. Following several victories against the rebels, the Qing emperor bestowed it with the title "Ever Victorious Army," and by 1862 the troops numbered 2,000 men. After Frederick Ward was killed in September 1863 at the Battle of Cixi, a British major, **Charles George Gordon**, took over the army. Collaborating with the **Anhui Army**, Gordon led the troops to storm the cities of Suzhou and Changzhou. Believing that there was no doubt about the final victory south of the Yangtze River, the Ever Victorious Army was disbanded in May 1864 in the town of Kunshan, near Shanghai.

EXAMINATION YUAN (*KAOSHI YUAN*). One of the five branches of the government of the Republic of China designed by **Sun Yat-**

sen. It was created by the constitutional theory of Sun Yat-sen and based on the Chinese tradition of the **civil service examinations**. The Examination Yuan was in charge of establishing the qualifications of government officials and consisted of two major institutions—the Examination Commission and the Ministry of Personnel. The former conducted different exams to recruit and evaluate civil servants, while the latter was in charge of civil service ratings.

EXECUTIVE YUAN (*XINGZHENG YUAN*). One of the five branches of the government of the Republic of China. The five-**yuan structure** stemmed from the Three Principles of the People and the constitutional theories of **Sun Yat-sen**. In 1928, as the **National Revolutionary Army** completed the **Northern Expedition** and reunified China, the Nanjing government issued the Organization Law, which stipulated that the Executive Yuan was the highest administrative institution, commonly dubbed the cabinet. The first president was **Tan Yankai**. It consisted of ten ministries, namely, internal affairs, foreign affairs, defense, finance, agriculture and mining, industry and commerce, education, communication, railway, and health. Some councils and committees were also included in the Executive Yuan, such as the Mongolian and Tibetan Affairs Committee. Different from Western practice, the Executive Yuan was responsible not to the legislative but to the ruling party and the president of the republic.

EXTRAORDINARY PARLIAMENT. In June 1917, **Zhang Xun** led 5,000 soldiers to Beijing to restore the Qing monarchy and disband the parliament. When Duan Qirui defeated Zhang's troops, he established his warlord government in Beijing. To protect parliamentarism and oppose the **warlord** regime, **Sun Yat-sen** called on the congressmen to leave the capital for the south. On 25 August, about 100 former members of the parliament arrived in Guangzhou, where they held an extraordinary parliament and elected Sun grand marshal of the Republic Protection Army. This parliament legitimized Sun Yatsen's revolutionary government in the south to oppose the warlord government in the north. *See also* CONSTITUTIONAL PROTECTION MOVEMENT; EXTRAORDINARY PRESIDENT.

EXTRAORDINARY PRESIDENT. In November 1920, **Sun Yat-sen** came from Shanghai to Guangzhou to resume the **Constitutional**

Protection Movement. The national parliament held an extraordinary session, proclaiming the establishment of the central government of the Republic of China in Guangzhou and electing Sun president. It resulted in the confrontation of the two central governments and two presidents, one in Beijing and another in Guangzhou. Since President Sun was elected by the extraordinary session of the congress, he was usually referred to as Extraordinary President. *See also* EXTRAORDINARY PARLIAMENT.

EXTRATERRITORIALITY. A legal term that meant that Westerners in China were exempt from the jurisdiction of Chinese law. The Chinese judicial institutions could not take any civil and criminal action against them; they might not be sued or arrested even if they committed homicide in the Chinese territory. Extraterritoriality was the extension of the power of Western laws to their citizens in China based on the belief that China, as an uncivilized state, was incapable of establishing justice. This privilege of Western diplomats, traders, missionaries, tourists, and their families was first imposed on China in 1842 by Great Britain in the **Treaty of Nanjing**. Following the British example, all Europeans, Americans, and Japanese obtained the privilege of immunity against Chinese jurisdiction through various unequal treaties. In 1924, the Soviet Union gave up this privilege, and the United States and Great Britain abandoned it in 1943. By the end of World War II, this nondiplomatic extraterritoriality had been finally abolished in China.

– F –

FABI (LEGAL TENDER). The legal tender issued by the Nationalist government in 1935. It was part of the financial reform of the government, which limited currency issuance to four major banks: **Bank of China**, Central Bank of China, **Bank of Communications**, and Farmers Bank of China. Beginning on 4 November 1935, the four banks issued a new currency, the fabi, which transformed the Chinese traditional monetary system from a silver standard to a gold standard. This change was made because since the 1920s the price of silver had appreciated in the international market, leading to a massive flow of silver out of China and endangering the Chinese national currency.

After the fabi was issued, the silver dollar coins were no longer allowed to circulate in the market and private ownership of silver was also prohibited. Fabi could be freely exchanged for foreign currencies. The exchange rate between fabi and British sterling was ¥1 for £1/1 and 2.5 pence. The fabi was backed by the gold and foreign exchange reserve of the Nationalist government, which stabilized its value for several years. Fabi circulated widely in both Nationalist and Communist-controlled areas during the **Second Sino-Japanese War**. After the war, however, China's financial situation worsened and the Nationalist government replaced the fabi with new currency, *jinyuan quan*, on 19 August 1948.

FEBRUARY TWENTY-EIGHTH INCIDENT (FEBRUARY TWENTY-EIGHTH UPRISING, 1947). An antigovernment revolt violently suppressed by the **Nationalist Party** (GMD) in Taiwan on 28 February 1947. The incident was touched off by a dispute between a female cigarette vendor and an officer of the Office of Cigarette and Wine Monopoly. The rough attitude of the officer triggered the resistance of local people, which finally developed into an open rebellion, including strikes, protests, and armed uprising. The military crackdown on the revolt resulted in bloodshed and the deaths of thousands of people. The incident also evolved into a conflict between people of different ethnic and provincial backgrounds. The major reason for the incident was the increasing tension between people in Taiwan and the GMD administration, which was plagued by corruption, nepotism, and economic failure. It was reported that there was Communist involvement, and that some leaders of the uprising, such as **Xie Xuehong**, were members of the Communist Party. This incident marked the beginning of the White Terror period in Taiwan. The February Twenty-Eighth Incident is now commemorated in Taiwan as Peace Memorial Day.

FEI XIAOTONG (1910–2005). Pioneering sociologist and anthropologist in modern China. Born into a landlord family in Wujiang, Jiangsu Province, Fei began to receive a formal education at the age of four at a nursery school founded by his mother, Yang Renlan. At age 18, Fei entered the two-year premedical program at Dongwu University in Nanjing. After graduating, he quit his medical studies and transferred to the Department of Sociology at Yenching University. Having obtained his bachelor's in sociology, he entered the graduate school at Tsinghua University majoring in anthropology. In 1935, he gained a government scholarship to study in Great Britain. Before leaving for England, Fei did fieldwork in Guanxi, where he stepped into a tiger trap that crushed his leg. His wife died going for help. Fei took a little time off to recover and continued his research. In 1936, Fei began his study with Professor Bronislaw Malinowski at the London School of Economic and Political Science and obtained his PhD in 1938. His dissertation was published and became the internationally famous book *Peasant Life in China*. Fei was also influenced by Dr. R. H. Tawney, who invited him to lecture at the London School of Economics from 1945 to 1946.

After returning to China, Fei taught at Tsinghua University and Yunnan University. He joined the Democratic League in 1944 and became a famous social activist. He published more than 20 books in the fields of sociogy, anthropology, and ethnic studies, and he was regarded as a founding father of Chinese sociology and anthropology. One of his most influential theories is that Chinese social relations work through social networks of personal relations with the self at the center and decreasing closeness as one moves out. In his later years, Fei held some important government positions, including vice-chairman of the **Chinese People's Political Consultative Conference** and vice president of the Chinese Congress.

FENG GUIFEN (1809–1874). Born in Wuxian, Jaingsu Province, Feng obtained the *jinshi* degree in 1840. He began his career as a compiler in the **Hanlin Academy** and the supervisor of the civil service examination (CSV) in Guangxi Province. While serving under **Li Hongzhang**, he suggested that Li use foreign troops to suppress the **Taiping Rebellion**. It was also due to his proposal that Li set up a school for Western languages and science in Shanghai, which was later incorporated into Li's **Jiangnan Arsenal**. Feng wrote a well-known book called *Protest from the Jiaobin Studio (Jiaobin lu kangyi)*. In it he advocated "learning Western technology, making foreign machines, accumulating capital for the country's development, and reforming the CSV system." These ideas were the basis of the **Self-Strengthening Movement (1861–1895)**.

FENG YUNSHAN (1822–1852). Early leader of the **Taiping Rebellion**. Born in Huaxian, Guangxi Province, Feng was a classmate of

Hong Xiuquan. Having failed the **civil service examination**, he served as a private tutor in his home village. In 1847, he founded the **God Worshipping Society** and supported Hong Xiuquan as its leader. He recruited thousands of believers among the **Hakka** coal-burning workers to join Hong's uprising. In 1851, when the Taiping Kingdom was established, he was granted the title "Southern Prince." In the next year, he led the Taiping forces and stormed the city of Quanzhou. Feng was wounded in the battle and died shortly thereafter.

FENG YUXIANG (1882–1948). Full general of the first class of the **National Revolutionary Army**. Born into a military family in Baoding, Hebei Province, Feng joined the Huai Army (**Anhui Army**) at the age of 14. In 1902, he transferred to **Yuan Shikai**'s **Beiyang Army** and was promoted by Yuan to brigade commander. Feng converted to Christianity in 1914, and he tried to govern his troops with a mixture of paternalistic Christian socialism and military discipline, thus earning the nickname "Christian General." Feng became a **warlord** in Northwest China after Yuan Shikai's death in 1916, and he was involved in several wars with other warlords. In October 1924, Feng launched a coup in Beijing to overthrow **Cao Kun**'s government. Feng accused the last emperor, **Puyi**, of being involved in a conspiracy of monarchical restoration and thus abolished the agreement on "**Articles of Favorable Treatments**" of the **Manchu** royal family. On 5 November 1924, his soldiers expelled Puyi from the Forbidden City. Afterward, Feng pronounced his breakaway from the **Beiyang warlord** clique and reorganized his troops as the National Army. He sent **Sun Yat-sen** a telegraph, inviting him to Beijing for negotiations on China's reunification. Due to opposition of the **Anhui Clique**, however, Feng could not realize his plan.

In 1925, Feng joined the war against the **Fengtian Clique**. He was defeated and forced to retreat to Northwest China. The next year, he traveled to the Soviet Union on a tour of investigation. After his return in August 1926, Feng brought his troops to join the **Nationalist Party** (GMD) and supported **Chiang Kai-shek**'s policy of purging Communists. In 1929 and 1930, with **Yan Xishan** and **Li Zongren**, Feng launched two military campaigns against Chiang Kai-shek, but all failed and he was forced to retire. In May 1933, he organized a new army in North China known as the Chahar People's Anti-Japanese Alliance Army. His troops quickly increased to 100,000 men, who drove the Japanese and the **Manchukuo** troops out of Chahar Province by July. During the **Second Sino-Japanese War**, Feng served successively as the commander in chief of the Third and Sixth War Areas, and between 1935 and 1938 he was made the vice president of the National Military Council. In 1946, Feng traveled to the United States to investigate water conservancy and made public speeches to criticize Chiang Kai-shek. He joined the anti–Chiang Kai-shek Revolutionary Committee of the GMD and was elected president of its Political Committee. In response to **Mao Zedong**'s call for establishment of a new **Political Consultative Conference** in Beijing, Feng took the Russian ship *Victory* to return to China. Unfortunately, when *Victory* arrived in the Black Sea, its shipboard caught fire. Feng and his daughter were killed in the accident on 22 August 1948.

FENG ZIKAI (1898–1975). Renowned artist, cartoonist, and essayist. Born in Tongxiang, Zhejiang Province, Feng enrolled at the First Normal School of Zhejiang, where he met **Li Shutong**, who taught him painting, calligraphy, and music. Under Li's influence, Feng also became a devoted lay Buddhist. In 1921, he traveled to Japan to study oil painting. After returning to China the following year, he began to teach art in Shanghai and served as an editor at the Kaiming Press. He engaged in making creative sketches and cartoons and also published art critiques and general essays. His special style was to use simple line brush drawings to portray people and social activities. The major subjects of his cartoons were children and children's life, reflecting his love of an innocent and guileless world.

FENGSHUI **(CHINESE GEOMANCY).** A Chinese system of geo-mancy for determining auspicious locations for human occupation of land. There are three principal considerations in the *fengshui* system. First, certain shapes of landscapes are considered auspicious or in-auspicious by their association or combination with various mythical beasts or objects. Second, all landscape elements have male (*yang*) and female (*yin*) characteristics that must be balanced in architectural designs. Third, *fengshui* incorporates numerological beliefs derived from the mystical proportions of nature, which determine an auspi-cious time and place for certain behaviors. It is a Chinese belief that basic aspects of nature are critical to a human being's success or failure, fortune or disaster, health or death. The practice of *fengshui* serves the purpose of locating the appropriate site for a project or finding a way to readjust an ill-omened site.

FENGTIAN CLIQUE. A clique of **warlords** in Manchuria. It was named after the city of Fengtian (Mukden), where its headquarters was located. The founder of the Fengtian Clique was **Zhang Zuolin**, known as the Grand Marshal; his son, **Zhang Xueliang**, was known as the Young Marshal. Zhang's military power grew out of a small bandit gang in Manchuria, and his rise is ascribed greatly to the support of the Japanese. In 1920, the **Fengtian Clique** moved from Manchuria to China proper, supporting the **Zhili Clique**'s war against the **Anhui Clique**, and began to share power in the **Beijing government**. Two years later, the Zhili Clique drove Zhang out of Beijing and prevented him from returning to North China until 1924, when Zhang led his troops to Beijing to resume power. He proclaimed himself Grand Marshal of the army, navy, and air forces of the Republic of China. In 1927, **Chiang Kai-shek** launched the **Northern Expedition** against Zhang and other warlords. In June 1928, as the **National Revolutionary Army** approached Beijing, Zhang Zuolin was forced to retreat to Manchuria. However, Manchuria was no longer a safe refuge because the Japanese had already planned to replace him with another figurehead. They assassinated Zhang Zuolin on the Beijing–Mukden railway. Nonetheless, his son, Zhang Xueliang, managed to return to the headquarters of the **Fengtian Clique** in Mukden, assemble his loyalists, and take over. On 19 December 1928, Zhang Xueliang announced that Manchuria would be incorporated into China proper and that he would obey the Nanjing government; this action marked the end of the warlord era in Manchuria.

FENGTIAN MILITARY ACADEMY. One of four leading military academies in early modern China. It was founded in 1906 by the Qing general Zhao Erzhuan. In 1911, as the **Republican Revolution** overthrew the **Manchu** monarchy, the academy was closed, but it was reopened by **Zhang Zuolin** in 1919. The reorganized academy began to use Western methods to train the cadets. Initially, the academy trained only junior officers, but it gradually developed various programs to train both lower- and higher-ranking officers. It opened branches in Beijing (1926) and in Heilongjiang (1930). The academy produced more than

8,900 officers. Almost all officers in the Dongbei Army (military forces in Manchuria), from its supreme commander **Zhang Xueliang** to company commanders and platoon leaders, graduated from this academy. It was closed after the Japanese occupied Manchuria.

FIELD ARMY. On 15 January 1949, the **Chinese Communist Party** Central Military Committee decided to reorganize the regional armies of the **People's Liberation Army** (PLA) into four field armies. The Communist military forces in Northwest China were referred to as the First Field Army, with **Peng Dehuai** as the commander and concurrent political commissar. The First Field Army was composed of the 1st Army Corps and the 2nd Army Corps. The overall force consisted of 134,000 men. After 1949, the First Field Army was posted in Northwest China and controlled five provinces, namely, Shaanxi, Gansu, Qinghai, Ningxia, and Xinjiang.

The PLA troops in central China were reorganized into the Second Field Army with **Liu Bocheng** as commander and **Deng Xiaoping** as political commissar. The troops were composed of the 3rd Army Corps, 4th Army Corps, 5th Army Corps, and a column of special technical troops. The overall force consisted of 128,000 men. After 1949, the Second Field Army was posted in Southwest China and controlled five provinces, namely, Yunnan, Guizhou, Sichuan, Xikang, and Tibet.

The PLA troops in eastern China were reorganized into the Third Field Army, with Chen Yi as the commander and concurrent political commissar. This field army was composed of the 7th Army Corps, 8th Army Corps, 9th Army Corps, 10th Army Corps, and the headquarters of the special technical troops. The overall force consisted of 580,000 men. After 1949, the Third Field Army remained on the east coast, controlling five provinces: Shandong, Jiangsu, Zhejiang, Anhui, and Fujian.

The PLA troops in China's Manchuria were designated the Fourth Field Army, with **Lin Biao** as the commander and Luo Ronghuan as its political commissar. The field army was composed of the 12th Army Corps, 13th Army Corps, 14th Army Corps, 15th Army Corps, the special technical troops, the Column of Guangdong and Guangxi, 50th Army, and 51st Army. The overall force consisted of 800,000 men at the beginning and increased to 1.5 million men by December 1949. The Fourth Field Army made the longest march, from the Chinese northern frontier in Manchuria to the southern tip, Hainan Island, and liberated huge territories. After 1949, it was posted in central and south China and controlled four provinces, namely, Hubei, Hunan, Guangdong, and Guangxi. The Fourth Field Army was the leading force of the Chinese People's Volunteers in the Korean War. In 1955, the designation of the four field armies was abolished.

FILIAL PIETY. Considered the first virtue in Confucian teachings. It means a love and respect for parents and ancestors. In practice, filial piety consisted of obeying parents' instructions, not being rebellious, displaying courtesy, taking care of old parents, showing sorrow for their sickness and death, and holding proper funerals and rituals. More importantly, it required bearing sons so as to continue the family line. The concept of filial piety also applied to the relations between rulers and the ruled, known as loyalty to an emperor. In the **New Culture Movement**, filial piety was sharply criticized as a tool to serve the patriarchal domination and stifle the younger generation as well as any new ideas, making China stagnant and backward. Beginning with Shi Cunze's essay "Decry Filial Piety," a crusade against **Confucianism** was initiated in the 1910s and 1920s.

FIRST ALL-CHINA SOVIET CONGRESS. Held between 7 and 20 November 1931 in Ruijin, Jiangxi Province, this congress proclaimed the establishment of the Provisional Government of the Chinese Soviet Republic. The delegates came from seven Communist rural bases (so-called Soviet areas), including the largest central base in Jiangxi. The delegates elected **Mao Zedong** chairman of the government and Xiang Ying and **Zhang Guotao** vice-chairmen. Since the township of Ruijin was located in a mountainous area and far from big cities, the First All-China Soviet Congress decided to make it the capital of the Soviet republic. Functioning as the Communist legislature, the congress worked out the outline of the constitution, land law, labor law, and marriage law. To consolidate this regime and promote the revolution, the congress decided to immediately launch a land revolution, confiscating landlords' land and distributing it among the peasants.

FIRST FRONT ARMY (FIRST FRONT ARMY OF THE CHINESE WORKERS' AND PEASANTS' RED ARMY). One of three major Communist military forces during 1928–36. The First

Front Army was also known as the Central **Red Army** because it consisted of the troops under the direct command of **Mao Zedong**, **Zhu De**, and **Lin Biao**. After the failure of the **Nanchang Mutiny**, Zhu De moved the remnants to southern Hunan, where he met Mao Zedong's guerrillas in the **Jinggangshan** mountains. The merging of the two army units resulted in the establishment of the Fourth Army of the Chinese Workers' and Peasants' Red Army, with Zhu as the commander and Mao as the representative of the **Chinese Communist Party** (CCP). The overall forces consisted of 10,000 men, but only a fifth were armed. These troops began to build a rural base around Jinggangshan, which developed into the **Jiangxi Soviet**.

In the fall of 1928, the Fourth Army was strengthened by the arrival of the Fifth Army led by **Peng Dehuai**, who had staged the Pingjiang Mutiny a few months earlier. In early 1929, Mao and Zhu were ordered to move some troops eastward. Peng planned to stay and defend the base, but he was forced to retreat shortly under enemy pressure. Ignoring the military inferiority of the Red Army, the CCP central leader, **Li Lisan**, instructed Peng to attack the city of Changsha and Mao to storm another city, Nanchang. Li's large-scale uprisings in major cities caused heavy casualties in the two troops.

In August 1930, both the First and Third army corps were evacuated from the urban areas to the county of Liuyan, Hunan Province, where their remnants merged to form the First Front Army, with Zhu as the commander and Mao the political commissar. In November 1931, the First Front Army was designated the Central Red Army (it reverted to the First Front Army during the **Long March**) and put under the direct command of the Central Military Committee. Zhu De was made commander; Mao Zedong and **Zhou Enlai** served as political commissars. The troops were organized into three army corps, commanded by Lin Biao, Peng Dehuai, and Dong Zhentan, respectively. The overall force consisted of some 70,000 men. The Central Red Army shattered **Chiang Kai-shek**'s four **Encirclement and Suppression Campaigns** but was defeated in the fifth campaign after Mao Zedong had been dismissed from the party and army leadership.

In October 1934, the First Front Army had to flee the Jiangxi Soviet and start the Long March. In January 1935, Mao resumed his command of the army. In June, Mao's First Front Army met with the **Fourth Front Army** led by **Zhang Guotao** at Maogong, Sichuan Province. A critical dispute arose between Mao and Zhang over the route and destination of the Long March. Following Mao, the First Front Army continued to push northward to Shaanxi. This army left Jiangxi with some 80,000 men, but only 8,000 had survived the Long March by the time it reached its destination. After the outbreak of the **Second Sino-Japanese War** in 1937, the First Front Army was reorganized as the 115th Division of the **Eighth Route Army**. Lin Biao was appointed commander and **Nie Rongzhen**, political commissar.

FIRST NATIONAL CONGRESS OF THE CCP. Held in July 1921 in Shanghai and Jiaxing. The congress first took place at 106 Wangshi Road in the Shanghai French concession on 1 July. On 3 July, the meeting was interrupted by French policemen, and the delegates decided to move to a tourist boat on the South Lake in Jiaxing, Zhejiang Province, the next day. The First Congress was attended by 12 formal delegates, representing six **Communist groups** from different provinces and cities. Two cofounders of the **Chinese Communist Party** (CCP), **Chen Duxiu** and **Li Dazhao**, were unable to attend, and only a personal representative of Chen Duxiu was present at the congress. The **Comintern**'s representative, **Hendricus Maring**, also participated in the congress. **Zhang Guotao** presided over the congress while **Mao Zedong** took the minutes. The congress came to a resolution on the formation of the CCP, approved the party's constitution, and elected Chen Duxiu, Zhang Guotao, and Li Da members of the CCP Central Bureau with Chen Duxiu as the general secretary.

FIRST PARLIAMENT. On 27 August 1912, **Yuan Shikai** issued the Organization Regulations of the Parliament of the Republic of China. The parliament was bicameral, with 274 senators and 596 representatives. On 8 April 1912, the first session of the parliament was called; it elected Yuan president of the Republic of China. The presidency would be formally inaugurated on 10 October 1913. On 31 October 1912, the parliament approved the Tiantan Constitution, which adopted the cabinet rather than the presidential system. Since the **Nationalist Party** (GMD) won the majority of seats in the parliament in 1913, it would organize a cabinet to deal with state affairs. However, the GMD's leader **Song Jiaoren** was assassinated and the GMD was dissolved by Yuan on 4 November 1913. The parliament thus could not meet for lack of a legal quorum in 1914. After Yuan's death in 1916, President **Li Yuanhong** ordered the restoration of the parliament. The parliament existed until it was disbanded in June 1917 by **Zhang Xun**.

In the following years, there were two parliaments in China: one was in Guangzhou, organized in August 1917 by **Sun Yat-sen**'s supporters and known as the **Extraordinary Parliament**. The other was in Beijing, established in August 1918 by the **Anhui Clique warlords** and known as the **Anfu Parliament**. In 1920, President **Xu Shichang** tried to organize the election of a new parliament. However, only 12 provinces held the local election, and their elected representatives did not come to Beijing for the national assembly. In 1922, the **Zhili Clique** warlords **Wu Peifu** and **Cao Kun** restored the old parliament, and Cao bribed the congressmen to elect him president of the republic on 5 October 1923. The bribery scandal led to the collapse of Cao's presidency and dismissal of the parliament on 24 November 1924.

FIRST SINO-JAPANESE WAR (1894–1895). War between Qing China and Meiji Japan, touched off by the issue of Korea. In the late 19th century, Korea remained one of China's tributary states, while Japan saw Korea as its first target of expansion. In June 1894, the Qing government, at the request of the Korean emperor, sent 2,800 troops under **Yuan Shikai** to Korea to aid him in suppressing the Tonghak Rebellion. The Japanese considered this action to be a violation of the Convention of Tianjin and sent an expeditionary force of 8,000 troops to Korea. The Japanese force landed on Incheon, moved to Seoul, seized the emperor, and set up a new pro-Japanese government on 23 July 1894. The Qing government decided to withdraw Yuan's troops but rejected recognition of the pro-Japanese government.

This government terminated all Sino-Korean treaties and granted the Imperial Japanese Army the right to expel the Chinese **Beiyang Army** from Korea. By July, about 3,000 to 3,500 Chinese troops still remained in Korea, and they could be supplied only by sea through the Korean Bay. On 25 July, the Japanese navy attacked and sank the steamer *Gaoshen* in the Korean Bay; the ship was carrying 1,200 Chinese troops plus supplies and equipment. This sneak attack occurred seven days before Japan's declaration of war on China. By 15 September 1894, the battle had moved to Pyongyang. The Chinese had 17,000 troops defending the city, while 16,000 Japanese soldiers converged on Pyongyang from several directions. Before the battle ended, the Chinese commander in chief, Ye Zhichao, lost the will to fight and ordered a retreat. His troops rushed to escape back to Manchuria, facilitating the Japanese takeover of Korea. The decisive battle was on the Yellow Sea. Although the Chinese **Beiyang Fleet** had 65 ships, outnumbering Japan's 32, it suffered from poor preparation and command. It was ironic that the Chinese Nanyang Fleet and two other warships remained "neutral" in the battle for self-preservation. After five hours of exchanging fire, the Beiyang Fleet lost four ships and suffered several thousand casualties. The Japanese flagship was damaged and stopped its attack, allowing the surviving Chinese ships to retreat to Port Arthur. Japan began to boast of the victory, while the Qing government, including **Li Hongzhang** and the **Dowager Cixi**, were terrified and attempted to avoid fighting and further losses. This mentality eventually led to more disastrous failures.

In October 1894, the Japanese army quickly pushed north toward Manchuria, and within three days it had broken the defense line of the Yalu River, where 30,000 Chinese troops failed to organize a strong resistance. The big victory for the Japanese was their capture of two strategic areas, the cities of Dalian and Port Arthur on 22 October. Li Hongzhang had invested several million taels in building these naval bases. However, as the Japanese approached, the major commanders abandoned their positions, leaving a few troops to fight. The last battle of the First Sino-Japanese War took place at the fort of Weihaiwei. Again, the defenders had to fight a lone battle without any reinforcement from Li Hongzhang. Believing that the fort was to be stormed, the Chinese commander Ding Ruchang committed suicide on 11 November 1894. Six days later, the Japanese landed on Weihaiwei and the Chinese troops surrendered, turning over 11 warships and all ammunition to the Japanese. From 17 January to 14 March 1895, the Chinese troops launched four counterattacks in the Liaodong Peninsula, but all ended in failure. The First Sino-Japanese War concluded with the **Treaty of Shimonoseki**. Li Hongzhang, the highest military commander of the Chinese troops, was appointed imperial commissioner to Japan to negotiate the treaty. The treaty required China to pay a huge indemnity and to cede Taiwan to Japan. Japan also gained a predominant position in Korea.

FIVE-YUAN STRUCTURE. The government structure of the Republic of China. It was designed by **Sun Yat-sen** in the 1911 Revolution and was finally established in 1928 in Nanjing. The five-yuan structure consists of the **Executive Yuan, Legislative Yuan, Judicial Yuan, Examination Yuan**, and **Control Yuan**. *See also* NATIONAL ASSEMBLY.

FLINT INCIDENT (1759). During the 18th century, Canton was the major Chinese port for foreign trade. Disappointed with high customs duties and maltreatment in Canton, some foreign merchants moved northward to find alternatives. In 1755, British traders Samuel Harrison and James Flint went to Ningbo and did good business with local tea and silk merchants. Many foreigners followed suit, and the calls of English ships at Canton decreased. The Qing court urged the foreigners to desist from going north. James Flint ignored the prohibition and continued to visit Ningpo in 1759. When he was refused admission, Flint went to Tianjin to submit to the **Qianlong Emperor** a **memorial** to complain about the corruption and irregular customs duties in Canton. This caused a government investigation of the Canton customs. In the meantime, the Qing court also argued that Flint had violated official protocol in trying to address the emperor directly and jailed him in Macao for three years. Flint's efforts eventually brought about a negative change, for the emperor issued a decree to formally make Canton the only port open to foreign trade. A series of follow-up restrictive regulations was announced, perpetuating the **Canton System** until 1842.

FLYING TIGERS. The nickname of the First American Volunteer Group (AVG) fighting Japanese forces in China in 1941–1942. The Flying Tigers was largely the creation of its commander, **Claire Chennault**, a retired U.S. Army Air Corps captain who had become the military aviation adviser to the Chinese generalissimo **Chiang Kai-shek** during the Sino-Japanese War. In 1940, when the Soviet Union called back their fighter and bomber squadrons from China, Chiang Kai-shek turned to the United States for help. Chennault tried to recruit his pilots from among former U.S. Army, Navy, and Marine Corps pilots and ground crews. Since the United States was not at war, President Franklin D. Roosevelt signed a secret executive order authorizing the pilots on active duty to resign from the U.S. military and sign up for the AVG. The pilots were officially employees of a private military contractor, the Central Aircraft Manufacturing

Company, which employed them for "training and instruction," and they volunteered to fly and fight for the Republic of China air force. The Flying Tigers consisted of three fighter squadrons that trained in Burma and first saw combat on 20 December 1941, 12 days after Pearl Harbor. In seven months, they destroyed almost 300 Japanese aircraft with a loss of only 14 pilots, thereby dominating the skies over southwest China, northern Burma, and the Assam Valley of India. The AVG was disbanded in July 1942, to be replaced by the U.S. Army 23rd Fighter Group, which was later absorbed into the U.S. 14th Air Force with General Chennault as commander. The AVG was then awarded a Presidential Unit Citation for "professionalism, dedication to duty, and extraordinary heroism." In 1996, the U.S. Air Force awarded the pilots the Distinguished Flying Cross, and the ground crewmen were all awarded the Bronze Star. Many activities are held to commemorate the Flying Tigers in China.

FOOTBINDING. A practice of **Han** Chinese of wrapping **women**'s feet to stop their normal growth. Manchu women and women of many other ethnic groups in China did not bind their feet. Footbinding became very popular among Han Chinese of all social classes except for the poorest families, who needed their daughters to work in the fields. This practice can be traced back to the Song dynasty in the 10th century. The girls were usually required to begin wrapping their feet in tight bandages when they were four or five years old. Their toes were broken and bent under the soles of the feet, and the feet became highly deformed. This process took 10 to 15 years, keeping the feet from growing more than four to six inches in length. Bound feet prevented women from doing physical labor outside the home and from walking long distances, limiting the women's activities to preparing meals, taking care of children, and serving husbands at home. The women suffered their whole lives from disabilities related to bound feet. From a man's perspective, however, bound feet were considered intensely erotic and necessary for a good marriage. It is obvious that the so-called feminine beauty, small feet, became the symbol of women's subservience. Due to efforts of the Chinese reformers and revolutionaries, the footbinding practice waned in the early 20th century and gradually disappeared in China in the 1950s. *See also* CHINESE FEMINISM; LITTLE, ALICIA ARCHIBALD; MENG BUYU.

FOREIGN CONCESSIONS. Chinese territories administered by foreign entities under foreign jurisdiction. The **Treaty of Nanjing** of 1842 and the Supplement Treaty of Humen of 1843 granted the British the right of residence in five cities—Canton (Guangzhou), Amoy (Xiamen), Fuzhou, Ningbo, and Shanghai. In 1845, the British councilor Sir George Balfour rented from the Chinese municipal government land in Shanghai and built the first foreign concession in China. There were eventually 25 foreign concessions and four international settlements in China. The foreign concessions were divided among Britain with seven; France, four; Japan, nine; Germany, two; Italy, one; Austria-Hungary, one; and Belgium, one. The last concession was granted to Austria-Hungary in 1902. All concessions were in treaty cities in coastal areas or on the banks of major rivers. In the early days, the foreign concessions set up the principle of segregation, but increasing numbers of Chinese employees and laborers worked for foreign companies and lived in the concessions, making up the majority of the population of the concessions. The Chinese municipal government gradually lost judicial power in the foreign concessions.

In Shanghai, for example, the Chinese government had judicial control over the foreign concessions at first. The Shanghai Land Lease Regulation of 1845 stated that the concession was leased, not sold, to foreigners. However, when the Taiping rebels approached Shanghai in 1853, the foreign councils organized militias to protect the concessions and established the Municipal Committee to maintain social order in the concessions, so that the Chinese government began to lose control. The Municipal Committee also refused to provide the Chinese government any information on the Chinese employees of the foreign companies. In 1864, a "mutual public trial" system was established, which meant that when any Chinese court reviewed civil or criminal cases in a foreign concession, it had to have a foreign judge participate in the trial. When the Taiping rebels attacked Shanghai, more than 500,000 Chinese refugees fled to the foreign concessions. The Municipal Committee refused to inform the Chinese government of the number and status of the refugees and also ordered these newcomers to pay taxes to the foreign administrator. In the 1920s, China began to take over the foreign concessions. In 1945, after the **Second Sino-Japanese War**, the Nationalist government announced the abolition of all foreign concessions, and China regained sovereignty over these lands.

FORMOSA. The Portuguese name of Taiwan, literally meaning "beautiful island." In the 16th century, the Portuguese arrived in East Asia, found Taiwan, and called it "Ilha Formosa." The name first appeared on the Portuguese map by Lopo Homem in 1554 and was used by many other Western scholars in the past centuries. It is prohibited to use the name Formosa in mainland China, where it is regarded as a colonial term.

FOURTH FRONT ARMY (FOURTH FRONT ARMY OF THE CHINESE WORKERS' AND PEASANTS' RED ARMY). One of three major Communist military forces during 1928–1936. The Fourth Front Army was established on 7 November 1931, with **Xu Xiangqian** as the commander and Chen Changhao as the political commissar. However, power was actually in the hands of **Zhang Guotao**, the party leader in the E-Yu-Wan Soviet base. In July 1932, the Nationalist government assembled 300,000 troops to attack the base. Unable to withstand the offensive, the Fourth Front Army decided to relinquish the base, leaving only one small troop to carry out **guerrilla warfare**. Soon after, the leading forces transferred to the border between Shaanxi and Sichuan, where they managed to establish a new revolutionary base. The year 1933 witnessed the rapid growth of the Fourth Front Army. Having defeated the poorly equipped local army, the Fourth Front Army expanded to 800,000 men and established the Shaan-Chuan Soviet.

In March 1935, this army was ordered to retreat from the Shaan-Chuan Soviet and start the **Long March**. Zhang's Fourth Front Army met Mao's **First Front Army** in June at Maogong, Sichuan Province. It was decided that the two units would move north in two columns. The First Front Army was the right wing and Zhang's was the left. After passing through the Songpan swampland, Zhang refused to continue the journey and led his troops back in an attempt to build a new base in Southwest China. The heavy casualties and many setbacks suffered by the Fourth Front Army were attributed to this decision. In July 1936, the **Second Front Army** met the Fourth Front Army in Ganzi. Most leaders of the Fourth Front Army decided to change their strategy and join the Second Front Army to move northward. Three months later they were reunited with the First Front Army in Huining, Gansu Province, thus completing the Long March.

Part of the Fourth Front Army was ordered to cross the Yellow River and launch a western expedition to open a communication avenue to the Soviet Union via Xinjiang. However, they were destroyed by Muslim cavalry en route, and only 436 survivors led by Li Xiannian arrived in Xinjiang. There they were captured and jailed by the local warlord, **Sheng Shicai**. In August 1937, the remnants of the Fourth Front Army and the 29th Army of the Red Army were reorganized into the 129th Division of the **Eighth Route Army**. **Liu Bocheng** was appointed commander and Zhang Hao, political commissar. In January 1938, **Deng Xiaoping** replaced Zhang Hao to serve as political commissar.

FRYER, JOHN (1839–1928). British missionary best known by his Chinese name, Fu Lan Ya. Born in Hythe, Kent, England, into the family of a poor pastor, Fryer graduated from the Highbury Training College in London. On 30 July 1861, he traveled to Hong Kong, where he became the dean of St. Paul College. Two years later, Fryer was invited to teach at the **Tongwenguan** in Beijing. In 1868, he began to work at the **Jiangnan Arsenal**, serving as director of the translation division for 28 years. His translations totaled 129 volumes, covering five fields: natural science, applied science, military science and navigation, history, and social science. Fryer was a pioneer scholar who introduced Western concepts, approaches, and scientific methodology in these fields to China. In the meantime, he engaged in building schools, opening science bookstores, and publishing science journals in China.

In May 1877, the Protestant missionaries held a conference in Shanghai and founded the School and Text Book Series Committee to edit textbooks for missionary schools in China. Fryer was in charge of the textbooks for the elementary and middle schools. This gave the Chinese educators and students, for the first time, an awareness of textbooks. Fryer edited 27 popular science books and recommended them as further readings for missionary schools. His elder son, J. R. Fryer, followed in his footsteps to work at the Jiangnan Arsenal as a translator, but unfortunately he died early. In 1896, Fryer retired from the arsenal and went to the United States. Fryer created the Department of East Asian Languages and Cultures at the University of California, Berkeley, and served as its first department chair. Fryer donated to the university his private library, including more than 2,000 books and his own manuscripts; this was the first collection of the East Asian Library of the university. After he left the

Jiangnan Arsenal, Fryer translated 14 more books for the institution. He donated 60,000 taels of silver to build a school for blind children in Shanghai and asked his younger son, G. Fryer, to serve as its principal. According to his last will, $50,000 from his property were donated to the establishment of a school for blind girls in Shanghai. On 2 July 1928, Fryer died in Oakland, California.

FU JEN CATHOLIC UNIVERSITY (FJU). Catholic school established in 1925 in Peking (Beijing) by Ildephonse Brandstetter. In 1912, Chinese Christian scholars Ying Jianzhi and Ma Xiangbo asked Pope Pius X to help establish a Catholic school in Beijing. The next year, Ying built the Fu Ren school and recruited students from among the Christian youth, but this school existed for only four years. In 1925, the Benedictines of St. Vincent Archabbey in Latrobe, Pennsylvania, at the request of the Holy See, formally established this college with four departments: Chinese Literature, English Literature, History, and Philosophy. The first group of students was made up of 23 young boys. The number of freshmen rose to 120 the next year. The first president of the FJU was the American missionary George Barry O'Toole. He was succeeded in 1929 by Chen Yuan, a Chinese Protestant and prominent historian, who remained the university's president until the school's forced closure in 1952. The FJU had become one of the four major universities in Peking when the Communists took over the city. In 1952, as the government was to abolish all missionary schools, the FJU's facilities were divided and assigned to Beijing Normal University, **Peking University**, and People's University, while the Beijing Normal University occupied the FJU campus. In 1960, FJU was reestablished in Taiwan.

FU SINIAN (FU SSU-NIEN, 1896–1950). Prominent historian, linguist, and educator. Born in Laocheng, Shandong Province, Fu began to study with a private Confucian tutor at the age of six. In 1913, he was enrolled in the Chinese Department of **Peking University**. In 1918, with Luo Jialun, he founded the monthly magazine *New Tide*, introducing new ideas and theories that were very appealing to university students. During the **May Fourth Movement**, he was one of the organizers of the student demonstration. From 1919 through 1926, he studied science and comparative linguistics in England and Germany. At the invitation of Zhongshan University, he returned to

Guangzhou and served as dean of the School of Liberal Arts in 1927. Fu founded the Institute of History and Philosophy first at Zhongshan University and then at the Academia Sinica. He also offered students courses on ancient Chinese history and ancient Chinese literature. He argued that a historian should not only look at documents but also pay attention to archeological discoveries and apply approaches of philology and other disciplines to historical studies. In 1933, he published his *East Yi West Xia* theory about the origin of prehistoric culture in current China. As an anti-Communist intellectual, he supported **Chiang Kai-shek** but sharply opposed the corruption of Chiang's government. As a congressman, he successfully impeached two presidents of the Executive Council, **H. H. Kung** and **T. V. Soong**, on corruption charges in 1938. In 1949, he followed the Nationalist government and retreated to Tiawan, where he served as president of Taiwan University. On 20 December 1950, when he made a speech at a hearing of the Taiwan Provincial Congress, he became so excited that a cerebral hemorrhage occurred, and he died in Taipei at the age of 55.

FU XIAO'AN (1872–1940). Mayor of Shanghai during the Japanese occupation. Born in Zhenhai, Zhejiang Province, into a poor family, Feng began his career as a child worker at a British shipbuilding factory in Shanghai. He went to night school to study English and technology and caught the eye of his employer. Three years later, he became a foreman. When he grew up, Fu left the factory and served as a comprador for foreign companies. He opened his own business in real estate and finance and worked as a manager in several Chinese banks. He gradually established extensive connections with powerful government officials and rich businessmen, including minister of communication **Sheng Xuanhuai**. With Sheng's support, he became a rising star in the Shanghai business world and a board member of the Shanghai Chamber of Commerce in charge of foreign affairs. In 1926, he was elected chairman of the Shanghai Chamber of Commerce and supported the **warlord** Sun Chuanfang's rule in Shanghai. He was on the wanted list of the Republican government and was forced to flee to Dalian for Japanese protection. In 1931, when the arrest warrant was rescinded, Fu returned to Shanghai and resumed his position as general manager of the Chinese Bank of Commerce, where he continued to be an agent of British and American companies. In 1937, after the Japanese troops captured Shanghai, Fu was appointed the first mayor of the Special City of Shanghai and worked for the occupiers. In 1938, he was appointed mayor of Shanghai. Two years later, the head of the Nationalist secret service agency, Da Li, managed to have Fu assassinated by his cook in his own home.

FU ZUOYI (1895–1974). Noted military commander and full general of the second class of the **Nationalist Party** army. Born in Ronghe, Shanxi Province, Fu studied successively at the Elementary School of the Army in Shanxi, Qinghe Cadet School in Beijing, and **Baoding Military Academy.** After graduating in 1918, Fu returned to Shanxi and served in **Yan Xishan**'s army. He rose from battalion commander to regiment, brigade, and division commander. In 1927, he earned a high reputation among Chinese generals by defending an isolated town, Zhuoxian, for three months. He was then promoted to army commander in 1929 and joined Yan's war against **Chiang Kai-shek**. Defeated by Chiang, he was transferred to Suiyuan Province. During the **Second Sino-Japanese War**, Fu held numerous commands in fighting the Japanese, including the battles of Xikou and Taiyuan. Defeated by the Japanese, he retreated to western Shanxi and began to cooperate with the Communist **Eighth Route Army** in the resistance movement. In 1936, his troops stormed the strategic post Beilingmiao, winning the battle of Suiyuan. During the civil war, Fu was made commander in chief of the North China Army, his army possessing 600,000 troops and controlling the cities of Tianjin and Beiping as well as the Suiyuan–Beiping corridor.

However, after the Lao-Shen Campaign, **Lin Biao** led a million troops into North China. Lin's troops stormed Tianjin, and Fu had to accept Lin's terms for the "peaceful liberation of Beiping." Fu's daughter, Fu Dongmei, was a secret party worker of the **Chinese Communist Party** (CCP) who provided the **People's Liberation Army** with information on her father's operations and helped the CCP persuade her father to surrender. After the founding of the People's Republic of China (PRC) in 1949, Fu was appointed vice-chairman of the National Defense Committee of the PRC, vice-chairman of the **Chinese People's Political Consultative Conference**, and minister of water resources. His daughter, Dongmei, was persecuted and committed suicide during the Cultural Revolution.

FUTIAN INCIDENT (1930). Military coup lunched by the 20th Army of the **Red Army** in December 1930 in Futian, Jiangxi Province. The coup was triggered by the cruel persecution of innocent Red Army officers and soldiers by Li Shaojiu, who was sent by **Mao Zedong** on 5 December 1930 to Futian to purge the "counterrevolutionary **AB League**" in the 20th Army. As soon as he and his working team arrived in Futian, Li used cruel methods to torture and murder innocents. Three days later, Mao sent his secretary Gu Bo with military forces to join Li and promote the massive arrests and executions. Consequently, more than 4,000 men were arrested and hundreds were executed, including a dozen regimental commanders. On the night of 11 December, Li and Gu executed 27 people, including a dozen members of the Provincial Committee of the **Chinese Communist Party** (CCP), and there were more people on his killing list. The next morning, the regimental commander Liu Di led his troops in revolt. They took control of the town of Futian, released more than a hundred people, denounced the atrocities, and shouted the slogan "Down with Mao Zedong." The next day, the 20th Army crossed the Gan River, announcing its separation from the **First Front Army** and establishing a CCP provincial committee.

The CCP Central Committee believed that the Futian Incident was a counterrevolutionary rebellion. The leaders of the incident sent Duan Liangbi to Shanghai to defend them before the CCP Central Committee. Having noticed the hostile attitude of the Central Committee, which did not want to listen or investigate, Duan escaped from Shanghai and disappeared forever. On 17 December, **Peng Dehuai** was ordered to lead the 3rd Army Corps to suppress the rebels. One of the CCP leaders, Chen Yi, still wanted to mediate. The 20th Army accepted Chen's suggestion and released Li Shaojiu and his team. However, when Liu and other leaders of the Futian Incident came for negotiation, they were arrested and executed by Mao's people. Xiang Ying, the acting secretary of the CCP Bureau of the Central Soviet Area, saw the Futian Incident as an internal conflict among revolutionaries and suggested they solve the problem by punishing the rebel leaders only. However, **Wang Ming**, the general secretary of the CCP Central Committee, condemned the incident as a counterrevolutionary mutiny, and Mao Zedong insisted on the suppression of the army.

The Red Army commanders, Peng Dehuai and **Lin Biao**, were sent to destroy the 20th Army. Since the officers and soldiers of the 20th

Army did not want to fight with another group of the Red Army, they were rapidly disarmed by Peng and Lin. All 700 officers at platoon level and above were executed. The designation of the 20th Army was abolished and its soldiers were incorporated into Peng's 7th Army in July 1931. After the Futian Incident, the campaign of purging the AB League gained more momentum, terminating the lives of about 70,000 Red Army soldiers and CCP workers in the **Jiangxi Soviet**.

FUZHOU DOCKYARD. Established in 1866 by Governor Zuo Zongtang in Fuzhou as an effort of the **Self-Strengthening Movement**. It was a government enterprise, making warships and cannons for the Qing Navy. There was also a naval academy attached that produced 628 navy officers. The courses on shipbuilding at the academy were given in French by French instructors, while the courses on navigation were given in English by British instructors. The academy offered a five-year program, including the internship in French or German shipyards and in the British Royal Navy. In 1875, the Qing government built the Beiyang Navy, whose officers, except for Commander Ding Ruchang, were all graduates of the Fuzhou Naval Academy. After the 1911 Revolution, the academy was turned into the Naval Engineer Institute, but its graduates continued to play an important role in the Republican naval force.

– G –

GAO GANG (1905–1954). One of the top leaders of the **Chinese Communist Party** (CCP) and the first to be purged in the inner-party struggle after 1949. Born in Hengshan, Shaanxi Province, Gao joined the Chinese Communist Party in 1926. Gao developed a party organization among the local militiary forces of the **Nationalist Party** and finally staged an uprising to form a Communist troop. He served as political commissar at various levels of the **Red Army** and was one of the founders of the Shan-Gan-Ning revolutionary base, which was the destination of the **Long March**. In Februry 1935, Gao was appointed general political commissar of the Communist troops in Northwest China and vice-chairman of the Military Committee of Northwest China. During the **Second Sino-Japanese War** and the civil war, Gao served first as the party secretary of the CCP Northwest Bureau and then as secretary of the CCP Northeast Bureau. Gao was one of Mao's strong supporters in the **Yan'an Rectification Movement** and contributed to the consolidation of the Communist base in Northwest China.

In 1949, when the People's Republic of China was founded, Gao Gang was elected vice president of the state. As a capable leader in Manchuria, he turned this region into the most energetic and robust part of China, an industrial base for the republic's economic development. Gao established a close relationship with Joseph Stalin, who gave more economic aid to Manchuria than to any other Chinese region. In November 1952, Gao was appointed chairman of the Central Planning Committee of the central government, which derived a great amount of power from Premier **Zhou Enlai**. Allied with Rao Shushi, the chief of the Organization Department of the CCP Central Committee, Gao began to criticize **Liu Shaoqi** and Zhou Enlai for their policies, and he initially received support from **Mao Zedong**. But his ambition of replacing Liu and Zhou, his sexual scandals, and his suspicious friendship with the Russians evoked criticism within the CCP Politburo. In February 1954, Mao instructed the CCP Central Committee to hold a special meeting, accusing Gao of being the head of an antiparty clique that had attempted to usurp the top power of the party and state. Gao refused to confess and committed suicide. He was purged from the CCP after his death.

GAO SHUXUN MOVEMENT. Gao Shuxun was the deputy commander of the Nationalist 11th War Zone. He revolted in Hanta, southern Hebei, and defected to the **Chinese Communist Party** (CCP), taking with him one corps and one column. To entice other Nationalist officers to follow Gao's example, the CCP Central Committee decided to start a propaganda campaign that was called the Gao Shuxun Movement.

***GELAOHUI* (SOCIETY OF BROTHERS AND ELDERS).** The most powerful secret society in the Yangtze River basin, known also as the Paoge or Hanliu. It originated in the early tradition of the *hongmen*, an organization devoted to the restoration of the Ming dynasty, but it evolved into a semimilitary association whose objective was mutual aid and community protection. It was banned by the Qing government because of its anti-**Manchu** inclination. Its membership consisted of people of various social classes, including peasants, gentry, craftsmen, and merchants, but the majority were poor people. Almost all *Gelaohui* members had their own jobs, according to which the society was divided into five sections named *ren* (love), *yi* (loyalty), *li* (rite), *zhi* (intelligence), and *xin* (trust). Most members of the *ren* section were gentry; the *yi* section, merchants; the *li* section, bandits, soldiers, and homeless people; the *zhi* section, poor farmers, craftsmen, and boatmen; the *xin* section was the smallest one, comprising actors and servants. The inauguration ritual for new leaders or new members included killing a rooster and drinking its blood, which symbolized establishing brotherhood and loyalty to the organization. Teahouses were a major place for the Gelaohui's daily gatherings and annual meetings. The Gelaohui emphasized **Confucian** moral codes (love, loyalty, filial piety, obligation, etc.) to hold its membership together. It was estimated that more than half the male adults in Sichuan were Gelaohui members in the late 19th century, and it had become a semiopen organization. The Gelaohu; did not have a national headquarters, but all members throughout the country shared the associational identity.

Using **anti-Manchu nationalism** to mobilize the Chinese to join the 1911 Revolution, **Sun Yat-sen** regarded the Gelaohui as a source of revolutionaries and recruited a large number of Gelaohui members for his **Tongmenghui**. Between 1906 and 1910, Sun launched several uprisings in western Sichuan, and the Gelaohui was the leading force. The Gelaohui also played a crucial role in the Sichuan Railroad Protection Movement, the founding of the Republic of China, and the **National Protection War**. The Nationalist government allowed the existence of the Gelaohui even after the government moved its capital to **Chongqing** during the **Second Sino-Japanese War**. Those Gelaohui members who established close connections with the Communists, known as Red Paoge, collaborated with the Communist **Eighth Route Army** during the war. In 1949, when the Nationalist government fled to Taiwan, some Gelaohui members continued an anti-Communist guerrilla warfare. They were soon crushed by the **People's Liberation Army** in the "elimination of bandits campaign." The Gelaohui was banned as a counterrevolutionary organization.

GENERAL STRIKE ON THE JING–HAN RAILWAY (1923). Known also as the Great February Seventh Strike. A general strike of the workers of the Jing–Han railways led by the Communist Party. On 2 February 1923, the railway workers held a meeting to establish a general trade union of the railway workers. Some leaders of the **Chinese Communist Party**, such as **Zhang Guotao**, Chen Tanjiu, and others also participated in the meeting. Because the police came to dismiss the meeting and drive the participants out of the conference hall, 20,000 workers launched a general strike, bringing the 1,200-kilometer-long Beijing–Hankou railway to a standstill and interrupting south–north communication. During the night of 7 February, the police arrested Lin Xiangqian, a member of the Communist Party and chairman of the Jiang'an Branch of the Federation of **Jinghan Railway** Workers. Because Lin refused to order the workers to return to work, he was executed. Another Communist Party member and leader of the strike, attorney Shi Yang, who was the legal adviser of the Hubei Trade Union, was executed with Lin. The Beijing–Hankou Railway was the major source of revenue of **warlord Wu Peifu**, who desperately needed it to be restored to operation. On his orders, the police and military opened fire on workers, which caused the deaths of 52 men and wounded more than 300 men. This incident sparked the Chinese labor movement.

GILES, HERBERT ALLEN (1845–1935). British diplomat and professor of sinology at Cambridge University. Giles traveled to China in 1867 and worked as a consular officer in Tianjing, Ningbo, and Shanghai. He resigned his office in 1893 to focus on academic studies of Chinese language and culture. In 1897, he became the second professor of sinology at Cambridge University. His publications included reference works, language textbooks, translations, and miscellaneous writings. He introduced the Chinese philosophy of Laozi to Western readers. His book *Chinese Sketches* was published in 1876. The book is based on his nine years of observations of China, providing Western readers with a fascinating narrative of etiquette, gambling, pawnbrokers, slang, superstitions, and torture. In 1892, he published the famous *Chinese-English Dictionary* (2nd ed. 1912), which was always cited as the locus classicus of the so-called Wade-Giles system of transcription of Chinese. The **Wade-Giles system** was widely used in the English-speaking world for most of the 20th century until it was replaced by the pinyin system in 1979.

GLOBE MAGAZINE (WANGUO GONGBAO). Known also as *A Review of the Times.* Originally called *Church News*, the magazine was established in Shanghai in 1868 by the American missionary **Young John Allen**. It was renamed *Globe Magazine,* or *A Review of the Times*, in 1874 and became devoted to the introduction of Western knowledge to China. The magazine nurtured several generations of Chinese intellectuals. The Qing reform leader, **Kang Youwei**, said that his reforms were greatly inspired by *Globe Magazine.* Sun Yatsen's reform proposal to **Li Hongzhang** was published in this journal. The well-known writer of 20th century China, **Lin Yutang**, said that *Globe Magazine* and Young Allen changed his whole life. Some prominent government officials, such as Li Hongzhang and **Zhang Zhidong**, were also readers of the magazine. In later years, *Globe Magazine* became the formal publication of the Christian Literature Society for China. Allen continued to edit the magazine, and the average print run was 4,000 copies for each issue. After Allen died in Shanghai in 1907, publication of the magazine ceased.

GLORIOUS CONSTITUTION (*HONGXIAN*). The name of **Yuan Shikai**'s short-lived dynasty, which lasted only 83 days. On 25 December 1915, the president of the Republic of China, Yuan Shikai, decided to restore the monarchy, proclaiming himself emperor of China. Yuan's betrayal immediately triggered military uprisings throughout the country. On the same day, **Cai E** declared the independence of Yunnan, and the provinces of Guizhou, Shanxi, Guangxi, Guangdong, Zhejiang, and others followed suit. Cai organized the Republic Protection Army for a punitive expedition. Yuan sent the **Beiyang Army** to suppress the Republic Protection Army, but it was quickly crushed by Cai E in Sichuan. In the meantime, foreign governments, including Japan, also opposed the restoration. Under all these pressures, Yuan had to proclaim the abolition of the monarchy on 22 March 1916. Two months later, Yuan died of uremia.

"GO WEST." An ideology of Chinese intellectuals in modern times that regarded Chinese traditional culture as the root of China's backwardness and humiliation. The leading scholars who urged the Chinese to "go West" were **Hu Shih** and **Chen Xujing**. They advocated Westernization in response to **Liang Qichao**'s criticism of the **New Culture Movement**—that the Chinese acceptance of Western learning would sacrifice their own spirit and undermine their destiny. Hu and Chen argued that China lagged behind the West not only in science and technology but also in politics, literature, arts, morality, research methodology, and physical stature. The slogan "Go West" required reexamining China's historical legacy.

GOD WORSHIPPING SOCIETY (*BAI SHANGDI HUI*). The early organization of the **Taiping Rebellion**, founded by **Hong Xiuquan** and **Feng Yunshan** in 1847 in the province of Guangxi. Hong began to organize the society after his failures in the **civil service examinations**. In the city of Guangzhou, where he took the exams, Hong and Feng happened to meet a missionary who handed Hong a booklet, *Good Words Exhorting the Age*, written by the Chinese minister **Liang Fa**. After reading it, Hong claimed that God was the only deity in the universe and that he was the younger son of God sent to the world to eliminate demons (**Manchus**). Hong used his own interpretation of Christianity to organize the God Worshipping Society and converted first his relatives and then a considerable number of **Hakka** coal-burning workers. Hong's followers numbered 10,000 by 1851, when he staged the Taiping Uprising. Hong created his own rituals for the God Worshipping Society, including praying, baptism, and holidays different from mainstream Christianity. The society saw foreign Christians as their brothers and sisters, but Western missionaries found that the religion of the Taiping rebels was not real Christianity. Hong refused the Christian teachings the missionaries tried to offer, instead working to promote his revolutionary programs and to build his own cult of personality. *See also* YANG XIUQING.

GOLD YUAN (*JIN YUAN JUAN*). Currency issued by the Nationalist government in 1948. This was part of **Chiang Kai-shek**'s monetary reform to stem the chaotic national financial slide. The reform was to issue 2 billion of the new currency, the gold yuan, to replace **fabi**, at a conversion rate of 3 million yuan to 1 gold yuan. All the old fabi were to be exchanged for the new currency, and any gold, silver, and foreign currency held privately by Chinese also had to be turned in to the bank in exchange for gold yuan. To ensure the success of the reform, the government froze market prices and forbade wage increases. Chiang also sent his son **Chiang Ching-kuo** to Shanghai as commissioner in charge of the reform. Chiang Ching-kuo mobilized criticism against corruption and speculation in order to stabilize the market and regain popularity. Nonetheless, as prices continued to rise, the government began to increase note printing, which soon exceeded the ceiling of 2 billion gold yuan. Inflation got out of control and 10 months later, the gold yuan had been devalued by 250,000 times. The gold yuan became wastepaper also because the government could not reduce its deficit spending, which was due mostly to its huge military expenses in the civil war.

GONG ZIZHEN (1792–1841). Reformist scholar and poet during the late Qing dynasty. He was born in Hangzhou into an official family and went to Beijing to study Han **Confucianism**. He obtained the *juren* degree at the age of 26, then failed five times in further **civil service examinations** until he finally received the *jinshi* degree at the age of 37. He remained a minor official but published extensively on philosophy, politics, and economy. Believing that China faced a major crisis, Gong proposed substantial reforms, including offering officials higher salaries to prevent corruption, reforming the contents of the exams and recruiting officials of various backgrounds and skills, curbing the concentration of landholdings, and banning the opium trade. To enhance China's control of Xinjiang, he suggested that the central government establish a province there and "station troops to cultivate wasteland and defend the frontiers." In his early years, he had supported the policy of "emphasizing agriculture and suppressing commerce," but his later works indicated his recognition of the importance of the market economy. His ideas were of great influence on late Qing reformers, such as **Kang Youwei** and **Liang Qichao**. In his later years, Gong became a devout Buddhist. He retired at the age of 48 and died two years later on his journey of teaching and traveling in the province of Jiangsu.

GONGCHE SHANGSHU. See STATEMENT OF PUBLIC VEHICLES.

GORDON, CHARLES GEORGE (1833–1885). A British military officer and diplomat, known as "Chinese Gordon." Born in Woolwich, England, Charles George Gordon was the son of Major General Henry William Gordon. Charles Gordon was educated at the Royal Military Academy and served as a second lieutenant in the Royal

Engineers. He was promoted to full lieutenant in 1854. Gordon volunteered to go to China in 1860, as the Second **Opium War** broke out. He participated in the battle in Beijing and the destruction of the Old Summer Palace (**Yuan Ming Yuan**). Gordon was in China during the **Taiping Rebellion**, and when the American commander of the **Ever Victorious Army**, Frederick Townsend Ward, was killed in the Battle of Cixi, Gordon took command of the force. The first operation he commanded was the successful relief of the strategically important city of Changsu; the operation won him a reputation with the troops. Collaborating with the **Anhui Army**, Gordon led his troops to storm the cities of Suzhou and Changzhou. Believing that there was no doubt about the final victory south of the Yangtze River, the Ever Victorious Army was disbanded in May 1964 in the town of Kunshan, near Shanghai. The emperor granted Gordon the title *tidu*, one of the highest grades in the Chinese army, and decorated him with the yellow jacket. Gordon accepted the title but refused the offer of 100,000 gold pieces by the emperor. The British promoted him to lieutenant colonel and he became a Companion of Honor. After he returned to Great Britain, he was sent to Africa, where he was killed in the Sudanese civil war on 26 January 1885.

GRAND COUNCIL (*JUNJI CHU*). The highest policymaking institution of the Qing regime, founded in 1729 by the Yongzheng Emperor. *Junji chu* literally means "office of military secrets," which was originally a temporary institution established for the war against the Dzungars, helping the emperor obtain direct military information and make quick decisions. The council worked directly with the emperor, avoiding bureaucratic inefficiency. After the war ended, it was not abolished; rather, it was expanded and it eventually outstripped the power of the Council of Advisor Princes and the **Southern Study**, marking an important shift of central power from bureaucrats to the emperor himself. Most of the officials in the council were **Manchu**, and a few **Han** officials were included in later years. The most senior official was the chief councillor. The major functions of the council included drafting the emperor's edicts and reviewing the memorials of government officials; offering suggestions on policies, military tactics, preachments, and punishments of government officials; reviewing important judicial cases; nominating candidates for important positions, such as ministers of the six boards, governors, viceroys, examiners for the **civil service examinations**, exam writers, and exam supervisors; being around the emperor and ready to respond to his questions on various issues; and being ready to serve as imperial commissioners to provinces to solve crucial problems. The power of the Grand Council gradually waned after the **Zongli Yamen** was established in March 1861, but it was not formally abolished until April 1911.

GRAND SECRETARIAT. An institution of the Qing government inherited from the preceding Ming dynasty that handled the routine matters of the state. The Grand Secretariat was the principal policymaking body during Ming times, but it became less important under the Qing and evolved into an imperial chancery, a part of the outer court. In fact, all important decisions were made in the inner court, which consisted of the emperor (in the later years, the Dowager Cixi) and the **Grand Council**.

GREATER EAST ASIAN CO-PROSPERITY SPHERE. The Japanese domination of East Asia. *See* NEW ORDER IN EAST ASIA.

GREEN GANG (*QING BANG*). The most powerful secret society in Shanghai during the first half of the 20th century. This organization could be traced back to the late Qing period, when the **Tributary Grain Shipment** was institutionalized. Some of the boatmen who were involved in the shipment of grain organized a brotherhood and tried to affiliate it to the *hongmen,* a well-known anti-**Manchu** organization. However, since they engaged in Qing government business, their organization was not recognized as part of *hongmen* (red gang), but was rather referred to as *qing bang* (green gang). The two colors red (*hong*) and green (*qing*) symbolized the boatmen's political differences. After the decline of the Tributary Grain Shipment, most crews left the grain boats and migrated to Shanghai and other cities.

Three major leaders of the Green Gang in Shanghai were Huang Jinrong, Zhang Xiaolin, and **Du Yuesheng**. They handled several Mafia-like enterprises, such as gambling dens, prostitution, and opium smuggling, which were rampant in the **foreign concessions** of Shanghai. More often than not, the foreign administrators in the concessions turned to the Green Gang to maintain social order and curb crime. In addition, the Green Gang had various connections with revolutionary parties. Some notorious revolutionary leaders, such as **Chen Qimei** and **Chiang Kai-shek**, were also members of the Green Gang. In 1927, the Green Gang contributed to Chiang Kai-shek's purge of the Communists in Shanghai, but during the **Second Sino-Japanese War**, Du Yuesheng also helped the Communist **New Fourth Army** by donating to them some military supplies.

The three leaders of the Green Gang had very different experiences during the war. Zhang chose to collaborate with the Japanese and was assassinated by the Nationalist Party (GMD). Huang pretended sickness to refuse Japanese offers and survived the war. Du organized the Green Gang followers to wage **guerrilla warfare** in southeastern China and continued to play an important political role after the war. The Communists defined the Green Gang as a "social evil" and were determined to eliminate it. In 1949, as the Communists took over Shanghai, Du fled to Hong Kong while Huang stayed. Huang made a public confession and got a pardon, but the Green Gang was outlawed in mainland China.

GREEN STANDARD ARMY (*LÜYINGJUN*). The professional army of the Qing government whose solders were recruited from ethnic **Han** Chinese. Once a man joined the army, he was registered as a professional soldier, serving in the army for his whole life. The army was built up by the first emperor of the Qing dynasty, Shunzhi, in the 17th century, and was divided into two parts: one joined the metropolitan banners to defend the capital; the other was stationed at strategic posts. The central government provided the officers and soldiers with stipends and military supplies, and the Green Standard Army was supervised and controlled by the **Manchu Eight Banners**. In the middle Qing, the Green Standard Army became the leading military force of the empire, which numbered 600,000 troops at its peak. In the later Qing, however, the **Opium War** and the **Taiping Rebellion** proved that this army was too weak to deal with domestic rebellions or foreign intrusion. The budget for this army was cut down and its size was reduced. By the 1860s, private regional armies like the **Hunan Army** and the **Anhui Army** had surpassed the Green Standard Army in both numbers and military importance.

GU SHUNZHANG (1903–1934). Special agent first working for the **Chinese Communist Party** (CCP) and then for the **Nationalist**

Party (GMD). Born in the suburbs of Shanghai, Gu was a worker at a tobacco factory. He joined the **Green Gang** and was promoted to foreman. Gu took an active part in the **May Thirtieth Movement** of 1925 and joined the CCP the same year. In 1926, Gu was sent to Moscow for espionage training with the KGB. Soon after his return, Gu was appointed chief commander of the worker pickets in the Shanghai Worker Uprising of 1927. At the **August Seventh Conference** of the CCP in Hankou, Gu was elected alternate member of the Politburo and head of the Central Communication Bureau. He was the head of the terrorist organization Red Team in Shanghai; this group performed assassinations and other covert missions. Gu was a corrupt person who indulged in drinking, gambling, and prostitution. In March 1931, Gu was arrested by the GMD. He quickly defected and began to work for the GMD; this move led to the destruction of the whole CCP secret organization in Shanghai and the deaths of the major Communist leaders Yun Daiying and Cai Hesheng. Viewing Gu as a dangerous traitor, the **Jiangxi Soviet** issued his death warrant on 1 December 1931. The Communists could not capture Gu, but **Zhou Enlai** led the Red Team in Shanghai and killed all Gu's family members, including a five-year-old girl. After a short time of cooperation with the GMD espionage agency, Gu tried to develop his own power by organizing a "new Communist Party." **Chiang Kai-shek** ordered Gu's execution in 1933.

GU WEIJUN (VI KYUIN WELLINGTON KOO, 1887–1985). Prominent diplomat of the Qing dynasty and Republic of China. Born in Jiading, Shanghai, Gu first received a traditional education and then enrolled at **Saint John's University** in Shanghai. He went to the United States at the age of 16 and studied at Columbia University, where he obtained his PhD in international law and diplomacy. When **Tang Shaoyi** visited Washington, Gu was the representative of the Chinese students in the United States at the welcome party. Tang was impressed by Gu, and when he returned to China, Tang recommended him to be **Yuan Shikai**'s secretary for foreign affairs. Strengthening this bond, Gu married Tang's daughter. In 1919, Gu led the Chinese delegation attending the **Paris Peace Conference**. He demanded that Shandong be returned to China. After his claims were turned down by the Western powers, he and the Chinese delegation refused to sign the Versailles Treaty.

Between 1922 and 1927, Gu successively served the **Beijing government** as minister of foreign affairs, minister of finance, and acting premier. In 1930, he joined the Nationalist government in Nanjing and continued his diplomatic career. In 1931, he represented China at the League of Nations in protest over the Japanese aggression in Manchuria. He served as China's ambassador to France and Great Britain during World War II. In 1945, he represented China at the signing of the Charter of the United Nations. Starting in 1946, Gu served for 10 years as ambassador to the United States. He retired in New York City and died there at the age of 98.

GUAN DU SHANG BAN (**GOVERNMENT-SUPERVISED MERCHANT UNDERTAKINGS**). A pattern of Chinese modern enterprises in the **Self-Strengthening Movement**. It began in the 1870s and became popular in the 1880s. The major enterprises included the **Kaiping Coal Mines**, Tianjin Telegraph Company, and **China Merchant Steamship Navigation Company**. Their capital was mainly private investment, with a little from the Qing government. They were run by merchants, but the government controlled the personnel, administration, and finances of the companies. These enterprises enjoyed certain privileges, such as tax exemptions or deductions, low-interest loans from the government, and a market monopoly. The merchants gained profits and took risks while the government gained a fixed bonus. Due to low productivity and tension between bureaucrats and private investors, this pattern became less effective. In the 1890s, merchants lost interest in investing in these enterprises. *See also* LI HONGZHANG.

GUANGDA COMPANY. Established in October 1933 in Shanghai by the Communist secret organization, it began by selling Western medicine and gradually expanded to importing medical equipment, hardware, chemical materials, and paper, and exporting tung oil and casings for sausages; it also dealt with grain shipments. Its original capital was $300 but increased to $2.5 million by 1941. The company established an extensive trading network by opening branches in some of China's big cities and in New York. After the Japanese occupied Shanghai, the headquarters was moved to China's wartime capital, **Chongqing**. The president of the board of trustees, Lu Xuzhang, and the other two managers of the company, Yang Yanxiu and

Zhang Ping, were all capable businessmen and secret members of the **Chinese Communist Party** (CCP). Besides submitting profits to the CCP organization, the company was also involved in illegal business, including money laundering for the CCP, smuggling medicine and military materials to the Communist rural bases, and other urgent assignments. After the **New Fourth Army Incident** in 1941, **Zhou Enlai** ordered the company to stop all its other activities and function solely as a moneymaking machine for the CCP. In March 1949, the company merged with the Huayun Company in Hong Kong. Lu Xuzhang was dispatched to Beijing and became the deputy minister of foreign trade of the People's Republic of China.

GUANGFUHUI. *See* RECOVERY SOCIETY.

GUANGHWA, TREATY OF (1876). The full name was the Korea-Japanese Treaty of Amity. In the late 19th century, Japan was determined to follow the Western powers to build up its domination over East Asia. In 1875, the Japanese government dispatched the warship *Unyo* to survey Korean coastal waters without Korean permission; this caused conflict with the Korean army. On 20 September, the ship approached Guanghwa Island and exchanged fire with the Korean coast guards. The *Unyo*'s superior firepower silenced the Korean guns. Having attacked another Korean port, the *Unyo* withdrew to Japan. The following year, the Japanese fleet led by Special Envoy Kuroda Kiyotaka came demanding an apology from the Joseon government and forced the Korean government to sign the Treaty of Guanghwa. The treaty granted **extraterritoriality** to Japanese citizens in Korea and opened Busan, Incheon, and Wonsan to Japanese trade and residence. Although Korea continued to pay tribute to China after the treaty, its foreign relations began to be controlled by Japan.

GUANGXI CLIQUE (GUI CLIQUE). One of the **warlord** cliques in southwest China. It was named after the clique's base of power, Guangxi Province, and it also controlled the provinces of Guangdong and Hunan. Its early leader was Lu Rongting, who began the military buildup when he was governor of Guangxi in 1912. He moved the provincial capital from Guilin to Nanjing and centralized all military, administrative, and financial powers in his own hands by promulgating "governing Guangxi by the Guangxinese." In 1916, he proclaimed Guangxi independence and led his troops to occupy Hunan and Guangdong. After being appointed by the **Beijing government** as viceroy of Guangdong and Guangxi, he wasted no time in expanding his troops to 50,000, making himself the most powerful warlord in southwest China. During the **Constitutional Protection Movement**, his officers controlled the military government in Guangzhou and expelled **Sun Yat-sen** from the leadership. In 1921, Sun led the military forces of the provinces of Guangdong, Yunnan, Guizhou, and Jiangxi in launching an expedition against Lu, and stormed the cities of Nanjing and Guilin. Lu fled to Shanghai but returned the next year, becoming "superintendent of military affairs in Guanxi."

However, Lu no longer had the predominant influence, since the Guangxi Clique itself had split. In January 1924, the younger generals of the Guangxi Clique, **Li Zongren** and Huang Shaohong, anounced their acceptance of the leadership of Sun Yat-sen's Revolutionary Government in Guangzhou. In the following years, Guangxi Clique troops took an active part in the **Northern Expedition** against the northern warlords. Its Seventh Army played a crucial role in several decisive battles, contributing greatly to the reunification of China. Nonetheless, Li Zongren, Huang Shaohong, and **Bai Chongxi** engaged in several campaigns against **Chiang Kai-shek** and the central government in Nanjing. Because of this, they were referred to as new warlords of the Guangxi Clique. In the war with Chiang in 1929, the Guangxi Clique was defeated and Li and Bai fled abroad. In the 1930s, Chiang reconciled with the clique and called Li and Bai back.

The Guangxi Clique joined Chiang's **Encirclement and Suppression Campaigns** against the Communists. On the other hand, the Guangxi Clique focused its efforts on the reconstruction of Guangxi during the period of 1930–1936, making it a "model" province in terms of efficient administration, social stability, and economic development. In addition, the Gaungxi Clique provided a large number of troops in the **Second Sino-Japanese War**, especially in the famous **Battle of Taierzhuang**. Li Zongren was elected vice president of the Republic of China in 1947, and then served as acting president when Chiang Kai-shek resigned the next year. As the **Central Army** under Chiang's command lost all the decisive battles north of the Yangtze River, Li asked for negotiations with the Communists to keep half of China under Nationalist control. But the negotiations went nowhere. The Guangxi Clique tried to fight one last battle, but its more than

100,000 troops were utterly destroyed in Guangxi. Li fled to the United States and Bai led a few remnants to retreat to Taiwan in 1949.

GUANGXU EMPEROR (1871–1908). Tenth emperor of the Qing dynasty. Born as Zaitian, his father was Prince Chu Yi and his mother was the **Dowager Cixi**'s younger sister. In January 1875, the **Tongzhi Emperor** died without a son, and Cixi chose Zaitian as successor to the throne. Since Guangxu was four years old when he became the emperor, Cixi served as regent, and **Weng Tonghe** was the imperial tutor. Guangxu began formal rule in 1889 but continued to live in the shadow of Cixi. During the **First Sino-Japanese War** (1894–1895), he repeatedly urged **Li Hongzhang** to fight but was obstructed by Cixi and some officials who stood for compromise with Japan. After China's defeat by Japan, the emperor was forced to approve the **Treaty of Shimonoseki**. This loss made him understand China's desperate need for a radical reform. On the recommendation of Weng Tonghe, he met **Kang Youwei** and was convinced by Kang's reform plan. In June 1898, Guangxu began the **Hundred Days' Reform** by issuing edicts for a massive number of far-reaching modernizing programs, and appointed Kang Youwei and other reformists to the **Zongli Yamen** and the **Grand Council**. Gaungxu's goal was to establish a constitutional monarchy in China like that in England and Japan. In the following 103 days, 40 decrees were issued on comprehensive reforms in the areas of government administration, education, industry, and foreign affairs. Because of this, Guangxu came into conflict with a large number of conservative **Manchu** nobles and their leader, the Dowager Cixi, who still held supreme power. Cixi had a loyal army commanded by Ronglu in Tianjin, while the emperor attempted to get help from a young general, **Yuan Shikai**. Guangxu issued Yuan a secret decree to kidnap Cixi, but Yuan exposed this plan to Ronglu. Cixi moved in to launch a coup, putting Guangxu under detention and announcing publicly that a serious illness had incapacitated the emperor. Guangxu was in fact dethroned. For years, he suffered from melancholy and other sickness. The emperor died under mysterious circumstances on 14 November 1908, one day before Cixi's death.

GUANGZHOU MUTINY (1927). One of the urban insurrections launched by the Communists in 1927. After the split of the **Chinese Communist Party** (CCP) and the **Nationalist Party** (GMD) in the spring of 1927, the Communist organizations had to withdraw from major cities. On 7 August 1927, the CCP's Politburo held an urgent meeting in Hankou. In the light of the **Comintern**'s instructions, the CCP decided to launch a series of insurrections to regain the cities, including Guangzhou. The leading forces of the Guangzhou uprising were the Cadet Regiment, which was controlled by the Communists, and the worker pickets. The mutiny began on 11 December 1927, when most Nationalist armies were not in Guangzhou. The Communists moved rapidly and controlled the city. A Soviet government, known as the **Canton Commune**, was established the next day. This uprising was led by prominent Communist leaders, including **Zhang Tailei**, **Ye Ting**, and **Ye Jianying**. Zhang was elected acting chairman of the Canton Commune, and Ye was the commander in chief of the uprising. The Nationalist armies in Guangdong Province organized a counterattack to regain the city. The fighting lasted two days and cost more than 5,000 Communists' lives. On 13 December, the Communists gave up the city and retreated. Some troops managed to break out of the encirclement and join the remnants who survived the failed Nanchang Uprising. These troops were finally led by **Zhu De** to meet **Mao Zedong**'s guerrillas in the **Jinggangshan** Mountain region.

GUERRILLA WARFARE. A military strategy developed by **Mao Zedong** and other Communist leaders during the Chinese Revolution. The Communists began guerrilla warfare after the failure of their urban mutinies in the late 1920s. Mao created the strategy and tactics of guerrilla warfare during the **Jinggangshan** period, which he summarized as "Enemy advances, we retreat; enemy encamps, we harass; enemy tires, we attack; enemy retreats, we pursue." This strategy proved to be successful, giving the Red Army victories in four of **Chiang Kai-shek**'s suppression campaigns. When the **Twenty-eight Bolsheviks** took over the party's leadership, they expelled Mao and changed the army's basic strategy from guerrilla warfare to conventional warfare, which led to the collapse of the **Jiangxi Soviet** base and disastrous casualties in the Red Army. Mao believed guerrilla warfare was necessary because the Chinese Revolutionaries were outnumbered and facing better-equipped, much stronger enemy troops. Mao's ideas were recognized at the **Zunyi Conference**, making him the supreme leader of the **Chinese Communist Party** (CCP).

During the **Second Sino-Japanese War**, Mao published many works, including *Guerrilla Warfare* (1934), *Questions of Strategy in the Anti-Japanese Guerrilla Warfare* (1938), and *On Protracted War* (1938), to formulate and elaborate his strategic ideas of guerrilla warfare, including how to organize and initiate flexible offensives within the defensive and protracted war; how to coordinate with regular warfare; how to establish base areas; and how to balance the centralized leadership on strategic issues with decentralized command in campaigns and battles.

The key to success of guerrilla warfare is political mobilization. Since most fighting is done either by armed peasants or by trained soldiers operating in small groups, it is vital to have mass support in terms of food supplies, covered positions, intelligence information, and troop mobility. Maoism sees guerrilla warfare as a people's war, which requires the Red Army not only to fight but also to launch social reforms to help the local populace. Guerrilla warfare greatly contributed to the growth of the CCP in much of North China, helping it establish rural bases and expand its troops from 80,000 men to 900,000 plus militia forces of 2.2 million by 1945. It was not until the civil war that the CCP began to move from guerrilla warfare to mobile and conventional warfare.

GUO MORUO (1892–1978). Poet, historian, archeologist, and government official. Born in Leshan, Sichuan Province, into a wealthy merchant family, Guo received a traditional education in his home village. In 1913, he abandoned his Chinese wife from a family-arranged marriage and went to Japan. He studied medicine at Kyushu Imperial University, where he married a Japanese woman who bore him five children. In Japan, his interest in Western literature grew and he began to translate the Western masterpieces into Chinese. In 1918, he published his first poem, and three years later he compiled his anthology *Nüshen* (*Goddess*), which was regarded as the cornerstone for modern Chinese poetry. In addition, his translation of Goethe's *Sorrows of Young Werther* gained enormous popularity among Chinese youth. Together with Yu Dafu and Cheng Fanwu, he founded the **Creation Society** (*chuangzao she*) to promote modern vernacular literature in China. He embraced Marxism and joined the **Chinese Communist Party** in the early 1920s. After his return to China with his wife, he took part in the **Northern Expedition**

and served as a political commissar in the **National Revolutionary Army**.

When **Chiang Kai-shek** purged the Communists from the Nationalist Party in 1927, Guo revolted with the Communists and participated in the **Nanchang Mutiny**. After the uprising was put down, he fled to Japan and cut off his connection with the Chinese Communist Party. He focused on academic work and spent 10 years studying history and archeology. He made important contributions to studies of inscriptions on oracle bones and bronze vessels. At the same time, he was an enormously prolific writer, publishing numerous poems, works of fiction, plays, autobiographies, and translations of great Russian and German writers. He declared that his works were part of Socialist literature, and he applied a Marxist approach to his academic studies.

In 1937, Guo abandoned his Japanese wife and children and returned to China. He went to Nanjing to see Chiang Kai-shek, who appointed him director of the Third Division of the Military Committee of the Nationalist government, in charge of cultural work in the **United Front** against Japanese aggression. In 1938, he began to cohabit with Yu Liqun (and got married the next year), who bore him six more children. In the post–World War II years, he joined a democratic movement against Chiang Kai-shek's political and economic policies. After 1949, as a representative of non-Communist intellectuals, Guo was given many important positions in the People's Republic of China, including deputy prime minister of the Communist government and president of the Chinese Academy of Sciences. Actually, he rejoined the Communist Party in 1958. Although his wife Yu Liqun and two of his sons committed suicide or were killed in the Cultural Revolution, he survived all political purges. He died of sickness in Beijing, holding the title of vice president of the Chinese Congress.

GUO SONGTAO (1818–1890). Official and diplomat of the Qing dynasty. Born in Xiangyin, Hunan Province, Guo obtained the *jinshi* degree in 1847 and was appointed to the **Hanlin Academy**. He worked under Zeng Guofan to build up the **Hunan Army** in the suppression of the **Taiping Rebellion**. In 1856, he went to Shanghai and was, for the first time, exposed to Western learning. He drafted a proposal for the development of shipbuilding facilities and the study of English language and Western science, but the proposal was rejected.

He served in several positions in the government, the highest being governor of Guangdong Province. In 1876, he was sent to London and became the first Chinese ambassador to a Western country. Two years later, he began to serve concurrently as the envoy to France. He was one of the major advocates for learning from the West. His diaries during the period of his stay in Europe illuminate his observation and analyses of Western economy, culture, and society, which had an important influence on the **Self-Strengthening Movement**. In 1879, the Qing court recalled him but offered no position. His works include *Mission to the Western Countries*, *Collected Works of the Yangzhi Study*, and *Guo Songtao's Diaries*.

– H –

HAKKA. A subgroup of the **Han** Chinese. Most still live in Jiangxi, Fujian, Guangdong, and Taiwan. Because their ancestors were immigrants from northern China, local people called the newcomers *hakka* (guest families). That was also the category they registered with the local governments since the Song dynasty. The Hakka witnessed five great treks. The first one began 1,700 years ago: when nomadic tribes invaded, they left their home in the provinces of Shanxi and Henan. Some arrived and settled down in the areas of the Hui River, while others went farther to reach the provinces of Jiangxi and Fujian. The second movement was triggered by the Huang Cao Rebellion in 875–884; the war taking place in central and eastern China pushed the Hakka to move southward. The majority of the Hakka moved to southern Fujian, while a few arrived in the provinces of Guangdong and Guangxi. In 1127, the Jurchen destroyed the northern Song regime, and great numbers of refugees from the north crossed the Yangtze River; the Hakka joined them to start the third trek to northern and eastern Guangdong. The fourth trek took place in the middle of the 17th century: when the **Manchus** conquered China, the Hakka moved in small groups to the provinces of Hunan and Sichuan. However, since their new home was poor and in mountainous areas and could not feed the increasing Hakka population, some of the Hakka started the last trek in the 19th century. They moved back to Guangdong and Fujian. Some crossed the Taiwan Strait to Taiwan and some migrated to Hong Kong, Macao, and Southeast Asia. The Hakka were agriculturally based, tough, and hardworking people who produced many important political leaders in modern China.

HAN. The largest ethnic group indigenous to China. Han Chinese constitute about 92 percent of the population of the People's Republic of China and about 19 percent of the entire global human population. The name *han* comes from the Han dynasty (206 BC–AD 220), which is considered a high point in Chinese civilization— its influence expanded as far as central and East Asia. In English-language writing, the Han Chinese are often referred to simply as Chinese, while from the Chinese perspective Han is but one of 56 ethnic groups of the Chinese nation. The majority of Chinese believe they belong to the Han group, due to thousands of years of assimilation of various regional ethnicities and tribes within China. The Han Chinese refer to themselves as "Descendants of the Dragon." Most of China's history witnessed a "majority rule" of Han people, except during the Yuan dynasty (Mongol rule, 1279–1368) and Qing dynasty (Manchu rule, 1644–1911).

HAN FUQU (1890–1938). Warlord of Shandong. Born in Baxian, Hebei Province, Han began to receive a traditional education at the age of seven and joined **Feng Yuxiang**'s army at the age of 20. Following Feng, he took part in the **Northern Expedition** against the **Beiyang warlords** and was rapidly promoted. In 1930, he was appointed governor of Shandong Province. He attempted to get rid of central government control and make the province his own kingdom. After the onset of the **Second Sino-Japanese War**, Japanese troops approached the city of Jinan, where Han abandoned the defense line without exchanging fire with the enemy. He escaped to Henan but was arrested by **Chiang Kai-shek**. He was charged with treason and executed in Wuhan.

HANLIN ACADEMY. A traditional government institution since the Tang dynasty (eighth century). It consisted of the most talented scholars who had obtained the *jinshi* degree. The academy did secretarial and literary work for emperors and the central government. More importantly, it offered an authoritative interpretation of the Confucian classics; this work was the basis of the **civil service examinations** that gave access to the higher levels of bureaucracy. The academy operated continuously until the collapse of the Qing monarchy in 1911.

HANYEPING COAL AND STEEL COMPLEX. The first modern iron-steelworks in China. It was established in 1908 through the merger of the Hanyang Steel Works, Daye Iron Mines, and Pingxiang Coal mines. Shen Xuanhuai was the general manager. It gradually transformed from a government-supervised merchant undertaking (*guan du shang ban*) to a pure private company, producing 600,000 tons of coal, 50,000 tons of iron ore, and 70,000 tons of steel, making up 90 percent of total steel production of Qing China. After 1911, the company suffered from debt and had to contract foreign loans, which enabled Japanese capital to penetrate and finally control the operation. During the **Second Sino-Japanese War**, the Nationalist government shipped most equipment for steel production to **Chongqing** and part of the equipment for the coal mining to Guangxi Province, while other equipment was taken by the Japanese. Because of war devastation, the company had no capital or equipment to continue production and finally went bankrupt by the end of the war.

HART, SIR ROBERT, 1ST BARONET (1835–1911). British diplomat and inspector-general of the Chinese customs bureau. Born into a devout Methodist family in Armagh, Ulster, Hart entered Queen's University at the age of 15 and graduated three years later. Hart traveled to China the next year and began his career as a student interpreter in the China consular service in Hong Kong. In September 1854, Hart was appointed to the British vice-consulate in Ningpo as a supernumerary interpreter. He served in the Chinese Customs as local inspector and acting inspector general, and was finally promoted to inspector general of China's Imperial Maritime Customs Service in 1863. He held this position until his retirement in 1907. In his 50 years of service, Hart designed and developed a comprehensive system of customs management, ensuring a stable source of government revenue. Under his supervision, the customs service also built China's first modern postal service. Hart regarded himself as an employee of the Chinese government. For this reason, when he was asked to become British minister plenipotentiary on the retirement of **Sir Thomas Wade**, he declined this appointment, arguing there would be a conflict of interest. Hart was a close friend of **Prince Gong**, the head of the **Zongli Yamen**; he strongly supported the prince's diplomatic reforms and sponsored the prince to establish China's first foreign language school, the **Tongwenguan**, in Peking.

Hart helped China purchase eight warships, which were the first fleet of the Beiyang Navy. Hart was involved in the negotations of the Treaty of Yantai, the Sino-French Treaty of 1885, and the **Boxer Protocol**. Hart received several Chinese honorific titles, including the button of the highest rank; he also received a baronetcy from Great Britain.

HARVARD-YENCHING INSTITUTE. An independent institute jointly founded by Harvard University and **Yenching University** in 1928. The institute was dedicated to the advancement of the humanities and social sciences in East Asia and Southeast Asia. It was initially funded by Charles Martin Hall. The institute was located on the Harvard campus, and its Peking branch office was located on the Yenching campus. In spite of the close connection between the two universities, the institute was financially and legally independent, with a board of trustees consisting of nine members: three each from the estate, Harvard University, and Yenching University. At Harvard, the institute developed a graduate program in Asian studies, established the Harvard-Yenching Library, and introduced the *Harvard Journal of Asiatic Studies* in 1936 to publish monograph-length scholarly articles focusing on Asian humanities. The Harvard-Yenching Institute supported Yenching and other Chinese universities in the 1930s and 1940s and engaged in academic programs in other countries in East Asia and Southeast Asia.

HE XIANGNING (1878–1972). Female revolutionary and artist. Born in Hong Kong, He married **Liao Zhongkai**, a left-wing leader of the **Nationalist Party** (GMD), in 1897. She followed her husband to Japan, where she met **Sun Yat-sen** and became the first female member of Sun's revolutionary party, the **Tongmenghui**, in 1905. She successively studied at Tokyo Mubal Women University, Women Normal School, and Women School of Arts. Influenced by Japanese modern paintings, He engaged in creating Chinese traditional ink paintings. Her favorite subject was the tiger. When the Republican revolutionaries began staging uprisings, He designed army flags for their troops. He and her husband took an active part in the 1911 Revolution, anti–**Yuan Shikai** campaigns, and the **Northern Expedition**. For her devotion to the revolution, the GMD Central Committee elected He a member of the Executive Committee and as women's minister.

As a woman who witnessed Sun Yat-sen's death and endorsed his last will, He felt strongly committed to Sun's policy of alliance with the **Chinese Communist Party** (CCP). Even after her husband was assassinated in 1925, she did not change her belief. When **Chiang Kai-shek** purged CCP members in 1927, He refused to continue to work with the Nationalist Party but focused on artistic work. She published several albums of paintings and held exhibitions of her works. During the **Second Sino-Japanese War**, she cooperated with Shen Junru in organizing the National Salvation League of All Circles. She sold her artistic work to donate money to the resistance movement. With senior GMD leader **Li Jishen**, in January 1948 he established the Revolutionary Committee of the Chinese Kuomintang, which became one of the major political parties cooperating with the CCP. After 1949, He Xiangming successively served as vice-chair of the **Chinese People's Political Consultative Conference**, chair of the Revolutionary Committee of the Chinese Kuomintang, honorary chair of the National Women's Federation, and chair of the China Association of Arts. On 1 September 1972, He Xiangming died in Beijing at the age of 94.

HE YINGQIN (1890–1987). Full general of the first rank of the Nationalist army. Born in Xingyi, Guizhou Province, He enrolled in the Guiyang Military Elementary School in 1907 and then transferred to the Wuchang Third Army Middle School the following year. Two years later, the Defense Department of the Qing dynasty sent him to study at Tokyo Shinbu Military Academy in Japan, where he joined the **Tongmenghui**. He returned to China in 1911 to join the revolution and worked in the government of the Shanghai military governor. In 1913, He went to Japan again and graduated from the Japanese Military Academy in 1916. When the **Whampoa Military Academy** was established with **Chiang Kai-shek** as its president, He was appointed the general instuctor.

When the **National Revolutionary Army** was set up, Chiang was the commander of the 1st Army Corps and He served as commander of the First Division, later becoming commander of the 1st Army Corps. He played a key role in Chiang's wars with the various **warlords**, including **Li Zongren, Feng Yuxiang**, and **Yan Xishan**. Beginning in 1930, he served as minister of the Military Administration Department. He was appointed general commander in the first and second **Encirclement and Suppression Campaigns** against the **Red Army**, but both ended in failure. To carry out Chiang's policy of "stabilizing the domestic situation before resisting Japanese aggression," He signed the notorious **Tanggu Truce** on 31 May 1933 and the **Ho-Umezu Agreement** on 10 June 1935, according to which the Chinese troops would evacuate Beijing and Hebei Province. When the **Xi'an Incident** occurred in December 1936, He stood for solving the problem by force, which might have endangered Chiang's life. For this reason, He lost Chiang's trust and thus his military power.

In 1944, his position as minister of war was taken over by Chiang's favorite, Chen Cheng. He was instead given the honorary title of general commander of the Chinese Military Area. On 9 September 1945, He was appointed as the representative of the Chinese Government to accept the surrender of the Japanese general **Yasuji Okamura**, the commander in chief of the Japanese forces in China. In 1946, he was sent to the United Nations Military Advisory Committee as head of the Chinese military delegation. Two years later, he was called back to take the position of minister of defense when it looked as though the **Nationalist Party** (GMD) was doomed to lose the civil war against the CCP. When Chiang resigned in 1949, He served as chairman of the **Executive Yuan** to work with the acting president, Li Zongren. When the Nationalist government retreated from Nanjing to Guangzhou, he resigned. After 1949, He faded from politics. He lost his membership in the Central Committee of the GMD and only gained a few honorary titles in Taiwan. With the nickname "Lucky General," he survived many bloody battles and power struggles, living longer than most GMD generals. On 21 October 1987, He died from apoplexy in Taipei at the age of 97.

HEAVEN AND EARTH SOCIETY (*TIANDIHUI*). One of many secret societies during the Qing dynasty. The name was derived from the belief that "heaven is the father, and earth is the mother." There are different explanations of its origin and its association with the *hongmen* and other secret societies. Nonetheless, it is a common belief that the Heaven and Earth Society was first organized by Ming loyalists and devoted to the overthrow of the **Manchu** regime. Most of the members were lower class, including boatmen, laborers, and jobless people, who made the society a mutual-aid association. In the beginning, it operated mainly in the provinces of Fujian, Taiwan, and eastern Guangdong, and then spread into southeast and central China. It revolted several times during late Qing period.

HEBEI-CHAHAR COUNCIL. The council was established in December 1935 by the **Nationalist Party** (GMD) under Japanese pressure. The Japanese troops had occupied a great part of the provinces of Hebei and Chahar and demanded "special administration for northern China." To compromise with Japan, the GMD government ordered the 29th Army to form the council and appointed General Song Zeyuan president and pro-Japan politicians Wang Yitang and Wang Kemin as members of the council. In name, the Hebei-Chahar Council was still under the leadership of the National Government, but the real power was in the hands of the Japanese. It was the Japanese belief that they would finally make northern China a second Manchukou. The establishment of the council provoked a massive student demonstration in the city of Beijing, known as the **December Ninth Movement** in 1935. On 20 August 1937, after the Japanese troops stormed Beiping and set up a puppet municipal government, the council was dismissed.

HONG KONG, CESSION OF. Hong Kong is a coastal island geographically located in southern China. Starting out as a fishing village, salt production site, and trading ground, Hong Kong would evolve into a military port of strategic importance. During the **Opium War** (1840–1842), the British navy landed on the island. On 25 January 1841, the Qing imperial commissioner **Qishan** signed the **Convention of Chuanbi** with the British, promising the cession of Hong Kong, but the treaty was not ratified by the **Daoguang Emperor**. On 29 August 1842, after China's defeat in the war, the Qing court and the British government signed the **Treaty of Nanjing**, formally ceding Hong Kong to Great Britain. On 18 October 1860, the Sino-British Convention of Beijing further ceded Kowloon (south of Boundary Street) to Britain, making it incorporated into Hong Kong. On 1 July 1898, China signed the second Convention of Beijing, leasing the **New Territories** (including New Kowloon) to Great Britain for 99 years. Since then, Hong Kong has consisted of the Hong Kong Island, Kowloon, and the New Territories. As the 99-year lease would soon expire, Britain undertook negotiations with China in the 1990s. As a result, the People's Republic of China resumed its authority over Hong Kong in 1997.

HONG KONG AND SHANGHAI BANKING CORP. (HSBC).
Known as Huifeng Bank in mainland China, the Hong Kong and
Shanghai Banking Corp. is referred to as the "Lion Bank" in Hong
Kong because a pair of lion statues stands outside its headquarters
and also appear on its banknotes. Founded in 1865 by Scott Thomas
Sutherland in Hong Kong to finance trade between China and Europe,
the HSBC first raised a capital of HKD$5 million and established its
first branch in Shanghai with branches in Tianjin, Beijing, Hankou,
and **Chongqing** in subsequent years. Within 26 years, the bank had
become a leader in Asia. Its business grew to range from personal finance and commercial banking to corporate and investment banking.
The bank handled international fund transfers, issued paper currency,
managed Chinese government bonds, and operated the accounts of
China's salt tax and customs duties. In anticipation of the Japanese
invasion of Hong Kong in 1941, the bank's headquarters moved to
London and did not return to Hong Kong until the end of World War
II. When the Communists took over mainland China in 1949, the
bank closed its offices in China. Thirty years later, on 4 October 1980,
the HSBC returned to the Chinese mainland.

HONGMEN **(HONG LEAGUE).** Secret society established in early
Qing, dedicated to the overthrow of the **Manchu** regime and restoration of the Ming dynasty. It had close connections with other
anti-Qing societies, such as the Elder Brother Society, the **Heaven
and Earth Society**, and others. Because of persecution by the Qing
government, the *hongmen* moved abroad and became the most influential organization among overseas Chinese. In the late 19th century,
90 percent of Chinese immigrants to the United States were members
of the Hongmen. In 1903, **Sun Yat-sen** joined the Hongmen in Honolulu and was elected *hong rod* (generalissimo). Sun revised the charter of the organization, retaining its original anti-Qing objective while
supplementing it with his program of "expelling the Manchu, restoring Chinese rule, establishing a republic, and equalizing the land." In
so doing, Sun's revolution gained great support from the Hongmen
and overseas Chinese, whom Sun referred to as the "mother of the
Chinese Revolution."

HONG RENGAN (1822–1864). Cousin of **Hong Xiuquan** and leader
of the **Taiping Rebellion** in its later years. Hong Rengan joined the

God Worshipping Society in 1843, but he was not with his cousin when Hong Xiuquan launched the uprising at the village of Jingtian. He fled to Hong Kong, where he received more education on Christianity and Western science. He did not travel to Nanjing until Hong Xiuquan called him for help in 1859. That was a crucial moment, when the massive purge and killings among the rebels seriously incapacitated the kingdom. Hong was granted the title Prince Gan and appointed to be in charge of routine affairs of the Taiping Kingdom. He initiated a number of reforms, including centralizing the administration, building railroads and banks, developing the mining industry, and improving communication facilities in the areas under Taiping rule. He also tried to enlist Western sympathy and support for the Taiping cause. Most of Hong Rengan's reforms, however, were never implemented, as his orders could not travel effectively beyond the city walls of Nanjing. In 1864, Hong Xiuquan committed suicide before the city was stormed by Qing forces. Hong Rengan planned to organize a counterattack in the name of Hong Tianguifu, the son of Hung Xiuquan, but he was captured in in the city of Nanchang, Jiangxi Province, and executed along with **Li Xiucheng**.

HONG XIUQUAN (1814–1864). Leader of the **Taiping Rebellion**. Born into a poor **Hakka** farming family in Huaxian, Guangdong Province, Hong Xiuquan was the only child in his family to receive an education, studying the Confucian classics in a private school. Between 1828 and 1843, he took the first-degree **civil service exam** four times but never passed. In the city of Guangzhou, he happened to meet a missionary who handed him a booklet, *Good Words Exhorting the Age*, written by a Chinese minister named **Liang Fa**. After reading it, Hong claimed that he was the younger son of God sent to the world to eliminate demons (**Manchus**). In 1844, he and **Feng Yunshan** organized the **God Worshipping Society**. Hong used his own interpretation of Christianity to mobilize his followers and converted a considerable number of **Hakka** coal-burning workers. Hong staged the uprising in 1851 in order to establish the *taiping tianguo* (Heavenly Kingdom of Great Peace), with himself as the **Heavenly King** (*tianwang*). He advocated a new culture and customs, banning prostitution, footbinding, opium smoking, and slavery. He expected all his subjects to believe only in the one Christian God. The most remarkable program was his **land reform**. All land belonged to the state, which was divided among all families according to their sizes, with men and women receiving equal shares. After a harvest, each family would keep what they needed for their sustenance and place the rest in state granaries. In 1853, the Taiping forces stormed Nanjing and made it the capital of their kingdom.

Hong gradually lost interest in state affairs but was infatuated with drugs and sensual pleasures. He demonstrated inefficiency and lack of mission. His major assistant, **Yang Xiuqing**, arrogated enormous power and thus threatened his authority. Hong first ordered **Wei Changhui** to kill Yang and then ordered others to kill Wei. The power struggle and slaughters among his earliest followers incapacitated the regime. Hong also failed in the countryside, where his reform remained unrealized and where his forces were attacked by militia organized by local gentry. Finally, his adventurous attack on Shanghai was shattered by the **Hunan Army** and the foreign "Ever Victorious Army." Hong had ruled this Nanjing-centered kingdom for 11 years, controlling 18 provinces of China. His war with the Qing forces caused huge damage to the economy and brought death to millions of people. In 1844, the Qing army destroyed the Taiping forces in Nanjing, and Hong committed suicide before the city was stormed. *See also* HONG RENGAN.

HO-UMEZU AGREEMENT (1935). On 6 July 1935, Ho Ying-chin sent a formal reply to Yoshijiro Umezu, commander in chief of the Japanese troops in Tianjin, informing him that the Chinese government had accepted all of his demands. This was known as the Ho-Umezu Agreement. According to this agreement, China would withdraw its military forces, including the Chinese Northeast Army and **Central Army**, from North China, disband or outlaw some organizations of the **Nationalist Party** (GMD), such as the **Blue Shirts** Society and Restoration Society, disband some government institutions, ban all anti-Japanese activities, and accept Japanese suggestions for appointing mayors of Beiping, Tianjin, and other Chinese local officials.

HU HANMIN (1879–1936). One of the early leaders of the **Nationalist Party** (GMD). Born in Fanyu, Guangdong Province, Hu obtained his *juren* degree at the age of 21. In 1902, Hu traveled to Japan for study, where he joined the **Tongmenghui** and served as editor of its formal publication, *Minbao*. Between 1907 and 1910, he was involved in several failed uprisings of the Tongmenghui in an attempt to overthrow the **Manchu** regime. After the 1911 Revolution, Hu was made governor of Guangdong and secretary of the Nanjing provisional government. In 1913, he participated in the **Second Revolution** against **Yuan Shikai**, and between 1917 and 1921 he followed **Sun Yat-sen** in Guangdong. He successively served as minister of communication and secretary-general of Sun's government. He supported Sun's policy of alliance with the Soviet Union and the Communists and was appointed political instructor at the **Whampoa Military Academy**. In September 1924, Hu served as the acting grand marshal of the Revolutionary Army when Sun was out of Guangzhou.

After the death of Sun Yat-sen, Hu was one of the three most powerful leaders in the GMD; the other two were **Wang Jingwei** and **Liao Zhongkai**. In August 1925, when Liao was assassinated, Hu was suspected of being the chief plotter and was detained by the party's investigation committee. Due to lack of evidence, Hu was soon released and sent to the Soviet Union for study. During the split between Nanjing and Wuhan in 1927, Hu supported **Chiang Kai-shek** and took an active part in the campaign to purge Communists. In September 1928, Hu was appointed president of the **Legislative Yuan** of the Nationalist government. However, his position on the promulgation of the constitution conflicted with Chiang's opinion, and he began to denounce Chiang as a "new warlord." In June 1935, he went to Europe on an investigation tour, and he made statements to reconcile with Chiang. Hu was elected president of the GMD Central Executive Committee while he was in France. In January 1936, he returned from Europe to Guangzhou, where he died of apoplexy four months later.

HU JUN (1898–1933). An early female leader of the **Chinese Communist Party** (CCP) and victim of the CCP's Anti–**AB League** Campaign. Born in Pingxiang, Hunan Province, into a rich merchant family, Hu liked both literature and the military in her childhood. She was married to Li Jiqi by family arrangement at the age of 19. In August 1924, she was enrolled in Pingjiang Female Normal School, where she met some Communist schoolmates and finally joined the CCP the next year. Hu participated in the **Northern Expedition** and was also admitted to the Wuhan branch of the Central Military Academy, becoming one of the first generation of Chinese female military officers. After **Chiang Kai-shek** began to purge the Communists, she returned to her home county and organized an anti-Chiang guerrilla troop. In 1928, her guerrillas joined the **Red Army** led by **Peng Dehuai**. These new troops stormed the town of Pingxiang and established a Soviet government, electing Hu chairperson of the government.

Hu demonstrated her military talent by serving as commander of the Independent Ganbei Regiment and commander of the Eighth Division of the Red Army. She led the troops in the battle of Changsha and built up a rural revolutionary base in Hubei. In 1931, the CCP established a provincial committee of Hunan, Hubei, and the Jiangxi border region, and Hu was elected executive member and director of the women's department. In 1933, after Mao Zedong and other radical leaders launched the Anti–AB League Campaign, Hu was accused as a member of the counterrevolutionary clique and executed the next year. It was not until 1945, 11 years after her death, that the seventh CCP national congress announced her rehabilitation.

HU QIAOMU (1912–1992). The major propagandist and bureaucrat of the **Chinese Communist Party** (CCP). Born in Yancheng, Jiangsu Province, Hu first studied history at Qinghua University between 1930 and 1932, then transferred to the Department of Foreign Literature at Zhejiang University and graduated in 1935. Hu joined the **Chinese Communist Youth League** (CY) in 1930 and the CCP in 1932. He served as secretary of the CY in the West Suburb District of Beijing and participated in student movements. In 1936, he became the general secretary of the Chinese Left-Wing Cultural League. From 1941, Hu served as **Mao Zedong**'s political secretary and drafted some important documents for the CCP, including the famous "Some Resolutions on Historical Issues of the CCP" (1941). After 1949, he was made the director of the Xinhua News Agency and deputy director of the CCP's Propaganda Department. He was assumed to be the authority on Marxist–**Mao Zedong Thought** and dominated the CCP's propaganda and the country's news censorship until his death.

HU SHIH (1891–1962). Prominent scholar, one of the leaders of the **New Culture Movement**, and diplomat of the Republic of China. Born in Shanghai, Hu began to receive the traditional Confucian education at the age of five. In 1910, Hu obtained the Boxer Rebellion Indemnity Scholarship to facilitate his trip to and study in the United States. Hu first studied agriculture and then changed his major to philosophy and literature. After receiving his undergraduate degree from Cornell University, Hu went to Columbia University to study philosophy, where he was greatly influenced by his professor, **John Dewey**. He became a lifelong advocate of Dewey's ideas about pragmatic evolutionary change. After he obtained his PhD in philosophy in 1917, Hu returned to China and taught at **Peking University**. When Hu was 13, his family arranged a marriage for him with Jiang Dongxiu, an illiterate girl with bound feet who was one year older than he was. Although Hu advocated Western liberalism, he accepted the traditional arrangement and married Jiang after he became a professor at Peking University.

With **Chen Duxiu**, the editor of the influential journal *New Youth*, Hu promoted vernacular Chinese in literature to replace classical Chinese. To initiate the literary revolution, Hu originally emphasized eight guidelines that all Chinese writers should take to heart when writing: (1) write with substance; (2) do not imitate the ancients; (3) respect grammar; (4) reject melancholy; (5) eliminate old clichés; (6) do not use allusions; (7) do not use couplets or parallelism; and (8) do not avoid popular expressions or popular forms of characters. During the **May Fourth Movement**, Hu supported the patriotic demonstrations of the students but also encouraged them to solve more concrete problems rather than talk abstract ideology. Hu made significant contributions to scholarship in a wide range of disciplines, including history, archeology, philosophy, literature, education, and ethical studies, thus becoming the most influential scholar in modern China. Hu served as ambassador of the Republic of China to the United States between 1938 and 1941, and chancellor of Peking University between 1946 and 1948. In 1949, Hu left China for the United States and then went to Taiwan, where he served as president of the Academia Sinica in Taiwan. He was criticized by the Communists in mainland China in the 1950s, but his scholarship was reevaluated in the post-Mao era. Hu died of a heart attack on 24 February 1962 in Taipei.

HUAI ARMY (*HUAIJUN*). *See* ANHUI ARMY.

HUAI-HAI, BATTLE OF (HUAI-HAI CAMPAIGN, NOVEMBER 1948–JANUARY 1949). One of the three campaigns in the civil war (the other two being the **Battle of Liao-Shen** and the **Battle of Ping-Jin**). It was known as the Battle of Hsupeng in the Nationalist literature. Huai-Hai refers to the area between the Hui River and the Yangtze River. The Battle of Huai-Hai was divided into three phases. In the first phase, the East China Army led by Su Yu and Chen Yi, and the Central China Army commanded by **Liu Bocheng** and **Deng Xiaoping**, cooperated in November 1948 to begin the Battle of Huai-Hai. After the assault started on 6 November, **Chiang Kai-shek** ordered the Nationalist troops to retreat to the eastern suburbs of Xuzhou. Two days later, two corps (with 23,000 troops) led by He Jifeng and Zhang Kexia, deputy commanders of the Third Pacification Zone of the Kuomintang army (who were actually secretly **Chinese Communist Party** [CCP] members), suddenly revolted on the battlefield; this exposed the flank of Huang Beitao's army corps to the Communists. When Chiang ordered Qiu Qingquan's troops to relieve Huang's army, Qing hesitated to take action. Consequently, the 100,000 troops of Huang's Seventh Army were annihilated on 22 November.

In the second phase, the troops of the **Nationalist Party** (GMD) in Xuzhou were ordered to give up the city and retreat south of the Yangtze River. However, as soon as they set out, Chiang Kai-shek changed the plan and assigned them to the southeast to relieve Huang Wei's Army Corps. Consequently, these troops found themselves marching into a trap set by the Communist troops. By 15 December, 34 GMD divisions were wiped out and another 22 divisions were also encircled. Seeing that victory was only matter of time, the Communist troops began a 20-day rest and reorganization period. In the last phase, the Communists tried to persuade **Du Yuming** to surrender, but Du refused. They then launched a general offensive on 6 January. The Communists quickly defeated the GMD's 13th Army Group, pushing its remnants toward the 2nd Army Group defense area. On 10 January, this defense line was broken and the 2nd Army Group was also annihilated. Commander Qiu Qingquan committed suicide and Du Yuming was captured. In all, 555,000 GMD troops were killed or reorganized by the Communist army, while the Communists' casualties amounted to 134,000 men.

HUANG JING (1912–1958). Communist leader. Born in Beijing as Yu Qiwei, Huang studied at Nankai High School in Tianjin. He engaged in the cultural movement in Shanghai in 1930. The next year, he enrolled at Qingdao University and majored in physics. He took an active part in the student movement, joined the **Chinese Communist Party** (CCP) in 1932, and served as director of the CCP's Qingdao Propaganda Department. In the city, Huang cohabited with **Jiang Qing** and introduced her to the CCP. Jiang later became **Mao Zedong**'s wife in **Yan'an**. Huang was jailed in the summer of 1933 and then rescued by the CCP. In 1935, he went to Beiping and enrolled at **Peking University**, majoring in mathematics. Huang had considerable experience in leading student movements and the party's secret work in the Nationalist Party (GMD)-controlled areas. He was one of the leaders of the **December Ninth Movement** and engaged in organizing the All-China Student Union for National Salvation. In February 1937, he was appointed secretary of the CCP Municipal Committee in Beiping. Huang held many important positions in the party and army during the **Second Sino-Japanese War** and the civil war. In 1949, he was appointed mayor of Tianjin and was later made minister of heavy industry. His son, Yu Zhensheng, is a member of the CCP Politburo and secretary of the CCP Municipal Committee in Shanghai.

HUANG XING (1874–1916). Revolutionary leader and the first commander in chief of the Republic of China. Huang Xing and **Sun Yat-sen** were referred to as the cofounders of the **Nationalist Party** (GMD) and the Republic of China. Born in the suburb of Changsha to a landlord family, Huang was supported by the viceroy of Huguang, **Zhang Zhidong**, who sent him to Japan to study on a government scholarship. Upon his arrival in Japan, he established a newspaper to introduce Western culture to China and disseminated revolutionary ideas among the overseas Chinese. In 1903, he returned to Hunan Province but was soon expelled from the province due to revolutionary speeches he made. In 1903, he founded the *huaxinghui* (**China Revival Society**), an organization devoted to the overthrow of the **Manchu** regime. He planned to stage an uprising, but the news was leaked and Huang had to flee to Japan. In 1905, he met Sun Yat-sen in Tokyo and shared the idea with him about joining together to form a unified organization. His *huaxinghui*, Sun's *xingzhonghui* (**Revive China Society**), and **Cai Yuanpei**'s *guangfuhui* (**Recovery Society**) merged into the *tongmenghui* (United League), and he was elected chief of the executive department. Huang turned his newspaper, *Twentieth Century China*, into the official publication of the Tongmenghui, and engaged in heated debate with the conservative faction headed by **Kang Youwei** and **Ling Qichao**, who attacked revolution and republicanism.

Huang Xing spent most of his energy recruiting revolutionaries and staging uprisings in China. All these revolts, however, ended in failure until 10 October 1911, when the revolutionaries succeeded in Wuchang. On 1 January 1912, the provisional government of the Republic of China was established and Huang was appointed commander in chief of the revolutionary army. In 1913, he led the **Second Revolution** against **Yuan Shaikai**. After the failure of the revolution, he fled to Japan. Huang disagreed with Sun Yat-sen's plan of transforming the Nationalist Party into the Chinese **Revolutionary Party** and left Japan. Nonetheless, he issued a public statement in the United States that he would continue to support Sun's leadership in the Nationalist Party, and he wasted no time in organizing new anti-Yuan campaigns, including doing fund-raising for general **Cai E**'s expeditionary army and shipping weaponry to the anti-Yuan forces in China. Huang died of complications caused by cirrhosis of the liver in Shanghai.

HUAXINGHUI. *See* CHINA REVIVAL SOCIETY.

HUNAN ARMY (*XIANGJUN*). Local military force of the Qing government built up by **Zeng Guofan**. In December 1852, when the **Taiping** rebels stormed the city of Hanyang, Zeng was ordered to command the **Green Standard Army** to quell the rebels. Zeng believed that the Green Standard Army was too weak to fight, so he decided to build a new army, known as the Hunan Army or Xiang Army. Most of the commanders of the army were local gentry, and soldiers were recruited among the peasants in Hunan. Zeng trained the troops in a special way, using Confucian concepts of loyalty and obedience to discipline the troops and using Western military tactics to guide them. He created a new pattern of army, according to which "soldiers belonged to the commander." What was established in this army was the loyalty of soldiers to commanders, subordinates to superiors, and all troops to Zeng himself. This provided a model for the personal armies of **warlords** in later years. When the training was completed in 1854, the Hunan Army had 6,500 infantry, 5,000 naval force, plus logistic troops, totaling 17,000 men. The troops were equipped with Western weaponry, and they set up their own arsenals to produce weapons. Early on, the Human Army was defeated by the Taiping rebels, but it quickly organized counterattacks and finally crushed the rebels. The Hunan Army stormed the capital of the Taiping Kingdom and brought the rebellion to an end. The Hunan Army significantly expanded in the war and thus controlled huge areas in southern and central China.

Understanding that the quickly expanding military power would arouse the suspicion of the emperor, Zeng began to decrease the size of the Hunan Army after 1864. He sent part of his troops to northern China to suppress the **Nian Rebellion** and reduced the rest to the size of the local Green Standard Army. His naval force was transferred to the Yangtze River. All of this meant that the Hunan Army was no longer the leading military force of Qing China, and Zeng managed to have a safe and honorable retirement. Nonetheless, the Hunan Army had produced a large number of military commanders who continued to play an important role in the Chinese army and politics.

HUNDRED DAYS' REFORM (1898). An institutional reform of 104 days from 11 June to 21 September 1898, initiated by **Kang Youwei** and **Liang Qichao** and supported by the young **Guangxu Emperor**. The major reforms included educational reform that abolished the eight-legged essay, established new schools and a university, and published an official newspaper; political reform that abolished sinecure and unnecessary offices, developed a new and simplified administrative procedure, revised Qing legal codes, and encouraged suggestions from private citizens; and economic reform that promoted railway reconstruction, encouraged invention, and promoted agricultural, industrial, and commercial development. The reform also promised protection of missionaries and dispatched high officials abroad for study. The reform met strong resistance from the conservative ruling elite, especially **Dowager Cixi**. The Qing officials disregarded or challenged the emperor's reform decrees, knowing that the real power of state was not in his hands but in those of the Dowager Cixi. The Guangxu Emperor sought support from military leaders to push the reform program. He ordered the reformers to meet **Yuan Shikai** for help. However, Yuan Shikai informed Cixi of the emperor's plan. She engineered a coup d'état on 21 September 1898, putting the emperor under house arrest within the Forbidden City and executing six reformist leaders, including **Tan Sitong** and Kang's brother. Kang and Liang fled to Japan. The reform ended in failure.

HUNDRED REGIMENTS OFFENSIVE (1940). From 20 August to 5 December 1940, the deputy commander of the **Eighth Route Army**, **Peng Dehuai**, organized and coordinated an offensive of 105 regiments to attack the Japanese troops stationed along the railway lines that separated the Communist base areas in North China. Preparations were started in the middle of July, including a survey of the terrain around the Japanese garrisons in Shanxi, the collection of intelligence on the enemy, the selection of road targets, the stockpiling of explosives and grain, and the mobilization of peasant support. The Eighth Route Army attacked the Japanese forces, who held well-fortified fixed positions. In the Jinjiyu District, according to a Communist source, total casualties reached 22,000. The offensive provoked a Japanese counterattack, forcing the Communists to change strategies from offensive warfare to "resistance to Japanese mopping-up" on 6 October. During the Hundred Regiments Offensive, the Eighth Route Army destroyed about 600 miles of railways and numerous Japanese garrisons. Despite some military accomplishments, the offensive was criticized by **Mao Zedong** because it violated Mao's strategies of **guerrilla warfare**. The offensive was intended to bolster the morale of the anti-Japanese troops. However, because it exposed the strength of the Communist military forces, the Japanese Army shifted its main forces away from the front of the **Nationalist Party** (GMD) and began concentrating on fighting the Communist guerrillas. The Communists believed that the offensive was a strategic mistake that brought about many serious problems for the Communist bases in the rear enemy areas.

HURLEY, PATRICK JAY (1883–1963). American general, statesman, and diplomat. In his early years, Hurley practiced law in Oklahoma and then served as secretary of war in the Hoover administration from 1929 to 1933. During World War II, Hurley traveled as a personal representative of General George C. Marshall and President Franklin D. Roosevelt, visiting the Near East, Middle East, China, and Afghanistan. Hurley arrived in China in August 1944 to help smooth over **Joseph Stilwell**'s relations with **Chiang Kai-shek**, but he found this was impossible and then supported the replacement of Stilwell with General **Albert C. Wedemeyer**. In August 1945, Hurley visited **Yan'an** to seek ways to bring about a reconciliation between the **Nationalist Party** (GMD) and the **Chinese Communist Party** (CCP). He escorted **Mao Zedong** to **Chongqing** for negotiations. Hurley tried to maintain neutrality and hoped the two parties would work out a detailed plan for peace. The bottom line of Hurley's policy still was to support Chiang to build a unified and democratic China. On 17 November 1944, Hurley was appointed ambassador to China, but he did not enjoy the complete support of the embassy staff. The State Department was openly critical of Chiang Kai-shek while Hurley stood for unconditional support of Chiang. In November 1945, as the GMD-CCP agreement was broken, Washington adopted a new China policy, which would continue to support the GMD government but not involve the United States in any direct military intervention. Disappointed with this policy, Hurley resigned in protest on 27 November.

– I –

IGNATIEV, NIKOLAI PAVLOVICH, COUNT (1832–1908). Russian diplomat. Ignatiev was sent to China as plenipotentiary in 1859. During the Second **Opium War**, after the British and French troops stormed Beijing and burned the Old Summer Palace (**Yuan Ming Yuan**), Ignatiev claimed that he would like to work as a mediator for the peace settlement between China and the Anglo-French alliance. Ignatiev persuaded the Qing court to accept the allied terms to end the destructive war. For his work, Ignatiev asked Beijing to sign several treaties, including the **Treaty of Tianjin** (1858) and the Supplementary Treaty of Beijing (1860), in which China gave Russia some 300,000 to 400,000 sq. m. of land.

ILI, TREATY OF (TREATY OF KULDJA, 1851). Also known as the Treaty of Saint Petersburg. In 1871, Russia took advantage of the **Muslim Rebellion** in Xinjiang and occupied the Ili basin. After **Zuo Zongtang** cracked down on the Muslim rebellion, China began to negotiate with Russia for resuming its authority over the Ili area. The negotiations were held in St. Petersburg and the treaty was signed on 24 February 1851. According to the treaty, Russia agreed to return to

China most of its occupied territory. The Chinese government agreed that the residents of the Ili area would be allowed to stay or return to the Russian Empire. In addition, China would give Russia 9,000,000 "metal rubles" as payment for the occupation costs, compensation for the Russian subjects, and their resettlement expenses. The treaty granted Russians the right to trade, build warehouses, and open consulates in Ili, Tarbagatai, and other cities in northwestern China. It also affirmed that Russian traders would be "temporarily" exempted from taxes in Mongolia and Xinjiang.

ILLUSTRATED TREATISE ON THE MARITIME KINGDOMS (*HAIGUO TUZHI*). The first significant Chinese work of Western studies. The original material was collected by **Lin Zexu** and compiled by his secretary **Wei Yuan**. Afther the first publication of the 50-volume book in 1844, the work was revised and enlarged in 1847 and 1852 into 100 volumes. The objective of the book was, as its preface expressed, "learning superior techniques of the barbarians to control the barbarians." The book is divided into four parts: part 1 deals with the geography, history, and recent conditions of Western countries; part 2, manufacturing and Western arms; part 3, shipbuilding, mining, and Western arts; and part 4 suggests a strategy and methods of dealing with the West. The book had an important influence on the leaders of the **Self-Strengthening Movement**, such as **Zuo Zongtang**.

IMPERIAL MARITIME CUSTOMS SERVICE. After the **Treaty of Nanjing** of 1842, China was forced to open five cities to foreign trade, and it gradually lost its control over Chinese maritime customs. In 1853, when the **Small Swords Society** revolted in Shanghai, the British, American, and French consulates helped the Qing government to quell the rebellion and organized a special committee to run the municipal customs office. The committee began to function the next year. In 1861, the Qing court formally appointed Horatio Nelson Lay the first general inspector of the Imperial Maritime Customs Service. Two years later, Irish-born **Robert Hart** succeeded him to run the office for 45 years. Hart's office was staffed by an international bureaucracy, which established branches in all treaty ports, fixed China's customs duties, and worked out comprehensive regulations and management systems for the institution.

INNER MONGOLIA. A border area of China inhabited by the Mongol-Chinese. Inner/Outer Mongolia is a geographic concept meaning South/North Mongolia. Both were territories of the Qing dynasty. In the Qing dynasty, the **Manchus** had much closer relations with the Mongols than with the **Han** Chinese. Inner Mongolia has an area of 1.18 million square kilometers occupying 12 percent of China's land area, about the same as France and Spain or Texas and California added together. In the east, Inner Mongolia adjoins the three provinces of Heilongjiang, Jilin, and Liaoning in Manchuria, and in the south it borders six provinces in north and northwest china. The name Inner Mongolia was used to create a distinction from the Mongolian People's Republic (**Outer Mongolia**), which claimed independence in 1924.

INTERNATIONAL MILITARY TRIBUNAL FOR THE FAR EAST (IMTFE). Also known as the Tokyo War Crimes Trial or Tokyo Trial. After the Japanese surrender in World War II, the IMTFE was conducted between 29 April 1946 and 16 April 1948, and its final judgments were delivered during 4–12 November 1948. A panel of 11 judges presided over the IMTFE, one from each of the victorious Allied powers (United States, Republic of China, Soviet Union, United Kingdom, the Netherlands, Provisional Government of the French Republic, Australia, New Zealand, Canada, British India, and the Philippines). Attorney Mei Ju-ao represented the Republic of China on the panel and another Chinese attorney, Hsiang Che-chun, served as one of the prosecutors. Twenty-eight Japanese former politicians, officials, and military leaders were put on trial. Some 419 witnesses appeared in person before the court, and an additional 779 submitted affidavits or depositions. Two of the 28 defendants died of natural causes during the trial. One defendant had a mental breakdown and was removed. The remaining 25 were all found guilty, many on multiple counts. Seven were sentenced to death by hanging, sixteen to life imprisonment, and two to lesser terms. Two former ambassadors were sentenced to seven and 20 years in prison; one died two years later in prison and the other was paroled in 1950.

INTERNATIONAL SETTLEMENT IN SHANGHAI. A **foreign concession** in Shanghai. On 8 November 1843, the first British consul, Sir George Balfour, arrived in Shanghai. Based on the right conferred by the **Treaty of Nanjing**, Balfour asked the Chinese municipal government to rent him land for foreign business and residence. As a result, Balfour signed an agreement with the government, known as the Shanghai Land Regulation, which rented the British 1,080 mu of land north of Yangjingbang, south of Lijiachang, and west of the Huangpu River. This was the first foreign concession in Chinese history: the British concession. In 1848, the concession expanded to include an additional 2,820 mu of land. In the same year, the Americans gained a concession in the north bank of the Suzhou Creek. The French consul Louis Charles Nicolas Maximilien de Montigny and the Shanghai *Daotai* Lingui signed a document, renting the French 2,385 mu of land to build the French concession. On 11 July 1854, the foreign residents in the three concessions held a conference. They decided to merge the three concessions into the International Settlement, establish the unified Shanghai Municipal Council, and organize the police forces to administer the concession. In 1866, the French concession asked for independence, working out the Règlement d'organisation de la commune municipale de la Concession Française de Changhai, and elected its own administration, the Conseil d'Administration Municipale de la Concession Française de Changhai. In 1869, the British, American, and French envoys to China approved the regulations and recognized the French council. The territory of the International Settlement now included only the previous British and American concessions.

– J –

JANUARY TWENTY-EIGHTH INCIDENT (1932). Battle between Chinese and Japanese troops in Shanghai, known also as the Shanghai War of 1932 or the Shanghai Incident. After the occupation of Manchuria, Japan made Shanghai one of its targets for further invasion. On 18 January 1932, a Japanese spy, Kawashima Yoshiko, organized the beating of five Japanese monks and blamed it on the Chinese. In revenge, the Japanese burned houses in the city, killed one Chinese policeman, and hurt more. This provoked an upsurge of anti-Japanese protests, calling for a boycott against Japanese goods. By 27 January, the Japanese military had finished their war preparations. They issued an ultimatum to the Shanghai municipal government, demanding a public condemnation and monetary compensation by the Chinese for any Japanese interests damaged in the monk incident and the suppression of all anti-Japanese protests in the city. Although the Shanghai municipal government accepted the demands, 3,000 Japanese troops entered the city. The Chinese **Nineteenth Route Army** put up a fierce resistance and the Japanese hastily retreated. **Chiang Kai-shek** sent his 5th Army to reinforce the troops. On 12 February, the fighting intensified. The Japanese were still not able to take the city, despite their increase in troop numbers to nearly 90,000, supported by 80 warships and 300 airplanes. On 2 March, the Nineteenth Route Army stated that they had to pull out of Shanghai due to lack of supplies and manpower. The next day, the Nineteenth Route Army and the 5th Army retreated from Shanghai, marking the official end of the battle. Through the mediation of the League of Nations, on 5 May China and Japan signed the Shanghai Ceasefire Agreement, which made Shanghai a demilitarized zone, forbidding China to garrison troops in areas surrounding Shanghai, Suzhou, and Kunshan but allowing the presence of a few Japanese military in the city. The agreement was widely regarded by the Chinese as a humiliation.

JARDINE, MATHESON & CO. The largest British company in China, founded in Guangzhou on 1 July 1832, by two Scotch traders, William Jardine and James Matheson. Jardine was a surgeon assistant on **British East India Company** vessels, sailing between Calcutta and Guangzhou. During this service, as the company allowed, he conducted business with the Chinese on his own. In 1819, he became a successful merchant working at Charles Magnica Co., the major opium dealer in Guangzhou. When Jardine and Matheson opened their own business, the company exported tea and silk to Europe and, in return, illegally traded Indian opium into China. The opium deals were the major source of their early profits. In 1842, the headquarters moved to Hong Kong. Jardine, Matheson & Co. had given up the opium trade by 1872 and diversified its business. Besides the import-export trade, the company invested in Chinese railways, shipyards, various factories, mines, and banks. The company built up China's first railway—the **Shanghai–Wusong Railway**—and introduced a great deal of Western machines and equipment to China. It moved its headquarters to Shanghai in 1912 and opened more than 15 branches in major Chinese cities. The largest ones were in Tianjin and Hankou.

After 1949, most properties of the company in mainland China were confiscated, and its last office there was forced to close in 1954, but it continued its activities in Hong Kong.

JIANG MENGLIN (1886–1964). Educator and former president of **Peking University** and National Zhejiang University. Born in Yuyao, Zhejiang Province, Jiang received both traditional Chinese and Western educations. In 1904, he obtained the *xiucai* degree in the imperial **civil service examination**, but he gave up seeking higher degrees and traveled to the United States for advanced education in 1909. Jiang obtained his PhD from Columbia University under **John Dewey**'s guidance in 1917. After his return to China, Jiang founded the journal *New Education* and published a number of articles attacking the Confucian school system and advocating Western-style education. Jiang was the president of Peking University for 17 years, helping the college survive its fiscal crisis, war destruction, and social chaos. During the War against Japanese Aggression, he helped some major universities move from Beijing and Tianjin to Southwest China, where he founded the **National Southwest Union University**. He succesively served as minister of education, general secretary of the Executive Council of the Republic of China (ROC), and president of the Red Cross Society of China. In 1949, he followed the Nationalist government to Taiwan. He served as chairman of the ROC Joint Commission for Rural Reconstruction and died of liver cancer in Taipei at the age of 79.

JIANG QING (1914–1991). The fourth wife of **Mao Zedong** and a radical leader of the **Chinese Communist Party** (CCP) during the Chinese Cultural Revolution. Born in Zhucheng, Shandong, into the family of a carpenter, Jiang was taken to Tianjin after the death of her father, where she worked as a child laborer at the Anglo-American Tobacco Company for three months. She received some training in drama performance in Jinan and then went to Qingdao University working as an assistant librarian. There she met **Huang Jing**, a physics student and Communist Party member. With Huang's recommendation, Jiang joined the CCP at the age of 19 and began to cohabitate with him. After Huang was arrested, Jiang fled to Shanghai, where she engaged in activities of the left-wing performers. She adopted a stage name—Lan Ping—and played various roles in films and plays, including *God of Liberty, The Scenery of City, Blood on Wolf Mountain, Big Thunderstorm,* and Henrik Ibsen's play *A Doll's House.* In 1937, after the **Second Sino-Japanese War** broke out, Jiang Qing left behind her life on the stage and went to **Yan'an**. She first studied at Kangda and then worked at the Lu Xun School of Arts. She was involved in creating the new Peking Opera, which was appreciated by **Mao Zedong**.

When Mao decided to marry Jiang, her records of previous marriages and divorces became an obstacle. The CCP Politburo approved her marriage with conditions, limiting Jiang's power and rights. Jiang worked as Mao's secretary, took care of his life, and shared risk and hardship with Mao in wartime, but she was not allowed to be proclaimed as Mao's formal wife. Jiang bore Mao a daughter in 1940. After 1949, due to illness, Jiang worked only for a short time and basically held minor positions in Chinese politics. In 1966, with Mao's support, Jiang became a radical leader of the Cultural Revolution. After Mao's death, Jiang was arrested and sentenced to death. She refused to confess and committed suicide at the Hospital of the Public Security Bureau in Beijing.

JIANGNAN ARSENAL. The major center for the manufacture of modern arms and the study of Western technology and languages in the 1860s and 1870s. It was opened in Shanghai in 1865 as part of China's **Self-Strengthening Movement**. The major advocates of the movement, including **Zeng Guofan**, **Li Hongzhang**, **Zuo Zongtang**, and **Zhang Zhidong**, served as its superintendents. An American, T. F. Falls, was its first chief engineer. The company included steelworks, machine making, shipbuilding, an arsenal, and other factories, employing more than 3,000 Chinese workers whose salaries were four to eight times higher than those of Chinese workers in other factories. Production and management of the arsenal depended greatly on foreign materials, foreign equipment, and Western experts. It produced muskets, artillery shells, large-caliber guns, Remington breech-loading rifles, and gunboats; it also successfully cast the first Armstrong breach-loading cannon in 1888. The arsenal also established a foreign school, translation bureau, and professional school for training technicians. The translation bureau of the Jiangnan Arsenal under the supervision of **John Fryer** translated and published hundreds of Western works, including William Chambers's *Homely*

Words to Aid the Government and Robert Phillimore's *Commentaries upon International Law*. Because the arms manufactured by the arsenal were of poor quality, Zeng Guofan's **Hunan Army** and Li Hongzhang's **Anhui Army** refused to accept them. In 1868, it began to make gunboats, but the cost was twice that of purchasing the same warships from Britain. The arsenal's early capital came from the military budget of Zeng's Hunan Army. Later, Zeng managed to get 10 percent of the Chinese customs revenue to support the arsenal and the fund increased to 20 percent of the revenue in 1869.

JIANGXI SOVIET (CHINESE SOVIET REPUBLIC). State founded after the Communists were forced to retreat from the cities and after the failure of a series of urban uprisings. In 1931, **Mao Zedong** and **Zhu De** consolidated their guerrilla base in Jiangxi Province. On 7 November 1931, the anniversary day of the Russian Bolshevik Revolution, the Chinese Communists held a National People's Delegates Conference in the town of Ruijin, Jiangxi Province. The conference proclaimed the establishment of the Chinese Soviet Republic with Ruijin as its capital. Mao Zedong was elected chairman of the Jiangxi Soviet. The Soviet controlled more than 30,000 sq. km, an area larger than many provinces in China. At its peak, its military force, the **Red Army**, numbered more than 140,000 men. Due to Soviet help, the Red Army was equipped with some modern weaponry and communication technology, such as telephones, telegraphs, and radios, which most Chinese **warlords'** armies did not have. The republic adopted a constitution and other laws, issued its own currency (paper bills, copper coins, and silver dollars), printed its own postage stamps, developed the local economy, and collected taxes. On 26 April 1932, the government made its first diplomatic statement, declaring war on Japan. The Jiangxi Soviet existed from 1931 to 1934, when it was finally suppressed by **Chiang Kai-shek** in his fifth **Encirclement and Suppression Campaign**.

JIAQING EMPEROR (REIGNED 1796–1820). The sixth emperor of the **Manchu** Qing dynasty, and the fifth Qing emperor to rule over China. Born in 1760, Jiaqing was the 15th son of the **Qianlong Emperor** and Qianlong's **Han** Chinese concubine of the second rank, Ling, who posthumously became Empress Xiao Yi Chun. Jiaqing was enthroned in February 1796, but for the next three years he lived under the shadow of his great father. After the death of his father, he arrested and executed Heshen, the infamously corrupt favorite of the Qianlong Emperor, and attempted to bring the country back to its 18th-century prosperity and power. He suppressed the White Lotus and Maio rebellions, quelled the pirates on the southern coast, and made great efforts in solving flood problems of the Yellow River. Despite being frugal, hardworking, and intelligent, Jiaqing faced an empty treasury and increasing outflows of silver from the country as payment for the opium importation. China's economy was in decline and governmental corruption became rampant. He continued an isolationist policy, refusing British demands for diplomatic relations, foreign trade, and residence. On 2 September 1820, the Jiaqing Emperor died mysteriously at the Traveling Palace in Rehe. The government version was that he died after being struck by lightning.

JING MIAO BU JING SHEN. *See* WORSHIP THE TEMPLE BUT NOT THE GODS INSIDE.

JING SHI ZHI YONG **(KNOWLEDGE FOR PRACTICE).** A new philosophy of study in the late Qing dynasty. In the late Qing era, there was a group of scholars who criticized the Confucian tradition of ignoring concrete social problems. These scholars addressed the commitment to the state and society and integration of knowledge and action. They argued that the purpose of education and study was to gain knowledge and skills to solve China's problems, and that ultimate truth exists in practice. The leading scholar of this school was **Wei Yuan**.

JINGBAO **(BEIJING DAILY).** Newspaper established in Beijing in November 1918 by **Shao Piaoping**. Three months earlier, Shao had founded China's first news agency—the News Translation and Editing Agency—which provided Chinese newspapers with fresh news from Western sources. As *Jingbao* was published, it not only used the news provided by this agency, but also required its correspondents to investigate and report local events. It reported on the student demonstrations during the **May Fourth Movement** and published articles criticizing **Yuan Shikai** and warlord politics. This clear-cut stance caused the paper to be very appealing to students and young intellectuals but also made it many political enemies. *Jingbao* issued various supplements, including *Drama Weekly*, *National Arts Weekly*, and *Women Weekly*. Some famous novelists worked for *Jingbao*: **Lu Xun**, for example, served as chief editor of its literary supplement. In 1926, the Fengtian **warlord Zhang Zuolin** took over the city of Beijing. Since *Jingbao* refused to cooperate with warlords, Zhang closed the editorial office and arrested and executed Shao Piaoping. Two years later, as Zhang's warlord government fell apart, Shao's wife, Tang Xiuhui, resumed the publication. An excellent journalist, Tang served not only as the general manager but as an active columnist for the newspaper. In July 1937, when the **Second Sino-Japanese War** interrupted the publication, Tang printed the last issue of *Jingbao* and left Beijing.

JINGGANGSHAN. Located in the border region between the provinces of Jiangxi and Hunan, Jinggangshan was a major rural base of the **Red Army** and was known as the cradle of the Chinese Communist Revolution. In 1927, after the failure of the Autumn Uprising in Hunan, **Mao Zedong** led the surviving troops to Jinggangshan, where they organized the Red Army's first regiment, the First Division of the 1st Workers and Peasants' Revolutionary Army, and persuaded the local bandit leaders Wan Zuo and Yuan Wencai to incorporate their troops into the Red Army. At the end of April 1928, **Zhu De** and his 1,000 remaining troops retreated from the abortive **Nanchang Mutiny** and joined Mao Zedong. Working from there, Mao and Zhu established the Chinese Soviet Republic in the province of Jiangxi in 1932. It was during this period that Mao developed his strategy of **guerrilla warfare** and his doctrine on the Chinese rural revolution. Mao defined three major tasks of the Red Army at the Jinggangshan: fight the Nationalist army, attack the landlords and distribute land, and mobilize the masses to establish a revolutionary government. Mao imposed three rules for the Red Army: obey orders in all actions, do not take anything from the masses, and turn in everything captured from the landlords. After the **Jiangxi Soviet** was established, Jinggangshan became its northwestern frontier, and several important battles took place there. Because of the defeat by **Chiang Kai-shek** in Chiang's fifth **Encirclement and Suppression Campaign**, the Red Army gave up this area and transferred to **Yan'an** in 1934.

JINGHAN RAILWAY (BEIJING–HANKOU RAILWAY). Railway line from Beijing to Hankou, constructed with a Belgian loan. In

April 1896, the Bureau of Railways was established under the Ministry of Navy, which was authorized to negotiate with Western powers on railway loans and **railway concessions**. On 22 October 1897, the general director of the Bureau of Railways, Shen Xuanhuai, signed the agreement of a loan with Belgium for the amount of 112.5 million francs with 5.5 percent interest to construct the Jinghan Railway. The Belgian bank was chosen because the Qing court believed that Belgium was a small country and might not have ambitions for China. At the end of 1897, the project started from both south and north terminals simultaneously and was completed on 1 April 1908. The railway extended southward to Guangzhou in 1936, forming the major avenue of the south–north communication in modern China, known as the Jingguang Railway (Beijing–Guangzhou Railway).

JINLING BUDDHIST PRINTING HOUSE (*JINLING KEJING CHU*). Center of Buddhist scripture studies, established in 1866 by lay Buddhist scholar Yang Renshan in Nanjing. The Jinling Buddhist Printing House was regarded as the source of the Buddhist revival movement in modern China. Yang taught Buddhist philosophy there for 40 years and was devoted to the preservation and publication of Buddhist literature. Under his guidance, the house printed millions of copies of Buddhist scripture and 10,000 Buddhist pictures. Yang also organized the Society for Buddhist Studies and invited distinguished monks, nuns, and lay Buddhists to offer lectures at the Jinling Buddhist Printing House, making it one of the global centers of Buddhist scripture studies.

JINSHI. The highest degree in the imperial **civil service examination** system. A *juren* degree holder who passed the national level examination could obtain the *jinshi* degree. The exam was held in the capital every three years. Usually, these candidates would also be interviewed by the emperor or his representatives to decide their ranks. The first rank was called *zhuanyuan*; the second, *bangyan*; and the third, *tanhua*, but all jinshi degree holders would get a position in the government. In the past 1,300 years, there were 98,749 Chinese students who gained the jinshi degree.

JUDICIAL YUAN (*SIFA YUAN*). One of the five branches of the government of the Republic of China, defined by **Sun Yat-sen**. Its duties included interpreting the constitution and laws and initiating pardons, reprieves, and the restitution of civil rights. It coordinated the court systems, which consisted of the supreme court, the high courts, the district courts, the administrative court, and the Commission on Disciplinary Sanctions of Public Functionaries. Although it was the highest judicial institution in China, it did not review concrete cases or interfere with the decisions made by courts at any level.

JUN PRINCE. Prince of Commandery. The second rank of **Manchu** princes. The title of peerage was conferred by the emperor on Manchu nobles and it could be inherited by the holder's descendants.

JUREN. The second degree in the imperial **civil service examination** system. A *xiucai* degree holder who passed a provincial level of exam would obtain the *juren* degree. The exam was held every three years and the provincial governor would be the examiner. After 1905, the **Guangxu Emperor** created a special exam for Chinese students returning from abroad. All who passed the exam would obtain the juren degree, and the best ones would be given a *jinshi* degree. Theoretically, the juren degree holders were qualified to hold positions in the government, but only very few obtained them.

– K –

KAIPING COAL MINES. An enterprise established in 1878 by **Li Hongzhang** during the **Self-Strengthening Movement**. It went into operation in 1881 with a daily output of 300 tons of coal. Two years later, this increased to 600 tons a day, and its highest annual output was 1.36 million tons. A canal and port at Qinghuangdao were available for coal movement. In addition, the Tang–Xu Railway was constructed to ship coal to Tianjin and Shanghai. Herbert Clark Hoover worked there as a mining engineer before he became the U.S. president. In 1900, the superintendent of the mines, Zhang Yi, was fooled into selling the mines to a British company. In 1904, **Yan Fu** accompanied Zhang to London to sue the company. The British court declared that the sale was illegal and the Chinese should get the mines back. However, the court's decision was never enforced. In 1912, the Kaiping Coal Mines expanded by merging with the Luanzhou Coal Mines and were renamed the Kai-Luan Coal Mines. In 1941, they were occupied by the Japanese, but the production never stopped. The Nationalist government took over the mines after the Japanese surrendered but soon handed them over to the British again. In 1948, the Communist army came to take over. All the mines and their properties were confiscated by the state in 1952.

KANG SHENG (1898–1975). Politician and radical leader of the **Chinese Communist Party** (CCP). Born into a wealthy landlord family in Zhucheng, Shandong, Kang was a countryman and political ally of **Jiang Qing**. Kang graduated from high school in 1917 and enrolled in the Department of Sociology at Shanghai University in 1924. Kang joined the CCP in 1925 and served as secretary of the district committee in Shanghai, where he participated in three workers' uprisings. He was made director of the CCP Central Organization Department. Kang was sent to Moscow as the major leader of the CCP delegation to the **Comintern**. After his return to **Yan'an** in 1937, he strongly supported **Mao Zedong** in the struggle against the Comintern-supported **Twenty-eight Bolsheviks**. He successively served as a member of the CCP Central Secretariat, director of the Society Department, and president of the Central Party School. In the Yan'an **Rectification Movement**, Kang was the major architect of the "rescue movement" in Yan'an, which arrested, tortured, and persecuted numerous party members and intellectuals coming from Nationalist or Japanese-controlled cities. Next, Kang became a head of the CCP's secret police. During the civil war, Kang was made secretary of the CCP Shandong Bureau, where he launched radical **land reform**s, causing the deaths of numerous people, including landlords as well as local CCP cadres. After 1949, Kang was once semiretired, but he took an active role during the Cultural Revolution, contributing to the 10-year chaos and disaster of the Chinese people. He was elected vice-chairman of the CCP in 1968, but after the death of Mao Zedong, Kang Sheng was expelled from the CCP.

KANG YOUWEI (1858–1927). Prominent scholar and political reformer in the Qing dynasty. Born into a gentry family in the township of Foshan, Guangdong Province, Kang began studying the Confucian classics with his grandfather. In 1879, he was first exposed to Western culture when he visited Hong Kong, and he was impressed by the cleanliness and orderliness of the city under Western administration. In 1882, Kang visited Shanghai and bought numerous Western works to study. He opened a school in Canton in 1891, offering his own interpretations of **Confucianism**, known as "New Text" scholarship. At the school, his students, including **Liang Qichao**, also studied mathematics, music, and even military drill. In 1893, he obtained the *jinshi* degree, and two years later he went to Beijing to succeed on the highest examinations. This was the year when the **First Sino-Japanese War** ended with the humiliating **Treaty of Shimonoseki**. Kang and Liang drafted a petition and acquired the signatures of nearly 1,300 jinshi degree candidates from various provinces. The petition proposed extensive governmental, educational, and economic reforms, but it failed to reach the emperor.

Between 1895 and 1898, Kang organized the Qiangguo Hui (Society for the Study of National Strengthening) and published extensively to elaborate on his ideas. In 1891, he published his first book, *A Study of the Gorged Classics of the Qing Period,* in which he sharply criticized the ancient texts, stimulated a spirit of doubt, and introduced new concepts to reappraise traditional scholarship. This work established him as the leader of scholars of the new generation. His political beliefs and ideals were clearly illuminated in his other book, ***Datong shu*** (*The Book of Universal Commonwealth*). Kang argued that mankind progresses from the primitive Age of Disorder to the Age of Approaching Peace and eventually reaches the Age of Universal Peace. In this process, he believed, human nature would be improved and human institutions should also evolve. In his view, the contemporary age was still in the stage of partial peace, not "universal commonwealth" (*datong*). According to his vision, in an ideal world there would be no nations, no families, no clans, and no autocracy. There would be public kindergartens, schools, homes for the elderly, hospitals, public dormitories, and dining halls; there would be cohabitation of men and women for the duration of one year, after which everyone would change mates; there would be fair division of labor and rewards for contributions. Kang believed that he was able to apply utopian socialism to China by a radical reform. Liang Qichao and his other students also shared his confidence and enthusiasm for his reform.

Thanks to the recommendation of Wen Tonghe, Kang finally won a chance to meet the reform-minded **Guangxu Emperor** in 1898.

Kang submitted memorials to elaborate on his platform and also wrote the emperor two short books, one on Russian reform by Peter the Great and the other on the Japanese Meiji Restoration. In June 1898, the Guangxu Emperor began the **Hundred Days' Reform** and appointed Kang Youwei to the **Zongli Yamen** and other reformists to the **Grand Council**. Kang and the emperor vigorously pushed reform in all areas of government administration, education, industry, and foreign affairs. On 21 September, however, the movement was cut short by the **Dowager Cixi** and her conservative supporters. Kang was forced to flee to Hong Kong on a British ship. For the next 14 years he lived in exile. Believing that a constitutional monarchy was the best political system for China, Kang founded the *baohuang hui* (Society to Protect the Emperor), bitterly opposing **Sun Yat-sen**'s revolution. From the perspective of his contemporary intellectuals, however, Kang had become a hopeless relic of the past and his influence gradually declined. After the Qing regime was overthrown, he and Liang Qichao continued to dream of its restoration. On 31 March 1927, Kang died in the city of Qingdao, Shandong Province.

KAOZHENG **SCHOLARSHIP.** Study of "practical evidential research." *Kaozheng* scholars focused their studies on Confucian texts and commentaries of the **Han** dynasty (206 BC–AD 220) rather than popular concerns for Confucian scholarship during the Song dynasty (960–AD 1279) and after. They explored the past with a sharp and penetrating skepticism and tried to make the study relevant to Qing reality. Their academic inquiries also moved beyond traditional classical studies to new realms of mathematics, geography, astronomy, hydraulics, and cartography. Emphasizing meticulous evaluation of data based on rigorous standards of precision, it sought to get away from studying the classical texts to root their studies in "hard facts." This approach might well have been influenced by Western learning and research approaches. The most famous *kaozheng* scholars included Gu Yangwu and **Dai Zhen**. During the middle Qing period, *kaozheng* scholarship became influential due to the support of new patrons, such as book dealers, publishers, printers, library owners, and professional teachers. Nonetheless, the evidential research was largely concentrated on Chinese territory and did not yet provide new knowledge or a perspective of foreign countries and people.

KARAKHAN MANIFESTO (1919). On 25 July 1919, the Soviet government annulled the unequal treaties imposed on China by imperial Russia, including the rights of **extraterritoriality**, economic concessions, and Russia's share of the **Boxer Rebellion** indemnity. The declaration was signed by Deputy Commissar of Foreign Affairs Lev M. Karakhan and known as the Karakhan Manifesto. Although the civil war in Soviet Russia prevented the formal delivery of this manifesto to China, the Beijing authorities soon learned of its particulars. The document was prepared in two versions, causing a controversy. One variant that was delivered to Chinese diplomats in February 1920 contained the statement that "the Soviet government returns to the Chinese people, without any compensation, the **Chinese Eastern Railway** [CER]." However, the version published in Moscow in August 1919 and in following years did not include this provision. Also, on 27 September 1920, the Soviet government ignored its previous promises and requested a new agreement on the joint administration of the CER by the two countries. The existence of two versions shows the ambiguity of Soviet policy toward China and its ambition for the control over the CER and Manchuria at large.

KONG XIANGXI. *See* KUNG, H. H.

KOO, VI KYUIN WELLINGTON. *See* GU WEIJUN.

KULDYA MILITARY GOVERNOR (*ILI JIANGJUN*). The highest military and administrative officer of the Qing government in Xinjiang. In 1759, the **Manchu** general Zhaohui's expeditionary army crushed the Zunghar forces and began to garrison Xinjiang (New Territory). Three years later, the **Qianlong Emperor** decided to establish the Office of the Kuldya Military Governor to rule the frontier area and build a new city, Huiyuan, on the northern bank of the Ili River for the headquarters of the first Kuldya military governor, General Mingrui, and his troops. In the following years, another eight cities were built and the local economy was developed. The major duties of the Kuldya military governor included defending the frontier, collecting taxes, organizing production, and arranging regular visits to the central Qing government in Beijing. In 1876, as the Muslims revolted in northwest China, Zuo Zongtang led his troops into Xinjiang to quell the rebellion and suggested making this area a province. In

1883, the Xinjiang provincial government was established in Dihua (present-day Urumqi), and Xinjiang Province began to be administered by a three-level government at province, prefecture, and county levels. Nonetheless, the region of the Ili military governor continued to act as the overseer of the border region. The Kuldya military governor was finally abolished after the 1911 Revolution.

KUNG, H. H. (KONG XIANGXI, 1880–1967). Banker and statesman of the Republic of China. Born in Taigu, Shanxi Province, Kung obtained his BA from Oberlin College in 1905 and an MS in chemistry from Yale University in 1907. Kung joined the 1911 Revolution and was elected commander in chief of the militia of Central Shanxi. After the North-South negotiations between **Sun Yat-sen** and **Yuan Shikai** started, he resigned his office and began to engage in business and local education. Kung founded the Xiangji Company as a special agency for the American Standard Oil Company in Shanxi; this company made the Kungs one of the richest families in China. In 1913, Kung traveled to Japan and served as the general secretary of the Association of Chinese Christians in Japan, and he also did fund-raising for Sun Yat-sen. Kung met Ai-ling Soong, an English-speaking secretary of Sun's in Tokyo, and married her in 1914. Since Ai-ling's two younger sisters were married to Sun Yat-sen and **Chiang Kai-shek**, respectively, H. H. Kung became a brother-in-law of Sun and Chiang. Kung was one of the few persons who witnessed Sun's death and endorsed his last will. In 1926, Kung began to work with Chiang Kai-shek. He successively served as mnister of industry and commerce (1928–1931), minister of finance (1933–1944), premier of the Republic of China (1938–1939), and president of the **Central Bank of China** (1933–1945).

Kung was also a member of the **Nationalist Party** Central Executive Committee. In his early years as the minister of finance, Kung initiated a monetary reform issuing **fabi** to replace the silver standard system; this reform greatly contributed to stabilizing the government's finances and the Chinese economy. In his later years, however, Kung was accused of using public power to raise money for his own family. Kung was forced to resign in 1944, but he held the presidency of the Central Bank until 1948. In 1947, Kung's wife went to the United States for medical treatment; Kung moved to New York to join her, and he died there on 16 August 1967.

KWANTUNG ARMY ("KANTŌ ARMY" IN JAPANESE). The Japanese army stationed in China's Manchuria. Established in 1906, this army took its name from its base on the Kwantung Peninsula ("Liaodong Peninsula" in Chinese). It was initially organized to defend the Japanese Leased Territory in Kwantung and the areas adjacent to the **South Manchuria Railway**. Composed of an infantry division and a heavy siege artillery battalion, the army consisted of 10,000 men in 1919. This number had increased to 700,000 troops by 1941. To speed up Japanese military expansion, the Kwantung Army plotted the assassination of **Zhang Zuolin** in 1928 and the Mukden Incident in 1931, which paved the way for the Japanese conquest of Manchuria and the establishment of the puppet regime of **Manchukuo** in 1932. The headquarters of the Kwantung Army was located in Xingjing (present-day Changchun). To put down the resistance movement in Manchuria, Inner Mongolia, and North China, the army killed large numbers of Chinese and Korean guerrillas and civilians.

In 1939, the army attacked the Soviet **Red Army** but was defeated, suffering heavy casualties. Because of this military failure, the commander in chief of the Kwantung Army resigned and the army was placed under the direct control of the Imperial General Headquarters. As the Pacific War broke out, much of the army's heavy weapons and ammunition reserves and best personnel were transferred from Manchuria to the Pacific islands. In August 1945, Soviet troops entered Manchuria and destroyed the leading force of the Kwantung Army. The Soviet Red Army also discovered secret labs with biological weapons at Unit 100 and Unit 731. However, the Kwantung Army had destroyed much of the evidence relating to biological and chemical weapons testing. The Kwantung Army was responsible for some of the most infamous Japanese war crimes. In 1948, the Tokyo Tribunal sentenced some of its commanders to death or to life imprisonment for their crimes against humanity.

– L –

LADY HUGHES. This was a British commercial ship from India. On 24 November 1784, the *Lady Hughes* approached Canton and fired a salute; the force of this blast inadvertently killed two Chinese fishermen and wounded another. Captain Williams of the *Lady Hughes* immediately sent the offending gunner into hiding because he knew that the Chinese authorities would impose the death penalty on the gunner even if they were convinced that the death had been accidental. The Chinese demanded that the captain surrender the gunner, but Williams refused. Then the municipal government in Canton arrested the ship's business manager, George Smith, as a hostage and threatened to enforce the implementation of imperial law and cancel all trade with the West. Among the American, French, Danish, and Dutch ships then trading at Canton, a few supported the British, but most did not want to get involved. The British had to compromise by bringing back the gunner and exchanging him for the hostage. The gunner of the *Lady Hughes* was executed by strangulation.

LAND LAW OF THE JIANGXI SOVIET. Law approved by the **First All-China Soviet Congress** in February 1931. The land law of the **Jiangxi Soviet** required that the government immediately confiscate all lands from landlords, rich peasants, **warlords**, bureaucrats, counter-revolutionaries, and rural communities and then redistribute it among the farmers according to family size. Land would not be granted to the old, sick, or disabled people who could not till land, but those people would be taken care of by the government. Although soldiers of the **Red Army** could not engage in agricultural production, the law stated that each of them should still get a share of land in his home village, and the local government should have someone cultivate the land for the soldier. It was a crucial principle of the law that "no land would be given to landlords and only poor land given to rich peasants." After the land redistribution, land could be sold, rented, or exchanged.

LAND REFORM. The heart of the Chinese Communist Revolution. It began in the late 1940s in the Communist bases and spread throughout mainland China, except Tibet, in 1950. The basic idea was similar to **Sun Yat-sen**'s ideal, "land to the tillers." The Communist methods were to confiscate all land and other properties of landlords and distribute them freely to landless peasants. The land reform aimed at destroying "the landlords' feudal land-ownership" and changing the traditional clan-lineage–centered community. Violence was an integral part of the process. On one hand, peasants attacked the wealthier farmers and killed the most hated; on the other, landlords who had been dispossessed and were spared death would expect to return in force and avenge. In the struggle, class sentiments were developed and a new demarcation of "us" and "them" was created. During the civil war, the **Chinese Communist Party** (CCP) changed its moderate rural program of "reduction of rent and interest rates" to radical land redistribution, which successfully mobilized peasants in the war against the **Chiang Kai-shek** government. After the CCP came to power, it promulgated the Agrarian Reform Law "so as to develop agricultural production and open the way for new China's industrialization." By the end of 1952, about 300 million peasants who had less or no land obtained about 700 million mu (about 117 million acres) of land and other productive materials.

LAND REGULATION OF THE HEAVENLY KINGDOM. A law of the Heavenly Kingdom of **Taiping** issued in 1853. It was a utopian program for land redistribution and social transformation. It classfied the land throughout the country into nine ranks and planned to distribute poor and fertile land by pairs to rural households. Per the law, each household would gain the land according to its size. Regardless of gender, every family member aged 16 or older could get one share of land, and those younger than 16 could get a half share. The land of landlords, temples, and the community would be confiscated and redistributed equally among the tillers. On this basis, the rural communities would be organized into the *liang* system. A liang consisted of 25 households. After a harvest, each household kept what it needed and submitted the surplus to the state. The head of the liang would be responsible for collecting the surplus and recruiting a soldier from each household. The Land Regulation of the Heavenly Kingdom was designed to abolish private ownership. It implied that no family needed surplus grain, and if a family needed more food for a pending ceremony or funeral, the state would provide it. The state would also take care of orphans, widows, and old and disabled people. The law addressed the equal rights of women in terms of size of land plot and participation in government and military service. However, the Land Regulation of the Heavenly Kingdom was never enforced in the areas under Taiping control.

LAND TO THE TILLERS. One of the revolutionary objectives of **Sun Yat-sen**, meaning "equalization of the landholdings." Sun saw it as an urgent task to change the situation that arable land in China had been concentrated in the hands of a small group of landlords. In 1905, Sun argued that to avoid the polarization between rich and poor, the land issue was vital for the Chinese Revolution. He showed a great concern for the sufferings of the majority of Chinese peasants who had little or no land. "Land to the tillers" was written into the Manifesto of the First Conference of the **Nationalist Party** in 1924.

LAO SHE (1899–1966). Pen name of Shu Qingchun, a prominent writer, educator, and social activist. Born into the family of a **Manchu** soldier in Beijing, Lao She grew up in poverty. At the age of 14, Lao She was enrolled at the Beijing Third High School, but he had to quit a few months later because of his family's financial difficulties. He transferred and graduated with honors from a tuition-free teachers school in 1918. After graduation, he was immediately appointed principal of the Seventeenth Public Elementary School of Beijing and thus began his teaching career. Lao She taught at elementary schools, middle schools, and universities. At the invitation of the School of Oriental Studies at the University of London, Lao She served as a lecturer in Chinese language from 1924 to 1929. During his stay in London, Lao She studied English literature and began his own creative writing. His famous novels, such as *Philosophy of Lao Zhang* and *Ma and Son*, came out during these years.

Lao She returned to China in 1930 and taught at several universities. In 1936, he resigned his teaching positions and focused on writing. He published numerous novels and short stories, including his masterpiece novel *Rickshaw Boy*, whose English version became a U.S. best seller in 1945. During the **Second Sino-Japanese War**, Lao She took an active part in the resistance movement. He was one of the leaders of the Federation of Literary and Art Circles in Wuhan and in **Chongqing**. His diligence, patriotism, and enthusiasm won him great support among the Chinese writers and intellectuals. Lao She advocated writing for the masses and peasants. He created new operas or new songs for the rural population, using traditional forms of performance to mobilize people.

In March 1946, Lao She was invited by the State Department to visit the United States. His other important work, *Four Generations under One Roof*, was written in an American house in New York. His play *Tea House* was performed in an American theater and was well received by both Chinese and American audiences. After 1949, Lao She held many leading positions in the organizations of Chinese writers and intellectuals, such as deputy chairman of the All-China Federation of Literary and Art Circles. During the Cultural Revolution, Lao She was persecuted, and he committed suicide in 1966.

LAY, HORATIO NELSON (1832–1898). British administrator and the first inspector general of Chinese customs. He was also known in China by his Chinese name, Li Tai Guo. In 1847, Lay was sent to China to study Chinese. Lay's proficiency in the Chinese language enabled him to serve as Lord Elgin's interpreter and participate in the negotiation of the Sino-British **Treaty of Tianjin**. Lay was appointed acting vice-consul in Shanghai in 1854. The same year, Lay took part in the founding of the Imperial Maritime Customs Service, and he became the first inspector general of the service the following year. In 1861, **Prince Gong**, the head of the **Zongli Yamen**, decided to purchase British gunboats and appointed Lay the Chinese representative to England for this business. With written instructions from Prince Gong, Lay bought seven steam cruisers and a supply ship to form the **Lay-Osborne Flotilla** and left London for China in 1863.

LAY-OSBORNE FLOTILLA. In 1861, the **Tongzhi Emperor** accepted the suggestion by the head of the **Zongli Yamen**, **Prince Gong**, to purchase British gunboats for building a Chinese navy. Prince Gong asked **Horatio Nelson Lay**, the inspector general of Chinese customs, to be in charge of the purchase. Lay left China for England on 14 March 1862, and Queen Victoria approved his purchase plan on 2 September. Consequently, he bought seven warships of different sizes for 650,000 taels. Lay appointed Captain Sherald Osborne commander of the flotilla. Although the Tongzhi Emperor had ordered that the Chinese flag be hung on all the warships, Lay designed the emblems for the flotilla. On 13 February 1863, the flotilla left London; it arrived in China in September. The flotilla claimed to obey orders from Lay and Osborne but refused any from Chinese officers, except those directly from the Tongzhi Emperor. Thus, the flotilla eventually became a personal naval force and was called the Lay-Osborne Flotilla. The Qing government could not accept this fact and decided to sell all the boats. The first effort in building a Chinese navy ended in failure. Osborne was forced to resign in 1863 and Lay was fired the next year. Robert Hart succeeded Lay as the inspector of Chinese customs.

LEAGUE OF LEFT-WING WRITERS. Association of Chinese left-wing writers organized by the **Chinese Communist Party** (CCP). In autumn 1929, the CCP ordered Feng Naichao, Xia Yan, and Feng Xuefeng to prepare to found a unified organization of revolutionary writers. Modeled on the All Russia Federation of Proletarian Writers, the League of Left-Wing Writers was established on 2 March 1930 in Shanghai with *Menya* (*Sprout*) as its formal publication. **Lu Xun** was included in its leadership. It adopted the Soviet doctrine of Socialist realism, which was that art and literature must focus on contemporary events in a realistic way to expose the evils in the old society and fight for China's future. The first group of members numbered 50 writers; the association then expanded to some hundred members, including teachers, students, and workers. Due to its obvious political inclination, the League of Left-Wing Writers was banned as soon as it was established, and some of its members/writers were arrested and executed by the Nationalist government. The league was also criticized by left-wing writers for its radicalism and sectarianism. In November 1930, the Chinese poet Xiao San participated in the Third Conference of the International Revolutionary Writers as the representative of the League of Left-Wing Writers. At this conference the Chinese League of Left-Wing Writers joined the international association and became its Chinese branch. In spring 1936, on the eve of the Chinese War against Japanese Aggression, the league voluntarily disbanded.

LEFTIST OPPORTUNISM. An ideology or policy criticized by **Mao Zedong** and his supporters during the Chinese Revolution. According to the documents of the **Chinese Communist Party** (CCP), leftist opportunism dominated the CCP between 1927 and 1935, when **Li Lisan**, **Qu Qiubai**, **Wang Ming**, and **Bo Gu** successively served as the top leaders of the CCP. Mao pointed out that leftist opportunism was a sort of subjectivism and utopianism. Their leaders took on the outward appearance of Marxists, but they were sham Marxists. They attempted to win the victory of the Communist Revolution overnight; they exaggerated the revolutionary forces, underestimated the strength of enemies, and ignored the serious difficulties in the revolution; they regarded themselves as pure Bolsheviks, expelling and attacking all comrades who disagreed with them; and they denied the significance of allying with the Chinese middle class. They put forth an adventuristic strategy to stage urban uprisings or to organize conventional war to fight the much stronger **Nationalist** troops; this strategy caused the **Red Army** and the CCP to suffer great losses. The **Zunyi Conference** in 1935 brought to an end to the domination of leftist opportunism over the CCP.

LEGISLATIVE YUAN (*LIFA YUAN*). One of the five branches of the government of the Republic of China, designed by **Sun Yat-sen**. It was the highest legislative organ of the government, consisting of 49 to 90 members elected from different provinces by popular vote for a two-year term. It was not a counterpart of the Western parliament but was essentially a law-drafting institution that translated the legislative principles adopted by the executive committee of the **Nationalist Party** (GMD) into law. It shared the legislative power with the **National Assembly** until the assembly was abolished in 2000. The Legislative Yuan deliberated on laws, budget, and amnesty; declared war; and signed treaties of peace. The National Assembly had the power to amend the constitution and formally elect the president and vice president of the Republic of China.

LI DAZHAO (1889–1927). One of the founders of the **Chinese Communist Party** (CCP). Born in Luoting, Hebei Province, into a peasant family, Li graduated from the Tianjin School of Political Science and Law. From 1913 through 1916, he studied political economy at Waseda University in Japan, where he learned Marxism. After his return to China, Li served as the head of the university library and professor in the departments of history and economics at **Peking University**. He founded an influential magazine, *Morning Bell*, and joined the editorial staff of *New Youth*, in which he published numerous articles to disseminate news on the Russian Bolshevik Revolution and the Soviet Union. Playing a leading role in the **New Culture Movement** in the 1920s, Li was the earliest and most influential mentor of young **Mao Zedong** when the latter worked at Peking University as a librarian's assistant. Following Li's Beijing Group for Marxist Studies, **Communist groups** were established in many provinces. The delegates of these Communist groups finally met in Shanghai and established the Chinese Communist Party. Therefore,

Li Dazhao was referred to as the cofounder (with **Chen Duxiu**) of the CCP and was elected as a member of the CCP Central Committee.

During the period of the CCP-GMD alliance, Li joined the **Nationalist Party** (GMD) and was elected as a member of the Executive Committee of the GMD Central Committee. In 1925, when the **warlord** government in Beijing suppressed the Communists, Li fled to the Russian consulate, where the warlord **Zhang Zuolin**'s military police arrested him. Li was executed with 19 other Communists in Beijing on 28 April 1927. His eldest son, Li Baohua, later became the CCP secretary of Anhui Province and president of People's Bank of the People's Republic of China.

LI DE. *See* BRAUN, OTTO.

LI HONGZHANG (1823–1901). Leading statesman and general of the late Qing dynasty. Born into a gentry family in Modian, nine miles northwest of the city of Hefei, Anhui Province, Li obtained the *jinshi* degree in 1847 and was appointed to the Hanli Academy two years later. In his early years, Li studied management skills with **Zeng Guofan**, who greatly admired his rare capacity of leadership. Zeng asked him to serve in the **Hunan Army** (Xiang Army) to suppress the **Taiping Rebellion**. Following the model of the Hunan Army, Li built up his personal **Anhui Army** (Huai Army). With the support of the Western mercenary army commanded by Charles Gordon, the Huai Army and Xiang Army defeated the Taiping force in decisive battles, including the capture of Suzhou and Nanjing. For his service, Li was granted the title of earl by the emperor. In the war with the Taiping, Li came to recognize the power of modern weaponry and began to build arsenals in Suzhou, Shanghai, and Nanjing. From 1865 to 1870, he served successively as acting governor of Liangjiang (provinces of Anhui, Jiangsu, and Jaingxi) and governor of Huguang (provinces of Hunan and Hubei), and he put down the **Nian Rebellion**. In 1870, he succeeded Zeng Guofan as the governor of Zhili and minister of Beiyang, thus establishing himself as the most powerful military leader in China for the next 25 years.

Li was one of the leaders of the **Self-Strengthening Movement**. In accordance with his approach, "government supervised and merchant managed," Li established several new factories and companies, including the Tianjin Machine Factory (1870), China Merchants'

Steam Navigation Company (1872), **Kaiping Coal Mines** (1877), **Shanghai Cotton Cloth Mill** (1878), Mo-ho Gold Mines (1887), Longzhang Paper Mill in Shanghai (1891), and others. He initiated and promoted programs to send Chinese students and officers abroad for study. Li also established a foreign-language school in Shanghai. Li's efforts contributed to China's drive toward modernization.

In 1888, Li founded the **Beiyang Fleet** with more than 20 warships. However, his relatively modernized troops and naval force were defeated by the Japanese in 1894; this defeat undermined his political standing and brought an end to the Self-Strengthening Movement. Li was actively involved in foreign trade and foreign affairs. He was the leading negotiator of the Qing government. Dealing with foreign powers, Li applied a basic principle of "compromising for the sake of general interest." He signed about 30 treaties, all of which were considered, from a Chinese perspective, unequal and humiliating. The Russian archives indicated that Russia offered Li a bribe to get the Sino-Russian treaty signed to Russia's advantage. What made Li the biggest target of public criticism was his responsibility for China's defeat in the **First Sino-Japanese War** and his signing of the treaty with Japan in 1895, which ceded Taiwan to Japan. The last negotiation Li conducted was the **Boxer Protocol**. Two months later, he died in Beijing, leaving huge bequests to his family.

LI JINGFANG (1855–1934). Adopted son of **Li Hongzhang**. He was Li Hongzhang's nephew and was adopted at the age of eight. Jingfang obtained the *juren* degree and was appointed to the Office of the Beiyang Minister. He also studied English, which enabled him to serve as his adoptive father's assistant for foreign affairs. From 1886 to 1892, he worked in the Qing legations in Great Britain and Japan. In 1895, when Li Hongzhang was sent to Japan for negotiations and was shot by a Japanese would-be assassin, Li Jing Fang continued the diplomatic talks under his father's guidance. On 23 March, he and Li Hongzhang cosigned the **Treaty of Shimonoseki**. A month later, he was sent to Taiwan as imperial commissioner and handed over Taiwan to Japan. The ceremony was held on a Japanese warship outside the port of Keelung on 7 May 1895.

LI JISHEN (1885–1959). Full general of the second class of the Nationalist army and one of the non-Communist leaders of the People's

Republic of China. Born in Cangwu, Guangxi, Li graduated from the Liaguang Military High School and the **Baoding Military Academy**. After graduating, he taught at the academy. Li was made division commander of the Guangdong Army. He persuaded Lin Zhongren and Huang Shaohong to join the **Nationalist Party** (GMD) and formed the **Guangxi Clique** in the GMD army. When the **Whampoa Military Academy** was established, Li was a major general and served as director of the training department of the academy. In 1925, he was promoted to full general in command of the Fourth Army and an independent regiment. During the **Northern Expedition**, Li was made chief of staff of the **National Revolutionary Army** and director of the Rear Office. In the meantime, he also served as governor of Guangdong. Li supported **Chiang Kai-shek** in the Wuhan-Nanjing split and led his troops in the crackdown on the Communist mutiny in Nanchang in 1927. However, because he launched an anti-Chiang military campaign, Li was expelled from the GMD after he was defeated by Chiang.

After the **Manchuria Incident** in 1931, Li regained his party membership. But he soon allied with Fang Dingying and Cheng Mingshu to organize a revolutionary committee, advocating an anti-Communist and anti–Chiang Kai-shek stance, and was thereby expelled from the GMD again. In November 1933, the **Nineteenth Route Army** revolted in Fujian and established the Revolutionary Government of the Chinese Republic, calling for collaboration with the **Chinese Communist Party** (CCP) against the Japanese. Li was elected chairman of the republic and chairman of its military committee. The rebellion of the Nineteenth Route Army was quickly suppressed by Chiang, and Li fled to Hong Kong. In 1937, when the **Second Sino-Japanese War** broke out, the Nationalist government cancelled Li's arrest warrant and he returned to the GMD.

In March 1947, Li published "My Opinion on the Current Situation" criticizing Chiang's policy, and he was expelled from the GMD for the third time. In January 1948, Li established the GMD Revolutionary Committee, which elected **Song Qingling** honorary chairman and Li chairman. Under an agreement with the CCP, Li and other leading members of the committee left Hong Kong and arrived in Beijing in September 1949. They attended the first **Political Consultative Conference**. Li became one of five vice presidents of the People's Republic of China on 1 October 1949. Li had many children. One of his sons, Li Peiyao, was elected vice president of the Chinese Congress.

LI LISAN (1899–1967). Early organizer of the Chinese labor movement and the top leader of the **Chinese Communist Party** (CCP) from 1928 to 1930. Born in Liling, Hunan Province, into the family of a Confucian teacher, Li went to Changsha for high school, where he met and made friends with **Mao Zedong** and Cai Hesheng. Sponsored by **Cheng Qian**, a **warlord** and his father's schoolmate, Li traveled to Beijing and then to France to study. He worked part-time as an assistant to a boilermaker to earn his tuition. Li's experience in Paris led him to accept Marxism. For his involvement in revolutionary activities in Paris, the French government expelled him in 1921. Li joined the CCP in Shanghai and engaged in the labor movement at the Anyuan Coal Mines, and thus began his revolutionary career. In 1925, he led the **May Thirtieth Movement** in Shanghai and won a reputation among workers and CCP members.

Beginning in 1928, Li was in charge of the CCP Politburo and advocated urban uprisings. On 16 October 1929, following the **Comintern**'s instructions, Li drafted for the conference of the CCP Politburo a resolution titled "A New Revolutionary Tide and the Victory in One or Several Provinces," which required the Communists and their supporters to attack major cities. His plan of urban uprisings, known as the **Lisan Route**, caused great casualties in the **Red Army** and the destruction of the party's organizations in cities, and it was denounced as a "leftist deviation" and an example of leftist opportunism. In 1930, when the Comintern recalled Li to Moscow, **Wang Ming** and his associates in the **Twenty-eight Bolsheviks** took over the party's leadership. Afterward, Li never played a crucial role in CCP politics again. After 1949, he served as minister of labor and deputy minister of industry and transportation. He was persecuted during the Cultural Revolution but was rehabilitated in 1980.

LI SHUTONG (1880–1942). Legendary figure in modern China. Born into the family of a rich salt merchant and banker in the city of Tianjin, Li was a prominent artist, poet, composer, calligrapher, dramatist, art teacher, and Buddhist master. Li began to study Chinese classical literature at the age of seven. He watched Peking Opera for the first time at the age of nine and immediately became interested in drama and music. In 1898, Li enrolled at the Nanyang Public School in Shanghai and joined the Shanghai Painting and Calligraphy Association and the Shanghai Scholarly Society. In 1905, Li traveled to Japan to study at Tokyo's Shangye Art and Music School, where he specialized in Western painting and music. While there, he married a Japanese girl. In 1906, Li with his schoolmates organized a student theatrical club and performed the French play *La dame aux camélias* (*The Lady of the Camellias*), making himself a pioneer in performing modern drama in China.

After his return with his wife to China in 1910, Li successively taught at the Beiyang Advanced Industry School in Tianjin, Shanghai's East Girl's School, Zhejiang Secondary Normal School, and Nanjing Advanced Normal School, and he was one of the most popular professors at all the schools. Li introduced Western art, music, and drama to China, being the first Chinese educator who used nude models in his art classes. Li was also a well-known composer and lyricist. Some of his compositions are still remembered and performed today. Due to his teaching excellence, some of his students, such as Feng Zikai and Liu Zhiping, became famous artists and composers.

Being a prestigious scholar in studies of Western culture and a modern educator, Li surprised his contemporaries by abandoning his family, property, and career to become a Buddhist monk with a new name, Master Hong Yi, in 1916. He chose to say good-bye to the secular world in China's most beautiful and prosperous city—Hangzhou—and began to live in seclusion at the Hupao Temple. He refused art, music, and drama, and only continued to practice calligraphy, developing a simple yet distinctive fine style to illuminate Buddhist teachings. His calligraphic work was of such high aesthetic and moral value that Chinese intellectuals such as **Lu Xun** and **Guo Moruo** took it as a great honor to have it. However, Li did not sell a single piece of the works and preferred living in poverty. In 1942, Master Hong Yi died peacefully at the age of 63 on a missionary trip to Quanzhou, Fujian Province.

LI WEIHAN (1897–1984). Leader of the **Chinese Communist Party** (CCP) and a specialist in **united front** work. Born in Changshan, Hunan Province, Li was **Mao Zedong**'s schoolmate at the Hunan First Normal School, where he, Mao, and Cai Hesheng organized the New People's Study Society. In 1919, he went to France to join the work-study program with **Zhou Enlai** and **Deng Xiaoping**. Li joined the CCP in 1922 and was elected a member of the Central Committee. He went to Moscow to study in 1931 and then traveled to the Jiangxi base two years later. Li held several posts in the party, including director of the Organizational Department, secretary of the CCP Mass Work Committee, and secretary of the Shan-Guan-Ning Border Region Government. The most important position, which he held for the longest time, was director of the United Front Department. The major activities of this department were to gain the allegiance of non-Communists, non-**Han** ethnic minorities, and overseas Chinese to the CCP's various political and military campaigns. Li continued to work in this capacity after 1949. His wife, Jing Weiying, was the second wife of Deng Xiaoping. Li and Jing got married when Deng was dismissed from office and divorced Jing in 1933. Li's son, Li Tieying, later became a member of the CCP Politburo after the Cultural Revolution.

LI XIUCHENG (1823–1864). An eminent military leader of the **Taiping Rebellion**, known as Loyal Prince Li. Born in Tengxian, Guangxi Province, Li joined **Hong Xiuquan**'s **Taiping Rebellion** and led the Taiping forces many military victories. In 1862, he commanded troops to attack Shanghai but could not storm it. He also failed to rescue Taiping's capital, Nanjing, from siege. Two years later, the Taiping kingdom collapsed and he was captured by the Xiang Army. Before **Zeng Guofan** executed him, Li wrote the famous "Self-statement of Li Xiucheng," expressing his wish to surrender, but the last part of the statement was destroyed and its contents remain unknown.

LI YUANHONG (1864–1928). President of the Republic of China (1916–1917 and 1922–1923). Born in Huangpi, Hubei (Hupei) Province, Li graduated from the Beiyang Naval Academy in 1889 and served as an engineer in the **Beiyang Fleet** during the **First Sino-Japanese War**. In the Battle of Bohai, his cruiser was sunk, but he was rescued. Admired by the viceroy of Huguang, **Zhang Zhidong**, Li was invited to Hubei to train a new army. During this period, he made three investigative trips to Japan. In 1906, Li was appointed commander of the 21st Mixed Brigade in Hankou, where the anti-Qing revolutionary movement had gained momentum. Although he was not involved in any antigovernment activities, Li appeared to be liberal and maintained good relations with the soldiers. During the Wuchang Uprising, because none of the revolutionary leaders were in the city, Li was chosen to be the head of the new provisional revolutionary government. Though reluctant at first, he agreed to take the position.

In 1912, Li was elected vice president of the Republic of China and continued to hold the position after **Yuan Shikai** replaced **Sun Yat-sen**. Li supported Yuan on various issues, including dismissing the **National Assembly**, offering unlimited power to the president, and suppressing Sun Yat-sen's **Second Revolution**. He also married his son to Yuan's daughter. However, he refused to support Yuan's monarchical movement and declined the noble titles offered by Yuan. In 1916, after Yuan died, Li became president of the republic, but the real power was in the hands of Premier Duan Qirui, who was a **warlord** of the **Anhui Clique**. In March 1917, Li argued with Duan over the issue of Chinese participation in World War I. After he dismissed Duan from office, the provinces controlled by the Anhui Clique declared independence in protest. Li invited General **Zhang Xun** to Beijing for mediation, but Zhang took the opportunity to restore the Qing monarchy. The Anhui Clique army crushed Zhang Xun's "**pigtail army**" and forced Li to resign. In 1922, the **Zhili Clique** defeated the Anhui Clique and asked Li to resume the presidency. Li became a figurehead again and was forced to resign the next year. After a failed attempt to regain power, Li retired to Tianjin.

LI ZONGREN (1891–1969). Statesman and military leader of the **Nationalist Party** (GMD) and the Republic of China (ROC). Born into the family of a rural teacher in Lingui, Guangxi Province, Li was elected vice president of the ROC in 1948 and acting president in 1949. He began his military career at the age of 17 as a cadet at the Guangxi Primary Army School. He joined the **Tongmenghui** in 1910 and the GMD in 1923. He participated in the **National Protection War** and **Constitutional Protection Movement**, serving as a junior officer in the Yunnan and Guangxi armies. His position as the new leader of the **Guangxi Clique** was established in the following events: he built an independent local troop in the mountainous area of Yulin in 1923; he defeated the old Guangxi **warlords** Lu Rongting (in 1924) and Shen Hongyin (in 1925); and he was appointed by **Sun Yat-sen** army commander of the First Guangxi Army.

Li participated in the **Northern Expedition** and destroyed the leading force of the Beiyang warlord Sun Chuanfang. He supported **Chiang Kai-shek**'s policy of purging the Communists from the Nationalist troops and governments. Together with **Bai Chongxi** and other Guangxi leaders, he built up their province as a model of economic development and social reform for the rest of China. But he failed in two anti-Chiang military campaigns in 1929 and 1930. As a result, he was dismissed from office, expelled from the GMD, and forced to flee abroad. After the **Manchuria Incident**, Chiang called him back for the Chinese resistance movement against Japan. Li commanded the Guangxi troops in several crucial battles, including the **Battle of Tai'erzhuang** (1928), which repulsed the Japanese assault in central China, annihilating about 16,000 of the Japanese troops and capturing numerous weapons, pieces of ammunition, and military vehicles. However, his troops paid the price with casualties of 30,000 men.

In the last year of the civil war, Chiang resigned because of the military failure and Li was made acting president without real power. He sued for peace negotiations with the Communists but could not accept the tough terms **Mao Zedong** demanded. As Chiang and his loyal GMD government fled to Taiwan, Li traveled to the United States for medical treatment. In 1965, he and his wife returned to mainland China, and four years later he died of pneumonia in Beijing.

LIANG FA (1789–1855). The first Chinese Protestant minister and evangelist. Born into a poor family in Zhaoqing, Guangdong Province, Liang went to Guangzhou to study printing skills at the age of 15. Despite the fact that printing materials related to Christianity were prohibited by Chinese law, his boss, **Robert Morrison**, managed to print a Chinese version of the Bible that he had translated; this act taught Liang about both printing technology and Christianity. In 1815, when Morrison's associate, William Milne, moved to Malaysia, he brought Liang with him and baptized him in Malacca a year later. When Liang returned to his home village in 1819, he married a rural woman named Li and made her China's first female Protestant. In December 1821 in Macau, Liang was ordained by Morrison as a minister with the London Missionary Society. He started evangelizing in Guangzhou, Singapore, and Malacca. In 1828, he opened China's first Christian school, teaching students not only Chinese but also English, Western science, and geography. The school also functioned as a Christian church. Liang wrote many missionary books and pamphlets. The most famous one was *Quanshi liangyan* (*Good Words Exhorting the Age*, published in 1832), which exposed **Hong Xiuquan** to Christianity and prompted him to use Chistianity to guide his **Taiping Rebellion**. In 1834, the Qing government ordered Liang's arrest, but he was able to flee to Macao and then to Singapore and Malaysia. He returned to Guangzhou five years later and began to travel back and forth between China and Southeast Asia to continue his missionary work. He died in Guangzhou and was buried in his home village. A memorial was dedicated to him in Hong Kong in 1963.

LIANG QICHAO (1873–1929). Scholar, journalist, and reformist leader during the **Hundred Days' Reform**. Born into a farm family in Xinhui, Guangdong Province, Liang began to study classical Chinese at the age of six and could write thousand-word essays by the age of nine. Liang obtained the *xiucai* degree at the age of 11 and *juren* degree at the age of 16, but he failed the *jinshi* examination in 1890. In the same year, he met another reformist leader, **Kang Youwei**, in Beijing. Five years later, Liang and Kang went to Beijing again for the national examination. They organized 1,000 provincial degree candidates to submit to the emperor the famous reform memorial, the *Statement of Public Vehicles*. Liang helped Kang organize the Society for National Strengthening and served as its secretary. Liang advocated constitutional monarchy and radical reforms. With the support of the **Guangxu Emperor**, Liang implemented the Hundred Days' Reform. After the **Dowager Cixi** suppressed the reform in 1898, Liang was exiled to Japan, where he and Kang organized the **Emperor Protection Society**, continuing to preach constitutional reform and opposing **Sun Yat-sen**'s revolutionary programs. In the following years, he visited Australia and the United States, giving lectures and raising funds for his reform campaign.

Liang was the most influential journalist in modern China. He believed that the newspaper was an educational program and could be used to communicate political ideas. He created "new journalism" for modern China by advocating the following tenets: journalism's first obligation is to the truth, newspapers' first loyalty is to the citizens, and journalists must maintain an independence from those they cover. His refined and convincing rhetoric about the importance of Chinese reform and modernization was most appealing to Chinese intellectuals and political leaders, including young **Mao Zedong**. Liang founded the newspaper *Qing yi bao* and edited two premier newspapers, *Zhongwai gongbao* and *Shiwu bao*. On 8 February 1902, Liang launched a popular biweekly journal, *Xinmin congbao* (New Citizen), in Yokohama, Japan. This journal published 96 issues, and its readership was estimated to be 200,000. Liang returned to China in 1912 and served in the cabinet of **Yuan Shikai**.

Liang retired from politics in 1917 to pursue academic studies and writings. He published scholarly monographs and wrote poems and novels. His major publications include *Chinese Academic History of the Past 300 Years*, *The Philosophy of Laozi*, and *The History of Buddhism in China*. His representative works in literature were collected and compiled in the 148-volume *Collected Works of Yinbingshi*. Liang had two wives in his life, Li Huixian and Wang Guiquan, who bore him nine children. Many of them, including his son Liang Sicheng, became successful scholars in China. Liang suffered from nephritis. Because of a botched surgery, he died in Beijing at the age of 55.

LIANG SHUMING (1893–1988). Prominent philosopher, educator, and thinker. Born into a gentry-official family in Beijing, Liang was a leading scholar of neo-**Confucianism**. Liang graduated from Shuntan High School. He joined the **Tongmenghui** in 1911 and served as editor and correspondent of the Tongmenghui's journal, *Republic Daily*. In 1916, he was appointed secretary of the Department of Law of the Republic of China in charge of its confidential archives, and he began to study and publish works on philosophy. At the invitation of **Cai Yuanpei**, Liang taught Indian philosophy at **Peking University** from 1917 to 1927. He spent three years exploring the essence of Buddhism and then moved to the field of Confucian studies. His book *Eastern and Western Cultures and Philosophies*, published in 1921, was regarded as the most important work in the field and was reprinted eight times.

Starting in 1928, he advocated the new village movement, opening rural schools, developing local economies, and other social reforms. In 1939, he organized the Society of Comrades for Unification and Reconstruction of China, which was renamed the **China Democratic**

League in 1944. Liang founded the *Guangming Daily* and served as president of the newspaper office. In 1947, he resigned and withdrew from the Democratic League to focus on academic research. He stated that Confucianism, Western philosophy, and medicine were the three fundamentals of his theories. He regarded the universe as akin to a human's life, a process in which a human being's demands gain satisfaction. He criticized the theory of **class struggle** and argued that social order could be maintained only through the restoration of the traditional legal and moral systems, and China's revival could be realized only through industry based on agricultural development. After 1949, he publicly argued with **Mao Zedong**. His theories were attacked, but he never gave up his beliefs.

LIANG SICHENG (1901–1972). Noted Chinese architect, known as the father of Chinese architecture. Sicheng's father was Liang Qichao, who was one of the leaders of the abortive **Hundred Days' Reform** of 1898 and who took refuge in Japan, where Sicheng was born. After the 1911 Revolution, Sicheng returned to China with his parents. He entered Tsinghua College at the age of 14. In 1923, he graduated from the college and in the next year, he went to the United States with his fiancée, **Lin Huiyin**, on a Boxer Rebellion Indemnity Scholarship to study architecture under professor Paul Cret at the University of Pennsylvania. Three years later, Liang got his master's degree in architecture and then went to Harvard University to study history. In 1928, Liang and Lin got married and the couple returned to China at the invitation of Northeastern University in Shenyang. They established a school of architecture there and developed the first curriculum for college education. In 1945, Liang began to teach architecture at Qinghua University in Beijing. Liang visited the United States in 1946 again as the Chinese representative in the design of the United Nations Headquarters Building.

Liang was determined to search and discover what he termed the "grammar" of Chinese architecture. He and his colleagues successively discovered some surviving traditional buildings, including the Temple of Buddha's Light (AD 857), the Temple of Solitary Joy (AD 984), the Yingzhou Pagoda (AD 1056), Zhaozhou Bridge (AD 589–617), and many others. Because of the efforts of these researchers, these structures managed to survive. In 1934, Liang published his first book, *Qing Structural Regulations*. In 1940, he began his monumental study of *Yingzao fashi* (*Treatise on Architectural Methods*, the Song dynasty), which spanned more than two decades and was published only after his death. All of Liang's books have become a solid basis for later scholars to explore the evolution and principles of Chinese architecture, and they are still valuable tools today. In 1947, Princeton University awarded him an honorary doctoral degree.

In 1949, Lin and Liang went to Xibeipo to meet the Chinese Communist leaders and suggest a peaceful settlement of the Beijing issue in order to preserve the traditional urban architecture in the city. After the People's Republic of China (PRC) was established, Lin was one of the designers of the national emblem of the PRC and was also involved, along with her husband, in the design of the Monument to the People's Heroes located in **Tiananmen Square**. During the Cultural Revolution, Liang suffered severe persecution and died. His posthumous manuscript *Chinese Architecture, A Pictorial History*, written in English and edited by Wilma Fairbank, was published by MIT Press in 1984 and won an American Institute of Architects Award.

LIAO ZHONGKAI (1877–1925). An early leader of the **Nationalist Party** (GMD). Born in San Francisco, Liao went to elementary and high school in the United States. After his move to China in 1896, he attended a village school in Guangdong to receive a traditional Chinese education. In October 1897, Liao married **He Xiangning** in Guangzhou and traveled with her to Japan to study economics and political science at Waseda University and Tokyo University. Liao was one of the founding members of the **Tongmenghui**, serving as its director of foreign affairs. In 1909, Liao returned to China and took the Qing government's **civil service exam**. He wanted to promote reform within the Qing bureaucracy. After the 1911 Revolution, Liao served as director of finance for **Sun Yat-sen**'s military government in Guangdong. In June 1922, he was arrested by the Guangdong **warlord**, **Chen Jiongming**, but he was soon rescued by his wife. They fled to Shanghai to meet **Sun**, who authorized Liao to negotiate with the Russian representative Adolf Joffe. Liao arranged a meeting between Sun and Joffe, which resulted in the **Sun-Joffe Manifesto**. Liao strongly supported Sun's policy of alliance with the Soviet Union and the **Chinese Communist Party** (CCP) and became the principal architect of the first GMD-CCP **united front** against **warlordism**.

After the GMD reorganization, Liao was elected a member of the GMD Central Executive Committee. He successively served as head of the Department of Workers, head of the Department of Peasants, minister of finance, and the GMD's party representative at the **Whampoa Military Academy**. As a left-wing leader, Liao borrowed democratic ideas from the United States and Switzerland. He advocated the notion of "citizen politics" to ensure the rights of every citizen to initiate and review laws and to elect and recall government officials. After Sun's death, Liao became one of three major leaders of the GMD (the other two were **Wang Jingwei** and **Hu Hanmin**). On 30 August 1925, Liao was assassinated in Guangzhou. He was survived by his wife; his daughter, Liao Mengxing; and his son, Liao Chengzhi, who later joined the Communist Party and became vice president of the Chinese People's Congress.

LIAO-SHEN, BATTLE OF (LIAOSHEN CAMPAIGN, SEPTEMBER 1948–NOVEMBER 1948). The first of three great campaigns in the civil war (the other two being the Battle of Ping-Jin and Battle of Huai-Hai). The Battle of Liao-Shen took place in Manchuria; it began on 12 September 1948 and ended on 7 November. Before the battle, the Communists evolved a policy of "strategic withdrawal and mobile warfare, abandoning the towns for the countryside." When they organized their counteroffensive and began the Liaoshen campaign, the Communist forces led by **Lin Biao** had 13 army columns of infantry, one artillery army, and 15 independent divisions, as well as three cavalry divisions—approximately 54 divisions totaling over 700,000 men, while the Nationalist troops commanded by Wei Lihuang had four armies consisting of 14 corps and 44 divisions, plus local security forces, totaling over 550,000 men.

The Liaoshen Campaign went through three stages. The first began on 3 October 1948, when Lin gathered 250,000 troops to lay siege on the city of Jinzhou. **Chiang Kai-shek** ordered the Nationalist defenders in Huludao and in Shenyang to reinforce and rescue Jinzhou, but these troops were blocked and destroyed by Lin's troops in the area of Taishan. On 14 October Lin stormed the city, killing and capturing its 100,000 defenders. The land route for the Nationalists to retreat from Manchuria to the North China Plain was thus cut off. In the meantime, Zeng Zesheng, the vice commander of the Nationalist forces defending Changchun, revolted, and Zheng Dongguo, the commander in chief, surrendered with 100,000 men on 21 October. In the second stage, the Nationalist troops tried to abandon Shenyang and go to the seaport Yinkou and return to North China by sea. However, they were unable to break through the Communist encirclement. Instead, 12 Nationalist divisions, including its elite New 1st Army, totaling up to 100,000 men, were destroyed and its commander, Liao Yaoxiang, was captured. The final stage began with the defense of Shenyang, which resulted in the annihilation of two Nationalist armies, totaling up to 134,000 men. In the following battle at Yinkou, the Nationalist 52nd Army lost 14,000 men, but its remnants managed to retreat to North China by sea. In the 52-day campaign, the Communists annihilated 472,000 Nationalist troops at the expense of 69,000 of their own men.

LIFAN YUAN (OFFICE OF BORDER AFFAIRS). An institution set up by the **Manchus** in 1638 to take charge of Korean and Mongolian affairs. After the Manchus conquered China in 1644, the Lifan Yuan also began to manage affairs relating to Tibet, Xinjiang, Russia, and other nations bordering China. It ranked directly after the Six Boards and was usually run by the Manchus and occasionally by Mongols. No Chinese was ever appointed a member. In 1687, the Regulations of Lifan Yuan were issued to clarify the office's organization, functions, and policies, which were revised four times in the following years. Besides the administrative offices, some research divisions, such as that for Mongolian studies and Russian studies, were attached to the institution. The Lifan Yuan would be comparable to an office of foreign affairs until the **Zongli Yamen** was established in 1861 to deal with other countries that did not border China's domain.

LI-FOURNIER AGREEMENT (1844). A treaty between Qing China and France on the issue of Vietnam. Since the period of Louis-Napoléon, France had the ambition to build a French Indo-Chinese empire and pose as a champion of Catholicism abroad. French influence in **Annam** (Vietnam) began to increase as it helped the overthrown emperor Gia-long regain power in 1802. As a token of appreciation, Gia-long signed two treaties with France in 1858 and 1874, granting the French the right to navigate on its interior river, the Red River, and to build concessions. The Qing government refused to honor the two treaties since it regarded Annam as a Chinese dependency and insisted that all the treaties had to be ratified by the Chinese emperor. A war broke out between China and France, and the former was defeated by the latter. The Chinese official **Li Hongzhang** stood for a peace settlement through negotiation. Under the approval of the **Dowager Cixi**, Li signed with the French navy captain F. E. Fournier a treaty known as the Li-Fournier Agreement.

This treaty required that China honor the other treaties signed by France and Annam and withdraw its troops. France promised to make no demand for indemnity, no invasion of China, and no undignified reference to China in future treaties with Annam. The Li-Fournier Agreement ended the first stage of the **Sino-French War**. However, the French parliament did not ratify the agreement, asserting that the treaty implied a recognition of the Chinese occupation of Annam. On the other hand, many Chinese government officials tried to continue the war and to impeach Li Hongzhang. Because of this, Li dared not inform the emperor about the Li-Fournier Agreement, especially his agreed-on date of withdrawal of Chinese troops. The stay of the Chinese troops in Annam gave the French a reason to resume military operations.

LIJIN. A form of local tax in the late Qing dynasty. First introduced in 1853, it was a surcharge on trading commodities instituted to collect money to support local armies in suppressing the **Taiping Rebellion**. It began at Yangzhou and spread to many towns, becoming a common and permanent practice throughout the country by 1862. There were two forms of *lijin*: one was levied on shops or points of a good's departure; the other was levied as a transit tax on a good during its movement. More often than not, the lijin was repeatedly levied in the process of production, transportation, and final sale. Farmers had to pay lijin according to their land and output because they might sell grain to traders. The shops engaging in long-distance trade were required to pay lijin on a volume basis. Finally, the commercial boats had to pay lijin at various lijin stations along the way. The Chinese merchants petitioned, foreign traders demanded, and some government officials suggested abolition or reform of the lijin. Their proposals, however, were never accepted, since lijin had become an important source of revenue for local governments. In 1860, due to lijin income, the revenue of the local governments in the southeast provinces increased by three or four times. All the provinces, except

Heilongjiang and Yunnan, had begun to collect lijin by 1862. In the last year of the Qing dynasty, the lijin income of the whole country was as high as 43.18 million taels silver. The existence of the lijin was regarded as a sign of the decentralization of state authority. The lijin was finally abolished by the Republican government on 1 January 1931.

LIN BIAO (1907–1971). Veteran military leader and vice-chairman of the **Chinese Communist Party** (CCP). Born into the family of a small landlord family in Huangung, Hubei Province, Lin received his primary education in his hometown. Two of Lin Biao's cousins, Lin Yutan and Lin Yuying, were also CCP members who later died for the revolution. They brought Lin Biao to Wuchang, exposing him to the Communist Revolution. Lin Biao joined the Socialist Youth League in 1923 and the CCP in 1925. That year, he enrolled in the **Whampoa Military Academy**. After graduating in 1926, Lin participated in the **Northern Expedition**. He was assigned to **Ye Ting**'s Independent Regiment, where he proved himself a talented military commander and was quickly promoted to battalion commander. As a junior officer, Lin joined the **Communist Nanchang Mutiny**, which was led by **Zhou Enlai**, He Long, **Ye Ting**, and **Zhu De**. After the failure of the uprising, Lin followed the small detachment led by Zhu De and moved to the **Jinggangshan**, where they met **Mao Zedong**'s guerrillas. Lin successively served as battalion commander, regiment commander, and army commander in the newly formed **Red Army**. He played a decisive role in building and defending the Communist rural base in Jiangxi.

When the **Long March** set out from the Jiangxi base, Lin was in command of the First Army Corps, one of two leading forces of the Red Army. His troops suffered great casualties in the first three months because of the poor command of the party's three-man leading group (**Otto Braun, Bo Gu**, and Zhou Enlai). Lin sharply criticized the three-man group and supported Mao Zedong's bid to resume his leadership of the army and party. Lin led his troops to win many of the decisive battles throughout the Long March, making himself a legendary hero. In June 1936, Lin was appointed president and political commissar of the Academy of the Red Army, which was renamed the **Anti-Japanese Military and Political University** (*kangda*) in 1937.

As soon as the **Second Sino-Japanese War** broke out, the Red Army was reorganized into the **Eighth Route Army**, composed of three divisions. Lin was appointed commander of the 115th Division of 15,000 men. The first notable victory in the war came when Lin's troops ambushed a Japanese division at Pingxing Pass, Shanxi Province. This victory provided a great morale boost for the Chinese troops and people. Nonetheless, the Communist troops returned to **guerrilla warfare**. Soon after this battle, Lin was seriously wounded and was sent to the Soviet Union for medical treatment. After Japan surrendered in August 1945, Lin led 30,000 men in marching to Manchuria, where his troops quickly expanded to a quarter of a million by the spring of 1946.

In the first year of the civil war, Lin adopted a strategy of "strategic withdraw, mobile warfare, and abandoning the towns for the countryside." He began his counteroffensive in 1947 and destroyed the **Nationalist Party** (GMD) leading forces in the **Battle of Liao-Shen** in 1948. Lin then led his troops south of the Great Wall and besieged the cities of Tianjin and Beiping (present-day Beijing). He stormed the former and took over the latter through peaceful negotiation. On 11 March 1949, Lin's troops were renamed the Fourth Field Army and numbered 800,000 troops. During the following months, the Fourth Field Army continued southward, hunting out and fighting the GMD armies, and finally liberating five provinces and Hainan island. Lin's troops became the largest military force of the **People's Liberation Army**, comprising 1.5 million men.

Lin was appointed to several important posts, including secretary of the CCP Central China Bureau, commander in chief of the Central China Military District, and chairman of the Military and Political Committee of Central-South China. After the founding of the People's Republic of China in 1949, Lin semiretired because of illness and his own strategy of self-protection. He was called back to replace **Peng Dehuai** as minister of defense in 1959. During the Cultural Revolution, Lin was elected vice-chairman of the CCP, and his position as Mao's successor was written into the CCP's party constitution. His wife, Ye Qun, also became a member of the CCP Politburo. However, Lin eventually lost Mao's trust and became a target of persecution. When he and his family attempted to escape from China, their airplane mysteriously crashed in Mongolia on 13 September 1971.

LIN HUIYIN (1904–1955). Prominent architect and poet. Born in Hangzhou, Zhejiang Province, Lin first received a good education from her father, who was a famous scholar and educator. In 1920, Lin followed her father to London and studied at St. Mary's College, where she became interested in architecture. In 1924, she went to the United States with her fiancé, **Liang Sicheng**, to study at the University of Pennsylvania. Because the school of architecture at the university did not admit female students, Lin had to enroll in the art school, from which she graduated with honors. In 1928, Lin married Liang Sicheng and returned to China. Lin wrote poems, essays, short stories, and plays. With her husband, she wrote *History of Chinese Architecture* and translated English works into Chinese. In the 1930s, she was referred to as the most beautiful and intelligent lady in China. Her house became a literary salon for notable scholars and social activists. In 1949, Lin and her husband went to Xibeipo to meet the Chinese Communist leaders, suggesting a peaceful settlement of the Beijing issue in order to preserve the traditional urban architecture of the city. After the People's Republic of China (PRC) was established, she was one of the designers of the national emblem of the PRC. She was also involved, along with her husband, in designing the Monument to the People's Heroes located in **Tiananmen Square**. On 1 April 1955, Lin died of pneumonia in Beijing.

LIN SEN (1868–1943). A leader of the **Nationalist Party** (GMD) and chairman of the National Government of the Republic of China from 1932 through 1943. Born in Minhou, Fujian Province, Lin began to study at an American missionary school at the age of nine. He first worked in the Telegraph Bureau of Taipei in 1884 and then served at the Shanghai customs office. Lin engaged in guerrilla warfare against the Japanese occupation of Taiwan and joined the **Tongmenghui** in 1905. After the 1911 Revolution, Lin was elected speaker of the first session in the **National Assembly** in April 1913. He joined the **Second Revolution**, and after it was suppressed Lin fled to Japan, where he joined **Sun Yat-sen**'s new organization, the Chinese **Revolutionary Party**. He followed Sun to Guangzhou and served as minister of foreign affairs, minister of reconstruction, and in other positions in Sun's government. In 1924, Lin was elected member of the Executive Committee of the GMD.

Lin was a political opponent of **Chiang Kai-shek**. He and Tsou Lu organized the right-wing GMD members to hold the Fourth Session of the GMD Central Committee against Chiang Kai-shek at the Western Hills in Beijing; they consequently were referred to as the Western Hills Clique. They opposed Sun Yat-sen's policy of alliance with the Soviet Union and Communists, demanding the purge of the Communists from the Nationalist army and government. Although the leading members of the Western Hills Clique were punished by the GMD Central Committee, this clique resumed its influence in the party after the GMD–**Chinese Communist Party** (CCP) split. In later years, Lin announced his support for the leadership of Chiang Kai-shek. During the **Second Sino-Japanese War**, as a senior GMD statesman, Lin was appointed chairman of the National Government, more an honorary position than one of real power. Lin died in the wartime capital, **Chongqing**, on 1 August 1943, two days after having a stroke.

LIN SHU (1852–1924). The most famous translator and writer in early 20th-century China. Born into a poor family in Fuzhou, Fujian Province, Lin did not receive a regular education. He audited at a private school and obtained the *juren* degree in 1882. However, Lin failed the highest level of **civil service examination** seven times and then turned his sights to literature. In 1897, a friend of his from France urged him to translate Alexandre Dumas' *La dame aux camélias*. Despite his ignorance of any foreign language, he collaborated with the friend to translate it into literary Chinese. The book was published in 1899 and was an immediate success, inspiring Lin to become a professional translator. In the following years, he translated more than 170 novels by great English and French writers. He was the first person to introduce Western literature and culture to the Chinese people. With his elegant Chinese and vivid imagination, he often "improved" the original works to make them more absorbing and appealing to Chinese readers. Despite all the mistranslations, his renditions were vigorous and popular. After 1913, however, his pen appeared to be dull. Sometimes, Lin also wrote in the vernacular language, but he opposed the total abolition of literary Chinese.

LIN YUTANG (1895–1976). Scholar and successful writer of both Chinese and English. Lin was born in Banzi, Fujian Province, into a

Christian family: his father was a Chinese Presbyterian minister. Lin graduated from **Saint John's University** in Shanghai and then taught at Qinghua University in Beijing. In 1919, with a half scholarship, he enrolled in the graduate program at Harvard University. Two years later, he obtained a master's degree in English literature and began to travel in France and Germany, where he obtained a PhD in Chinese literature from the University of Leipzig. From 1923 to 1926, Lin taught at **Peking University** and Peking Female Normal University and served as dean of the School of Letters at Xiamen University. In 1927, he also worked as a secretary in the Ministry of Foreign Affairs. In 1932, Lin founded China's first Western-style satirical magazine, *Yusi*, and became its leading columnist. Three years later, he published his first English book, *My Country and My People*. His charming and witty writing style immediately brought him international fame.

After 1936, Lin mainly lived in the United States, where he translated Chinese classics into English, attempting to bridge the cultural gap between the East and West. He published eight novels, more than 20 essay collections, and many other books in Chinese and English. Lin was a man of many talents, enabling him to formulate a new method for romanizing the Chinese language, creating an indexing system for Chinese characters, and inventing a Chinese typewriter. He wrote and edited several Chinese–English dictionaries and grammar books, and completed his *Chinese–English Dictionary of Modern Usage* at the age of 78. He died in Hong Kong at the age of 81 and was buried at his home in Yangmingshan, Taiwan.

LIN ZEXU (1785–1850). Known as Commissioner Lin, he fought against the smuggling of opium into Guangzhou, which touched off the First **Opium War** of 1840–1842. The Chinese now see Lin as a symbol of China's resistance to imperialism and as a national hero. He advocated Western studies and was thus called "the first person to see the world with open eyes." Lin was born in the city of Fuzhou, Fujian Province. In 1811, he obtained the *jinshi* degree and was appointed to the prestigious **Hanlin Academy**. He was sent out to various provinces to undertake water conservancy, salt administration, and famine relief. He served in various official capacities and became governor-general of Hunan and Hubei in 1837. He resolutely opposed opium trade and submitted many memorials to the **Daoguang**

Emperor, advocating the banning of opium. In 1839, he was sent to Guangdong to halt opium smuggling. Lin confiscated more than 20,000 chests of opium from the British dealers and ordered their destruction. He later blockaded the port to European ships and prepared for war. When the British warships moved northward to attack the province of Zhejiang and approached Tianjin, near Beijing, many other officials of the Qing government blamed Lin for provoking the British into military action.

The emperor dismissed Lin and sent him into exile in Ili, Xinjiang. As a result of the Opium War, China was forced to sign the **Treaty of Nanjing** and it lost its territorial authority over **Hong Kong**. Nonetheless, the emperor still admired Lin's uprightness and incorruptibility. In 1845, he was called back to engage in suppression of various rebellions. Lin addressed the need of a better knowledge of the world. He initiated projects to translate foreign books and newspapers. He collected much material on world geography, which was later compiled and published by **Wei Yuan** in 1844 as *Illustrated Treatise on the Maritime Kingdoms*.

LINEAGE. A Chinese descent group including all relatives living in the same community who share a common surname, claim a common pedigree, and trace their patrilineal descent to one ancestor. In rural China, the residents of an entire village often belonged to one lineage. With patrilineal descent, individuals belong to their father's lineage, and sometimes a lineage might consist of 2,000 to 3,000 members. Lineage organization and institutions were stronger in south China than in the north. The unity of lineage was often symbolized by an ancestral hall, and lineage elders had powerful moral and ethical control over the committee, making traditional China to a great extent a self-governed society. The **Chinese Communist Party** used the theory of **class struggle** and political campaigns to undermine the influence of lineages and establish Communist control in China.

LISAN ROUTE (1930). A revolutionary strategy made by **Li Lisan**, the Communist leader in 1930. On 16 October 1929, the **Comintern** sent a letter to China, instructing the **Chinese Communist Party** (CCP) to mobilize the masses to promote the revolution and "to build the Soviet-style dictatorship of workers and peasants." When the letter came, **Chiang Kai-shek** was involved in a military conflict with **Yan**

Xishan. Li Lisan, being in charge of the CCP Central Committee, believed that the Comintern's instructions were timely, and he drafted a resolution for the conference of the CCP Politburo titled "A New Revolutionary Tide and the Victory in One or Several Provinces." Accordingly, the CCP planned urban uprisings and assembled all **Red Army** units to attack major cities. It established a national operation committee and operation committees at various local levels. The Lisan Route was later denounced as a "Left deviation" and an example of opportunism, which caused great casualties when the Red Army attacked the cities. In addition, most of the CCP's secret organizations in urban areas were exposed and destroyed by the **Nationalist Party**.

LITTLE, ALICIA (ALICIA BEWICKE, 1845–1926). English feminist writer and early leader of the **Antifootbinding Movement** in China. Her full maiden name is Alicia Helen Neva Bewicke. Born in Madeira, England, in 1845, Little published her first novel, *Flirts and Flirts; or, A Season at Ryde*, at the age of 23. She then produced another nine novels, all focusing on the position of women in society. In 1886, at the age of 41, Alicia Bewicke married Archibald Little (1838–1907), a successful businessman and writer who published a number of nonfiction books on China, including *Through the Yangtse Gorges: Or Trade and Travel in Western China* (1888). Little arrived in China in 1887. The Littles first lived in **Chongqing** and later moved to Shanghai. Little studied Chinese and traveled extensively along the Yangtze River and in interior areas, visiting Chinese families, taking photographs, and beginning to write on China. In 1896, she published her best novel, *A Marriage in China*. Knowing the suffering of Chinese women, she founded the first Natural Foot Society in Shanghai in 1895 and was elected its president. The society published more than 30 pieces of literature, including edicts, proclamations, posters, poems, and folders of photographs, and even sent a petition to the **Manchu** emperor, vigorously campaigning for the abolition of the inhumane custom of **footbinding**. The Littles returned to Britain in 1907, and Archibald died in Cornwall the following year. Alicia moved to London, where she continued her active life until 31 July 1926, when she died at the age of 81. *See also* CHINESE FEMINISM.

LIU BOCHENG (1892–1986). Prominent military leader of the **Chinese Communist Party** (CCP) and one of 10 marshals of the

People's Liberation Army (PLA). Born in Kaixian, Sichuan Province, Liu received an early traditional education from his father, who was a Confucian scholar and traveling musician. In 1911, Liu graduated from middle school and immediately joined the Boy Scouts in support of the Xinhai Revolution. The next year, he enrolled in the Chongqing Military Academy. In 1914, Liu joined **Sun Yat-sen**'s Chinese **Revolutionary Party** and participated in the **National Protection War** against **Yuan Shikai**. Liu rose quickly in the army from company commander to regiment commander and then to chief of staff of a brigade. In March 1916, he lost his right eye in the Battle of Fengdu and was later nicknamed "one-eyed general." In 1923, during a war against the **warlord Wu Peifu**, Liu was appointed commander of the Eastern Route, during which his military talents gained wide recognition.

In May 1926, Liu joined the CCP and planned an uprising in Luzhou and Nanchong, but his troops were defeated by the warlords in Sichuan. On 1 August 1927, Liu joined the Communist-led **Nanchang Mutiny** as one of the leaders along with He Long, **Ye Ting**, **Zhou Enlai**, and **Zhu De**. The mutiny's poor preparations resulted in swift defeat, and Liu became a fugitive. In 1928, Liu was sent to the Soviet Union and studied at the Frunze Military Academy. That summer, he attended the Sixth CCP National Congress in Moscow and presented an additional report on Chinese military affairs. After graduating in 1930, Liu returned to China and served as a member of the CCP Central Military Committee and military secretary of the CCP Yangtze River Bureau. In January 1932, Liu traveled to the **Jiangxi Soviet** and was made chief of staff of the **Red Army**. Because he opposed the strategic plans of the **Comintern**'s adviser **Otto Braun**, Liu was dismissed from office. In October 1934, Braun's leadership against **Chiang Kai-shek**'s suppression campaigns led to the failure of the Red Army, and the Communists had to begin a strategic retreat known as the **Long March**.

During the Long March, Liu was appointed chief of the general staff of the Red Army and commander of the Central Column. At the famous **Zunyi Conference**, Liu strongly supported **Mao Zedong**, who resumed his command of the Red Army in January 1935. In May, Liu led the Red Army through regions controlled by ethnic minorities. During this time, he took oaths of brotherhood with a local chief of the *yi* ethnicity, ensuring the safe passage of the Red Army troops.

During the **Second Sino-Japanese War**, Liu was appointed divisional commander of the 129th Division of the **Eighth Route Army**. With **Peng Dehuai**, Liu commanded the **Hundred Regiments Campaign**, breaching the blockade by Japanese forces under **Yasuji Okamura**. In September 1943, Liu was called back to **Yan'an** to participate in the **Rectification Movement**. In criticizing **Wang Ming** and other political leaders supported by the Comintern, Liu showed his allegiance to Mao, and he was elected a member of the CCP Central Committee at the **Seventh National Congress** in 1945.

During the civil war, Liu served as the commander in chief of the Second Field Army, commanding various decisive battles and defeating the Nationalist Party's (GMD) troops. His troops, in coordination with **Lin Biao**'s Fourth Field Army, moved swiftly to encircle the GMD army in Southwest China and destroyed Chiang Kai-shek's last leading forces on the mainland, marking the end of the civil war. In December 1949, Liu was appointed chairman of the Southwest China Military and Administration Committee. After the establishment of the People's Republic of China, Liu served as vice-chairman of the CCP Central Military Committee and as president of the PLA Military Academy.

LIU KUNYI (1830–1902). Famous general of the **Hunan Army**. His courtesy name is Xiangzhuang. Born in Xinging, Hunan Province, Liu was a holder of the senior licentiate degree. He began government service under **Li Hongzhang** during the suppression of the **Taiping Rebellion**. Beginning in 1865, he successively served terms as governor of Jiangxi, governor of Guangdong and Guangxi, and governor of Jiangsu, Anhui, and Jiangxi. In 1891, he was appointed assistant to navy affairs in charge of military operations in the **First Sino-Japanese War** in 1894–1895. He opposed the deposition of the **Guangxu Emperor** in the aftermath of the failure of the **Hundred Days' Reform**. He was also active in the **Self-Strengthening Movement**, advocating applying Western methods for the rejuvenation of the Qing dynasty.

LIU MINGCHUAN (1836–1895). The first governor of Taiwan in the Qing dynasty. Born into a poor family in Hefei, Anhui Province, Liu joined **Li Hongzhang**'s Huai Army in 1857. Because of his efforts in the suppression of the **Taiping** and **Nian rebellions**, he was rapidly promoted and became a major general of the Huai army. The heavy workload and tough life in northwest China hurt his health and forced Liu to retire to his hometown at the age of 32. In 1884, as the war between China and France broke out, Liu was called back to defend Taiwan. He shattered the French landing attempt on Taiwan, forcing them to give up the attack. After the war, he was appointed the first governor of the newly established province of Taiwan. During his tenure as governor, he completed important projects, including strengthening fortifications, constructing railways, setting up the Taiwan Post, and opening modern schools. He encouraged people to move from the mainland to Taiwan and helped them to settle down and develop the local economy. Liu is regarded as a forerunner in developing modern capitalism in Taiwan.

LIU SHAOQI (1898–1969). A leader of the **Chinese Communist Party** (CCP) and president of the People's Republic of China (PRC) who was purged by **Mao Zedong** during the Cultural Revolution. Born into a rich peasant family in Ningxiang, Hunan Province, Liu joined the Socialist Youth League in 1920 and the CCP in 1921. That year, he traveled to Moscow and studied at the Communist University of the Toilers of the East. In 1922, Liu returned to China and began to work at the secretariat of the Chinese Labor Union. With **Li Lisan**, he led the general strike of the Anyuan Mine and Railroad Workers and then engaged in the **May Thirtieth Movement**, **Solidarity Strikes**, and Takeover of Foreign Concessions in Wuhan. In 1930, Liu attended the Fifth Congress of the International Red Laborers and was elected a member of the executive bureau. He was also elected an alternate member of the CCP Politburo and chairman of the **All-China Federation of Labor**. Liu participated in the **Long March** as the head of the Political Department of the Third Army Corps. He strongly supported Mao Zedong's leading position in the party and army.

In 1936, Liu was appointed secretary of the CCP's North China Bureau, and one of his major tasks was to lead secret party organizations and their activities in enemy-controlled areas, including the cities of Beijing and Tianjin. For many of the following years, Liu tried to increase the efficiency of the Communist operations in these "white areas" by developing the new strategy of "mobilizing masses, making party organization secret and small, accumulating forces, and sending new recruits to rural bases," for which he received singularly high praise at the **CCP Seventh Congress** in **Yan'an**. It was Liu who created the important concept of **Mao Zedong Thought** for sinicized Marxism; this made him a loyal ally of Mao Zedong and got him appointed one of the top five leaders of the CCP (five members of the party's secretariat). His booklets, *How to Be a Good Communist* and *On the Intra-Party Struggle*, were required readings for the CCP members in the **Rectification Movement**.

In Yan'an, Liu married his sixth wife, **Wang Guangmei**, daughter of a rich industrialist in Tianjin and a graduate of a Christian college. She bore him one son and three daughters. Liu had five other children from his previous marriage. Liu's leading position in the CCP was well established by the resolution of the party's Seventh Congress, "Resolution on Certain Questions in the History of Our Party," which affirmed his strategy in the "white areas" and his contribution to the theory of the Chinese Revolution. During the **Second Sino-Japanese War**, when cooperation between the **Nationalist Party** (GMD) and the CCP had deteriorated and the Communist **New Fourth Army** was destroyed by the GMD troops, Liu was sent to Jiangsu to rebuild the New Fourth Army, and he worked there as political commissar. He emphasized the necessity to mobilize mass support to fight the Japanese and anti-Communist forces.

By the end of the war, Liu had already become a towering figure in the party, and when Mao went to **Chongqing** for negotiations with **Chiang Kai-shek**, Liu functioned as acting chairman of the CCP. During the civil war, the CCP secretariat was divided into two, one led by Mao and the other headed by Liu. Liu's team, known as the Working Committee of the Central Committee, was in charge of the party's routines, especially **land reform**, in the Communist-controlled areas. Liu was elected vice president of the PRC in 1949 and president in 1959. Because of policy differences and inner-party power struggles, Liu was purged from the party during the Cultural Revolution. He was accused of being a renegade, traitor, and scab and was tortured to death on 12 November 1969. He was rehabilitated in February 1980 and a belated state funeral was held to commemorate his name.

LIU ZHIDAN (1903–1936). Prominent commander of the **Red Army** and one of the founders of the Communist Shanbei base. Born in Bao'an, Shanxi Province, Liu began his revolutionary career by organizing a student movement in nearby Shaanxi Province. Liu joined the Socialist Youth League in 1924 and the **Chinese Communist**

Party (CCP) in 1925. That year, he enrolled in the **Whampoa Military Academy** and, after graduating, became the party's representative in **Feng Yuxiang**'s Fourth Route Army. In April 1928, with Xie Zhichang and Tang Shu, Liu led the Weihua Uprising and founded the Northwest Revolutionary Army of Workers and Peasants. In 1932, this troop was designated the 26th Army with Liu as the commander. Liu established in Northwest China a solid revolutionary base consisting of 20 counties and thus providing the Central Red Army a foothold after it completed the **Long March** and arrived in Shanbei. In August 1935, Xu Haidong led the 25th Army to Shanbei and merged with Liu's troops to form the 15th Army Corps with Liu as the deputy commander. Two months later, Liu was dismissed from office and arrested by radical leaders in the "Wiping-Out Counterrevolutionaries Campaign." He was not released until the arrival of the Central Red Army. **Mao Zedong** announced his rehabilitation and appointed Liu army commander of the 28th Army again. In April 1936, Liu was ordered to cross the Yellow River for the Eastern Expedition. His troops were ambushed by the Nationalist army and Liu was killed in the battle at Sanjiao, Shanxi Province. To commemorate Liu Zhidan, the CCP Central Committee renamed Bao'an County Zhidan County.

LONDON KIDNAPPING. In the fall of 1896, **Sun Yat-sen** traveled to London. On 11 October, Sun was kidnapped by officials of the Qing legation to Great Britain. They placed Sun under house arrest and planned to ship him back to China. Sun's teacher, Dr. James Cantlie, found out about the kidnapping on 17 October and attempted to rescue Sun. Cantlie reported to the British police and contacted the British Ministry of Foreign Affairs. Before hearing anything from the British government, Cantlie released the story to the *Times* and hired a private detective to keep watch on the Chinese embassy. On 20 October 1896, the British press exposed this news and showed great concern over Sun's condition. The Qing embassy had to release Sun the next day. This event made Sun a well-known revolutionary leader in European countries.

LONG MARCH (OCTOBER 1934–OCTOBER 1935). Strategic retreat of the **Chinese Communist Party** (CCP) from the **Jiangxi Soviet** base to Northwest China, which traversed some 25,000 *li* (6,000 miles). The Long March resulted from the defeat of the **Red Army**

by **Chiang Kai-shek** in his fifth **Encirclement and Suppression Campaign**. On 10 October 1934, the CCP quickly decided to give up the Jiangxi Soviet on the eve of Chiang's final offensive against the Communist headquarters in Ruijin. The **First Front Red Army** in the Jiangxi Soviet base, known also as the Central Red Army, was the first troop to begin the Long March. The order to retreat was also sent to other Communist bases, from which the **Second** and **Fourth Front armies** set out shortly thereafter. When the Central Red Army of 86,000 men and the government employees and porters of 11,000 men embarked on the journey, they did not have a clear destination. Their leaders, including the **Comintern** military adviser **Otto Braun** and the Russian-trained leader **Bo Gu**, were eager to escape and had no strategic plan. Although they broke through several of Chiang's military blockades, the Red Army paid a great toll in human lives. After the Central Red Army crossed the Xiang River on 1 December, it had only 30,000 men left. Bo Gu and Otto Braun decided to lead the army to the Western Hunan to join the Second and Sixth Corps of Army, but Chiang discovered their intention and set up defenses to block their way. **Mao Zedong**, who was not a member of the Politburo, suggested giving up this plan and moving to the remote province of Guizhou. His suggestion was accepted. On New Year's Day 1935, the Red Army crossed the Wu River, and a week later it stormed the city of Zunyi, where the CCP held an enlarged Politburo conference. The **Zunyi Conference** criticized the impotent leadership of Bo Gu and Otto Braun and reshuffled the party's Politburo, breaking out of the party's reliance on instructions from Moscow and establishing Mao Zedong's position as the de facto supreme leader of the CCP. This conference is regarded as a landmark in Communist history.

Employing his **guerrilla warfare** skills, Mao maneuvered to avoid direct confrontation with Chiang's forces and led the Red Army to break out of the encirclements of local **warlord** troops. Then the Red Army penetrated into areas of ethnic minorities hostile to all **Han-Chinese** troops, tramped over snowy mountains, crossed swamps, and in the meantime, fought against Chiang's pursuing troops and local warlords. More than half the troops were lost when the First Front Army met the Fourth Front Army in Sichuan. Soon the Communist leaders were divided. Mao insisted on marching north while **Zhang Guotao** and the Fourth Front Army decided to move to southwest Sichuan. Mao's First Front Army reached the border area between

Gansu and Shaanxi and won the last battle against the Nationalist troops on 19 October 1935, ending the Long March at the town of Wuqi, Shaanxi Province.

About 100,000 men started the **Long March**, but only some 8,000 survivors ultimately made it. Also, not all the Red armies arrived at their destination at the same time. The Fourth Front Army under the command of Zhang Guotao took a different route. His troops were largely destroyed by Chiang's army or Muslim attacks. The remnants joined the Second Front Army led by He Long, who began the Long March on 19 November 1935. Driven by Chiang's troops even farther west, He Long's troops had to march to the south first and then north to meet Mao. On 22 October 1936, the three front armies of the Red Army finally assembled at Bao'an, Shaanxi Province. Afterward, a new revolutionary base was established in Northwest China with its headquarters at **Yan'an**.

LONG YUN (LUNG YUN, 1884–1962). Military commander of modern China. Born in Zhaotong, Yunnan, Long graduated from the Yunnan Military Academy and joined the local army in 1911. He rose quickly from junior officer to army commander. In 1928, he was appointed governor of Yunnan. He ruled the province for 17 years and was called the king of Yunnan. During the **Second Sino-Japanese War**, Long participated in the **Battle of Taierzhuang**. His troops defeated the Japanese but also suffered heavy casualties. Long established contacts with the **Chinese Communist Party** (CCP) and secretly joined the **China Democratic League**. In October 1945, Long was transferred to Nanjing. He was appointed president of the Military Consultative Yuan, a position with no real power. He fled to Hong Kong, where he met with CCP representatives and decided to cross over to Beijing. After 1949, Long held several positions, including vice-chairman of the National Defense Committee, vice-chairman of the Southwest China Military and Administrative Committee, and standing member of the **Chinese People's Political Consultative Conference**. Because he criticized the CCP's foreign policy, Long was persecuted in the Antirightist Campaign. Two years later he died in Beijing and was not rehabilitated until 18 years after his death.

LU BICHENG (1884–1943). Feminist journalist and pioneer of women's education in China. Born in Jinde, Anhui Province, into the family of a scholar-official, Lu was famous from childhood for her talent in painting and poetry writing. When her father died in 1895, his relatives attempted to grab her family property, but Lu brought a lawsuit on behalf of her mother and sisters. When this 11-year-old girl managed to win the case, she scared her fiancé, who believed that Lu was too strong to control and broke off the engagement. In 1903, Lu went to Tianjin to live with her uncle. Because her uncle forbade her to study at Western schools, Lu left him and worked for the local newspaper, *Dagong bao*, as an editor on probation. In September 1904, she served as the chief instructor of the Beiyang Women's School. Two years later, the school was renamed Beiyang Women's Normal School and Lu served as its first president. Between 1904 and 1908, Lu published many articles advocating women's education and emancipation; during that time, she also became a good friend of **Qiu Jin**, a female revolutionary. On 15 July 1907, she published an English-language article, "Biography of the Brave Revolutionary Woman—Qiu Jing," in American newspapers. Her anti–**Yuan Shikai** stance got her placed on the wanted list of Yuan's government.

In 1918, Lu traveled to the United States and studied English literature and arts at Columbia University. In the meantime, she worked as special correspondent of *Shibao* (Shanghai Times). After graduating in 1922, Lu visited Europe. She published travelogues, essays, and poems that were very appealing to Chinese readers. Nonetheless, all her works were written in classical Chinese, and Lu opposed vernacular writing. She engaged in the campaign for animal protection and became a vegetarian in Geneva. In 1940, Lu returned to China and moved to Hong Kong, where she became a devoted lay Buddhist and stopped her writing and social activities. She regretted that she did not find a male soul mate and thus stayed unmarried her whole life. In the spring of 1943, Lu died in Hong Kong at the age of 60. *See also* CHINESE FEMINISM.

LU DINGYI (1906–1996). Longtime head of the Propaganda Department of the **Chinese Communist Party** (CCP). Lu was born in Wuxi, Jiangsu Province, where his father was a small landlord and ran a textile factory. Lu participated in the **May Thirtieth Movement** in 1925 as a student at Shanghai Nanyang University (later known as Communication University). That same year, Lu joined the Socialist Youth League and the CCP. In 1927, he was made head of the Propaganda Department of the Youth League and chief editor of *Zhongguo qingnian* (China Youth). The next year, he traveled to Moscow as the Chinese **Communist Youth League** representative to the **Comintern**. Two years later, Lu returned to China but was dismissed from office by ultraleftist leaders. He participated in the **Long March** and was appointed head of the Propaganda Department of the **First Front Army** under **Lin Biao**'s leadership. Lu worked for the **Eighth Route Army** during the **Second Sino-Japanese War** and edited *Jiefan ribao* (Liberation Daily), the organ of the CCP in **Yan'an**. In 1945, Lu was elected a member of the CCP Central Committee and held the position of head of the Propaganda Department until the Cultural Revolution in 1966.

LU XIAOMAN (1903–1965). A legendary woman in modern China. Born into a rich family in Beijing, Lu was famous for her beauty, talent, and hospitality in the social circles of the upper class. Her father was director of the Tax Division of the Ministry of Finance and then resigned to become general manager of the Zhenhua Bank. Her first husband was Wang Geng, a promising air force officer who graduated from Princeton and West Point. But Lu did not love him. In 1926, Lu divorced Wang and married the famous poet **Xu Zhimo**. This romance made headlines in Beijing newspapers. After her second marriage, Lu's house became a center of social life for the city's celebrities because it was such an enjoyable experience to talk with Lu if the conversation touched on any topics of Chinese poetry, arts, music, or Western culture. Lu lived a very luxurious life, so her husband had to earn more to meet the extremely high expenses. Xu published more works, taught at three universities in Shanghai and Beijing, and flew back and forth between the two cities every week. Lu was surrounded by her worshippers, including a malicious friend who seduced Lu and addicted her to opium smoking. Her private life and new romances were always hot subjects for local papers. In 1931, when Xu died in a plane crash, Lu became the target of public criticism and many friends left her. Without other sources of income, she sold the copyrights of her husband's works to maintain her life. Besides being lonely and poor, she ruined her health with drugs. In 1956, the Communist mayor of Shanghai, Chen Yi, offered her a job as research fellow of the Shanghai Institute of Literature and Historical Studies. Lu tried to change her lifestyle, but she was still often frustrated by a lack of money. She translated several English novels, but they were not published. On 3 April 1965, Lu died in Shanghai leaving no last will.

LU XUN (1881–1936). The pen name of Zhou Shuren, the most influential Chinese writer of the 20th century, considered the founder of modern vernacular literature. He was born in Shaoxing, Zhejiang Province, into an impoverished noble family. Lu's grandfather held posts in the **Hanlin Academy**, but being accused of corruption, he was dismissed from office and arrested. Lu's father suffered from sickness and died early. Lu first studied at Jiangnan Naval Academy and the School of Mines and Railways, where he was exposed to Western learning. Both schools were established during the **Self-Strengthening Movement** to train new-style government officials. However, Lu's original interest was in medicine. In 1902, on a Qing government scholarship, Lu Xun left for Japan. He first attended the Kobun Gakuin, a preparatory language school for Chinese students attending Japanese universities. The next year, he was called home by his family to marry Zhu An, an illiterate gentry girl with bound feet who was picked by his mother. In 1904, Lu again traveled to Japan to study medicine. However, troubled by what he saw as the spiritual malaise of the Chinese people, Lu quit medical studies to pursue literature in an attempt to awaken his countrymen with his pen.

Lu became one of the leading vernacular writers in the **May Fourth Movement**. He worked with **Chen Duxiu** to edit the popular magazine *New Youth*, in which he published his first major vernacular short story, "Kuangren riji" ("A Madman's Diary") in May 1918. In it, he referred to **Confucianism** as cannibalism, and hoped the young generation would stop "eating people." Another of his well-known stories was "A Q zhengzhuan" ("The True Story of Ah Q"), which produced an image of the Chinese peasant who cheated himself and viewed personal failure as success up to his execution. Lu believed that self-deception and fear of the truth were part of the Chinese character and the reason for China's national weakness.

In 1927, he married his student Xu Guangping, who bore him a son. Lu Xun's major accomplishments were his numerous volumes of satirical essays. With his wry and incisive style, his societal commentary revealed grim realities and produced harsh criticism of social problems. Lu was thus regarded as an unbending fighter against injustice and a dauntless voice for the oppressed. In 1930, he published *Zhongguo xiaoshuo lueshi* (*A Concise History of Chinese Fiction*), a landmark piece of 20th-century Chinese literary criticism. He translated numerous European novels, especially works by the Russian writer Nikolai Gogol. He also introduced German expressionist prints to China and initiated the Creative Print Movement. Lu taught at various universities, edited several literature magazines, and was one of the founders of the **League of Left-Wing Writers**. Lu Xun died of tuberculosis in Shanghai on 19 October 1936. He never joined the Communist Party, but his radicalism helped bring many young people to support Communist thought. He was therefore hailed as "commander of China's cultural revolution" by **Mao Zedong**.

– M –

MA HUALONG (1810–1871). The leader of the **Muslim Rebellion** in northwest China (1863). Born in Lingzhou, Ningxia Province (today's Ningxia Hui Autonomous Region), Ma became the leader of the Jahriya school of Sufism in 1849. In 1863, he led the Hui people of 500 villages in a revolt. The Qing government sent General **Zuo Zongtang** to suppress the rebellion. In 1870, he defeated the rebels but did not catch Ma, so Zuo ordered his soldiers to kill all Hui people who helped Ma. To avoid further slaughter, Ma and his son decided to surrender. In line with his strategy of "pacification before elimination," Zuo first welcomed Ma's surrender, but months later he killed Ma by the method known as slicing. Zuo also made the decision to "not leave one alive" and massacred all 1,800 war prisoners.

MACAO. The oldest Portuguese colony in China. It is a peninsula of 28.6 sq. km, located to the west of the mouth of the Pearl River, 60 km east of **Hong Kong**. Portuguese traders settled in Macao in the 16th century, and merchants from other European countries who came afterward to do business with China also lived in Macao. For Western missionaries, Macao was the first working station and gateway to China. After the **Opium War**, many foreigners moved to Hong Kong and Macao began to decline. In 1887, Portugal and the Qing government signed the Sino-Portuguese Draft Minutes and the **Beijing Treaty**, in which China conferred on Portugal the right to "perpetual occupation and government of Macao." Macao's economy regained momentum, but the city's economy greatly depended on supply from the market in Hong Kong and the Pearl River Delta in China. For centuries, Macao has been known for its casino and tourist industry. The Portuguese government administered Macao until it was handed over to the People's Republic of China in 1999.

MAHJONG (MAJIANG). A classic Chinese game for four people. One of the myths of the origin of mahjong indicates that the game was invented by Confucius. The truth is that for thousands of years the Chinese have played mahjong for fun or for gambling. Mahjong is played with 72 tiles (sometimes it can also be played using cards). In the game, each player is given 13 to 16 tiles for a hand. Then she or he can draw a tile and discard one when her or his turn comes to make the best set of tiles or pairs in hand. Success in the game requires skill, strategy, calculation, and good luck. It was very popular during the imperial and republican periods, being a favorite pastime mainly for middle-class women but also for some men. When all gambling activities became outlawed, mahjong was banned in mainland China in 1949 but was revived after the Cultural Revolution in the late 1970s. Mahjong is also played in Hong Kong, Macao, Taiwan, and the United States.

MANCHU. A Tungusic people who originated in Manchuria. In 1644, they conquered Ming China and founded the Qing dynasty, which ruled China until collapsing in 1912. During their rule of China, the Manchu ethnicity was largely assimilated with the **Han** Chinese in terms of political participation and cultural integration. On one hand, Han Chinese adopted the Manchu hairstyle, formal dress, and most customs and traditions; on the other, the Manchu identified with Chinese culture, including its Confucian scholarship, institutions, language, arts, and social values. The Manchus were not allowed to marry Han Chinese until the constitutional reforms in 1910. The Manchus speak Chinese, but they have their own language, which is now almost extinct and spoken only by a few groups or in remote rural areas. *See also* BANNERMEN.

MANCHU ABDICATION. After the Wuchang Uprising on 10 October 1911, most southern provinces quickly proclaimed independence from the **Manchu** empire, but the Qings' **Beiyang Army** led by **Yuan Shikai** still retained control over North China. Yuan Shikai, as the last premier of the Qing government, urged the Qing court to abdicate to complete his deal with **Sun Yat-sen** and the revolutionaries in Nanjing. The six-year old **Xuantong Emperor** and his mother depended desperately on Yuan's support and were forced to agree with Yuan's arrangement. On 12 February 1912, Empress Dowager Longyu signed the Act of Abdication of the Emperor of the Great Qing on behalf of the boy emperor. On the same day, Yuan announced the formal abdication of the Xuantong Emperor (**Puyi**), indicating that the 268-year Qing rule had come to an end. To welcome the emperor's abdication, the Republicans offered the royal family the **Articles of Favorable Treatments**, allowing Puyi to retain his imperial title and the royal family to continue to stay in the Forbidden City, and requiring the Republican government to provide them with a ¥4 million annual stipend.

MANCHUKUO. A Japanese puppet regime in China's Manchuria established on 1 March 1932 with its capital at Xingjing (today's Changchun). Its territory included the provinces of Liaoning, Jilin, Heilongjiang, Eastern Inner Mongolia, and Northern Hebei. The head of state was **Puyi**, the dethroned last emperor of the Qing dynasty. On 1 March 1934, Manchukuo was renamed the Great Empire of Manchuria and Puyi became emperor. Soon after Manchukuo was founded, it was forced to sign a treaty with Japan. According to the treaty, Japan recognized Manchukuo and kept Japanese troops stationed in Manchukuo to defend Puyi's regime. The treaty also stipulated that Japan would administer the railways, navigation, seaports, and airlines in Manchuria, while Manchukuo had a responsibility to provide the Japanese troops with military supplies. In addition, Japanese citizens had the right to immigrate to Manchuria, explore its mines, and serve in Manchukuo's government. Puyi had no political power or personal freedom. In August 1945, as Japan surrendered, Manchukuo fell apart. On 19 August Puyi tried to flee to Japan, but he was captured by the Soviet Red Army at the airport. *See also* KWANTUNG ARMY.

MANCHURIA INCIDENT (MUKDEN INCIDENT). Military conflict that occurred on 18 September 1931 between the Japanese **Kwantung Army** and the Chinese troops in Manchuria, known also as the September Eighteenth Incident. As early as 31 May 1931, some Japanese junior officers of the Kwantung Army, including Colonel Itagaki Seishiro, Lieutenant Colonel Kanji Ishiwara, Colonel Kenji Doihara, and Major Takayoshi Tanaka, had planned the incident. On the afternoon of 18 September they arranged for sappers to place explosives near the tracks on the South Manchurian Railway. At around 10:20 p.m., the explosives blew up a small section of the track. The Japanese accused the Chinese troops of destroying the Japanese-owned railway and began to attack the Chinese troops at Beidaying, near Mukden. The fighting lasted less than one day and the Japanese occupied Mukden. The Manchuria Incident provided a pretext that would justify Japanese military invasion. Since the Nationalist government adhered to the nonresistance policy, **Zhang Xueliang**, the commander in chief in Manchuria, ordered his troops not to return fire. **Chiang Kai-shek** attempted to have the Japanese withdraw through diplomatic methods, but his hope proved to be an illusion. Although some Chinese local military forces put up resistance, Chiang's nonresistance policy and Zhang's retreat helped Japan conquer the whole of Manchuria by February 1932.

MANDATE OF HEAVEN (*TIANMING*). A traditional Chinese belief regarding the legitimacy of rulers. It argued that the power of an emperor came from heaven with a responsibility. If a ruler could not perform his duty, the ruled had the right to revolt and the Mandate of Heaven would transfer to those who would rule best. This concept was first recorded as the order of an ancient ruler, the Duke of Zhou (?–1095 BC), and was then developed into major Confucian teachings. The Chinese Mandate of Heaven is different from the Japanese notion of an unbroken line of the imperial house and the European notion of the divine right of kings, both of which granted the rulers unconditional legitimacy. The Mandate of Heaven was conditional on the performance of the ruler, serving as a justification for transference of power to new rulers who were not necessarily of noble birth. This political philosophy legitimated the overthrow of unjust rulers, leading to many dynastic replacements in Chinese history. *See also* CONFUCIANISM.

MAO DUN (1896–1981). The pen name of Shen Yanbin, a prominent writer of 20th-century China and minister of culture of the People's

Republic of China. He was born in Tongxiang, Zhejiang Province, into a scholar family. Mao's father obtained the *xiucai* degree in the Qing dynasty but was more interested in Western science. His mother was an educated lady who provided Mao's early education after the death of his father. In 1913, Mao Dun was enrolled at the preparatory school at **Peking University**. Due to the financial difficulties of his family, he gave up a college education and began to work at the **Commercial Press**. He began to translate English books into Chinese and then write his own novels. He became active in the **New Culture Movement** in 1919, editing *Fiction Monthly*, publishing creative works, and introducing new literary theories. In 1921, he joined the **Chinese Communist Party** (CCP) and took part in the **Northern Expedition** in 1926. After the **Nationalist Party** (GMD) broke with the CCP, he fled to Japan and lost connection with the Communists.

In 1927, he published his first novel, *Huanmie* (*Disillusion*, as the first volume of his trilogy *Eclipse*), and gradually gained popularity among urban readers. He established a close relation with **Lu Xun**, with whom he became a founding member of the **League of Left-Wing Writers**. Mao Dun established himself as the leading writer of modern China by publishing his masterpiece work, *Ziye* (*Midnight*) in 1933, unfolding a great picture of Chinese society, including worker strikes, peasant revolts, compradors' experiences, speculators in stock markets, and the success and frustration of the Chinese new middle class and their family lives. This work was referred to as "the first successful novel of realism" by the Communist leader **Qu Qiubai**. Mao also published short stories about silkworm raisers and small shopkeepers.

In the spring of 1939, Mao Dun left for Xinjiang and taught at the Xinjiang College, but he was forced to leave the next April. He traveled to **Yan'an** and lectured at the Lu Xun Institute of Arts. In the 1940s, he engaged in various cultural activities organized by the Communists or pro-Communist organizations. In May 1948, he coordinated with other writers, artists, and intellectuals to issue an open letter that called for support of the Communist **Political Consultative Conference**. After 1949, he was appointed president of the All-China Society of Writers and minister of culture.

MAO ZEDONG (1893–1976). The paramount leader of the Chinese Communist Revolution. One of the founders of the **Chinese Com-**

munist Party (CCP) and its supreme leader after January 1935. He formally held the position of chairman of the party from 1945 to his death in September 1976. Born in Shaoshan, Hunan Province, into a rich farmer family, Mao received a traditional Confucian education at his home village. In 1908, his family arranged his marriage to Luo Yixiu, a rural girl four years older than him. Mao never acknowledged this marriage. In 1912, he enrolled in the Hunan Provincial High School and then transferred to the Hunan First Normal School the next year. At this school, he met Professor Yang Changli and his daughter Yang Kaihui, who later became his second wife. Mao and his classmate Cai Hesheng established the *xinmin xuehui* (Society of New People). Most of its members later became Communists. Mao published two influential journals among the students, *Xiang River Review* and *New Hunan*. He led a student protest against the governor and was therefore compelled to flee Hunan. In April 1917, Mao wrote an article for *New Youth* edited by **Chen Duxiu** and thus established the first contact with Chen. Under Chen's influence, Mao began to study Marxism.

In 1918, Mao traveled with Yang Changli to Beijing. He worked as a librarian's assistant at **Peking University**. He audited some lectures by Chen Duxiu, **Hu Shih**, and Qian Xuantong, but the most influential figure for him was Professor **Li Dazhao**, the head of the university library and future cofounder of the CCP. Mao turned down an opportunity to study in France because he believed that China's problems could be resolved only by those who knew China better. In 1920, Mao returned to Hunan and organized a local Marxist studies group. In July 1921, he and He Shuheng went to Shanghai as the representatives of the Marxist studies groups in Hunan to participate in the **First Natio- nial Congress of the CCP**. At the suggestion of the representative of the Comintern, **Grigori Voitinsky**, the 13 delegates decided to found the Chinese Communist Party. In 1923, Mao was elected one of the five members of the CCP Central Committee. During the First **United Front**, Mao was also elected as an alternate executive member of the Central Committee of the **Nationalist Party** (GMD). Mao lectured at the Peasant Movement Training Institute in Guangzhou, and in 1927, he published "The Report on the Peasant Movement in Hunan," in which he, for the first time, put forward the concept of a violent "ru- ral revolution," referring to the peasants, the majority of the Chinese population, as the most dynamic revolutionary force.

In spring 1927, as the GMD-CCP alliance fell apart and **Chiang Kai-shek** tried to wipe out the Communists in Shanghai, forcing the CCP to leave the cities and retreat to the countryside. Mao believed that "political power grows out of the barrel of a gun," and launched the **Autumn Harvest Uprising** in Hunan. After the failure of the uprising, he led the remnants of his army to **Jinggangshan** Mountain in the border area between Hunan and Jiangxi. Mao began to build the **Red Army** in line with the principle "the Party commands the gun." His force was reinforced by survivors of the Nanchang Uprising led by **Zhu De**. In the border area, they established the Chinese Soviet Republic, known as the **Jiangxi Soviet**, and Mao was elected chairman of its government. In autumn 1928, Mao began to cohabit with He Zhizhen, though he did not divorce Yang Kaihui, whom he left in Changsha. Yang was later caught by the GMD and executed by the end of 1930. Mao developed his guerrilla war strategy, enabling the Red Army to defeat four campaigns of Chiang Kai-shek for elimination of the "Communist bandits." However, Mao's success was not complete. The Central Committee of the CCP was controlled by the **Twenty-eight Bolsheviks**, a group of CCP leaders trained in Moscow, who accused Mao of "protecting the interests of rich peasants" and "being an opportunist." Mao lost his command of the army. In 1934, Chiang Kai-shek won the final encirclement campaign and the Red Army had to retreat to Northwest China. This was known as the **Long March**.

In January 1935, during the Long March, the CCP Politburo held an extraordinary conference in **Zunyi**, at which Mao reassumed control over the Communist military forces. Although **Zhou Enlai** and **Zhang Wentian** held higher formal positions in the party, Mao became de facto supreme leader and had the final say on the party's affairs. His position was consolidated after their arrival at **Yan'an**, especially during the **Rectification Movement** (1942), which ended the political influence of the Twenty-eight Bolsheviks and promulgated Mao's personality cult. In 1937, Mao and Chiang came to an agreement to form the Second United Front to fight against Japan. The Red Army was reorganized into the **Eighth Route Army** and the **New Fourth Army** under Chiang Kai-shek's command. Mao, however, never gave up the CCP's control over the military forces. In addition, he criticized some Communist commanders who preferred "conventional war" to "mobile war," and ordered the Communist army to follow his **guerrilla strategy**. In 1945, the Seventh Party Congress elected Mao chairman of the party and pronounced that Mao's sinicization of Marxism, known as **Mao Zedong Thought**, was the only ideology meeting Chinese conditions and would lead the Chinese Revolution to victory. In Yan'an, as his third wife, He Zhizhen, went to Moscow for medical treatment, Mao married **Jiang Qing**, an actress from Shanghai.

At the end of World War II, the American ambassador **Patrick Hurley** escorted Mao to **Chongqing** for negotiations with Chiang Kai-shek. These negotiations resulted in a peace agreement. However, soon after this, civil war broke out. Again, Mao chose to give up the cities, including his headquarters in Yan'an, and retreated to the rural areas. Mao launched the **land reform** programs to win support from the peasants, while the financial crises in the postwar period incapacitated Chiang. Within three years, the **People's Liberation Army** under Mao's command defeated Chiang in several decisive battles and took over the whole of mainland China in 1949. Mao was elected chairman of the People's Republic of China. Mao resigned from this position in 1957 but kept his chairmanship of the CCP until his death.

MAO ZEDONG THOUGHT (MAOISM, BEFORE 1949). Sinicized Marxism-Leninism and the official doctrine of the **Chinese Communist Party** (CCP), derived from **Mao Zedong**'s teachings on the Chinese revolution and military strategy. Mao Zedong Thought as a theory emerged primarily from Mao's engagement in the Hunan peasant movement of the 1920s, in which Mao explored the revolutionary potential of poor farmers. Mao shared many Communist theories on **class struggle** and proletarian dictatorship. However, he rejected an urban-based revolution of orthodox Marxism-Leninism, addressing the peasantry as the main revolutionary force and emphasizing **land reform** and the creation of rural bases as the first vital step of the Chinese Revolution. Mao pointed out that the urgent task for Chinese Communists was to fight landlords, imperialism, and comprador bourgeoisie and that violent struggle was the only form for the Chinese Revolution. Mao established the principle of the unchallengeable control of the military force by the Communist Party. He created a series of strategies and tactics of **guerrilla warfare** and put forward a notion of the people's war in the CCP's fight with much stronger enemies, the Nationalist armies and the Japanese invaders. Mao argued that the Chinese native bourgeoisie might be friends of the revolution, and he worked out some tactics to win the support from the native bourgeoisie and urban residents. The dominant position of Mao and Mao Zedong Thought within the CCP was first established during the **Long March** and confirmed in the **Rectification Movement** of 1943 in **Yan'an**. Mao's contributions to the Chinese Communist Revolution before 1949 also included his guiding the CCP's transition from guerrilla to conventional warfare and from rural bases to capture of cities so as to finally take over the whole of China.

MAO ZETAN (1905–1935). Younger brother of **Mao Zedong** and junior leader of the **Chinese Communist Party** (CCP). Influenced by Mao Zedong, Zetan joined the Socialist Youth League at the age of 16 and the CCP at 18. He engaged in the labor movement in Hunan and then served as the secretary of the political department of the 4th Army of the **National Revolutionary Army** in 1925. Zetan participated in the **Nanchang Mutiny**. After the mutiny's failure, he was sent to **Jinggangshan** to contact his brother Mao Zedong, and thus helped **Zhu De** lead his troops to meet Mao. The following year, Zetan served as director of the political department of the 3rd Army, political commissar of the 5th Independent Division, and secretary of the Central Bureau of the **Jiangxi Soviet**. With **Deng Xiaoping** and other leaders, Zetan was persecuted in the campaign against the "Luoming Line." When the **Long March** set off in October 1924, he was ordered to stay behind and engage in **guerrilla warfare**. On 26 April 1935, his guerrilla team was ambushed by the **Nationalist Party** troops, and Zetan was killed in the battle at the age of 29.

MAOISM. *See* MAO ZEDONG THOUGHT.

MARCO POLO BRIDGE INCIDENT (1937). Known also as the July Seventh Incident. A military conflict between Chinese and Japanese troops. After occupying Manchuria, the Japanese moved to North China and approached the suburbs of Beiping. On 7 July 1937, the Japanese military was outside of the city of Beiping; they claimed that a soldier was missing and asked to enter the city to search for him. The Chinese administration refused the demand. At 8:00 p.m., the Japanese began to bomb the Marco Polo Bridge, which was located in the suburb south of Beiping, and attacked the Chinese defense troops. Colonel Ji Xingwen, commander of the 219th Regiment of the 29th Army, ordered his soldiers to fight back. Although the Chinese asked for a settlement, the Japanese intensified military operations and stormed Beiping and Tianjin. Soon after the incident, the **Chinese Communist Party** sent an open telegraph urging **Chiang Kai-shek** to declare war on Japan, and on 17 July, Chiang expressed his determination for resistance. The Marco Polo Bridge Incident was the beginning of the Chinese War against Japanese Aggression.

MARING, HENDRICUS (1883–1942). Originally named Hendricus Josephus Franciscus Marie Sneevliet but known in China by the pseudonym Hendricus Maring or just Maring. Born in Rotterdam, the Netherlands, Maring started working for the Dutch railways in 1900 and became a member of the Dutch Labor Party as well as the railway union in 1902. He went to the Dutch East Indies and took an active part in the struggle against Dutch colonial rule. After the Russian Revolution of 1917, Maring's influence grew among the local population and Dutch soldiers. This made the Dutch colonial authorities nervous and they expelled him from the Dutch East Indies in 1918. After his return to Europe, Maring joined the Dutch Communist Party and attended the second congress of the **Comintern** in Moscow. Maring's experiences and political views impressed the Comintern leader Vladimir Lenin, who decided to send him as a Comintern representative to China to help the formation of the **Chinese Communist Party** (CCP). Maring arrived in China in 1921 and worked with the leaders of the various Chinese **Communist groups**. This led to the **First National Congress of the CCP**, which was held in July 1921. Maring established personal contacts with **Sun Yat-sen** and tried to persuade him to cooperate with the Communists. In 1923, Maring was recalled to Moscow and then returned to the Netherlands the next year. He established his own party, the Revolutionair Socialistische Partij. During World War II, Maring started his resistance activities, engaging in producing propaganda for socialism and opposing the German occupation of the Netherlands. Maring was arrested and executed by the Nazis on 12 April 1942.

MARRIAGE LAW OF THE CHINESE SOVIET REPUBLIC (1931). The first marriage law issued by the **Chinese Communist Party** (CCP), announced on 26 November 1931. Its main regulations included freedom of marriage and the abolition of family-arranged, forced, and mercenary marriages; abolition of child brides; monogamy; freedom of divorce; protection of the marriages of **Red Army** soldiers; and protection of the rights of women and children. The law's most important article concerned the rights of divorced women. After a divorce, the man was responsible for bringing up any children (to the age of 16); family property should be divided between the man and woman, while family debts were the man's responsibility; and the man should provide for the woman a living stipend until she remarried. These regulations were even more favorable for women than the marriage law the Communists issued in the 1950s.

MARSHALL MISSION. A U.S. mediation mission led by George Marshall at the end of World War II. After the Japanese surrendered, the **Nationalist Party** (GMD) and the **Communist Party** (CCP) were immediately involved in conflicts. The American China policy was to assist the Nationalist government in restoring its authority but not to involve the United States in a military intervention. U.S. president Harry Truman decided to send General George C. Marshall to China as presidential ambassador for mediation between the two sides. Marshall arrived in China in mid-December 1945. His immediate objects were a cease-fire between the GMD and CCP; a **Political Consultative Conference** to discuss a coalition government; and the integration of the GMD and CCP forces into a unified national army. At first, Marshall made encouraging progress. Both the GMD and CCP endorsed a cease-fire; the Political Consultative Conference was convened and there was also agreement on military cuts and reorganization. However, neither the GMD nor the CCP trusted the other, and they did not stop preparations for further military conflict. Fighting in Manchuria became even more bitter, marking the prologue of the civil war. All agreements, especially the resolution of the Political Consultative Conference, thus remained unrealistic dreams. In July 1946, the Nationalist government unilaterally called the **National Assembly** while the CCP and the **China Democratic League** proclaimed their boycott. **Chiang Kai-shek** told Marshall that he was ready to wipe out the CCP in six months, and **Mao Zedong** called for a war of self-defense. Marshall realized that his mission had become impossible, but he continued to work in China until President Truman recalled him on 6 January 1947.

MARTIN, WILLIAM ALEXANDER PARSONS, DD, LLD (1827–1916). American Presbyterian missionary in China known by his Chinese name, Ding Wei-liang. Born into a Christian family in Indiana, Martin graduated from Indiana State University in 1846 and studied theology at the Presbyterian Seminary in New Albany, Indiana. He obtained his DD degree from Lafayette College (1860) and LLD from the City University of New York (1870). He was sent by the Foreign Mission Board to China and arrived in Ningbo in 1850. Martin was hired by the American minister William B. Reed as an interpreter in negotiating the **Treaty of Tianjin** in 1858, and he contributed to the drafting of the sections on a fixed tariff rate and opening more ports to foreign trade. In 1862, he began to translate Henry Wheaton's *Elements of International Law*. He saw it as a necessary book for the Chinese because it was required reading for the British civil service exam. Before Martin finished the translation, **Anson Burlingame** introduced some of the chapters to the **Zongli Yamen**. **Prince Gong** admired Martin's work and sent him four assistants to finish the job. Martin served as the head instructor at the **Tongwenguan** (Beijing foreign-language school) and **Peking University**. He died at home in Beijing and was buried in a private cemetery in a suburb of the city.

MASS LINE. A basic revolutionary strategy of the **Chinese Communist Party** (CCP), developed by **Mao Zedong** in the **Yan'an** years. Mao summarized it as "from the masses, to the masses." It refuses a top-down administrative approach but advocates a process in which a revolutionary leader should first investigate the conditions of people, learn about and participate in their struggles, gather ideas from the masses, and work out a plan of action based on the ideas and concerns of the people. Mao criticized Joseph Stalin's ignorance of the strength and creative ability of the peasantry and the masses of people. Mao also emphasized giving heed to the daily needs and will of the masses before educating them to raise their political consciousness. The mass line proved to be an effective and democratic method for mobilizing people in the **Second Sino-Japanese War** and the Chinese civil war.

MAY FOURTH MOVEMENT (1919). An anti-imperialist political and cultural movement, beginning with a student demonstration in

Beijing on 4 May 1919. During World War I, China entered the war on the side of the Allied Triple Entente. It was expected that the German concessions, such as Shandong, would be returned to China after the war ended. The **Paris Peace Conference** in 1919, however, proposed to grant Shandong Province to Japan. On the afternoon of 4 May, over 3,000 students of **Peking University** and 13 other schools gathered together in **Tiananmen Square** and held a demonstration in protest of the resolution of the Paris conference and urged the government to punish those Chinese diplomats who were willing to accept the resolution. Their slogans included "Struggle for the sovereignty externally, get rid of the national traitors at home," "Do away with the **Twenty-one Demands**," and "Don't sign the Treaty of Versailles." They demanded punishment for three pro-Japan diplomats, Cao Rulin, Zhang Zongxiang, and Lu Zongyu. The enraged students marched to Cao Rulin's residence and burned down his house. The **Beijing government** arrested 30 students on the spot. The president of Peking University, **Cai Yuanpei**, and many professors took action to rescue the students.

The government, however, ordered the suppression of the student movement. This sparked student demonstrations all over the country. After 5 June, workers and businessmen first in Shanghai and then in Nanjing, Tianjin, Wuhan, Hanzhou, and many other cities also went on strike. The Beijing government was shocked. It released all the students, "accepted" the resignation of the three pro-Japan diplomats, and ordered the Chinese delegation not to sign the Versailles Treaty. The May Fourth Movement made the Chinese intellectuals see that China's crises had been rooted in its cultural tradition. The student protest and workers' strikes marked the upsurge of Chinese nationalism and also promoted an intellectual revolution, the **New Culture Movement**.

MAY THIRTIETH MOVEMENT (1925). Labor movement led by the Communists first in Shanghai and then throughout the country. On 14 May 1925, a Japanese boss suddenly closed his textile mill in Shanghai and refused to pay the workers' salaries. A worker named Gu Zhenghong, who was a secret member of the **Chinese Communist Party** (CCP), led workers to rush into the factory and argue with the owner. The owner ordered his security officers to open fire, killing Gu and wounding several workers. This slaughter provoked a strike in 11 Japanese textile mills. On 30 May, when more than 2,000 students went to the **foreign concession** and held a demonstration, the police arrested a hundred of them. As urban dwellers came to rescue the students, the Shanghai municipal policemen opened fire, killing a dozen demonstrators and wounding many more. In protest, the Shanghai General Trade Union was established with **Li Lisan** as president, and a general strike was staged. Consequently, 200,000 workers and all merchants in the foreign concession participated in this movement. Beijing, Tianjin, Nanjing, Hankou, Changsha, and other cities held similar demonstrations to support Shanghai. The strikes lasted for three months.

MCCARTNEY MISSION (1793). British mission of 84 members headed by Lord McCartney and dispatched on 26 September 1792 to visit China. The mission arrived in Canton on 19 June 1793 and then went to Beijing to congratulate the **Qianlong Emperor** on his birthday. Before meeting the emperor, there was a dispute between the mission and the Chinese officials about whether the British should follow the Chinese ritual, including performing the kowtow in front of the emperor. Finally, a compromise was made that McCartney would fall on one knee during the audience as he would do for his own king. He would also be exempt from the English custom of kissing the emperor's hand. McCartney presented to the Qianlong Emperor 590 exquisite gifts indicating the high level of British science and technology. In return, the emperor bestowed on him 3,000 pieces of gifts, including silk, porcelain, and jade articles. The most impressive one was a whitish jade scepter that was about a foot and a half long and symbolized peace and prosperity, with a good wish to the British king.

The imperial audience seemed to please both sides, but the substantial issue remained unsolved. The British mission required the Qing government to allow a British legation in Beijing; to open Zhoushan, Ningbo, and Tianjin as trading ports; to allow English traders a warehouse in Peking; to assign a small unfortified island near Zhoushan for the residence of English traders and the storage of goods; to assign a small place near Canton for the same use; to abolish the transit dues between Macao and Canton or reduce them to the tariff of 1782; and to make the imperial tariff and regulations available to English traders. The Qianlong Emperor believed that China did not need any European manufactured goods, so he saw no benefit in developing trading relations with the British and still less in having their diplomats in the capital. He refused all of McCartney's demands, and the mission was a complete diplomatic failure.

MCMAHON LINE. A demarcation line between India and China's Tibet drawn on a map attached to the **Simla Convention**. It was named after Sir Henry McMahon, foreign secretary for British India and the chief British negotiator of the convention. The convention was signed by Great Britain and Tibet in 1914 at Simla. Although the Chinese delegation attended the negotiation, it refused to sign the treaty or accept the McMahon Line. The McMahon Line extends along the crest of the Himalayas for 550 miles from Bhutan in the west to the great bend of the Brahmaputra River in the east. India refers to the line as a legal national border, while Chinese maps show some 56,000 sq. mi. of territory south of the line as Chinese. In 1915, the British recognized Tibet as "under Chinese suzerainty" and admitted that "the Simla convention has not been signed by the Chinese government and is, therefore, for present invalid." The McMahon Line was forgotten until 1937, when the Survey of India (India's central map agency) published a map showing the McMahon Line as the official boundary. The boundary dispute between New Deli and Beijing provoked the Sino-Indian War of 1962–1963.

MEMORIAL. Formal report of a government official to the emperor. The memorials were statements of the country's political and economic situation, petitions, impeachments of government officials, or suggestions on state policy or personnel appointments. They were usually submitted through the imperial bureaucracy, and some of them would be discussed in the regular morning meeting between the emperor and his ministers.

MEMORIAL ARCHWAY OF HONORABLE WOMEN (*ZHENJIE PAIFANG*). This was a Confucian practice wherein a woman who committed suicide after her husband's death or lived as a widow for more than 20 years was honored by the government and community. In the era of the **Daoguang Emperor**, the Board of Rites worked out sophisticated rules rewarding women. First, local scholars had to write a detailed report of the woman's deeds and send them to the county government; then the county government had to submit a formal report with request to the Board of Rites. The Board of Rites would review each case, inform the departments concerned, and offer 30 taels of silver to erect a memorial archway for the woman. It was also possible to build an archway for a group of honorable women. In 1827, the Board of Rites gave permission to two counties in Jiangsu Province, Wujin and Yanghu, to build an archway for 3,018 local honorable women with all their names carved on the stone.

MENG BUYU (1867–1932). An early advocate of women's emancipation. Born into a merchant family in Qixian, Shanxi Province, Meng began to work as an apprentice in a small firm. Soon he quit this business career and turned to the study of the Chinese classics. In 1894, he obtained the *juren* degree and began to advocate for the abolition of the practice of **footbinding**. In 1903, he created in Shanxi a provincial women's school that admitted only girls with natural feet. He asked his wife to release her feet and serve as the school's instructor. His daughter, who never bound her feet, became the first student of the school. Meng also organized the Provincial Association for Women's Natural Feet of Shanxi and served as its president. Despite opposition and criticism from conservative people, he insisted on promoting women's education. He established several elementary and high schools exclusively for female students. He used his own money and did fund-raising to send rural girls to high schools and colleges in cities. His efforts were finally recognized by the Republican government. Meng was referred to as a pioneer in women's education. A good scholar, he also published several books on astronomy and mathematics. In 1932, Meng died in Beijing at the age of 66. *See also* CHINESE FEMINISM.

MILLARD'S REVIEW OF THE FAR EAST WEEKLY. The oldest American weekly in the Far East. Founded in June 1917 in Shanghai by a senior American journalist, Thomas Millard, who was a correspondent for the *New York Herald*. The purpose of the publication was to provide people in the United States with reports on what was going on in the Far East. Millard was against British imperialism and sympathized with China's revolution. *Millard's Review of the Far East Weekly* was therefore the only Western publication opposing foreign intervention of China's **Northern Expedition** against **warlordism** in 1927. The next year, John Benjamin Powell succeeded Millard to serve as the publication's editor in chief; he followed Millard's policy. After the Japanese bombed Pearl Harbor, Powell was arrested and put into a camp of war prisoners by the Japanese. *Millard's Review* was also closed. After the Japanese surrendered, Powell was released and his son J.W. Powell resumed the publication of *Millard's Review* in October 1945 in Shanghai. *Millard's Review* was the only Western magazine allowed to be published after the Communists took over China. In September 1950, this weekly changed to a monthly. *Millard's Review* tried to continue Millard's tradition of speaking without reservation. The publication was forced to close in June 1953.

MINBAO. *See PEOPLE'S JOURNAL.*

MO XIONG (1891–1980). Born in Yingde, Guangdong Province, Mo joined the **Tongmenghui** at the age of 16 and became a close friend and loyal follower of **Sun Yat-sen**. Mo participated in the **National Protection War** and the **Northern Expedition** and was promoted to divisional commander. Disliking **Chiang Kai-shek**, Mo was involved in **Zhang Fakui**'s campaign against Chiang. Because of the failure of the campaign, Mo was dismissed from office. With the help of **T. V. Soong**, Mo got a job in the Ministry of Finance in Shanghai, where he met Liu Yafo, a member of the **Chinese Communist Party** (CCP). Mo wanted to join the Communist Party, but Li Kenong convinced Mo that he would be more valuable to the party by remaining a non-Communist. On the recommendation of Chiang's secretary-general Yan Yongtai, Mo was appointed administrator and commander in chief of the De'an District, Jiangxi Province. In 1934, Chiang launched the fifth **Encirclement and Suppression Campaign** against Communists and called a military meeting in Mo's district. As Chiang's major generals came to discuss the operation plan named Iron Bucket Plan, Mo managed to obtain a copy. Mo wasted no time in forwarding the document to Communist leaders, informing them of the looming danger and helping them make an urgent decision to abandon the Jiangxi revolutionary base and start the **Long March** in a hurry. **Mao Zedong** said that it was Mo Xiong who saved the Chinese Communist Party and the Chinese revolution. In 1949, Mo was appointed vice-chairman of the Guangdong Provincial Political Consultative Conference.

MODERN TEXT MOVEMENT. A cultural campaign initiated by **Kang Youwei** before his constitutional reforms. "Modern text" referred to the classics of the Qin (221–206 BC) and Han (206 BC–AD 220) periods as opposed to the ancient text (before Qin). For a long time, the ancient text scholars dominated the learned world. In 1891, Kang published his book *A Study of the Gorged Classics of the Qin Period*, in which he sharply criticized the ancient texts, stimulated a spirit of doubt, and introduced new concepts to reappraise traditional scholarship. This work marked the beginning of the Modern Text Movement, which established Kang as the leader of scholars of the new generation.

MORRISON, ROBERT (1782–1834). The first Protestant missionary in China. Morrison was born into a family of farming laborers in Bullers Green, near Morpeth, Northumberland. His parents were both active members of the Scottish Presbyterian Church. He married Mary Morton in 1809 and had three children with her. After Mary died in 1821, Morrison married Eliza Armstrong, who bore him five more children. Morrison joined the Presbyterian Church at the age of 16. To become a missionary, he started learning Latin, Greek, and Hebrew in private. In 1803, he entered George Collison's Hoxton Academy in London to study theology, astronomy, and Chinese. In January 1807, he became a minister in London and left for China in May of that year. Because no ship was willing to take him to China, he had to go to America first and then to Macao. This journey took eight months. He was not allowed to do missionary work in Guangzhou, and he was only able to gain legitimate residency as a Chinese translator for the **British East India Company**. Even so, his wife was not allowed to stay with him in Guangzhou. Despite the ban of Christian books by the Qing government, Morrison published his translation of the Bible in 1813.

Eleven years later, he worked with his assistant, William Milne, to translate and publish a second Chinese version of the Bible. He also compiled the *Chinese Dictionary* and *Introduction to Chinese Grammar* for use by Westerners. In 1820, Mary brought their younger daughter to China for a family reunion. Unfortunately, she contracted malaria and died. Afterward, since the Chinese government continued to prohibit materials relating to Christianity, Morrison and Milne moved to Malacca, Malaya, where they established a printing house and a school named the Anglo-Chinese College. In 1843, the school was moved to Hong Kong and continues to operate today. In 1824, Morrison returned to Great Britain for a vacation. Impressed by his talks on his missionary work in China, his countrymen received him warmly; the British king, George IV, also met with him. Two years later, Morrison brought his new wife to China. During his 27 years of service in China, he published books on Christian theology and Chinese history. He converted only 10 Chinese to Christianity, but every one of them was a devoted Christian, including **Liang Fa**, the first Chinese Protestant minister and evangelist. Morrison died in Guangzhou at the age of 52; his influence became even greater among the Chinese after his death.

MOSCOW SUN YAT-SEN UNIVERSITY. Officially named the Communist Sun Yat-sen University of the Toilers of China, this school was founded in 1925 by the Soviet Union and was devoted to the training of revolutionary cadres for both the **Chinese Communist Party** (CCP) and the **Nationalist Party** (GMD). Many CCP and GMD leaders, including **Wang Ming, Bo Gu, Deng Xiaoping**, and **Chiang Ching-kuo**, studied at this university. At the 66th session of the Political Conference of the GMD Central Committee in October 1925, the Soviet adviser **Mikhail Borodin** announced the establishment of Moscow Sun Yat-sen University and began to recruit Chinese students. All the Chinese students admitted were given Russian names and had their personal files classified. The university offered a two-year program teaching students basic theories of Marxism and Leninism, methods of mass mobilization, and military strategies. In addition to regular courses, the Russian leaders, including Joseph Stalin and Leon Trotsky, were invited to give lectures on campus. In 1927, after the CCP-GMD split, most GMD students withdrew from the program, but a few, such as Chiang Ching-kuo, were detained in Russia as hostages. There were factional struggles among the CCP students: one group was associated with Stalin and Pavel Mif, the university president, and was known as 28-and-a-half pure Bolsheviks; another group was labeled the Trotskyites. The Moscow Sun Yat-sen University closed in 1930. *See also* RETURNED BOLSHEVIKS; TWENTY-EIGHT BOLSHEVIKS.

MOST FAVORED NATION (MFN). This clause is normal in trade relations within international law but had a different meaning for China in the 19th century. The MFN was first conferred on Great Britain in 1843 by the **Treaty of Bogue**, which stipulated that China would grant to Great Britain whatever privileges might be conceded to other powers. In later years, the other European countries, the United States, and Japan also obtained the MFN status through their treaties with China. This MFN was unilateral and extended beyond trading and commercial matters, since the privileges that all the Western powers automatically gained included **extraterritoriality, foreign concessions**, navigation on Chinese interior rivers, management of Chinese customs, and so forth.

"MOUNTAIN STRONGHOLD" MENTALITY (*SHANTOU ZHUYI*). A type of factionalism within the **Chinese Communist Party** (CCP). "Mountain stronghold" mentality was a tendency to form cliques within the party and army. This arose mainly out of the circumstances of the protracted guerrilla war in which rural revolutionary bases were scattered and cut off from each other. Most of these bases were first established in mountain regions. Each tended to regard itself as a compact unit, like a single mountain stronghold. The members of each mountain stronghold trusted, protected, and promoted each other. In the meantime, they discriminated against those from other guerrilla teams or other revolutionary bases.

MR. DEMOCRACY, MR. SCIENCE. A slogan during the **May Fourth Movement** and the **New Culture Movement**, advocating learning Western science and Western ideas of democracy. It was a common belief of the Chinese intellectuals that only the Western advanced science and democratic systems could save China. The introduction of Western science and democracy provoked a sharp criticism of Chinese traditions. In 1918, the leader of the New Culture Movement, **Chen Duxiu**, pointed out that "to stand for Mr. Democracy and Mr. Science, the Chinese people had to oppose Confucian values, laws, customs, chastity, ethics, and institutions; to support Mr. Democracy and Mr. Science, the Chinese had to cast off old art and religion and abandon the cult of **Chinese quintessence**." In the New Culture Movement, Mr. Democracy and Mr. Science served as a synonym of progress, civilization, and social revolution.

MUKDEN INCIDENT. Known also as the September Eighteenth Incident and the **Manchuria Incident.**

MUSLIM REBELLION (DUNGAN REVOLT, 1862–1877). A group of Chinese Muslims living in northwest China, known as the Hui people, revolted in 1862 in response to the **Taiping rebels** who approached Shaanxi Province. The Hui people staged several uprisings against the Qing government and local **Han** landlords, but they lacked a central leadership and coordination. The three strongest groups of the Muslim rebels were led by **Ma Hualong** in southern Ningxia, Ma Wenyi in eastern Qinghai, and Ma Wenlu in western Gangsu. The Qing government sent General **Zuo Zongtang** to quell these rebellions. In 1871, Ma Hualong was defeated. To avoid further slaughter, Ma and his son decided to surrender. In line with his strategy of "pacification before elimination," Zuo first accepted Ma's surrender but months later ordered Ma's execution by slicing. Zuo also decided "not to leave one alive" and massacred all 1,800 war prisoners. Zuo led his troops westward along the caravan trade route to the city of Lanzhou, where he built an arsenal and planted more grain to feed his armies. Zuo destroyed Ma Wenyi's troops the next year and stormed the capital of Qinghai—the city of Xining—after bloody fighting. In 1873, the leader of the last group of rebels, Ma Wenlu, surrendered but was also executed by Zuo. Only a small number managed to flee to Xinjiang. The Muslim Rebellion in northwest China lasted for 15 years and was brought to an end in 1877.

– N –

NANCHANG MUTINY (NANCHANG UPRISING, 1927). The Nanchang Mutiny was launched by the **Chinese Communist Party** (CCP) on 1 August 1927. After **Chiang Kai-shek** and **Wang Jingwei** purged the Communists from the **Nationalist Party** (GMD) in Shanghai and Wuhan, the CCP Central Committee decided to stage a serious counteroffensive. The leaders of the Nanchang Mutiny included He Long (army commander of the 20th Army), **Ye Ting** (deputy army commander of the 11th Army), **Zhu De** (head of the police bureau in Nanchang), and the representative of the CCP Central Committee **Zhou Enlai**, who served as the chairman of the rebels' revolutionary committee. The insurgents first achieved quick success in disarming local troops, but they were soon defeated by GMD reinforcements commanded by **Zhang Fakui** and Zhu Peide. Three days later, they were forced to retreat and move to Guangdong. On the way to the south, over one-third of the original 20,000 troops were lost to illness and desertion. A few survivors managed to arrive at **Jinggangshan**, where they met **Mao Zedong**'s guerrillas and formed the 4th Army of the **Red Army** in April 1928. The Nanchang Mutiny is regarded as the beginning of the armed struggle of the Chinese Communist Revolution, and 1 August is celebrated as Army Day in the People's Republic of China.

NANJING, TREATY OF (1842). Treaty between China and Great Britain that ended the **Opium War**. The Treaty of Nanjing consisted of 13 articles and was signed on 29 August 1842. The main points included an indemnity of 21 million taels to Britain; the abolition of the **Canton System**; opening five ports to trade and residence of British merchants, consuls, and their families—namely, Guangzhou, Fuzhou, Amoy, Ningbo, and Shanghai; cession of **Hong Kong** island; and a fixed tariff to be set shortly thereafter. This treaty did not mention the opium trade, but in fact, it implied the British freedom to smuggle opium. In the follow-up supplementary **Treaty of Bogue**, Great Britain was also granted the **most favored nation** status, meaning the British would obtain whatever privileges China might concede to other powers in the years to come. The treaty was approved by the Daoquang Emperor on 15 September and Queen Victoria on 28 December 1842. The treaty marked the beginning of the so-called unequal treaty system and Western aggression against China.

NANJING MASSACRE. Also known as the Rape of Nanking. An infamous war crime committed by the Japanese military in and around Nanjing during World War II. The massacre lasted more than 40 days, from the middle of December 1937 to early February 1938. After the Japanese troops stormed the Chinese capital of Nanjing on 13 December 1937, they began killing civilians under the order of General Iwane Matsui and Lieutenant General Hisao Tani. The atrocities included rape, looting, arson, and the execution of war prisoners. The slaughter began with shooting the war prisoners to the "clean street" campaign. Estimates of the number killed range from 100,000 to 300,000, and 20,000 women were raped, their ages ranging from infants to the elderly (as old as 80). In addition, one-third of the houses in the city were destroyed. In November 1948, the International Military Tribunal for the Far East completed its review of the case and charged leaders of the massacre with Class A war crimes. *See also* INTERNATIONAL MILITARY TRIBUNAL FOR THE FAR EAST.

NANYANG BROTHERS TOBACCO COMPANY. The largest tobacco company run by overseas Chinese in the 20th century. It was opened by the Jian brothers (Jian Zhaonan and Jian Yujie) in 1905 but had to close shortly thereafter because of competition from the Anglo-American Tobacco Company. Four years later, with financial support from their uncle, the two brothers resumed efforts by creating the famous brands Flying Horse, Double Happiness, and White Pigeon, and using slogans like "Only Chinese cigar for Chinese," and "No American cigar" in the advertisements. The tactics proved successful, and the company won a large market, especially among lower-class Chinese. In 1919, it became a shareholding company with a capital of HK$15 million. The company also set up factories and wholesale companies in some coastal cities and in Hong Kong. Although its cigarettes continued to be welcomed by a considerable number of Chinese consumers, the company went into debt after 1927. Ten years later, it sold 50 percent of its shares at a low price to **T. V. Soong**, and the Jian brothers lost control of the business. In 1949, the company was moved to Taiwan by the Soong family. The Nanyang Brothers Tobacco Company became a joint state-private enterprise in 1951.

NAPIER MISSION (1834). On 10 December 1833, Lord William John Napier was appointed chief superintendent of British trade in China. The British government had placed the **British East India Company** in charge of dealing with China as regarded trade and other diplomatic relations. In September 1834, Lord Napier was sent to China in an attempt to establish good and friendly relations with China and to look into the possibility of extending the Sino-British trade beyond Canton. Napier was instructed to adjudicate cases involving British subjects in China but not to offend the Chinese and not to use military force unless absolutely necessary. Napier ignored the Chinese demand that all foreigners wait in Macao for permission to enter Canton; instead he went straight to the city and moved into the British factory. He did not contact local *co-hong* merchants but addressed the governor-general directly, and he did not use the humble word "petition" in his letter. His letter was rejected and Napier was ordered to leave Canton. Taking this as insult, Napier accused the governor-general of ignorance and obstinacy, stating that although his government did not want war, he was perfectly prepared for it. The Qing government withdrew all Chinese employees from the British factory, cut off its food supply, and stopped all business with the British. Napier asked for military support from the British government. The Chinese troops surrounded the factory and declared that Napier was the culprit, and that his departure would reopen trade. Some British merchants began to ask Napier to leave. Feeling betrayed by his countrymen, Napier was frustrated and left for Macao on 11 September 1834. He fell ill and died there a month later.

NATIONAL ASSEMBLY. A parliamentary body that existed in the history of the Republic of China. After the 1911 Revolution, a general election yielded the first bicameral parliament in 1913. However, less than 1 percent of the Chinese people participated in this election due to gender, property, tax, residential, and literacy requirements. During the era of **warlordism** (1916–1927), the parliament was resurrected and disbanded more than once as different warlords in Beijing attempted to manipulate the legislature. In 1937, a parliament was formally reestablished and renamed the National Assembly. In light of the Election Law and the Government Organization Regulations of the Republic of China, the National Assembly shared legislative power with the **Legislative Yuan**. The Legislative Yuan deliberated on laws and the budget, paid amnesty, declared war, and signed treaties of peace, while the National Assembly had the power to amend the constitution and formally elect the president and vice president of the Republic of China. In 1949, when the Nationalist government fled to Taiwan, the National Assembly was abolished in mainland China. Although it continued to exist for five more decades in Taiwan, its parliamentary powers were totally transferred to the Legislative Yuan in 2000.

NATIONAL CITY BANK OF NEW YORK. The first American bank operating in China. The bank was founded in 1902 in Shanghai and was nicknamed *"Huaqi* Bank." *Huaqi* literally means a colorful flag, implying the American national flag. Many Chinese government officials and industrialists, such as **T. V. Soong** and Rong Zhongjing, were its customers. Besides the regular banking business for American and Chinese merchants and enterprises, it was also authorized to issue paper currency, which circulated throughout China, except in a few cities. In the city of Harbin, for example, the Chinese Chamber of Commerce criticized the American control over China's monetary affairs and called on urban residents to refuse the bills issued by the City Bank. Circulation of this currency, however, continued in many other cities until 1934.

NATIONAL CONSULTATIVE CONFERENCE OF DEFENSE. A consultative institution of the Nationalist government during the **Second Sino-Japanese War**. It consisted of 200 delegates representing the Nationalist Party, Communist Party, Youth Party of China, All-China Salvation Society, and other political organizations, as well as social celebrities. It was inaugurated in the city of Hankou on 6 July 1938. In 10 years, 13 meetings were held. This institution was supposed to have the right to listen to government reports, investigate special cases, and question and suggest government policy. However, the institution had no power to enforce the implementation of its resolutions. Many sessions of the conference were devoted to the discussion of constitutional reform, but the participants never came to agreement. It was legally replaced by the **National Assembly** and automatically dismissed when the assembly opened in March 1948.

NATIONAL ESSENCE SCHOOL. A group of scholars in the late Qing dynasty who studied Chinese language, literature, traditional institutions, and regulations and deeds of noble people. They advocated the following: to disseminate patriotism through the study of Chinese learning and promote the **anti-Manchu** revolution; to separate national learning from imperial learning and abolish the monarchy; to find grounds for democratic reforms; and to emphasize the need to develop an indigenous Chinese culture while learning from the West. The establishment in February 1905 of the Society for the Preservation of National Learning marked the rise of the National Essence School. The leading members included Zhang Bingyan, Deng Shi, Ma Xulun, Liu Yazi, and others. They published the *Journal of*

National Essence and *Bulletin of Politics and Methodology.* The major contributors to the journals were all famous scholars of national learning. This school was very influential prior to **Sun Yat-sen**'s **Republican Revolution.**

NATIONAL GENERAL LABOR UNION. Founded on 11 August 1921, the National General Labor Union was the early leading institution of the Communist-led labor movement. The first director was **Zhang Guotao**, and **Mao Zedong** was the director of its Hunan branch. On 1 May 1922 it held the first National Convention of Chinese Labor and elected **Deng Zhongxia** as its general secretary. In 1925, it was replaced by newly established **All-China Federation of Labor.**

NATIONAL HUMILIATION DAY. The two days (7 May and 9 May) formerly called "Humiliation Days" during the early Republican period. In January 1915, Japan sent a set of demands to the **Yuan Shikai** government, asking for recognition of Japan's supremacy in Shandong, Japan's special position in Manchuria and Inner Mongolia, Sino-Japanese joint operation of China's iron and steel industry, control by Japan of several of China's important domestic administrations, and nonalienation of China's coast areas to any third country. On 7 May 1915, Japan presented Yuan with an ultimatum, demanding that he respond within two days. In order to get Japanese support for his monarchical restoration, Yuan accepted the infamous **Twenty-one Demands** on 9 May 1915. Afterward, the Chinese Education Association decided to name 9 May National Humiliation Day to remind the Chinese public of foreign intrusion. In later years, some Chinese called for a national Humiliation Day on 18 September, which was the start of Japan's invasion of China's Manchuria in 1931. Others saw it more meaningful to remember the date of the **Nanjing Massacre** as the Humiliation Day. Still others suggested that China name 7 September, the date when China was forced to sign a humiliating Internal Protocol (Xinchou Treaty) with 11 foreign powers in 1901, as the Humiliation Day. There is no public agreement or formal decision on which specific day should be National Humiliation Day.

NATIONAL LIBRARY OF BEIPING. The library was founded in 1909 as part of the **Xinzheng Reform**, but it was not open to the public until 27 August 1912. The founding of the Beijing Library was first officially proposed by **Zhang Zhidong**. In 1908, Zhang commissioned the governor-general of Jiangsu, Jiangxi, and Zhejiang, Duan Fang, to buy up two wealthy scholars' private libraries and ship them to Beijing. They were later placed together with the collections of the library of the **Grand Secretariat** and the Imperial Academy to establish the new library at the Gaunghua Temple. After the Nationalist government decided to move the capital to Nanjing and Beijing was renamed Beiping in 1928, the name of the library also changed accordingly. In August 1929, the National Library of Beiping began to be sponsored by the Foundation of Chinese Education and Culture and function as a state library under the Ministry of Education. In 1931, a new building of the National Library of Beiping was erected, costing 2.4 million silver dollars, which all came from the Boxer Indemnity returned by the United States. The equipment and facilities were not inferior to any other state library in the world. It was open to the public, providing free reading, but all books and materials were not in circulation. The library had a strict dress code—only neatly dressed readers could enter. On 12 June 1950, the library was renamed the Beijing Library. It remains the largest and only state library in the People's Republic of China.

NATIONAL PACIFICATION ARMY. Some Chinese military forces collaborating with the Japanese troops during the **Second Sino-Japanese War**, known also as the Collaborationist Chinese Army. By 1938, it consisted of some 78,000 men. After the previous leader of the **Nationalist Party** (GMD), **Wang Jingwei**, launched the **Peace Movement** and established a puppet government in Nanjing, the number of the National Pacification Army reached 145,000 troops. Most of them were previous GMD troops; the largest troops were commanded by Pang Binxun and Sun Dianying, who surrendered to the Japanese on 14 May 1943. Wang not only recruited new soldiers but also opened a military academy to train officers for the army. Besides a few who were assigned to big cities, most of the National Pacification Army was dispatched to North China to join the "wipe-out" campaigns and conduct war atrocities as the Japanese troops did. According to the estimate of the Chinese military authority, this army had 118,600 men at the end of the war in 1945. After the Japanese surrendered, a few troops of the National

Pacification Army were dismissed, but most were incorporated into the GMD troops.

NATIONAL PROTECTION WAR. On 12 December 1915, **Yuan Shikai** restored the monarchy, proclaiming himself the emperor of a new Empire of China. This provoked widespread rebellions in many provinces. On 25 December, the former governor of Yunnan Province, **Cai E**, and the Yunnan general Tang Jiyao declared Yunnan's independence. Joined by the former governor of Jiangxi Province, Li Liejun, they formed the Republic Protection Army and declared war on Yuan's regime. Many southern provinces followed suit. Yuan sent troops to crack down on the Republic Protection Army, but the officers and soldiers of Yuan's army did not want to fight and were quickly routed in Sichuan. On 22 March 1916, Yuan had to abolish the monarchy and died soon after the Republican government resumed its authority in Beijing.

NATIONAL RESOURCE COMMITTEE (NRC). An institution of the Nationalist government responsible for industrial development and management of state enterprises. The NRC was established in November 1932 with the original name National Defense Planning Committee; it was renamed in April 1935 under the Military Committee of the **Nationalist Party** (GMD). The NRC was staffed by economic experts and technocrats and played a leading role in China's war economy. **Chiang Kai-shek** was the concurrent president and **Weng Wenhao** the secretary-general, so that the committee could report directly to Chiang. The committee drafted a five-year development plan for Chinese heavy industry, planning a government investment of CH$270 million in iron-steel, mining, mechanics, electricity, chemical, and fuel industries. During the **Second Sino-Japanese War**, the committee moved some factories from the coastal cities to interior provinces or built new factories there. The NRC made great efforts in surveying and exploiting natural minerals and ores and sent a considerable number of people abroad for advanced technical training.

In 1938, the NRC became a part of the Ministry of Economy, with Wong Wenhao, minister of economy, as the concurrent chairman of the committee. By July 1945, the NRC had 115 industrial, mining, and electric enterprises. By 1947, the NRC had a staff of 33,000 and supervised 230,000 workers. From 1937 through 1948, the NRC invested ¥8.82 million in and controlled 70 percent of China's industry. The committee was finally disbanded in 1949. Some of its staff stayed in mainland China while the rest fled to Taiwan with the GMD government.

NATIONAL REVOLUTIONARY ARMY (NRA). The NRA was the national standing army of the Republic of China from 1925 until 1949. Its flag was the "white sun and blue sky" bordered with a wide red fringe. In 1924, **Sun Yat-sen**, with Soviet help, founded the **Whampoa Military Academy** in Guangzhou. Using the Soviet model of "the party-commanded military academy and the academy-created army," the **Nationalist Party** (GMD) created the leading army of the revolutionary military forces. On 18 August 1925, the Military Committee of the National Government issued the order that the names of local armies be abolished and incorporated into a unified National Revolutionary Army. The officers who graduated from the Whampoa Military Academy constituted the first army commanded by **Chiang Kai-shek**; the previous **Hunan Army** became the second army; the Yunnan Army, the third; the Guangdong Army, the fourth; and the Fujian Army, the fifth. The commandant of the Whampoa Military Academy, Chiang Kai-shek, was appointed commander in chief of the NRA. Like the Soviet army, all five armies established political departments at the army and division levels with political commissars appointed by the Military Committee.

The NRA grew in the **Northern Expedition** against **warlords**, and after the reunification of China, it also absorbed other local military forces. The NRA included an air force, which was built during World War II with American help, and a navy, rebuilt in the postwar period. The NRA was supposed to be the unified state's military force, but it was largely controlled by the GMD. Also, various local military forces and their commanders did not always obey the orders of the central government. Between 1927 and 1937, the NRA engaged in military campaigns against the Communist **Red Army**. During the **Second Sino-Japanese War**, Communist forces became part of the NRA, reorganized as the **Eighth Route Army** and the **New Fourth Army** under Chiang Kai-shek's command. When the Japanese surrendered, due to the American mediation, the **Chinese Communist Party** (CCP) and GMD signed an agreement on reorganization of the

NRA. Accordingly, the GMD's troops (about 3 million) were to be reduced to 90 divisions and the CCP's troops (about 1.3 million) to 18 divisions, and after six months both were to be further reduced to 50 and 10 divisions, respectively. However, this agreement was soon broken. In 1947, the Communists began to refer to the NRA as the "bandit army of Chiang," and the GMD called the CCP troops the "Communist bandits." After Chiang's defeat by the Communists in 1949, the NRA fled to Taiwan, where it was renamed the Republic of China Army and exists to this day.

NATIONAL SALVATION ASSOCIATION. On 31 May 1936, some leading intellectuals and cultural literati, including Sheng Junru, Zhang Naiqi, **Tao Xingzhi**, and Zhou Taofen, established this association. It was followed by the establishment of the Shanghai Women's Salvation Association and salvation associations of professors, students, and urban dwellers in Shanghai, Nanjing, Tianjin, and other cities. More than 70 delegates from 20 cities and provinces attended the inaugural meeting of the National Salvation Association. They drew up the association's charter and the Primary Political Program for National Salvation and Anti-Japanese Movement, calling for the end of the civil war and peace negotiations to establish a united government to lead the Chinese resistance movement. The inaugural meeting also elected **Song Qingling**, **He Xiangning**, and 38 other people as members of the executive committee. The association expended all its efforts to promote the program of anti-Japanese national salvation during the **Second Sino-Japanese War** and disbanded on 18 December 1949 in Beijing.

NATIONAL SOUTHWEST UNION UNIVERSITY. A Chinese university established in April 1938 in Kunming, Yunnan Province. During the **Second Sino-Japanese War**, the leading universities in north China moved to the south. **Peking University**, Tsinhua University, and Nankai University merged into one university, first in Changsha, known as the Temporary University, and then in Kunming, renamed the National Southwest Union University. It consisted of five schools: humanities; science; law and commerce; engineering; and education. All the schools opened on 4 May 1938. Despite the different teaching styles and traditions of the three universities, all faculty shared a commitment to teaching excellence and academic pursuits. In the eight years of the war, the university produced 2,000 graduates, including many notable scholars and scientists. Some of the students joined the army and died in battles against the Japanese aggression. In 1946, the university was disbanded and each of the three universities moved back and resumed its own operations.

NATIONALIST PARTY. *See* CHINESE NATIONALIST PARTY (GUOMINDANG).

NATIVE BANK (*QIANZHUANG*). Financial agency that appeared in the 18th century to meet the increasing need of long-distance traders for credit. It created a mechanism that eased the transfer of funds and safety of large business. The native banks accepted deposits, made loans, and issued banknotes that could be cashed in associated banks locally or beyond their own regions. Some small native banks cashed only the notes issued by big banks. Because of the complex currency system and the changing exchange rate between silver and silver dollars and between other circulating currencies, the jobs at native banks required professional training and experience. The native banks were small in size and in business volume. They often relied on support from chambers of commerce or local governments. They also needed protection from local secret societies. In the late Qing and Republican years, modern banks gradually replaced the traditional native banks, though a few still existed up until 1949.

NAVY YAMEN. The Ministry of Navy in the late Qing dynasty. It was founded in October 1885 after the **Sino-French War**. Prince Chu was appointed minister, and Prince Qing and **Li Hongzhang** were his associates. Before the establishment of the Navy Yamen, Li had built the Beiyang Navy (Fleet of the Northern Ocean). The later-built Nanyang Navy (Fleet of the Southern Ocean) was much smaller and could not compete with the Beiyang Navy in terms of fighting ability and supply. Li remained the de facto supreme commander of China's naval forces and controlled the Navy Yamen. In February 1895, the **Beiyang Navy** was destroyed by Japan and the Navy Yamen was disbanded the following month.

NERCHINSK, TREATY OF (1689). In the 1680s, Russian settlers quickly expanded to the east, and the Qing emperor Kangxi dispatched an expedition to stop them at the Chinese border area. In 1687, the Qing troops crushed the Russian army at Albazin, and Russia had to accept China's suggestion for a peace settlement. It was against this background that the **Treaty of Nerchinsk** was signed on 7 September 1689 in the city of Nerchinsk by the Chinese envoy Prince Songgotu and Russian representative Fedor Golovin. The most important article was on the demarcation of the Siberian-Manchurian border along the Argun River and **Amur River** to the mouth of the Kerbechi, and along the Outer Xing'an Mountains to the sea. Nonetheless, the frontier between Mongolia and Siberia remained unsettled. Both sides agreed that all fortifications in Albazin would be demolished and that Russian residents in that area would be repatriated with their properties. The treaty also stipulated that both Chinese and Russians could enter each other's territories for free trade. The treaty served as the basis of Russo-Chinese relations until the mid-19th century.

NEW ARMY. Known also as the **Beiyang Army**. Established in 1895, the New Army had modernized troops trained and equipped according to Western standards. After China's defeat by Japan, the **Dowager Cixi** ordered **Yuan Shikai** to train a new army at Xiaozhan, near the city of Tianjin. This army of 4,000 men was formally organized on 8 December 1895 and further expanded to 75,000 troops. It became the major military force of the Qing dynasty. Many officers of the army later became famous warlords and politicians of the Republic of China. Like Yuan Shikai, most officers of this army came from **Li Hongzhang**'s **Anhui Army**. Yuan kept a tight grip on the command of the army by installing officers loyal to him only. Republican revolutionaries also tried to penetrate the New Army. As Yuan was promoted to minister of Beiyang on 25 June 1902, people began to call this army the Beiyang Army.

NEW CULTURE MOVEMENT. An enlightenment movement, known as China's Renaissance, that began in 1915, culminated in the **May Fourth Movement**, and continued into the early 1920s. It opposed traditionalism and **Confucianism** and advocated Western science and democracy. The major objectives of the movement were opposing Confucian moral codes while advocating individual freedom and equality; opposing superstition and the worship of Confucian tradition while advocating scientific spirit; opposing the dull classical Chinese writings while advocating a new literature and vernacular writings; and opposing the patriarchal clan system while advocating the emancipation of women. **Chen Duxiu** was the key figure in starting the New Culture Movement in 1915. He edited the journal *New Youth*, making it the first forum for Chinese intellectuals to introduce new ideas and theories. Before the May Fourth Movement, there were only a few magazines in China; by 1920, the number of various kinds of magazines had shot up to 400. Wu Yu vigorously attacked Confucian morality, and **Hu Shih** initiated writing in vernacular Chinese. **Lu Xun** was the first novelist to write short stories in the vernacular language, such as "The Madman's Diary" and "The True Story of Ah Q."

The New Culture Movement exposed the Chinese to two main philosophies. One was **John Dewey**'s pragmatism, espousing an evolutionary approach to social improvement. The other was the Marxist revolutionary approach modeled after the Bolshevik Revolution in Russia. The May Fourth scholars were divided in a heated debate. Hu Shih advocated pragmatism and the study of concrete social problems, while Chen Duxiu and **Li Dazhao** argued for revolution to change all of China's political and economic systems. In addition, Western liberalism, **social Darwinism**, and anarchism also became appealing to the Chinese people. The New Culture Movement led to a drastic change in society that fueled the birth of various political organizations, including the **Chinese Communist Party**.

NEW DEMOCRACY. A Maoist concept. Different from orthodox Marxism, **Mao Zedong** argued that the Chinese Communist movement was not a revolution of one class, namely, the workers, but required the collective efforts of four social classes: workers, peasants, petty bourgeoisie, and national bourgeoisie. The goal of the **Chinese Communist Party** (CCP) before 1949 was not a Communist revolution but an antifeudalist, anti-imperialist, democratic revolution. It is referred to as a "new democratic revolution" because the leadership of the revolution was the Communist Party, making it distinct from the "old" democratic revolution led by **Sun Yat-sen**. New Democracy was also a political system in the early years of the People's Republic of China, described by Mao as "a joint dictatorship of the four classes with the Chinese Communist Party as the leader." However, this system quickly collapsed as Mao launched the Socialist transformation and adopted Joseph Stalin's economic model in 1955.

NEW FOURTH ARMY. A Communist military force in central and southeast China during the **Second Sino-Japanese War**. After its defeat by the **Nationalist Party** (GMD) troops in the fifth **Encirclement and Suppression Campaign**, the **Red Army** retreated from the **Jiangxi Soviet** to China's northwestern provinces. Only a few small Red Army troops continued **guerrilla warfare** to the south of the Yangtze River. According to the agreement between the GMD and the **Chinese Communist Party** (CCP) on the **United Front** against the Japanese aggression, the Communist guerrilla troops in southern China were reorganized as the New Fourth Army with the non-Communist general, **Ye Ting**, as commander and a Communist leader, Xiang Ying, as political commissar. In November 1937, its headquarters was in Wuhan; then it moved to Nanchang and finally settled down in Shexian, Anhui Province. The New Fourth Army was controlled by Xiang Ying, who led the troops to build up a revolutionary base and expand the influence of the CCP.

In December 1940, the GMD government ordered the New Fourth Army to evacuate the southern portion of Anhui and Jiangsu and move to the north. In the process of this transfer, the New Fourth Army was ambushed and defeated by the GMD troops. This was the notorious **New Fourth Army Incident**. The GMD government accused the New Fourth Army of failing to follow the evacuation instructions and disbanded the army on 17 January 1941. The CCP denounced the incident as an anti-Communist conspiracy with the purpose of destroying anti-Japanese military forces. Three days later, the CCP announced the reestablishment of the New Fourth Army with Chen Yi as commander and **Liu Shaoqi** as political commissar. The leading forces of the army were transferred to the north of the Yangtze River, engaging the Japanese in some battles as it regrouped and expanded. In 1947, the New Fourth Army merged with the **Eighth Route Army** and became part of the People's Liberation Army in the civil war against the GMD.

NEW FOURTH ARMY INCIDENT (DECEMBER 1940–JANUARY 1941). An armed clash between the **Nationalist Party** (GMD) and the **Chinese Communist Party** (CCP) during the **Second Sino-Japanese War**. As a result of the negotiations between the GMD and CCP on the **United Front** against Japanese aggression, the Communist **Red Army** guerrilla troops in southern China were reorganized as the **New Fourth Army** with non-Communist general **Ye Ting** as commander. The CCP appointed a Communist leader, Xiang Ying, as political commissar to control this army. From 1937 to 1940, the leading forces of the New Fourth Army were stationed to the south of the Yangtze River. This army spent a lot of time building and expanding the Communist revolutionary bases, thus arousing the suspicion of the GMD government. In December 1940, **Chiang Kai-shek** ordered the New Fourth Army to evacuate the southern portion of Anhui and Jiangsu provinces and to move to the north of the Yangtze River to fight against the Japanese. The New Fourth Army obeyed the order but moved slowly because its leaders disagreed on the destination and route of the transfer.

However, after Xiang Ying reported to the GMD government its finalized operation route and schedule, the New Fourth Army fell into a trap set by the GMD. After a seven-day bloody fight, Ye Ting went to negotiate with the government, but he was detained. Xiang Ying was murdered by his bodyguard as they tried to escape. Only 2,000 Communist troops broke out of the encirclement, and the remaining 7,000 men were either killed or disarmed. The GMD government justified its action by accusing the New Fourth Army of failure to follow the evacuation instructions, while the CCP denounced the incident as a conspiracy of eliminating the CCP military force. Six days later, the CCP proclaimed the rebuilding of the New Fourth Army with Chen Yi as commander and **Liu Shaoqi** as political commissar. The New Fourth Army Incident seriously undermined the anti-Japanese United Front between the GMD and CCP.

NEW LIFE MOVEMENT. Referred to as the Campaign for Citizen Education initiated by **Chiang Kai-shek** and his wife **Soong Mayling** in February 1934. The New Life Movement aimed to revive traditional Chinese values to counter both Communist ideology and government corruption. The New Life Movement began with collective efforts against such uncivilized and undisciplined acts as spitting, public urination, smoking opium, adultery, and wearing provocative clothing. It was designed in a way that the movement began by addressing hygienic practices, promptness, and courtesy, to finally realize the goal of the "social regeneration of China." For this purpose, Chiang Kai-shek urged the Chinese people to cultivate the four traditional virtues of politeness (*li*), righteousness (*yi*), integrity (*lian*), and self-respect *(chi)*, calling on people to create a civilized, productive, and militarized life. The movement advocated "one country, one doctrine, and one leader," implying an anti-Communist ideology and absolute loyalty to Chiang Kai-shek. The movement's ideology mixed **Confucianism**, nationalism, and authoritarianism in a way that finally led to Chiang's personal authoritarian rule and fascism. The New Life Movement took place throughout the country, and all major government officials were required to be involved. Nonetheless, it failed to create an appealing and cogent ideology. Chiang's failure in the civil war in 1949 brought the New Life Movement to an end.

NEW ORDER IN EAST ASIA. A Japanese plan to dominate East Asia. On 3 November 1938, in commemoration of the birthday of the Japanese emperor Meiji, the Japanese premier Fumimaro Konoe proposed a "New Order in East Asia." He argued that this was to end white colonialism, and it was referred to as the Japanese Monroe Doctrine. It also attempted to create a Greater East Asian Coprosperity Sphere based on six principles: permanent stability, neighborly amity and international justice, joint defense against communism, economic cooperation, new East Asian culture, and world peace. The New Order in East Asia was designed by Japan for the brutal exploitation of East Asia for its military needs and served as an instrument to woo and suppress the Chinese resistance movement.

NEW TERRITORIES. A district of **Hong Kong**. The New Territories was leased by the Qing government to Great Britain in 1898 for 99 years. The New Territories consisted of territory north of the Lion Rock and south of the Shenzhen River (Sahm Cun River), and also outlying islands. Since Hong Kong and Kowloon were ceded to Britain in 1842 and 1860, respectively, the population of Hong Kong had increased rapidly, making the city overcrowded. In 1898, the British government negotiated with the Qing court in Beijing and signed the Convention for the Extension of Hong Kong Territory to possess the New Territories. In the 1980s, as the lease of the New Territories would soon expire, the British government and the People's Republic of China (PRC) began to negotiate over Hong Kong's future. According to the Sino-British Joint Declaration (1984), the whole of Hong Kong, including Hong Kong Island, Kowloon, and the New Territories, would be returned to China in 1997.

NEW YOUTH (**1915–1926**). The most influential journal during the Chinese **New Culture Movement** in the early 20th century. *New Youth* was founded as *Youth Monthly* on 15 September 1915 by **Chen Duxiu** in Shanghai. It was renamed *New Youth* after the second volume. The journal did not call for contributions, and all articles published in the journal were written by the editorial board, including Chen Duxiu, Qian Xuantong, Gao Yihan, **Hu Shih**, **Li Dazhao**, Shen Yimo, and **Lu Xun**. In the early days, the journal focused on the introduction of Western science and democracy, initiating the anti-**Confucianism** campaign. *New Youth* announced its mission to "save China from all political, moral, academic, and intellectual darkness." *New Youth* appealed to and influenced a great number of Chinese youngsters, including social activists of various political beliefs. Beginning with issue 5 in 1918, *New Youth* began to publish a series of articles by Li Dazhao to propagate the Russian Bolshevik Revolution and socialism. It also engaged in a heated debate with anarchists and non-Marxist Socialists. The magazine published short stories by Lu Xun written in vernacular Chinese with Western punctuation. In 1920, Hu Shih suggested that the journal not discuss politics, but his idea was opposed by Chen Duxiu, Li Dazhao, and Lu Xun. After the founding of the **Chinese Communist Party** (CCP) in 1921, *New Youth* became a formal publication of the CCP with Chen as the chief editor. In July 1922, the publication of *New Youth* was formally ceased. A year later, **Qu Qiubai** resumed its publication in Guangzhou and continued to print the journal until 1926.

NG CHOY. *See* WU TINGFANG.

NIAN REBELLION (NIEN REBELLION). Large peasant uprising that took place in central and northern China between 1853 and 1868. The rebellion went through two stages of development. The first was from the spring of 1853 to March 1863. As the flood of the Yellow River devastated hundreds of thousands of acres of farmlands and caused an immense loss of life in 1851, peasants in the provinces of Henan and Anhui began to revolt and organize into small bands against local governments. In 1853, inspired by the **Taiping Rebellion**, these small groups of rebels merged into the Nian armies and stormed the cities of Wuhan and Anqing. Unlike the Taiping, however, the Nian had no clear political program and no centralized leadership, and most did not want to leave their homeland to fight. Nonetheless, several Nian armies assembled in 1855 to form a coalition army, electing Zhang Luocing as their leader; this brought the number of troops to 40,000. In 1875, the Nian troops coordinated with the Taiping in several battles, and Zhang was granted the title Prince Wo by Taiping Heavenly King. Zhang accepted the title but refused to incorporate the Nian into the Taiping army. In fact, he could command only part of the Nian armies to the south of the Huai River because the rest of the Nian army had returned to the north. Zhang's troops were defeated by Qing troops led by General Senggelinqin (**Sengge Rinchen**) in northern Anhui in 1862. Zhang was captured and executed in April 1863.

The second stage of the Nian Rebellion was between April 1863 and August 1868, during which the remnants of the Nian armies continued to fight in even wider areas of the provinces of Henan, Hubei, and Shaanxi. Some Taiping rebels joined and strengthened the Nian. In a battle in Shandong, the Nian cavalry crushed Senggelinqin's Mongolian infantry-based army and killed Senggelinqin. The Qing government appointed **Zeng Guofan** as the new commander to quell the rebellion. Zeng began to dig canals and trenches to hem in the Nian cavalry. The Nian troops were divided into the eastern and western wings. In 1867, when the eastern wing failed to break out of the encirclement of the **Anhui Army**, the western wing rushed to reinforce it but was too late to help. The western army had to return to Henan, but it was crushed by the Qing troops led by **Zuo Zongtang** in August 1868.

NIE RONGZHEN (1899–1992). One of the ten marshals of the **People's Liberation Army** (PLA) and a leader of the **Chinese Communist Party** (CCP). Born into a wealthy family in Jiangjin, Sichuan Province, Nie received a traditional education in his hometown and joined the work-study program of Chinese students in France in 1920. He studied engineering in France and Belgium, where he met **Zhou Enlai** and became a protégé of Zhou's. With Zhou's recommendation, Nie joined the **Communist Youth League** in 1922 and the CCP in 1923. Then he traveled to Russia and graduated from the Soviet Red Army Military Academy. After his return to China, he served as a political instructor at the **Whampoa Military Academy**, working with Zhou, who was the deputy director of its Political Department. Nie participated in the **Northern Expedition** in 1926. After **Chiang**

Kai-shek began to purge the Communists from the **National Revolutionary Army** (NRA), Nie participated in the **Nanchang Mutiny** in August 1927, serving as the party representative of the 11th Army of the NRA. He was involved in establishing the **Canton Commune** in December. After the failure of these uprisings, Nie was assigned to Shanghai and other cities to lead the CCP's secret organizations. In December 1931, he went to the **Jiangxi Soviet** and began to work with **Lin Biao** under **Mao Zedong**'s leadership. During the **Long March**, Nie strongly opposed the **Returned Bolsheviks** and supported Mao to resume military leadership of the **Red Army**. He led his troops to cross the Jingsha River and fought the decisive battle in Northwest China, gaining a foothold for the CCP.

During the **Second Sino-Japanese War**, the Red Army was reorganized as the **Eighth Route Army**, consisting of three divisions. Nie was appointed the deputy division commander of the 115th division, with Lin Biao as its commander. He led the troops to penetrate into the Japanese-occupied area and established the CCP's first anti-Japanese rural base. During the civil war, he was made the commander in chief of the North China Field Army and party secretary of the CCP Central Bureau in the provinces of Shanxi, Chahar, and Hebei. After 1949, he held several important positions, including acting chief of staff of the PLA, mayor of Beijing, vice-chairman of the People's Congress, and vice president of the CCP Military Committee. Nie was also a member of the CCP Politburo. Nie was the leader of the PLA's military modernization, initiating and completing various important projects, including China's development of nuclear weapons.

NINE-POWER TREATY (1922). Treaty signed by nine countries, namely, Belgium, Britain, China, France, Japan, Italy, the Netherlands, Portugal, and the United States, at the Washington Naval Conference on 6 February 1922. The **Beijing government** of the Republic of China sent a 130-man delegation, including Shi Zhaoji, **Gu Weijun**, and Wang Chonghui as plenipotentiaries to Washington to demand the abolition of **extraterritoriality** and **foreign concessions**, the resumption of authority over Chinese maritime customs, and the withdrawal of foreign troops from China. The U.S. delegation seconded this motion. In fact, American secretary of state John Hay had issued the Open Door Notes of September–November 1899, followed by a diplomatic circular in July 1900, asking that all the major world powers respect China's territorial integrity and maintain an "open door" to allow all nations to have equal rights and equal access to the treaty ports within their spheres of influence. Hay believed that the major powers had a consensus in principle, but he was leery of Japanese ambitions for Manchuria and its **Twenty-one Demands**.

During the **Washington Conference** of 1921–1922, the United States again raised the **Open Door Policy** as an issue, adding it to the draft of the treaty that China proposed. Finally, all the attendees signed the treaty, which affirmed the sovereignty and territorial integrity of China and made the Open Door Policy international law. However, the Nine-Power Treaty lacked any enforcement regulations, and Japan soon violated it by invading Manchuria and, soon after, China proper.

NINETEENTH ROUTE ARMY. A military force of the **Nationalist Party** (GMD), best known for its brave defense of Shanghai in 1932. It was a Cantonese army that originated in the **Whampoa Military Academy** and the **Northern Expedition**. Its commander in chief was Chiang Guannai and its field commander, **Cai Tingkai**. Having conquered Manchuria, Japan attempted to seize Shanghai. In January 1932, the Japanese mobilized nearly 90,000 troops, supported by 80 warships and 300 airplanes, to attack the city. Despite inferior military equipment and heavy casualties, the Nineteenth Route Army put up a fierce resistance, and the Japanese were unable to overrun the city. The officers and soldiers of the army became well-known national heroes. On 2 March, due to a lack of ammunition and manpower, the Nineteenth Route Army had to pull out of Shanghai. After the cease-fire of the Shanghai War of 1932, **Chiang Kai-shek** reassigned the army to Fujian to suppress the Communist insurrection.

In Fujian, however, the Nineteenth Route Army conducted peace negotiations with the Red Army and established the Fujian People's Government, opposing both Japan and Chiang Kai-shek. The new government did not gain sufficient support from local people, and the radical Communist leaders, the **Comintern**-supported **Twenty-eight Bolsheviks**, hesitated to ally with the Nineteenth Route Army. The Fujian People's Government was quickly suppressed by Chiang Kaishek's armies in January 1934. Cai and Jiang fled to Hong Kong. The Nineteenth Route Army's designation was abolished, all officers of the rank of lieutenant colonel or higher were replaced, and the troops were absorbed into the army of **Li Zongren**.

NORTHERN EXPEDITION (1926–1927). Revolutionary war against **warlords** to unify China under the Nationalist banner. The 100,000-member **National Revolutionary Army** (NRA) with **Chiang Kai-shek** as its commander in chief took the oath of the Northern Expedition in Guangzhou on 9 July 1926. Ten days later, **Feng Yuxiang** from northern China also joined Chiang in the military campaign. The main targets of this expedition consisted of three notorious warlords: **Wu Peifu** (200,000 troops), who controlled almost five provinces in North China; Sun Chuanfang (200,000 troops), who ruled five provinces on the eastern coast; and **Zhang Zuolin** (350,000 troops), who governed Manchuria and also occupied the cities of Beijing and Tianjin. The Communists took an active part in the campaign, marking the first **united front** between the **Chinese Communist Party** (CCP) and the **Nationalist Party** (GMD). The **Comintern** showed great enthusiasm by sending the famous Russian general Vasily Blyukher, known as Galen, to China as the NRA's military adviser. The NRA was far better organized and equipped than the warlord armies, and it decided to defeat these warlords one by one: first Wu, then Sun, and finally Zhang. It was not surprising that the expedition was supported by ordinary Chinese people, and the NRA quickly increased to 250,000 troops. The decisive battle took place in Wuchang, where the NRA destroyed 20,000 troops of **Wu Peifu**'s. Chiang's troops also moved quickly, defeating Sun Chuanfang and storming Shanghai and Nanjing.

The progress, however, was interrupted by the split between the CCP and the GMD as well as the disruption between Chiang Kai-shek and **Wang Jingwei**. Nonetheless, after both Chiang and Wang expelled the Communists from the army and government, they reunited and resumed the military campaign, which is called the Second Northern Expedition. The capture of Beijing on 8 June 1928 marked the victory of the Second Northern Expedition, which provided a nominal reunification of China and won Chiang Kai-shek prominence on the political stage.

– O –

OCTOBER TENTH AGREEMENT. This was the "Summary of Conversations" signed by representatives of the **Chinese Communist Party** (CCP) and the **Nationalist Party** (GMD) on 10 October 1945.

As a result of the negotiations between **Chiang Kai-shek** and **Mao Zedong** at the end of the **Second Sino-Japanese War**, both sides agreed to the "basic policy of peace and national reconstruction." The Summary of Conversations proclaimed to "accept long-term co-operation on the basis of peace, democracy, solidarity and unity . . . resolute avoidance of civil war and the building a new China, independent, free, prosperous and powerful." This summary also included an agreement on the convening of a **Political Consultative Conference**. Nonetheless, the CCP and GMD did not come together on more concrete details of these general principles and disagreed on measures for their implementation.

OCTOBER REVOLUTION (1917). The Russian Bolshevik Revolution in October 1917 led by Vladimir Lenin. The October Revolution overthrew the Russian czarist regime and established the first Communist state in the world. The October Revolution exposed the Chinese to Marxism-Leninism and the Russian pattern of revolution. It proved Lenin's hypothesis that a Communist revolution could take place in a less-developed country, such as Russia; this brought new hope to Chinese revolutionaries. In 1918, a professor at **Peking University**, **Li Dazhao**, began publishing a series of articles in *New Youth* to introduce Chinese readers to the Bolshevik Revolution, which provoked enthusiasm in Chinese radical intellectuals for studying Marxism. The members of the early Marxist study societies became the pioneer Chinese Communists. Li's articles and the activities of young Chinese revolutionaries attracted the attention of the **Comintern**, which sent representatives **Grigori Naumovich Voitinsky** and **Hendricus Maring** to China to help establish the **Chinese Communist Party** (CCP). The CCP was formed on the model of the Russian Bolshevik Party and followed its instructions. The Russian pattern of Communist revolution, including urban uprisings and an urban-centered labor movement, was the model for the early Chinese revolution. After the Chinese Communists failed in the urban areas and retreated to the countryside, they continued to imitate the Russian Bolsheviks by establishing the **Jiangxi Soviet** in the rural base areas.

OKAMURA, YASUJI (1884–1966). Born in Tokyo, Okamura entered Waseda University in 1897, then transferred to Tokyo Junior Army School and the Imperial Japanese Army Academy. He finally graduated from the academy in 1904. From 1923 to 1927, he was the military adviser of the **warlord** Sun Chuanfan. In 1928, he was made commanding officer of a Japanese infantry regiment and took part in the Battle of Jinan. In 1932, he served as deputy chief of staff of the Japanese Expeditionary Force that attacked and occupied Shanghai. He played a role in the recruitment of comfort women from Nagasaki prefecture to serve in military brothels in Shanghai. Okamura represented Japan in signing the **Tanggu Truce**, which sped up the Japanese plan of conquering the whole of China. He also served as military attaché to **Manchukuo** from 1933 to 1934.

Okamura was promoted to lieutenant general in 1936. From 1937 to 1945, he was the commander of, successively, the Japanese 11th Corps, the Northern China Front Army, and the 6th Front Army. In April 1940, he was promoted to the rank of full general. In July 1941, he was appointed commander in chief of the Northern China Area Army. Okamura enforced the extremely brutal policy of "burn all, kill all, and loot all" in North China. On 9 September 1945, Okamura represented the Imperial Japanese Army in the China-Burma-India theater at the official ceremony of surrender held at Nanjing. He was charged as a war criminal but was declared not guilty in January 1949 and then sent back to Japan by the Nationalist government. In 1950, he was invited by **Chiang Kai-shek** to be a senior training officer in the Research Institute of Revolutionary Practice.

ON PROTRACTED WAR. A speech by **Mao Zedong** at the Conference on Anti-Japanese War in **Yan'an** from 26 May to 3 June 1938. The speech was soon translated into English. Mao argued that the **Second Sino-Japanese War** was a life-and-death struggle between semifeudal and semicolonial China and imperial Japan. Japan had advantages in terms of military strength but suffered from a shortage of manpower and resources, while China was a weak but huge country with international support. Mao criticized arguments on both "quick victory" and "doomed to failure" and pointed out that China would finally win the protracted war.

OPEN DOOR POLICY. A principle of American foreign policy, especially toward China in the late 19th and early 20th centuries. It was established by the American government during the scramble by the Western powers for concessions that followed the **First Sino-Japanese**

War. In September 1899, U.S. secretary of state John Hay sent notes to the major powers, namely, Britain, France, Germany, Italy, Russia, and Japan, suggesting that they declare the recognition of China's territorial and administrative integrity and open the treaty ports within their spheres of influence. This idea was first suggested by a British "Old China Hand," A. E. Hippisley, to his American friend, W. W. Rockhill, a former minister in China and adviser to John Hay. Although John Hay announced that the European powers had granted their consent in principle, none would commit themselves until they were sure that the other countries would do the same thing. The principle was affirmed by the **Nine-Power Treaty** at the **Washington Conference** in 1922, but there was no provision for its enforcement. This principle finally ceased to exist after the Japanese invasion of Manchuria in 1931.

OPIUM WAR (1840–1842). In the 18th century, China's trade with the Western countries was allowed to take place only in one city—Canton—and conducted only through the imperially sanctioned *co-hong*. This trade was heavily one sided in China's favor. The Europeans came to buy Chinese tea and silk while the Chinese showed little interest in purchasing any European commodities. Huge amounts of silver flowed from Great Britain into China. The balance did not shift the other way until the British began to ship opium in large amounts to China in 1781. The rapid rise in opium imports caused serious financial and social problems for Qing China. Some statesmen, like **Lin Zexu**, suggested a ban on the opium trade, and the **Daoguang Emperor** agreed. But as the legal market was abolished, drug smuggling became rampant.

On 31 December 1838, the emperor appointed Lin imperial commissioner to suppress the Canton opium traffic. Lin eventually forced the British merchants to surrender all stocks of opium (21,306 chests, 120 lbs. each) for destruction on 4 June 1839. On December 6, the trade between China and Britain was stopped "forever." The British merchants petitioned the British government to take steps to protect their interests. In June 1840, the British expeditionary force reached Guangdong from Singapore under Rear Admiral George Elliot. It consisted of 15 barracks ships, 4 armed steamers, and 25 transports with 4,000 marines. The British demanded reimbursement for the surrendered opium and compensation for their losses from the interrupted trade. The Qing government refused and the British attacked. Due to good war preparations by Lin, it was difficult to storm Guangzhou.

The British moved northward. They seized Zhousan and blocked the port of Ningbo and then advanced to Tianjin, directly threatening the security of Beijing. Not only local officials but the emperor criticized Lin for provoking the British into war and for his mismanagement. The Daoguang Emperor dismissed Lin and appointed a new commissioner, **Qishan**, to negotiate with the British. This resulted in the **Convention of Chuanbi**, which provided for the **Cession of Hong Kong** and an indemnity of 6 million taels. The emperor was enraged by the terms of the convention. He argued that Qishan was not authorized to sign any treaty. Qishan was dismissed and sent into exile.

The emperor appointed Yisan as barbarian-suppressing general to resume the war, but his troops were quickly defeated. The British took the Bogu port near Guangzhou and besieged the city. The emperor sued for peace again. The British demands were similar to the previous ones, except for asking that the indemnity of 6 million taels be paid within a week. When a compromise appeared possible as the new representative Isan signed the Convention of Canton and the British troops began to retreat, 10,000 Chinese organized by local gentry attacked the British at Sanyuanli, near Canton. The British government was not satisfied with the treaties Elliot signed with the Chinese either. It sent Sir Henry Pottinger to **Macao**, ushering in a new phase of the war.

Pottinger led the troops to storm several important coastal cities, including Amoy, Ningbo, Zhenhai, Dinghai, and Shanghai, finally arriving in Nanjing. Qiying, tatar-general of Canton, was made a commissioner and rushed to Nanjing for peace negotiations. The Qing government proved incapable of dealing with Western powers either militarily or politically. There was no room for Qiying to bargain, so he had to accept Pottinger's terms. On 29 August 1842, the **Treaty of Nanjing** was signed. The war indemnity was increased to 21 million taels, Hong Kong was ceded to Britain, five ports were opened to foreign trade, the **Canton System** was abolished, and a fixed Chinese tariff would be decided shortly. *See also* ARROW WAR.

ORACLE BONE SCRIPT (*JIAGUWEN*). Ancient Chinese texts first found in 1899 on oracle bones by Wang Yirong in Beijing, when he bought some oracle bones thinking they were medicine. As the highest administrator of education in the Qing dynasty and an expert in the study of ancient Chinese characters, Wang wasted no time in purchasing all the oracle bones (about 1,500 pieces) from the pharmacies in the city, and he began to study them in earnest. It was proved that these turtle shells were used in shamanistic divinatory practices in ancient China. The script on the oracle bones recounted the records of the divination activities of ancient Chinese kings. The oracle inscriptions are the oldest known form of Chinese writing. The leading scholars on the oracle bone script included Wang Xiang, Luo Zhenyu, Dong Zhuobin, and **Guo Moruo**. In later years, archeologists discovered 154,600 pieces of oracle bone with 4,500 Chinese characters, and about 2,000 of them have been decoded.

OUTER MONGOLIA. A Chinese term referring to the territory of today's Mongolia (a sovereign state), as opposed to Inner Mongolia, today's autonomous region of the People's Republic of China. It was an administrative region of the Qing dynasty and early Republican China. Referring to the northern part of the region as "outer," and the southern portion, closer to the Chinese capital (Beijing), as "inner" is regarded by some scholars to be a sinocentric perspective. Nonetheless, the term is used as a geographic concept; for example, in Western slang it denotes a stereotypically remote place. In 1911, as the **Republican Revolution** took place in China, Mongolia declared its independence. Two years later, the **Yuan Shikai** government signed a treaty with Russia, claiming that Outer Mongolia was part of China but enjoyed local autonomy. Outer Mongolia became a special administrative region of the Republic of China beside 22 regular provinces under the **Beijing government**. In 1919, with Soviet help, the Communists in Mongolia established an independent government. The Chinese Nationalist government did not recognize that independence until 5 January 1946. China and Mongolia established formal diplomatic relations on 13 February 1946. Beginning in the 1920s, the **Chinese Communist Party** supported the Mongolian Communist revolution, and as soon as the People's Republic of China was founded, the two Communist states established diplomatic relations on 16 October 1949.

– P –

PARIS GROUP, COMMUNIST. In March/April 1921, five Chinese students, Zhang Shengfu, Liu Qingyang, **Zhou Enlai**, Zhao Shiyan, and Cheng Gongbo established a Communist group in Paris. Zhang

Shengfu was the head of the group. The Communist Paris Group did not send its representatives to the First Congress of the **Chinese Communist Party** (CCP). Instead, Zhao Shiyan and Zhou Enlai also established the Chinese Youth Communist Party on 28 June 1922 in a suburb of Paris. Zhao was elected president. Most of the members of the Chinese Youth Communist Party transferred to the CCP in later years. This group produced a large number of the CCP leaders, including Zhou Enlai, **Deng Xiaoping**, Cai Heshen, Cai Chang, Chen Yi, **Nie Rongzhen**, and others.

PARIS PEACE CONFERENCE (1919). Conference held in January 1919 by the Allies at Versailles, Paris, known also as the Versailles Peace Conference. The conference was to discuss the post–World War I world order, especially the issue of previous German colonies. In 1897, Germany obtained China's Shandong Province as its concession area. Because China joined the war in 1917, all treaties with Germany had been abrogated. As one of the victorious nations in World War I, China had the right to ask for the restoration of its sovereign authority over Shandong. At the Paris Peace Conference, when Japan asked to take over Shandong, the Chinese delegation pleaded that because Shandong was the birthplace of Confucius, China could not give up this holy land just as the Christians could not give up Jerusalem. The Chinese delegation pointed out that although the Chinese **Yuan Shikai** government accepted Japan's **Twenty-one Demands**, recognizing Japan's interest in Shandong in 1915, the treaty was never ratified by the Chinese parliament and was thus invalid.

However, Great Britain was bound by a secret deal with Japan and persuaded most Western powers to reject China's demands. U.S. president Woodrow Wilson first championed China and then compromised. He believed that it was more important to establish the League of Nations and have Japan join it than to secure justice for China. On 28 April 1919, the conference decided to hand over Shandong to Japan. This news reached Beijing and triggered a series of massive protests, known as the **May Fourth Movement**. China eventually withdrew from the Versailles Treaty.

PARKER, PETER (1804–1888). An American physician and pioneer medical missionary to China. Born in Framingham, Massachusetts, into an orthodox Congregational family, Parker received his BA from

Yale University in 1831 and his Doctor of Medicine from Yale Medical School in 1834. At Yale, Parker also studied Chinese language and was determined to do missionary work in China. Having completed his theological studies, Parker was ordained as a Presbyterian minister in Philadelphia in January 1834. The next month, Parker departed for Canton as the first Protestant medical missionary to China. One year after his arrival, he opened the first Christian hospital in China, the Canton Boji Hospital (Ophthalmic Hospital, 1835). Parker was an ophthalmologist, but he also helped patients in many other ways, including removing tumors. Parker served as the major interpreter in the Sino-American negotiations in 1844, which resulted in the Treaty of Wanghia, a guiding document for U.S.-China relations in the 19th century.

PARLIAMENTS OF THE EARLY REPUBLIC OF CHINA. From 1912 to 1928, China witnessed several parliaments, including the first and second **Provisional National Assemblies**, **First Parliament**, **Extraordinary Parliament**, **Anfu Parliament**, and **Provisional Consultative Yuan**.

PEACE MOVEMENT. Wang Jingwei's collaboration campaign with Japan during the **Second Sino-Japanese War**. On 3 November 1938, the Japanese premier Fumimaro Konoe proclaimed a "**New Order in East Asia**," promising political stability, economic cooperation, new culture, and joint defense against communism in East Asia under Japanese domination. **Wang Jingwei**, who once urged resistance against the Japanese, had lost confidence in China's war of resistance and saw hope for a peaceful solution from Fumimaro Konoe's statement. He flew out of **Chongqing** to Hanoi on 18 December 1938 and started his peace movement. **Chiang Kai-shek** denounced Wang's behavior and purged him from the Chinese government. The Japanese offered Wang a promise of no demands for territory or indemnity and also of abolishing **extraterritoriality** and returning to China all concessions and leased land. Then Wang went to the French concession in Shanghai for further negotiations. Finally, Wang signed eight agreements with Japan, including the recognition of **Manchukuo**, permission for Japan to station its army in China, and mutual efforts against communism. Wang also acknowledged Japanese control over Chinese resources, education, and cultural affairs. In March

1940, Wang established his puppet government in Nanjing. Although he found that the Japanese would neither return to China any land nor abolish the unequal treaties, Wang had passed the point of no return and served the Japanese throughout the war.

PEACE-PLANNING SOCIETY (*CHU'ANHUI*). Established on 23 August 1915 to restore the monarchy in China. The society was registered as an academic organization and was initiated by Yang Du and five other scholars. **Yan Fu**, the famous translator of Western literature on social progress and democracy, was also listed. The Peace-Planning Society argued that the current chaos in China was caused by the republican system, and a constitutional monarchy was the only suitable system of government for China. It published numerous articles to push **Yuan Shikai**'s monarchical movement. The society sent open telegraphs to each province, asking them to send representatives to Beijing to discuss China's political system. Six days later, it announced that all the representatives had agreed to abolish democracy and establish a constitutional monarchy. Beginning on 1 September, the society organized various people to submit petitions to the congress. The Peace-Planning Society was accused of cheating people and destroying China. After the death of Yuan Shikai in 1916, the members of the society were listed as criminals.

PEASANT MOVEMENT TRAINING INSTITUTE. Founded by the **Chinese Communist Party** in Guangzhou during its alliance with the **Nationalist Party**. Between July 1924 and September 1926, it held six terms of workshops, training rural cadres to support the **Northern Expedition** and promote the peasant movement. For the first five terms, all the peasant students came from the nearby three provinces, while the sixth term enrolled students from 26 provinces and thus made it the most influential school of Communist rural cadres. **Peng Bai** was the founder of the institute, and **Mao Zedong** was the director of the last term.

PEASANT NATIONALISM. A concept created by Chalmers Johnson to explain the key to Communist victory in China. He argues that the primary cause of the success of the **Chinese Communist Party** (CCP) in North China during the Anti-Japanese War and its subsequent takeover of the whole of China was neither its participation in an international Communist conspiracy nor the overwhelming appeal of the CCP's economic programs, but its ability to use peasant nationalism to mobilize popular support in response to the Japanese invasion and misrule. Peasant nationalism was different from that which the **Nationalist Party** advocated; the latter appealed mainly to intellectuals and the inhabitants of the treaty ports, who asked for cultural identity or economic independence. Peasant nationalism was provoked by the Japanese invasion, and it came with a belief in a myth that only the Chinese Communists could provide the peasants with organizational assistance and ideological "instruments for helping the rural masses attain a political understanding of the war to serve as a gloss on their personal experience."

PEKING MEDICAL UNION HOSPITAL. The best-known hospital in China. It was founded in 1921 by the China Medical Board of the Rockefeller Foundation. Before the hospital opened, the Rockefeller Foundation had already established the Peking Medical Union College in 1917. The Rockefeller Foundation invested several tens of millions of U.S. dollars in this hospital and its attached medical school over the following 30 years. The hospital was built in the previous residence of Prince Yu; therefore, it was called "The Rockefeller Institute in a Chinese Palace with a Medical School." The buildings of the hospital were designed by Charles Coolidge, who was involved in building the Harvard Medical School and the Rockefeller Institute. Franklin McLean was appointed the first president. In September 1921, the first group of female students in China were admitted by the Peking Medical Union College. In 1924, the first group of graduate students, three doctors and one nurse, obtained their degrees from the college. Afterward, more Chinese who graduated from the medical school began to work at the hospital. In 1928, the Nanjing government issued a law stipulating that presidents of Chinese universities must be Chinese citizens, and the majority of their boards of trustees must also be native Chinese. In April 1929, the American board members resigned and elected Chinese people as their successors.

In 1937, as the **Second Sino-Japanese War** broke out in Beijing, the American government suggested that all Americans return to the United States, but all American doctors and nurses chose to stay. During the war, most of them were detained by the Japanese in camps of war prisoners, and they were not released until Japan surrendered. In 1950, because of the Korean War, all U.S. connections with Peking Medical Union Hospital were cut off, the Rockefeller Foundation could no longer provide funds and personnel to support the institution, and the Communists took over the hospital and college.

PEKING UNIVERSITY. A top university in China. It was founded in 1888 as the Imperial University of the Capital and was the first modern university in China. After the **civil service examination** was abolished in 1905, most students saw the university as an alternative avenue to produce bureaucrats. The Imperial University of the Capital was renamed National Peking University in 1912. The fundamental reform of the university was initiated by the prominent scholar **Cai Yuanpei**, who was appointed university president on 4 January 1917. Cai encouraged diversity, tolerance, and academic freedom on this campus, making it an institution of teaching excellence and a center of academic research. In 1920, Peking University began to accept female students. The university was the birthplace of the **May Fourth Movement**, the **New Culture Movement**, and many student demonstrations. Respect for scholarship and patriotism became its tradition.

During the **Second Sino-Japanese War**, Peking University moved to Changsha and then Kunming, and along with Tsinhua University and Nakai University formed the National Southwestern Union University. In 1946, the three universities returned to their original sites and resumed their names. In the 1950s, Peking University merged with **Yenching University**, an American-sponsored private college, and moved from downtown Beijing to the former Yenching campus.

PENG DEHUAI (1898–1974). Prominent communist military leader and a victim of the inner-party struggle. He was born in Xiangtan, Hunan province, and his parents died when he was nine years old. Peng lived with his grandmother, who was a beggar. He worked in coal mines when he was a child before joining the Hunan warlord's army at the age of 16. In 1926, Peng was made a brigade commander and joined the **Chinese Communist Party** (CCP) in the next year. In 1928, he launched an uprising at Pingjiang, then led his troops to join **Mao Zedong**'s **Red Army**. When the **Long March** set out, Peng was in command of the Fifth Army Corps, one of two leading forces of the Central Red Army. He helped Mao resume his leadership at the **Zunyi Conference**. He also employed Mao's **guerrilla warfare** skills to break out of the encirclements of local warlord troops and led the army to arrive in Shanbei.

During the **Second Sino-Japanese War**, Peng served as deputy commander-in-chief of the **Eighth Route Army**. He launched the **Hundred Regiments Offensive**, which destroyed about 600 miles of railways and numerous Japanese garrisons. Despite these accomplishments, the offensive was criticized by Mao because it violated his strategies of guerrilla warfare. During the **Civil War**, Peng led the First **Field Army** to take over northwest China. He was appointed commander-in-chief of the Chinese troops in Korea during the Korean War, and he was elected vice chairman of the CCP Central Military Committee, serving as defense minister of the PRC. For his criticism against Mao's economic policy Peng was purged, and during the Cultural Revolution he was jailed and tortured to death.

PENG MING-MIN (1923–). Scholar of international law and noted Taiwanese independence activist. Born into a wealthy landlord family in Taizhong, Taiwan, Peng was a fifth-generation immigrant from Fujian to Taiwan. With a rich family background, Peng could afford to go to a Japanese-style school in Taiwan. He then traveled to Japan and studied political science at Tokyo Imperial University in 1942. World War II interrupted his studies, and he lost his left arm in an American air attack on Tokyo. Peng returned to Taiwan in 1946 to continue his education and graduated from Taiwan University in 1948. Later, he obtained his MA from McGill University and a PhD in law from the University of Paris. Peng witnessed the **February Twenty-Eighth Incident**, in which his father was badly hurt. Peng had been employed by the **Nationalist Party** in high government levels, but he decided to break with the Nationalist government. He published a manifesto claiming Taiwanese independence and was therefore arrested and exiled. Peng was an early leader of the Democratic Progressive Party.

PENG PAI (1896–1929). An early Communist leader and pioneer organizer of the Chinese rural revolution. Born into a wealthy landlord family in Haifeng, Guangdong Province, Peng traveled to Japan to study political economy in 1917 and graduated from Waseda University four years later. Peng joined the Chinese Socialist Youth League in 1921. In the same year, he returned to his home village and tried to establish a peasant association. Because of his landlord family background, Peng had difficulty winning the peasants' trust. To show his devotion to the rural revolution, Peng burned all his family's land deeds and distributed the land to landless villagers. His rebellious actions inspired a large number of peasants, who then joined Peng's association. By December 1922, 12 peasant associations were established in his home county with more than 16,000 members. For this, **Mao Zedong** referred to him as "the king of the peasant movement."

In July 1924, Peng built up the **Peasant Movement Training Institute** and organized peasant militia of the province of Guangdong. He joined the **Chinese Communist Party** (CCP) in 1924 and was elected an alternate member of the CCP Politburo in 1927. Peng participated in the **Northern Expedition** and the **Nanchang Mutiny**. After the failures of these urban insurrections, he embarked on **guerrilla warfare** in rural areas. By October 1927, a month before Mao Zeng set up the **Jiangxi Soviet**, Peng had established the first Soviet government and a Communist troop in Hailufeng, Guangdong Province. However, he was defeated by **Chen Jiongming**'s troops. Peng escaped to Guangzhou to join the **Canton Commune**. Afterward, Peng went to Shanghai, where he was arrested and executed by the **Nationalist Party** at the age of 32.

PENG ZHEN (1902–1997). Leading member of the **Chinese Communist Party** (CCP). Born in Quwo, Shanxi Province, Peng joined the CCP in 1923 and immediately organized local branches in the province. In 1929, Peng was arrested by the **Nationalist Party** (GMD) and stayed in jail for six years until being rescued by the CCP in 1935. Peng participated in the party's urban work and labor movement, and he was one of the major Communist leaders in North China and Manchuria. After 1949, he served as first secretary of the CCP in Beijing and mayor of the city. Peng was in charge of legal affairs of the new republic and served as the major assistant to **Deng Xiaoping** in the CCP Central Secretariat. During the Cultural Revolution, Peng was purged, but he returned to power in 1979 and was elected president of the Chinese Congress in 1983.

PEOPLE'S JOURNAL (MINBAO). The official publication of the **Tongmenghui**, founded on 26 November 1905 by **Sun Yat-sen** and

Huang Xing in Japan. The official publication of the **China Revival Society**, *20th-Century China,* was its predecessor. In the preface of the journal, Sun put forward his famous revolutionary theory, the **Three People's Principles**. The *People's Journal* pronounced the revolutionary ideas and engaged in a heated debate with the Constitutionalists headed by **Liang Qichao**. The *People's Journal* was a monthly, published in Japan. The Chinese students in Japan were its first group of readers, but most copies were smuggled to China for wider circulation. After the publication of issue 24, the journal was banned by the Japanese government. However, **Wang Jingwei** secretly edited and printed two more issues.

PEOPLE'S LIBERATION ARMY (PLA). The military arm of the **Chinese Communist Party**. Its flag consists of a yellow star and the Chinese characters for "Eight One," referring to 1 August, its founding day. After the split between the **Chinese Communist Party** (CCP) and the **Nationalist Party** (GMD), the Communists launched an uprising in the city of Nanchang on 1 August 1927. Although the uprising was quickly put down, its remnants joined **Mao Zedong**'s guerrilla fighters on **Jinggangshan** Mountain and formed the **Red Army**. In the following decade, **Chiang Kai-shek** launched several campaigns to encircle and eliminate the Red Army, and the Communists had to transfer from Jiangxi to northwestern China. This was known as the **Long March**. When the Long March started, the Central Red Army had 100,000 troops, but only 8,000 survived the journey to the destination. It was during the Long March that **Mao Zedong**'s de facto leadership of the army was established.

The Japanese aggression toward China brought the CCP and GMD together. The Red Army was integrated into the **National Revolutionary Army**, forming the **Eighth Route Army** and the **New Fourth Army** in 1937. During the war, they insisted on guerrilla tactics and recruited large numbers of peasants for quick expansion. By the end of the war, the Communists had 1.3 million troops. In 1946, due to the United States' mediation, the CCP and GMD signed an agreement that the GMD's troops (about 3 million) should reduce to 90 divisions and the CCP to 18 divisions; after six months, both would make a further reduction to 50 and 10 divisions, respectively.

In January 1947, after the civil war broke out, the Communist military forces were renamed the People's Liberation Army (PLA). It defeated the GMD's National Army and took over the whole of mainland China. Leadership by the Communist Party is always the fundamental principle of the military command system, and it was required that the party establish its branches in every company since the Red Army era. Since 1949, there have been Central Military Committees in the party and in the government. Although most members of the two committees are identical, the CCP Central Military Committee is the real headquarters of the PLA, while the state's Central Military Committee is only an honorary institution with some members who were previous GMD generals but transferred their allegiance to the CCP. The PLA's chief of staff is the secretary of the Central Military Committee of the CCP, and he is in charge of daily affairs of the military.

PEOPLE'S WAR. A theory and strategy developed by the Communist leader **Mao Zedong** for the Chinese Revolution. The Maoist theory of People's War emphasizes the power of the broad masses of people and argues that, from this perspective, the Chinese Revolution should go through three stages of development: first, it should mobilize the rural population, gaining their support through propaganda and social reforms; second, it should build Red armies to wage **guerrilla warfare** to attack the government's military forces and develop rural bases; finally, it should change from guerrilla warfare to mobile and conventional warfare, destroy the enemy, and seize cities.

PERIODIC MARKET SYSTEM. A model created by William Skinner on an economic hierarchy of rural markets in China. The first level in the hierarchy was the standard market, where the village households sold what they produced but did not consume, and they bought what they needed but did not produce. Because the consumption level of Chinese peasants was low, the standard market was frequently operated on a periodic basis, usually once or twice a week. The standard market had only a limited range of goods available. Itinerant merchants would travel to and from the next level, the intermediate market. At the top of the rural hierarchy were the central markets, which were the most rarified and had the most exclusive items available. Through this hierarchically ascending marketing system, goods moved from producers to wholesalers to retailers and to individual consumers. Intermediate and central markets performed large wholesale functions and handled more specialized and exotic goods that the lower markets could not provide. On the other hand, the intermediate and central markets also functioned as standard markets in their own areas.

PERMANENT REVOLUTION. The theory of permanent revolution was first formulated by the Russian Bolshevik leader Leon Trotsky in 1905. Trotsky pointed out that the proletariat in countries like Russia had to make two revolutions: the democratic revolution to overthrow feudal regimes and the Socialist revolution to build a proletarian dictatorship. **Mao Zedong** and the **Chinese Communist Party** (CCP) shared this idea with Trotsky but opposed Trotskyism for two reasons. First, Joseph Stalin initiated a war against Trotsky and purged him and other old Bolsheviks from the Russian Communist Party, denouncing Trotskyism as a counterrevolutionary theory. Second, Mao criticized Trotskyism for its ignorance of the revolutionary potential of the peasants and denial of a possible **united front** between the CCP and the Chinese national bourgeoisie. Mao emphasized the necessity to uphold the leadership of the working class in the Chinese democratic revolution so that the CCP would not waste time launching a Socialist revolution after it took over the whole of China. Mao's theory of permanent revolution was regarded as his contribution to orthodox Marxism, which developed into a theory of "continued revolution under the proletarian dictatorship," eventually leading to China's Great Proletarian Cultural Revolution in 1966–1976.

PIDGIN (PIGEON) ENGLISH. The lingua franca of the Chinese trading communities on the southern coast. A mixture of English, Portuguese, and Indian words, organized in Chinese syntax without regard for English grammatical rules.

PIGTAIL ARMY. Some 3,000 troops led by the **warlord** general **Zhang Xun**. The soldiers kept the **Manchu** hairstyle (pigtail) to show their loyalty to the abdicated **Xuantong Emperor**. In 1915, President **Li Yuanhong** and Premier Duan Qirui engaged in a conflict over the issue of China's participation in World War I. Li invited Zhang to come to Beijing to mediate. Zhang took this opportunity to lead the 3,000-strong pigtail army into the city, dismissing the Republican government and restoring Xuantong to the throne. Li Yuanhong fled to the Japanese embassy and ordered all provinces to attack Zhang, while

Duan Qirui organized an expeditionary army and stormed Beijing. Zhang Xun escaped and the pigtail army was quickly destroyed.

PING-JING, BATTLE OF (PINGJING CAMPAIGN, DECEMBER 1948–JANUARY 1949). One of the three campaigns in the civil war (the other two being the **Battle of Liao-Shen** and **Battle of Huai-Hai**). The term *Ping-Jin* refers to the cities Bei*ping* and Tian*jin*. In the closing weeks of 1948, **Lin Biao** led his Northeast Field Army south of the Great Wall and, in combination with the North China Army commanded by **Nie Rongzhen**, began to close the Communist net around the Suiyuan area and cities of Tianjin and Beijing. The Communist troops numbered over 1 million, while the commander in chief of the **Nationalist Party** (GMD) army, Fu Zuoyi, had about 500,000 troops. **Chiang Kai-shek** asked Fu to evacuate to South China, but Fu did not trust Chiang and remained in North China. The Communist troops first adopted the strategy of "besieging but not attacking" and cut off the connections between the GMD-defended cities.

Lin Biao created three models for finishing the job. The first was called the Suiyuan model. In the Suiyuan area, the **People's Liberation Army** (PLA) destroyed part of the GMD's military force, about 60,000 troops at Xinbaoan and Zhangjiakou, and had part of the troops led by Dong Qingwu cross over to the Communists. The second was the Tianjin model. On 13 January 1949, they launched an attack on Tianjin, and after 29 hours of fighting, wiped out the defenders' 62nd Army and 86th Army, totaling 10 divisions of 130,000 men. They also captured the Tianjin garrison commander, Chen Changjie. The third model was known as the Beiping model of peaceful settlement. Under immense pressure, Fu negotiated with the Communists and accepted their terms for surrender. Fu's 260,000 troops inside the city were reorganized by the PLA. On 31 January 1949, the Communists took over Beiping.

PINGXINGGUAN, BATTLE OF (1937). In September 1937, the 115th Division of the **Eighth Route Army** under **Lin Biao** found a chance to attack the Japanese, who had just defeated **Yan Xishan**'s troops in the Battle of Nankou and invaded the province of Shanxi. Lin Biao led the 115th Division to ambush the Japanese 21st Brigade at Pingxingguan, Shanxi Province. The battle began in the morning of 25 September and lasted until the afternoon. All the Japanese soldiers fought to the death, and no prisoners were captured. The 115th Division annihilated about 1,000 Japanese men but also paid high costs of its own. The Battle of Pingxingguan was the first victorious battle for the Chinese troops in the **Second Sino-Japanese War**, which inspired the Chinese in the resistance movement. It was on behalf of the National Government that **Chiang Kai-shek** sent Lin Biao a special citation.

POLITICAL CONSULTATIVE CONFERENCE (1946). Organized by the **Nationalist Party** (GMD) in 1946, it was referred to as the "old" Political Consultative Conference, as opposed to the "new" Political Consultative Conference organized by the **Chinese Communist Party** (CCP) in 1949. After the **Second Sino-Japanese War**, the CCP and GMD were immediately involved in several conflicts. With U.S. mediation, **Mao Zedong** and **Chiang Kai-shek** met in **Chongqing** and signed a peace agreement on 10 October 1945 that called for a political consultative conference to discuss further cooperation between various political forces. The conference opened on 10 January 1946 and closed on 31 January 1946. Thirty-eight delegates attended the conference, including eight representatives of the GMD, seven of the CCP, nine of the **China Democratic League**, five of the Youth Party, and nine nonpartisan individuals.

The participants discussed and came to agreement on five issues: the Plan for Enlarging the National Government, which would increase the Committee of National Affairs by one-third (most of the new members would be non-GMD members, but the GMD would still remain the majority in the committee); nationalization of military forces (especially the Communist troops; a three-person group would be organized to discuss the methods and steps); Outline of the Peaceful State Building Program; the addition of 150 representatives from Taiwan and Manchuria to the **National Assembly**, bringing the number of assembly seats to 2,050; and agreement on the constitutional draft, confirming the Chinese political system, including the parliament, cabinet, and local autonomy. However, these resolutions were not implemented due to the outbreak of the civil war.

POLITICAL RESEARCH GROUP. A political faction in the **Nationalist Party** (GMD). After the death of **Yuan Shikai**, the parliament was divided into different groups. A group of the GMD members, including Zhang Yaozeng, Li Genyuan, and Du Zhongxiu, supported the **Anhui Clique warlord**, Duan Qirui. They allied with the Society of European Studies and other intellectuals and formed the research group in parliament. Zhang, Li, and Du all became members of Duan's cabinet. In 1918, **Sun Yat-sen** launched the Protect the Constitution Movement, calling on congressmen to go to Guangzhou. Most members of the Political Research Group went to Guangzhou and formed the **Extraordinary Parliament**. The research group disappeared when the parliament was dissolved in 1923.

In the 1930s, the group resurfaced with Yang Yongtai as its leader and Xiong Shihui, Huang Fu, Zhang Qun, and Wu Tiecheng as its core members. During the **Encirclement and Suppression Campaigns** against the Communists, Yang was appointed chief secretary of **Chiang Kai-shek**'s headquarters in Nanchang and Xiong was appointed director of the General Office. They were Chiang's major assistants in forming the GMD's military strategy in the Suppression Campaigns, establishing new political orders in previously Communist-controlled areas, and promoting the **New Life Movement** throughout the country. Chiang's headquarters in Hanchang was the de facto **Executive Yuan** of the National Government, and the Political Research Group controlled the daily operations of the GMD. However, Yang was assassinated by his rivals in 1936, and the influence of the group quickly waned.

POTSDAM CONFERENCE. After Nazi Germany had agreed to unconditional surrender on 8 May 1945, three Allied countries, the United States, Great Britain, and the Soviet Union, held a conference at Cecilienhof, the home of the Crown Prince Wilhelm Hohenzollern, in Potsdam, Germany, from 17 July to 2 August 1945. The heads of state of the three countries, U.S. president Harry S. Truman, British prime minister Winston Churchill (later Clement Attlee), and chairman of the Soviet Council of People's Commissars Joseph Stalin attended the conference and discussed issues regarding the peace treaties and the postwar world order, especially how to administer the defeated Nazi Germany. On 26 July, the conference adopted the **Potsdam Declaration**, announcing that "the terms of the Cairo Declaration would be carried out," meaning that the Japanese-occupied Chinese territories, including Manchuria, Taiwan, and the Pescadores, must be returned to China. The declaration gave Japan an ultimatum, calling on the government of Japan to proclaim the unconditional surrender of all its military forces; "the alternative for Japan [was] prompt and utter destruction."

POTSDAM DECLARATION (PROCLAMATION DEFINING TERMS FOR JAPANESE SURRENDER). Statement issued on 26 July 1945 by Harry S. Truman, Winston Churchill, and **Chiang Kai-shek**. On 8 August, the Soviet Union entered the war against Japan and signed the Potsdam Declaration. This declaration called on the government of Japan to proclaim the unconditional surrender of all Japanese armed forces; otherwise, Japan would face "prompt and utter destruction." It also outlined the terms of surrender for Japan. The major points included the following: militarism in Japan had to end; Japan would be occupied until the basic objectives set out in this proclamation were met; the terms of the Cairo Declaration would be carried out, which meant that Japan had to return to China its occupied Chinese territories, including Manchuria, Taiwan, and the Pescadores; the Japanese army would be completely disarmed and allowed to return home; war criminals would be tried and punished; Japan would be permitted to maintain a viable industrial economy but not industries that would enable it to rearm for war; and freedom of speech, religion, and thought, as well as respect for fundamental human rights would be established in postwar Japan. The treaty was not intended to enslave the Japanese as a race or as a nation, and the Allied forces promised to withdraw from Japan as soon as these objectives were accomplished. *See also* POTSDAM CONFERENCE.

POTTINGER, HENRY ELDRED CURWEN (1789–1856). British military officer and administrator. Born in Mountpottinger, Ireland, Pottinger traveled to India in 1804. He first served in the army and then joined the **British East India Company** two years later. In August 1841, he participated in the **Opium War** against China, leading the British troops to defeat the Qing army and storm the cities of Amoy, Dinghai, Ningbo, and Shanghai. In August 1842, when Pottinger's troops besieged the city of Nanjing, the Qing court asked for peace. As an envoy of Great Britain, Pottinger negotiated with commissioners Qiying and Ilipu, who signed the **Treaty of Nanjing** on the British ship *Cornwallis*, which ended the first Opium War. On

26 June, Pottinger was appointed the first governor of Hong Kong. He continued the negotiations with China and persuaded Qiying to sign the supplementary Treaty of Nanjing on 22 July and the **Treaty of Humen** on 8 October 1843. Pottinger returned to England the next year and was then sent to South Africa. He died in retirement in Malta.

PRINCE CHUN. The title of peerage created by the **Xianfeng Emperor** for his seventh brother, Yi Xuan, in 1850. Yi Xuan was the second-rank prince (Prince of the Commandery), and then he was promoted to the first rank (Prince of Blood) in 1871. His son **Zai Feng** inherited the title of Prince Chun in 1891 and held it until the collapse of the Qing dynasty in 1911.

PRINCE GONG (1833–1898). The formal title of Prince Yixin. The sixth son of the **Daoguang Emperor**, known as the Sixth Prince. His nickname was Devil Number Six, in reference to his frequent contacts with Westerners. His mother was the Imperial Consort Jing, a daughter of a Mongol official in the government. She was made posthumously Empress Xiao Jing Cheng. In 1850, when his father, the Daoguang Emperor, died, Yixin's older half brother Yizhu acceded to the throne, becoming the **Xianfeng Emperor** and assuming the title Prince Gong of the First Rank. Prince Gong did not play a major role in government until the **Arrow War** in 1860, when British and French armies approached Beijing and the emperor fled to Rehe. Prince Gong was ordered to negotiate the **Convention of Peking** and thus won a reputation for dealing with foreign affairs.

In 1861, the Xianfeng Emperor died in Rehe. His only heir, a five-year-old son, came to the throne as the **Tongzhi Emperor**, and five powerful ministers became his regents. Prince Gong supported the **Dowager Cixi** in staging the Xinyou Coup, which purged the five regents and made Cixi the first and only Qing dynasty empress to rule China from "behind the curtains." Yixin was named prince-regent and appointed to a variety of important posts in the government. In 1861, on his recommendation, the **Zongli Yamen** was established; it functioned as a de facto foreign ministry. As the longtime head of the Zongli Yamen, Prince Gong engaged in many reforms, including opening a foreign-language school (the **Tongwenguan**). He attempted to be the sole regent, but the Dowager Cixi kept him from taking complete power. In 1862, his influence waned because of chastisements by the Dowager Cixi. The title Prince Gong was inherited by Yixin's son and grandson.

PRINCE YI. Title of peerage first given to Yin Xiang, the 13th son of the Kangxi Emperor, then subsequently inherited by his descendants for five generations. Zai Yuan, the sixth Prince Yi, was appointed regent for the **Tongzhi Emperor.** After the Xinyou Coup, however, Zai Yuan was put to death by the **Dowager Cixi** and the title was abolished.

PROBLEMS VERSUS "ISMS." A debate between Chinese liberal and Communist intellectuals in the 1920s. On 20 July 1919, **Hu Shih** published an article in *Weekly Critic* titled "More Study of Problems and Less Talk of 'isms.'" Hu criticized the intellectuals who embraced "isms" but ignored how to solve concrete problems. He stood for gradual evolution and step-by-step improvement. **Li Dazhao**, the leading Marxist, replied that the "isms" were necessary to provide a general direction for fundamental solutions, and then people could have hope of solving concrete problems one by one. Li also took Russia as an example to show that as the czarist regime was overthrown, every problem in Russia would be solved. Hu's rebuttal was that there was no panacea for all the ills of China, while Li insisted that solving the economic problem was fundamental. Nonetheless, Li agreed with Hu's criticism of the vague talks of anarchism and bolshevism. Li's Communist colleague, **Chen Duxiu**, conceded that it would be important to promote a concrete movement for the education and emancipation of workers. However, it was also impossible for the Chinese intellectuals in the 1920s to totally ignore "isms." Even Hu Shih could not help but talk about liberalism, pragmatism, and experimentalism. For the debate, Hu published four articles; Li also wrote four, but his last article was banned by the **warlord** in Beijing; this brought the debate to an end.

PROVISIONAL CONSULTATIVE YUAN. In November 1924, the parliament was dismissed by the **warlord Feng Yuxiang**. The leader of the **Anhui Clique**, Duan Qirui, came to power, and he called the Aftermath Resolution Meeting from 1 February through 21 April 1925. The meeting decided to elect the Provisional Consultative Yuan to excise the power of parliament. The Consultative Yuan existed for only one year and was dismissed after the collapse of Duan's government.

PROVISIONAL NATIONAL ASSEMBLY. Founded in 1912 as the first legislative institution of the revolutionaries after the Qing dynasty fell apart. On 29 December 1911, delegates from 17 provinces held a conference in Nanjing, electing **Sun Yat-sen** provisional president and designating 1 January 1912 as the first day of the republic. On 28 January, the Provisional National Assembly was established based on the conference of the provincial delegates, and **Lin Sen** was elected president of the assembly. On 6 March 1912, the Provisional National Assembly accepted the resignation of Sun Yat-sen and elected **Yuan Shikai** to succeed him. On 8 April 1913, the first Parliament of the Republic was inaugurated, and the provisional assembly was dismissed.

PURGE COMMITTEE. First established on 10 April 1927 by **Chiang Kai-shek** to dissolve the political department of the **National Revolutionary Army**. On 12 April 1927, Chiang Kai-shek dissolved the Communist-controlled Shanghai General Trade Union, disarmed the workers, and arrested and executed leaders in Shanghai. Three days after the incident, Chiang called a meeting with members of the **Nationalist Party** (GMD) Central Committee and Central Supervision Committee in Nanjing. The attendees passed a resolution on the wholesale liquidation of the Communists in the GMD party, army, and government. Following this, purge committees were set up in the provinces of Zhejiang, Fujian, Guangdong, Guangxi, Anhui, and Sichuan. The purge committees were authorized to use police, military force, and secret agents to raid Communist cells, disarm workers' pickets, shoot down suspects, eliminate trade union leaders, and persecute political dissidents to wipe out the influence of the **Chinese Communist Party**.

PUYI, AISIN-GIORO (1906–1967). Known as the Last Emperor of China, Puyi belonged to the **Manchu** Aisin-Gioro family and was the son of the **Prince Chun** Zai Geng. In 1908, when the **Guangxu Emperor** died without an heir, the **Dowager Cixi** handpicked Guangxu's cousin Puyi to succeed him. Puyi became the **Xuantong Emperor** at the age of three, and his father served as regent. When Puyi was five, the **Republican Revolution** took place and Puyi's mother, the

Empress Dowager Longyu, was forced to sign the Act of Abdication of the Emperor of the Great Qing on his behalf on 12 February 1912. In return, the Republicans offered the royal family the **Articles of Favorable Treatment**, allowing Puyi to retain his imperial title and continue to stay in the Forbidden City.

On 1 July 1917, the **warlord** general **Zhang Xun** led his **pigtail army** to Beijing and restored Puyi to the throne, but this lasted only 12 days. Believing that Puyi had violated the Act of Abdication, the Republican government abolished the Articles of Favorable Treatment and thus drove Puyi out of the palace. With Japanese help, Puyi fled to Tianjin and then moved to Manchuria, where he was installed by the Japanese as the "head of state" of **Manchukuo** in 1932. Two years later, he was officially crowned under the reign title Kangde. However, Puyi never held any real power and could do only what the Japanese advisers told him to do. His personal life was also closely watched by the Japanese. At the end of the **Second Sino-Japanese War**, the Soviet Red Army captured him before the Japanese could remove him to Japan. In 1946, he was asked to testify at the war crimes trial in Tokyo, and in 1950 he was repatriated from Russia to China. With other war criminals of Manchukuo, he lived in jail for 10 more years until his release in 1959. Puyi married five times but had no children.

– Q –

QIANLONG EMPEROR (REIGNED 1735–1796). The fifth emperor of the **Manchu** Qing dynasty, and the fourth Qing emperor to rule over China. Born in 1711, Qianglong was the fourth son of the Yongzheng Emperor and Empress Xiao Sheng Xian of the Niuhuru Clan. The Qianlong Emperor was a successful military leader, and his reign was one of the longest in Chinese history. Under Qianlong, the Qing dominated **Outer Mongolia**, incorporated Xinjiang into the dynasty's rule, sent armies into Tibet, and firmly established the Dalai Lama as ruler, with a Qing resident and garrison to preserve Chinese suzerainty. In addition, the Qing court enrolled dozens of Asian states in the Chinese tributary system.

Qianlong promoted several important cultural programs, including the compilation of the Complete Library of the Four Treasuries (*Siku qiuanshu*), which contained more than 36,000 volumes, arranged in the four main categories: classics (*jing*), history (*shi*), philosophy (*zu*), and belles-lettres (*ji*). At the same time, the emperor ordered the destruction of 13,862 volumes of works containing **anti-Manchu** sentiments and other "unacceptable" content. Qianlong believed in isolationism and refused the **McCartney Mission**, continuing to limit foreign trade to the one city of Canton. In his later years, Qianlong indulged in luxuries and hunting, leaving state affairs in the hands of his favored minister Heshen, who was corrupt and impotent. Qianlong's early military expeditions and increasing corruption of his government permanently harmed the dynasty, sowing the seeds of destruction. In 1795, Qianlong officially announced that he would pass the crown to his son, the **Jiaqing Emperor**, but he kept a tight grip on state power; Jiaqing was kept out of the limelight until his father's death in 1799.

QIN PRINCE. Prince of Blood. The first rank of **Manchu** prince. The title of peerage was conferred by the emperor on Manchu nobles, and it could be inherited by his descendants.

QIN-DOIHARA AGREEMENT. In June 1935, Japan began to push the plan of demilitarizing and controlling northern China. On 5 June 1935, Chinese troops arrested four Japanese spies in Zhangbei, Chahar. The Japanese military intelligence chief Doihara Kenji protested and demanded the punishment of the Chinese commanders and an in-person apology by the 29th Army Corps chief Song Zheyuan. The governor of Chahar, Qin Dechun, requested negotiations to settle the issue. On 17 June, the Kwantung Army devised a "negotiation guideline" that raised further demands, including moving the 29th Corps to the southwest of the Great Wall. On 27 June, Qing conceded to Japan in the Qin-Doihara Agreement, dismissing the commanders who arrested the Japanese spies, banning anti-Japanese organizations, pulling back the 29th Army Corps to the east of the Great Wall and to the north of Kalgan, and accepting Japanese advisers in the local administration in Chahar.

QINGYIBAO **(QINGYI JOURNAL).** Newspaper founded on 23 December 1898 by **Liang Qichao** after he was exiled to Japan; its purpose was to introduce Western political theories and democratic ideas to China. *Qingyibao* was published every 10 days. Each issue included political editorials, news, translations, and book reviews.

Qingyibao criticized the Qing conservatives headed by **Dowager Cixi** and praised the **Guangxu Emperor**, who supported radical reform. The mission of the newspaper was to advocate Liang's ideal of constitutional reform. On 21 December 1901, a fire destroyed the paper's offices and publication ceased.

QINGYIPAI (QINGYI PARTY). *Qingyi* was a traditional practice in which intellectuals used Confucian moral codes to evaluate and criticize government officials. Those officials who became the targets of qingyi criticism might be dismissed from their offices and forced to return to their home villages. This practice could be traced back to the Eastern Han period and it became a general mode of the independent intellectuals during the Ming dynasty. In the 19th century, the Qingyi Party consisted of a group of brilliant young scholars who attacked the "appeasement and defeatism" of **Li Hongzhang** and other Qing government officials, especially Li's compromise with France in the **Sino-French War**. They condemned appeasement as a sure way to encourage greater demands from the insatiable powers. Their speeches won public acclaim and imperial attention. Li Hongzhang complained that he was plagued by the irresponsible talk of the Qingyi Party. Although the party included some prominent officials, such as **Zhang Zhidong**, it was labeled as a group of people having no practical experience or genuine knowledge of foreign and military affairs. Facing foreign challenges, the Qing court vacillated between war and peace, but the dominant feeling was a fear of fighting the Western powers. Therefore, the Qing court, especially the **Dowager Cixi**, ignored qingyi criticism against Li Hongzhang and supported Li's various deals with foreigners.

QISHAN (1790–1854). Manchu noble and government official. Born into a family of the first-class Marquis, Qishan began to serve in the government at the age of 16. In 1819, Qishan was promoted to the position of governor of Henan but was soon dismissed due to a dereliction of duty. The **Daoguang Emperor** reinstated him shortly afterward in Shandong Province. Qishan successively served as governor of Sichuan and Zhili, and as a member of the **Grand Secretariat**. Qishan was one of the advocates for the legalization of the opium trade. When the first **Opium War** broke out, Qishan accused **Lin Zexu** of misunderstanding the opium issue, and he argued for a cease-fire and peace settlement. On 28 September 1840, Qishan replaced Lin Zexu as the imperial commissioner and viceroy of Liangguang to negotiate with the British. Qishan signed the **Convention of Chuenpeh**, ceding **Hong Kong** to Britain. The cession of the Chinese island enraged the Daoguang Emperor, who dismissed Qishan and confiscated his family properties. Years later, the emperor forgave Qishan again and appointed him minister to Tibet and governor of Sichuan. In 1853, Qishan was ordered to build a base camp in the north of the Yangtze River to confront the Taiping Kingdom in Nanjing. Qishan died in a battle against the rebels the next year.

QIU JIN (1875–1907). Revolutionary feminist, known as the Woman Knight of Mirror Lake. She was born in Shaoxing, Zhejiang Province. Well educated but unhappily married, Qiu was exposed to the new ideas brought about by Western learning, which eventually led her to leave her husband's family. In 1904, she sold her jewels and traveled to Japan. She studied at a women's school in Tokyo, where she joined the United League led by **Sun Yat-sen** in 1905. Having returned to China, she founded the *Chinese Woman's Journal* in Shanghai, speaking out for women's rights, including freedom of education, marriage, profession, and the abolition of footbinding. She served as headmistress of the school for girls in Shaoxing. In 1905, she and her cousin, **Xu Xilin**, planned to launch anti-Qing uprisings simultaneously, but Xu started earlier. After Xu's uprising failed, the government arrested Qiu. She was tortured and executed at the age of 32. Qiu is also remembered in China for her poetry, written in elegant language and mixing classical mythology and vivid imagination along with revolutionary rhetoric.

QIU YUFANG (1871–1904). The first female journalist in modern China. Born in Wuxi, Jiangsu Province, into a scholar family, Qiu began to study with her uncle at the age of 11 and then went to a Western-style school to study English. In 1898, Qiu and local liberal intellectuals organized the Society for Vernacular Literature and she worked with her uncle to create the *Wuxi Vernacular Journal* (*Wuxi baihua bao*). Qiu served as the major editor and columnist. *Wuxi Vernacular Journal* was a weekly journal that advocated political reform in China. As Qiu emphasized, this journal was devoted to radical reform by introducing "Western learning, Western affairs, and Western literature." Soon after she took up the journalist's life, she joined the editorial board of the first woman's newspaper—*Women Learning Post* (*Nüxue bao*) in Shanghai. After the failure of the **Hun-**

dred Days' Reform, the *Wuxi Vernacular Journal* was banned by the government after issue 29, and *Women Learning Post* also closed in October 1898. Qiu died of cholera at the age of 33.

QU QIUBAI (1899–1935). Marxist writer, journalist, and one of the early leaders of the **Chinese Communist Party** (CCP). Born in Changzhou, Jiangsu Province, Qu graduated from the Beijing School of Russian Language. He took an active part in the **May Fourth Movement** in 1919 and joined the Society for Marxist Studies organized by **Li Dazhao**. In 1920, Qu was dispatched by *Chengbao* (Morning Daily) to Moscow as its correspondent to report on the Soviet Union. His report and commentary were influential in exposing the Chinese to the Bolshevik Revolution and Soviet Russia. Having returned to China in 1923, Qu edited the CCP's journals, including *New Youth*, *Vanguard*, and *Guide*. On 7 August 1927, he presided over the urgent CCP meeting in Hankou, which elected him to replace **Chen Duxiu** as the acting chair of the CCP Politburo. According to **Comintern** instructions, Qu led several abortive urban uprisings. He was blamed for these failures and was removed from the party leadership in 1931 by **Wang Ming** and the **Twenty-eight Bolsheviks**.

As an excellent Marxist writer, Qu began to work with **Lu Xun** and lead the left-wing cultural movement in Shanghai. During this period, he published extensively on Marxist philosophy and Russian literature. In 1934, he was dispatched to the Communist Central base in Jiangxi and served as both chief editor of *Red China* and president of the Soviet University. When the Communists embarked on the **Long March**, however, Qu was not allowed to follow the **Red Army** in retreat. He was ordered to stay and carry out **guerrilla warfare**. His poor health made him incapable of successfully carrying out this assignment, and Qu was arrested on 23 February 1935 by **Chiang Kai-shek**'s troops in Changting, Fujian Province. He was executed three months later at the age of 36.

– R –

RAILWAY CONCESSION. A privilege granted to foreign countries or foreign companies by the Qing government in the 19th century that permitted them to invest in and construct railways in China.

Coincidentally, a wide belt of land along the railway lines was also ceded to the foreign countries or companies, so that the foreigners could live, open businesses, own properties, and build churches, schools, and hospitals in the railway concessions. More importantly, the railway concessions were entirely under foreign jurisdiction. The typical railway concessions were the Russian China Eastern Railway and the Japanese Southern Manchurian Railway. Both established their home states within the Chinese state.

RAILWAY PROTECTION MOVEMENT. Protests against the nationalization of railways mainly in Sichuan and also in the provinces of Hubei and Guangdong. The movement took on an antigovernment and antiforeign nature, feeding into the 1911 Revolution. By the turn of the century, the Chinese had shown enthusiasm in constructing railways with their own funds. In 1904, Xiliang, the governor of Sichuan, formed the Sichuan–Hankou Railway Company, which turned into a joint venture between the government and merchants the next year. He decided to collect railway levies for the construction of a provincial railway, which made all the landed gentry and most merchants in Sichuan shareholders in the company. Nonetheless, the company did not raise enough funds, and the railway project made slow progress. In May 1911, at the recommendation of the general director of the Bureau of National Railways, **Sheng Xuanhuai**, the Qing government proclaimed the nationalization of all railway projects. Sheng's idea was to take out foreign loans to speed up construction. The new policy meant that all private efforts would be in vain. Not only would money be lost, but also all hope of local autonomy.

The opposition to nationalization and foreign loans gave birth to the Railway Protection Movement. On 17 June 1911, more than 2,000 people held a rally in the city of Chengdu to show public anger and denounce the Qing court. The rally was followed by demonstrations and general strikes of students and merchants throughout the province. As the movement turned increasingly violent in Sichuan, tax bureaus and police offices were destroyed in the riots. Hubei and Guangdong followed suit. As the Qing government sent troops from Wuchang to quell the disturbance, the conflicts triggered armed uprisings. First in Wuchang, as soon as the troops were dispatched to Sichuan, the revolutionaries seized the opportunity to take control of the city on 10 October, and then people in the cities and counties of

Sichuan Province revolted, attacking local Qing governments. Following the other provinces, Sichuan declared independence on 27 October 1911, marking the collapse of the Qing dynasty.

RECOVERY SOCIETY (*GUANGFUHUI*). One of the revolutionary organizations in the late Qing period. Founded in the winter of 1904 by **Cai Yuanpei** in Shanghai, it was devoted to **anti-Manchu nationalism**. Many members were from Zhejiang Province, and their leaders included **Qiu Jin**, **Xu Xilin**, and Tao Chengzhang. In 1905, it was incorporated into the **Tongmenghui** in Tokyo, while continuing to operate in China. After massive arrests, followed by the execution of Xu Xilin and Qiu Jin, this organization ceased to exist. In February 1910, the Recovery Society was reestablished. **Zhang Binglin** was elected its new president and Tao Chengzhang its vice president. The Recovery Society played a leading role in the Shanghai Uprising in 1911. However, after Tao Chengzhang was assassinated on 14 January 1912, the organization ceased operations once again.

RECTIFICATION MOVEMENT. A political campaign launched by the **Chinese Communist Party** (CCP) in **Yan'an** in 1942 with the purpose of bringing Communist cadres and intellectuals to a uniformity of spirit to focus on the party's mission. In the beginning, the cadres were given 22 required readings, including six articles by **Mao Zedong**. It was an attempt to indoctrinate party members, especially those who joined the CCP after 1937, to help them have a better understanding of **Mao Zedong Thought**. In theory, this movement would eliminate the influence of **Wang Ming** and his supporters who blindly imitated Soviet experience and followed Moscow's directives. The participants were divided into small study groups, in which they discussed party documents, engaged in self-criticism, and confessed their errors. The discussions eventually evolved into personal attacks and a massive purge. The most famous victim of the purge was **Wang Shiwei**, who criticized the corruption and bureaucracy in Yan'an and was thus labeled a Trotskyite and arrested by the Central Social Department. Wang was executed in 1947.

Mao Zedong was the architect of the movement, and the leading group consisted of **Peng Zhen**, **Liu Shaoqi**, and **Kang Sheng**. Kang Sheng was in charge of a so-called Rescue Campaign, in which intellectuals and young people from coastal cities became suspected spies or Trotskyites. They were attacked, tortured, and forced to confess. Some survived the campaign, but many did not. Kang thus created a model of purges for the antirightist movement in 1957 and the Cultural Revolution in 1966–1976. It was also in this movement that Mao asserted that art and literature should serve politics and entertain workers, peasants, and soldiers. The Rectification Movement consolidated Mao Zedong's dominance as party leader and ensured the independence of CCP ideology from Moscow's control.

RED ARMY (CHINESE WORKERS' AND PEASANTS' RED ARMY). The Communist military force founded in 1927. After the failure of the Communist-led **Nanchang Mutiny** on 1 August 1927, **Zhu De** moved the remnants to the **Jinggangshan**, where he met **Mao Zedong**'s guerrillas. The merging of the two army units resulted in the establishment of the Chinese Workers' and Peasants' Red Army with Zhu as the commander and Mao as the CCP representative. During the **Second Sino-Japanese War**, the Red Army was organized into the **Eighth Route Army** and the **New Fourth Army**. Then these troops became the **People's Liberation Army** in March 1947 after the civil war broke out. Except during a short period of time (October 1932–January 1935), the Communist military force remained under the direct control of Mao Zedong until his death in 1976.

REED TREATY. The formal name is the U.S.-China Treaty of Tianjin of 17 June 1858. For details, see TIANJIN, TREATY OF. For the Supplemental Reed Treaty (1868), known as the Burlingame Treaty, see BURLINGAME, ANSON.

REORGANIZATION CLIQUE. A left-wing organization within the **Nationalist Party** (GMD). It was founded in 1928 by **Wang Jing-wei**'s supporters after Wang lost his leadership position to **Chiang Kai-shek** in the National Government. This clique regarded Wang Jingwei as its spiritual leader while daily operations were directed by **Chen Gongbo**. When Chen left for Paris, Wang Leping succeeded him. It had its headquarters in Shanghai and branches in 18 provinces and overseas. Appealing to students and young party members, its membership once exceeded 10,000. It published the magazines *Revolutionary Review* and *Forward*, calling on a revival of the spirit of the 1924 party reorganization. It instigated a series of military campaigns against Chiang Kai-shek, but all of them ended in failure. In August 1930, Wang even established another national government in Beijing to coordinate with **Yan Xishan**, **Feng Yuxiang**, and **Li Zongren** in a nationwide anti-Chiang expedition. This revolt was crushed by Chiang. In 1931, Wang announced that the Reorganization Clique had been dismissed, but the connections among its previous members remained, as well as its influence within the party.

REORGANIZATION LOAN. In February 1912, the **Yuan Shikai** government applied for a loan from the Five Power Banking Consortium for the reconstruction of China. The negotiations between his government and the consortium lasted 14 months, and in April 1913, his representatives finally signed the Reorganization Loan Contract with five countries: Great Britain, France, Germany, Russia, and Japan. The total loan amount was 25 million at 5 percent interest, to be paid off in 47 years. The Chinese salt tax and customs duty served as security. Because of these tough terms, this loan was opposed by the **Nationalist Party** and other political parties, and four provincial governors sent open telegraphs questioning the decision. Yuan proclaimed that his application for the loan had been secretly authorized by the senate in 1912, and he refused to submit the loan to parliament for discussion and ratification. Yuan used this loan for military purposes and to expand his personal army to crack down on **Sun Yat-sen**'s **Second Revolution**.

REPUBLIC PROTECTION CAMPAIGN (1915–1916). A campaign against **Yuan Shikai**'s monarchist movement. On 12 December 1915, Yuan declared the restoration of monarchy, calling it the **Glorious Constitution**. On 23 December, the Yunnan revolutionaries sent him an ultimatum, demanding that Yuan cancel this plan within two days. When Yuan refused, Yunnan declared its independence, and many other provinces followed suit. Yunnan leader **Cai E** organized the Republic Protection Army (RPA) dedicated to the "elimination of the country's thief, defense of the republic, upholding democracy, and developing the spirit of popular sovereignty." Yuan ordered an expedition against the RPA, but two of his major generals, Duan Qirui and Feng Guozhang, declined the post of commander. The foreign governments, including the Japanese, did not support Yuan's new reign. Finally, Yuan's troops were defeated by Cai E on 17 March 1916 in

Sichuan. The Republic Protection Campaign forced Yuan to abandon monarchism on 22 March 1916.

REPUBLICAN REVOLUTION (*XINHAI GEMING*, 1911 REVO-LUTION). Revolutionary movement that overthrew the **Manchu** monarchy and established the Republic of China. The decisive uprising occurred in the city of Wuchang on 10 October 1911. Because the year 1911 was Xinhai in the Chinese calendar, the 1911 Revolution is also called the Xinhai Revolution. After China's defeats by the Western powers and Japan in the 19th century and the failures of all the different reform efforts, many Chinese turned their sights to a radical revolution. Early revolutionary organizations included the **Revive China Society** led by **Sun Yat-sen**, the China Revival Society led by **Huang Xing**, and the **Recovery Society** led by **Cai Yuanpei**. These societies were merged into the United League (**Tongmenghui**) in Japan in 1905, defining their revolutionary objectives as "expelling the Manchus, restoring China for the Chinese, establishing a republic, and equalizing land holdings." The United League gained strong support among overseas Chinese and the secret organization—Hong Meng. Between 1900 and 1911, Sun Yat-sen, Huang Xing, and other leaders organized 10 uprisings in China, but all were suppressed by the Qing government.

On 10 October 1911, a group of **New Army** soldiers and low-ranking officers led by Xiong Bingkun and Wu Zhaolin decided to revolt and attacked the governor's residence. After the governor fled, they gained control over the cities of Wuchang, Hankou, and Hanyang. Since no revolutionary leader of the Tongmenghui was in Wuchang, they decided to elect a liberal senior commander, **Li Yuanhong**, as the military governor of Hubei Province. Soon after the success of the uprising, 15 provinces sent open telegrams supporting the revolution and proclaiming their independence. Sun Yat-sen and other leaders returned to China and established the Republic of China. Sun was elected provisional president by the provincial representatives on 25 December 1911. Nonetheless, the Qing court still controlled northern China, and power was in the hands of the military leader of the **Beiyang Army**, **Yuan Shikai**. Foreign consuls presented a note to both sides asking them "to establish a peaceful resolution at all speed." Sun negotiated and reached a compromise with Yuan. Yuan promised to support the republic and force the emperor to abdicate; in return,

Sun resigned the presidency and persuaded the provisional assembly to elect Yuan president. On 12 February 1912, the last emperor's mother signed the Act of Abdication on behalf of the **Xuantong Emperor**. With this act, the several-thousand-year-old monarchal system in China came to end.

RETURNED BOLSHEVIKS. Students who were trained by Russia at **Moscow Sun Yat-sen University** or the **Communist University of the Toilers of the East** between 1926 and 1930. After their return to China, they assumed the leadership of the **Chinese Communist Party** (CCP), hewing to the **Comintern**'s line and opposing **Mao Zedong**'s revolutionary strategy in the 1930s and 1940s. *See also* TWENTY-EIGHT BOLSHEVIKS.

REVIVE CHINA SOCIETY (*XINGZHONGHUI*). One of the revolutionary organizations during the late Qing period. It was led by **Sun Yat-sen**. As Sun was in exile, the society was founded in Honolulu, Hawaii, on 24 November 1894 with an initial membership of 112. Many of its early members were Overseas Chinese, secret society members, Christian converts, and missionaries. At the first meeting of the society, Sun put forward the platform "Expel the Manchus, restore China to the Chinese, and establish a republic." In 1904, Sun added "equalizing land" to the platform. On 16 March 1895, Lu Haotong designed for the Revive China Society a "Blue Sky, White Sun" flag, which became the national flag of the Republic of China in 1912. This organization was merged into the United League (**Tongmenghui**) in 1905.

THE REVOLUTIONARY ARMY (GEMINGJUN). Book advocating republican revolution in China. It was referred to as "the first textbook for national education." Published in May 1903 by the Datong Press in Shanghai, the book was written by **Zou Rong**, a Chinese student studying in Japan. He believed that the Chinese had become slaves of the Manchus. He argued that **Manchu** tyranny was the source of China's humiliation, frustration, and suffering. In his book, Zou called on Chinese to reject the Manchu yoke and seize their own destiny. To reach this goal, the Chinese had to learn from Western examples, make revolution, and build a Chinese republic. Qing officials arrested Zou in the **International Settlement in Shanghai** and tried to kill him. Due to Chinese protest and opposition from Western governments, Zou was tried by a Chinese-foreign mixed court in the **foreign concession** and was only sentenced to two years' imprisonment with hard labor. Following illness and torture by prison guards, Zou died at the age of 20.

REVOLUTIONARY COMMITTEE OF THE CHINESE KUOMINTANG (RCCK). One of eight registered minor "democratic parties" in the People's Republic of China (PRC). It was founded in 1948 by left-wing leaders of the **Nationalist Party** (GMD) in **Hong Kong**. As the **Second Sino-Japanese War** approached its end, the relations between the **Chinese Communist Party** (CCP) and the GMD turned sour. The left-wing GMD members criticized **Chiang Kai-shek**'s anti-Communist policy and the civil war. They established the Association of the Comrades of the **Three People's Principles** in 1945 in Chongqing and the Association for Promoting the GMD's Democracy in 1946 in Guangzhou. In November 1947, the left-wing GMD members held the first congress and decided to found the united organization. The congress announced the formal establishment of the RCCK on 1 January 1948. Madame Sun (**Song Qingling**) was elected honorary president and **Li Jishen**, president. The other RCCK leaders included **He Xiangning** and Liu Yazhi. In 1949, the representatives of the RCCK were invited by the CCP to attend the first **Chinese People's Political Consultative Conference** in Beijing. It worked with the CCP and other parties to draft the **Common Program**, electing the leaders of the PRC. Some of the RCCK members began to serve as vice-chairs or ministers of the new government. The RCCK had over 53,000 members and held 30 percent of the seats in the People's Political Consultative Conference, being the second-largest party next to the CCP. The RCCK had numerous assets in mainland China. It recruited members mainly among the social elite and intellectuals who had some connections with Taiwan.

REVOLUTIONARY PARTY OF CHINA. Founded in Japan by **Sun Yat-sen** in 1914, its predecessor was the **Chinese Nationalist Party**. In 1913, the **Second Revolution** ended in failure. Sun believed that the reason was the Nationalist Party was poorly organized and its leaders did not have a consensus on the anti–**Yuan Shikai** revolution. To transform the Nationalist Party into a more disciplined and devoted organization, Sun created the Revolutionary Party of China. All the members had to reregister with fingerprints and swear an oath of loyalty to Sun Yat-sen. **Huang Xing** and some other leaders disagreed with Sun and did not join the new party. By May 1914, the party had only 400 to 500 members, and the journal *Republic* was created as its formal publication. Between June 1914 and December 1915, the Revolutionary Party of China organized more than 40 abortive uprisings and succeeded in four assassinations. It coordinated with **Cai E** in the **National Protection War**. In July 1916, as the war approached its end, the Revolutionary Party of China proclaimed to restore the name Chinese Nationalist Party in October 1919.

RICHARD, TIMOTHY (1845–1919). Best known by his Chinese name, Ma Lixun. A British Baptist missionary sent to China by the Baptist Missionary Society (BMS), which had established three Christian district parishes in the provinces of Shandong, Shanxi, and Shaanxi in China. Born into a devout Baptist farming family in Carmarthenshire, Wales, Richard was inspired by the Second Evangelical Awakening to become a missionary. In 1865 Richard entered Haverfordwest Theological College, where he decided to devote himself to missionary work in China. In 1869, Richard arrived in Yantai (Chefoo), Shandong Province, where he did missionary work and engaged in a famine relief program. He established close connections with many government officials, including Zen Guoquan, **Zhang Zhidong**, and **Li Hongzhang**. It was his belief that "as long as we changed the minds of the noble officials, other people would be following in herd like sheep." In 1890, he became the editor in chief for the Chinese version of the *Chinese Times* and a major contributor to *Globe Magazine*. In his later years, he spent most of his time working for the **Society for the Diffusion of Christian and General Knowledge (SDCK)**. The SDCK published 2,000 books and pamphlets, including Richard's most influential book, *New Views on Current Affairs*. Richard's book not only introduced Western science and Christianity to the Chinese but also promoted China's institutional reform. **Kang Youwei** listed Richard as one of the two missionary writers who inspired him to initiate the **Hundred Days' Reform**. In May 1916, Richard resigned as general secretary of the SDCK and returned to England. He died in London three years later.

RIGHTIST OPPORTUNISM. An ideology or policy criticized by **Mao Zedong** and his supporters during the Chinese revolution. According to Mao, rightist opportunism opposes the basic principle of Marxism and cannot push the revolutionary movement forward. The major representatives of rightist opportunism in the **Chinese Communist Party** (CCP) were **Chen Duxiu** in 1924–1927 and **Wang Ming** during the **Second Sino-Japanese War**. Both gave up the proletarian leadership in the **United Front** between the CCP and the **Nationalist Party** (GMD). This was because they overestimated the enemy's strength and underestimated the power of the broad masses of the people. They took a pessimistic view of the Chinese Communist Revolution, feared the mass movements, and compromised with the enemy. Finally, they followed their immediate interests at the expense of long-term political goals.

Chen and Wang were both early leaders of the CCP. Chen's rightist opportunism offered **Chiang Kai-shek** an opportunity to launch on 12 April 1927 an anti-Communist coup in which many Communists were arrested and killed. Consequently, the CCP lost its foothold in the urban areas. Chen was criticized in the **August Seventh Conference** of the CCP Politburo and dismissed from office in 1927. Wang was a left opportunist in the 1930s, but he went to another extreme during the Second Sino-Japanese War. He advocated absolute obedience to Chiang Kai-shek during the war. His rightist opportunism prevented the CCP from maintaining an independent status in the second United Front with the GMD and would impede the CCP's development. Wang lost his influence after the **Rectification Movement** in **Yan'an** in the 1940s.

RONG DESHENG (1875–1952). An industrialist of modern China. Born in Wuxi, Jiangsu Province, Rong first worked as an apprentice at a native bank in Shanghai and then became an accountant. In 1896 with his elder brother, Rong Zhongjing, he opened his own native bank. They also invested in wheat flour and the textile industry by building 12 flour mills and four textile mills in Shanghai, Wuxi, Hankou, Jinan, and other cities. Rong thus became the biggest industrialist in China. Rong imported advanced equipment from abroad, recruited professional experts and technicians, and established a new managerial system to run his factories. He was enthusiastic about social welfare and was elected a member of the National Congress. During the **Second Sino-Japanese War**, Rong refused to collaborate with the Japanese, and most of his factories in Shanghai were destroyed or confiscated. Nonetheless, his enterprises in Hankou continued to be profitable. Production was restored and expanded after the Japanese surrendered. In 1949, as the Communists approached Shanghai, some of his family members left for Hong Kong, but he decided to stay. In 1950, Rong was appointed a member of the **Chinese People's Political Consultative Conference**. One of his sons, Rong Yiren, became vice president of the People's Republic of China in 1993.

ROY, MANABENDRA NATH (1887–1954). An Indian Communist and the **Comintern** representative to China in 1927. Born into a landed Brahmin family in Bengal, India, Roy joined the Indian Independence Movement at the age of 18. In 1917, Roy went to Mexico. He established close relations with local political leaders and was elected general secretary of the Mexican Socialist Party. After the Russian Bolshevik Revolution, Roy accepted communism and worked with **Mikhail Borodin** to found the Mexican Communist Party. At the invitation of Russian Communist leader Vladimir Lenin, Roy went to Moscow to attend the Second Congress of the Comintern and presented a report on revolutionary movements in colonial countries. In 1922, he became one of the leaders of the Far East Bureau of the Comintern.

In early 1927, Roy was sent to China as the head of the Comintern delegation to guide the Chinese Revolution. After **Chiang Kai-shek** purged the Communists in 1927, Roy had a sharp debate with Borodin and **Chen Duxiu**, who attempted to ally with the left-wing members of the **Nationalist Party** (GMD) to oppose Chiang. Roy advocated an agrarian revolution against Chiang and his rightist allies. On 23 May, the Comintern sent a secret telegraph to the **Chinese Communist Party** (CCP), instructing the CCP to launch a land revolution and urban mutiny, and to infiltrate the GMD's military forces. Roy showed this telegraph to the left-wing GMD leader **Wang Jingwei**. Wang was shocked and decided to change his policy from a peaceful separation from the CCP to suppression of the Communists. In August, Roy was called back to Moscow. Roy openly criticized the Comintern's policy as an ultraleftist fantasy and was therefore expelled from the Comintern. In 1930, he returned to India and was arrested by the British colonial government. He was jailed for six years, during which he wrote a 3,000-page manuscript, *The Philosophical Consequences of Modern Science*. During World War II, he advocated an alliance with Great Britain to fight fascism. He foresaw that India would attain independence following the defeat of the Axis powers, and he drew up a draft constitution for a free India. In his later years, he became disillusioned with communism but formulated an alternative philosophy, which he called "radical humanism."

RUAN LINGYU (1910–1935). The most famous Chinese movie star in the 1920s and 1930s. Born in Shanghai, Ruan began her acting career at the age of 16. Her father died early, and her mother was a domestic servicewoman. Ruan became known to nationwide audiences when she starred in *The Flower and Weeds* in 1930. She successfully starred in 29 films, being cast in diverse roles: rural woman, urban worker, young student, prostitute, schoolteacher, and housewife. Her films grossed big profits for the producers, making her the most successful actress in terms of box office receipts. Ruan had two unsuccessful love experiences and did not get married. After she became famous, her private life became a hot subject of the newspaper reporters and paparazzi. Various rumors about her romances and scandals spread quickly. Unable to endure the insults and pressure from the local media, Ruan committed suicide by taking an overdose of sleeping pills. On 8 March 1935, Ruan died in a hospital at the age of 25. The news shocked her colleagues and thousands of fans. **Lu Xun** wrote an article pointing out that it was gossip in the newspapers that killed Ruan Lingyu. Ruan's story was adapted into many novels, dramas, talk shows, operas, and movies.

RURAL EDUCATION MOVEMENT. Begun in the 1920s by a group of Chinese educators who believed that the "modern" Chinese education system simply imitated the Western model, which did not fit Chinese conditions. These scholars advocated "going to rural areas" and "going to people in an attempt to renew village life through educating peasants." However, the participants in the movement had differing goals and approaches to rural reforms. Some focused on rural schools, some on agricultural production, and others on political organizations. In October 1923, Yan Yangchu was elected general secretary of the China Society for the Promotion of Mass Education. He was first devoted to literacy education in cities and then turned his sights to the countryside. In 1926, the society chose Hebei Province as its experiment ground, beginning with Zecheng County. It designed a "four educations on livelihood, arts, health, and citizenship" program through school, community, and family. It also promoted political, educational, economic, hygienic, and customs reconstruction so as to solve the four major problems in the Chinese rural areas: poverty, ignorance, weakness, and selfishness. **Tao Xingzhi**, **Liang Shuming**, and other prominent educators engaged in these programs with great enthusiasm, and some leading universities, such as **Yenching University**, Nankai University, and Jingling University, were also involved. The movement made some progress in Sichuan Province during the **Second Sino-Japanese War** but finally lost its momentum after 1949.

RUSSELL & CO. An American trading company, also known as Qichang Co. in China. It was founded by Samuel Russell from Middletown, Connecticut, who came to China in 1818 and engaged in trading tea, silk, and opium on behalf of the Providence firm of Edward Carrington & Company. With the profits made in the business, Russell founded the company in Canton, and Wu Bingjian, one of the **Thirteen Hongs**, served as its major Chinese trading agent. In 1845, John Murray Forbes, Russell's partner, withdrew his capital to invest in the American transcontinental railway, but the company continued to thrive, moving its headquarters to Shanghai and opening Fuzhou as its trading port. In 1862, the company established the first navigation subcompany—Shanghai Steam Navigation Company—opening the navigation line between Shanghai and Hankou and controlling 80 percent of China's navigation business on the Yangtze River. Five years later, it opened another line between Shanghai and Tianjin.

The years between 1862 and 1877 were called the "era of Russell & Co." in the history of Chinese navigation. However, in the following years, the Shanghai Steam Navigation Company lost to the British China Navigation Company and the Chinese China Merchants' Steam Navigation Company. To pay his debts, Russell had to sell the company and its business to the China Merchants' Steam Navigation Company for 2.2 million taels in 1877. The next year, Russell opened a silk factory in Shanghai, which proved to be another failure. Russell was forced to stop production and he sold the factory to a French merchant. In sum, the middle 19th century was the golden age of Russell & Co., during which the company played a principal role in politics. Most American consuls in Shanghai were from this company. One of Russell's partners, Edward Cunningham, served as the American consul in Shanghai; it was he who suggested merging the British and American concessions to build the **International Settlement**.

RYUKYU ISLANDS. "Nansel Islands" in Japanese, but more commonly known as Okinawa. It is a chain of islands in the western Pacific Ocean at the eastern limit of the East China Sea. The islands have warm winters and hot summers. Precipitation is high and often affected by typhoons. Ryukyu was once an independent kingdom and became a member of China's **tributary system** in 1372. In 1609, the Japanese lord of Satsuma invaded and occupied the islands. In 1879, as the Japanese government announced the annexation of Ryukyu, the Ryukyuan king went to Beijing for help. The Qing government was too weak to send troops and offered him only diplomatic support. Despite China's objections, Japan finally annexed the islands. At the end of World War II, the United States occupied Okinawa. Nonetheless, in accordance with the San Francisco Peace Treaty, sovereignty was returned to Japan in 1972. Traditionally, the Ryukyus speak various indigenous languages (as members of the Japonic language family). Since 1879, Japanese has been the official language.

– S –

SAIFUDIN EZIZ (1915–2003). Prominent Uighur statesman and leader of the People's Republic of China. Born into a Muslim merchant family in Artush, Xinjiang, Saifudin received both traditional religious training and a modern education, and he could speak Chinese, Russian, and his native Uighur language. Saifudin traveled to the Soviet Union and studied at the Central Asian Political Institute in Tashkent from 1935 to 1937. In September 1944, he participated in the Soviet-supported **Three Districts Revolution** and served as minister of education in the revolutionary government (Yili regime). While most leaders of the Yili regime had a pro-Turkic sentiment, Saifudin distinguished himself for his socialist belief and close relations with the Russians. He joined the People's Revolutionary Party of the Three Districts in 1946. When the Nationalist government sent General **Zhang Zhizhong** to negotiate and reconcile with the rebels, Saifudin supported the peace agreement and joined the coalition government, serving as minister of education. He supported the Communist "peaceful liberation" of Xinjiang and joined the **Chinese Communist Party** (CCP) on 27 December 1949. After 1949, Saifudin was one of the major leaders of the local Communist government and military forces in Xinjiang. He was promoted to lieutenant general of the **People's Liberation Army**, member of the CCP Central Committee, alternate member of the CCP Politburo, and vice-chairman of the Chinese Congress.

SAIJINHUA (1872–1903). The pseudonym of Fu Yulian, a legendary woman in the late 19th and early 20th centuries. She was the first Chinese lady diplomat in Europe and a popular prostitute in Shanghai. But what made her more notorious was the story about her efforts to avoid a massacre in Beijing during the **Boxer Rebellion**.

Born into a poor family in Qianxian, Anhui Province, Fu was sold to a brothel in Suzhou when she was a child. In January 1886, she met Hong Jun, who was the number-one scholar in the imperial exam. Impressed by her beauty, Hong bought Fu freedom and made her his third concubine. The following spring, Hong was appointed Chinese ambassador to Russia, Germany, Austria, and the Netherlands. Hong saw Fu as the smartest among his wives and concubines and decided to bring her to Europe. In her three years' stay in Europe, Fu performed well in her new role, quickly picking up European languages and making friends with the German queen and various diplomats. In 1892, Hong was called back to China and died of sickness the next year. Fu gave up the title of noble lady of Hong, as well as her inheritance, and escaped from the Hong family.

Fu renamed herself Saijinhua and returned to a brothel in Shanghai. Her personal charm and "wife of ambassador" title made her the most popular prostitute in the city. The government worried about her influence and forced her to leave Shanghai. Saijinhua moved to Tianjin and then Beijing. The major controversy of her life was her performance during the Boxer Rebellion. When European expedition troops fought the Boxers and stormed Beijing, Saijinhua arranged meetings with some officers she had become acquainted with in Germany, including the commander in chief, Alfred Graf Von Waldersee.

It was said that she persuaded the German general to stop sacking the city and killing the people. For this reason, Saijinhua was referred to by ordinary Chinese as a "real ambassador." No official document supports this story, which seemed to have embarrassed the government. However, after the government secretly expelled Saijinhua from the city in 1900, more people began to give credence to the story. Three years later, the government accused her of abusing child prostitutes and put her in jail. She was released a month later and sent to Suzhou. She had two more marriages and both of her husbands died. In her later years, with nothing but the support of a few friends, she lived in poverty. In 1936, Saijinhua died in Beijing. After her death, her story was adapted into many novels and dramas.

SAINT JOHN'S UNIVERSITY. An Anglican university located in Shanghai, China. The university was founded in 1879 as Saint John's College by Samuel Isaac Joseph Schereschewsky, bishop of Shanghai, by combining two preexisting Anglican colleges in Shanghai. The university is located on a bend of the Suzhou Creek, and its architecture was designed to incorporate Chinese and Western elements. Saint John's began with 39 students, and the courses were given in both the Mandarin and Shanghai dialects. The college was originally designed and opened as a secondary school. Gradually, more college courses were added. In 1881, a young American missionary, Francis Lister Hawks Pott, began to teach courses in English, making Saint John's the first college offering courses in English in China. In 1886, when he was 24, Pott began to serve as president of Saint John's. He held the presidency for 52 years, and his teaching philosophy and devotion to education greatly contributed to the development of the school.

In 1905, Pott transformed Saint John's College into Saint John's University, consisting of schools of humanities, science, medicine, and divinity. It granted its first bachelor's degree in 1907. Saint John's University was registered in Washington State of the United States, and its diploma was recognized by American institutions of higher education. During the first half of the 20th century, Saint John's University produced several influential figures, including **Wellington Koo**, **Lin Yutang**, **T. V. Soong**, Yen Chia-kan, and **Rong Yiren**. After 1949, the Communist government decided to close all missionary schools or universities receiving foreign donations. Saint John's University was broken up in 1952, and its faculty were transferred to several universities, including East China Normal University, Fudan University, Shanghai Second Medical College, and the University of Communication, while the campus of Saint John's University became occupied by East China University of Politics and Law.

SCRAMBLE FOR CONCESSIONS. The policies and efforts of the Western powers to create their respective spheres of influence in China during the late 19th century. The Western powers had a strong intention to seek cheap raw materials, favorable markets, and investments in China. Prompted by the Sino-Japanese **Treaty of Shimonoseki** of 1895, the powers worried that China would be partitioned and began to compete with each other. The British mainly intended to keep the status quo in its commercial predominance. In the meantime, Great Britain was aggressive in the scramble for concessions, leasing the **New Territories** for 99 years and Weihaiwei for 25 years to contain Russian expansion, and fostering its holding of the Yangtze Valley to counterbalance German occupation of the Jiaozhou Bay. The Russians gained more territories from China—including the **railway concession** along the **Chinese Eastern Railway** from Siberia via Harbin to Vladivostok—in order to contain the Japanese expansion in Manchuria. Japan was waiting for an opportunity to deprive the Russians of southern Manchuria, and it forced the Qing government to promise the nonalienation of Fujian Province to pave the way for its intrusion into southeastern China. The most important area for France was south China, where France gained the 99-year lease of Guangzhou Bay and a nonalienation clause over Hainan Island, which also contributed to the consolidation of French Indochina. The United States, involved in the Spanish-American War, did not participate in the scramble. Instead, it insisted on the concept of an "**open door**" to allow the free movement of trade and commerce.

SECOND FRONT ARMY (SECOND FRONT ARMY OF THE CHINESE WORKERS' AND PEASANTS' RED ARMY). One of three major Communist military forces during 1928–1936. After the failure of the urban uprisings in Nanchang, He Long and Zhou Yiqun were sent to Hunan to organize peasant guerrilla forces. He and Zhou recruited the first group of soldiers mainly from among the **Gelaohui** and then organized partisan units in the Hunan-Hubei border areas. These were known as the 2nd Army of the **Red Army**. In the meantime, Zhou cooperated with Duan Dechang and established the 6th Army in western Hubei. The two units were brought together to form the 2nd Army Corps, and the area under its control became known as the Xiang-E-Xi Soviet. In October 1934, the 2nd Army Corps was joined by the 6th Army led by **Ren Bishi** and **Xiao Ke** from the Hunan-Jiangxi border base. With this merger, the Second Front Army was established. He Long was made the commander and Ren Bishi, the political commissar. When the **First Front Army** left the **Jiangxi Soviet** on the **Long March** in the fall of 1934, the Second Front Army was still in northwest Hunan.

The Nationalist troops' focus on hunting, blocking, and fighting the First Front Army tentatively released the pressure on He Long. In April 1935, however, the Second Front Army could no longer withstand the **Nationalist Party** attacks and had to move to northwest Hunan. After the First Front Army arrived in Shaanxi, the Nationalist troops initiated a new offensive against He's men. The Second Front Army finally set out on its own leg of the Long March. In June 1936, He Long's troops met the **Fourth Front Army** led by **Zhang Guotao** and **Xu Xiangqian** in Ganzi, Xikang Province. Having noticed that Zhang had a strategy different from the Central Committee of the **Chinese Communist Party**, He persuaded most commanders of the Fourth Front Army to follow him. He Long brought the combined forces north and finally joined **Mao Zedong**'s First Front Army at Huining, Gansu Province, in October 1936. The overall force of the Second Front Army consisted of 40,000 men at the beginning of the Long March, but by the time it arrived at Huining, that number had been reduced to 15,000. The Second Front Army was then posted in the northern section of Shaanxi Province. After the outbreak of the **Second Sino-Japanese War** in 1937, the Second Front Army was reorganized into the 120th Division of the **Eighth Route Army**. He Long was made the commander and Guan Xiangying, the political commissar.

SECOND PROVISIONAL NATIONAL ASSEMBLY. On 13 June 1917, taking advantage of the conflict between President **Li Yuanhong** and Premier **Duan Qirui**, General **Zhang Xun** led his **pigtail army** to Beijing and restored the **Manchu** monarchy. This provoked great protests all over China. Duan and his ally **Cao Kun** gathered their **Beiyang Army** against Zhang's troops. After Duan drove Zhang out of Beijing, he organized the Second Provisional National Assembly, which was a transitional institution before Duan managed to establish the **Anfu Parliament** under his control in August 1918. *See also* NATIONAL ASSEMBLY.

SECOND REVOLUTION (1913). An abortive anti–**Yuan Shikai** campaign launched by **Sun Yat-sen**. In February 1913, the Nationalist Party won the majority of seats in the Congress of the Republic of China, and its leader, **Song Jiaoren**, was to be the premier. Since Song advocated republicanism and opposed the dictatorship of President Yuan Shikai, Yuan's people sent an assassin to Shanghai and murdered Song at the railway station. Sun Yat-sen urged an immediate military expedition against Yuan, while other leaders preferred to protest by legal methods. The military campaign was postponed until Yuan began to dismiss republican commanders and governors from their offices. On 12 July, Sun ordered General Li Liejun to declare the independence of Jiangxi Province. Five other provinces and the city of Shanghai followed suit. Three days later, **Huang Xing** arrived in Nanjing to embark on a nationwide expedition. However, the poorly organized troops of Sun and Huang's revolutionaries were quickly crushed by Yuan's **Beiyang Army**. On 1 September 1913, General **Zhang Xun** led troops to storm Nanjing, and all six provinces surrendered. Sun and Huang fled to Japan and the Second Revolution concluded in failure.

SECOND SINO-JAPANESE WAR (1937–1945). A war between China and Japan, known also as the War of Resistance against Japanese Aggression, or the Eight Years' War of Resistance, or simply the War of Resistance in China. This was part of World War II, or the Asian front of World War II against global fascism. On 18 September 1931, young officers of the Japanese Kwantung Army detonated a bomb on the Southern Railway track outside Mukden and claimed that the bombing was a Chinese conspiracy. They began to attack the Chinese troops in Mukden. **Chiang Kai-shek** warned **Zhang Xueliang**, the commander of the Chinese troops in Manchuria, not to engage the Japanese, and appealed to the League of Nations for help. Chiang ordered all Chinese troops to retreat to China proper, which allowed the Japanese to easily occupy the whole of Manchuria.

On 28 January 1932, the Japanese besieged Shanghai but met strong resistance from the **Chinese Nineteenth Route Army**. In

February, the Japanese army established the puppet state of **Manchukuo** in Manchuria. When the League of Nations refused to recognize Manchukuo's legality, Japan withdrew from the league. In Japanese imperial propaganda, the invasion of China was part of the "holy war" (*seisen*), the first step of the *hakko ichiu* (eight corners of the world under one roof). After the seizure of Manchuria, the Japanese forces began to move into North China. Believing in "domestic pacification before resistance against foreign invasion," Chiang spent all his energy staging military campaigns to wipe out the Communists.

On 12 December 1936, Zhang Xueliang kidnapped Chiang, forcing him to agree to stop the civil war and fight against Japan. Chiang's government finally engaged in the war after the **Marco Polo Bridge Incident** on 7 July 1937. Chiang organized an anti-Japanese front with the Communists, and the Communist **Red Army** was reorganized into the **Eighth Route Army** and **New Fourth Army** under his command. On 13 December 1937, the Japanese stormed Nanjing and began to conduct the Rape of Nanjing, massacring 200,000 to 300,000 people in the following months. The Nationalist government retreated to the temporary capital **Chongqing**, but guerrilla fighting still went on in the Japanese-conquered regions. The Chinese won few but important battles, such as the battles at **Pingxingguan**, **Tai'erzhuang**, and Changsha, and also organized strong resistance in the Japanese-occupied areas, which made victory seem impossible to the Japanese.

In November 1938, the Japanese premier Fumimaro Konoe proclaimed a **New Order in East Asia**, urging China to surrender. In response to his call, one of the **Nationalist Party** (GMD) leaders, Wang Ching-wei, initiated a **peace movement** and established a puppet government in Nanjing in March 1940. On the other hand, the Japanese employed the Three Alls Policy (kill all, loot all, and burn all) in an attempt to wipe out the guerrilla fighters and their supporters. However, as they successfully mobilized millions of peasants to join the guerrillas and undertook democratic reforms in their controlled areas, the Communists not only survived the war but also greatly expanded.

After the attack at Pearl Harbor, the United States increased its support to the Chinese resistance movement. In 1942, the visit of Madame Chiang (**Soong May-ling**) to the United States and her speech before the U.S. Congress won public understanding of and support for the Chinese resistance movement. The U.S. Lend-Lease aid to China had passed the $1.54 billion mark by the end of the war. General **Stilwell** served as Chiang's chief of staff and commanded U.S. troops in the China-Burma-India theater. A group of American "volunteer" pilots joined the war, forming the famous **Flying Tigers**, with **Claire Chennault** as their commander.

In August 1945, as the United States dropped atomic bombs on Japan and the Soviet troops destroyed the Japanese Kwantung Army, Japan announced its unconditional surrender to the Allied powers. On 9 September 1945, Yasuji Okamura, representing the Japanese headquarters, signed the Instrument of Surrender and submitted his sword to **He Yingqin**, commander in chief of the Chinese troops. By the provisions of the Cairo Declaration, Manchuria, Taiwan, and the Pescadores were restored to China. Chinese sources indicate that the total military and nonmilitary casualties of the war totaled 35 million.

SELF-STRENGTHENING MOVEMENT (1860–1895). Chinese efforts to make a rich country and strong army by learning Western technology and building Western-style industry. The movement was motivated by an urgent need to deal with the increasing threat of domestic rebellions and foreign intrusions. It produced China's first group of modern enterprises but concluded with China's defeat by Japan in 1895. By the middle of the 19th century, most scholars and officials had reached a consensus on "learning barbarians' superior technology to control the barbarians." It was assumed that China could employ Western technology while retaining traditional Chinese values and philosophy. The *Ti-Yong* **formula**, meaning "Chinese learning for essence and Western learning for practical use," thus became the guiding principle of the movement.

On March 11 1861, the Qing court established a new office for foreign affairs, the **Zongli Yamen** headed by **Prince Gong**, marking the beginning of the Self-Strengthening Movement. The first foreign-language school, **Tongwenguan**, opened in Beijing and a total of 120 teenage boys were sent to the United States for study. Prince Gong tried to promote cooperation with the powers and made large orders of Western firearms. Some provincial officials transformed their local militias along the lines of Western military models to suppress the **Taiping Rebellion**. The Western gunfire proved to be shockingly powerful in battle. After the Taiping rebels were eliminated, serious military projects were immediately launched in the southern and southeastern provinces, creating the Anqing Arsenal by **Zeng Guofan**, the **Jiangnan Arsenal** and Jinling Arsenal by **Li Hongzhang**, the **Fuzhou dockyard** by Zuo Zongtang, and the Tianjin Machine Factory by Chonghou. The court showed great interest not only in purchasing Western firearms and equipments but also in dispatching officials and students abroad to discover the secret of Western armament and shipbuilding so as to develop China's own military industry.

In the first stage of the Self-Strengthening Movement (1861–1872), all the programs were government undertakings, operating in old ways and plagued by bureaucratic inefficiency and official nepotism. As the movement's leaders recognized that military industry was capital consuming and could not quickly enrich the country, they shifted their attention to profit-oriented enterprises, such as railways, shipping, mining, and telegraph.

The main accomplishments in the second stage (1872–1884) included the inauguration of the **China Merchants' Steamship Navigation Company**, the **Kaiping Coal Mines**, the **Shanghai Cotton Cloth Mill**, and the Imperial Telegraph Administration. A new managerial approach was also employed, known as "government supervised and merchant managed." The government offered the enterprise licenses and provided some funds or loans, but profit and loss were entirely the responsibility of the merchants. The government also adopted some measures, if necessary, to suppress competition and help these enterprises monopolize business. In the meantime, Western-style schools mushroomed throughout the country, and more students traveled to the United States to study science, military training, and foreign languages. Although new enterprises trained and employed Chinese engineers and technicians, they relied heavily on foreign equipment and personnel.

During the third stage (1885–1895), textile and other light industry gained momentum. The Daye Iron Mines, the Pingxiang Coal Mines, the Hanyan Ironworks, and the Guizhou Ironworks were established. The major enterprises created at this stage were "joint government and merchant undertakings," which meant that government and merchants shared managerial responsibility and profit. It was also at this stage that the government continued to emphasize the military buildup by establishing the **Navy Yamen** (1885) and the **Beiyang Fleet** (1888), which possessed the two largest warships in East Asia: the *Dinyuan* and the *Zhengyuan*.

The Self-Strengthening Movement did not have a national leader or coordinator; the major planners included Prince Gong and provincial officials—**Zeng Guofan, Zhang Zhidong, Zuo Zongtang**, and **Li Hongzhang**. The conservatives at court often criticized them and refused to cooperate. In 1894, the Beiyang Fleet was destroyed by Japan; this showed the Self-Strengthening Movement to be a dismal failure and taught the Chinese the necessity of moving beyond tradition and transforming the country not only economically but also politically and culturally.

SELF-STRENGTHENING SOCIETY (*ZIQIANGHUI*). One of the revolutionary organizations before the 1911 Revolution. It was founded by Wu Gu in Japan and merged with the **Tongmenghui** in 1905.

SENGGE RINCHEN (SENGGELINQIN, 1811–1865). Mongol nobleman and general of the Qing dynasty. Sengge Rinchen was a descendant of Genghis Khan, and his personal name consists of the Tibetan words for "lion" and "treasure." Adopted by the Mongolian prince Kererxin, Sengge Rinchen inherited the title of Imperial Prince of the Second Degree in 1825. During the Second **Opium War**, he was appointed imperial commissioner to defend the **Dagu Forts**. Sengge Rinchen once defeated the Anglo-French alliance troops in 1859, but his troops were finally crushed by the alliance army the next year. He abandoned his army and escaped from the battlefield. Because of this, Sengge Rinchen was dismissed and his title was revoked. However, the Qing soon reinstated him, dispatching him to quell the **Nian Rebellion** while restoring his title and rank. In May 1865, his troops were ambushed by Nian rebels and Sengge Rinchen was killed in the battle at Heze, Shandong Province.

SERVICE, JOHN STEWART (1909–1999). An American diplomat, one of the "China hands" prior to and during World War II. Service was born in Chengdu, Sichuan Province, where his father was working as a missionary for the Young Men's Christian Association. Service attended the Shanghai American Middle School and then followed his family to California, where he graduated from Berkeley High School at the age of 15. He then enrolled at Oberlin College in 1927, majoring in art history and economics. In 1933, Service took and passed the Foreign Service Exam. His first assignment was a clerkship position at the American consulate in Kunming; two years later, he was promoted to foreign service officer. In 1938, he was assigned to the Shanghai Consulate General under Clarence E. Gauss. When Gauss was promoted to ambassador, he made Service third and then second secretary of the American Embassy in **Chongqing**.

Service was an important member of the U.S. Army Observation Group, also known as the **Dixie Mission**, which traveled to **Yan'an**, where he met and interviewed many of the top Communist leaders, such as **Mao Zedong** and **Zhou Enlai**. Over the next four months, he sent back many reports that were highly positive about the Chinese Communists. In the meantime, he wrote critically of the Nationalists under **Chiang Kai-shek**, whom he considered hopelessly corrupt and incompetent. He argued for American support of the **Chinese Communist Party** during the **Second Sino-Japanese War** and predicted that a civil war between the CCP and the **Nationalist Party** was inevitable and that the Communists would triumph. He also suggested that the United States could work constructively with the Communists. His recommendations were rejected by the new U.S. ambassador to China, **Patrick Hurley**.

Service returned to Washington in 1945 and was soon arrested, being accused of passing top-secret documents to Communist sympathizers at the magazine *Amerasia*, but he was found innocent by a grand jury by a vote of 20–0. In 1950, Joseph McCarthy launched an attack against Service. From 1952 on, Service worked for a steam trap company in New York and also appealed against his dismissal from the State Department. The Supreme Court found that Service's dismissal had violated U.S. State Department procedures, but this did not clear Service of security violation charges. Service returned to the State Department in 1957 but held no important assignments. After his 1962 retirement, he pursued a master's degree in political science at the University of California, Berkeley. After graduation, Service worked as library curator for the school's Center for Chinese Studies into the 1970s. In 1971, preceding President Richard Nixon's visit to China, Service was one of a handful of Americans who were invited back to China. He met again with Zhou Enlai, and he and his wife Caroline appeared on the cover of *Parade Magazine*. In 1977, Oberlin College awarded him an honorary degree. Service died on 3 February 1999 at the age of 90 in Oakland, California.

SEVEN GENTLEMEN. The Seven Gentlemen were seven democratic activists—Sheng Junru, Zhang Naiqi, **Zou Taofen**, **Shi Liang** (female), Li Gongpu, Wang Zhaoshi, and Sa Qianli—who were arrested by the **Nationalist Party** (GMD) in 1936. After the **Manchuria Incident** of 1931, China witnessed a great anti-Japanese movement. In May 1936, Madam Sun, **He Xiangning**, and some senior GMD leaders and nonpartisan intellectuals initiated the formation of the National Salvation Association in Shanghai. The Seven Gentlemen were among the initiators and were deeply involved in the activities of the association. On 15 July, they issued an open statement demanding an end to the civil war, the release of political prisoners, and the creation of a unified anti-Japanese government. On 12 November, the Seven Gentlemen organized a rally propagandizing their program to mobilize the urban masses. On the morning of 23 November 1936, GMD agents arrested the seven. Since they were all prominent scholars and professionals in their fields, they were referred to as the Seven Gentlemen. In 1937, the government decided to try them, which provoked a nationwide campaign to rescue the Seven Gentlemen. Madame Sun (**Song Qingling**) even warned the government that she would ask to be jailed with the Seven Gentlemen. Under the pressure of public opinion, the government released the Seven Gentlemen on 31 July 1937.

SHANDONG ISSUE. Shandong was a former German concession in China. After World War I, as one of the victorious nations, China wished to restore its sovereign authority over Shandong. However, Japan asked the Allied powers to allow it to replace Germany and colonize the province. On 23 August 1914, Japan declared war on Germany, and after 70 days fighting, on 7 November Japan stormed the German concession in Shandong. In January 1915, Japan raised the **Twenty-one Demands**, including the recognition of Japan's position in Shandong, which were accepted by the **Yuan Shikai** government. However, the Twenty-one Demands were never ratified by the Chinese parliament. In 1917, the **Beijing government** declared war on Germany, and Japan provided a military loan to help China build up its forces for the war. This loan was not spent for military buildup but was instead used by Duan Qirui to bribe congressmen to support his cabinet. In offering China the loan, the Japanese government prepared a "loan contract," known as the Sino-Japanese Secret

Treaty, which granted Japan some privileges in Shandong, such as Sino-Japanese comanagement of the Jiao-Ji Railway. The secret treaty later became the major basis for Japanese demands for taking over Shandong after World War I. In 1919, the Chinese delegation attended the **Paris Peace Conference** and announced China's position. The Chinese representative **Wellington Koo** (Gu Weijun) argued that Shandong was the birthplace of Confucius, and the Chinese could not give up this holy land, just as Christians could not give up Jerusalem. However, the conference decided to compromise with Japan and hand over the former German colony to Japan. The Shandong issue provoked the **May Fourth Movement** and anti-Japanese boycott in China. The Chinese delegation headed by Koo refused to sign the Versailles Treaty.

SHAN-GAN-NING BORDER REGION. A "sparsely populated and bandit-ridden badlands" in the border area between three provinces, Shanxi, Gansu, and Ningxia in Northwest China. In October 1935, the **First Front Army** under the command of **Mao Zedong** arrived in this area, making it the central revolutionary base of the **Chinese Communist Party** (CCP) during the **Second Sino-Japanese War**. The headquarters of the reorganized **Red Army**, the **Eighth Route Army** and the **New Fourth Army**, were located in this region. It consisted of 23 counties and the town of **Yan'an**, with a population of 2 million. In the Shan-Gan-Ning Region, Mao rebuilt the Communist military forces, organized the resistance movement, launched a "reduction of rent and interest rates" program, established a "**three-thirds**" regional government and thus gained popular support among the Chinese peasantry and set up a model for a Communist regime.

SHANGHAI COTTON CLOTH MILL. The first Chinese spinning mill, established in 1878 by **Li Hongzhang** and **Shen Baozhen**. The Shanghai Cotton Cloth Mill was a government-supervised merchant undertaking that used cheap female labor to cut costs. The mill enjoyed monopoly rights under the patronage of Li Hongzhang to hinder the advance of foreign capital into China. In addition, no other Chinese merchants were allowed to open cotton cloth mills to compete with it. The mill did fund-raising among Chinese merchants and gained a primary investment of 500,000 taels. The machines and equipment were imported from England. However, with local cotton, it could not produce high-quality cloth. The general manager was a government official, Peng Ruzhong, who knew little about production. Because of poor management, the mill's products could not find a market, and the mill suffered a serious deficit. In 1893, a fire turned the whole factory into ashes.

SHANGHAI TARIFF CONFERENCE (1858). The conference between China and Great Britain held in October 1858. After the Sino-British **Treaty of Tianjin** was signed, the Chinese emperor worried that the "barbarians" would erect high buildings in the capital and from there use binoculars to spy on him in the palace. The emperor asked to abrogate the article of the Treaty of Tianjin that granted foreign envoys the right of residence in Beijing. In return, he wanted to offer a reduction or exemption of customs dues for the British commodities. To seek a compromise, the British representative, Lord Elgin, suggested that the British ambassador reside in a place other than Beijing, and his visits to the capital would be only for business if the emperor ratified the Treaty of Tianjin. The Shanghai Tariff Conference was held against this background and finally came to the following agreements on the tariff: 5 percent ad valorem for both imports and exports, except for opium, tea, and silk; legalized opium importation at 30 taels per picul (about 7–8 percent of the value); the tariff on tea would be 2.5 taels per picul (15–20 percent of the value); the tariff on silk would be 10 taels per picul (5 percent of the value). Compared with the British tariff, the Chinese duties were rather low. For example, the tariff on tea was 1.5 pence per pound in China and 1 shilling 5 pence in England.

SHANGHAI UNIVERSITY. University cofounded by the **Chinese Communist Party** (CCP) and the **Nationalist Party** (GMD) in 1922 in Shanghai. After the CCP was founded in 1921, **Chen Duxiu**, **Li Dazhao**, and other leaders decided to set up a university to train revolutionary cadres. They tried to reorganize the old Southeast Normal College and make it Shanghai University. The GMD decided to support this plan and to be the major sponsor. On 23 October 1922, Shanghai University was inaugurated, and the senior GMD leaders, **Yu Youren** and **Shao Lizi**, were appointed its president and vice president. In January 1924, the first National Congress of the GMD passed a resolution to provide the university with 1,000 silver dollars each year to cover its administrative expenses. In the next year, the GMD promised to offer 20,000 more silver dollars to build new buildings for the university. Nevertheless, the CCP had gained a prevalent influence among the faculty and students, and its campus was thus referred to as a "red base" of the CCP. The CCP leader, **Deng Zhongxia**, served as provost, and **Qu Qiubai** as a board member—he also created China's first Department of Sociology at Shanghai University. Shanghai University comprised four departments: Chinese, English, arts, and sociology. Many leading scholars were invited to be faculty members or give lectures. Enrollment increased from 160 to 400, and most of them were CCP members who took an active part in the **May Thirtieth Movement** and Communist campaigns. When **Chiang Kai-shek** began to purge the Communists on 12 April 1927, a considerable number of the students were arrested, and the university was ordered to close on 3 May.

SHANGHAI WAR OF 1932. Known also as the Shanghai Incident or the **January Twenty-eighth Incident**.

SHANGHAI–WUSONG RAILWAY. The first Chinese railway, constructed in 1876 by the British company **Jardine, Matheson & Co**. Construction of this nine-and-a-quarter-mile narrow-gauge railway in Shanghai was technically successful, and it appeared to create new commercial opportunities in the area from downtown Shanghai to the suburb township of Wusong. When the railroad began to operate on 1 July 1876, thousands of locals were curious to meet the train and roared with great excitement. The Qing government worried about the growing foreign influence, arguing that this project was never legally approved. There was also a complaint by the local gentry, who argued that the train, as a foreign monster, destroyed the local geomantic environment. In December 1877, the Chinese government purchased the railway for 185,000 taels silver and then ordered the workers to dig up the track, level over the roadbed, and tear down the station.

SHANGWU YINSHU GUAN. *See* COMMERCIAL PRESS.

SHAO PIAOPING (1884–1926). Prominent journalist in modern China. Born in Jinhua, Zhejiang Province, Shao first received a traditional Confucian education and obtained the *xiucai* degree at the age of 14, later graduating from the Western-style Zhejiang High School. In 1912, Shao established the *Hanmin Daily* in Hangzhou. Because he published articles against **Yuan Shikai**'s dictatorship, Shao was arrested three times and was finally forced to flee to Japan. Shao created the News Editing Society in Tokyo and became a columnist of *Shenbao*. Shao's major accomplishment was the very influential newspaper *Jingbao* (Beijing Daily). While most early Chinese newspapers just copied the news scripts offered by foreign news agencies, Shao required that his correspondents report news through their own observation and investigation. Shao asked to increase the length of news reports from 200 words to 500, covering what happened locally. He opposed government censorship and called on journalists to fight for freedom of the press. Before the first issue of *Jingbao* was published, Shao asked his staff to have "iron shoulders and skillful hands." As China was under the control of authoritarian governments, Shao hoped his newspaper would be able to withstand pressure and criticize social injustice. He created a new style of news writing, making *Jingbao* the most popular newspaper in China.

In spring 1925, Shao secretly joined the **Chinese Communist Party** on the recommendation of **Li Dazhao** and Luo Zhanglong. In 1926, the **Fengtian Clique warlord Zhang Zuolin** attacked the **Zhili Clique** and attempted to take over the **Beijing government**. Zhang sent Shao ¥300,000, asking for cooperation. Shao returned the money and refused his request. On 18 April 1926, Zhang Zuolin's troops stormed Beijing and closed *Jingbao*. Accusing the newspaper of Communist propaganda, Zhang ordered the arrest and execution of Shao in Beijing. Shao was survived by his wife, Tang Xiuhui, who resumed the publication of *Jingbao* two years later and continued her husband's work until 1937 when the Japanese occupied Beijing.

SHEN BAOZHEN (1820–1879). High-ranking official of the Qing government and son-in-law of **Lin Zexu**. Born in Minhou, Fujian Province, Shen obtained the *jinshi* degree in 1847 and was appointed to the **Hanlin Academy**. In 1854, he was assigned to southeast China to engage in suppression of the **Taiping Rebellion**. Shen captured the son of the rebel king and was highly rewarded by the Qing government. At **Zeng Guofan**'s recommendation, he was promoted to be the governor of Jiangxi. Shen became actively involved in the **Self-Strengthening Movement** and succeeded **Zuo Zongtang** as administrator of the shipyard in Fuzhou, where he built 15 warships and trained a number of Chinese naval officers. In 1874, when the Japanese soldiers landed on Taiwan, Shen led troops to the island, negotiated with Japan, and finally obtained a peace settlement. To improve the administration, Shen moved the Fujian provincial government to Taiwan and helped the local people develop agriculture and education.

SHEN CONGWEN (1902–1988). The pen name of Shen Yuehuan, the greatest lyric novelist of modern China. Shen was born Shen Yuehuan in Fenghuang, Hunan Province, into a farming family of the Miao ethnic group. At the age of 14, he joined the army and traveled throughout the border areas of southern China. This early experience later became the subject of his writing. He began his literary career in 1924 and wrote six novels, along with numerous short stories, that were compiled into 30 collections before 1950. Influenced by both Western literature and the oral tradition of Miao nationality, Shen created a special loose, vernacular, and beautiful writing style. His works, combining his doubts about modern urbanization with an idealized view of the beauty of rural life, were translated into more than 40 foreign languages. During the **Second Sino-Japanese War**, he taught at various Chinese universities and was a professor at **Peking University** from 1947 through 1949. In the 1950s, his works were criticized in **Mao Zedong**'s "thought reform" campaign, and he was forced to leave the institutions of higher education. After that, he never again wrote fiction. He was given a staffing post at the Palace Museum at the Forbidden City in Beijing, where he began to do research and publish on ancient Chinese costume and dress, making himself a prominent historian and archeologist.

SHENBAO **(SHANGHAI NEWS).** The first and most influential private newspaper in modern China. *Shenbao* was a Chinese newspaper established by the British merchant Ernest Major in Shanghai on 30 April 1872. In 1909, *Shenbao* was sold to a Chinese comprador and handed over to **Shi Liangcai** in 1912. Shi required that the newspaper report more local news. In 1922, for instance, its news coverage was 96 percent domestic and 4 percent foreign. For this reason, *Shenbao* became a synonym for Shanghai newspapers. In addition, *Shenbao* published serial novels in its literary supplements and also issued a special "Pictorial Weekly" to satisfy the readers' interest in illustrated material and entertainment news. In 1933, *Shenbao* had a daily circulation of 150,000, the largest in China. After the Japanese invaded Manchuria, this newspaper sharply criticized the Nationalist government's nonresistance policy; this criticism resulted in the assassination of Shi in 1934. When the Japanese stormed the city of Shanghai, *Shenbao* moved to the International Settlement and gained a British license to continue publication. But *Shenbao* could not throw off Japanese control in the following years. After the Japanese surrendered, *Shenbao* was taken over by the Nationalist government and was greatly influenced by the **CC Clique**. On 27 May 1949, when the Communist military force entered Shanghai, *Shenbao* ceased publication. The newspaper had existed for 77 years and published 25,000 issues.

SHENG MANYUN (1869–1915). Banker and revolutionary. Born into the Sun family in Wuxi, Jiangsu Province, Manyun was taken into the Sheng family as its son-in-law with the condition of following the family name of his wife. He obtained the *juren* degree at the age of 20 but soon gave up academic pursuits and began to learn how to run factories. In 1906, he took over his in-laws' family business and, in cooperation with friends, created the Xincheng Savings Bank, the first commercial bank in China. In 1910, he joined the United League founded by **Sun Yat-sen**. He did fund-raising among overseas Chinese to facilitate Sun's revolutionary programs. Sheng organized China's National Chamber of Commerce and was elected its vice president. Sheng organized a militia for the Shanghai Chamber of Commerce, which launched the uprising in Shanghai in response to the October 10 uprising in Wuchang. He then served as minister of finance of the Shanghai military government. In 1913, he took part in the **Second Revolution** against **Yuan Shikai**. After the failure of the revolution, he and his family were exiled to the city of Dalian, where he was assassinated at the age of 48.

SHENG SHICAI (1897–1970). Warlord who ruled Xinjiang from 2 April 1933 to 29 August 1944. Born in Kaiyuan, Liaoning Province, Sheng graduated from the **Fengtian Military Academy** and joined the army of the **Fengtian Clique warlord** after his graduation. He traveled to Xinjiang to work for Governor Jin Shuren and served as the general military instructor to train Jin's army. He suppressed the

Kumul Uprising with support from the Soviet Union and won the trust of the Nationalist government. In 1933, he served as acting military inspector of Xinjiang and was formally appointed governor by the central government a year later. Shen launched a series of reforms with the support of the Soviet Union. At Joseph Stalin's request, Sheng joined the Communist Party of the Soviet Union in August 1938. In 1942, sensing the Soviet Union's threat, he turned anti-Soviet, expelling Soviet advisers and executing many Communists, including Mao Zemin, a brother of **Mao Zedong**. He controlled the government, army, culture, education, finance, foreign trade, and all the resources of Xinjiang; he persecuted and murdered all dissidents and political rivals, making the province his own kingdom so that the **Nationalist Party** central government was finally forced to remove him in August 1944. Sheng later held the position of minister of agriculture and forestry in the Nationalist government. In 1949, he fled to Taiwan, where he died of a cerebral hemorrhage in 1970.

SHENG XUANHUAI (1844–1916). Government official of the Qing dynasty and one of the leaders of the **Self-Strengthening Movement**. Born into the family of a government official in Wujing, Jiangsu, Sheng first worked with **Li Hongzhang**, who was his father's friend. In 1871, he was appointed mayor of Tianjin. That year North China witnessed a serious flood, and his father donated food and clothing for Sheng to distribute among the homeless people, thus beginning his first charitable business. In 1872, Sheng suggested to Li the development of the shipbuilding industry, and Li accepted the idea, which led to establishment of the **China Merchants' Steamship Navigation Company** with Sheng as its general manager. In 1875, Li assigned him to Hubei to administer the new coal mines. Sheng proposed the development of a telegraph company and the building of a telecommunication network from Shanghai to Guangdong, Ningbo, Fuzhou, and Amoy. In 1883, Sheng was made inspector of the Tianjin customs office, where he diverted customs income to subsidize the telegraph company; this act violated the custom service's regulations. Because some powerful people pleaded for mercy for him, he was not dismissed from office. After 1892, Sheng began to supervise the textile industry in Shanghai.

Sheng advocated modern education. On 2 November 1895, the **Guangxu Emperor** approved one of his proposals, enabling Shen to build the Tianjin Beiyang School for Western Studies. It was later renamed Beiyang University (today's Tianjin University), the first public university in China. A year later, he founded the second Western-style school in Shanghai—Nanyang Public School, the predecessor of today's University of Communication. Sheng also set up the China Commerce Bank in Shanghai and the **Hanyeping Coal and Steel Complex**. Sheng opposed Cixi's policy of supporting the Boxers and encouraged the governors in southeast China to sign a treaty with foreigners to suppress the Boxer Movement and maintain order in the areas of the Yangtze River delta. In his later years, Sheng handed over the management of the railways to Tao Shaoyi and helped the **Communication Clique** become an important political force in early modern China. **Yuan Shikai** admired Sheng's abilities and appointed him minister of communication and the postal service. Sheng was involved in the suppression of **anti-Manchu** uprisings in several provinces. After the 1911 Revolution, he fled abroad. In 1912, he returned to Shanghai to run the **China Merchants' Steamship Navigation Company** and the Hanyeping Coal and Steel Works. On 27 April 1916, Sheng died in Shanghai and his magnificent funeral hit the headlines of the local newspapers.

SHI CUNTONG (1890–1970). Social activist and early leader of the Chinese **Communist Youth League** (CY). Born in Jinghua, Zhejiang Province, Shi began studying at a Confucian school at the age of 9. He became notorious in the **May Fourth Movement** for his article, *Fei Xiao* ("Decry Filial Piety"), published in a local radical journal, which criticized **filial piety** and Confucian morality as a whole. Believing in an anarchist program of social transformation, he moved to Beijing for a utopian experiment of the Working-Study Corp. After the failure of the program, he converted to Marxism and founded the Marxist Group in Tokyo. He joined the Chinese Socialist Youth League and the **Chinese Communist Party** (CCP). He was elected secretary-general of the CY. During the CCP–**Nationalist Party** (GMD) alliance, he served as an instructor and director of the political department at the Wuhan branch of the Nationalist Central Military Academy. Upon the split of the CCP and GMD in 1927, he withdrew from the CCP and began to focus on scholarly work, translating Marxist works and publishing books on Marxism. In 1945, along with Huang Yanpei and Zhang Naiqi, Shi founded the China

Democratic National Construction Association and was elected vice-chairman. In 1949, as a non-Communist social activist, he was given several positions, including first deputy minister of labor. Shi was persecuted and died during the Cultural Revolution, and he was posthumously rehabilitated in late 1970s.

SHI DAKAI (1831–1863). An eminent military leader of the **Taiping Rebellion**, Shi was known as the Prince Wing. Born into a half-**Hakka** and half-Zhuang family, he joined **Hong Xiuquan's God Worshipping Society** at the age of 16. He led Taiping forces to win many decisive battles. Disappointed with Hong's massive purges of innocent Taiping commanders and soldiers, Shi led an army of 100,000 men out of Nanjing in 1875. He continued to fight against the Qing troops for six years throughout central and south China. Later, his army began to sustain losses, and some of his generals left with their battalions. In 1863, when his troops attempted to march to Sichuan, a flood stopped them on the bank of the Dadu River. This allowed the larger army of the Qing government to catch up with them. In this desperate situation, Shi put down his weapons and asked for mercy for his soldiers, to which the government agreed. After Shi surrendered, however, he was dismembered and his 2,000 men were all massacred.

SHI LIANG (1900–1985). Famous lawyer and social activist. Born in Changzhou, Jiangsu, Shi graduated first from the Wuji Female Normal School and then Shanghai University of Law and Government. She began to practice law in Shanghai in 1931. Shi served as a defense attorney for many liberal intellectuals and Communist Party members who engaged in the democratic movement but were arrested by the **Nationalist Party** (GMD). She was a devoted participant in the Chinese resistance movement. She denounced the civil war and called for a **united front** against Japanese aggression. As one of the **Seven Gentlemen** involved in the activities of the National Salvation Association, Shi was arrested in 1936. She was the only woman of the seven prominent social activists, who were persecuted for their patriotic actions. In 1937, she was rescued by Madame Sun (**Song Qingling**) and other friends. She joined the **China Democratic League** in 1942 and, as its representative, attended the first **Chinese People's Political Consultative Conference** on 21 September 1949.

After the Communists came to power, she was appointed minister of law. She was also elected vice president of the Chinese Congress. Shi died on 6 September 1985 in Beijing.

SHI LIANGCAI (1880–1934). Newspaper magnate in Shanghai. Born in Nanjing, Jiangsu Province, Shi graduated from Hangzhou School of Sericulture. After graduation, Shi opened the Women's School of Sericulture in 1904. Four years later, however, Shi took an interest in journalism. In 1912, Shi found that due to poor management, *Shenbao*'s market was shrinking, which offered him an opportunity to manifest his talents and rebuild the newspaper. Shi bought the newspaper, serving as its general manager, and transformed it into a forum for metropolitan affairs in Shanghai by covering more local news, discussing social issues, and publishing serial novels for urban readers. His newspaper had a "Pictorial Weekly" to satisfy the readers' interest in illustrated material and entertainment news. In 1933, *Shenbao* had a daily circulation of 150,000, the largest in the country. After the **Manchuria Incident**, Shi engaged in many anti-Japanese activities, and his newspaper sharply criticized the Nationalist government's nonresistance policy. For this reason, Shi received many warnings and was assassinated when he and his family were on vacation.

SHI PINGMEI (1902–1928). Female journalist and activist of the early feminist movement. Born in Pingding, Shanxi Province, into an intellectual family, Shi began to study classical Chinese at the age of four with her father, who was a *juren* degree holder. After the 1911 Revolution, her father got a job as a librarian at the provincial library and brought her to the city of Taiyuan. Shi studied at the Taiyuan Female Normal School and became a leader of the student movement on campus. After graduating in 1919, she was admitted to the Beijing Female Normal University, where she met a young revolutionary, Gao Junyu, who found her to be very talented and encouraged her to write for newspapers and journals. In 1923, she organized female students to travel in southern China and wrote long travelogues, which were published in the *Morning Daily* from 4 September to 7 October 1923. With another woman journalist, Lu Jingqing, Shi edited and published *Women's Weekly*, which was a supplement of *Jingbao* (Beijing Daily). She participated in a mass demonstration against Western demands for the disarming of the **Dagu Forts**. When the Du

Qirui government suppressed the demonstration, Shi was injured, and her friend Ms. Liu Hezhen was killed. She published "Cry for Hezhen" in the supplement of *Jingbao*. The 1925 death of her boyfriend, Gao, was a big shock for her. Shi wrote more than 10 essays in his memory. She began to edit the *Rose Weekly* for the *World Journal* in 1926 and continued to publish poetry and essays. In 1927, Shi published her first novel, *A Horse Neighs in the Storm*. On 18 September 1928, she suddenly fell sick; 12 days later, Shi died of cerebritis in Beijing at the age of 26. *See also* CHINESE FEMINISM.

SHIMONOSEKI, TREATY OF (1895). The treaty ended the **First Sino-Japanese War** of 1894–1895. In the war, the **Chinese Beiyang Fleet** was destroyed and its armies defeated. The terms of the **Treaty of Shimonoseki** were tougher than any other treaties China had signed with foreign powers in the 19th century. It consisted of 11 articles that provided for recognition of Korean independence and the termination of tributary relations between Korea and China. It required that China pay an indemnity of 200 million taels and cede Taiwan, the Pescadores, and the Liaodong Peninsula to Japan. China was also forced to open four cities, **Chongqing**, Suzhou, Sashi, and Hangzhou, as trading ports. It also granted the Japanese the right to open factories in Chinese coastal areas. The Qing representative **Li Hongzhang** tried to bargain with Japan but finally compromised. Nonetheless, due to the **Triple Intervention** of Russia, Germany, and France, the Japanese withdrew their claim to the Liaodong Peninsula in return for an increased war indemnity of 30 million taels from China. The treaty was signed by Count Ito Hirobumi and Viscount Mutsu Munenitsu for Japan and Li Hongzhang and his son **Li Jingfang** on behalf of China on 24 March 1895. Chinese scholars and officials vigorously opposed these terms, but the treaty was ratified by the **Guangxu Emperor**. Li Jingfang was sent to Taiwan to turn the island over to Japan, but the cession met with strong resistance by the local populace. The Japanese did not take over the island until they had bloodily suppressed the local opposition in October 1895.

The Republic of China formally declared war on Japan on 9 December 1941, announcing the abolition of the Treaty of Shimonoseki. At the end of the **Second Sino-Japanese War**, Japan surrendered and both countries signed the Peace Treaty between the Republic of China and Japan on 28 April 1952, reaffirming that all treaties signed before 9 December 1941 between China and Japan, including the Treaty of Shimonoseki, were null and void.

SICHUAN CLIQUE. A clique of **warlords** during the Republican period. In 1913, Sichuan responded to **Sun Yat-sen's Second Revolution** and formed the anti–**Yuan Shikai** Expedition Army led by General Xiong Kewu. But it was soon crushed by Yuan's **Beiyang Army**. In 1916, **Cai E** led his Republic Protection Army to march on Sichuan and defeated the Beiyang Army, helping Sichuan rebuild its military forces. In 1918, Xiong Kewu decided to divide the province into several defense districts; in each district, the military leader was authorized to collect taxes to feed his own troops. These military leaders not only required the locals to provide them with military supplies but also controlled civil affairs by appointing officials, creating new taxes, and making each district an independent kingdom. Coinciding with the emergence of these various states within the state, numerous small warlords built their spheres of influence and fought each other. From 1912 through 1933, the province witnessed more than 470 military clashes, pitting one warlord against another. In the second half of 1926, the Sichuan warlords began to ask the central government for intervention and accepted the authority of the Nanjing government to reorganize the provincial troops. Afterward, the military power in the province was comparatively centralized.

In the following decade, five warlords—Liu Xiang, Yang Sen, Liu Wenhui, Deng Xihou, and Tian Songyao—dominated Sichuan. In 1935, the **Central Army** entered Sichuan to hunt the Communist **Red Army** during the **Long March**. The presence of the Nationalist and Communist troops weakened the power of local warlords. Liu Xiang, as chairman of the government of Sichuan Province, issued a series of orders to abolish the defense districts. His major rival, Liu Wenhui, was transferred to Xikang Province by **Chiang Kai-shek**. Nonetheless, the warlords in each former defense district remained predominant until the central government moved into Sichuan during the **Second Sino-Japanese War**.

SILVER PURCHASE ACT. On 19 June 1934, the United States issued the Silver Purchase Act, requiring the American treasury to buy silver to make its silver stockpiles equal to a third of its gold reserves, or enough that the price of silver reached $1.29 per ounce. This led to the outflow of a great amount of silver from China. To stabilize the Chinese currency, the Chinese government decided to give up the silver-standard monetary system and issue a new currency—**fabi**. This monetary reform started on 4 November 1935. In May 1935, China had signed an agreement on fixing the exchange rate of one Chinese dollar to US$0.2975. However, China's serious inflation problems quickly devaluated the fabi, which contributed to the **Nationalist Party** government's continuing financial crisis.

SIMLA CONVENTION. International conference held on 3 July 1914 in Simla, India. Delegates from India, China, and Tibet participated in the Simla Convention. Disputes between the Chinese and Tibetan delegates cropped up on two major issues: the borders between China and Tibet, and the degree and nature of Chinese suzerainty over the **Dalai Lama**'s government. The Chinese government insisted that Tibet was part of China, and its delegate Ivan Chen refused to sign any agreement on the two issues and walked out of the conference room. The British and Tibetan delegates signed the Simla Agreement. In the following years, the two signatory parties, India and Tibet, carried on trade and religious pilgrimages under the terms of the Simla Convention. However, China rejected the right of the Tibetan delegates to sign or ratify such an agreement without authority from Peking. Both the **Chinese Communist Party** (CCP) and the **Nationalist Party** (GMD) saw the agreement as illegal and refused to recognize the **McMahon Line** attached to the Simla Agreement. In 1915, the British recognized Tibet as "under Chinese suzerainty" and admitted that "the Simla convention has not been signed by the Chinese Government . . . and is, therefore, for present invalid."

SINICIZATION OF MARXISM. The term literally means "transposition of the theory and practice of Marxism to apply to Chinese conditions." Since the inception of the Chinese revolution, **Mao Zedong** emphasized the necessity to modify the Russian version of Marxism according to China's own requirements. Sinicization of Marxism was a process in which Mao struggled with and triumphed over the early party leaders, such as **Chen Duxiu** and **Wang Ming**, who blindly followed the **Comintern**'s instructions and ignored China's conditions. Mao clarified the goals and tasks of the Chinese revolution and created a new strategy and approach to the Communist success. The term *sinicization of Marxism* came into use after Mao's position as a supreme leader of the party was established in **Yan'an**. His sinicized version of Marxism, known as Maoism, or **Mao Zedong Thought**, was accepted and became orthodox for the **Chinese Communist Party** in the 1940s. *See also* DEMOCRATIC CENTRALISM; GUERRILLA WARFARE; MASS LINE; NEW DEMOCRACY.

SINO-AMERICAN COMMERCIAL TREATY (1946). The formal name of the treaty is the Treaty of Friendship, Commerce, and Navigation. On 11 January 1943, the United States announced that it was relinquishing its extraterritorial rights in China. Two years later, both China and the United States expressed the hope of signing a new treaty to facilitate their commercial relations. The negotiations began on 5 February 1946 in **Chongqing**, and the treaty was signed on 4 November 1946 in Nanjing. The tenor of the treaty is as follows: "national treatment" and "**most favored nation**" treatment for both Chinese and American citizens (for example, the nationals of one country have full rights to form corporations or associations in the other country); most favored nation treatment for nationals or corporations of one country participating in corporations of the other country; safeguarding the corporations' personnel and properties in the territory of the other signatory; "most favored treatment" with respect to internal taxes; most favored nation rights concerning the acquisition and disposal of real estate and immovable properties; mutual protection of patents and copyright properties; most favored nation treatment for nationals or corporations of one country engaging in mining, navigating internal rivers, and taking part in coastal trade in the other country; right of the ships of one country to access the ports, territories, and inland waters of the other country; and most favored nation treatment regarding customs duties, other taxes, and loading-unloading. It was the intention of the Republic of China to encourage foreign investment and technological exchange, but as Foreign Minister Wang Shih-chieh pointed out, China would be unable to administer many of the provisions as effectively as the United States. The treaty might allow American capital to infiltrate and eventually capture and control the entire Chinese economy. It was for this reason that the Sino-American Commercial Treaty was referred to as the last unequal treaty China signed with foreign countries in modern times.

SINOCENTRISM. An ethnocentric perspective regarding China as the center of the world. Sinocentrism viewed China as the only civilized country in the world and foreign nations or ethnic groups as barbarians. It saw neighboring countries as mere cultural offshoots and refused to recognize the uniqueness and variety of other cultures. Based on sinocentric beliefs, China treated these countries as vassals and thus established a **tributary system** between China and other countries, including Korea, Vietnam, Siam, Cambodia, and other Southeast Asian countries. Sinocentrism was seriously challenged by the European powers in the 19th century. After China's defeat in the wars with Western powers and Japan, the sinocentric model rapidly collapsed.

SINO-FRENCH WAR (1883–1885). In an attempt to build a French Indochina empire, France began its military presence in Saigon in 1859. A treaty was imposed on **Annam** in 1874 by France, confirming the French possession of Cochin China, the right to direct Annamese foreign relations, and navigation on the Red River. To counter the treaty, Annam strengthened its ties with China and asked the irregular Chinese military force, the Black Flags, for help. A conflict between the **Black Flag Army** and French forces occurred in 1882. **Li Hongzhang** suggested negotiation, while other officials in the Qing court advocated war to defend China's honor and the Chinese dependency on Annam. In December 1883, the French army defeated the Black Flags and Qing regular troops in Tongking. The **Dowager Cixi** ordered Li to seek a settlement. The negotiations took place on 11 May 1884 between Li and F. E. Fournier, resulting in the **Li-Fournier Agreement**, which called for China's recognition of all French treaties with Annam and the withdrawal of Chinese troops from Tongking. The war seemed over at this point. On 17 May, Fournier informed Li of the required date for the removal of the Chinese garrison. Li did not report the date of Chinese withdrawal to the court. When the French troops came to take over the garrison on 23 June, the Chinese troops refused to withdraw since they had not received the order. This resulted in the expansion of the war.

The decisive battle was the Battle of Foochow, 23 August 1884, which lasted less than an hour. The French navy, under the command of Admiral Amédée Courbet, utterly destroyed the anchored Chinese naval fleet. The French occupied Keelung (Jilong), and from 29 March 1885 the Pescadores, and they blockaded the Taiwan Straits. However, the Chinese troops continued to fight, and France could not occupy Taiwan. In the land battle, the French army was defeated by the Chinese troops commanded by the governor of Guangxi, Feng Zicai, at the Zhennan Pass. In subsequent fighting at Lang Son, the French brigade commander was wounded and the brigade fell back in disarray toward the Red River Delta, abandoning all gains they had made during the previous campaigns. Chinese troops turned the defeat into victory. The defeat, which the French called the "Tonkin affair," contributed to the collapse of the French cabinet. Nonetheless, Li Hongzhang insisted that China had not reached the point where it could fend off France. In the previous two years, the Dowager Cixi had vacillated between war and peace and now supported Li to make a deal with France. In June 1885, China and France finally concluded a formal agreement: China recognized all the French treaties with Annam and saw Annam as a French protectorate; China opened two ports to French trade; China cut its import tax on French goods; China agreed to consult with French companies on future railway projects in south China; and France evacuated its troops from Taiwan and the Pescadores. The treaty signaled the failure of China's **Self-Strengthening Movement** and ended Annam's tributary relationship with China.

SINO-RUSSIAN SECRET ALLIANCE (1896). Disappointed with the British failure to intervene on China's behalf during the **First Sino-Japanese War**, China resorted to an alliance with Russia in 1896. Russian czar Nicholas II invited **Li Hongzhang** to Moscow, where Li held secret negotiations with Count Sergei Witte and Prince Lobanov-Rostovskii. On 3 June 1896, the Chinese and Russian representatives signed the Sino-Russian Treaty of Alliance, also known as Li-Witte Agreement. The major terms of the treaty included the following: China and Russia would provide mutual aid in terms of munitions, food, and other assistance if Japan invaded China, Korea, or Russian far Eastern possessions, and during this war with Japan, all Chinese ports would be open to Russian warships; China would grant Russia permission to construct a railway along the **Amur River** via Harbin to Vladivostok, and Russia would have the right to ship military personnel, armaments, and food on this railway both in war- and peacetime; and China would cede a strip of land sufficient for the building and operation of the railway, and this land would be under the complete jurisdiction of Russia. It was reported later that Li Hongzhang accepted a bribe of $1.5 million from the Russians and promised to have the treaty ratified by the Chinese emperor. From Li's perspective, the Sino-Russian Secret Alliance was a success of his policy of playing the barbarians (Russia and Japan) against each other.

SMALL SWORDS SOCIETY (*XIAODAOHUI*, 1853–1855). An organization that staged an anti-**Manchu** uprising in Shanghai. The Small Swords Society was a branch of the **Heaven and Earth Society**, and its major members were workers and small shopkeepers originally from Fujian Province. Inspired by the **Taiping Rebellion**, the society revolted on 7 September 1853 and quickly gained control of the old Chinatown of Shanghai and adjacent counties. The society elected Liu Lichuan, a worker from Guangdong Province, its leader. Liu wrote a letter to **Hong Xiuquan**, showing his willingness to join the Taiping rebels and accept Hong's leadership. The Qing government sent troops to quell the Small Swords Society rebellion. Although the Qing troops regained the adjacent counties, the Small Swords Society managed to keep the walled Chinatown and most parts of Shanghai, where they promised three-year tax exemption, minted copper currency, and tried to stabilize the market and improve the grain supply. They did not, however, invade the **foreign concessions**. At first, the British and American authorities remained neutral. While the French supported the imperial government, some British and American sailors even joined up with the Small Swords Society. However, the Westerners were soon ordered by their governments to take the side of the Qing army. The Small Swords Society was not a well-organized political force. Because of provincialism, the rebels split between the Fujian and Guangdong groups; this split significantly weakened their combat effectiveness. On 17 February 1855, the society tried to break out of the encirclement, but its troops were crushed by the Qing and foreign armies, and Liu Lichuan and other leaders were killed in the battle.

SNOW, EDGAR PARKS (1905–1972). American journalist. Born in Kansas City, Missouri, Snow graduated from the University of Missouri, majoring in journalism. He traveled to China in 1928, working as an assistant editor of *Millard's Review of the Far East Weekly*. After the September 18 Incident of 1931, he went to Manchuria and reported on the Japanese invasion and Chinese resistance movement.

Snow met **Lu Xun** and **Sun Yat-sen**'s widow, **Song Qingling**, in Shanghai. It was Lu and Song, as Snow said, who helped him understand China. On Christmas day of 1932, he married Helen Foster in Tokyo and brought her to China. In 1934, Snow began to teach journalism at **Yenching University** and was involved in the student movement. He made his house a meeting place for student activists, including the Communist leaders Huang Hua (**Yenching University**), Yao Yiling (Tsinghua University), and **Huang Jing** (**Peking University**).

With the arrangements made by Song, Snow visited **Yan'an**, where he met and interviewed a number of Communist leaders, including **Mao Zedong**. This trip provided the material for his famous book, *Red Star over China*, which was first published in October 1937 in London and came out in its Chinese version in February 1938 in Shanghai. Snow was the first person who reported on the Chinese Revolution, educating the world about Yan'an and the Communist resistance movement. In the 1950s, Snow was persecuted by Joseph McCarthy. He kept his American citizenship but moved to Switzerland. In 1960 and 1972, Snow revisited China and forwarded Mao's message of Sino-American rapprochement to Washington. Snow died of cancer on 15 February 1972 in Geneva. According to his last will, a portion of his ashes was buried on the campus of Peking University.

SOCIAL DARWINISM. An application of Charles Darwin's theory to social science. The theory of social Darwinism draws on the work of many authors, including Herbert Spencer, Thomas Malthus, and Francis Galton. Social Darwinism argues that as competition between individual organisms drives biological evolutionary change (speciation) through "survival of the fittest," competition between individuals, groups, nations, or ideas follows the same logic and drives social evolution in human societies. Social Darwinism was introduced to China in the late 19th century by **Yan Fu** in his translation of Thomas Huxley's *Evolution and Ethics*. Yan summarized the theory arguing that in the struggle between one social group and another, the weak invariably became the prey of the strong and the stupid invariably became subservient to the clever. Social Darwinism led the Chinese to ponder problems of race and racial strength. Optimist intellectuals, such as **Liang Qichao**, believed that the Chinese could strengthen their race to engage in the struggle for survival. Social Darwinism served as a source for both China's 19th-century reforms and radical revolutions in the 20th century.

SOCIETY FOR THE DIFFUSION OF CHRISTIAN AND GENERAL KNOWLEDGE (SDCK). The full name of the society is Society for the Diffusion of Christian and General Knowledge among the Chinese. Founded in 1887 by a group of American and British Methodist missionaries in Shanghai, its initiator was the Scottish Protestant missionary Alexander Williamson, and leading members included **Young John Allen**, **William Alexander Parsons Martin**, and **Timothy Richard**. The establishment of the society marked a shift of the missionaries from pure religious work to introducing the Chinese to both Christianity and Western science. The SDCK sponsored or organized the translation of Western books, public speeches, magazines, and Western-style education so as to prompt legal and institutional reform in China. The secretary of the society, Richard, published the book *New Views on Current Affairs*, describing the reforms of Peter the Great and the Meiji Emperor, which had a great influence on prominent officials such as **Prince Gong** and **Li Hongzhang** and the radical reformers headed by **Kang Youwei** and **Liang Qichao**.

SOLIDARITY STRIKES. General strikes of workers in Hong Kong and Guangzhou from June 1925 to October 1926 organized by both the **Chinese Communist Party** (CCP) and the **Nationalist Party** (GMD). In May 1925, a labor upheaval in Shanghai caused bloodshed and the deaths of workers. To support the Shanghai workers, the Communist leaders **Deng Zhongxia** and Su Zhozheng established the League of All Hong Kong Worker Organizations and staged a general strike. The strike started with workers in public transportation, printing houses, and steamship companies on 10 June 1925. More than 20,000 workers left Hong Kong for Guangzhou within three days. On 23 June 1925, the workers, students, and some peasants held a demonstration in the **foreign concession**, Guangzhou. They battled with the police, who opened fire on the demonstrators, killing 50 people. This incident became known as the Sanji Massacre. The Nationalist government in Guangzhou decided to support the strike and help Hong Kong workers return to Guangzhou. By 8 July, about 130,000 to 140,000 Hong Kong workers had returned, and this greatly influenced the city's economy. The municipal government of Guangzhou also blocked the transportation. The import-export volume of Hong Kong in 1925 was only half that of the previous year. The Hong Kong colonial authority suffered a huge deficit and had to borrow £3 million from London.

By the end of 1925, the confrontation had softened, and a new governor of Hong Kong arrived in November to negotiate with the Nationalist government. In the meantime, the political situation changed unfavorably for the laborers in Guangzhou. The left-wing leader **Liao Zhongkai** was assassinated, and the worker pickets were disarmed by the conservative government. In April 1926, the **Northern Expedition** was initiated and the GMD's attention shifted to this military campaign. In June 1926, the Nationalist government sent **T. V. Soong** and **Chen Gongbo** to Hong Kong to discuss the restoration of production. As the negotiation progressed, the Nationalist government announced that the blockade of Hong Kong would be lifted on 10 October 1926. On the same day, the Strike Committee was disbanded, marking the end of the solidarity strikes.

SONG JIAOREN (1882–1913). A major organizer and leader of the **Chinese Nationalist Party**. He was born in Taoyuan, Hunan Province. Along with **Huang Xing**, Song founded the *huaxinghui* (**China Revival Society**) in Changsha in 1904. This organization was dedicated to the overthrow of the **Manchu** monarchy. Song studied at Seaside University and in 1905, together with **Sun Yat-sen**, he established the **Tongmenghui** (United League), which was transformed into the **Guomindang** (GMD) after the founding of the Republic of China. He served as acting general secretary of the party and was also appointed president of the legislative council and minister of agriculture and forestry. Song advocated a cabinet system and opposed the dictatorship of **Yuan Shikai**. In February 1913, the GMD won China's first general election, and according to the constitution, its secretary-general would hold the premiership and organize a new cabinet. Unfortunately, Song was assassinated on 20 March 1913 by Yuan Shikai's people at the Shanghai railway station. *See also* SECOND REVOLUTION.

SONG QINGLING (SOONG CH'ING-LING, OR ROSAMOND SOONG, 1893–1981). Distinguished lady of modern China, prominent social activist, and wife of **Sun Yat-sen**, also known as Madame

Sun. Born into a wealthy businessman and missionary family in Shanghai, Song first studied at Motyeire School for Girls in Shanghai, and then traveled to the United States and graduated from Wesleyan College in Macon, Georgia. In 1914, Song Qingling went to Japan and served as Sun's English secretary. She fell in love with Sun and married him in Tokyo on 25 October 1915. In 1924, when the Guangdong **warlord Chen Jiongming** attacked Sun's residence, she miscarried and never got pregnant again. In 1925, Song accompanied Sun to Beijing for the North-South peace negotiations, but Sun died on the way.

The next January, Song was elected as a member of the Central Executive Committee of the **Nationalist Party** (GMD). Song insisted on Sun's policy of alliance with the Soviet Union and Communists and opposed **Chiang Kai-shek**'s purge. She also opposed the marriage between her sister and Chiang. In July 1927, she published a statement accusing Chiang of violating the revolutionary principles of Sun Yat-sen. She went into exile in Moscow and lived in Europe for many years. After the **Xi'an Incident**, Song stood for the **United Front** against the Japanese. She firmly supported the Outline for the War of Resistance and Reconstruction of China, adopted by the GMD National Congress in 1938, and urged its full implementation. In 1939, she founded the China Defense League, which later became the China Welfare Institute. In the wartime capital **Chongqing**, she was often present on public occasions with her sisters (Madam Chiang and Madam Kong), signaling her reconciliation with the GMD.

After 1949, she stayed on the mainland and was elected vice president of the People's Republic of China (PRC) and honorary president of the All-China Women's Federation. She was not active in politics but engaged in various activities such as education, child care, and other charitable institutions. She created the Children's Foundation of China. In May 1981, Song, critically ill and near death, was admitted to the **Chinese Communist Party** (CCP) and named honorary president of the PRC. She was the only woman ever to hold this title. On 29 May, Song died of leukemia in Beijing at the age of 88. *See also* REVOLUTIONARY COMMITTEE OF THE CHINESE KUOMINTANG; SOONG, CHARLIE JONES; SOONG SISTERS.

SOONG, CHARLIE JONES (1863–1918). Missionary, businessman, and loyal supporter of the 1911 Revolution. Born into a **Hakka** family in Hainan, Guangdong Province, Charlie Soong was the third son in his family. His sonless uncle adopted him and took him to Boston when he was 12. Three years later, Soong converted to Christianity. In 1880, he became the first Chinese student at Trinity College and later transferred to Vanderbilt University, where he obtained a degree in theology. In January 1886, he returned to Shanghai as a Chinese minister and married a Christian woman, Ni Kwei-tseng, who bore him three daughters and three sons. Most of their children, including **Song Qingling, Soong Meiling**, and **T. V. Soong**, were important figures in modern China. Soong resigned his missionary position at 26 and opened his own business. He was very successful in printing and selling Chinese Bibles. In summer 1894, he met **Sun Yat-sen** in Shanghai and was deeply impressed by Sun's revolutionary programs. He donated over US$20,000 to the **Tongmenghui**, and two of his daughters, **Ai-ling** and Qingling, worked as Sun's secretaries. Soong also secretly published anti-Qing revolutionary material along with his Bibles. Seven years after the victory of the revolution, Soong died of stomach cancer in Shanghai.

SOONG, T. V. (SONG ZIWEN, 1894–1971). A statesman of the Republic of China, T. V. Soong was born in Shanghai into a Chinese Christian family. His father, **Charlie Soong**, was educated in the United States and worked first as a missionary in China and then as a successful businessman who generously financed **Sun Yat-sen**'s revolutionary activities. One of T. V. Soong's sisters, **Song Qingling**, married Sun Yat-sen; the other, May-ling, married **Chiang Kai-shek**. T. V. Soong graduated from **Saint John's University** in Shanghai and then traveled to the United States to study economics at Harvard University. After returning to China in 1917, he began to do fund-raising to facilitate Sun's military program, the **Northern Expedition**. Soong held many important positions in the Nationalist government, including president of the **Central Bank of China** (1924–1925, 1932), minister of finance (1925–1928, 1932), acting president of the **Executive Yuan** (1933), president of the Bank of China (1934), minister of foreign affairs (1941–1947), and president of the Executive Yuan (1945–1947).

Soong contributed to a peaceful settlement of the **Xi'an Incident**, which led to the Second **United Front** between the **Chinese Communist Party** (CCP) and the **Nationalist Party** (GMD) in the War against the Japanese Aggression. During 1940–1942, Soong served as Chiang's resident representative in the United States to seek American support for China's anti-Japanese war. He also engaged in negotiations with the Western powers on the abolition of **extraterritoriality** and regaining sovereignty over **foreign concessions** in China. In April 1945, Soong and the Communist representative, Dong Biwu, led a joint Chinese delegation to the first United Nations Assembly in San Francisco, making China one of the founders of the United Nations. Soong was regarded as one of the wealthiest men in the world and also as a typical corrupt bureaucrat of the Nationalist government who used state power to raise money. In January 1949, Soong resigned all government positions and lived in seclusion in San Francisco until his death.

SOONG AI-LING (NANCY SOONG, 1890–1973). The eldest of the **Soong sisters** and wife of **H. H. Kung**. Born in Shanghai, Soong traveled to the United States at the age of 14. She enrolled at Wesleyan College in Macon, Georgia. After her graduation from Wesleyan, she returned to China in 1909 and began to work two years later as a secretary for **Sun Yat-sen**, who was leader of the Chinese **Republican Revolution** and a good friend of her father's. She married Kung in 1914 in Yokohama, Japan, and helped her husband become one of the leaders of the Republican government. In later years, Soong worked as an English teacher in China and engaged in child welfare work. It was her suggestion to arrange the meeting and marriage between her younger sister, **Soong May-ling**, and **Chiang Kai-shek**, which made the Soong family the most influential family in modern China. In the late 1940s, Kung was forced to resign from the National Government. Following her husband, Soong moved to the United States. On 18 October 1973, Soong died in the New York–Presbyterian Hospital at the age of 83.

SOONG MAY-LING (SOONG MEI-LING, 1897–2003). The first lady of the Republic of China, also known as Madame Chiang. May-ling was born into a wealthy Christian family in Shanghai. Her father, **Charlie Soong**, was educated in the United States and became a Chinese Methodist minister and successful businessman. At the age of 11, May-ling traveled with her second sister, **Song Qingling**, to the United States. After graduating from high school in Georgia, she attended Wesleyan College and then transferred to Wellesley College, graduating with honors in 1917. She majored in English literature and minored in philosophy. After her return to China, May-ling had to relearn the Chinese language and Chinese culture.

In 1927, she met the political rising star **Chiang Kai-shek** and married him on 1 December. As a dedicated Christian, Madame Chiang made her husband get baptized in 1930. With her husband, Madame Chiang initiated the **New Life Movement** and became actively engaged in Chinese politics. She was made a member of the **Legislative Yuan** from 1930 to 1932, served as secretary-general of the Chinese Aeronautical Affairs Commission from 1936 to 1938, and was elected a member of the Central Executive Committee of the **Nationalist Party** (GMD) in 1945. Involved in China's foreign affairs, Madame Chiang acted not only as her husband's secretary and interpreter but also as a skillful negotiator and adviser of the Chiang government. Her role was so important that when Chiang met with Franklin Roosevelt, Winston Churchill, and Joseph Stalin during World War II, Madame Chiang made the cover of *Time* magazine twice as the lady of the year in 1938 and 1943. On 18 February 1943, she became the first Chinese national and the second woman to address the U.S. Congress. In 1949, Madame Chiang followed her husband to Taiwan. After the death of Chiang Kai-shek in 1975, she moved to New York, living first in Long Island and then in Manhattan. Madame Chiang died peacefully in her apartment in 2003 at the age of 106.

SOONG SISTERS (SONG SISTERS). Three prominent sisters of the Soong family who had a profound influence on modern China. Their father was **Charlie Jones Soong**, a Chinese Christian minister and successful businessman, who traveled to the United States to study and graduated from the Divinity School at Vanderbilt University. He sent his daughters to study in the United States as well. After returning to China, the three sisters began to engage in Chinese politics through their marriages and family influence. The eldest of the Soong sisters, **Soong Ai-ling**, was the wife of **H. H. Kung**, the richest man in China, who served as finance minister and premier of the Republic of China. The second of the Soong sisters, **Song Qingling** (Soong Ching-ling), married **Sun Yat-sen** and served as an important assistant to her husband in the 1911 Revolution and the anti-**warlord**

campaigns. She supported the Chinese Communist movement and became vice president of the People's Republic of China in 1949. The youngest sister, **Soong May-ling**, was a prominent Nationalist political leader and social activist. She married **Chiang Kai-shek**, the leader of the **Nationalist Party** (GMD) and president of the Republic of China. After the GMD's failure in mainland China, May-ling followed her husband and fled to Taiwan. The Soong sisters also had three brothers, **T. V. Soong**, T. L. Soong, and T. A. Soong. One was a politician and the other two successful businessmen.

SOUTH MANCHURIA RAILWAY COMPANY LTD. (NANMAN-ZHOU TIEDAO ZHUSHI HUISHE, SMRC). Japanese railway company that operated in China's Manchuria. It was founded by Japan in 1906, after the Russo-Japanese War (1904–1905), with its headquarters in Dalian and with Baron Shinpei Goto as its first president. The primary capital of the company was ¥200 million (Japanese dollars), one-half of which was government funded, and the rest of which was private investments of the Japanese royal family, aristocrats, and military leaders. After it was founded, the SMRC took over the South Manchuria branch of the China Far East Railway from Russia and also began to run Korean railways (until 1925). The SMRC also owned the 16.7–3,000 meter-wide area of land along both sides of the railway line, known as the Japanese **railway concession** (totaling 482.9 sq. km) under the company's jurisdiction. Through the concessions, the SMRC possessed farms, forests, mines, iron-steel works, power stations, schools, hospitals, and hotels in Manchuria. The SMRC also opened an air line between Manchuria and Korea. As the company expanded, its capital quickly increased to ¥1.4 billion by 1940.

After the **Manchuria Incident** in 1931, the Japanese troops, known as the **Kwantung Army**, occupied the whole of Manchuria and put the SMRC under the supervision of the army. In the next year, the SMRC was ordered to hand over its administrative power to the Japanese puppet government, **Manchukuo**. In 1938, its power was further reduced by transferring the iron-steel works and chemical industry to other Japanese enterprises, and it started focusing on transportation, coal mining, and intelligence operations. The SMRC's Investigation Department was Japan's largest intelligence agency in China, conducting surveys and research of the Manchurian geography, demography, mineral resources, and political and social conditions. The collected data greatly contributed to the Japanese occupation and development of Manchuria. By the end of the **Second Sino-Japanese War**, the total capital of the SMRC was ¥4.2 billion and its employees totaled 398,000. When the Japanese army surrendered, China planed to expropriate the company's property. However, a great deal of the SMRC's equipment and movable properties were shipped by the Soviet Red Army to Russia. With all these difficulties, the company's accounts were not cleared until 1957.

SOUTHBOUND CADRE. In 1948, the military situation was proving that the Communists were on their way to taking over all of China. The Central Committee of the **Chinese Communist Party** (CCP) decided to recruit a large number of cadres and "quickly and systematically train them to administer military, political, economic, Party, cultural and educational affairs" in the newly liberated areas. All these Communist cadres were from the northern rural revolutionary bases and were assigned to take over south and southeast China; therefore, they were referred to as southbound cadres.

SOUTHERN STUDY. An institution of the emperor's personal advisers during the Qing dynasty. It was established in 1677 to replace the **Council of Advisor Princes** as a new policymaking institution until it was abolished in 1898. The Kangxi Emperor built up this institution in the Forbidden City for close consultation of state affairs. All members came from the **Hanlin Academy** and worked closely with the emperor to offer him policy advice. After the establishment of the **Grand Council** in 1861, it became more of an honorable position and had less influence on the emperor.

STANDARD VACUUM OIL CO. INC. (MEIFU OIL CO.). The Chinese branch of the American Standard Oil Co. of New York (established 1866). The company began its business in China by exporting kerosene to Canton in 1894. For centuries, Chinese families had used vegetable oil lamps, and as kerosene replaced vegetable oil as the main source of light, cooking, and heat, it fundamentally changed the life of the Chinese people. Since the Standard Vacuum Oil Co. Inc. monopolized China's market for kerosene, its Chinese name, Meifu, became a household word. In 1905, the company had over US$18 million of total assets in Asia, most of which were in China. To expand its business, the company opened the Chinese market to petroleum, asphalt, and aviation fuel. Great commercial success was attained when automobiles, modern war vehicles, and aircraft were introduced into China. The company established an intensive purchasing and marketing network. When young **H. H. Kung** returned from the United States, he began his career as a comprador for the Standard Vacuum Oil Co. In his later years, Kung kept close relations with the Standard Vacuum Oil Co. when he served as the minister of finance. In the first half of the 20th century, China's energy consumption depended on the oil supplied by the company. More often than not, China's relations with the oil company were an issue of nationalism and foreign affairs. In the meantime, the Standard Vacuum Oil Co. played an important role in the formulation of U.S. petroleum policy in China and East Asia, especially during the **Second Sino-Japanese War**.

STATEMENT OF PUBLIC VEHICLES (*GONGCHE SHANGSHU*). Petition for war with Japan and constitutional reform. In 1895, **Kang Youwei** and **Liang Qichao** submitted to the Qing court a **memorial** with the signatures of about 1,200 provincial degree candidates protesting the **Treaty of Shimonoseki**. Since the provincial candidates came to Peking for the imperial exam by public transportation, they were nicknamed "public vehicles." The memorial urged the Qing court to reject the Treaty of Shimonoseki, to move the capital to an interior province and continue the war against Japan, and to initiate constitutional reform. On 2 May, the degree candidates led by Kang and Liang went to the Censorate to address their demands. As the Censorate officials refused to present the memorial to the emperor, Kang and Liang began to publicize their memorial. The Statement of Public Vehicles provoked nationwide repercussions.

STILWELL, JOSEPH WARREN (1883–1946). Four-star general of the United States Army. Born in Palatka, Florida, Stilwell grew up in New York under the strict supervision of his father. After graduating from Yonkers High School, Stilwell planned to study at Yale University, but his father sent him to the United States Military Academy. In 1926, Stilwell arrived in China for the first time and served as a battalion commander of the 15th Regiment. He was then promoted to lieutenant colonel in 1929. Stilwell's infantry regiment was stationed in Tianjin, where he studied the Chinese language. He continued to travel or work in China and was appointed military attaché at the U.S. Embassy from 1935 to 1939.

In 1942, Stilwell was promoted to lieutenant general and was dispatched to China to serve as the commander of the China-Burma-India theater. He was responsible for all Lend-Lease supplies going into China and later was appointed deputy commander of the South East Asia Command. Stilwell organized the Burma Expedition, but both British and Chinese troops were defeated by the Japanese. Nonetheless, he led the troops to overcome numerous difficulties and constructed a shortcut, the Ledo Road, to supply China by land. This road was later renamed the Stilwell Road in acknowledgment of Stilwell's efforts. Stilwell also established a training center for two divisions of Chinese troops in India. He was promoted to four-star general during World War II. In attempting to press **Chiang Kai-shek** to fight against the Japanese, Stilwell came into conflict with the Chinese leader. Stilwell wanted to use the supplies to prosecute the war, while Chiang was interested in hoarding Lend-Lease supplies for later use in fighting the Chinese Communists. To put up a stronger resistance against the Japanese, Stilwell suggested reforming the Chinese Army, which Chiang saw as a challenge to his power. Stilwell noted that about $380,584,000 of American aid had been wasted due to Chiang's procrastination. Infuriated by what he regarded as Chiang's corruption, incompetence, and timidity, Stilwell constantly filed reports to Washington against Chiang.

In July 1944, Stilwell visited **Yan'an** and began calling for cooperation with the Communists in the war against the Japanese. This offended Chiang, who demanded that Washington recall Stilwell. In October 1944, Stilwell was relieved of his command by President Franklin Roosevelt. He continued to serve in the U.S. Army and received the Distinguished Service Cross, Distinguished Service Medal with oak leaf cluster, Combat Infantryman Badge, and many other awards. On 12 October 1946, Stilwell died of stomach cancer at the Presidio of San Francisco, while still on active duty. His ashes were scattered over the Pacific Ocean. In recent years, a museum and research center were built in Chongqing to commemorate General Stilwell.

STRONG, ANNA LOUISE (1885–1970). American journalist, well known for her extensive reporting on both the Soviet Union and the

Chinese Communists. Born into the family of a Social Gospel minister in Friend, Nebraska, Strong first studied at Bryn Mawr College in Pennsylvania, then graduated from Oberlin College in Ohio. In 1908, she received a PhD in philosophy from the University of Chicago. As an advocate for child welfare, Strong organized an exhibit and toured it extensively throughout the United States and abroad. Strong became openly involved in the labor movement, writing forceful prolabor articles for the labor-owned daily newspaper in Seattle, the *Union Record*. In 1922, she was made Moscow correspondent for the International News Service. Drawing on her observations, she became an enthusiastic supporter of socialism and the Soviet Union.

In the late 1920s, Strong traveled in China and became friends with **Song Qingling** and **Zhou Enlai**. Strong reported on the Chinese Revolution in her books, *China's Millions: The Revolutionary Struggles from 1927 to 1935* (1935), *One Fifth of Mankind* (1938), and three other books on the success of the **Chinese Communist Party** (CCP). During the **Second Sino-Japanese War**, Strong visited **Yan'an** and met and interviewed **Mao Zedong**. In his talks with Strong, Mao argued the important point that "American imperialism and all reactionaries are paper tigers." Although Strong published many works praising the Soviet Union, she was accused by the Russians of espionage and arrested in Moscow in 1949. After she was released, she returned to the United States, but she expressed her willingness to live in China. In 1958, she finally managed to move to China at the age of 72. She visited Tibet and wrote a book, *When Serfs Stood Up in Tibet*. Strong settled permanently in China until her death in 1970 at the age of 85.

STUART, JOHN LEIGHTON (1876–1962). The first president of **Yenching University** and ambassador of the United States to the Republic of China. Born into an American missionary family in Hangzhou, Zhejiang Province, Stuart considered himself Chinese more than American. At the age of 11, Stuart went to America for his education. He first attended Hampden-Sydney College in Virginia and then Union Theological Seminary, where he aspired to be a missionary. After returning to China, Stuart began a mission in a northern suburb of Hangzhou, where his parents had worked for many years. He picked up the local dialect and enjoyed communicating with the illiterate masses. As a missionary from the Presbyterian Church in the United States, Stuart did not see any clash between Christianity and the local culture and strongly believed that Christianity would be highly beneficial to China when combined with Confucian ethics and values. When Stuart left Hangzhou, the city congress presented him with a gold key to the city and bestowed on him the title "honorable citizen of Hangzhou."

In 1908, Stuart became a Greek language lecturer in Nanking Theological Seminary in Nanjing, and the next year he was appointed president of Yenching University in Beiping. As a devoted academic leader and enthusiastic fund-raiser, he quickly made Yenching University one of the top universities in China. On 11 July 1946, at the crucial moment of the **Nationalist Party** (GMD) and the **Chinese Communist Party** (CCP) military conflict, Stuart was appointed U.S. ambassador to China. The deterioration of the situation in China required "an American of unquestionable character and integrity and with long experience in China" for mediation efforts to achieve some peaceful settlement. However, Stuart's efforts to bring both sides to end the hostilities were in vain. He was actively involved in projects of "the U.S. relief assistance to Chinese people." During the civil war, Stuart stood for economic aid to the GMD government but urged substantial reforms.

As the **People's Liberation Army** stormed the Nationalist capital Nanjing and most foreign embassies, including the Soviet one, followed the GMD government's move to Guangzhou, Stuart and his embassy stayed. Believing in the possibility of new relations between the United States and Chinese Communists, he tried to arrange a meeting with **Zhou Enlai** through a student at Yenching University, Huang Hua, who later became foreign minister of the People's Republic of China. However, his proposal was rejected by the U.S. State Department. On 2 August 1949, Stuart left China. **Mao Zedong** published "Farewell, Leighton Stuart" and five other articles to criticize Stuart and American China policy.

SUBAO **CASE (1903).** *Subao* was one of five leading Chinese newspapers in Shanghai during the late Qing era. Starting in May 1903, it published a number of anti-Qing articles, including "Rebuttal on **Kang Youwei**'s Comments on Revolution" by **Zhang Binglin** and "The Revolutionary Army" by **Zou Rong**. At the request of the Qing government in Shanghai, the Municipal Committee in the Shanghai International Settlement arrested Zhang, and Zou and closed the newspaper office on 30 July 1903. According to the agreement between the Qing government and the administration of the **foreign concession**, all civil and criminal cases in the International Settlement should be reviewed by Chinese officials in conjunction with the foreign judges. On one hand, the Chinese officials would make judgments based on instructions of the Qing government; on the other, they could not ignore the foreign administration. The Qing government asked the court to extradite Zang and Zou to Chinatown or offer them lifetime imprisonment. This provoked objection by Shanghai newspapers and a massive protest throughout the country. The British and American governments also voiced their concerns. Ten months later, the court pronounced its verdict that Zhang's sentence be three years' imprisonment, Zou's two years, and both with hard labor. Zou was tortured to death in the jail. Zhang left for Japan to continue his anti-**Manchu** activities after he was released in June 1904.

SUN YAT-SEN (1866–1925). The preeminent leader of China's **Republican Revolution**, referred to as the Father of Modern China. Sun was born in Xiangsha, Guangdong Province, into a peasant family. After receiving a few years' training in the Chinese classics at a village school, he was sent to Honolulu in 1879, at the age of 13. There he stayed with his elder brother, Sun Mei, who had emigrated to Hawaii as a laborer and had become a prosperous merchant. Sun Yat-sen studied first at the Anglican missionary Iolani School and graduated from Oahu College in 1883 at the age of 17. Although he attempted to continue to study in the United States, he was sent home to China as his brother was becoming afraid that Sun would convert to Christianity. In 1883, Sun returned to China and, a year later under family arrangement, married Lu Muzheng, who bore him one son and two daughters. The son, Sun Ke, followed his father's path and later became the president of the Executive Council of the Republic of China.

In the winter of 1883, Sun Yat-sen went to **Hong Kong** to study medicine and was baptized by an American missionary of the Congregational Church of the United States. Hong Kong was a source of inspiration and instruction for the young medical student, who had been exposed to Western ideologies and models of administration. Sun began to make new friends who shared his ideas of transforming China. In 1892, he graduated from the Hong Kong College of Medicine for Chinese and went to Macao and Guangzhou to practice medicine.

In 1894, Sun wrote to **Li Hongzhang** suggesting political reform, but the proposal was rejected. Disappointed with the Qing government, Sun went to Honolulu to raise funds to facilitate his revolutionary activities, and in February 1985 in Hong Kong, he established his first revolutionary organization, *xingzhonghui* (**Revive China Society**). The "Blue Sky, White Sun" designed by Lu Haotong became its formal flag. All its members took the oath to "expel the **Manchus**, restore China to the Chinese, and establish a republic." Sun thus began to use **anti-Manchu nationalism** to mobilize the Chinese for his revolution. The Revive China Society plotted to launch an uprising and take Guangzhou as their revolutionary base. However, the uprising failed and Sun was expelled by Hong Kong authorities.

For the next 16 years, Sun was an exile in Europe, the United States, and Japan, recruiting adherents among overseas Chinese and raising money for further uprisings in China. In 1896, he was kidnapped by the Chinese legation in London. The *London Globe* exposed the news, and the British Foreign Office forced the Qing legation to release Sun. The **London kidnapping** made Sun Yat-sen an internationally known revolutionary leader. In 1903, Sun set up a military school in Japan to train young revolutionaries. He also added the idea of "equally distributing land among the people" to his revolutionary program. In 1904, he joined the *hongmen* in Honolulu and was elected *hong rod* (generalissimo). Under Sun's influence, the *hongmen* changed its original dedication (revive the Ming dynasty) to a republican revolution.

In 1905, Sun met **Huang Xing** in Tokyo, and they unified all revolutionary groups into one organization, the *tongmenghui* (the Chinese United League). Sun was elected chairman and Huang chief of the executive department. In the foreword to Tongmenghui's formal journal *Minbao* (***People's Journal***), Sun for the first time illuminated his **Three People's Principles**: nationalism, democracy, and the people's livelihood; the principles were his revolutionary program and also the guideline for the Republic of China. *Minbao* propagandized Sun's program and attacked the monarchists headed by **Kang Youwei** and **Liang Qichao**, the previous leaders of the abortive **Hundred Days' Reform**, who continued to advocate a legitimate constitutional monarchy. From 1907 through 1911, Sun and Huang led 10 uprisings, but none of them succeeded.

On 10 October 1911, a military uprising at Wuchang was staged by local army officers and responded to by revolutionaries throughout the country. Sun learned of the successful revolt in Denver, Colorado. Before returning to China, however, Sun decided to travel to New York and Europe to solicit much-needed diplomatic support for the revolutionary regime. Upon his final arrival in Shanghai on 25 December 1911, Sun was warmly welcomed and elected provisional president of the Republic of China four days later by representatives from 14 provinces. The urgent task of the provisional government was to achieve national unification. However, the Qing government still controlled most northern provinces, and its leading force, the **Beiyang Army**, was in the hands of **Yuan Shikai**. The provisional government sent Wu Tingfan as its representative to negotiate with Yuan's representative, **Tang Shaoyi**.

As a compromise, the revolutionaries elected Yuan president, and Yuan swore to join the republicans and force the Qing emperor to abdicate. After the Qing dynasty was terminated, however, Yuan Shikai betrayed the republic rather quickly and proclaimed himself emperor. In 1913, Sun led the **Second Revolution**. But the poorly organized revolutionary army was crushed and Sun had to flee to Japan. In order to build a strictly disciplined party, Sun transformed the Tongmenghui into the Chinese **Revolutionary Party**. On 25 October 1915, Sun married **Song Qingling**, a daughter of Sun's longtime supporter, **Charlie Soong**.

In 1916, Yuan died and Sun returned to Shanghai. The next year, as Duan Qiren dismissed the parliament to build a new dictatorship, Sun launched the Protection of the Constitution Movement, known as the Third Revolution. He called all congressmen to travel south to Guangzhou, where he established a military government and prepared for a northern expedition. In 1921, Sun was elected **extraordinary president** and generalissimo. Sun urged a **northern expedition** against the **warlords** to reunify China. This caused a conflict with the Guangdong military leader, **Chen Jiongming**, who stood for provincial autonomy. In June 1922, Chen's troops attacked the residence of the generalissimo. **Chiang Kai-shek** rushed to rescue Sun, who retreated to Shanghai.

In 1923, Sun began to seek Soviet aid. On 26 January, he met the Soviet envoy, Adolf Joffe, who promised to help Sun reorganize the **Chinese Nationalist Party** (GMD) and complete his Republican

Revolution. Although he accepted the Soviet support, Sun refused to substitute communism for his Three People's Principles or to establish communism or the Soviet system in China. Sun reinterpreted his Three People's Principles and elaborated the Five-Yuan Constitution as the future political system of the Republic of China. At the First National Congress of the GMD in 1924, Sun pronounced his new policy of alliance with the Soviet Union and the **Chinese Communist Party** (CCP). He explained the possibility and necessity for the GMD and CCP to join hands in the struggle against imperialism and **warlordism**. With Russian help, Sun established the **Whampoa Military Academy** near Guangzhou. He appointed Chiang Kai-shek as its commandant and **Wang Jingwei** and **Hu Hanmin** as political instructors. The representative of the **Comintern**, **Gregory Borodin**, served as his adviser, and a CCP member, **Zhou Enlai**, worked as the director of the political department of the academy. Sun was eager to resume the Northern Expedition, but he did not give up efforts for a peaceful settlement.

On 10 November 1924, **Feng Yuxiang** overthrew **Cao Kun**'s warlord government in Beijing and invited Sun to come north for negotiations. Despite his deteriorating health, Sun accepted the invitation to travel with Soong Qing-ling to Beijing. Suffering from advanced-stage liver cancer, Sun's condition worsened on the way, and he died shortly after his arrival in Beijing on 12 March 1925 at the age of 58. *See also* SUN-JOFFE MANIFESTO.

SUN-JOFFE MANIFESTO. In January 1923, the special envoy of the Soviet Union, Adolf Abramovich Joffe, flew to Shanghai to meet the premier of the **Chinese Nationalist Party** (GMD), **Sun Yat-sen**. Sun elaborated a new policy stance of the Nationalist Party. Their meeting resulted in the Sun-Joffe Manifesto of 26 January 1923, which included the following main points: consensus on the impossibility of the building of Soviet-style communism in China at present; agreement on the current urgent task of the Chinese Revolution, which was to reunify China and win China's full independence, and a promise of Soviet support; confirmation by the Soviet government to give up all special rights and privileges in China; understanding that the future administration of the **Chinese Eastern Railway** by the Russians and reorganization of the administration should be arranged through further negotiations; Soviet disavowal of imperialistic intention in Outer Mongolia; and China's agreement to not require the immediate withdrawal of Soviet troops from Outer Mongolia. This joint manifesto was the basis of the GMD's cooperation with the Soviet Union and the **Chinese Communist Party** (CCP). On 27 January, Joffe left for Japan, and Sun sent **Liao Zhongkai** to Japan to continue to discuss with Joffe follow-up programs, including Soviet aid in building a military academy and revolutionary army, reorganizing the GMD, and promoting the GMD-CCP **United Front** against **warlordism.**

"SUPPORT THE QING, DESTROY FOREIGNERS." The slogan of the Boxers during the Boxer uprising of 1899–1900. As early as October 1898, Zhao Sanduo and Yan Shuqin had led peasant revolts in Guanxian, Shandong Province. They first raised a flag with the slogan, "Support the Qing, Destroy Foreigners," when they attacked local Christian churches. It was intended to revive China by expelling foreigners. The **Boxer Rebellion** gained momentum with this slogan because the disaffected and dispossessed peasantry, who used to aim squarely against the **Manchu** government, had now found a more attractive target and had gained support from local gentry. The **Dowager Cixi** and the Qing court decided to ally with the Boxers in their antiforeign and anti-Christian violence in northern China.

SUSHUN (1816–1861). One of the regents for the **Tongzhi Emperor**. Sushun was the sixth son of Wurgongga, the Prince Zheng. He joined the army early and was promoted to general in the late years of the **Daoguang Emperor**'s reign. He then became the closest aide of the **Xianfeng Emperor** and held numerous important positions, including president of the **Lifan Yuan**, minister of civil affairs, and member of the **Grand Council**. To suppress the **Taiping Rebellion**, he suggested that **Han** officials, such as Hu Lingyi and **Zeng Guofan**, be put in important positions. During the Second **Opium War**, he was in charge of negotiation with foreigners. He signed several treaties, including the Sino-Russian **Treaty of Aigun**. When the Xianfeng Emperor died, his successor was only five. Sushun and seven other prominent ministers were appointed as regents for the boy emperor, and they were thus involved in a power struggle with the emperor's mother, the **Dowager Cixi**. In November 1861, the Dowager Cixi staged a coup and arrested the regents. Sushun was charged with treason and beheaded in public.

– T –

TAI'ERZHUANG, BATTLE OF (1938). China's first victorious battle in the conventional war with the Japan. On 24 March, the Japanese 10th Division commanded by Rensuke Isogai launched an attack on Tai'erzhuang. After three days of fighting, the Japanese troops with the support of the air force rushed into the town, and the Chinese troops began street-to-street fighting. The commander in chief of the 2nd Army Group, Sun Zhonglian, advanced forces five times larger than Rensuke's to encircle the enemy but could not annihilate them quickly, and the Chinese troops were almost completely exhausted. On 29 March, Itagaki Seishiro led the 5th Division to relieve Rensuke, but he was blocked on the way.

On 4 April, when Sun asked **Li Zongren** to permit him to retreat, Li ordered him to fight to the death and told him that "victory will be decided in the last five minutes." Finally, the Chinese reinforcements led by Tang Bo'en arrived and began to attack Rensuke from behind, and the Chinese troops inside Tai'erzhuang organized dare-to-die squads launching frontal attacks. Rensuke led his remnants in retreat to Yixian. The **Nationalist Party** troops repulsed the Japanese assault at Tai'erzhuang, annihilating about 16,000 of the Japanese troops and capturing numerous weapons, ammunition, and military vehicles, but they paid the casualty of 30,000 men.

TAIPING REBELLION (1851–1864). The largest revolt against the Qing government in China, which established the Heavenly Kingdom of Great Peace. The war between the Taiping rebels and the Qing troops killed about 20 million people and destroyed numerous towns and villages. At its peak, the rebels had over 1 million troops. The Taiping regime lasted for 13 years, and its power reached into 14 provinces of south and southeast China. The leader of the Taiping Rebellion was **Hong Xiuquan**, a failed examination candidate, who happened to get a Christian booklet and declared himself to be God's son given a divine mission to kill all demons (**Manchus**). Hong, **Feng Yunshan**, and **Yang Xiuqing** worked together to found the **God Worshipping Society**, the basis of the Taiping movement. Hong's followers grew from the early conversions of friends and relatives to the participation of tens of thousands of impoverished peasants. Finally, the revolt began in Guangxi Province, in early January

1851, and seven months later, Hong proclaimed the establishment of the Heavenly Kingdom of Peace with himself as *tian wang* (king). The revolt rapidly spread northward. In March 1853, the Taipings stormed Nanjing, killing 30,000 imperial soldiers and slaughtering thousands of civilians, making the city their Heavenly Capital.

The Taiping rebels traveled throughout south China, but they did not establish any rural bases. They left huge rural areas to local gentry who organized militias to fight the Taiping and also launched cultural crusades against the Taiping's heathenism. After they seized Nanjing, the Taiping did not organize new campaigns to attack the already-weakened Manchu troops in north China, but gave them the much-needed time to organize a counterattack. The Taiping Kingdom tried to carry out many new policies. Imitating the Western calendar, it created a solar calendar to replace the Chinese lunar calendar. It required the study of Hong's version of Christianity and designed new exams to replace the traditional **civil service examination**, testing not with Confucian classics but the Christian Bible. The Taiping also banned footbinding, opium smoking, gambling, tobacco, alcohol, concubinage, slavery, and prostitution. The most remarkable program was **land reform**. According to the Land Regulation of the Taiping Kingdom, all land belonged to the state, which then divided the land between all families based on their size, with men and women receiving equal shares. After a harvest, each family would keep what it needed for its sustenance and place the rest in state granaries. However, these policies were never effectively implemented.

After seizing Nanjing, Hong quickly lost interest in state affairs, being infatuated with medication and his harem, while his most ambitious followers engaged in brutal power struggles. In 1856, the second most important leader, **Yang Xiuqing**, was murdered by Hong's trusted follower, **Wei Changhui**. Yang's family and thousands of adherents were also massacred. This massacre aroused the ire of many officers, so Hong ordered the execution of Wei Changhui. Wei resisted. As the slaughter continued, more than 20,000 innocent Taiping soldiers and urban residents became its victims. Disappointed with Hong, one of the major military commanders, **Shi Dakai**, led an army of 100,000 men out of Nanjing in 1857. All these problems incapacitated the Taiping regime. In its later years, Hong Xiuquan called his cousin **Hong Rengan** from Hong Kong. Hong Rengan initiated a number of reforms, including centralization of the administration, development of the economy, and improvement of relations with the Western powers. But it was too late to make any substantial changes.

Hong Xiuquan appointed young military commanders, such as **Li Xiucheng** and Chen Yucheng, to lead new military campaigns. When the Taiping troops attempted to take Shanghai, they were defeated by the "Ever Victorious Army" and the Qing forces under the command of **Zeng Guofan** and **Li Hongzhang**. At the third Battle of Nanjing in 1864, more than 100,000 soldiers from both sides were killed in three days. A month before the capital fell into the hands of the **Hunan Army** and **Anhui Army**, Hong committed suicide. His elder son succeeded him and escaped from Nanjing but was soon captured and executed.

TAIWAN DEMOCRATIC SELF-GOVERNMENT LEAGUE (TDSL). One of the eight legally recognized non-Communist parties in Communist China. After the **February Twenty-Eighth Uprising** was suppressed in Taiwan, **Xie Xuehong** and other leaders of the uprising fled to Hong Kong, where they founded the Taiwan Democratic Self-Government League on 12 November 1947. In May 1948, the TDSL issued the Letter to the Compatriots in Taiwan, expressing its cooperation with the **Chinese Communist Party** (CCP) in the civil war and the Chinese Revolution. In September 1949, when the **Chinese People's Political Consultative Conference** was held in Beijing, the TDSL sent its representatives to attend. The TDSL announced that it accepted the leadership of the CCP and held the **Common Program** as its own political program. Some of the TDSL leaders gained positions in the Communist government. The TDSL now has about 2,100 members, all originally from Taiwan.

TAN PINGSHAN (1886–1956). Early leader of the **Chinese Communist Party** (CCP). Born in Gaoming, Guangdong Province, into the family of a tailor, Tan graduated from the Liangguang Normal School in Guangzhou and went to **Peking University** to study philosophy. Tan joined the **Tongmenghui** in 1917 and then organized a **Communist group** in Guangzhou. Tan served as a member of the CCP Central Executive Committee and as minister of peasants. During the CCP–**Nationalist Party** (GMD) alliance, Tan was appointed head of the GMD's Organization Department and minister of peasants. After the CCP-GMD split, he led the **Nanchang Mutiny** and was elected chair of the Revolutionary Committee. After the failure of the uprising, Tang fled to Hong Kong. Accusing him of making a policy mistake in the uprising, the **Comintern** instructed the CCP to expel Tan from the party. As soon as the **Second Sino-Japanese War** broke out, Tan advocated the three principles of "resistance, unity, and progress" and returned to serve the GMD government. In 1948, he worked with **Li Jishen, He Xiangning**, and other senior GMD members to establish the Revolutionary Committee of the GMD against **Chiang Kai-shek**'s policy. In September 1949, Tan attended the **Chinese People's Political Consultative Conference** and began to cooperate with the CCP.

TAN SITONG (1865–1898). An eminent scholar and reformer in the late Qing dynasty. Born into a noble family in Liuyang, Hunan Province, Tan was greatly influenced by the works of Gong Zhizhen and **Wei Yuan**. After China's defeat in the **First Sino-Japanese War**, he gave up Confucian studies and turned to the West for China's salvation. Through **Liang Qichao**, Tan got to know the reformist leader **Kang Youwei**, whom he respected as a teacher. In 1897, Tan returned to Hunan Province and helped the governor, **Chen Baozhen**, promote local reforms, including opening new schools, constructing the Guangzhou–Wuhan Railway, and mining local coal. Tan also organized the *nanxuehui* (Society of Southern Scholars) and published *Xiangbao* (*Hunan Daily*) to propagandize new ideas. Tan was deeply involved in the **Hundred Days' Reform** in 1898 and was one of the four liberals appointed by the Quangxu Emperor to the **Grand Council**. In the same year, the **Dowager Cixi** launched a coup, placing the emperor under house arrest and hunting out all reform leaders in Beijing. Tan refused to flee and was determined to sacrifice himself for the reform. He was executed in public in Beijing on 28 September 1898. His coffin was moved to his home village one year later.

TAN YANKAI (1880–1930). Politician and military leader of the Republic of China. Born in Hangzhou, Zhejiang Province, Tan obtained his *jinshi* degree in 1904 and was appointed to the **Hanlin Academy** of the Qing court. During the **constitutional reform**s of the Qing government, he was elected president of the Hunan provincial consultative council and thus became a reform leader. After the 1911 Revolution, Tan supported the republicans and joined the

Nationalist Party (GMD) in 1912. Tan took an active part in the anti–**Yuan Shikai** campaigns and was dismissed from office. In the Protect the Republic War, Tan put forward the slogan "Return Hunan to the Hunanese," which won him much acclaim among the local communities. Tan served as both the military and civilian governor of Hunan between 1916 and 1918, but in 1920 he was driven out of the province by the **warlord** Zhao Hengti.

Tan then followed **Sun Yat-sen** to Guangzhou and served as his minister of internal affairs. In July 1922, he was appointed commander in chief of the **Hunan Army**, which grew to more than 10,000 men. These troops defeated **Chen Jiongming** and stabilized the political situation in Guangdong. As a rising star, Tan was elected a member of the GMD Central Executive Committee. Tan then led the Second Army of the **National Revolutionary Army** in the **Northern Expedition** against the warlords. In 1926, Tan was elected chair of the Central Political Committee of the GMD. During the conflict between **Wang Jingwei** and **Chiang Kai-shek**, Tan was the chairman of Wang's Wuhan government and initiated negotiations with Chiang's Nanjing government. Later, Tan was involved in an anti-Chiang campaign that forced Chiang to resign, but when Chiang Kai-shek regained power, Tan soon showed his support for Chiang's new government. Tan served Chiang as chairman of the National Government and president of the **Executive Yuan**. With solid training in traditional scholarship, Tan was good at Chinese classical literature and the Yang-style **calligraphy**. It was said that none in the 20th century could compare with his calligraphic works. After his death, Tan was buried next to Sun Yat-sen's tomb in Nanjing.

TANG SHAOYI (1859–1938). The first premier of the Republic of China. Born in Xiangshan, Guangdong Province, to a family of tea merchants, Tang was sent to the United States to study at the age of 14. After graduating from Yale University, he was called back to China. He worked as **Yuan Shikai**'s major assistant in Korea and then was appointed consul general to Korea. After this service, Tang became inspector of customs in Tianjin on Yuan's recommendation. As the plenipotentiary of the Qing government, Tang was in charge of two negotiations with Great Britain over the Tibetan issue, concluding with the Supplementary Treaty on the Indo-Tibetan Issue.

He successively served as governor of Fengtian, deputy minister of foreign affairs, and minister of the postal service in the Qing government. From December 1911 through February 1912, Tang negotiated on Yuan Shikai's behalf with the representative of the revolutionary army, **Wu Tingfang**, in Shanghai, which concluded with an agreement on the abdication of the Qing emperor and the recognition of Yuan as president of the Republic of China.

Tang became the first prime minister of the Republic of China. On March 25, 1912, he organized the first cabinet in Shanghai and moved it to Beijing in April. Despite his close relations with Yuan, he opposed Yuan's restoration of the monarchy, and for this reason he was forced to resign from office. He then went to Shanghai to establish a life insurance company. Tang joined **Sun Yat-sen**'s United League early, and in 1917, he served as minister of finance in Sun's military government in Guangzhou. In 1931, he was appointed a member of the Supervision Committee of the Nationalist Party. When the Japanese troops stormed Shanghai in 1938, Tang stayed in Shanghai but sent his family to Hong Kong. Because of his reputation, the Japanese attempted to make him the head of a Japanese puppet government in the city. They set up a special committee to approach him, but Tang refused to cooperate. Tang was assassinated shortly thereafter at his home. *See also* BEIJING GOVERNMENT.

TANG SHENZHI (1889–1970). Prominent military commander of modern China. Born in Dongan, Hunan Province, Tang graduated from the **Baoding Military Academy**. He participated in all the important movements and wars in early 20th-century China, including the 1911 Revolution, Anti–**Yuan Shikai** Expedition, Constitution Protection War, and **Northern Expedition**. In the early years, Tang served in the local **warlord** army in Hunan, but in 1926 he joined the **National Revolutionary Army** and was appointed commander of the 8th Army. His troops stormed Changsha in June 1926, and he became the governor of Hunan. Tang was involved in two anti–**Chiang Kai-shek** campaigns. He first sided with the Wuhan government against Chiang's Nanjing regime. Afterward, he was forced to flee to Japan. Two years later, he joined Chiang's troops in fighting the Guangxi warlords, but in December 1929, Tang collaborated with Shi Yousan to attack Chiang again. This time he had to go into exile until after the **Manchuria Incident**.

Tang returned to the Nanjing government to fight the Japanese and was made the president of the Military Consultative Council. In April 1935, Tang was conferred the title of full general of the first class. As the Japanese approached Nanjing in November 1937, he advocated defense to the death and became the commander in chief of the municipal defense. Tang destroyed all roads and boats, making it impossible for people to evacuate, and organized a strong resistance for about one month. However, on 12 December, he gave up the city and escaped. Having lost their commanders, the Chinese troops were quickly crushed by the Japanese, who then slaughtered 200,000 to 300,000 civilians and war prisoners. This was known as the **Nanjing Massacre**. During the civil war, Tang suggested peace negotiations with the **Chinese Communist Party** (CCP) and sent an open telegraph saluting the Communist takeover of Hunan Province. After 1949, Tang was appointed deputy governor of Hunan and a member of the China Committee of National Defense.

TANGGU TRUCE (1933). Cease-fire agreement between China and Japan before the formal declaration of the **Second Sino-Japanese War**. In 1933, the Japanese occupied the province of Rehe and continued to march southward. The 29th Army commanded by Song Zheyuan put up strong resistance against the Japanese but could not stop their advance. The Nationalist government negotiated with the Japanese and signed the Tanggu Truce at Tanggu, Hebei Province. This cease-fire agreement stipulated that the Chinese troops retreat to the south, and it made 100 km of territory south of the Great Wall a demilitarized zone. From the perspective of the Nationalist government, the truce not only created a buffer zone between the Japanese- and Chinese-controlled areas but also legitimized the Japanese occupation of Manchuria and Rehe Province. In fact, it opened the door for Japan's entry to China's heartland. **Wang Jingwei** directed the day-to-day negotiations and encouraged **Chiang Kai-shek** to accept the Japanese terms. As soon as the truce was signed on 31 May 1933, Chiang Kai-shek ratified it. However, the 19th Army, the Chinese troops stationed in the Great Wall area, strongly opposed the Tanggu Truce. Also, the Defense Conference of the Nanjing government on 2 June 1933 referred to the truce as "unauthorized and illegal." The Chinese troops, therefore, did not retreat to the line designated by the truce.

TANSHAN–XUGEZHUANG RAILWAY (TAN-XU RAILWAY).
The first commercial railway constructed by the Chinese. The
Tanshan–Xugezhuang Railway, a seven-mile railroad, is a section of
today's railway from Beijing to Shenyang. In 1876, **Li Hongzhang**
discovered rich coal deposits in the area near the city of Tangshan and
decided to construct a commercial railway to transport coal from the
mines to the city, from where coal could be shipped by boats to Tianjin and Shanghai. The Tanshan–Xugezhuang Railway was underwrit-
ten by a Guangdong merchant, Tang Jingxing, and designed by British engineer C. W. Kinder in accordance with British standard gauge
railways. Li found additional support for this project in the capability
of the rail line to efficiently ship military supplies to the newly built
Chinese Beiyang Navy. The proposed trunk line passed the foot of
Mount Malanyu, where the Royal Eastern Tomb was located, and
the Qing court believed that the snorting of the steam engines would
startle sleeping royal ancestors in the Eastern Tomb. Because of this,
the Qing court approved the project with an ironic condition that no
locomotive could be used; thus the trains had to be drawn by mules.
The project was completed in 1881, but locomotives were not put into
daily use on this line until 1882.

TAO XINGZHI (1891–1946). Prominent educator in modern China.
Born in Shexian, Anhui Province, Tao graduated from Jingling University in Nanjing and then traveled to the United States to study. In
1915, he obtained a master's degree in political science at the University of Illinois and then transferred to Columbia University and
obtained a second master's in education. After returning to China,
he was appointed provost of Nanjing Advanced Normal School. He
urged the development of a new Chinese school system different
from Western models, which advocated popular education, especially education in rural areas. In 1926, he published the *Manifesto
of Transforming Rural Education in China* and founded the world-
famous Xiaozhuang School (Rural Teacher School). This school
not only trained rural teachers but also promoted rural reforms for
renewing village life. The experiment was a success in terms of the
improvement of rural economy, living standards, and peasant education. However, the National Government found that some students at
the Xaiozhuang School were Communists and, for this reason, closed
the school and hunted Tao.

In 1934, Tao founded a semimonthly, *Living Education*, creating a theory on "living education." Tao looked on society as a school and proposed the unity of learning and reflective acting. His teaching philosophy combined education with social practice and made education serve the broad masses of the people. Tao was involved in the resistance movement during the **Second Sino-Japanese War**, serving as a people's ambassador to visit many European and Asian countries to tell the world about China's war against the Japanese. Tao published extensively on educational theory and pedagogical studies, greatly contributing to the modernization of the Chinese education system. In 1939, he created China's first school for talented children, and in January 1946, he created a community college to promote popular education. Six months later, Tao died of a cerebral hemorrhage in Shanghai at the age of 55.

TAO ZHIYUE (1892–1988). Lieutenant general of the **National Revolutionary Army** and full general of the **People's Liberation Army** (PLA). Born into a wealthy gentry family in Nanning, Hunan, Tao began to receive a Confucian education at the age of six. During his time at a high school in Changsha, the 1911 **Republican Revolution** occurred, and Tao joined the *tongmenghui* in 1912 and the **Nationalist Party** (GMD) in 1927. He graduated from a military school and participated in the **Northern Expedition**, during which he was promoted to regiment commander. After the **Marco Polo Bridge Incident**, Tao was sent to reinforce the 19th Army to defend Shanghai. Outnumbered by Japanese troops, he held the position for 22 days. Then Tao was transferred to Shaanxi, serving as army commander of the 1st Army and as commander in chief of the 37th Group Army. In 1946, he was made commander of the Xinjiang garrison. In 1949, Tao wanted to cross over to the the PLA. He worked with the governor of Xinjiang, **Burhan Shahidi**, and made a plan for an uprising. He persuaded the GMD hard-liners in Xinjiang to leave China with their money, avoiding a military conflict in the area. On 25 September 1949, Tao sent the open telegraph announcing that he and his army had "cut off all relations with the Nationalist government," making the Communist takeover of Xinjiang a "peaceful liberation." After 1949, he was promoted to full general and his troops were reorganized as the 22nd Army Corps. Tao was also elected vice-chairman of the **Chinese People's Political Consultative Conference**. He died on 26 December 1988 in Changsha.

THIRTEEN HONGS (THIRTEEN FACTORIES). Known also as Co-hong, it was the Chinese guild of companies with licenses for foreign trade in Guangzhou. The term Thirteen Hongs also referred to an area in the city where foreign trade was allowed in the 18th century. The Thirteen Hongs performed a dual duty: to pay the Chinese government tariff and various taxes on behalf of foreign merchants and to manage foreign trade on behalf of the Chinese government. The foreign traders could do business only with licensed Chinese companies. When foreign merchants needed to contact the Chinese government, they had to ask the Co-hong to forward their messages. Despite the name Thirteen Hongs, the licensed companies did not number exactly 13. In fact, 16 Chinese companies in Guangzhou obtained licenses and organized the guild called the Co-hong in 1720. The Co-hong monopolized foreign trade, offering foreign merchants services or recommendations when they needed compradors, interpreters, silver masters, scribes, and clerks. The Co-hong also represented foreigners in lawsuits. The Co-hong was disbanded with the abolition of the **Canton System** by the **Treaty of Nanjing** in 1842.

THREE ALLS POLICY. A Japanese scorched-earth policy adopted in China during the **Second Sino-Japanese War**. Generally considered a Japanese war atrocity, it was a policy that encouraged killing all the people, burning down all the villages, and looting all the grain and other properties in guerrilla-active areas. This policy was also referred to as "the burn to ash strategy" in Japanese literature. It was designed to uproot the guerrillas in northern China. On 10 July 1941, General Yasuji Okamura was appointed commander in chief of the Japanese Army in North China, and he decided to implement the Three Alls policy. Approved by Imperial Headquarters as Army Order Number 575 on 3 December 1941, the policy was the objective of more than a hundred military campaigns launched by Okamura. The Three Alls policy was responsible for the deaths of more than 2.7 million Chinese civilians.

THREE AND A HALF STRATEGISTS. Four prominent military commanders of the **Chinese Communist Party** and the **Nationalist Party** troops. The three were **Lin Biao**, **Bai Chongxi**, and **Liu Bocheng**, and the half referred to Su Yu.

THREE AXIAL AGES. Theory by **Kang Youwei**, a leader of the **Hundred Days' Reform** in the late 19th century. This theory was elaborated in his book ***Datong shu*** (*The Book of Universal Commonwealth*). The theory argues that mankind progresses through three ages, from the primitive Age of Disorder to the Age of Approaching Peace, and eventually reaches the Age of Universal Peace. In the process, Kang believed, human nature would improve and human institutions would also evolve. In his view, the contemporary age was still in the stage of partial peace, not the "universal commonwealth" (*datong*). According to his vision, an ideal world would be established during the third stage: there would be no nations, no families, no clans, and no autocracy. There would be public kindergartens, schools, homes for the elderly, hospitals, public dormitories, and dining halls. Men and women would cohabit for the duration of one year, after which everyone would change mates; there would be fair labor division and rewards for contributions.

THREE DISTRICTS REVOLUTION (1944–1945). An uprising that took place in Xinjiang. It was a revolt against the domination of the **Nationalist Party** (GMD) in three districts of Xinjiang: Ili, Taicheng, and Altai. In November 1944, the rebels proclaimed the establishment of the "Eastern Turkestan Republic" (ETR). The Ili rebellion was initially merely a spontaneous uprising bred in the general disillusionment among the local population, but the Russians were deeply involved in an attempt to turn the rebellion into a pro-Soviet Socialist revolution. With the Soviet military support, the ETR quickly expanded its territory. Its military force, the Ili National Army, defeated the GMD troops and had advanced to within 70 miles of Urumchi by the fall of 1945. However, the Russians soon discovered a strong Pan-Islamic and Pan-Turkish tendency among the Ili rebel leaders. Believing that the Muslim independence movement would pose challenges to the legitimacy of Soviet domination over Russia's own Muslim minorities, Moscow turned to support the GMD's government and called for a cease-fire and negotiations.

The negotiations between the ETR and the GMD began in October 1945, and the peace treaty was finalized in June 1946. As a result, the Ili rebels agreed to disband the ETR in exchange for a provincial coalition government. The representatives of the Ili regime would join the coalition government, and the Ili National Army was permitted to continue to exist as the Peace Preservation Corps. Moscow also urged the **Chinese Communist Party** (CCP) to take over the leadership of the Ili regime. After **Mao Zedong** decided to march to Xinjiang, he sent a telegraph to the Ili leaders, recognizing that the Three Districts Revolution was "part of our Chinese People's democratic revolution," and he invited their representatives to join the **Chinese People's Political Consultative Conference** in Beijing. In the meantime, the Peace Preservation Corps was incorporated into the **People's Liberation Army**.

THREE PEOPLE'S PRINCIPLES. The political philosophy of **Sun Yat-sen**, championing nationalism, democracy, and the people's livelihood. Sun's nationalism, the first principle, meant freedom from imperialist domination. However, to make the 1911 Revolution, Sun once referred to it as **anti-Manchu nationalism** and restoration of **Han** Chinese rule. After 1911, Sun began to emphasize harmonious coexistence and equality among the different ethnic groups in China. He opposed all forms of ethnocentrism and advocated self-determination, thus defining nationalism as anti-Western imperialism. By democracy, the second principle, Sun meant "government of the people, by the people, and for the people." He believed in a system of checks and balances and suggested that the Chinese republican government be divided into five branches: legislative, executive, judicial, supervision, and examination. The third principle, that of people's livelihood, may be understood as social welfare—that a government should take care of people's "food, clothing, housing, and transportation." People's livelihood also consisted of two policy orientations. One was "equalization of landholdings and" another was "limiting private capital" to avoid economic monopolies.

Sun's political philosophy was influenced by both Western democratic thinkers and Chinese Confucian ideology. The Three People's Principles were also Sun's revolutionary program, which first appeared in the *Manifesto of the Tongmenghui* in 1905. The last clarification could be seen in 16 talks that Sun made in Guangzhou in 1924, when he reinterpreted the principles and added new ideas, including anti-**warlordism** and alliance with the **Chinese Communist Party** (CCP). Despite the 1927 split between the **Nationalist Party** (GMD) and the CCP, both the Nationalists and Communists claimed that they were upholding the true Three People's Principles.

THREE PEOPLE'S PRINCIPLES YOUTH LEAGUE. A short-lived youth organization under the leadership of the **Nationalist Party** (GMD). To mobilize more Chinese youngsters to join the War against Japanese Aggression and to develop their loyalty to **Chiang Kai-shek**, the youth league was founded in Wuchang on 9 July 1938. Chiang Kai-shek was its first chairman, and Chen Cheng served as the secretary-general. It recruited members mainly among students and young intellectuals. The **CC Clique** and other factions of the GMD all tried to penetrate the youth league and control it. Finally, **Chiang Ching-kuo** made it his base of power, and some of the youth league activists became the second generation of GMD leaders. The Fourth Plenary Session of the Sixth Central Committee of the GMD passed a resolution to merge the youth league, and all the members of the Three People's Principles Youth League were registered as GMD members in September 1947.

THREE RULES AND EIGHT POINTS. Discipline laid down by **Mao Zedong** for the Communist military forces. The three main rules of discipline are: obey orders in all your actions, don't take a simple needle or piece of thread from the masses, and turn in everything captured. The eight points for attention are: speak politely, pay fairly for what you buy, return everything you borrow, pay for anything you damage, don't hit or swear at people, don't damage crops, don't take liberties with women, and don't ill-treat captives.

THREE-THIRDS SYSTEM. A form of government created by the Chinese Communists during the **Second Sino-Japanese War**. In March 1940, **Mao Zedong** published an article on behalf of the Central Committee of the **Chinese Communist Party** (CCP) pointing out that the governments at various levels in the CCP-controlled areas should be coalition governments. These should consist of three groups of people: Communists, progressive non-Communists, and representatives of the bourgeoisie and landed gentry. Each group should occupy one-third of government positions. This policy was designed to consolidate the **United Front** in the war against the Japanese. It was reported that the three-thirds system had been established by 1942. After 1944, this principle also applied to public enterprises and cultural institutions. Nonetheless, this form of government ceased to exist when the Communists launched the **land reform** and engaged in civil war with the **Nationalist Party**.

TIAN WANG (HEAVENLY KING). The title of **Hong Xiuquan**, the leader of the **Taiping Rebellion**. After Hong founded the Taiping Kingdom in 1851, he proclaimed himself *tian wang* and appointed his major assistants as princes. The term *tian* (heaven) was different from the Chinese traditional concept; instead, it denoted the Christian paradise. Tian Wang was the emperor of the utopian paradise created by the Taiping rebels on earth.

TIANANMEN (GATE OF HEAVENLY PEACE). The front entrance to the Forbidden City originally built in 1417 and reconstructed in 1651. The Tiananmen is located in the center of the city of Beijing and along the northern edge of Tiananmen Square. Many important rallies and demonstrations in modern Chinese history have taken place in the square, including the **May Fourth Movement** of 1919, the **December Ninth Movement** of 1935, and the proclamation of the People's Republic of China by **Mao Zedong** on 1 October 1949. Because of this, the Tiananmen has become the symbol of the People's Republic of China. The annual celebration ceremony and government-sponsored rituals were held in this square. It was also in the streets to the west of the square and adjacent areas where a democratic demonstration took place and slaughter occurred in 1989.

TIANANMEN SQUARE. The largest city square in the world. Located in the center of Beijing, Tiananmen Square was opened in 1417 and expanded several times during the periods of the Republic of China and the People's Republic of China. It was named after Tiananmen, the gate to the imperial Forbidden City, which is on the northern edge of the square. Many important mass rallies and demonstrations took place in the square, including the **May Fourth Movement** of 1919 and the **December Ninth Movement** of 1935, as well as major Communist rituals. The founding ceremony of the People's Republic of China was also held there on 1 October 1949. One day earlier, the **Chinese People's Political Consultative Conference** passed the resolution to build the Monument to the People's Heroes in the center of Tiananmen Square. The monument was finally erected by April 1958.

TIANJIN, TREATIES OF (1858). These were several treaties the Qing government signed in 1858 with Russia (13 June), the United States (18 June), Great Britain (26 June), and France (27 June) in Tianjin in the middle of the Second **Opium War**, June 1858. The treaties were almost identical regarding Western demands and China's offers. The military failure of the war forced the Qing court to accept the terms by the four powers to grant them the right to station legations in Beijing, navigate freely (including their warships) on the Yangtze River, and travel in the internal regions of China for commercial or missionary purposes. China had to open 11 more ports to foreign trade and pay a war indemnity of 2 million taels to Britain and France, as well as a compensation of 2 million taels to British merchants. In addition, the Qing government promised to ban references to Westerners as *yi* (barbarian). From these treaties, all four powers gained **most favored nation** status. The treaties of Tianjin were ratified in the Beijing Convention in 1860, after the end of the Second Opium War.

TIANJIN MASSACRE (1870). Notorious slaughter of missionaries and foreigners in the late Qing dynasty. In June 1870, an epidemic disease killed a large number of children at the orphanage run by the French church Notre Dame des Victoires in Tianjin. Rumor spread that the church bewitched the children, mutilated their bodies, and extracted their hearts and eyes to make medicine. Also, a criminal who kidnapped children claimed that he was paid by the church. On 21 June, the magistrate Liu Jie brought the criminal to the church for investigation while the French consul Henri Fontanier had his chancellor M. Simon travel there to demand justice for the French sisters. When they got there, the church had already been surrounded by an enraged mob. In a conflict with a few people, Fontanier opened fire and wounded the magistrate's servant. The mob then burst out of control. They killed Fontanier, his assistant, 10 sisters, two priests, two French officials, and three Russian traders who happened to pass the church. They burned the French church and the orphanage. At the same time, four British and American churches were also destroyed.

After the massacre occurred, seven Western ministers lodged strong protests, demanding redress and punishment of the rioters, and foreign gunboats quickly anchored off Tianjin. The Qing court appointed the governor-general of Zhili, Zeng Guofan, to investigate the case. Based on the truth he discovered, Zeng asked to restore the reputation of the French nuns and suggested heavy penalties for those involved in the riot. As a result, 16 men were executed, 25 were exiled, and the Chinese government paid 400,000 taels of silver for the loss of lives and property. The Qing court also sent to France a mission of apology headed by Chonghou; the mission met the French provisional president Aldolphe Thiers on 23 November 1871. Thiers, on behalf of the French government, accepted the letter of apology from the Qing emperor.

TIANJIN MILITARY ACADEMY. Also known as the Tianjin Beiyang Military Academy. Established in 1885 in Tianjin by **Li Hongzhang**, it was the earliest modern military academy of China. The academy invited German officers to use German textbooks (translated into Chinese) to teach the cadets, making itself a model for other Chinese military academies in the years to come. The Tianjin Military Academy offered a three-year regular program and also some short-term workshops. The academy was designed to train cadets in both intellectual and military areas. They were required to study astronomy, geography, mathematics, chemistry, and military tactics, as well as the German language. During the **Boxer Rebellion** in 1900, when the **Eight-Nation Alliance** stormed Tianjin, the academy became one of the major targets of attack because it possessed a large amount of munitions and was located near the German concession. The academy dismissed all the cadets in June, but 90 of them refused to leave. On 17 June, the alliance bombarded the academy and all the cadets were killed. In 1906, **Yuan Shikai** tried to rebuild the academy. He spent one year doing fund-raising, land clearing, and other preparations. However, according to the **Boxer Protocol**, no military force was allowed to stay around Tianjin. The new academy had to move to Baoding and it became the Baoding Military Academy.

TI-YONG **FORMULA.** A Chinese attitude toward Western learning. The *ti-yong* formula was invented by a conservative reformer, the viceroy of Huguang, **Zhang Zhidong**, who attempted to learn Western technology and build modern industry to make China strong and rich. At the same time, Zhang placed emphasis on Chinese values as the essence, refusing to change China's cultural tradition or political system. As Zhang argued, the formula meant that Chinese learning was the foundation (*ti*) while Western learning was for practical application (*yong*). This formula was associated with **Wei Yuan**'s slogan "Learning superior techniques of the barbarians to control the barbarians," which served as a guideline for the **Self-Strengthening Movement** in the late 19th century. On one hand, the ti-yong formula was a way to justify borrowing Western culture and was thus welcomed by Chinese pragmatists; on the other, the formula was also used to preserve political institutions of the Qing regime and was therefore criticized by radical reformers, who believed that the formula was doomed to failure because the persistence of Chinese *ti* inhibited Chinese acceptance of Western *yong*. Although China's defeat by Japan in 1895 proved that any reform guided by the ti-yong formula could not lead to the revitalization of China, this formula remained influential even among the Chinese Communists.

TONGMENGHUI (CHINESE UNITED LEAGUE). Revolutionary party and underground movement organized on 20 August 1905 by **Sun Yat-sen**, **Huang Xing**, **Cai Yuanpei**, and **Song Jiaoren** in Tokyo. It was created through the unification of Sun's *xingzhonghui* (**Revive China Society**), Huang Xing's *huaxinghui* (**China Revival Society**), Cai Yuanpei's *guangfuhui* (**Recovery Society**), and other Chinese revolutionary organizations. At the founding meeting, Sun was elected president and Huang chief of the executive department. The meeting turned *Twentieth-Century China* into the official publication of the Tongmenghui and changed its name to *Minbao* (**People's Journal**). The original political platform of the Tongmenghui was "to overthrow the **Manchu** empire and to restore China to the Chinese, to establish a republic." Then Sun Yat-sen added another objective, "distributing land equally among the people."

When the Tongmenghui was founded, 400 Chinese students in Japan and more people in China joined, and its secret branches began to cover all major cities and provinces. In 1904, Sun Yat-sen joined the *hongmen* in Honolulu and was elected *hong rod* (generalissimo). The Tongmenghui thus gained the support of the largest organization of overseas Chinese in the United States. Two years later, the Tongmenghui formed a branch in Singapore, followed by other branches in Europe and the United States. The Tongmenghui played a leading role in the **Republican Revolution**, which led to the collapse of the Qing dynasty. To become a majority party in the parliament of the

Republic of China, the Tongmenghui decided to absorb other political parties and organizations in the parliament and to transform itself into a larger party. On 25 August 1912, the Tongmenghui completed this task and was reorganized as the **Nationalist Party** (Guomindang). *See also* REVOLUTIONARY PARTY OF CHINA.

TONGWENGUAN. Founded on 24 August 1862, the Tongwenguan was the first foreign-language school in China. It was set up by **Prince Gong** and was attached to his **Zongli Yamen**. In the early days of the school, the Tongwenguan taught only English, French, and Russian. Gradually, the curriculum was developed to include German, Japanese, astronomy, chemistry, natural science, and mathematics. The length of schooling was five years, and all students enjoyed free tuition, accommodation, and monthly stipends. The school hired a foreign provost and Western instructors, including **John Fryer** and **William A. P. Martin**. Because of the **Boxer Rebellion**, the Tongwenguan was suspended for two years, and it was incorporated into the Imperial University of the Capital (present-day **Peking University**) in 1902.

TONGZHI EMPEROR (REIGNED 1862–1874). Born in 1856, Tongzhi was the ninth emperor of the **Manchu** Qing dynasty and the eighth Qing emperor to rule over China. He was the only surviving son of the **Xianfeng Emperor** and **Empress Dowager Cixi**. Tongzhi was enthroned at the age of five. His mother, the Dowager Cixi, attended the state meetings behind the scene and made decisions on state affairs. This practice was referred to as *chuilian tingzheng*. In the Tongzhi era, a series of reforms was initiated in his name. These reforms, known as the **Tongzhi Restoration**, included the establishment of the **Zongli Yamen**, the **Tongwenguan**, and the **Self-Strengthening Movement**. Without political power, Tongzhi indulged in sensual pursuits. He died of smallpox (rumors say syphilis) on 12 January 1874, three months before his 19th birthday.

TONGZHI RESTORATION. Efforts to bring **Manchu** China back to previous prosperity in the era of the Tongzhi Emperor (1862–1874). After the Convention of Beijing in 1860 and the suppression of the **Taiping Rebellion** in 1864, China witnessed a period of relative peace and political stability. Several programs were engineered in the emperor's name by his mother, **Empress Dowager Cixi**, including enhancing Confucian education and the **civil service examinations**, reducing rural taxes to promote agricultural production, and advocating "practical knowledge" and Western learning. The Qing court also established a new office, the **Zongli Yamen**, to direct foreign affairs. Although the restoration was not yet a genuine program of modernization, it paved the way for the **Self-Strengthening Movement** and other institutional reforms in the later years. The leading players involved **Prince Gong**, **Zeng Guofan**, **Zuo Zongtang**, **Li Hongzhang**, and Hu Lingyi.

TREATIES. See names of individual treaties, for example, AIGUN, TREATY OF.

TRIADS (*SANHEHUI*, THREE HARMONIES SOCIETY). One of many secret societies in China. The Triads were a branch of the *tiandihui* (**Heaven and Earth Society**), founded in the 1760s with the purpose of "resisting the **Manchus** and restoring the Ming dynasty." The name *sanhehui* literally means "Three Harmonies Society," referring to the unity between heaven, earth, and human being. The Triads once offered **Sun Yat-sen** help in his revolution to overthrow the **Manchu** monarchy. Over the centuries, however, it gradually evolved from a Nationalist society into a criminal organization. Its activities include drug trafficking, contract murder, money laundering, gambling, prostitution, and various forms of racketeering. The Triads are active in **Hong Kong** and **Macao**, and among overseas Chinese as well as in China.

TRIBUTARY GRAIN SHIPMENT (*CAO YUN*). A shipment of grain from south and southeastern China to Beijing by river or by sea. The purpose of the tributary grain shipment was to supply the royal family, central government officials, military, and urban residents in the capital. The tributary grain shipment administration was in charge of collecting government and military grain (as part of the agricultural tax), building or purchasing grain boats, recruiting boatmen, and maintaining the Grand Canal. In 1855, the Yellow River changed course and the Grand Canal silted up, which made the shipments very difficult. On the other hand, shipment by sea appeared unsafe. The government, therefore, began to order local governments to pay in silver rather than grain. In the 20th century, as the grain market had become well developed, the tributary grain shipment became unnecessary, and it was finally abolished in 1901.

TRIBUTARY SYSTEM. As a traditional Chinese system for dealing with neighboring countries, it was built on Chinese cultural hegemony and military power. China received tribute from the states under its influence and gave them gifts in return. The tributary states recognized China's authority, and China promised their protection. More ritual and cultural connections were involved than military occupation. Sometimes, political marriages were also arranged between the Chinese empire and tributary states in order to strengthen bilateral ties. During the Ming dynasty, China had 65 tributary states; the number decreased to seven by the middle Qing era. In 1793, Lord McCartney visited China to ask for the establishment of modern diplomatic and commercial relations, which caused the first conflict between the Chinese tributary system and the Western treaty system. In the later 19th century, Qing China became too weak to protect itself and still less its tributary states. Finally, the Sino-French **Treaty of Tianjin** in 1885 and the Sino-Japanese **Treaty of Shimonoseki** in 1895 brought China's tributary system to an end.

TRIPLE INTERVENTION (TRIPARTITE INTERVENTION, 1895). This was a diplomatic intervention by Russia, Germany, and France on 23 April 1895 over Japan's demand for China's Liaodong Peninsula. In March 1895, China signed the **Treaty of Shimonoseki**, ceding the Liaodong Peninsula to Japan. Since the peninsula was in Russia's sphere of influence, Russia expressed great concern. France had financial interests in Russia while Germany needed Russian support in demanding concessions from China. Both joined Russia to apply diplomatic pressure on Japan to return the peninsula to China in exchange for a larger indemnity. Although it finally compromised with Russia, Japan did not give up its ambition for the Liaodong Peninsula and for Manchuria as whole. The Triple Intervention inspired the Qing court to seek a secret Sino-Russian alliance to contain Japanese expansion, which became the main cause of the Russo-Japanese War in 1904–1905.

TROTSKY CLIQUE, CHINESE. In 1927, **Chiang Kai-shek** launched a coup in Shanghai to arrest and execute Communists. Some Chinese

Communist leaders, such as **Chen Duxiu** and Pen Shuzhi, ascribed the failure of the Chinese Communist movement to the arbitrary leadership of the Russian-controlled **Comintern**. The Comintern associated this group of Chinese with Leon Trotsky, labeling them the Trotsky Clique. The criticism against Chen Duxiu and the attack against the Chinese Trotsky Clique coincided with the Soviet "great purges" of all anti-Stalin Russian Bolsheviks and the Chinese students who criticized Joseph Stalin at the **Moscow Sun Yat-sen University**. The purge of the Trotsky Clique became the major tool for the Russian-trained party leader **Wang Ming** to attack those who had not supported his leadership. It was also used by **Mao Zedong** and other Chinese Communist leaders in the later power struggle.

Chen was prohibited from attending the **August Seventh Conference** in 1927 and was thrown out of the party when he criticized Soviet chauvinist policy regarding the China Eastern Railroad. Two major supporters of Chen, Peng Shuzhi and **Zheng Chaolin**, were expelled by the **Chinese Communist Party** (CCP) and began to engage in the activities of Trotsky's followers. Peng joined the Fourth Communist International, an organization supporting Trotsky's political theory. Zheng translated Trotsky's *History of the Russian Revolution* and organized the Chinese Internationalist Party of Workers. The Chinese supporters of Trotsky believed that they were upholding true Marxism and revolutionary spirit. Nonetheless, most of the CCP members who were labeled as members of the Trotsky Clique and victimized in inner-party struggles did not really know Trotsky's theory, much less have any organizational connections with Trotsky. *See also* TWENTY-EIGHT BOLSHEVIKS; WANG SHIWEI.

TWENTY-EIGHT BOLSHEVIKS. A group of early leaders of the **Chinese Communist Party** (CCP) who were trained by Moscow. They studied at **Moscow Sun Yat-sen University** from 1925 to 1930 and then returned to China. The establishment of the university resulted from **Sun Yat-sen**'s alliance with the Soviet Union. It was designed to train officials of the **Nationalist Party** (GMD) but also educated many Chinese Communists. The Twenty-eight Bolsheviks were CCP members who supported Stalin in his power struggle against Leon Trotsky and followed Moscow's instructions regarding the Chinese Revolution. This group included **Wang Ming**, the de facto highest leader of the CCP in the 1930s, **Bo Gu**, Kai Feng, **Yang**

Shangkun, Wang Jiaxiang, **Zhang Wentian**, and others. Because of the poor and impotent leadership by Bo Gu and the **Comintern** adviser, **Otto Braun**, the Communists were almost destroyed by **Chiang Kai-shek** in the fifth **Encirclement and Suppression Campaign** and forced to begin the **Long March**. During the Long March, **Mao Zedong** replaced the Twenty-eight Bolsheviks and led the **Red Army** to **Yan'an** to build a new revolutionary base in Northwest China.

Nonetheless, because of Moscow's support, the Twenty-eight Bolsheviks and their policies remained influential in the CCP until the Yan'an **Rectification Movement**, during which Wang Ming, Bo Gu, and their political and military policies were sharply criticized. Afterward, most members of the Twenty-eight Bolsheviks no longer played an important part in the Chinese Revolution. In fact, the Twenty-eight Bolsheviks as a group had disintegrated after they returned to China with a surrender to Chiang Kai-shek. Wang Ming was exiled and died in Moscow. Other members, such as Wang Jiaxiang and Zhang Wentian, changed their allegiance and helped Mao Zedong to consolidate his dominant position in the party. Yang Shankun served as the director of the CCP Central Office for many years and was elected president of the People's Republic of China after the death of Mao. Those who died in battle, including Bo Gu, who died in an airplane crash, were granted the title of martyr. However, for their anti–Mao Zedong records, the survivors of the Twenty-eight Bolsheviks were all persecuted during the Cultural Revolution in 1966–1976. *See also* COMINTERN.

TWENTY-ONE DEMANDS. A set of demands that Japan sent to **Yuan Shikai**'s government on 18 January 1915. The major points included Chinese recognition of Japan's supremacy in Shandong, Japan's special position in Manchuria and Inner Mongolia, Sino-Japanese joint operation of China's iron and steel industry, control by Japan of several of China's important domestic administrations, and nonalienation of China's coastal areas to any third country. In order to bargain with Japan, Yuan sent his minister of foreign affairs, Lu Zhengxiang, and deputy minister, Cao Ruling, to Tokyo for secret negotiations. Yuan also had the content of the negotiations leaked to Western powers in the hope of having their help to contain Japan. The United States criticized Japan's rejection of its **Open Door Policy**, and Great Britain expressed concern. No Western country, however, took any substantial action against Japan.

The Chinese press reported the Japanese demands from the Western sources, which provoked wide protests. Under pressure, Yuan did not accept the original Japanese proposal. Japan revised the terms by deleting some demands, including the appointment of Japanese advisers to the Chinese central government and the Japanese administration of the Chinese police force, and sent them back to Yuan. On 7 May 1915, Japan presented Yuan with an ultimatum, demanding he respond within two days. Worrying about a military conflict with Japan and eager to gain Japanese support for his monarchical restoration, Yuan accepted the infamous Twenty-one Demands and signed the treaty with Japan on 25 May 1915. Continuing protest against the Twenty-one Demands resulted in an upsurge of Chinese Nationalist sentiment and paved the way for the **May Fourth Movement** in 1919. *See also* NATIONAL HUMILIATION DAY.

– U –

ULANFU (ULANHU, 1906–1988). The most important non-**Han** Chinese revolutionary leader. His other name was Yun Ze. Born in the Tumet Banner of the Bayan Tala League, **Inner Mongolia**, Ulanfu received a Chinese education during his childhood. He joined the Chinese Socialist Youth League in 1923 and the **Chinese Communist Party** (CCP) in 1925. He traveled to Moscow and studied at **Moscow Sun Yat-sen University**. His classmates included **Chiang Ching-kuo**, **Deng Xiaoping**, and Wang Ruofei. He returned to China in 1929 and served as secretary of the CCP West Mongolia Work Committee. He worked under Wang Ruofei, the secretary of the CCP North China Bureau. Wang sent Ulanfu to West Mongolia to mobilize the masses and collect intelligence information on the Japanese invaders. In May 1933, Ulanfu attended the inaugural meeting of the Anti-Japanese Allied Army in Chahar, where he met with General **Feng Yuxiang** to discuss the anti-Japanese movement and establish CCP organizations in Feng's army. In the winter, he returned to Suiyuan and worked as a schoolteacher to continue secret party work.

During the **Second Sino-Japanese War**, Ulanfu staged the Bailingmiao Mutiny, reorganizing the troops of the Japanese-supported Mongolian prince and making it an anti-Japanese military force. Ulanfu came to **Yan'an** in 1940 and began to train party workers of ethnic minority backgrounds. Ulanfu was the major leader of the government and military forces in Inner Mongolia. He served as the chairman of the Inner Mongolian Autonomous Region after 1947. He was a full general of the People's Liberation Army and vice-premier of the central government. In 1983, he was elected vice president of the People's Republic of China.

UNITED FRONT, FIRST (1924–1927). The first alliance between the **Nationalist Party** (GMD) and the **Chinese Communist Party** (CCP) against **warlordism**. After the founding of the Republic of China, power fell into the hands of the **Beiyang warlords** in Beijing. **Sun Yat-sen** launched several anti-warlord campaigns, but all concluded in failure. Sun resorted to Soviet support and decided to ally with the CCP. Moscow believed that due to the lack of a large enough number of workers, China could not achieve a Communist revolution. The CCP had to ally with the Chinese bourgeoisie to make a democratic revolution against feudalism and imperialism. In January 1923, the Soviet representative Adolf Joffe came to Shanghai to meet Sun Yat-sen. The meeting led to a joint manifesto released on 26 January. Sun sent **Liao Zhongkai** to Moscow for further negotiations, dispatched **Chiang Kai-shek** to Russia to study Soviet political and military systems, and finally invited the **Comintern**'s representative **Mikhail Borodin** to advise him on reorganizing the GMD, making it a Bolshevik-style revolutionary party. In June 1923, the CCP held its Third National Congress and accepted the instructions of the Comintern, letting CCP members join the GMD as individuals. On 20–30 January 1924, Sun Yat-sen called the First GMD Congress in Guangzhou and finalized the GMD-CCP collaboration.

A dozen leading CCP members, including **Li Dazhao**, **Tan Pingshan**, **Mao Zedong**, and **Qu Qiubai**, were elected members of the GMD Central Committee. Tan Pingshan was appointed director of the GMD Organizational Department and Mao Zedong acting director of the Propaganda Department. With Soviet help, the **Whampoa Military Academy** was established. Chiang Kai-shek was appointed the commandant; the left-wing GMD leader, Liao Zhongkai, served as director of the Political Department, and the Communist leader, **Zhou Enlai**, was deputy director of the Political Department. More often than not, there were conflicts and clashes between the two parties on the campus of the military academy and in the government of the

GMD. The First United Front brought the GMD and CCP together in the **Northern Expedition** of 1926–1927, which led to military victory over the warlords and reunified China. However, the parties had competing long-term goals and profound disagreements over social policy, which undermined and ended their alliance in April 1927.

UNITED FRONT, SECOND (1937–1945). The alliance between the **Nationalist Party** (GMD) and the **Chinese Communist Party** (CCP) during the **Second Sino-Japanese War**. When the Japanese invaded Manchuria in 1931, the GMD government did not organize resistance. Instead, **Chiang Kai-shek**, who saw the CCP as a greater threat, continued his military campaign against the Communists. As the Japanese moved into North China, their menace loomed so large that Chiang's internal policies were opposed by increasing numbers of people. On 12 December 1936, GMD generals **Zhang Xueliang** and Yang Hucheng kidnapped Chiang and forced him to subordinate the CCP-GMD rivalry to national resistance. After this event, known as the **Xi'an Incident**, the CCP and GMD held six negotiations and agreed to form the Second United Front.

The Communist **Red Army** was reorganized as the **Eighth Route Army** and the **New Fourth Army**, Chiang recognized the Communist local government in **Yan'an**, the Communists gave up radical programs, and some Communist leaders joined the newly created People's Political Council. On 23 September 1937, Chiang Kai-shek formally proclaimed that the GMD and CCP had started to collaborate in the face of Japanese aggression. The GMD engaged the Japanese in major battles while the CCP proved efficient in guerrilla warfare. The Japanese defeated the GMD's leading armies and occupied vast Chinese territories, forcing the GMD government to retreat to the mountainous province of Sichuan. The Communists began to infiltrate behind the Japanese lines and build up new bases from which to promote their revolutionary programs. Within the United Front, conflicts between the CCP and the GMD occurred with increasing frequency. The biggest clash was the **New Fourth Army Incident**, in which the GMD troops ambushed and disarmed the Communist New Fourth Army in January 1941. The Communists denounced the GMD's violation of the United Front agreement and rebuilt the New Fourth Army. Although this incident did not entirely destroy the United Front, both the CCP and GMD began to exert more effort preparing for a future confrontation following the Second Sino-Japanese War.

– V –

VERSAILLES TREATY. *See* PARIS PEACE CONFERENCE.

VOITINSKY, GRIGORI NAUMOVICH (1893–1956). Comintern representative to China. After being sent to China in 1920, Voitinsky met various Chinese political activists, including anarchists, social Darwinists, trade unionists, and Socialists. He reported to the Comintern that **Chen Duxiu** and his supporters were the most promising political force in China. Voitinsky met Li Dazho in Beijing and Chen Duxiu in Shanghai, discussing with them the establishment of the **Chinese Communist Party** (CCP). With his support, Chen organized the first **Communist group** in Shanghai. The actual process of forming the CCP, as a branch of the **Comintern**, was attributed mostly to the influence of the Comintern representatives Grigori Naumovich Voitinsky and **Hendricus Maring**. Voitinsky traveled to China six times, contributing to the alliance between the CCP and the **Nationalist Party** (GMD) in the 1920s. After the split of the two parties, Voitinsky was called back to Moscow and blamed for the setback of the Chinese Revolution. He faded from politics and became a professor of economics, but he continued to watch China and publish works on the Chinese Revolution. Voitinsky fortunately survived Joseph Stalin's Great Purges and other inner-party struggles. He died in Moscow at the age of 60, being the only one of the early Comintern representatives in China who died a natural death.

– W –

WADE, THOMAS FRANCIS (1818–1895). British diplomat and sinologist. Wade arrived in China in 1842, following the British army after the **Opium War**, and lived in China for 43 years. Wade began his Chinese career as a Cantonese interpreter at the Supreme Court of Hong Kong in 1845. Seven years later, he was appointed British deputy consul in Shanghai. During the **Taiping Rebellion**, the Western powers believed that the Chinese government could not effectively administer its maritime customs, and Great Britain, the United States, and France took over the Chinese customs, in 1854. Wade became the director of the tariff division. From 1869 through 1882, he served as British plenipotentiary envoy and engaged in negotiations for British rights in Tibet and Mongolia, which resulted in the Yantai Convention (**Chefoo Convention**). Wade returned to England in 1883, and three years later he donated his 4,304 volumes of Chinese books to Cambridge University. In 1888, he became the first professor of sinology at Cambridge University. He created a spelling system of Chinese for Western readers. This was a good effort to romanize the Chinese language, but it rendered pronunciation and not the written characters. This system was later improved by another sinologist, **Herbert Allen Giles**. The **Wade-Giles system** became widely used in English-language books on China.

WADE-GILES SYSTEM. The main system of romanization of Chinese based on its pronunciation. The Wade-Giles system was widely used in the English-speaking world for most of the 20th century. The system was mostly replaced by the pinyin system in 1979, but it remains in use in Taiwan. This system was created in 1867 by **Thomas Francis Wade**, a British plenipotentiary envoy to China and the first professor of Chinese at Cambridge University. In 1892, another British diplomat and sinologist, **Herbert Allen Giles**, published his famous Chinese-English dictionary (second edition published in 1912), in which he refined Wade's work. Giles was also Wade's successor, teaching Chinese language at Cambridge. Since then, the dictionary has been cited as the locus classicus of the so-called Wade-Giles system.

WANG GUANGMEI (1921–2006). Secretary and wife of **Liu Shaoqi**. Born into a wealthy industrialist family in Tianjin, Wang graduated from **Fu Jen Catholic University** and obtained her master's degree in physics in 1945. After graduating, she became an assistant professor in the Department of Physics at Fu Jen Catholic University. The next year, she served as English interpreter for the Three-Man Group for military mediation in Beiping, which consisted of a representative from the United States, the **Chinese Communist Party** (CCP), and the **Nationalist Party** (GMD). After this mission she went to **Yan'an** and continued to work for the CCP as an English interpreter; she also took part in **land reform**. In 1948, Wang joined the CCP, married **Liu Shaoqi**, and began to work for Liu as his secretary. Wang accompanied Liu in making successful visits to Indonesia and other Asian countries in the 1960s. She was accused of being a spy of the American Central Intelligence Agency and was jailed during the Cultural Revolution. She was rehabilitated in 1979 and began to initiate "poverty reduction" programs, especially to help poor mothers. She died of heart failure at the age of 85 in Beijing.

WANG GUOWEI (1877–1927). Historian, linguist, and poet. Born in Haining, Zhejiang Province, Wang went to Shanghai to work as a proofreader for a newspaper at the age of 22 and then became a protégé of Luo Zhenyu. Sponsored by Luo, Wang traveled to Japan in 1901 to study natural sciences. He returned to China one year later and began to teach at various colleges, including **Peking University**. In the meantime he worked as editor in chief of the journal *Education World*. He published intensively on ancient Chinese history and became the authority on the study of oracle bone inscriptions (16th–11th century BC). In 1924, he was appointed professor at Tsinghua University. As a versatile scholar, he made important contributions to the studies of ancient history, epigraphy, philology, vernacular literature, and literary theory. He was one of the early scholars who introduced Western philosophy, psychology, and aesthetics to China. He believed in a traditional monarchical system and supported the abdicated emperor. In 1927, when the **National Revolutionary Army** approached Beijing, he drowned himself mysteriously in Kunming Lake at the Summer Palace.

WANG JINGWEI (1883–1944). Politician and leader of the Japanese collaborationist government during the **Second Sino-Japanese War**. Born in Sanshui, Guangdong, Wang obtained his *xiucai* degree at the age of 18. In 1903, he was awarded a government scholarship to study in Japan. He then enrolled at Tokyo University of Politics and Law, majoring in political science, and began to publish anti-**Manchu** articles. He joined the **Tongmenghui** in 1905 and served as editor in chief of its formal publication, *Minbao* (**People's Journal**). In March 1910, Wang attempted to assassinate the Manchu regent, Prince Zaifeng, but he was caught and sentenced to life imprisonment. Released after the 1911 Revolution, Wang contributed to the peace negotiations between **Sun Yat-sen** and **Yuan Shikai** and supported

Yuan as president of the Republic of China. When Sun launched the anti-Yuan campaign, Wang followed Sun to Guangzhou and served as his chief adviser. He supported an alliance with the Soviet Union and the **Chinese Communist Party** (CCP) but disagreed with the policy of allowing the CCP members to join the **Nationalist Party** (GMD). As a left-wing leader of the GMD, Wang opposed Chiang's bloody anti-Communist coup in Shanghai, but he also began to purge the CCP members shortly thereafter. In 1930, with the aid of local **warlords**, Wang attempted an abortive coup against Chiang. After its failure, he fled to **Hong Kong**.

The **Manchuria Incident** brought Chiang and Wang together again, and Wang finally gained the position of chairman of the GMD Political Committee. Wang once advocated a resistance movement against the Japanese, but he saw no prospect for victory and thus initiated his **peace movement**. In December 1938, Wang flew to Hanoi and announced that he planned to collaborate with the Japanese. In March 1940, his puppet government was established in Nanjing. He recognized the other Japanese puppet regimes in Manchuria and Mongolia and launched a pro-Japanese "citizen's education" campaign, and his troops joined the Japanese to suppress the resistance movement and slaughter Chinese people. In 1944, Wang went to Japan for medical treatment and died of pneumonia in Nagoya.

WANG MING (CHEN SHAOYU, 1904–1974). Early leader of the **Chinese Communist Party** (CCP) and head of the Russian-supported **Twenty-eight Bolsheviks**. Born in Liuhe, Anhui Province, Wang began his revolutionary career as a student leader at the Third Agricultural School of the Anhui Province, and he joined the CCP in 1924. The next year, Wang was sent to Moscow to study the Russian language and Marxist-Leninist theory at **Moscow Sun Yat-sen University**. Wang was in the good graces of Pavel Mif, who was a member of the executive committee of the **Comintern**, head of the Eastern Department, and president of the university. In January 1927, when Mif visited China as the head of the Soviet delegation, Wang served as his interpreter. For Wang's loyalty and service, Mif nominated Wang secretary of the CCP's Propaganda Department. After the July 15th Coup in Wuhan, Wang returned with Mif to Moscow Sun Yat-sen University.

Wang began to recruit orthodox Marxists among his schoolmates and founded the famous Twenty-eight Bolsheviks group. In 1929,

Wang and other members of the Twenty-eight Bolsheviks returned to China. At first, they were not assigned to important positions because of resistance from local Chinese leaders. Nonetheless, with Comintern support, Wang became a member of the politburo in 1931. Although **Xiang Zhongfa** was the party's general secretary, he was manipulated by Wang and Mif. When Xiang was arrested, Mif on behalf of the Comintern appointed Wang as acting general secretary. In June 1932, when Wang was called to Moscow as the CCP's representative to the Comintern, he appointed **Bo Gu** to succeed him. Wang Ming and Bo Gu glorified the Russian model of revolution and emphasized the need to obey the Comintern's instructions on Chinese revolution. They urged urban uprisings and repudiated **Mao Zedong**'s rural revolution and **guerrilla warfare** model. They deprived Mao of power in the **Red Army** and the party; this action led to the failure of the **Jiangxi Soviet** and great losses during the **Long March**.

At the **Zunyi Conference** in 1935, Bo Gu was dismissed from office, and some key members of the Twenty-eight Bolsheviks, including **Zhang Wentian**, Wang Jiaxiang, and **Yang Shangkun**, defected to Mao's side. In the early years of the **Second Sino-Japanese War**, Wang was the secretary of the CCP Changjiang Bureau. He advocated a policy of "making everything serve the **United Front**," which was regarded as a sort of capitulationism. Wang was called back to **Yan'an** and was criticized as a representative of dogmatism in the **Rectification Movement**. Wang made his confession and apology. Although he managed to keep his position as a member of the Central Committee, he lost influence in the party. After 1949, he was assigned to some ceremonial jobs. In 1956, Wang went to Moscow for medical treatment and stayed there until he died on 27 March 1974.

WANG SHIH-CHIEH (1891–1981). Educator and government official of the Republic of China. Born in Chongyan, Hubei Province, Wang graduated from Beiyang University in 1911, majoring in mine engineering. When the **Republic Revolution** broke out, Wang quit his advanced studies and returned to Hubei to join the local revolutionary army. In 1913, Wang traveled to Europe for further education. He obtained a BA in political economics from the University of London in 1917 and a PhD in law from the University of Paris in 1920. In Paris, Wang took part in the demonstration of Chinese laborers and students against the Chinese delegation signing the Paris Treaty, which handed over the Chinese province of Shandong to Japan. After his return to China, he taught at **Peking University** and was involved in founding the *Xiandai Pinglun* (Modern Review Weekly) with **Hu Shih**.

Wang began his political career by joining the **Nationalist Party** (GMD) in 1912. He served successively as minister of education, minister of the Propaganda Department, and secretary of the Central Planning Bureau. In 1945, he was appointed foreign minister and signed the Treaty of Sino-Soviet Friendship, recognizing the independence of Mongolia. In 1947, he was elected a member of Academia Sinica. In 1949, Wang followed the Nationalist government to Taiwan and served as secretary of the president's office in 1950. Wang died in Taipei at the age of 91. Wang was the first president of Wuhan University in mainland China, and in his last will he donated all his collections of books and artistic works to the university. To commemorate President Wang Shih-chieh, a statue was erected on the campus.

WANG SHIWEI (1906–1947). Journalist, translator, and victim of the **Rectification Movement** in **Yan'an**. Born into the family of a poor rural schoolteacher in Huangchuan, Henan Province, Wang felt social inequality from his childhood. In 1923, he joined the American Exchange Studies program in Henan Province. Two years later, he got a chance to study at **Peking University**, where he took an active part in the student movement. Due to financial problems, however, he was forced to quit school in 1927. In the early 1930s, Wang traveled to Moscow and studied at the Marx-Engels Institute. In 1937, he traveled to Yan'an and became involved in translating works of Karl Marx and Vladimir Lenin and working for the Communist newspaper *Jiefang ribao* (Liberation Daily). In 1942, during the Rectification Movement in Yan'an, Wang published his famous series of critical essays titled *Wild Lilies*, in which he criticized the Communist bureaucracy, gender discrimination, and unjustified privileges of the CCP leaders. Wang was therefore accused of three categories of crimes: "counterrevolutionary," "Trotskyite spy," and "hidden GMD spy." In 1947, when the Communists retreated from Yan'an, Wang was secretly executed.

WANG TAO (1828–1897). Reformist thinker, political columnist, and publisher. His original name was Wang Libin. Born in Puli,

Jiangsu Province, Wang received a traditional Confucian education and obtained the *xiucai* degree in 1845. At the age of 21, he began to work at the London Missionary Society Press, assisting the British missionary Walter Henry Medhurst in his translation of the New Testament into Chinese. During his 13 years of service at the press, Wang translated many English books into Chinese in collaboration with missionaries Alexander Wylie and Joseph Edkins, including *Pictorial Optics*, *An Elementary Introduction to Mechanics*, *A Concise History of Sino-British Trade*, and *A History of Astronomy of the Western Countries*. In 1862, upon being accused of having contacts with **Taiping** rebels, Wang was placed on the wanted list of the Qing government. He took refuge in the British consulate and was then exiled to Hong Kong. He lived in Hong Kong for 22 years and changed his name to Wang Tao.

In 1867, Wang made a trip to Great Britain and wrote *Jottings from Carefree Travel*, the very first travel book about Europe by a Chinese scholar. He was also invited by the chamberlain of Oxford University to deliver a speech, the first speech by a Chinese scholar in Oxford, in which he talked about the importance of cultural exchange between East and West and elaborated his belief in the Confucian concept of the great unity of the world. By the spring of 1870, he had completed the translation of various Chinese classics, including *The Book of Songs*, *I Ching*, and *The Book of Rites*. In the winter, he returned to Hong Kong, where he founded the Zhonghua General Printing House and published *Xuanhuan ribao* (Universal Circulating Herald), the first daily newspaper in Chinese history. The accomplishment won him the honor of being "Father of the Chinese Newspaper." As the chief editor of the newspaper, he called for the reform of the Chinese political system, education, and the establishment of textile, mining, railway, and machinery industries. His reformist editorial articles reached a wide audience. In 1879, at the invitation of Japanese literati, Wang Tao spent over four months in Japan and wrote a book, *Japan Travel*. In the spring of 1884, Wang and his family returned to Shanghai. He founded the Tao Garden Publishing House in the city and became the principal of a Western-style school, Gezhi College. Wang died in Shanghai at the age of 70.

WANGXIA, TREATY OF (1844). The first diplomatic agreement between China and the United States. The Treaty of Wangxia was signed on 3 July 1844 by Caleb Cushing, an American lawyer, and Qiying, the governor-general of Guangdong and Guangxi, in the village of Wangxia, northern **Macao**. The treaty granted the United States **most favored nation** treatment and **extraterritoriality**, which meant that U.S. citizens in China were exempted from local law and the United States would enjoy any privileges that China granted to a third country. Nonetheless, the treaty specified the prohibition of the opium trade, and the United States agreed to hand over any American offenders of this law to Chinese officials. The treaty granted the Americans the right to buy land in the five treaty ports and to erect churches and hospitals facilitating Christian missionary activities and social welfare services. Both sides agreed to abolish the traditional Chinese law that forbade foreigners from learning the Chinese language.

WARLORDISM. A period during the Republic of China in which China witnessed civil wars and chaos, and state power fell in hands of local military leaders/**warlords**. The rise of warlordism could be traced to the later years of the Qing dynasty, when the Qing court allowed local governments to use local resources to build their own military forces. Most of the provincial or regional troops, such as the **Hunan Army** led by **Zeng Guofan** and the **Anhui Army** led by **Li Hongzhang**, were loyal only to their local military commanders and not to the central government. These commanders became warlords who had de facto control of subnational areas. Warlordism in the early Republican years was ascribed to **Yuan Shikai**, who built up his personal army—the **Beiyang Army**—and produced many military strongmen. After Yuan's death in 1916, his subordinates divided and engaged in periodic military conflicts. In 1927, the **Northern Expedition** launched by the Nationalist Party destroyed the leading force of the **Beiyang warlords** and brought the period of warlordism to an end. *See also* ANHUI CLIQUE; FENGTIAN CLIQUE; ZHANG ZUOLIN; ZHILI CLIQUE.

WARLORDS. Military strongmen in modern China who had great authority beyond the control of central authority. The legitimacy of their power was based on their personal armies, whose soldiers and officers were bound by loyalty to the warlords. After the death of **Yuan Shikai** in 1916, national disintegration and the militarization of politics gave rise to **warlordism**, accompanied by violence, chaos, and oppression. The most powerful warlords were three cliques of the **Beiyang warlords**: the **Zhili Clique** headed by Feng Guozhang, who controlled Beijing and several provinces in northern China; the **Anhui Clique** headed by Duan Qirui, whose sphere of influence was the provinces in southeastern China; and the **Fengtian Clique** led by **Zhang Zuolin**, whose power base was Manchuria. The three cliques often engaged in war for expansion of their territories and hegemony in China. Most presidents and heads of the **Beijing government** came from these cliques. Three were from the Zhili Clique: Feng Guozhang (1917–1918), Xu Shichang (1918–1922), and **Cao Kun** (1923–1924); one from the Anhui clique: Duan Qirui (1924–1926); and one from the Fengtian Clique: Zhang Zuolin (1926–1928). In 1927, the **National Revolutionary Army** destroyed the troops of the Zhili and Anhui cliques, and a few months later the Fengtian warlord **Zhang Xueliang** retreated from Beijing and announced acceptance of the leadership of **Chiang Kai-shek**'s Nationalist government. Although the completion of the **Northern Expedition** reunified the country, warlordism remained a problem until the Communist take-over of the whole of China.

In 1922, the Gongdong warlord **Chen Jiongming** insisted on full autonomy for his province and opposed any form of central government. He revolted in Guangzhou. His rebellion was suppressed by Chiang Kai-shek's Eastern Expedition three years later. In April 1930, the warlords of the Northwest Clique, **Feng Yuexiang** and **Yan Xinshan**, cooperated with the warlord of the **Guangxi Clique**, **Li Zongren**, who had launched anti–Chiang Kai-shek campaigns. Their troops were defeated by Chiang in central China by November. Feng and Yan accepted Chiang's appointment and began to work for the Nanjing government. Li was forced to flee abroad, but Chiang soon called him back. Although almost all local warlords had joined the **Nationalist Party** and recognized the central Chinese government by the 1930s, they continued to make their regions states within the state. The major regional warlords included Yang Xishan in Shanxi; Ma Hongkui and Ma Bufan in their provinces of Gansu, Ningxia, and Qinghai; Liu Xiang and Liu Wenhui in Sichuan; Yun Long in Yunnan; **Han Fuqu** in Shandong; and **Sheng Shicai** in Xinjiang.

Warlord troops received fewer supplies from the central government, and most of them were poorly equipped. In military conflicts with the **Chinese Communist Party** (CCP), the warlords would preserve their strength and let Chiang's central army fight the **Red Army**. This strategy helped the CCP survive the **Long March** and win several battles in the civil war. Although **Mao Zedong** believed Communist power grew out of the barrel of a gun, he emphasized that the gun must be surbservient to the party. The highly centralized CCP control of military forces brought warlordism to an end.

WASHINGTON CONFERENCE (1921–1922). International conference held in Washington, D.C., from 12 November 1921 to 6 February 1922. It was also known as the Washington Naval Conference. Nine powers—Belgium, China, France, Great Britain, Italy, Japan, the Netherlands, Portugal, and the United States—attended the conference, making it the first disarmament conference in history. The Chinese delegation consisted of 130 members, with Alfred Sao-ke Sze, **Vi Kyuin Wellington Koo**, and Wang Ch'ung-hui as plenipotentiaries. Three important international treaties were concluded at the conference. One was the Four-Power Treaty of 13 December 1921, which stipulated that any dispute in the Pacific should be settled by Britain, the United States, Japan, and France through peaceful consultations. This treaty actually abrogated the Anglo-Japanese alliance. The second one was the Five-Power Naval Treaty of 5 February 1922, which fixed the naval ratio of capital ships of Britain, the United States, France, Japan, and Italy. The ratio was 5 for Britain and the United States, 3 for Japan, and 1.75 for France and Italy. It allowed Britain and the United States to possess 15 capital ships of 525,000 tons each, Japan capital ships of 315,000 tons, and France and Italy 175,000 tons each.

The Chinese delegation presented a nine-point proposal. With American support, the Chinese demands were consolidated into four general principles of the third treaty, the **Nine-Power Treaty** of 6 February 1922. The seven Western powers and Japan agreed to respect China's territorial integrity and political independence, to renounce further attempts to seek concessions or spheres of influence, to respect China's neutrality in times of war, and to honor the **Open Door Policy** in China so as to ensure equal commercial opportunities for the powers. Although the Nine-Power Treaty was a success of Chinese diplomacy, it did not invalidate the existing privileges of the foreign powers in China, and it lacked enforcement power to defend Chinese independence.

WEDEMEYER, ALBERT COADY (1897–1989). Full general of the U.S. Army and commander in chief of the American troops in the China theater during World War II. Born in Omaha, Nebraska, Wedemeyer graduated from the U.S. Military Academy at West Point in 1919. At the outbreak of World War II, Wedemeyer was a lieutenant colonel serving as a staff officer to the War Plans Division of the U.S. Department of War. In February 1942, he was promoted to colonel, and a year and half later to major general. This was in recognition of his contribution to the Victory Program and Normandy Invasion in the European front. In 1943, Wedemeyer was assigned to the South-East Asia theater to be chief of staff to the supreme allied commander of the South-East Asia Command, Lord Louis Mountbatten. In October 1944, Wedemeyer replaced General **Joseph Stilwell** as chief of staff to Generalissimo **Chiang Kai-shek** and commander of American forces in China.

Wedemeyer's service in China lasted to March 1946, and his major contribution was the training of the Chinese army and improving their equipment and logistic supply. He proposed an alliance with the **Chinese Communist Party** (CCP) during the war, but it was ignored by the State Department. After Japan's surrender, Wedemeyer led the American forces to swiftly occupy five key strategic points: Shanghai, Dagu, Canton, Qingdao, and Pusan (in Korea). More importantly, he organized the airlift of the **Nationalist Party** (GMD) troops from Sichuan to north and east China to accept the Japanese surrender. In the summer of 1947, President Harry Truman sent Wedemeyer back to China on a fact-finding mission. Wedemeyer was disappointed by the corruption and impotence of Chiang's government. He pointed out that military force could not solve China's problems and that Chiang needed to institute urgent military, economic, and political reforms. He predicted that the CCP would win the civil war and suggested sufficient and prompt American military and economic aid to Chiang under American supervision. His report, however, was not taken into serious consideration by either Chiang Kai-shek or the American government. After 1949, Wedemeyer became associated with the **China Lobby** and openly criticized those responsible for the "loss of China." In 1951, Wedemeyer retired but was promoted to four-star general in 1954. He died on 17 December 1989 at Fort Belvor, Virginia, at the age of 92.

WEI CHANGHUI (1823/1824–1856). One of the leaders of the **Taiping Rebellion**. Born into a rich farming family in the village of Jingtian, Guangxi Province, Wei joined the **God Worshipping Society** in 1848 and donated all his family holdings to facilitate the preparation of the Taiping Rebellion. Wei took part in the Jingtian uprising and was granted the title North Prince. In the power struggle between Taiping's two top leaders, **Hong Xiuquan** and **Yang Xiuqing**, he took Hong's side, leading 3,000 troops from Jiangxi Province to Nanjing to kill Yang Xiuqing and his family in 1856. As the slaughter continued and the number of victims reached more than 20,000 innocent Taiping soldiers and urban residents, indignation among the Taiping rebels grew, and Hong decided to execute Wei in Nanjing.

WEI YUAN (1794–1856). One of the leading scholars of Western studies in the Qing dynasty. Born in Shaoyan, Hunan Province, he went to Beijing to study Han **Confucianism** at the age of 21. In 1831, Wei moved with his family to Yangzhou, Jiangsu Province, where he remained for the rest of life. He obtained a *juren* degree at the age of 29 and the *jinshi* degree at the age of 52. Wei held minor positions in the government only for a short time and spent most of his life serving several prominent statesmen as their secretary or adviser. He sketched a number of proposals for reforms in maritime transportation, water conservancy, salt administration, and the currency system. Wei was mostly known for his work *Illustrated Treatise on the Maritime Kingdoms* (*Haiguo tuzhi*), published in 1844.

In the 100-volume book, he combined Western material collected by **Lin Zexu** with his own research findings to introduce the Chinese to world geography and history. Wei was impressed by Western technology but still called Westerners uncivilized barbarians. He advocated "learning superior techniques of the barbarians to control the barbarians." He emphasized that for state security in the new world, China had to develop a modern defense industry. As a vocal member of the statecraft school, he attempted to combine traditional Chinese scholarship with Western technology to solve the problems plaguing the **Manchu** government. While he firmly stood for a ban on the opium trade, Wei opposed isolationism and called for promotion of foreign trade. After the **Opium War**, he published the book *Records of Warrior Sages* (*Shèngwu ji*), in which he tried to inspire the Chinese by the military history of the early Qing rulers who led a small group of Manchu to conquer the huge territories of China. It was his belief that the warrior tradition was most needed in dealing with the foreign threat. Wei's ideas were an important influence on the leaders of the **Self-Strengthening Movement**, like **Zuo Zongtang**.

WENG TONGHE (1830–1904). Eminent official and imperial tutor in the late Qing era. Born in Changsu, Jiangsu Province, Weng obtained the *jinshi* degree and the *zhuan yuan* title (conferred on the scholar who came in first in the highest **civil service examination**) in 1856 and immediately became a member of the **Hanlin Academy**. For his excellent scholarship, he was appointed as imperial tutor of the **Tongzhi Emperor** and the **Guangxu Emperor**. In the meantime, he also held a number of prominent positions, including member of the **Grand Council**. He emphasized the basic values of **Confucianism** but also advocated Western learning. In his 20 years of teaching experience, his ideas greatly influenced the emperors. First, reform programs were initiated in the era of the Tongzhi Emperor, and then the Guangxu Emperor supported a radical **Hundred Days' Reform**. It was Weng who introduced the reformist leader, **Kang Youwei**, to the Guangxu Emperor and recommended other reformers to important government positions. After the abortive **Hundred Days' Reform**, Weng was stripped of his ranks and forced to retire. He was also a great calligrapher in the Qing dynasty.

WENG WENHAO (1889–1971). Geologist, educator, and politician. Born into the family of a wealthy merchant in Ningbo, Zhejiang, Weng obtained his *xiucai* degree in 1902 at the age of 13. He then went to Shanghai and studied at a French-speaking Catholic school. Weng traveled to Europe and obtained his PhD in geology from the Catholic University of Leuven in Flanders, Belgium, in 1912. He was one of the earliest geologists of modern China. As the founder of Chinese geology, he counted many famous geologists as his students. Under his guidance, China found the first oil field in Xinjiang, and for this reason he is referred to as the father of China's oil industry. After returning to China, Weng served as the minister of mine industry and the minister of agriculture and commerce in the **Beijing Government**. He also taught at **Peking University** and Tsinghua University. In July 1931, he was appointed acting president of Tsinghua University and served as minister of education (1932–1933). In

1934, when Weng was seriously injured in a car accident, **Chiang Kai-shek** ordered the doctors to spare no effort in saving his life.

After his recovery, Weng agreed to work for the government of the **Nationalist Party** (GMD). He successively served as general secretary of the **Executive Yuan** (1935–1937), minister of industry (1937–1938), and minister of economy (1938–1947). On 25 May 1948, Chiang appointed him president of the Executive Yuan and encouraged him to initiate monetary reform by issuing jinyuan quan to replace the **fabi**, which led to hyperinflation and financial crisis. Weng took the blame and resigned on 26 November. When **Li Zongren** became acting president of the Republic of China, Weng was made general secretary of the president's office. On the eve of the collapse of the GMD government, Weng went to Europe. In 1951, he returned from Europe to mainland China and was made a member of the **Chinese People's Political Consultative Conference**. He died in 1971 in Beijing.

WEST HILL GROUP. Right-wing faction of the **Nationalist Party** (GMD). On 23 November 1925, 14 members of the GMD Central Committee held the GMD Fourth Plenary Session of the First Central Committee at the Biyun Temple on the west hill in Beijing. The participants included some major GMD leaders, such as **Lin Sen**, Ju Zheng, Zou Lu, Xie Chi, and others. The plenary session proclaimed that the **Chinese Communist Party** (CCP) was an illegal organization and it passed several resolutions on purging the Communists and expelling the **Comintern**'s adviser, **Mikhail Borodin**. The West Hill Group changed **Sun Yat-sen**'s policy of alliance with the Soviet Union and the Communists. It established its headquarters in Shanghai and challenged the left-wing GMD leaders **Liao Zhongkai** and **Deng Yanda**. In January 1926, the Second GMD National Congress passed a resolution to expel the members of the West Hill Group from the party. Nonetheless, after **Chiang Kai-shek** began to purge Communists in Shanghai in April 1927, he cancelled this resolution and restored the membership of the West Hill Group.

WHAMPOA, TREATY OF (1844). The first treaty between China and France in modern history. Modeled after the Sino-American **Treaty of Wangxia**, the **Treaty of Whampoa** was signed on 24 October 1844 by the governor-general of Guangdong and Guangxi, Qiying, and the French envoy, Théodore de Lagrené. The treaty granted France **most favored nation** status, **extraterritoriality**, and the right to build and maintain churches and hospitals in the five trading ports. In addition, the treaty legalized a free propagation of Catholicism in China. Through this treaty, France gained all the rights and privileges that Great Britain and the United States had obtained, and made China finally lift the ban on Catholicism on 8 February 1845.

WHAMPOA MILITARY ACADEMY. The formal name was the **Chinese Nationalist Party**'s Army Officer Academy. The Whampoa Military Academy was founded in Guangzhou on 16 June 1924 by **Sun Yat-sen**, under the sponsorship of the Soviet Union. Sun was premier of the academy, and his favorite officer, **Chiang Kai-shek**, was appointed the first commandant. The motto of the academy, as Sun proclaimed at the inauguration ceremony, was Fraternity and Honesty. The academy imitated the Soviet model to establish a political department headed by a party representative. The famous leftist leader of the Nationalist Party, **Liao Zhongkai**, served as the chief party representative; **He Yingqin** was appointed the head military instructor; and the Communist **Zhou Enlai**, right-wing leader **Hu Hanmin**, and left-wing leader **Wang Jingwei** served as instructors in the Political Department. Many military instructors came from Russia, including Soviet Red Army officers and ex-officers of the Russian White Armies who switched to the Soviet side. The first two terms of graduates became the core of the First Army of the **National Revolutionary Army** (NRA), and the commandant of the academy, Chiang Kai-shek, was appointed commander in chief of the NRA and concurrently served as the commander of the First Army in the **Northern Expedition**.

The Whampoa Military Academy produced a great number of prominent generals who served in various armies during the **Second Sino-Japanese War** and the civil war between the **Chinese Communist Party** (CCP) and the Nationalist Party. The most prestigious on the Nationalist side included Hu Zhongnan and **Du Yuming**; on the Communist side were **Lin Biao** and **Xu Xiangqian**. The original Whampoa Military Academy existed from 1924 to 1926, and over six terms it supplied more than 7,000 officers to the NRA. With the advance of the Northern Expedition, the academy was relocated to Nanjing in 1928 and renamed the Central Army University; it then moved to Chengdu during the Second Sino-Japanese War and finally to Taiwan in 1950.

WHITE LOTUS REBELLION (1796–1804). Anti-**Manchu** uprising taking place in the provinces of Hubei, Sichuan, and Shaanxi. The White Lotus was a folk religion originating from the Pure Land Buddhism. The White Lotus members organized an antigovernment secret society with religious overtones. In 1796, they rose up in protest, using as a pretext that "official oppression forced people into revolt." The movement quickly spread and crushed the corrupt **Green Standard Army**. The local gentry organized militia and constructed fortresses. The Qing government transferred troops from 16 provinces and spent 200 million taels (about four years' revenue) suppressing the rebellion.

"WORSHIP THE TEMPLE BUT NOT THE GODS INSIDE." Traditional policy of the local government in Xinjiang toward the central government during the Republican era. In the 1910s and the 1920s, the central power quickly changed hands in Beijing. The first Republican governor of Xingjiang, Yang Zengxin, looked down on all the warlord governments in Beijing. He decided to recognize any new government that came to power in Beijing or Nanjing but to avoid a dependence on any of them. Following the tenet "Worship the temple but not the gods inside," Yang and his successors managed to get support from the central government in ruling the indigenous non-**Han** people and legitimizing the persecution of their rivals and political dissidents.

WU PEIFU (1874–1939). Warlord of the **Zhili Clique.** Born in Penglai, Shandong Province, into a merchant family, Wu initially obtained the *xiucai* degree but gave up further intellectual pursuits and took up a military life. Wu studied at the **Tianjin Military Academy** and **Baoding Military Academy**. He joined the **Beiyang Army** under **Yuan Shikai** and rose quickly in the ranks. After Yuan's death in 1916, the Beiyang Army split into several mutually hostile factions, or cliques. Wu engaged in several wars with other warlords and became the most powerful military leader of the Zhili Clique. In 1919, he supported the **May Fourth Movement** and suggested that the Chinese government reject the **Versailles Treaty**. He allowed the Communists to organize trade unions among railwaymen. He defeated the **Anhui Clique** in 1920, and the **Fengtian Clique** in 1922, helping the Zhili Clique control the **Beijing government**. In 1923, he changed his labor policy. Wu ruthlessly suppressed the workers' strike on the Jing–Han railways and executed labor leaders, conducting the notorious February Seventh Massacre. During the **Northern Expedition**, his troops were destroyed by the **National Revolutionary Army**, and this event ended his political career. Nonetheless, Wu shared the Nationalist sentiment with the Chinese people. During the **Second Sino-Japanese War**, he denounced **Manchukuo** and refused to cooperate with the Japanese. Wu died under suspicious circumstances in Beiping after a Japanese dentist performed an operation.

WU TINGFANG (NG CHOY, 1842–1922). Prominent diplomat and politician in the later Qing and Republican periods. Born in Singapore, Wu was taken by his father back to China at the age of three. He graduated from the Anglican St. Paul's College in Hong Kong and went to England in 1874 to study law at Lincoln's Inn. After he obtained his law degree, Wu became the first ethnically Chinese barrister and member of the Legislative Council of the colony. In 1882, **Li Hongzhang** invited him to be his assistant of foreign affairs. Wu began his diplomatic career by participating in China's treaty negotiations with France and Japan, and he then served as minister to the United States, Spain, and Peru in 1896–1902 and 1907–1909. Afterward, he resigned and returned to Shanghai.

Wu supported **Sun Yat-sen**'s revolution and served as minister of law of the provisional government of the Republic of China. In December 1912, he negotiated in the name of the provisional government with **Yuan Shikai**'s representative, **Tang Shaoyi**, which resulted in the peace settlement of the North-South conflict. In June 1916, **Li Yuanhong** succeeded Yuan Shikai and appointed Wu minister of foreign affairs. It was also on Li's recommendation that Wu served as acting prime minister the next year. However, when Li Yuanhong asked him to sign an order to dismiss the parliament, Wu refused and resigned his office. After Sun Yat-sen's call to congressmen to move to Guangzhou for a new parliament, Wu traveled southward to join them. In 1921, when Sun took the position of **extraordinary president**, Wu served concurrently as his minister of foreign affairs, minister of finance, and governor of Guangdong. He died in his second year of service. His son, Wu Zhaoshu, was also a diplomat of the Republic of China and served as ambassador to the United States.

WU YUZHANG (1878–1966). Political activist and prominent philologist, historian, and educator in modern China. Born in Rongxian, Sichuan Province, Wu traveled to Japan to study and became one of the founding members of the **Tongmenghui**. In 1911, he was sent back to Sichuan to launch an uprising that was part of the 1911 Revolution. After the revolution, he was involved in the anti–**Yuan Shikai** movement and was forced to flee to France, where he initiated a work-study program to bring Chinese students to study abroad. In 1923, Wu established the Chinese Youth Communist Party, and two years later he joined the **Chinese Communist Party** (CCP). He engaged in planning the Nanchang Mutiny and served as the general secretary of the Nanchang Revolutionary Committee. After the failure of the mutiny, Wu went to Moscow and served as the director of the Chinese division of **Moscow Sun Yat-sen University**, where he managed to conduct solid research on Chinese linguistics and history and engaged in different activities for the **Comintern**. Soon after the **Second Sino-Japanese War** broke out, Wu returned to **Yan'an** and was appointed dean of the **Lu Xun** School of Art and president of Yan'an University. In 1949, Wu became the first president of the People's University in Beijing and chairman of the All-China Language Reform Committee.

WU ZHIHUI (WU JINGHENG, 1865–1953). Politician and theorist. Born in Wujin, Jiangsu Province, Wu received a traditional Confucian education and obtained the *juren* degree. At the turn of the 20th century, Wu was exposed to Western culture and began to advocate new scholarship and ideologies, especially anarchism. He participated in **Sun Yat-sen**'s 1911 Revolution. Believing that communism was going to destroy Chinese culture and hurt China, he strongly supported the purging of Communists in 1927 and firmly attacked the **Chinese Communist Party** (CCP) and Communist ideology throughout his whole life. Wu took an active part in the **New Culture Movement**, advocating the phonetic notation of Chinese characters and promoting the unification of the Chinese spoken language. He was the first member of the Humanities Division of the Academia Sinica and a representative of the Nationalist People's Delegate Conference. **Chiang Ching-kuo** respected Wu as his teacher. Wu was a prominent calligraphist. In 1949, he followed the Nationalist government's move to Taiwan and died there in 1953. A bronze statue was erected to commemorate him at the intersection between the North Dunhua and East Nanjing streets of Taipei; however, it was removed by the Democratic Progressive Party in 1990.

WUHAN-NANJING SPLIT (1927). Split of the Nationalist leadership between the Nanjing government headed by **Chiang Kai-shek** and the Wuhan government headed by the left-wing leader of the **Nationalist Party** (GMD), **Wang Jingwei**. The first conflict was over the choice of capital of the Republic of China. In 1926, the **National Revolutionary Army** (NRA) stormed Wuhan, and most GMD leaders moved from Guangzhou and established the new government in Wuhan. In the meantime, as the commander in chief of the NRA, Chiang Kai-shek led his troops to occupy Nanchang, insisting that the capital of the republic should be located there. In May 1927, Wang called the Third Plenum of the GMD Second Central Executive Committee, which stripped Chiang of much of his authority. Responding to this, Chiang established his headquarters and new government in Nanjing in April, challenging the authority of the Wuhan regime.

Another issue causing the split was the policy of alliance with the Soviet Union and the **Chinese Communist Party** (CCP). Wang criticized the bloody massacre of the Communists in Shanghai. Nonetheless, Wang also felt threatened by the Communist-led peasant and worker movements, which had caused an economic crisis in the Wuhan-controlled area. In addition, the **Comintern** representative M. N. Roy informed Wang of the Comintern's instructions on land revolution, urban mutinies, and the development of CCP organizations within the GMD's military forces. This made Wang change his policy from a peaceful separation from the CCP to suppression of the Communists. Therefore, Wang and Chiang reconciled; the reconciliation led to the establishment of the unified National Government in Nanjing, making the confrontation between the CCP and GMD complete.

– X –

XIA YAN (1900–1995). Modern Chinese writer, playwright, and one of the founders of China's film industry. Born in Hangzhou, Zhejiang Province, into a poor family, Xia studied at Zhejiang Industrial School at the age of 15. In 1919, he was involved in the **May Fourth Movement** and founded a student magazine, *New Tide of Zhejiang*. In the next year he traveled to Japan, where he was exposed to Marxism and participated in the Japanese labor movement. Xia joined the **Nationalist Party** (GMD) in 1924 and the **Chinese Communist Party** (CCP) in 1927. He translated Maxim Gorky's novel *The Mother* from Russian to Chinese and published his influential reportage titled *Indentured Laborers*. More importantly, he wrote a number of dramas and scenarios. Xia organized the Shanghai Society of Arts and advocated development of proletarian drama. He was elected an executive member of the **League of Left-Wing Writers** in Shanghai. Beginning in 1933, he worked for the CCP secret organization in Shanghai, being in charge of film production and the party's cultural programs. He founded the most influential newspaper during the **Second Sino-Japanese War**—*Jiuwang ribao* (National Salvation Daily). Because of the Japanese attack, the newspaper had to move from Shanghai to Guangzhou and then to Guili, but he kept publishing it until it was banned by the GMD in 1941. After 1949, Xia was made deputy minister of culture of the new republic and vice-chairman of the Association of Film Producers. Xia died on 6 February 1995 in Beijing at the age of 95.

XI'AN INCIDENT (1936). Coup initiated by **Zhang Xueliang** to force **Chiang Kai-shek** to fight the Japanese on 12 December 1931. On 19 September 1931, the Japanese **Kwantung Army** blew up a small section of the **Southern Manchuria Railway** and used this as an excuse to attack the Chinese troops in Manchuria. Since he was busy with fighting the Communists, Chiang Kai-shek ordered not to resist. This move allowed the Japanese to easily occupy the whole of Manchuria. Zhang, as the commander in chief of the Northeast Army in Manchuria, had to retreat to south of the Great Wall. Believing in "domestic pacification before resistance against foreign invasion," Chiang dispatched Zhang's troops to suppress the **Red Army** in Shaanxi, where Zhang worked with Yang Hucheng, the commander in chief of the Northwest Army.

Both Zhang and Yang did not want to fight the Red Army. They began to contact the Communists and signed a secret agreement on a cease-fire in June 1936. On 4 December 1936, Chiang flew to Xi'an to push a new suppression campaign against the Communists. Zhang and Yang tried to persuade Chiang to change his policy but had no result. Then they decided to use force. At dawn on 12 December, Zhang's troops stormed Chiang's headquarters, disarmed his bodyguards, and kidnapped Chiang. On the same day, Zhang and Yang sent an open telegraph, demanding that he reorganize the Nanjing government to include all political parties and forces for the national salvation; stop all civil wars; release immediately the patriotic leaders who were arrested in Shanghai; release all political prisoners; allow a mass patriotic movement; ensure the people's political freedom, including freedom of assembly; implement the last will of **Sun Yat-sen**; and immediately call a conference for national salvation.

This incident shocked China. There were great disagreements within the **Nationalist Party** (GMD) on how to handle the crisis. **He Yingqin** and a few GMD leaders advocated solving the issue by force and ordered two armies to attack Xi'an. Madame Chiang and other leaders believed that the military action would endanger Chiang's life and asked for negotiations to rescue Chiang. On 22 December, Madame Chiang (**May-ling Soong**) and her brother **T. V. Soong** arrived in Xi'an. Zhang and Yang met them at the airport and had substantial negotiations with them. The **Chinese Communist Party** saw the incident as a good opportunity to change Chiang's policies. It accepted the **Comintern**'s suggestion for peaceful settlement and sent **Zhou Enlai** to Xi'an to join the Chiang-Zhang negotiations. On 24 December, Chiang accepted Zhang's major demands, especially promising to alter his "suppression of the Communists" policy and to ally with the Red Army in the resistance movement. On 25 December, Zhang escorted Chiang to leave Xi'an for Nanjing. Chiang saw the Xi'an Incident as the greatest humiliation in his life. As soon as Zhang arrived in Nanjing, he was sent to a special court-martial for a trial. Zhang was charged with "rebellion" and sentenced to 10 years' imprisonment. Then he was put under house arrest for almost his whole life (54 years). Zhang was not released until 1990, after Chiang and his son died. Yang was arrested and sent to a concentration camp. In 1949, when the GMD had to retreat to Taiwan, Chiang secretly ordered Yang's execution. *See also* MANCHURIA INCIDENT.

XIANFENG EMPEROR (REIGNED 1851–1861). Eighth emperor of the **Manchu** Qing dynasty, and the seventh Qing emperor to rule over China. The name Xianfeng means "universal prosperity." Born in 1831 in Beijing, he was the fourth son of the **Daoguang Emperor** and the imperial concubine Quan of the (Manchu) Niuhuru clan, who was made empress three years later. Xianfeng was enthroned in 1851, when the **Taiping Rebellion** began in southern China. The young emperor was faced with a countrywide rebellion and increasing foreign intrusion. Xianfeng was unable to deal with the overwhelming crises, leaving more decision making to his ministers and his favorite concubine, Yi. During the Second **Opium War**, when the British and French attacked Beijing, Xianfeng and his imperial entourage fled to Rehe, where he died in the next year. When he was dying, he gave his concubine Yi the title of **Empress Dowager Cixi** to assist his four-year-old son, the **Tongzhi Emperor**. Subsequently, Cixi ruled China for the next 47 years.

XIANG ARMY (*XIANGJUN*). *See* HUNAN ARMY.

XIANG JINGYU (1895–1928). Early leader of the **Chinese Communist Party** (CCP) and pioneer leader of China's women's movement. Born in Xupu, Hunan Province, into the family of a rich merchant, Xiang first studied at her brother's school and then went to Changsha and enrolled at the First Female Normal School of Hunan. After graduation, Xiang returned to her home county and founded an elementary school for local girls. In 1918, she went to Beijing, where she met Cai Heseng, who became her husband two years later. Xiang joined the Xinmin Society organized by **Mao Zedong** and thus began her political career. In July 1919, with Cai's sister, Cai Chang, Xiang initiated and organized the Association of Female Students for the Work-Study Program in France and went to Europe in December. She studied Marxism in Paris, wrote articles on women's liberation for Chinese journals, and played a leading role in student demonstrations in Paris. She was accused of "disturbing public order" by the French police and repatriated to China.

Xiang joined the CCP in 1922 and was made the first director of the CCP's Women's Department. In the same year, she drafted the Resolution on the Women's Movement for the Third National Congress of the CCP. Xiang organized China's first group of women's organizations and led a general strike of women workers of 14 silk mills in Shanghai. Nonetheless, Xiang was not satisfied with engaging in the women's movement. She saw the argument for liberation as an insult implying that women were weaker and less competent than men. Believing that women could make substantial contributions to the Communist revolution, she began to hold more important positions in the party. In 1925, Xiang was elected a member of the CCP Politburo and was sent to Moscow to study at the **Communist University of the Toilers of the East**. She returned to China in March 1927, a month before **Chiang Kai-shek** began to purge and kill the Communists. Despite all risks, Xiang insisted on staying in Wuhan, serving as editor in chief of the party's formal newspaper, *Dajiang Daily*, and leading the CCP's urban operations. On 20 March 1928, she was arrested in the French concession and executed on 1 May in Hankou, leaving a six-year-old daughter and a four-year-old son. *See also* CHINESE FEMINISM.

XIANG ZHONGFA (1879–1931). Paramount leader of the **Chinese Communist Party** (CCP) in 1928–1931. Born in Hanchuan, Hubei Province, Xiang was a worker at the Hanyang Arsenal, and he began his revolutionary career by participating in the labor movement in Wuhan. Xiang joined the CCP in 1922 and served as vice president of the General Trade Union of Hanyeping and chief commander of the worker pickets. In 1927, Xiang was elected a member of the CCP Central Committee and the Politburo. In October, he went to Moscow as the CCP's representative to the **Comintern**. In 1928, Xiang wrote two letters to Joseph Stalin criticizing **Qu Qiubai**'s leftist and **Zhang Guotao**'s **rightist opportunism**. The letters attracted the attention of the Comintern leaders. At the first session of the Sixth Conference of the CCP Central Committee in Moscow, Xiang made a speech titled "The Resolution of the Comintern on Chinese Issues," in accordance with the opinions of Stalin and Nikolai Bukharin. Because of the Comintern's emphasis on the principle of "letting workers dominate the party," Xiang's worker background made him an ideal candidate for the position of general secretary of the CCP. In 1930, Xiang supported **Li Lisan**'s plan of urban uprisings that ended in great failure.

In 1931, Xiang returned to China and still held the party's leading position, but the real power of the CCP had already fallen into the hands of **Wang Ming** and the **Twenty-eight Bolsheviks**. When he was transferred to the rural base in Jiangxi, Xiang refused to go, staying instead in the French concession in Shanghai. Xiang was betrayed by his previous subordinate, and he and his mistress were captured by the Nationalist policemen at a jewelry store on 22 June 1931. Although Xiang defected from the CCP rather quickly, **Chiang Kai-shek** saw no reason to keep this useless person alive. After a brief interrogation, Xiang was executed the next evening.

XIAO CHAOGUI (?–1852). One of the early leaders of the **Taiping Rebellion**. Born in Wuxuan, Guanxi Province, Xiao was a brother-in-law of **Hong Xiuquan**. In 1845, he joined the **God Worshipping Society**. In order to establish a reputation among the followers and hold them together, Xiao claimed that he was able to serve as a mouthpiece for Jesus Christ. It was Xiao who held the members together when other leaders of the society were arrested. In 1851, when the Taiping Kingdom was established, he was granted the title Western Prince. He pressed the siege of Changsha and was killed in battle the next year.

XIAO HONG (1911–1942). Famous woman writer of modern China. Born in Hulan, Heilongjiang Province, into a landlord family, Xiao ran away from her family to escape her parent-arranged marriage in 1930. She spent two years wandering from place to place until she met a young writer, Xiao Jun. She fell in love with Xiao Jun and began to cohabitate with him. Xiao Jun appreciated her talent and inspired her to pursue a literary career. In 1933, Xiao published her first short story, "Death of Sister Wang," which made her a rising star in the literary world. With the help of **Lu Xun**, she published her novel *The Place of Life and Death* and became a left-wing writer. Most of the time, Xiao Hong and Xiao Jun lived in poverty, but they were very happy. In 1934, when they settled down in Shanghai and their financial situation was improved, the couple began to quarrel. One year later they parted, and Xiao Hong married another writer, Duanmu Hongliang, in 1938. Revealing social injustice and criticizing traditional ignorance, Xiao attempted to use her novels to remold the "nation's soul." Although she suffered from pneumonia, Xiao continued to produce a great deal of work (millions of Chinese words). She was pregnant once but had a miscarriage. Xiao died in Hong Kong at the age of 30. She continued to be deeply loved by both Xiao Jun and Duanmu Honglian, the two men who entered her life and helped her become a prominent writer.

XIAO KE (1907–2008). Full general of the **People's Liberation Army (PLA).** Born in Jiahe, Hunan Province, Xiao joined the army at the age of 18 and was promoted to army commander at the age of 25. He joined the **Chinese Communist Party** (CCP) in 1927 and participated in the **Northern Expedition** and the **Nanchang Mutiny.** With He Long and Ren Bishi, Xiao established a revolutionary base in the Hunan-Hubei-Sichuan-Guizhou border area. At the age of 27, commanding the 6th Army Corps, he launched the Western Expedition, which paved the way for the final transfer of the **Red Army** to Northwest China. During the **Long March,** Xiao was made the deputy chief commander of the **Second Front Army.** As the **Second Sino-Japanese War** broke out, he was appointed deputy commander of the 120th Division of the **Eighth Route Army,** and during the civil war, he served as chief of staff for the Fourth Field Army. After 1949, Xiao served as director of the Military Training Department of the PLA and deputy minister of national defense. He was pushed out of important positions and persecuted in several political campaigns, but his optimism helped him survive these crises and remain in good health. Xiao died on 24 October 2008 in Beijing at the age of 101.

XIE XUEHONG (1901–1970). A leader of the **February Twenty-eighth Uprising** in Taiwan and a female Communist leader in China. Born in Zhanghua, Taiwan, into a family of poor workers, Xie became an orphan at the age of 12 and was sold as a child bride to pay the family debt and bury her mother. In 1917, Xie escaped from the family and went to southern Taiwan, where she worked in a sugar plant. Later, she met a rich landlord, Zhang Shumin, and became his concubine. In 1919, Xie traveled to Japan, where she studied Chinese and Japanese literature and was exposed to revolutionary ideas. She then went to Shanghai and studied at the Department of Sociology at **Shanghai University** in 1925. Xie also participated in the **May Thirtieth Movement** and joined the **Chinese Communist Party** (CCP). In October 1925, she was sent to study at the **Communist University of the Toilers of the East** in Moscow. Two years later, Xie returned to China and founded the Taiwan Communist Party (TCP) in Shanghai; the TCP was a Taiwan branch of the Japanese Communist Party. The program of the TCP was to throw off Japanese colonial domination and establish an independent Taiwan Republic. Xie was made a representative of the TCP to Japan. In 1931, she was arrested and put into prison by the

Japanese government for almost 10 years. She was severely tortured in jail and was not released until 1939. In 1945, after Japan's surrender, Xie tried to restore Communist activities and organized the People's Association and the Peasant Association in Taiwan. In 1947, when the February Twenty-eighth Incident occurred, she led the local revolt in Taizhong, attacking the police bureau and establishing a people's government on 2 March. She organized a small troop and served as its commander in chief. After the uprising was suppressed by the **Nationalist Party** (GMD), Xie fled to Shanghai and then went to Hong Kong. With Su Xin and other Taiwanese leaders, she founded the **Taiwan Democratic Self-Government League** (TDSL) in Hong Kong and was elected chairperson of the TDSL. She resumed her CCP membership and joined the Communist government as the representative of the TDSL. After 1949, Xie served as vice president of the China Women's Federation, a member of the Chinese Congress, a member of the Political Committee of the State Council, and a member of the **Chinese People's Political Consultative Conference**. However, she was persecuted in various Communist political campaigns, especially in the Cultural Revolution. Xie died of cancer on 5 November 1970 in a hospital corridor in Beijing. Her rehabilitation was not announced until 1986, 16 years after her death.

XINYOU COUP. Palace coup during the Qing dynasty that made the **Dowager Cixi** the real ruler of **Manchu** China for more than three decades. *Xinyou* is the Chinese name for the year 1861 in the sexagenary cycle. In that year, China was defeated by the allied Franco-British army, and the Qing court fled to Chengde, a city hundreds of miles away from the capital, Beijing. The **Xianfeng Emperor** became seriously ill and died before the negotiations between China and the European powers were concluded. His four-year-old son, known as the **Tongzhi Emperor**, came to the throne, and eight veteran ministers headed by **Sushun** were appointed as his regents. The Empress Cixi had begun to deal with state affairs on behalf of the Xianfeng Emperor when he was sick, and now she did not want to hand over the power to the regents. Tensions grew between the eight regent ministers and the Empress Dowager Cixi, who aligned herself with Dowager Ci'an, **Prince Gong**, and **Prince Chun** in the power struggle. When Xianfeng's funeral was to be planned in Beijing, Cixi managed to return to the capital before the eight regents, which allowed her to launch a coup. Consequently, the regents were arrested and charged with having carried out incompetent negotiations with the "barbarians," causing the death of the Xianfeng Emperor in Chengde. All the regents were dismissed, and three of them were executed. The two dowagers began to "listen to politics behind the curtains" (*chulian tingzheng*). Since the Dowager Ci'an was not interested in state affairs, Cixi was in charge of the court's routines, reading ministerial reports, asking questions, and making decisions. Prince Gong was appointed prince-regent as a principal "aide to the emperor."

XINZHENG REFORM (XINZHENG REVOLUTION). The political and economic reforms instituted by the Qing court in the last decade of the Qing dynasty. It developed through two stages: the Qing reform from 1901 to 1905 and the constitutional movement from 1905 to 1911. After the suppression of the **Boxer Rebellion**, the Qing court was determined to initiate reform and instituted the superintendent of political affairs to formulate the programs. The programs were to abolish old government institutions and terminate the sale of offices; to create new offices, such as new ministries of foreign affairs, mining, commerce, military training, education, and modern police; and to create military academies and train a new army. The most influential reform was on education, which included abolition of the **civil service examinations**, the opening of Western-style schools, and the sending of students abroad. The Qing court would allow intermarriage between **Manchu**s and **Han** Chinese and it prohibited opium smoking and footbinding. Other new measures included the collection of a tax on tobacco and liquor, promoting railway construction, and reducing the expenses of the royal family.

Some of the reforms were of great importance. For example, the newly built military academies produced the major military and political leaders of late Qing and early Republican China; the abolition of the civil service examinations reshaped social mobility, which led to the **Republican Revolution**. The Qing reforms by and large, however, did not make any substantial progress and failed to solve the urgent problems of the dying regime. The second stage of the Xinzheng Reform was the constitutional movement advocated by a group of intellectuals and institutionalized by the Qing court. **Liang Qichao** published *New People's Miscellany*, in which he advocated a responsible parliamentary government, legal reform to ensure judiciary independence, a balance of power between central and local governments, and China's equal status in the international community. The Chinese belief in constitutionalism was ascribed not only to the persuasive voice of Liang but also to the influence of Japan's successful Meiji reforms. In 1905, Japan defeated czarist Russia in the Russo-Japanese War, which took place in China's Manchuria. The Chinese intellectuals saw it as a victory of Japan's constitutionalism over Russia's monarchism. In 1905, a research mission of five Qing ministers was sent to Europe, the United States, and Japan. The ministers concluded that the Japanese constitutional monarchy was more suitable to China. The mission leader absorbed some ideas of Liang Qichao and proposed constitutional reform, with the tacit consent of the **Dowager Cixi**.

On 27 August 1908, the *Outline of the Constitution* was issued, declaring that the constitution would take effect in nine years. Although the outline confirmed some democratic principles, such as freedom of speech, press, assembly, property, and the citizen's right to vote, the emperor's absolute power in executive, legislative, and judicial affairs remained intact. The emperor was described as a divine ruler who would rule China in an unbroken family line. Parliament could suggest and discuss, but not decide, state affairs; any law passed by the parliament could not become effective unless approved by the emperor. In 1909, **Prince Chun** ordered the establishment of provincial assemblies and the inauguration of a National Consultative Assembly by the next year. However, when the provincial representatives petitioned for an early convocation of parliaments, they were reprimanded for interfering in state affairs. On 8 May 1911, the royal cabinet was established; in it the imperial relatives and **Manchu** and Mongolian nobles were the overwhelming majority. Chinese intellectuals, including most constitutionalists, began to shift their sympathy toward revolution. It was not until three weeks after the Wuchang Uprising in 1911 that the Qing court announced a lifting of the ban on political parties and promised to organize a new cabinet without appointing imperial relatives as government ministers. This was too late, however, to rescue the abortive **constitutional reform** of the Qing regime.

XIUCAI. The first degree in the imperial **civil service examination** system. The *xiucai* degree was obtained by exams at a county level held every year. A xiucai degree holder had certain privileges, such as access to local government, immunity from corporal punishment, and the waiving of the *kowtow* (kneeling down to pay respect) in meeting with local government officials. More often than not, xiucai played a role in local lawsuits or communication between the government and local people. *See also JINSHI; JUREN.*

XU SHICHANG (1855–1939). President of the Republic of China from 10 October 1918 to 2 June 1922. Xu was born in Jixian, Henan Province, to a family of low-ranking government officials. To form an alliance, Xu and **Yuan Shikai** became sworn brothers in 1879. Under Yuan's sponsorship, Xu went to Beijing to take the **civil service examination**. He obtained the *jinshi* degree in 1886 and was appointed to the **Hanlin Academy**. He successively served in the Qing government as viceroy of Manchuria, minister of the postal service, and a member of the **Grand Council**. In the meantime, Yuan became a powerful military commander of the **Beiyang Army**. In 1911, when Yuan was forced to retire to his home village, Xu urged the Qing court to recall Yuan to deal with the revolutionaries. In 1914, Yuan, as president of the Republic of China, appointed Xu as prime minister. Xu did not support Yuan's restoration of the monarchy and resigned the office. As a senior politician with close ties with the Beiyang Army, Xu had played the role of mediator in the conflicts between the various **warlords** and political parties. In 1918, with the support of the warlords of the **Anhui Clique**, Xu was elected president of the **Beijing government**. In 1922, as the **Zhili Clique** defeated the Anhui Clique and came to power, they claimed that Xu's presidency was illegal. Xu was thus forced to step down.

XU XIANGQIAN (1902–1990). Major military leader, one of ten marshals of the **People's Liberation Army** (PLA). Born into a landlord family in Wutai, Shanxi Province, Xu graduated from a normal school. He participated in a student protest against the Japanese **Twenty-one Demands**. To escape his father's control, he left home for Guangzhou, where he first joined the **Nationalist Party** (GMD) and enrolled in the **Whampoa Military Academy** in 1924. Xu took part in the **Northern Expedition** against the **warlords** and joined the **Chinese Communist Party** (CCP) in 1927. After the split between the GMD and the CCP, he managed to work covertly in

Zhang Fakui's army and later was dispatched to Shanghai for new assignments. In the early 1930s, Xu worked with **Zhang Guotao**, serving as the major military commander of the **Red Army** in the E-Yu-Wan base and as one of the commanders of the **Fourth Front Army** during the **Long March**. After his troops met with the **Mao Zedong**–led **First Front Army**, Mao and Zhang split on the issues of march line and destination of the Long March. Mao insisted in continuing to march northward, while Xu followed Zhang Guotao to move west into Xikang Province. The campaign led by Xu and Zhang later proved to be a disaster, and the Fourth Front Army was forced to redirect the march to catch up with Mao.

In 1936, Xu was ordered to lead 20,000 troops of the Fourth Front Army for the western expedition in order to open a corridor between the **Yan'an** and Moscow. His troops suffered a series of disastrous setbacks that left him with only 2,000 men to retreat with to Yan'an in mid-1937. When the **Second Sino-Japanese War** broke out, the Red Army was reorganized into three divisions. Xu was made deputy commander of the 129th Division. Coordinating with local guerrilla units, he established the south Hubei Military District, which proved to be of particular value as a communication route connecting several Communist bases. Xu was elected one of the 44 full members of the CCP Central Committee in 1945. During the civil war, he was one of the major commanders in northwestern China. He commanded some extraordinarily bitter battles, including the Battle of Taiyuan, in which he had to fight against both GMD troops and thousands of Japanese mercenaries. Finally, his 100,000 troops destroyed the enemy's numerically and technically superior force of 130,000 men and stormed the city on 24 April 1949. After the establishment of the People's Republic of China, Xu held several important positions, including general chief of staff of the People's Liberation Army, vice president of the CCP Military Committee, and member of the CCP Politburo. Xu died on 21 September 1990 in Beijing.

XU XILIN (1873–1907). Revolutionary leader. Born in Shaoxing, Zhejiang Province, Xu obtained the *xiucai* degree at the age of 20. He traveled to Japan in 1903 to visit the Osaka International Fair, where he made friends with Chinese revolutionaries. In 1904, he joined the **Recovery Society** in Shanghai on the recommendation of **Cai Yuan-**

pei. The next year, Xu set up the Datong Normal School in Shaoxing and developed a local network for revolutionaries. He pretended to be loyal to the Qing government and was appointed dean of the Anhui Police Academy in Anqing. In 1907, Xu and his cousin, **Qiu Jin**, worked out a plan to assassinate the governor of Anhui at the inauguration ceremony of the police academy, after which he and Qiu Jin would launch uprisings simultaneously in Anhui and Zhejiang. The plan leaked, however, and he had to take action early. Xu led a group of students of the Anhui Police Academy to attack the local arsenal. The battle raged for four hours before his army surrendered. Xu was captured and executed at dawn the next day.

XU ZHIMO (1897–1931). Romantic poet and pioneer of modern Chinese literature. Born in Xiashi, Zhejiang Province, Xu first studied law at **Peking University** and then traveled to the United States to study political science. He graduated from Columbia University with an MA in political science in 1920. Afterward, he went to England and changed his major again and studied economics at Cambridge University. There, Xu found that his true love was English and French romantic poetry, and he turned to a literary career. He began to translate European romantic literature into Chinese and to write his own poetry. In 1922, Xu went back to China and became a leader of the modern poetry movement. He wrote in vernacular Chinese, promoting a new form of modern Chinese poetry. He taught at several universities and edited *Xinyue* (Crescent Moon), a literary monthly featuring liberal ideas and Western literature. In 1923, he organized the **Crescent Moon Society** (*xingyue she*), one of the most influential literary associations. Working with the society members, Xu tried to break the shackles of the traditional poetic mode: he emphasized free expression and formal beauty, making a great contribution to modern Chinese poetry. Like his poetry, his personal life was full of his pursuit of love, freedom, and beauty. He married twice, but neither marriage was a happy one. He died in a plane crash on the way from Shanghai to Beijing, in order to attend a lecture by **Lin Huiyin**, a woman whom he deeply loved.

XUANTONG EMPEROR. Aisin-Gioro Puyi. The last emperor of the Qing dynasty. Born in 1906, the Xuantong Emperor reigned between 1908 and 1912. *See* PUYI.

XUE FUCHENG (1838–1894). Diplomat and reformer during the late Qing dynasty. Born in Wuxi, Jiangsu Province, Xue was not successful in the **civil service examinations**. However, his petition on reform impressed **Zeng Guofan**, who offered him a job as personal assistant. He drafted many memorials on foreign affairs for Zeng and followed Zeng's **Hunan Army** to engage in the suppression of the **Nian Rebellion** in the 1860s. During the **Sino-French War** of 1884, Xue successfully pushed the French naval forces back at the port of Ningbo, Zhejiang Province, showing his capacity for dealing with foreigners in negotiations. In 1890, he was appointed minister to Great Britain, France, Italy, and Belgium. In his four and a half years of service abroad, Xue examined European development and concluded that the key to the West's prosperity was railway transportation. He argued that modern industry would solve China's problem of overpopulation. His reformist ideas were similar to those of **Wang Tao**. Xue published numerous books and articles, the most famous work being *Chushi riji* (*Journal of a Diplomatic Mission*).

– Y –

YAKUB BEG (MUHAMMAD YAQUB BEG, 1820–1877). Born in the town of Tashkent, Uzbekistan, Yakub Beg was the commander in chief of the army of Kokand. Taking advantage of the Muslim uprising in northwestern China, Yakub Beg made himself the ruler of Kashgaria with its capital in Kashgar, and occupied part of Xinjiang by 1870. He signed treaties with the Russians and British to offer them trade privileges in exchange for diplomatic recognition. The Qing court gave **Zuo Zongtang**, the governor-general of Shaanxi and Gansu, the special assignment of suppressing the Muslim rebels. After he pacified the two provinces, Zuo poised to strike into Xinjiang. Yakub Beg was soundly defeated and died in exile. Yakub Beg's son tried to lead the remnants to continue the resistance, but his troops were quickly destroyed. Thus, the Qing government reestablished its authority in Xinjiang.

YALTA CONFERENCE (1945). Important international conference before the end of World War II, also known as the Crimea Conference. The Yalta Conference was held from 4 February 1945 to 11

February 1945 and was attended by U.S. president Franklin D. Roosevelt, British prime minister Winston Churchill, and Soviet premier Joseph Stalin. The participants passed a resolution regarding the unconditional surrender of Nazi Germany and the postwar arrangements for Germany. They also came to an agreement on the issues of Poland, the Far East, and the United Nations. The Soviet Union promised to enter the fight against Japan within 90 days after the defeat of Germany. In exchange, the Soviet Union would gain the southern part of Sakhalin and the Kuril Islands after the war was over. At the conference, Stalin also asked for the comanagement of the **Chinese Eastern Railway**; internationalization of the Chinese trading port, Dalian; and occupation of the Chinese-owned Port Arthur to make it a Russian naval base. The Yalta Conference met all the Russian demands. It decided to establish the UN Security Council with the United States, the Soviet Union, Great Britain, France, and China as the five permanent members, and each would have veto power.

YAN FU (1853–1921). An influential scholar and translator during the late Qing dynasty, Yan is most famous for his introduction of Charles Darwin's ideas of "natural selection" and "survival of the fittest." Born in Minxian, Fujian Province, he graduated from the Fujian Arsenal Academy in 1871. Yan did a five-year internship on Chinese warships and then went to England for advanced studies. From 1877 to 1879, he studied at the British Royal Naval Academy and became a close friend of the Chinese ambassador to England, **Guo Songtao**. Upon his return to China, Yan was unable to pass the **civil service examination** to get a position in the government. Instead, he taught at the Fujian Arsenal Academy and the Beiyang Naval Officers' School. Yan translated Thomas Huxley's *Evolution and Ethics*, Adam Smith's *Wealth of Nations*, John Stuart Mill's *On Liberty*, and Herbert Spencer's *Study of Sociology*. He exposed the Chinese people to the idea of survival of the fittest, arguing that the evolutionary theory could "explain the origin of human relations and of civilization." He made **social Darwinism** appealing to Chinese intellectuals, who began to ponder problems of race and racial strength, and of progress and the stagnation of Chinese civilization. Yan established three standards for translation, "faithfulness, understandability, and elegance," which were regarded as the pinnacle that all translators dreamed to reach.

After the **First Sino-Japanese War**, Yan published numerous articles, advocating radical reform and the buildup of a strong national defense. In 1896, he created China's first Russian-language school. He became the first president of the National **Peking University** in 1912. His ideal political system was a constitutional monarchy. After the **Republican Revolution**, Yan supported **Yuan Shikai**'s attempt to restore the monarchy. After Yuan's death, Yan was put on the wanted list of China's parliament and had to flee to the **foreign concession** in Tianjin. He returned to his hometown, Fuzhou, and died shortly thereafter.

YAN HUIQING (1877–1950). Politician and diplomat of modern China. Born in Shanghai, Yan graduated from the Shanghai Foreign Language School in 1895 and the University of Virginia in 1900. He taught English at **Saint John's University** in Shanghai, worked at the **Commercial Press** (*Shangwu yinshuguan*), and edited the *English-Chinese Dictionary*. In 1906, Yan passed a special exam offered by the Qing government to the Chinese returned students and obtained the *jinshi* degree. Two years later, Yan was dispatched to the United States as a consul. During his stay there, he audited courses on diplomatic theories and international law at George Washington University. After the 1911 Revolution, he served the Republic of China as deputy minister of foreign affairs, and was envoy to Germany, Sweden, and Denmark, successively. After 1920, he began to work in the **Beijing government**, serving five times as prime minister and once as acting president. In 1926, he was forced to resign his office by the Fengtian **warlord Zhang Zuolin**, and he fled to the **foreign concession** in Tianjin.

After the **Manchuria Incident** in 1931, Yan was recalled by the Nationalist government in Nanjing and appointed as the first Chinese representative to the League of Nations, where he made a motion demanding the league punish Japan. He also engaged in secret diplomacy with the Soviet Union. In 1933, Yan was appointed China's first ambassador to the Soviet Union. Yan visited the United States many times and met with President Franklin D. Roosevelt to seek American support for the Chinese anti-Japanese war. During the civil war between the **Nationalist Party** (GMD) and the **Chinese Communist Party** (CCP), Yan joined the delegation of the Nanjing Nationalist government, going to Xibeipo and Beijing for peace negotiations with the CCP. After the failure of the negotiations, he stayed with the Communists in Beijing. When the People's Republic of China was founded, he was given a few honorary positions, including vice-chairman of the Political and Military Committee of East China. His English autobiography, *East-West Kaleidoscope,* was translated into Chinese and published in mainland China in 2005, 55 years after his death.

YAN XISHAN (YEN HSI-SHAN, 1883–1960). Warlord and politician of the Republic of China. Yan was born in Wutai, Shanxi Province, into the family of a gentry merchant who went bankrupt when Yan was 17 years old. His father sent him to Taiyuan to avoid creditors, and there Yan was admitted into the Shanxi Military Academy. In 1904, he traveled to Japan for formal military training on a government scholarship at the Imperial Japanese Army Academy. In Japan, Yan joined the **Tongmenghui,** but he did not attend many of its activities. In 1909, he graduated from the Imperial Japanese Army Academy and returned to China. Yan took a special imperial exam offered by the Qing court for the returned students and obtained the *juren* degree. In 1911, Yan participated in the anti-**Manchu** uprising in the city of Taiyuan and was elected governor of Shanxi. Yan joined the **Beiyang Army,** affiliating with the **Anhui Clique,** but he remained neutral in the wars between the warlords and took advantage of the political chaos to develop his own troops. Yan's home province of Shanxi built up a major arsenal and manufactured field artillery, which helped Yan expand his military forces. In 1926, Yan pledged his loyalty to **Chiang Kai-shek,** but in 1929 he joined **Feng Yuxiang** and **Wang Jingwei** to fight against Chiang. Yan was defeated and fled to the Japanese-controlled city of Dalian.

After the **Manchuria Incident** in 1931, Chiang and Feng were reconciled, and Yan managed to return to Shanxi as the highest officer of the province. During the **Second Sino-Japanese War,** Yan collaborated with the Communists and staged several important battles to check the Japanese coming from North China. After the provincial capital Taiyuan was lost, Yan relocated his headquarters to the remote corner of the province in order to continue the resistance. Yan was referred to as the "model governor" who utilized Confucian teachings to control the people and published a number of books and pamphlets to promote his social reforms. In fact, he was a military dictator, ruling the province by cruel laws and military police. Yan organized all male adults between ages 18 and 48 into groups, forcing one-third of them to serve in his army. As soon as the Japanese surrendered, he opened fire on the Communists in an attempt to rid Shanxi of Communist influence. But in less than a month, he lost 13 divisions of his best troops. In the latter days of the civil war, Yan shipped much of the provincial treasury to Shanghai, preparing for the retreat. On 29 March 1949, he escaped from Taiyuan before the city was stormed by **Xu Xiangqian**'s troops. In June, he was appointed president of the **Executive Yuan** and minister of defense of the Republic of China in Guangzhou. In December, Yan fled to Taiwan, where he died at the age of 77.

YAN'AN (YEN-AN). A small township located in Shaanxi Province, northwest China. Yan'an was the endpoint of the **Long March** and the center of the Chinese Communist revolution from 1935 to 1948, where the Communists rebuilt their military forces and carried out moderate social reform programs. Yan'an symbolizes an idealistic society, the so-called **Yan'an Way**, a magnet for many youthful supporters from other parts of China. It was in Yan'an that **Mao Zedong** initiated the **Rectification Movement**, which established the authority of his sinicized Marxism. During World War II, some Western journalists, including **Edgar Snow** and **Anna Louise Strong**, visited Yan'an and met with and interviewed Mao Zedong and other important leaders. The United States Army Observation Group, known as the **Dixie Mission**, visited Yan'an, thus establishing official ties with the Communists. The Americans had a presence in Yan'an from 1944 to 1947. During the civil war, Yan'an was once again occupied by the Nationalist army after the Communist headquarters were moved out.

YAN'AN FORUM ON LITERATURE AND ART. A conference of Chinese writers and artists held in May 1942 at the headquarters of the Communist movement, **Yan'an**. **Mao Zedong** presided over the meeting. During the **Second Sino-Japanese War**, a great number of writers, artists, actors, and actresses left the Japanese-occupied or Nationalist-controlled cities for Yan'an. This conference was to educate these intellectuals in Mao's theory on revolutionary culture and to reorient the cultural movement in the rural bases and China at large. Mao's theory on revolutionary culture argued that literature and the arts should serve Communist politics and serve the workers, peasants, and revolutionary soldiers. It required that creative writers and actors go to the broad masses of people, experience their lives, understand their feelings, and write on them and for them. It also emphasized the necessity for the intellectuals to remold themselves before doing revolutionary artistic work. After 1949, this theory became the cultural orthodoxy of the People's Republic of China.

YAN'AN WAY. The Yan'an Way refers to a series of highly innovative, heroic, and protodemocratic programs launched by the **Chinese Communist Party** (CCP) in its rural bases around **Yan'an** during the **Second Sino-Japanese War**. These programs included the Reduction of Rent and Interest Rates, the **three-thirds system**, Production Campaign, and **Rectification Movement**. According to Mark Selden, a scholar on East Asia, the Yan'an Way was the key to the CCP's success in the 1940s. The Yan'an Way thesis has been challenged by the argument that it is unrepresentative of the Communist movement as a whole and by incontrovertible evidence of the powerful elitist, authoritarian, and repressive strains within Chinese communism.

YANG SHANGKUN (1907–1998). A leader of the **Chinese Communist Party** (CCP) and president of the People's Republic of China (1988–1993). Born in Tongnan, Sichuan Province, Yang graduated from the Chengdu Normal School and, influenced by his elder brother, joined the Communist Youth League in 1925 and the CCP in 1926. Yang traveled to Moscow and studied at **Moscow Sun Yat-sen University**, where he followed **Wang Ming** and joined the radical Marxist group the **Twenty-eight Bolsheviks**. In 1931, Yang returned to China and first worked at the All-China Federation of Workers and then in Jiangsu Province. In 1933, he went to the **Jiangxi Soviet**, serving as deputy director of the Political Department of the CCP Central Committee. Jiang participated in the **Long March** as the political commissar of the Third Army Corps. He attended the **Zunyi Conference** in January 1935 and supported **Mao Zedong** as the new leader of the **Red Army** and CCP. During the **Second Sino-Japanese War**, Yang was deputy secretary and then secretary of the CCP North China Bureau, leading the **guerrilla war** and the party's secret activities in the Japanese-occupied areas.

After 1941, he served as director of the CCP Central Office until 1966, when he was purged on the eve of the Cultural Revolution. In 1978, Yang was rehabilitated and appointed party secretary of Guangdong Province. He was elected president of the PRC in 1988. On 14 September 1998, Yang died in Beijing at the age of 92. His brother, Yang Baibing, was a full general of the People's Liberation Army and member of the CCP Politburo.

YANG XIUQING (1821–1856). A major leader of the **Taiping Rebellion**. Born in Guiping, Guangxi Province, Yang was an orphan brought up by his uncle. Yang worked as a firewood burner and salesman before he joined the Taiping Rebellion. In 1848, he followed the founder of the **God Worshipping Society**, **Feng Yunshan**, and converted to Christianity. When Feng was arrested, Yang claimed that he had experienced visions of God and was authorized to deliver messages from God. This statement was confirmed by **Hong Xiuquan** so that Yang was recognized as the most powerful leader next to Hong. In 1851, when Hong Xiuquan took the title of Heavenly King for himself, Yang was granted the title Eastern Prince, serving as commander in chief of the army and then prime minister of the government.

Yang was the real commander in the battle of Nanjing and became de facto leader of the kingdom after the city was captured. Once Hong Xiuquan lost interest in state affairs, Yang took over routine administration and his power expanded. The tension grew between Yang and Hong. Yang made all decisions that the Heavenly King could only approve. This made Yang believe he could easily replace Hong. In order to depose the Heavenly King, Yang sent Hong's trusted commander, Northern Prince **Wei Changhui**, away from Nanjing. Having recognized the danger, Hong secretly called Wei Changhui and his troops back. On 2 September 1856, Wei broke into the residence of Yang Xiuqing and massacred Yang with his family and thousands of his adherents.

YE JIANYING (1897–1986). One of the ten marshals of the **People's Liberation Army** and a leader of the People's Republic of China. Born into a wealthy **Hakka** merchant family in Meixian, Guangdong Province, Ye graduated from the Yunnan Military Academy in 1919. He joined the Guangdong Army in support of **Sun Yat-sen**. When the **Whampoa Military Academy** was established, **Liao Zongkai** invited him to work there as deputy director of the training department. Ye joined the **Chinese Communist Party** (CCP) and participated in the failed **Nanchang Mutiny** in 1927. In December he helped to organize the **Canton Commune**, which also ended in disaster. Ye was forced to flee to Hong Kong, but he was not blamed for these failures and was subsequently sent to Moscow to study at the **Communist University of the Toilers of the East.**

In 1932, Ye returned to the **Jiangxi Soviet** and served as both a member of the executive committee of the Soviet central government and chief of staff of the Fifth Front Army. After meeting with **Zhang Guotao's Fourth Front Army** during the **Long March**, the two front armies established a unified headquarters, and Ye was made chief of staff. When Zhang and **Mao Zedong** disagreed on the destination and route of the Long March, Ye stood with Mao. He informed Mao of Zhang's conspiracy to divide the **Red Army** and endanger Mao, thus helping the **First Front Army** get rid of Zhang's control and successfully arrive in Shanbei. During the **Second Sino-Japanese War**, Ye was appointed chief of staff of the **Eighth Route Army** and elected a member of the CCP Central Committee in 1945. Before the outbreak of the civil war, Ye joined the CCP delegation headed by **Zhou Enlai** to negotiate with the **Nationalist Party** (GMD), and served as a member of the U.S.-GMD-CCP mediation group to supervise the cease-fire. Ye was the first CCP mayor of Beijing in 1948 after it was taken over by the People's Liberation Army. After 1949, Ye was subsequently made mayor of Guangzhou, commander of the Guangdong military district, and vice-chairman of the CCP Central Military Committee. Ye was also elected to the CCP Politburo. In 1978, he became president of the Chinese Congress.

YE TING (1896–1940). Prominent military leader of both the Nationalist and Communist troops. Born in Huiyang, Guangdong Province, Ye graduated from the **Baoding Military Academy** in 1918. He joined the **Nationalist Party** (GMD) in 1919 and served as the commander of **Sun Yat-sen**'s guard battalion. Ye first won recognition among the soldiers at the Battle of Huangpijing, when he defeated an enemy four times larger than his own troops. When the Guangdong **warlord**, **Chen Jiongming**, attacked Sun's residence in 1921, Ye escorted Madame Sun (**Song Qingling**) out of Guangzhou. Three years later, Ye traveled to Moscow to study at the **Communist University**

of the Toilers of the East and Military Academy of the Red Army. There, he joined the **Chinese Communist Party** (CCP).

Ye's position as a talented commander was well established during the **Northern Expedition**, in which he led an independent regiment to break the warlords' defense line and storm the city of Wuchang. After the battle, he was promoted to deputy army commander of the 11th Army. On 1 August 1927, along with **Zhou Enlai**, He Long, and **Zhu De**, Ye led the **Nanchang Mutiny**, and with **Zhang Tailei**, Yun Daiying, and Ye Jianying, he organized the **Canton Commune** in December. Made a scapegoat for the two military failures by **Wang Ming** and **Li Lisan**, Ye decided to withdraw from the CCP and go into exile in Europe. When the **Second Sino-Japanese War** broke out, Ye returned to China and was appointed army commander of the Communist **New Fourth Army**. Nonetheless, the CCP appointed Xiang Ying the political commissar to control these troops. In 1938–1939, Ye smashed all Japanese attempts to encircle and eliminate the New Fourth Army and built several bases along the Jin–Pu Railway. During the **New Fourth Army Incident** in 1941, Ye attempted to negotiate a peaceful resolution, but he was detained by GMD forces. **Chiang Kai-shek** labeled the New Fourth Army traitors and jailed Ye Ting for five years. After he was released, Ye rejoined the CCP and participated in the CCP-GMD peace negotiations. On 8 April 1946, Ye flew from **Chongqing** to **Yan'an** but was killed with his family and several other Communist leaders in an airplane crash.

YEN, Y. C. JAMES (YAN YANGCHU, 1893–1990). Prominent educator and promoter of the rural reconstruction program. Born in Baozhong, Sichuan Province, Yen first received a traditional Confucian education from his father, a Confucian tutor and medical practitioner, and then began studying at a missionary school at the age of 13. In 1913, he enrolled at St. Paul College in Hong Kong and then studied at Yale University, where he took courses including those offered by William Howard Taft and Woodrow Wilson. After graduating from Yale, Yen went to France and served as a labor volunteer during World War I, helping the illiterate Chinese laborers write letters to their families. Yen was impressed by the experiences of the Chinese laborers and began to think about education for laborers. He created the first labor newspaper, *Chinese Labor Weekly*. A couple of months later, he received a letter of appreciation from a

Chinese worker who donated all his wartime savings of 365 francs to support the newspaper. Yen was deeply moved and said that the triple-C (Confucius, Christ, and coolies) greatly influenced his ideals and life. In 1920, Yen obtained his master's degree at Princeton and returned to China.

Yen worked for the Young Men's Christian Association (YMCA) in Shanghai and edited some teaching materials for mass education. He traveled throughout the country to promote the mass education program and was elected general secretary of the China Society for Mass Education. He was first devoted to literacy education in cities and then turned his sights to the countryside. In the early 1930s, the Nationalist government recognized Yen's accomplishment and decided to spread his movement to the other parts of China. This plan, however, was interrupted by the **Second Sino-Japanese War**. At the end of the war, Yen tried to persuade **Chiang Kai-shek** to invest in rural education, but his proposal was not accepted. Nonetheless, he successfully got the American president Harry Truman and the U.S. Congress to pass the James Yen Clause, stipulating that no less than 5 percent and no more than 10 percent of the American aid to China should be spent reconstructing Chinese villages. The **Chinese Communist Party** (CCP) was not supportive of Yen's mass education and rural reconstruction programs. Yen went to Taiwan in 1949 and soon left for the United States, where he was involved in mass education programs in South America, Africa, and Southeast Asia. Yen died in the United States, but part of his ashes were brought back to China and buried in his home country, according to his last will.

YENCHING UNIVERSITY. A notable university in Peking. It was established in 1919 in the royal gardens of the Qing court by integrating three old Christian colleges. **John Leighton Stuart** served as the first university president. Stuart engaged in fund-raising worldwide and obtained generous support from Charles Martin Hall and Alcoa Aluminum to fund the university's early development. In 1921, the American architect Henry K. Murphy designed the Chinese palace-style buildings with all modern heating, bathing, and toilet facilities for the university. When Murphy's project was completed in 1926, Yenching became the largest and most beautiful modern campus in China. That year, Yenching University consisted of law, medical, and divinity schools as well as schools of arts and sciences. In 1928, the

Harvard-Yenching Institute was jointly founded by the two universities to promote education in the humanities and social sciences in East Asia and Southeast Asia. Yenching invited prominent scholars to join the staff; they trained a new generation of talented student-scholars, including Lei Jiequn, Bing Xi, **Fei Xiaotong**, and Hu Renzhi. During the **Second Sino-Japanese War**, Yenching University was moved to southwest China. After 1949, a major part of Yenching was merged into **Peking University**, while its science faculty was transferred to Tsinghua University. Peking University is located on the Yenching campus.

YI MIN ZHI YI **(USE THE PEOPLE TO CONTROL THE BARBARIANS).** The strategy of the Qing court to resist foreign intrusion during and after the reign of the **Daoguang Emperor**. Although the Qing government signed numerous treaties with the Western powers, it did not want to comply with them, though it dared not fight the foreigners. In 1842, after the **Treaty of Nanjing** was signed, the city of Guangzhou was opened to the British, but the local Chinese residents spontaneously took actions to check foreign entry. The Qing court believed that this would be a good way to make the international treaty a mere scrap of paper. The government encouraged the people to follow the Guangzhou example to deny the treaty rights of the foreigners. It was the government's belief that, on one hand, the foreigners would be deprived of these rights of residence, mining, and missionary work, while on the other, the government would not be responsible for the violation of the treaties. The idea of *yi min zhi yi* was to instigate the xenophobic sentiment of the Chinese people and incite mass violence. It was also used by the **Dowager Cixi** during the **Boxer Rebellion**, which caused and sharpened the conflict between Chinese people and foreigners and eventually brought about more failures and humiliation on the Chinese state. *See also YI YI ZHI YI* (USE BARBARIANS TO CONTROL THE BARBARIANS).

YI YI ZHI YI **(USE BARBARIANS TO CONTROL THE BARBARIANS).** This was a traditional Chinese tactic in dealing with the nomadic tribes in the Chinese northern border areas. The phrase refers to the use of conflicts among these tribes to divide and control them in order to ensure China's security along its frontiers. During the 19th century, although China continued to call foreigners barbarians, the Qing court was terrified of Western military power and hoped to use one Western country to check or balance another. The typical example was China's efforts for a secret Sino-Russian alliance to contain the Japanese expansion in Manchuria. In the 19th century, *yi yi zhi yi* was reiterated by **Wei Yuan**, who emphasized the advantage of modern Western science and technology, which offered China accessible models to learn and emulate in order to deal with the increasing challenge from the Western powers. Yi yi zhi yi treated foreign countries as barbarian enemies. Many Qing government officials, such as **Li Hongzhang**, believed that China could not change its disadvantaged position in international politics but had to depend on the support of a friendly foreign power in dealing with its external crises. They held up yi yi zhi yi as the guiding line in foreign-policy-making and diplomatic activities.

YI ZONG (1831–1889). Dun Prince (of blood). The fifth birth son of the **Daoguang Emperor** and adopted by Prince Mian Kai, the fifth son of the **Jiajing Emperor**. Yi Zong was president of the Ministry for Imperial Affairs.

YU DAFU (1896–1945). Popular short-story writer and poet. Born in Fuyang, Zhejiang Province, Yu began his literary career by writing poetry in classical Chinese but soon became a vernacular novelist. He was first enrolled at Zhejiang University in 1912 but was expelled because of his participation in the student movements. In 1914, he traveled to Japan to study economics at Japanese Imperial University. In 1921, he and **Guo Moruo**, Cheng Fangwu, and other Chinese students in Japan founded the *chuangzao she* (**Creation Society**), an organization of young writers devoted to vernacular and modern literature. In the same year, Yu published *Ch'en-lun* (Degradation), which shocked the Chinese literary world with its frank descriptions of sex and psychic suffering.

After returning to China, Yu published many short stories, travel writings, and poems. His sensational narrative of physical and spiritual experiences of the human being eventually appealed to young readers. He edited a literature quarterly for the Creation Society and also taught Chinese literature at **Peking University**, Wuchang Normal University, and Guangdong University. Yu was one of the initiators of the **League of Left-Wing Writers** in Shanghai. He took an active part in the Chinese resistance movement and was hunted by the Japanese. In 1938, for family reasons, he moved to Singapore, where he worked as a literary editor for the newspaper *Sin chew jit poh*. After the Japanese invaded Singapore, he quit writing and changed his identity. The Japanese military police, however, finally discovered and murdered him at the end of the war.

YU QIAQING (1867–1945). Industrialist and social activist. Born into a very poor family in Zhenhai, Zhejiang, Yu began his career in 1893 as a comprador for a German company in Shanghai. He also worked for Russian and Dutch banks. In 1905, Yu's voluntary defense of a Chinese woman in the International Settlement made him a household name in Shanghai. In 1906, Yu opened his own business by building the Siming Bank and forming the Ning-Shao Steamship Company. He supported the 1911 Revolution and served as general director of civil affairs in Zhabei District. Yu expanded his business by buying a British navigation company in 1918 and building a shipyard in 1922. Two years later, he was elected president of the Shanghai Chamber of Commerce, which supported the Chinese workers' general strikes and demonstration against the Japanese in the **May Thirtieth Movement**. Yu did fund-raising for **Chiang Kai-shek** during the **Northern Expedition** and firmly supported Chiang's bloody purge of the Communists. Yu lost some ships in the early years of the **Second Sino-Japanese War**, but he managed to register his fleet with foreign countries and continue his business. When Shanghai suffered from food shortages, he organized rice shipments from Southeast Asia to the **foreign concessions** in Shanghai and thus earned a great profit. He was criticized by the mass media for taking advantage of the war to make money. Disappointed with public opinion, Ye left Shanghai for **Chongqing** in 1941 and died there on 24 April 1945.

YUAN MING YUAN (OLD SUMMER PALACE). The imperial garden of the Qing dynasty destroyed by the Anglo-French troops in 1860. Located five miles northwest of the city walls of Beijing, Yuan Ming Yuan was initially constructed in 1709 by the Kangxi Emperor and expanded by two successive emperors. It was a place where the Qing emperors resided, received foreign diplomats, and discussed government affairs. Due to its extensive collection of art, hundreds of halls, pavilions, temples, galleries, gardens, lakes, towers in Tibetan and Mongol styles, and a group of Western-style palaces, Yuan Ming Yuan was referred to as the "garden of gardens." During the Second **Opium War**, when the Anglo-French allied troops stormed Beijing in August 1860, the **Xianfeng Emperor** fled to Rehe. On 6 October, the Anglo-French allied troops occupied the Yuan Ming Yuan. The next day, the British general, Lord Elgin, ordered his soldiers to loot and burn the palace. This action was partly in retaliation for the Qing officials' violation of international law by kidnapping, imprisoning, and executing some British diplomats and journalists. The treasure was gone rather quickly, but it took three more days for the palace to burn. In 1862–1874, the **Dowager Cixi** tried to reconstruct the palace, but the project was not completed due to financial difficulties. In 1900, the Yuan Ming Yuan was looted again by Chinese mobs and the **Eight-Nation Alliance** troops during the **Boxer Rebellion**. Yuan Ming Yuan remains in ruins today to remind the Chinese of this humiliation.

YUAN SHIKAI (1859–1916). Military official of the Qing dynasty and first president of the Republic of China. Born to a locally prominent family in Xiangcheng, Henan Province, Yuan grew up in Beijing under the supervision of his uncles until 1878. After failing the **civil service examinations** twice, Yuan began to work for Wu Changqing, a friend of Yuan's uncle's. Wu took Yuan to Korea as his assistant and promoted Yuan to be the imperial resident-general of Seoul. In 1884, Yuan was placed in command of three Chinese divisions in Korea. At the request of the Korean king, Yuan smashed the king's political enemies, helping the king survive a military coup planned by the Japanese. In the **First Sino-Japanese War**, both the Chinese navy and army were defeated by Japan, but Yuan retreated earlier to Tianjin, where he retrained his troops on **Li Hongzhang**'s recommendation. The troops were equipped with Western weaponry and organized along Western lines with infantry, cavalry, artillery, and engineering units. Yuan fostered in the new army a sense of personal loyalty to him.

During the **Hundred Days' Reform**, the **Guangxu Emperor** plotted with Yuan against the **Dowager Cixi**. Yuan, however, exposed the emperor's plot to his superior, General Ronglu, who was in Cixi's party. Cixi performed a coup, placing Guangxu under detention and suppressing the reforms. In 1899, Yuan was appointed governor of

Shandong, and he tried to drive the Boxers out of the province. When the **Eight-Nation Alliance** launched the expedition and destroyed Ronglu's troops, Yuan's right-wing army survived. In addition, Yuan took advantage of the suppression of the Boxers and recruited soldiers for himself, making his **Beiyang Army** the largest military force in North China. In 1901, when Li Hongzhang died, Cixi made Yuan the viceroy of Zhili and minister of Beiyang. After the death of Cixi, Yuan's career declined. The regent **Prince Chun** distrusted him for his betrayal of the Guangxu Emperor and forced Yuan to resign his office in 1908. Although he returned to his home village in Henan, Yuan kept in close touch with his protégés and continued to influence the Beiyang Army.

When the Wuchang Uprising started, the Qing court had no choice but to summon Yuan back and grant him the office of prime minister. On one hand, Yuan accepted the order to suppress the revolutionaries; on the other, he began to negotiate with **Sun Yat-sen**. Yuan promised to force the **Manchu** emperor to abdicate and support the **Republican Revolution**. In return, the **National Assembly** elected Yuan president of the Republic of China in 1912.

However, Yuan soon dismissed the National Assembly, replacing it with a political council that produced a new constitution granting unlimited power to the president. Yuan also ordered the abolition of the **Nationalist Party** (GMD), and he was responsible for the assassination of its leader, **Song Jiaoren**. In 1915, to gain political and financial support from Japan, he accepted the Japanese **Twenty-one Demands**. Yuan also signed agreements with Russia and Great Britain recognizing their special interests in Outer Mongolia and Tibet, drastically curtailing Chinese sovereignty. In 1913, Sun Yat-sen launched the **Second Revolution** in southern China. Yuan moved quickly to crush Sun's poorly equipped revolutionary army. The easy suppression of the opponents elevated Yuan's ambitions, and he wasted no time in pushing his monarchical movement. On 11 December 1915, he proclaimed himself emperor and 1916 to be the first year of a new reign, the **Glorious Constitution**.

This move met with defiance and revolts even from his subordinates. Yunnan was the first province that formed a Republic Protection Army to fight against him. Many provinces declared their independence. Facing this political crisis, Yuan had to end his monarchical dream on 23 March 1916. After less than a month, desperate and ill,

Yuan died of uremia. His military dictatorship laid the groundwork for the **warlordism** in the decade that followed his death.

YUANYANG HUDIE PAI. *See* BUTTERFLIES FICTION.

YUDIE. Genealogy of the **Manchu** royal family. It was first compiled in 1656 and updated every 10 years. By the end of the Qing dynasty, it had been revised 26 times. Containing 1,070 volumes, the *yudie* was arranged into four categories: emperor families, prince families, clans, and remote relatives. This is the largest genealogy of a family in the world.

YUNG WING (RONG HONG, 1828–1912). The first Chinese student to study at an American university. He was born in Zhuhai, Guangdong Province, to a very poor farmer. Yung was offered his early education by the local church school and then studied at **Robert Morrison**'s missionary school in Macao and Hong Kong. When the Amercian missionary S. R. Brown took him and two other Chinese boys to the United States, Yung was 19 years old. Yung was the only one of the three Chinese boys who completed his education in American schools. In 1854, he graduated from Yale College and returned to China and worked with Western missionaries as an interpreter. In 1859, he went to Nanjing to see the leaders of the **Taiping Rebellion** and suggested reforming the Chinese school system and the economy, but his proposals were rejected. Afterward, Yung worked in the Supreme Court of Hong Kong, the Shanghai Customs, and the American consulate in Guangzhou. In 1863, Yung persuaded **Zeng Guofan** to buy machinery from the United States, and these machines and equipment were shipped from the United States to Shanghai two years later. Beginning with these machines and equipment, Zeng Guofan and **Li Hongzhang** established the **Jiangnan Arsenal**.

Yung also suggested that the Qing government send Chinese children to the United States to study Western science and engineering. This program, known as the **Chinese Educational Mission**, included 120 young Chinese students from the ages of 12 to 14 who would study in the United States for 15 years. In 1872, the first group of Chinese boys began their studies in New England. Some of them enrolled in and graduated from American colleges. Although the mission was disbanded in 1881, many of the students returned to

China and made significant contributions to China's modernization. Yung Wing was naturalized as an American citizen and married an American woman, Mary Kellogg. He died in Hartford, Connecticut, and was buried in Cedar Hill Cemetery outside the city. *See also* SELF-STRENGTHENING MOVEMENT.

YUNNAN MILITARY ACADEMY. One of the four major military academies in early modern China. The Yunnan Military Academy was founded in 1909 in Kunming, Yunnan Province, with Li Genyuan as the first commandant. The Yunnan Military Academy divided the cadets into four majors: infantry, cavalry, artillery, and engineering. In the early 20th century, the Qing government planned to build two new divisions in Yunnan in order to defend the southern border and suppress the **Republican Revolution**. The academy was originally established to train officers for this purpose. More than half the instructors graduated from the Japanese Military Academy. They either joined the **Tongmenghui** in Japan or sympathized with **Sun Yat-sen**'s revolution. Influenced by these military instructors, many cadets later participated in the 1911 Revolution and became famous generals of the **National Revolutionary Army**. The graduates of the academy, totaling 22 terms, also included some Communist leaders, such as **Zhu De** and **Ye Jianying**. For the 15th term, the academy also admitted cadets from Korea and Vietnam. In 1935, the Yunnan Military Academy was renamed the Fifth Branch of the Central Army University, and the academy closed in 1945.

– Z –

ZAI FENG (1883–1951). The second **Prince Chun**. The younger brother of the **Guangxu Emperor** and father and regent of the **Xuantong Emperor**. Zai Feng was the second son of the first Prince Chun, Yi Huan, and he inherited the title of first-rank prince at the age of eight. His mother was a **Han** Chinese woman, the second concubine of the first Prince Chun, and her Chinese name Liu was changed to the **Manchu** clan's name Lingiya, which was required in order to marry a Manchu prince. In 1901, Zai Feng was appointed ambassador extraordinary to Germany to convey the Qing government's regrets for the murder of the German ambassador

Baron von Ketteler by the Boxers. This trip made him the first member of the Manchu royal family ever to travel abroad. He also served as a member of the **Grand Council**. In 1908, the Guangxu Emperor died without an heir. The **Dowager Cixi** designated Zai's son **Puyi** emperor and appointed Zai as regent. After the Wuchang Uprising in 1911, he negotiated with the revolutionaries, announcing the **Manchu abdication**, and handed over power to the Republican government.

ZAI XUN (?–1901). The second son of Prince Zhuang IX, Yi Ren. In 1875, Zai inherited the title Prince Zhuang. In June 1900, the **Dowager Cixi** decided to support the Boxers and declared war on the eight Western powers. Zai Xun supported the Dowager's idea to facilitate the Boxers who moved to Beijing to fight against foreigners. He hosted the headquarters of the Boxers at his residence, asking all Boxers to register with him. He ordered some government troops to join the Boxers in besieging the foreign legations. In August, Zai escaped from Beijing when the **Eight-Nation Alliance** stormed the city. His residence became the major target of the military attack. In a fierce battle, his residence was burned and 1,700 people in the family compound were killed. As the war ended and the foreign governments demanded the punishment of the Boxers' supporters, Zai Xun was charged as one of the major offenders. At the Dowager Cixi's order, he committed suicide in Puzhou, Shanxi Province.

ZAI YI (1855–1920). Prince Duan of Commandery. The second son of **Prince Yi** Zong, Zai was adopted by Prince Mian Hien, the fourth son of the Jiajing Emperor. Zai married the niece of the **Dowager Cixi** and was bestowed the title of second-rank prince in 1894. During the **Boxer Rebellion**, Zai was the head of the **Zongli Yamen** and suggested that the Dowager Cixi use the Boxers to expel the foreigners. He was appointed as a member of the **Grand Council**. After the Boxer Rebellion was put down, he was accused of collaborating with the rebels and was dismissed in 1901. He and his family were exiled to Xinjiang the next year. The Dowager Cixi once attempted to designate his son, Fu Jun, emperor to replace the Guangxu, but the Western powers refused to recognize the new monarch whose father was a supporter of the Boxers. The Dowager Cixi retracted the order and sent Fu Jun and his father, Zai Yi, into exile.

ZENG GUOFAN (1811–1872). Statesman, general, and Confucian scholar during the late Qing dynasty. His original name was Zeng Zicheng. Born into a farmer's family in Xiangxiang, Hunan Province, Zeng married a woman from the Ouyang family, with whom he had eight children. He obtained the *jinshi* degree in 1838 and was appointed to the **Hanlin Academy**, where he changed his name to Zeng Guofan. He served as deputy secretary of the Board of Rites and as secretary of other boards. In 1852, observing the customary three years of mourning for his mother at home, he was ordered to command the government army to fight the Taiping rebels. Believing that the old standing armies, including the Eight Banners and the **Green Standard Army**, were ill disciplined and unable to fight the Taiping rebels, Zeng decided to rebuild the **Hunan Army**. He recruited officers and soldiers locally, emphasizing strict discipline and the soldiers' loyalty to their commanders. In doing so, he created a model of the personal army, which eventually contributed to the growth of **warlordism** in the 20th century.

In 1860, Zeng was appointed governor of Liangjiang (the provinces of Jiangxi, Jiangsu, and Anhui) and military commissioner. After several military failures, his Hunan Army finally stormed Nanjing and crushed the Taiping forces. After this, Zeng was sent to Shandong to put down the **Nian Rebellion**. To avoid suspicion of his growing military power by the Qing court, he began to decrease the size of the Hunan Army. He advocated the military self-strengthening of China and sponsored the building of the **Jiangnan Arsenal** in Shanghai. Under Zeng's influence, his pupil, **Li Hongzhang**, later became an eminent military commander and one of the leaders of the **Self-Strengthening Movement**. He and Li initiated a program to send Chinese children to the United States to study. Zeng was one of the most influential Confucian scholars and a great interpreter of the Chinese classics. His works were compiled into a 156-volume book, *Zeng wenzheng gong quanji* (Complete Works of Zeng Wen Zheng). The most famous was *Zeng wenzheng gong jiashu* (Letters to Home by Mr. Zeng Wen Zheng), edited by Li Hongzhang. His writing style and moral teaching had a great influence on the later reformers and revolutionaries. Zeng was granted the title First Marquis of Prowess for his great feats and was posthumously honored as "Wen Zheng."

ZHAN TIANYOU (1861–1919). Engineer known as the father of China's railroad. Born into the family of a tea merchant in Nanhai near Guangzhou, Zhan was chosen by the government to be sent to the United States for study at the age of 12. In 1881, Zhan graduated from Yale University, majoring in civil engineering with a concentration on railroads. In that year, he was recalled to China and assigned to the newly formed imperial navy to be retrained as a seaman. In 1888, he finally found an opportunity to work as a railroad engineer. He worked with the British engineer Claude W. Kinder as an intern engineer in the Tianjin–Tangsha Railway, which was later turned into the Peking–Mukden Railway. He was soon promoted to full engineer, and six years later, Zhan was elected as a member of the British Engineering Research Society. In 1905, Zhan was appointed chief engineer of the Jiang–Zhang Railway (Beijing–Zhangjiakou). This was the first railway surveyed, designed, and constructed completely by Chinese. He designed a zigzag upward railway by switching back the line to overcome the steep gradient. He was also responsible for the adoption of standard gauge and Janney couplers in all railroads. Zhan died in Hankou but was buried at the Qinglongqiao railway station, where the first Chinese railway passed, and a museum was built nearby to commemorate his accomplishments.

ZHANG AILING (EILEEN CHANG, 1921–1995). Prominent writer in modern China. Zhang was born into a renowned family in Shanghai; its members included Zhang Peilun, **Li Hongzhang**, and other famous imperial officials. In 1931, Zhang enrolled in Saint Maria Girl's School in Shanghai, where she displayed great talent in literature by publishing essays and short stories in the school journal and other journals. In 1939, she went to Hong Kong University to study literature. After the Japanese occupied Hong Kong, she returned to Shanghai, focusing on creative writing. In the years 1943 and 1944, Zhang was the hottest writer in Shanghai, and her most acclaimed work, *The Golden Cangue,* was published during this period. Unlike most other contemporary writers, her subject was everyday life, and she provided the readers with vivid descriptions of urban experiences of ordinary people and impressive psychological portrayals of human relationships. After 1949, Zhang's works were ignored in mainland China but still remained a great influence in Taiwan and among overseas Chinese. In 1952, she left Shanghai for Hong Kong and then went to the United States three years later. Zhang had two marriages, but neither of them left her any children. She died alone at her apartment in Los Angeles.

ZHANG BINGLIN (1868–1936). Philologist and revolutionary, also known as Zhang Taiyan. Born into a scholarly family in Yuhang, Zhejiang Province, Zhang joined **Kang Youwei**'s New Text Movement and supported the **Hundred Days' Reform**. After the failure of the reform, Zhang fled to Taiwan with the help of a Japanese friend. In September 1898, he worked as a reporter for the *Taiwan Daily News (Riri Xinbao)*. In May 1899, Zhang went to Japan and was introduced to **Sun Yat-sen** by **Liang Qichao**. He joined the United League in 1906 and served as the editor in chief of its official newspaper, *Minbao*. Zhang published several articles advocating the anti-**Manchu** revolution. Based on his study of Chinese philology, he created a system of "mnemonic alphabets" (*zhuyin zimu*), the basis of China's modern spelling system. He did not like vernacular literature and opposed the **New Culture Movement**. Knowing he disagreed with Sun Yat-sen's policies, **Yuan Shikai** invited Zhang to be his adviser, but Zhang refused. He denounced Yuan for the assassination of **Song Jiaoren** and opposed Yuan's restoration of the monarchy. Consequently, he was put into jail by Yuan Shikai for three years. After his release in June 1917, he accepted an appointment as general secretary to Generalissimo Sun Yat-sen and went to Guangzhou to join the revolutionaries. In later years, he became critical of **Chiang Kai-shek** and the **Nationalist Party** (GMD). In 1924, Zhang left the GMD, labeled himself a loyalist to the Republic of China and the true spirit of Sun Yat-sen's doctrine, established the National Studies Society, and edited the magazine *Moral Code (Zhiyan)*. In 1936, he urged Chiang Kai-shek to stop the military campaign against the Communists and to declare war on Japan. Zhang died in Suzhou on 14 June 1936 and was buried on the bank of West Lake in Hangzhou. The Nationalist government held a state funeral for him.

ZHANG DAQIAN (CHANG DAI-CHIEN, 1899–1983). The Buddhist monastic name of Zhang Zhengquan, a great artist, known as China's Picasso of the 20th century. Born into a gentry-scholar family in Neijiang, Sichuan Province, Zhang traveled to Japan to study the technology of textile weaving and dyeing. After his return to China in 1919, he became a Buddhist novice and took the Buddhist monastic name Daqian. Three months later, Zhang resumed his secular life but kept his monastic name. He began to study Chinese ink painting in Shanghai, spending most of his time copying ancient Chinese masterpieces. He had become a famous artist by the 1930s and was invited to be an art professor at the Nanjing Central School of Art in 1936. Zhang was known for his singular ability to mix traditional techniques and styles with contemporary ideas and currents. He was also a connoisseur and successful art dealer. During the **Second Sino-Japanese War**, Zhang refused to accept the Japanese appointment and was thus put in jail. In 1942, he decided to move his family to Dunhuang, Gansu Province, spending three years copying Buddhist wall paintings at the Dunhuang caves. Thereafter, his artistic style changed to be full of power and grandeur. His most famous work in mainland China is the *Picture of the Thousand Li Yangtze River*. In 1948, Zhang left China for Mogi das Cruzes, Brazil, and in 1976 he settled in Taipei, Taiwan. Zhang died on 2 April 1983 at the age of 84.

ZHANG DONGSUN (1886–1973). Philosopher and social activist. Zhang was born in Hanghzhou, Zhejiang Province, into a gentry-official family. In 1905, he traveled to Japan and studied epistemology and the ethics of Immanuel Kant. He returned to China on the eve of the Republican Revolution and advocated a "third way" between the revolutionaries and monarchists. He edited several philosophy journals and taught at Yanjing University. He tried to reinterpret **Confucianism** along Kantian lines and engaged in the heated debate on "science and metaphysics." When the Japanese occupied Beijing, he refused to cooperate with the invaders. Zhang was arrested and tried to commit suicide in prison. He was then released on bail through the efforts of his friends. He was one of the founders of the **China Democratic League**, a political party that did not support the Communists but also opposed **Chiang Kai-shek's** dictatorship during the civil war. In 1948, when the **People's Liberation Army** (PLA) besieged Beijing, Zhang was asked to be the representative of the Nationalist troops to negotiate with the Communists. The success of the negotiation led to a peaceful takeover of the city by the PLA. After 1949, as a non-Communist intellectual, he was given some positions in the government but was soon accused of selling intelligence to the American Central Intelligence Agency (CIA) and purged from the government and his own party. The Cultural Revolution (1966–1976) ruined his whole family. He was arrested with his elder son. He died in jail, his elder son became deranged, and his two other sons and a daughter-in-law committed suicide.

ZHANG FAKUI (1896–1980). Four-star general of the Nationalist army. Born in Shixing, Guangdong Province, Zhang joined the army at the age of 15. He then enrolled in the Second Officer Preparatory School of Wuchang and graduated in 1916. Having returned to the Guangdong Army, Zhang gradually rose from platoon leader to brigade commander. During the **Northern Expedition**, he was a divisional commander and was then promoted to commander of the 4th Army of the **National Revolutionary Army**. In April 1927, when left-wing leader **Wang Jingwei** broke with **Chiang Kai-shek**, Zhang supported Wang. In July, however, Zhang joined Chiang's purge of the Communists and suppressed the Canton Mutiny in December. Zhang was involved in several failed anti-Chiang campaigns and slowly faded from the Nationalist government.

In 1937, Zhang was appointed commander in chief of the Eighth Group Army and he commanded the army in the Battle of Shanghai in 1937. Zhang's troops also fought the Japanese in the battle of Wuhan and several battles in both Guangdong and Guangxi. In 1945, as the chief commander of the Chinese troops in south China, Zhang accepted the surrender of the Japanese troops in Guangzhou. In March 1949, Zhang was appointed commander in chief of the Nationalist army, but he resigned three months later. Zhang moved to Hong Kong, where he formed an anti–Chiang Kai-shek organization and served as president of a **Hakka** provincial association. While he was anti-Chiang, Zhang refused to cooperate with the Communists and never returned to mainland China.

ZHANG GUOTAO (1897–1979). Early leader of the **Chinese Communist Party** (CCP) and one of the major rivals of **Mao Zedong**. Born in Pingxiang, Jiangxi Province, Zhang studied at **Peking University**, where Mao Zedong worked as a librarian's assistant. Taking an active part in the **May Fourth Movement**, Zhang became a prominent student leader and founding member of the CCP in 1921. Zhang was elected by the first party congress as one of three members of the Central Bureau of the CCP. He also served as director of the secretariat of the China Labor Union and chief editor of its formal journal, *Labor Weekly*. Zhang was devoted to the labor movement and led several important strikes of railway and textile workers. In 1924, he was arrested by the **warlord** government in Beijing but was released shortly. Zhang held many important posts in the party, including director of the organizational department, secretary of the Military Department, head of the CCP delegation to the **Comintern**, vice-chairman of the Chinese Soviet Republic, and general political commissar of the **Red Army**.

In 1931, he was sent to the Er-Yu-Wan base as secretary of the CCP Central Bureau and chairman of the military committee of the Er-Yu-Wan area. At Er-Yu-Wan, Zhang staged a cruel "cleansing campaign" to persecute dissidents and establish his absolute authority. In 1934, when **Chiang Kai-shek** launched the fifth **Encirclement and Suppression Campaign**, Zhang led the **Fourth Front Army** in evacuating the base and beginning the **Long March**. Because the **First Front Army** had suffered large casualties due to the inept leadership of the "three-man group," it was much smaller than Zhang's Fourth Front Army. When Zhang met Mao Zedong in Sichuan in June 1935, Zhang had 80,000 troops while Mao had fewer than 10,000. Zhang arrogantly opposed Mao's plan to continue the march northward and insisted on moving west to the regions dominated by Tibetan and other ethnic minorities. Zhang declared the establishment of a new CCP Central Committee and made himself chairman. However, his military campaign ended with disastrous results, and he lost three-quarters of his troops. Zhang was forced to give up his plans and follow He Long's **Second Front Army** to catch up with Mao's troops in Gansu in October 1936.

The final blow to Zhang was that his remaining troop of 21,800 men, sent to open a "corridor" between the CCP's base and the Soviet Union, was destroyed by Ma Bufang's Muslim cavalry and only 427 survivors returned to **Yan'an**. In 1937, the CCP held the Extended Meeting of the Politburo to criticize Zhang. Zhang thereafter defected to the **Nationalist Party** (GMD). He first worked with **Dai Li** and then with Zhu Jiahua. In 1949, he went into exile in Hong Kong and then Toronto. His autobiography is an important source on the early Chinese Communist movement.

ZHANG JIA'AO (1889–1979). Banker and government official of the Nationalist government. Born into the family of a famous local gentry in Baoshan, near Shanghai, Zhang traveled to Japan in 1904 to study. Five years later, he returned to China and worked as the chief editor of the *Bulletin of Communication*. After the 1911 Revolution, he and his brother **Zhang Junli** formed the Democratic Party and invited **Liang Qichao** to be its leader. When Liang became the minister of finance of the **Beijing government** in 1913, Zhang was assigned to the **Bank of China**, serving successively as deputy manager of the Shanghai branch and vice president and general manager of the Bank of China. In 1916, the Beijing government ordered the Bank of China and the **Bank of Communication** to stop cashing their banknotes. Zhang refused to obey this order and continued the regular money-transfer business of the Bank of China, which enhanced the bank's credibility.

After the **Second Sino-Japanese War**, Zhang was appointed chairman of the Economic Committee of Northeast China and president of the Bureau of the East Chinese Railways. In March 1947, Zhang was appointed president of the Central Bank and president of the Central Trust Bureau, but he resigned a year later. In May 1949, he left China for Australia and the United States, doing research and giving lectures at several universities. His publications included *China's Current Economic Problems and Treatment in the Future* (1936), *Railway Construction in China* (1945), *The Diagram of Inflation: A Chinese Lesson in 1939–1950* (1958), and several articles on China's economic development.

ZHANG JIAN (1853–1926). Scholar, entrepreneur, and educator in modern China. Born in the city of Nantong, Jiangsu Province, Zhang was the last *zhuan yuan* (title conferred on the scholar who came first in the highest **civil service examination**) of the Qing dynasty and was appointed to the **Hanlin Academy** in 1894. After China's defeat by Japan in 1895, he came to believe that only industrialization could save China. He resigned his office and began to engage in building and managing factories and other enterprises. He believed that the key to national economy was textile and iron industries. The enterprises that he built up included textile mills, ironworks, flour mills, navigation companies, saltworks, and also the Haihai Shiye Bank. The total capital volume of his enterprises passed the ¥40,000,000 mark. Zhang engaged in opening new-style schools, calling on entrepreneurs to invest in education. He argued that developing China's education had to begin with elementary schools, and improving elementary education had to begin with normal schools. He established the Tongzhu Normal School (the first normal school in China), Tongzhi Female Normal School, and some medical, agricultural, and professional schools. He built China's first school for deaf-mutes and its first modern museum. He supported **Yuan Shikai**'s monarchical attempt and in 1913 served as minister of agriculture and commerce in Yuan's government. Although he advocated a constitutional monarchy, Zhang was soon disappointed with Yuan Shikai's performance and resigned his office. In later years, his enterprises were heavily in debt and finally went bankrupt in July 1925. Zhang died on 24 August 1926 in Nantong.

ZHANG JINGJIANG (1877–1950). A leader of the **Nationalist Party** (GMD). Born into a very wealthy merchant family in Xiuning, Anhui Province, Zhang suffered from several childhood diseases, and for this reason, his father allowed him to withdraw from the **civil service examination**. Zhang gave up the study of Confucian texts and began to study the arts and **calligraphy**. When Zhang was 19, his father bought him a position in the imperial government and married him to a daughter of the academic administrator of Shandong, Yao Hui. In 1900, Zhang went to France as Chinese commercial consul in Paris, where he opened his own business selling Chinese silk, tea, and antiques. His business was so profitable that he opened branches in London and New York. In 1905, Zhang was exposed to anarchism. With Wu Zhihui, Li Shizhen, and **Cai Yuanpei**, he set up the anarchist organization Global Society and published *New Century Weekly* and *Global Pictorial*, criticizing the **Manchu** monarchy and introducing Western culture. In 1906, Zhang happened to meet **Sun Yat-sen** on his trip to Singapore, and he was impressed by Sun's idealism and revolutionary efforts. After 1907, Zhang began donating his commercial income to support Sun's revolution. From that time forward, Zhang always responded to Sun's urgent demands as soon as he could, becoming a major supporter of the revolution.

After the 1911 Revolution, Zhang returned to Shanghai, where he became **Chiang Kai-shek**'s sworn brother and his major political supporter. Zhang witnessed Sun Yat-sen's death and was one of the first readers of Sun's will. In May 1926, Zhang was elected chairman of the GMD Central Political Committee. Two months later, Zhang resigned for health reasons and Chiang succeeded him. Zhang supported Chiang's anti-Communist policy and served as governor of Zhejiang to purge the Communists from various levels of government. In 1928, when Chiang stepped down, Zhang left Zhejiang. After Chiang returned to power, Zhang resumed the position of governor. Zhang was the chief witness at Chiang's second wedding and helped Chiang make arrangements for the separation with his first wife. After Chiang formally married **Song May-ling**, the relations between Zhang and Chiang became sour. In his term of governor, Zhang initiated several important projects to promote the local economy, including building power stations, constructing railways, improving local transportation, opening coal mines, and developing communication facilities. Zhang had two marriages that gave him two sons and 10 daughters, none of whom were involved in politics. In his later years, Zhang faded from politics and devoted himself to Buddhism. On 2 September 1950, Zhang died of heart failure in New York and was buried at the Ferncliff Cemetery, Ardsley, New York.

ZHANG JUNLI (1887–1968). Confucian scholar and social activist. Zhang was born in Jiading, Jiangsu Province; his father was a Chinese doctor who also engaged in some business activities. Zhang began to study **Confucianism** at the age of six and obtained the *xiucai* degree 10 years later. He then traveled to Japan to study law and political science at Waseda University. During his stay in Japan, he became acquainted with **Liang Qichao** and joined Liang's Society for Political Reform. Zhang obtained a bachelor's degree in political science from Waseda University in 1910 and returned to China. Because he was persecuted by **Yuan Shikai**, Zhang left China for Germany to study philosophy. Having published numerous books and articles on Chinese culture and philosophy, Zhang was regarded as a prominent scholar of neo-Confucianism.

Zhang was an active social activist. He was a founding member of the Chinese National Socialist Party, Chinese Democratic Party, and **China Democratic League**. He served as a member of the National Senate and the **Political Consultative Conference** (1946) and drafted the **Constitution of the Republic of China**. Zhang criticized **Chiang Kai-shek** but also strongly opposed communism. His life was full of controversies. He advocated women's emancipation but prohibited his younger sister's remarriage. He criticized Chiang Kai-shek and was thus kidnapped by Chiang's secret policemen and placed under house arrest for two years, but he still supported Chiang's anti-Communist civil war. He made friends with **Zhou Enlai**, but he was listed as a war criminal by **Mao Zedong**. In 1949, Zhang moved to the United States; he died there at the age of 81.

ZHANG LAN (1872–1955). A leader of the **China Democratic League** and vice president of the People's Republic of China. Born in Nanchong, Sichuan Province, Zhang received a traditional Confucian education from his father and obtained the *xiucai* degree. In 1902, Zhang went to Japan on a government scholarship to study. He was sent back to China under escort for suggesting the retirement of the **Dowager Cixi**. After his return, Zhang began his career as a devoted educator, opening elementary, middle, and women's schools and also teaching at universities. Some Communist leaders, such as **Zhu De** and Luo Ruoqing, were students of Zhang Lan's. Zhang took part in the **constitutional reform** movement and led the **Railway Protection Movement** in Sichuan, which undermined **Manchu** control over the province.

After the 1911 Revolution, Zhang served as governor of Sichuan for a short time and then went to Beijing to serve as the executive trustee of *Morning Daily*, a newspaper devoted to the dissemination of science and democracy. During the **Second Sino-Japanese War**, Zhang worked with Huang Yanpei and leaders of several other political parties to form the **China Democratic League**. He served as its chairman for 14 years until his death. In 1949, because he refused to follow the Nationalist government to Taiwan, Zhang was placed under house arrest in Shanghai. Rescued by the **Chinese Communist Party**'s secret organization, he went to Beiping to join the **Chinese People's Political Consultative Conference**. After the establishment of the People's Republic of China in 1949, Zhang was elected president of the state, vice president of the Chinese Congress, and vice-chairman of the Chinese People's Political Consultative Conference.

ZHANG TAILEI (1898–1927). The leader of the Canton Communist Mutiny. Born in Changzhou, Jiangsu Province, Zhang enrolled in Beiyang University, where he took an active part in the **May Fourth Movement** and joined the Beijing **Communist group**. Zhang took part in the labor movement and opened a night school for the railway workers in a suburb of Beijing. In 1921, Zhang went to Moscow and served as the director of the China Division of the **Comintern**'s Far East Bureau. Zhang accompanied the Comintern's representatives to meet **Li Dazhao** and **Chen Duxiu** to discuss the founding of the **Chinese Communist Party** (CCP). Zhang was also the founder of the Chinese **Communist Youth League** and served as its general secretary. In 1927, Zhang attended the **August Seventh Conference** of the CCP Politburo, which criticized Chen Duxiu's compromise with the **Nationalist Party** (GMD) and passed a resolution to launch a series of urban insurrections. Zhang was elected as an alternative member of the CCP Politburo and appointed secretary of the CCP South China Bureau. Zhang was also chair of the military committee in Guangdong Province and in charge of preparations for an uprising in Guangzhou (the Canton Mutiny). The insurrection was staged in December 1927, and a Soviet government was soon established. Zhang was elected acting chair of the Guangzhou Soviet. On 12 December, his office was attacked by GMD troops, and Zhang was killed in battle at the age of 29.

ZHANG XUELIANG (1901–2001). General of the first class of the **Nationalist Party** (GMD) army and a patriotic military leader. Born into a **warlord** family in Haicheng, Liaoning Province, Zhang succeeded his father (**Zhang Zuolin**) to become the ruler of Manchuria, nicknamed the "Young Marshal." Zhang graduated from **Fengtian Military Academy** in 1918, majoring in artillery. He went to Japan to observe military maneuvers, and there he developed a special interest in aircraft. Two years later he began to develop Manchuria's naval and air forces. In his father's army, Zhang served successively as commander of a battalion, regiment, brigade, army, and army corps. After his father was assassinated in 1928, Zhang was made the commander in chief of the army, navy, and air force of Manchuria and he proclaimed his allegiance to the Nationalist government in Nanjing. During the **Manchuria Incident** in 1931, Zhang followed **Chiang Kai-shek**'s order of nonresistance and gave up Manchuria to the Japanese. Having retreated to Rehe Province, Zhang continued the policy of nonresistance, allowing the Japanese to swiftly occupy North China. Chiang and Zhang were denounced by the Chinese mass media, and Zhang was forced to resign.

In 1936, Zhang and his troops (Northeast Army) were assigned to Northwest China to join the Northwest Army led by Yang Hucheng in a suppression campaign against the Communists. Both Zhang and Yang disagreed with Chiang's policy of "stabilizing China before resisting Japan." When Zhang stopped the **Red Army** blockade, Chiang flew to Xi'an to push his new plan of "bandit suppression." Zhang and Yang were unable to persuade Chiang to change his mind. At dawn on 12 December, Zhang's army stormed Chiang's headquarters and arrested Chiang and his entourage. The incident greatly enhanced the possibility of a civil war. The government in Nanjing was torn between choosing military reprisals or conciliatory negotiations. The **Comintern** denounced the incident as a Japanese conspiracy—Japan would have loved to have Chiang killed. With the help of **Zhou Enlai**, Zhang and Yang worked on a peaceful settlement. Chiang's adviser, the Australian W. H. Donald; Madame Chiang (**Soong May-ling**); and her brother **T. V. Soong** traveled to Xi'an to join the negotiations. After promising to cooperate with the Red Army to fight the Japanese, Chiang was released. Zhang escorted Chiang and his entourage to Nanjing. The **Xi'an Incident** had obviously revived Chiang's popularity as a national leader and Zhang as a patriotic hero. Zhang was charged with insubordination by a military tribunal in Nanjing and placed in jail and then under house arrest for most of his life.

Zhang was detained first in Zhejiang, then moved to Jiangxi, Hunan, Guizhou, and finally to Taiwan. His girlfriend, Miss Zhao, accompanied Zhang in house arrest for more than 50 years, marrying him in 1964. Zhang and Zhao regained their freedom in 1990 and moved to Hawaii in 1995. On 15 October 2001, Zhang died of pneumonia in Honolulu at the age of 101. *See also* FENGTIAN CLIQUE.

ZHANG XUN (1854–1923). Born in Fenxin, Jiangxi Province, Zhang joined the **Hunan Army** in Changsha. Promoted in the suppression of the **Boxer Rebellion**, Zhang became a powerful general in **Yuan Shikai**'s new army. In later years, Zhang was promoted to governor of Liangjiang and minister of Nanyang affairs. Several times, Zhang served in the entourage of the **Dowager Cixi** and the **Guangxu Emperor**. Maintaining his loyalty to the **Manchu** emperor, Zhang ordered his soldiers to keep their pigtails after the Qing dynasty was overthrown. In March 1917, in conflict with Premier Duan Qirui, President **Li Yuanhong** invited Zhang Xun to Beijing for mediation. Zhang took this opportunity to lead his **pigtail army** to Beijing and overthrow the Republican government. Zhang put **Puyi** back on the throne and restored the Qing monarchy. However, Duan organized a counterattack and destroyed Zhang's troops. The imperial regime Zhang restored existed only 11 days. Zhang fled to the **foreign concession** in Tianjin.

ZHANG WENTIAN (1900–1976). Also known as Luofu. General secretary of the **Chinese Communist Party** (CCP) from 1935 to 1943. Born into the family of a rich farmer in Nanhui, Jiangsu Province, Zhang participated in the **May Fourth Movement** in 1919 and joined the CCP in 1925. He traveled to Russia and studied at **Moscow Sun Yat-sen University**, where he met **Wang Ming** and **Bo Gu** and joined their group, becoming one of the **Twenty-eight Bolsheviks**. In 1930, he returned to China and was appointed the CCP's minister of propaganda and a standing member of the Politburo. He was also made government head of the **Jiangxi Soviet** when **Mao Zedong** was expelled from leading positions in the army and party.

However, at the **Zunyi Conference** during the **Long March**, Zhang supported Mao Zedong in criticizing the political leadership of Bo Gu and the military adviser from the **Comintern**, **Otto Braun**. The conference reshuffled the party's Politburo, breaking out of the party's reliance on instructions from Moscow and establishing Mao Zedong's position as the de facto supreme leader of the CCP. Zhang was elected the party's general secretary, a top leader of the CCP in name. Although he gave his allegiance to Mao, Zhang was finally removed from the leading position when Mao was elected chairman of the CCP Central Committee in 1945. During the civil war, he was sent to Manchuria, where he worked with **Lin Biao**, **Gao Gang**, and **Chen Yun**. After 1949, Zhang did not hold any important positions in the party. He was appointed China's ambassador to the Soviet Union and deputy minister of foreign affairs. In 1957, he criticized Mao's economic policies and was therefore charged with "anti-CCP conspiracy" and dismissed from office. Zhang died of a heart attack in 1976 and was not rehabilitated until two years after his death.

ZHANG ZHIDONG (1837–1909). An eminent Chinese politician and reformer, known as one of the "Four Famous Officials of the

Late Qing." Born in Nanpi, Hebei Province, Zhang earned the *jinshi* degree in 1863 and was appointed to the **Hanlin Academy** in 1880. He was appointed governor of Shanxi in 1881 and promoted to governor of Huguang (the provinces of Hubei and Hunan) in August 1889. He also served as the viceroy of Liangjiang in 1901 and as a member of the **Grand Council** in 1906. In 1898, Zhang published his work *Exhortation to Study*, opposing the **Hundred Days' Reform** and insisting on a conservative reform based on his famous *ti-yong* **formula** (Chinese learning for fundamental principles and Western learning for practical application). During the **Boxer Rebellion**, as the **Eight-Nation Alliance**'s troops entered Beijing, Zhang began to negotiate with the Western consuls in Shanghai and drafted the Mutual Defense of the Southeast agreement, ensuring cooperation between the European powers and the local governments in southeast China in suppression of the Boxers.

When China was defeated in the **First Sino-Japanese War** and **Li Hongzhang** was dispatched to Tokyo to negotiate the peace treaty, Zhang vigorously opposed Li's compromise over the cession of Taiwan and sought British aid to protect the island. As one of the leaders of the **Self-Strengthening Movement**, he promoted railway construction in southern China, sponsored the **Hanyeping Coal and Steel Complex**, created a new-style army, opened schools in the provinces of Hubei and Jiangsu, and sent students to Japan and Europe to study Western science. Zhang was the first government official who suggested borrowing money from Western banks to facilitate China's military buildup and industrial development.

ZHANG ZHIZHONG (1890–1969). Full general of the second class of the Nationalist army and statesman of modern China. Born in Caoxian, Anhui Province, Zhang joined the Boy Scouts while attending middle school in Shanghai. Zhang graduated from the **Baoding Military Academy** in 1916 and served in several provincial armies, including Guangdong, Yunnan, Guangxi, and Sichuan. In 1924, he served as regiment commander of the Cadets Regiment and Officers Regiment at the **Whampoa Military Academy** and made friends with the Communists **Zhou Enlai** and Yun Daiying. During the **Northern Expedition**, he was made director of staff at the headquarters of the **National Revolutionary Army**, where he established close relations with **Chiang Kai-shek**. He served as provost of the

Central University of the Army from 1929 to 1937. During this period he also joined Chiang's expeditions against **warlords Feng Yuxiang** and **Yan Xishan**, and **Cai Tingkai**. On 8 December 1932, as the army commander of the Fifth Army, he led his troops to fight the Japanese in Shanghai, crushing the Japanese plan to occupy the city. In 1937, as the commander in chief of the Nanjing-Shanghai garrison, Zhang oversaw the second defense of Shanghai. In November 1937, he was appointed governor of Hunan and then director of the Political Department of the Military Committee of the Republic of China. Zhang advocated cooperation with the **Chinese Communist Party** (CCP) during the **Second Sino-Japanese War**. He stood for a peaceful settlement of the **Xi'an Incident** and remained allied with the CCP after the **New Fourth Army Incident**.

In 1946, Zhang was appointed representative of the **Nationalist Party** (GMD) in the Three-Man Group (the United States, GMD, and CCP) to supervise the cease-fire between the GMD and CCP. He foresaw the GMD's failure in the civil war as early as 1948. In 1949, he was made the chief negotiator of the GMD for peace talks with the CCP in Beiping. After the failure of the **Beiping Peace Negotiation**, he remained in Beijing and announced his withdrawal from the GMD. Since he was the chief administrator of Northwest China and governor of Xinjiang, Zhang persuaded the GMD leaders in Xinjiang defect to the CCP in 1949. After the establishment of the People's Republic of China (PRC), Zhang was appointed vice-chairman of Northwest China Military and Administrative Committee and vice-chairman of the National Defense Committee of the PRC. He was also elected vice president of the Chinese Congress.

ZHANG ZIZHONG (1891–1940). Full general of the **National Revolutionary Army** and commander in chief of the 33rd Corps Army, Zhang was the highest-ranked officer who died in the **Second Sino-Japanese War**. Born into the family of a gentry-official in Liqing, Shandong Province, Zhang received a traditional education at home. At the age of 20, he traveled to Tianjin and Jinan to study at the schools of politics and law, where he became a secret member of the **Tongmenghui**. In 1914, he began his military career as a 23-year-old soldier in the army of the **Fengtian Clique**. This army supported **Yuan Shikai**'s monarchist movement and was defeated by **Cai E**'s

Republic Protection Army. Zhang soon left the Fengtian army and joined **Feng Yuxiang**'s troops, who were incorporated into **Chiang Kai-shek**'s National Army in 1931. He was gradually promoted from first lieutenant to general and also served in the Nationalist government as governor of Chahar and mayor of Tianjin. After the **Marco Polo Bridge Incident** in 1937, Zhang was made the commander of the 59th Army. He called an oath-taking rally, saying: "This is the time for us to kill the enemy and find the place to die." He led the 59th Army to participate in the famous **Battle of Tai'erzhuang**. In May 1939, he commanded the troops and defeated the Japanese in northern Hubei. In the next year, the Japanese assembled 150,000 troops and launched a fierce offensive against his garrison area. Zhang led the 47th Division to cross the Xiang River and check the enemy. He was shot down at the battle in Zaoyi on 1 May 1940. Both the **Nationalist Party** and the **Chinese Communist Party** honored him, holding grand funeral ceremonies in **Chongqing** and **Yan'an**. Some roads in the cities of Beijing, Tianjin, and Wuhan are named after him.

ZHANG ZONGCHANG (1881–1932). **Warlord** of Shandong. Born into poverty in Yexian, Shandong Province, Zhang joined a bandit gang in Manchuria at the age of 18. After the 1911 Revolution, he led his bandit followers to join the army of the governor of Shandong, and gained a position in the Republican troops. In later years, his troops moved to Shanghai, and Zhang was appointed a regiment commander. Zhang pledged to participate in **Sun Yat-sen**'s **Second Revolution** but betrayed the revolutionary army on the eve of battle. Zhang sought refuge with the **Fengtian Clique** and was put in an important position by **Zhang Zuolin**. In the war between the **Zhili** and **Fengtian cliques**, Zhang stormed Shanghai and was appointed governor of Shandong, where he established his own kingdom. Zhang engaged in opium smuggling and had more than 20 concubines. Zhang killed numerous innocents to maintain his rule in his kingdom. In 1927, his troops were defeated by the **National Revolutionary Army**, and Zhang fled to Japan. Zhang returned to Shandong in 1932, and on 2 September, **Zhang Xueliang** asked him to return to Beiping. The next day, Zhang was to take the train but was assassinated at the railway station by a young officer, Zheng Jichen, who was avenging his father's death.

ZHANG ZUOLIN (1875–1928). Warlord of the **Fengtian Clique.** Born into poverty in Haicheng, Liaoning Province, Zhang tried various jobs to support his family, including peddler, woodworker, and veterinarian's assistant. At the age of 12, Zhang eavesdropped on a class at a private school; he was found and a tutor offered him free lessons. In 1894, Zhang avenged his father by killing a bandit, and then he became a bandit himself. Zhang recruited the homeless to join his gang and won himself a Robin Hood–like reputation in Manchuria. During the Russo-Japanese War in 1904–1905, Zhang's men were hired by the Japanese army as mercenaries, and thus he established a close connection with the Japanese. In 1900, he managed to make his troops a regiment of the Qing standing army. When the 1911 Revolution started, Zhang led his troops to fight against the revolutionaries and was rewarded by the Qing government. Zhang gradually expanded his troops and became the largest warlord in Manchuria, founding the group known as the Fengtian Clique.

In Manchuria, his warlord government initiated several important reforms, including issuing new currency, improving the tax collection system, advocating reclamation of land for agriculture, investing in textile and other industries, bringing more laborers from China proper, and encouraging those workers to come with women and children for permanent settlement. In the late 1910s and early 1920s, when China proper suffered from wars and chaos, Manchuria experienced good development. Zhang's rise has been ascribed to Japanese support, but he did not want to be their puppet and his relations with the Japanese turned out to be tense in later years. Zhang attempted to become a figure of national prominence and expand into North China. He engaged in several wars with the **Zhili** and **Anhui cliques** and finally became the highest ruler of the **Beijing government** in 1927, proclaiming himself the grand marshal of the Chinese army, navy, and air forces. His troops, however, were quickly defeated by **Chiang Kai-shek** in collaboration with other local regional forces. Zhang's military campaigns also led to the collapse of Manchuria's economy. When Zhang retreated from Beijing to Shenyang, the Japanese colonel Komoto Daisaku of the **Kwangtung Army** had a bomb placed on the railway line. When Zhang's train passed, the bomb exploded and killed him. His son, **Zhang Xueliang**, succeeded him and announced his recognition of Chiang Kai-shek's National Government in Nanjing.

ZHENG CHAOLIN (1901–1998). An early leader of the **Chinese Communist Party** (CCP) and member of the **Trotsky Clique**. Born in Zhangping, Fujian Province, Zheng traveled to France and joined the work-study program, where he and 18 other Chinese students, including **Zhou Enlai**, organized the Communist Youth Party in June 1922. Zheng was sent to the Soviet Union to study at the Eastern Labor University the next year. Zheng returned to China in 1924 and served as chief editor of the CCP's formal publication, *Bolshevik*. In 1929, he was purged from the party because he supported **Chen Duxiu**, who was blamed by the **Comintern** for the failure of the Chinese Communist movement in the 1920s. Zheng was soon arrested by the GMD and sentenced to 15 years' imprisonment. Because of the outbreak of the **Second Sino-Japanese War**, Zheng was released before seven years had passed. In the following years, Zheng published extensively on Marxist theories and translated a large number of Western works of political science, including Leon Trotsky's *The Revolution Betrayed* and *History of the Russian Revolution* (volumes 2 and 3). Zheng organized the Chinese International Party of Workers to promote a "real Communist revolution" in China. On 22 December 1952, Zheng was arrested by the Communist government on charges of engaging in Trotskyite activities. The Communist adherent Zheng Chaolin spent 27 years in a Communist jail until released in June 1979. Zheng died on 1 August 1998 in Shanghai at the age of 97.

ZHENG GUANYING (1842–1922). An influential leading reformer during the late Qing dynasty. Zheng was born into an intellectual family in Xiangshan, Guangdong Province. In 1858, after he failed the lowest level of the **civil service examination**, Zheng gave up academic pursuits and moved into business. Zheng first worked at the age of 17 in his uncle's firm in Shanghai. In his free time, he took evening classes at the Anglo-Chinese School in Shanghai, studying English and Western technology. Zheng then worked as a comprador with the British company **Butterfield & Swire**. Having accumulated enough capital, Zheng opened his own business and was actively involved in various public services. In 1880, he published his first book, *Yiyan* (On Change). In it, he advocated Western learning, calling for the translation of more Western books and the application of Western machines. He suggested a series of policies promoting mining, shipbuilding, and railway construction. Appreciating the Western representative system, he proposed that a constitutional monarchy be established in China. **Li Hongzhang** invited Zheng to work at the China Merchants' Steam Navigation Company as an assistant manager in 1882 and promoted him to general manager the next year. In 1884, during the **Sino-French War**, Zheng was commissioned by the chief of defense in Guangdong to be in charge of logistic supply of Taiwan when the French attacked it.

In the following years, Zheng was involved in several exhausting lawsuits and had to retire to Macao. He then focused on writing and published the book *Shenshi weiyan* (Words of Alarm in Times of Peace) in 1894, elaborating his reformist ideas in a systematic way. He put forward the famous concept of "commerce war," arguing that in order to defeat the Western powers, China had to promote commerce. The book was admired by the **Guangxu Emperor** and was also well received by reformer officials such as **Zhang Zhidong** and Li Hongzhang. It even influenced later revolutionaries such as **Sun Yat-sen** and **Mao Zedong**. In his late years, Zheng resumed his commercial activities, serving as the general manager of the **Kaiping Coal Mines** (1891), general manager of the **Hanyeping Coal and Steel Complex** (1896), and president of the board of trustees of the Yue-Han Railway Company (1897).

ZHENG YUXIU (1891–1959). Female diplomat, legalist, and activist of the **Chinese feminist** movement. Born in Xinan, Guangdong Province, into the family of a gentry-official, Zheng demonstrated an independent personality from childhood. At the age of five, she forced her family to give up binding her feet. At the age of 13, after hearing that her family had arranged her marriage, she wrote a letter to the "fiancé" to break the engagement. This rebellious action created a big problem for her at home, but she decided not to compromise. In 1905, Zheng enrolled in a missionary school in Tianjin, and two years later she traveled to Japan, where she joined **Sun Yat-sen**'s **Tongmenghui**. In 1909, Zheng engaged in **Wang Jingwei**'s plan of assassinating **Yuan Shikai**. She delivered bombs to Wang at the Beijing railway station. Although this plan failed, Zheng was involved in the assassination of another imperial official, Liangbi, and this time she succeeded. In 1914, Zheng herself became a target of assassination by Yuan Shikai, and this forced her to leave China for Europe. She studied law at the University of Paris, obtained her MA in law in 1918, and then worked for the Chinese Diplomatic Committee in Paris. In 1919, Zheng participated in the **Paris Peace Conference** as a member of the Chinese delegation. She criticized the conference resolution on China's Shandong issue and strongly opposed China's signing of the treaty. The next year, Zheng returned to China and organized the Chinese female students to Europe for the work-study program. The Chinese students in France totaled 1,000, and more than 30 of them were girls.

Zheng proposed to write women's rights into Chinese laws and established a united league for women's political participation. In 1925, Zheng was appointed president of the Beijing Female Normal University. As a prominent legalist, she published *Introduction to International Organization* and *Comparative Studies of Constitutions*. In 1926, she married her schoolmate Wei Daoming and opened a law firm in Shanghai. Zheng served successively as president of the Shanghai court, chief procurator of Jiangsu Province, a member of the Shanghai municipal committee of the Nationalist Party, a member of the political committee of Jiangsu Province, a member of the Republican Senate, and a member of the Drafting Committee of Civil Law. In 1942, her husband, Wei, was appointed Chinese ambassador to the United States, and Zheng accompanied him to Washington, D.C. The next year, Zheng published her autobiography, *My Revolutionary Years: The Autobiography of Madame Wei Tao-Ming*, in New York. In 1947, she followed her husband to Taipei, where he was made governor of Taiwan. A year later, after Chen Cheng replaced Wei, the couple moved back to the United States and faded out of the political scene. In 1954, Zheng was diagnosed with cancer and one of her arms was amputated. As Zheng was suffering from this illness, she and Wei hoped to return to China. However, neither the mainland nor Taiwan welcomed them back. On 16 December 1959, Zheng died in Los Angeles at the age of 68.

ZHENJIE PAIFANG. *See* MEMORIAL ARCHWAY OF HONORABLE WOMEN.

ZHILI CLIQUE. One of several factions that split from the **Beiyang Army** in the early Republican years. The Zhili Clique was named after the clique's base of power, Zhili Province (today's Hebei). The Zhili Clique also dominated the provinces of Jiangsu, Jiangxi, and

Hubei for a long time. Its major leaders included Feng Guozhang, **Cao Kun**, and **Wu Peifu**, were **Yuan Shikai**'s important military officers in the Beiyang Army. In 1913, Feng Guozhang was sent by Yuan to quell the **Second Revolution** and occupied Nanjing. Later, **Cao Kun** led troops to fight against the Republic Protection Army but was defeated by General **Cai E** in Sichuan. The Zhili Clique engaged in military conflict with **warlords** of other cliques for control of the **Beijing government**, including the Zhili-Anhui War (1920), the First Zhili-Fengtian War (1922), and the Second Zhili-Fengtian War (1924). All these wars had huge costs in terms of human life and economic destruction. In 1927, the **Nationalist Party** launched the **Northern Expedition** against **warlordism**. The leading force of the Zhili Clique was destroyed by the **National Revolutionary Army**, and the political power of the clique was eliminated by the Northern Expedition.

ZHOU ENLAI (1898–1976). Prominent statesman, diplomat, and military leader of the People's Republic of China (PRC). Born in Huai'an, Jiangsu Province, into a family of low-ranking government clerks, Zhou was taken by his uncle to Manchuria at the age of 12 for education. In 1913, Zhou was admitted to the famous Nankai School in Tianjin but traveled instead to Japan and studied at Meiji University, where he was exposed to Marxism. Returning to Nankai in 1919, Zhou enrolled in the literature department but did not attend classes. Instead, he was actively involved in the **May Fourth Movement**, organized the Tianjin student union, and edited its newspaper. He made it the union's mission "to struggle against warlords, imperialism and [to] save China." On Nankai's campus, Zhou established a revolutionary organization, the Awareness Society, with 12 men and eight women. A 15-year-old girl, Deng Yingchao, was one of its members and later became Zhou's wife. In 1920, Zhou joined the work-study program in France. Two years later, Zhou joined the **Chinese Communist Party** (CCP) in Paris and was elected secretary of the European branch of the Chinese Socialist Youth League. In 1924, when **Sun Yat-sen** established his policy of alliance with the CCP, the **Comintern** recommended Zhou for the post of deputy director of the political department at the **Whampoa Military Academy**. During the **Northern Expedition**, Zhou served as the director of the political department in the First Army of the **National Revolutionary Army**.

In 1927, Zhou led a worker uprising in Shanghai in preparation for the arrival of the National Revolutionary Army. When **Chiang Kai-shek** began to purge the Communists in Shanghai, Zhou and other Communist leaders led the **Nanchang Mutiny** on 1 August 1927. Afterward, Zhou engaged in secret work in Shanghai, including espionage and assassination. By the end of 1931, Zhou was transferred to the **Jiangxi Soviet**, serving as the secretary of the CCP Bureau of the Central Soviet Region and the general political commissar of the **Red Army**. In October 1934, after the defeat by Chiang Kai-shek in the fifth **Encirclement and Suppression Campaign**, the Red Army embarked on a great retreat, known as the **Long March**; Zhou Enlai, **Otto Braun**, and **Bo Gu** formed a leading group in charge of political and military affairs. This group proved to be incompetent and caused great losses to the Red Army.

In January 1935, the CCP Politburo held a conference at Zunyi, Guizhou Province, at which Zhou made self-criticisms and took responsibility for the setbacks. **Mao Zedong** became the de facto leader of the CCP. Afterward, Zhou always supported Mao. In 1936, **Zhang Xueliang** and Yang Hucheng kidnapped Chiang Kai-shek in Xi'an. Zhou went to Xi'an for a peace settlement. He successfully persuaded Zhang, Yang, and Chiang to agree on a **united front** to fight the Japanese.

During the **Second Sino-Japanese War**, Zhou served as the resident representative of the CCP in **Chongqing**. At the end of the war, Zhou accompanied Mao to negotiate with Chiang Kai-shek and sign a peace agreement on 10 October 1946. In addition, he worked with the representative of the **Nationalist Party**, Zhang Qun, and American general George Marshall to supervise the cease-fire operations. After the failure of the peace efforts, Zhou returned to **Yan'an**. When the CCP leaders were divided into two working teams, Zhou assisted Mao in commanding the military campaigns of the People's Liberation Army. Zhou showed his great loyalty to Mao. After the establishment of the PRC, Zhou became the head of the government. Zhou served as premier of the PRC from 1949 to his death in 1976 and as concurrent foreign minister from 1949 to 1958.

ZHOU FOHAI (1897–1948). Politician and major Japanese collaborator during the **Second Sino-Japanese War**. Born in Hunan, Zhou traveled to Japan, where he was exposed to communism. In July

1921, Zhou attended the First Congress of the **Chinese Communist Party** (CCP) as a representative of the **Communist group** in Japan, but three years later he withdrew from the CCP and joined the **Nationalist Party** (GMD). Zhou returned to Japan to graduate from the Department of Economics at Kyoto University. He became a follower of **Wang Jingwei** as early as 1927 when Wang opposed **Chiang Kai-shek**'s Nanjing government. After Chiang and Wang reconciled, Zhou served as chief instructor of Chiang's Central Military University. He also served as Chiang's deputy director and deputy minister and acting minister of the GMD Central Propaganda Department.

When the **Second Sino-Japanese War** broke out, Zhou saw no possibility for victory and decided to follow Wang Jingwei to collaborate with the Japanese. He became the number two leader in Wang's puppet government. He held the positions of vice president of the **Executive Yuan**, minister of finance, and mayor of Shanghai. After 1943, Zhou believed that Japan was doomed to lose the Pacific War, and he began to contact Chiang's **Chongqing** government via **Dai Li** and **Du Yuesheng**, promising to atone for his crimes by serving the GMD. He assumed that he could gain a pardon by helping Chiang take over Shanghai after Japan surrendered. However, he was tried as a traitor and sentenced to death, which was then commuted to life imprisonment. He died in jail at the age of 51.

ZHU DE (1886–1976). Communist leader and military commander. Born in Yilong, Sichuan Province, Zhu joined the **Tongmenghui** in 1909. After he graduated from the Yunnan Military Academy in 1913, he served in the Yunnan army and rose from battalion commander to brigade commander. In 1922, Zhu traveled to Germany to study and joined the **Chinese Communist Party** (CCP) in Europe. Three years later, Zhu went to the Soviet Union to receive military training and returned to China the next year. Zhu and other Communist leaders led the first urban insurrection, the **Nanchang Mutiny** on 1 August 1927, and helped to create the Communists' first military force. Zhu was therefore called one of the founders of the **Red Army**. After the failure of the mutiny, Zhu led the remnants to the mountains of **Jinggangshan** to meet **Mao Zedong**'s guerrilla fighters. During the **Jiangxi Soviet** period, Zhu and Mao were so closely associated with each other that peasants referred to "Zhu-Mao" as one person. When the **Returned Bolsheviks** expelled Mao from the leading positions of the Red Army and the party, Zhu remained commander in chief of the Red Army; but the real power fell into the hands of a new "three-man group" headed by the Comintern representative **Otto Braun**. In 1934, Zhu took part in the **Long March**. At the **Zunyi Conference** of 1935, Zhu helped Mao resume his leadership of the army and party. During the **Second Sino-Japanese War**, Zhu was appointed commander in chief of the newly organized Communist troops, the **Eighth Route Army**. Although he was the paramount military leader of the CCP in name, Zhu actually was one of the major assistants of Mao Zedong in commanding the Communist troops. Seeking neither fame nor wealth, Zhu was not involved in any inner-party power struggles. After 1949, Zhu's position as commander in chief of the **People's Liberation Army** became an honorary title; the real headquarters of the Communist military force was the Military Committee of the CCP Central Committee, with Mao Zedong as chair. Zhu concurrently served as one of the vice-chairs of the Military Committee and the president of the Chinese People's Congress.

ZONGLI YAMEN. The office for foreign affairs of the Qing dynasty established in 1861. Literally meaning "office in charge of affairs of all nations," the Zongli Yamen was the first significant institutional innovation made in response to Western impact. It was designed to be a temporary office to centralize the direction of foreign affairs, functioning like a subcommittee of the **Grand Council**. It was divided into five bureaus: British, French, Russian, American, and Coastal Defense. Under the leadership of **Prince Gong**, it played a crucial role in directing foreign relations with the Western powers in the 1860s. Its budget came mainly from the revenue of Chinese customs. The Zongli Yamen was not a policymaking body but an institute of policy execution. The ultimate power in foreign policy and reform programs still rested in the hands of the **Dowager Cixi** and the Grand Council. Nonetheless, the Zongli Yamen designed and promoted a number of modern projects, such as new schools and communication facilities. Its influence rose with the success of Prince Gong, and its members had more chance to be promoted. However, the Zongli Yamen waned after Prince Gong lost power in the 1870s. Its position was further weakened by influential officials such as **Zeng Guofan** and **Li Hongzhang**, who not only controlled military troops but were also deeply involved in foreign affairs. In 1901, the Zongli Yamen was replaced by the Qing Foreign Office.

ZOU RONG (1885–1905). Born into the family of a rich merchant in Baxian, Sichuan Province, Zou was expelled from school because he openly criticized the traditional education system. He then studied English, Japanese, and Western sciences with private Japanese tutors in China and became an active advocate of reform. He traveled to Japan in 1901 for advanced studies, and there he established contacts with revolutionaries. He founded the Association of Chinese Students in Japan and wrote *The Revolutionary Army*, which was published in Shanghai after his return to China in 1903. The book emotionally denounced the **Manchu** rulers, referring to them as the source of China's sufferings and humiliation, thus inspiring the Chinese to revolt. When this book was reprinted in the newspaper *Subao*, it struck a strong chord among readers. The Qing government arrested Zou in the **International Settlement in Shanghai.** Thanks to public protests and the intervention of foreign authorities, the Chinese court in the **foreign concession** imposed on him only a light penalty of two years' imprisonment with hard labor. Due to illness and torture by prison guards, however, Zou died in the jail shortly thereafter at the age of 20.

ZOU TAOFEN (1895–1944). Prominent journalist and political columnist of modern China. Born in Yongan, Fujian Province, Zou graduated from Saint John's University in Shanghai. He began his career as a journalist by editing the *Education and Profession Monthly* in Shanghai. Beginning in November 1926, Zou served as chief editor of *Life Weekly*. He changed the editing policies and made the journal focus on the discussion of social issues. After the **Manchuria Incident** in 1931, this weekly devoted a great deal of space to the anti-Japanese struggle and China's salvation movement, becoming the most popular journal in the country: its circulation reached 155,000 copies. Zou was the first journalist who wrote and published articles on Japanese atrocities and criticized **Chiang Kai-shek's** nonresistance policy. He appealed in the journal for donations to the soldiers fighting the Japanese. Zou opened the Life Hospital for soldiers and civilians wounded in the Shanghai War of 1932. He set up the Life Bookstore Press, translating and publishing revolutionary books. Influenced by *Life Weekly* and books published by Zou, a large number of young readers took part in the Chinese resistance movement and even joined the army or guerrillas.

Zou participated in China's resistance movement with great enthusiasm. On 22 November 1936, Zou and six other intellectuals were arrested by the Nationalist government for organizing the National Salvation Association. He was not released until the war against Japan formally started in 1937. The next year, Zou was made a member of the **National Assembly**, but because he continued to criticize the Chiang Kai-shek government, he was forced to flee to Hong Kong. In January 1942, Zou went to the Communist guerrilla base in Guangdong and was then escorted by the Communists to their northern Jiangsu base, where he continued to write for newspapers. In 1943, he went to Shanghai for medical treatment but died of cancer in spring 1944. According to his last will, he was admitted into the **Chinese Communist Party**. His son, Zou Jiahua, later became vice-premier of the People's Republic of China.

ZUNYI CONFERENCE (1935). An enlarged meeting of the Politburo of the **Chinese Communist Party** (CCP) during the **Long March**. After the **Red Army** retreated from the **Jiangxi Soviet** and started the Long March, it was not able to end the cycle of military failures. In October 1935, the Central Red Army, which consisted of 86,000 men, and the government employees and porters, who numbered 11,000 men, embarked on the journey, but in three months the Communists lost more than 40,000 troops and all the civilian porters. The CCP had to reexamine its military strategy and change its leadership. In early 1935, after the Red Army took over the city of Zunyi, Guizhou, it called an urgent meeting that took place on 15–17 January. The Zunyi Conference witnessed a heated debate on the military strategies and political leadership of the CCP. The majority of the participants criticized the impotent leadership of the three-man leading group, namely the **Comintern**'s adviser **Otto Braun**, **Bo Gu**, and **Zhou Enlai**, and blamed them for the failure of the Jiangxi Soviet and the heavy losses incurred during the Long March. The conference believed that these setbacks in the Chinese Revolution were due to the incorrect guidance of the Comintern and the **Twenty-eight Bolsheviks** who had refused **Mao Zedong**'s military strategies and expelled Mao from his leading positions. The conference elected new leaders of the party, restoring Mao's leadership on the most urgent military affairs.

The Zunyi Conference was Mao's victory over the Twenty-eight Bolsheviks. However, in order to get the recognition of the Comintern, Mao suggested that **Zhang Wentian** (one of the Twenty-eight Bolsheviks) be the party's general secretary. Bo Gu and Braun were dismissed from office and Zhou maintained his position, while Mao became one of the new three-man leading group (with Zhou Enlai and Wang Jiaxiang). The majority of the participants praised Mao Zedong's guerrilla strategy and political programs, believing it necessary to accept Mao's leadership. After the conference, Mao became the de facto supreme leader of the party and army.

ZUO ZONGTANG (1812–1885). General and statesman during the late Qing dynasty. Born in Xiangyin, Hunan Province, Zuo obtained the *juren* degree in 1832 but could not pass the highest level of the **civil service examination**. He served as secretary for several government officials and won the admiration of **Zeng Guofan**, who recommended Zuo for the post of governor of Zhejiang Province. Afterward, Zuo served successively as the governor-general of Fujian and Zhejiang, governor-general of Shaanxi and Gansu, and grand minister of state. His early military career began with the suppression of the **Taiping Rebellion**. In 1860, he commanded 5,000 soldiers recruited in Hunan to form the Chu Army. The army expanded quickly, defeated the Taiping troops, and drove them out of the provinces of Hunan and Guangxi. Four years later, he and Zeng Guofan put down the rebellion. Following Zeng Guofan's plan for military modernization, Zuo established the **Fuzhou dockyard**, which purchased machines from France and hired French engineers. In addition, a naval school was attached with two divisions: one taught the French language and offered courses on shipbuilding, and another taught the English language and courses on navigation.

In 1875, Zuo was appointed military commissioner of Northwest China. For the next 12 years, he engaged in the suppression of several **Muslim rebellion**s in this area. Despite the objection of some high officials in the Qing court, such as **Li Hongzhang**, who emphasized coastal defense only, Zuo insisted on the strategic importance of the western frontiers and launched a military campaign in Xinjiang. He adopted as his military strategy "proceeding slowly but fighting quickly" and finally regained the imperial sovereignty over Xinjiang in 1877. He prompted the Qing court to establish a province in

Xinjiang and advocated the long-standing Chinese practice of "stationing troops to develop wasteland and defend the frontier" (*tunken shubian*) in Xinjiang. He was called back to the city of Fuzhou when the **Sino-French War** broke out, but he was too ill to command troops in battles and died shortly before the two countries signed a treaty. He was posthumously honored as "Wen Xiang." His works were compiled into *Zuo wenxiang gong quanji* (Complete Works of Mr. Zuo Wenxiang).

Appendix 1

Emperors of the Qing Dynasty

Emperor	Name	Birth Year	Ruling Years
Tianming (天命)	Nurhachi (努爾哈赤)	1559	1616–26
Tiancong (天聰)	Huangtaiji (皇太極)	1592	1627–43
Shunzhi (順治)	Fulin (福臨)	1633	1644–61*
Kangxi (康熙)	Xuanye (玄燁)	1654	1662–1722
Yongzheng (雍正)	Yinzhen (胤禛)	1678	1723–35
Qianlong (乾隆)	Hongli (弘歷)	1711	1736–95
Jiaqin (嘉慶)	Yongyan (顒琰)	1760	1796–1820
Daoguang (道光)	Minning (旻寧)	1782	1821–50
Xianfeng (咸豐)	Yining (奕寧)	1831	1851–61
Tongzhi (同治)	Zaichun (載淳)	1856	1862–74
Guangxu (光緒)	Zaitian (載湉)	1871	1875–1908
Xuantong (宣統)	Puyi (溥儀)	1906	1908–12

* Shunzhi was the first emperor of the Qing dynasty after the Manchu conquered China.

Appendix 2

Presidents of the Republic of China (1912–1950)

Time	Name	Title
Jan.–April 1912	Sun Yat-sen (孙中山)	Provisional President
April–Dec. 1912	Yuan Shikai (袁世凯)	Provisional President
1913–Dec. 1915	Yuan Shikai (袁世凯)	President
Dec. 1915– March 1916	Yuan Shikai (袁世凯)	Emperor
March–June 1916	Yuan Shikai (袁世凯)	President
June 1916–17	Li Yuanhong (黎元洪)	President
1917–18	Feng Guozhang (冯国璋)	President
1918–22	Xu Shichang (徐世昌)	President
1921–23	Sun Yat-sen (孙中山)	Extraordinary President
1922–23	Li Yuanhong (黎元洪)	President
1923–24	Cao Kun (曹锟)	President
1924–26	Duan Qirui (段祺瑞)	Provisional Executive
1926–28	Zhang Zuolin (张作霖)	State Head (in the north)
1927–28	Tan Yankai (谭延闿)	Chairman (in the south)
1928–31	Chiang Kai-shek (蒋介石)	Chairman
1931–43	Lin Sen (林森)	Chairman
1931–Jan. 1949	Chiang Kai-shek (蒋介石)	President*
1949–50	Li Zongren (李宗仁)	Acting President

* Chiang Kai-shek was the supreme leader of the Republic of China with different titles: chairman of the Nationalist Government of China (1928–1931), president of the Executive Committee of the Nationalist Party (GMD) (1931–1938), chairman of the National Government (1943–1948), president of the GMD (1938–1975), and president of Republic of China (20 May 1948–21 January 1949, 1950–1975).

Appendix 3

Major Early Universities

By July 1948, China had established 210 institutions of higher education. Of them, 31 were national universities; 25, private universities; 23, national normal and medical schools; 24, provincial colleges; 32, private colleges; 20, national professional schools; 32, provincial professional schools; and 23, private professional schools.

Founding Year   **Name**

FIRST COMPREHENSIVE UNIVERSITY

1898   Imperial University of the Capital (IUC), 京师大学堂[1]

PROFESSIONAL AND NORMAL SCHOOLS

1897   Teachers School of Nanyang College, 南洋公学师范院
1898   Beiyang Railway School, 北洋铁路官学堂
1902   Teachers School of IUC, 京师大学堂师范馆
1902   Sanjiang Normal College, 三江师范学堂
1905   Imperial Polytechnic College, 上海高等实业学堂
1907   Tongji German Medical School, 同济德文医学堂

MILITARY ACADEMIES

1885   Tianjin Military Academy, 天津武备学堂
1906   Beiyang Military Academy, 天津北洋讲武堂
1906   Fengtian Military Academy, 奉天东北讲武堂
1909   Yunnan Military Academy, 云南陆军讲武堂
1912   Baoding Military Academy, 保定陆军军官学校
1924   Whampoa Military Academy, 黄埔军校

MISSIONARY UNIVERSITIES

1900	Soochow University, 东吴大学
1903	Aurora University, 震旦大学
1905	Saint John's University, 圣约翰大学
1910	West China Union University, 华西大学
1910	Central China Union University, 华中大学
1910	Private University of Nanking, 金陵大学
1914	Hangchow Christian College, 之江大学
1914	Hwa Nan College, 华南女子文理学院
1914	Hsiang-Ya Medical College, 湘雅医学院
1914	University of Shanghai, 沪江大学
1915	Ginling College for Women, 金陵女子大學
1916	Canton Christian College, 岭南大学
1917	Cheeloo University, 齐鲁大学
1918	Fukien Christian University, 福州协和大学
1919	Yanching University, 燕京大学
1929	Fu Jen Catholic University, 辅仁大学

OTHER MAJOR UNIVERSITIES

1902	Beiyang University, 北洋大学[2]
1911	Tsinghua College, 清華學堂[3]
1912	Northwest University, 西北大学
1919	Nankai University, 南开大学
1920	University of Communication, 交通大学
1923	Northeast University, 东北大学
1926	Shandong University, 山东大学
1926	Sun Yat-sen University, 中山大学[4]
1927	Chekiang University, 浙江大学
1928	Central University, 中央大学
1928	Wuhan University, 武汉大学
1937	Southwestern Union University, 西南联合大学[5]

NOTES

1. Imperial University of the Capital was renamed Peking University, 北京大学, in 1912.

2. Beiyang University grew out of China's earliest college, Beiyang College, 北洋西学堂(1895).

3. Tsinghua College was a preparatory school for studying abroad. It became a four-year college and was renamed Tsinghua University, 清華大学, in 1925.

4. Sun Yat-sen University grew out of Guangdong University, 广东大学, founded by Sun Yat-sen in 1924.

5. During the Sino-Japanese War, the Japanese troops occupied Northern China. Peking University, Tsinghua University, and Nankai University moved to Southwest China. They united in Kunming to form the Southwest Associated University.

Appendix 4

Early Newspapers and Journals (before 1930)

MAJOR CHINESE NEWSPAPERS

Year	Title	Founder	Place
1860	*Chung Ngoi San Po* (中外新报)	Wu Tingfang	Hong Kong
1862	*Shanghai Xinbao* (上海新报)[1]	M. F. Wood	Shanghai
1872	*Shenbao* (申报)	Frederick Major[2]	Shanghai
1873	*Tusnwan Yat Po* (循环日报)	Wang Tao	Hong Kong
1886	*Guangbao* (广报)	Kuang Qizhao	Guangzhou
1893	*Xinwenbao* (新闻报)	A.W. Danforth	Shanghai
1895	*Zhong Wai Gongbao* (中外公报)	Liang Qichao	Beijing
1896	*Shi Wubao* (时务报)	Huang Zhunxian	Shanghai
1896	*Subao* (苏报)	Wu Zhang	Shanghai
1898	*Wuxi Baihuabao* (无锡白话报)	Qiu Yufang	Wuxi
1899	*Zhongguo Ribao* (中国日报)	Chen Shaobai	Hong Kong
1902	*Tainan Ribao* (台南日报)	Lian Yatang	Taiwan
1902	*Da Gongbao* (大公报)	Ying Lianzhi	Tianjin
1904	*Shibao* (时报)	Di Baoxian	Shanghai
1907	*Shenzhou Ribao* (神州日报)	Yu Youren	Shanghai
1909	*Dajiangbao* (大江报)	Zhan Dapei	Hankou
1916	*Minguo Ribao* (民国日报)	Chen Qimei	Shanghai
1918	*Jingbao* (京报)	Shao Piaoping	Beijing
1920	*Shangbao* (商报)	Tang Jiezhi	Shanghai
1926	*Central Daily News* (中央日报)[3]	GMD	Guangzhou

MAJOR ENGLISH NEWSPAPERS IN CHINA

1850	*North China Herald* (北华捷报)	Henry Sherman	Shanghai
1857	*Daily Press* (孖剌西报)	G. M. Ryder	Hong Kong

1864	*North China Daily News* (字林西报)	Henry Morris	Shanghai
1879	*The Shanghai Mercury* (文汇报)	J. D. Clark	Shanghai
1897	*L'Écho de Chine* (中法新汇报)	J.-Em. Lemière	Shanghai
1903	*South China Morning Post* (南华早报)	A. Cunningham	Hong Kong
1910	*Peking Daily News* (北京英文日报)	Yan Huiqing	Beijing
1911	*China Press* (大陆报)	Wu Tingfang[4]	Shanghai

MAJOR JOURNALS

1867	*Far Eastern Review* (远东评论)	William H. Donald	Shanghai
1874	*Globe Magazine* (万国公报)	Young J. Allen	Shanghai
1898	*The China Discussion* (清议报)	Liang Qichao	Japan
1902	*Xinmin Congbao* (新民丛报)	Liang Qichao	Japan
1904	*Gongfang Zazi* (东方杂志)	Jiang Weiqiao	Shanghai
1905	*Minbao* (民报)	Tongmenghui	Tokyo
1915	*New Youth* (新青年)	Chen Duxiu	Shanghai
1917	*Weekly Review of the Far East* (密勒氏评论)	Thomas Millard	Shanghai
1919	*Xin Chao* (新潮)	Fu Sinian	Beijing
1919	*Jianshe* (建设)	Sun Yat-sen	Shanghai
1922	*Xiang Dao* (向导)	CCP	Shanghai
1922	*Chuangzao* (创造)	Chuangzao Society	Shanghai
1924	*Yusi* (语丝)	Yusi Society	Beijing
1926	*Liang You* (良友)	Wu Liande	Shanghai
1928	*Xinyue* (新月)	Xinyue Society	Shanghai

MAJOR WOMEN'S NEWSPAPERS AND JOURNALS

1898	*Nüxuebao* (女学报), every 10 days	Li Yun	Shanghai
1899	*Nübao* (女报), monthly	Chem Jifen	Shanghai
1904	*Nüzi Shijie* (女子世界), monthly	Ding Chuwo	Shanghai
1905	*Beijing Nübao* (北京女报), daily	Zhang Zhanyun	Beijing
1907	*Zhongguo Nübao* (中国女报), monthly	Qiu Jin	Shanghai
1907	*Shenzhou Nübao* (神州女报), monthly	Chen Yiyi	Shanghai

1911	*Funü Shibao* (妇女时报), monthly	Di Pingzi	Shanghai
1912	*Nü Quan* (女权), monthly	Tongmenghui	Shanghai
1913	*Wanguo Nüzi Canzhenghui Xunbao* (万国女子参政会旬报), every 10 days	Zhang Hanying	Shanghai
1914	*Mei Yu* (眉语), monthly	Gao Jianhua	Shanghai
1915	*Funü Zazhi* (妇女杂志), monthly	Hu Bingxia	Shanghai
1917	*Nü Duo* (女鐸), monthly	Le Liangyue	Shanghai
1922	*Funü Sheng* (妇女声), bimonthly	Li Da	Shanghai
1923	*Funü Zhoubao* (妇女周刊),[5] weekly	Xiang Jingyu	Shanghai
1926	*Xin Nüxing* (新女性), monthly	Zhang Xichen	Shanghai
1930	*Funü Gongming* (妇女共鸣), monthly	Chen Yiyun	Nanjing

NOTES

1. It was the Chinese edition of *North China Herald*.
2. Shi Liangcai bought this newspaper in 1912.
3. This is the official publication of the Nationalist Party (GMD) and it moved to Nanjing in 1929.
4. Wu's partners were B. W. Fleisher and Thomas Millard. The newspaper was sold to Edward Ezra in 1917.
5. *Funü Zhoubao* was a supplement of *Minguo Ribao*.

Appendix 5

Chinese Economy

CHINESE POPULATION AND CULTIVATED LAND (1771–1947)

Year	Cultivated Land*	Population**	Per Capita Cultivated Land*
1771	794,020	214,600	3.70
1800	1,067,323	335,211	3.19
1811	846,317	358,610	2.36
1821	770,200	379,409	2.03
1833	679,986	398,942	1.70
1851	756,287	432,164	1.75
1863	751,762	404,946	1.86
1872	755,536	329,563	2.29
1887	840,842	337,590	2.49
1900	874,784	366,810	2.31
1910	1,455,236	368,147	3.95
1916	1,276,894	509,500	3.12
1934	1,228,367	462,153	2.66
1947	1,410,731	462,798	3.05

* Unit = one thousand mu (one mu equals 1/6 acre).
**Unit = one thousand people.
Source: Ma Yuping and Huang Yuchong, eds., *Zhongguo zuotian yu jintian: 1840–1987 guoqing shouce* [China's Yesterday and Today: A Factbook, 1840–1987] (Beijing: Jiefanjun Chubanshe, 1989), 2.

CHINESE MODERN INDUSTRIES (1895–1920)

Industry	No. of Factories	Capital (in Thousands)	No. of Workers
Before 1895			
Textile	59	7,859	45,268
Chemical	16	2,050	3,571
Food Processing	4	2,016	328
Machinery	14	20,618	3,571
Printing	2	60	300
Metallurgy	2	25,000	3,000
Mintage	2	5,000	647
Ordnance	18	120,000	27,000
Total	117	182,603	83,685
Before 1913			
Textile	231	32,547	157,150
Food Processing	105	18,620	13,700
Printing	25	8,280	8,460
Machinery	101	31,219	18,450
Metallurgy	8	28,100	7,532
Chemical	153	20,127	28,687
Public Service	38	53,700	5,640
Ordnance	23	128,000	28,500
Mintage	5	10,000	1,447
Others	9	231	1,151
Total	698	330,824	270,717
Before 1920			
Textile	475	82,750	358,110
Food Processing	280	63,246	43,150
Printing	51	10,821	11,825
Machinery	252	38,885	25,720
Metallurgy	12	32,150	8,990
Chemical	383	47,558	61,955
Public Service	243	85,377	15,190

Ordnance	23	128,000	28,500
Mintage	5	10,000	1,447
Others	35	1,833	2,735
Total	1,759	500,620	557,622

Source: Calculation based on data in Ma Yuping and Huang Yuchong, eds., *Zhongguo zuotian yu jintian: 1840–1987 guoqing shouce* [China's Yesterday and Today: A Factbook, 1840–1987] (Beijing: Jiefanjun Chubanshe, 1989), 54–55.

THE INDUSTRIAL GROWTH OF CHINA (1895–1949)

Year	Cotton Yarn Spindles (Tons)	Output of Coal (Tons)	Output of Iron (Tons)
1895	174,564	—	—
1913	484,192	12,879,770	267,513
1914	544,780	14,182,330	300,000
1919	658,748	20,146,818	407,743
1920	842,894	21,318,825	429,548
1921	1,248,282	20,507,390	399,413
1922	1,506,634	21,139,918	401,844
1924	1,750,498	25,780,875	360,804
1925	1,866,232	24,255,042	363,836
1927	2,018,588	24,172,009	436,815
1936	2,746,392	39,902,985	809,996
1949	5,200,000	32,000,000	250,000

Source: Ma Yuping and Huang Yuchong, eds., *Zhongguo zuotian yu jintian: 1840–1987 guoqing shouce* [China's Yesterday and Today: A Factbook, 1840–1987] (Beijing: Jiefanjun Chubanshe, 1989), 261–62.

Appendix 6

Chinese Foreign Trade and Foreign Investment in China

FOREIGN TRADE UNDER THE CANTON SYSTEM (VALUE IN SILVER DOLLARS)

Year	Exports from Canton	Imports into Canton	Trade Balance
1817	15,566,461	18,693,440	–3,126,979
1821	20,518,936	21,430,018	–911,082
1825	22,229,791	23,269,060	–1,039,269
1830	17,602,365	26,814,660	–9,212,295

Source: Cheng, Yu-kwei, *Foreign Trade and Industrial Development of China* (Washington, DC: University Press of Washington, D.C., 1956), 6.

OPIUM IMPORTS BEFORE THE OPIUM WAR (VALUE IN SILVER DOLLARS)

Year	Imported Opium (Chests)	Value of the Opium
1830–31	21,849	14,960,695
1831–32	16,225	13,022,703
1832–33	21,609	14,079,600
1833–34	21,177	13,748,916
1834–35	21,885	14,225,250
1835–36	26,000	16,900,000
1836–37	28,307	19,814,900
1837–38	30,000	19,500,000
1838–39	35,500	23,075,000
1839–40	15,619	14,057,100
Total	238,171	163,384,164

Source: Ma Yuping and Huang Yuchong, eds., *Zhongguo de zuotian he jintian: 1840–1987, guoqing shouce* [China's Yesterday and Today: A Factbook, 1840–1987] (Beijing: Jiefanjun Chubanshe, 1989), 6–7.

OPIUM IMPORTS AFTER THE OPIUM WAR (VALUE IN SILVER TAELS)

Year	Imported through Volume (Chests)	Hong Kong Value	Imported through Volume (Chests)	Other Ports Value
1865–69	400,005	181,110,084	288,925	133,297,070
1870–74	450,638	181,367,683	315,321	131,128,282
1875–79	478,673	176,852,531	358,454	152,431,445
1880–84	461,159	176,111,286	351,023	148,178,987
1885–86	186,493	61,348,246	134,433	50,427,475
Total	1,976,968	776,789,830	1,448,156	615,463,259

Source: Ma Yuping and Huang Yuchong, eds., *Zhongguo de zuotian he jintian: 1840–1987, guoqing shouce* [China's Yesterday and Today: A Factbook, 1840–1987] (Beijing: Jiefanjun Chubanshe, 1989), 6–7.

FOREIGN TRADE, 1864–1936 (VALUE IN SILVER TAELS)

Year	Net Export	Net Import	Total Value	Balance
1864	48,655	46,210	94,865	2,445
1865–69	278,822	315,739	594,561	–36,917
1870–74	333,600	341,111	674,711	–7,511
1875–79	356,662	364,338	721,000	–7,676
1880–84	372,020	395,248	767,268	–23,228
1885–89	417,422	513,610	931,032	–96,188
1890–94	535,413	709,664	1,245,077	–174,251
1895–99	792,697	1,051,443	1,844,140	–258,746
1900–1904	996,675	1,465,537	2,462,212	–468,862
1905–9	1,344,379	2,086,435	3,430,814	–742,056
1910–14	1,888,224	2,546,970	4,435,194	–658,746

1915–19	2,480,282	2,722,293	5,202,575	−242,011
1920–24	3,322,462	4,555,036	7,877,498	−1,232,574
1925–29	4,566,310	5,546,766	10,113,076	−980,456
1930–34	3,033,189	5,317,031	8,350,220	−2,283,842
1935–36	822,561	1,194,323	2,016,884	−371,762

Source: Calculation based on data in Cheng Yu-kwei, *Foreign Trade and Industrial Development of China* (Washington, DC: University Press of Washington, D.C., 1956), 258–59.

FOREIGN INVESTMENT IN CHINA
(1900–1948) (VALUE IN MILLION U.S. DOLLARS)

Country	1900	1914	1930	1936	1941	1948
Britain	344.1	664.6	1,047.0	1,045.9	1,095.3	1,033.7
USA	79.4	99.1	285.7	340.5	482.4	1,393.3*
France	211.6	282.5	304.8	311.9	285.1	297.3
Germany	300.7	385.7	174.6	136.4	137.0	—
Japan	53.6	290.9	1,411.6	2,096.4	6,826.0	—
Russia	450.3	440.2	—	—	—	—
Others	69.6	92.7	263.9	354.3	333.0	374.6
Total	1,509.3	2,255.7	3,487.6	4,285.4	9,158.8	3,098.9*

*This does not include the American economic aid to China, totaling $470,920,000.

Source: Ma Yuping and Huang Yuchong, eds., *Zhongguo zuotian yu jintian: 1840–1987, guoqing shouce* [China's Yesterday and Today: A Factbook, 1840–1987] (Beijing: Jiefanjun Chubanshe, 1989), 283.

Glossary

AB tuan (AB团): Anti-Bolshevik League

bai shangdi hui (拜上帝会): God Worshipping Society

baihuawen (白话文): vernacular Chinese

baoyi (包衣): house clave of Manchu nobles

Beijing nübao (北京女报): Beijing Women's News

biantong qizhi chu (变通旗制处): Banner Reorganization Office

caoyun (漕运): tributary grain shipment

changmao (长毛): nickname for the Taiping rebels

chou'anhui (筹安会): Peace-Planning Society

chuangzaoshe (创造社): Creation Society

chuilian tingzheng (垂帘听政): Listening to politics behind the silk curtain

dadaohui (大刀会): Big Swords Society

Datong shu (大同书): *The Book of Universal Commonwealth*

fabi (法币): legal tender

fengshui (风水): Chinese geomancy

gelaohui (哥老会): Society of Brothers and Elders

guan du shang ban (官督商办): government-supervised merchant undertakings

guangfuhui (光复会): Recovery Society

Haiguo tuzhi (海国图志): *Illustrated Treatise on the Maritime Kingdoms*

hongmen (洪门): Hong League

hongxian (洪宪): Glorious Constitution

huaxinghui (华兴会): China Revival Society

huaijun (淮军): Anhui Army

Ili jiangjun (伊犁将车): military governor of Ili

jiaguwen (甲骨文): oracle bone script

jiancha yuan (监察院): Control Yuan

jing miao bu jing shen (敬庙不敬神): worship the temple but not the gods inside

jing shi zhi yong(经世致用): knowledge for practice
Jingbao (京报): *Beijing Daily*
Jinling kejing chu (金陵刻经处): Jinling Buddhist Printing House
jinyuanjuan (金元券): gold yuan
junjichu (军机处): Grand Council
jinshi (进士): highest degree in the civil service examination
juren (举人): middle degree in the civil service examination
Kangda (抗大): Anti-Japanese Military and Political University
kaoshi yuan (考试院): Examination Yuan
kaozheng (考证): eventual research
keju (科举): civil service examination
lifa yuan (立法院): Legislative Yuan
lifan yuan (理藩院): Office of Border Affairs
lijin (厘金): transportation tax
lüyingjun (绿营军): Green Standard Army
majiang (麻将): mahjong
Minbao (民报): People's Journal
qianzhuang (钱庄): native bank
qingbang (青帮): Green Gang
qingyipai (清议派): Qingyi Party
Qingyibao (清议报): Qingyi Journal
ruxue, rujiao (儒学, 儒教): Confucianism
shangwu yinshu guan (商务印书馆): Commercial Press
shantouzhuyi (山头主义): "Mountain Stronghold" mentality
Shenbao (申报): Shanghai News
sifa yuan (司法院): Judicial Yuan
taiping tianguo (太平天国): Heavenly Kingdom of Great Peace
tianming (天命): Mandate of Heaven
tiandihui (天地会): Heaven and Earth Society
tianwang (天王): Heavenly King
tianzuhui (天足会): Natural-Foot Society
tongmenghui (同盟会): United League
tongwenguan (同文馆): School of Foreign Language
Wanguo gongbao (万国公报): Globe Magazine
xiangjun (湘军): Hunan Army
xiaodaohui (小刀会): Small Swords Society
xinhai geming (辛亥革命): Republican Revolution
xingzheng yuan (行政院): Executive Yuan
xingzhonghui (兴中会): Revive China Society
xinyueshe (新月社): Crescent Moon Society

xiucai (秀才): primary degree in the civil service examination
yi min shi yi (以民制夷): use the people to control the barbarians
yi yi zhi yi (以夷制夷): use barbarians to control the barbarians
yuan ming yuan (圆明园): Old Summer Palace
yuanyang hudie pai (鸳鸯蝴蝶派): Butterflies fiction
zhenjie paifang (贞节牌坊): Memorial Archway for Honorable
    Women
Zhongguo nübao (中国女报): Chinese Women's Journal
ziqianghui (自强会): Self-Strengthening Society
zizheng yuan (咨政院): Consultative Assembly
zongli yamen (总理衙门): Office for General Management

Bibliography

CONTENTS

INTRODUCTION

This selected bibliography directs the reader to major English-language writings on modern China, 1800–1949. Works on Chinese politics, economy, military, foreign relations, society, and culture during this period have been abundant, and more literature continues to appear each year. Included in the bibliography are the most important monographs by university and commercial publishers and some scholarly articles on refereed journals. They are selected for various reasons. First, priority is given to recent scholarship—the works that speak to academic and popular concerns for new facts and interpretations. The rich collection of these works is due to the new approach to China's modernization process during the late Qing period and a revisionist perspective on the Republican history. Second, the bibliography includes classics in their fields that stand the test of time. The reader can always benefit from these original and substantial research works. Third, while some books on important subjects require updating, they are included because no new research works are available. These works are highly provocative, suggesting directions for further exploration.

In a sense, the bibliography shows both our historical heritage and the fruits of new academic inquiries. This is reflected in the coverage of the bibliography, in which more works on politics, military, and foreign relations indicate the efforts of scholars in past years, but other collections indicate their shifting attention from previous foci of research to a study of the economic, social, and cultural dimensions of modern China. More importantly, an increasing number of interdisciplinary studies are introduced in the list. Although each title is put into one subsection, they discuss wider issues than the headings or subheadings indicate. In an attempt to provide the reader with a brief guide to general information on modern China, purely theoretical discussion and technique-oriented books are excluded. For the same purpose, only a few works on fiction, arts, and cinema are listed. Moreover, the bibliography does not cover the Chinese-language literature published in mainland China, Taiwan, and Hong Kong, except for those that have been translated into English.

The bibliography is topically divided into several sections and subsections with headings and subheadings. In each subsection, books and articles are arranged alphabetically by author. The list begins with major reference books, bibliographies, encyclopedias, dictionaries, and survey histories, which provide the reader with the necessary background knowledge and research sources for modern China. More often than not, some works in different sections approach the same subject from different angles, so the reader should use cross-referencing skills to get related information and further analyses of the given event, person, or issue. For example, the reader can find the full body of material treating Sun Yat-sen in the subsections of Sun Yat-sen, The Public, Law and Constitution, Revolutionary Theory, and others.

The works in this list are available in most research libraries or can be obtained through library loans by the reader. The most important archival collection of materials for the study of Manchu dynasty are the First National Historical Archives in the Forbidden City, Beijing, and for the Republican period, the Second Historical Archives in Nanjing and the National Archives of the Republic of China in Taipei. In addition, numerous local and private archives have recently been opened to the public in mainland China. As is known, the Library of Congress possesses the most valuable English- and Chinese-language collections in the United States. Finally, so many electronic resources have been developed, including digital libraries, websites, databases, e-journals, and so on, that the reader can easily find user-friendly launching pads for further search and reading.

GENERAL WORKS

Bibliography and Sourcebooks

Chan, Wing-tsi, trans. *A Sourcebook in Chinese Philosophy.* Princeton, NJ: Princeton University Press, 1969.

Brook, Timothy. *Geographical Sources of Ming-Qing History.* Ann Arbor: Center for Chinese Studies, University of Michigan, 2003.

Cheng, Pei-kai, Michael Elliot Lestz, and Jonathan D. Spence, eds. *The Search for Modern China: A Documentary Collection.* New York: W. W. Norton, 1999.

Clubb, O. Edmund. *Twentieth Century China.* New York: Columbia University Press, 1978.

de Bary, William Theodore, and Richard J. Lufrano. *Sources of Chinese Tradition: From 1600 through the Twentieth Century.* New York: Columbia University Press, 2001.

Hayford, Charles W., comp. *China.* World Bibliographical Series, vol. 35. Oxford: Clio Press, 1997.

Hutchings, Graham. *Modern China: A Guide to a Century of Change.* Cambridge, MA: Harvard University Press, 2001.

Skinner, G. William, and Winston Hsieh. *Modern Chinese Society and Analytic Bibliography.* Stanford, CA: Stanford University Press, 1973.

Ye, Wa, and Joseph W. Esherick. *Chinese Archives: An Introductory Guide.* Berkeley: University of California Press, 1996.

Zurmdorfer, Harriet T. *China Bibliography: A Research Guide to Reference Works about China Past and Present.* Leiden: Brill, 1995.

Dictionaries and Encyclopedias

Boorman, Howard L., ed. *Biographical Dictionary of Republican China.* New York: Columbia University Press, 1970.

Brandon,-James R., ed. *The Cambridge Guide to Asian Theatre.* Cambridge: Cambridge University Press, 1993.

Copper, John F. *Historical Dictionary of Taiwan (Republic of China).* Lanham, MD: Scarecrow Press, 2007.

Guo, Jian, Yongyi Song, and Yuan Zhou. *Historical Dictionary of the Chinese Cultural Revolution.* Lanham, MD: Scarecrow Press, 2007.

Hook, Brian, ed. *The Cambridge Encyclopedia of China.* Cambridge: Cambridge University Press, 1991.

Hummel, Arthur, ed. *Eminent Chinese of the Ch'ing Period (1644–1911).* Washington, DC: U.S. Government Printing Office, 1944.

Hucker, Charles O. *A Dictionary of Official Titles in Imperial China.* Stanford, CA: Stanford University Press, 1985.

Klein, Donald W., and Anne B. Clark, eds. *Biographic Dictionary of Chinese Communism, 1921–1965.* Cambridge, MA: Harvard University Press, 1971.

Lamb, Malcolm. *Dictionary of Officials and Organizations in China: A Quarter Century Guide.* Armonk, NY: M. E. Sharpe, 1994.

Leung, Pak-Wah. *Historical Dictionary of the Chinese Civil War.* Lanham, MD: Scarecrow Press, 2002.

Schoppa, R. Keith. *The Columbia Guide to Modern Chinese History.* New York: Columbia University Press, 2000.

Sullivan, Lawrence R. *Historical Dictionary of the People's Republic of China.* 2nd ed. Lanham, MD: Scarecrow Press, 2007.

Atlases and Photographs

Donald, Stephanie Hemelryk, and Robert Benewick. *Pocket China Atlas: Maps and Facts at Your Fingertips.* Berkeley: University of California Press, 2008.

Gamble, Sidney D. *Sidney Gamble's China Revisited: Photographs by Sidney D. Gamble from 1917 to 1931.* New York: China Institute, 2004.

Harris, David, and Lyman Van Slyke. *Of Battle and Beauty: Felice Beato's Photographs of China.* Berkeley: University of California Press, 2000.

Hsieh, Chiao-min, and Jean Chine Hsieh. *China: A Provincial Atlas.* New York: Macmillian, 1995.

Lucas, Christopher J., ed. *James Ricalton's Photographs of China during the Boxer Rebellion: His Illustrated Travelogue of 1900.* Lewiston, NY: Edwin Mellen, 1990.

Pearce, Nick. *Photographs of Peking, China 1861–1908: An Inventory and Description of the Yetts Collection at the University of Durham, N.C.: Through Peking with a Camera.* Lewiston, NY: Edwin Mellen, 2005.

Spence, Jonathan D. *The Chinese Century: The Photographic History of the Last Hundred Years.* New York: Random House, 1996.

Survey Histories and Historiography

Bailey, Paul John. *China in the Twentieth Century.* Oxford: Blackwell, 2001.

Cohen, Paul A. *China Unbound: Evolving Perspectives on Chinese Past.* New York: Routledge Curzon, 2003.

———. *Discovering History in China: American Historical Writing on the Recent Chinese Past.* New York: Columbia University Press, 1984.

Dirlik, Arif. "Post Modernism and Chinese History." *Boundary* 28, no. 3 (2001).

———. "Reversals, Ironics, Hegemonies: Notes on the Contemporary Historiography of Modern China." *Modern China* 22, no. 3 (1996).

Duara, Prasenjit. *Rescuing History from the Nation.* Chicago: University of Chicago Press, 1995.

Esherick, Joseph W. "Harvard on China: The Apologetics of Imperialism." *Bulletin of Concerned Asian Scholars* (November–December 1972).

Fairbank, John K. *The Great Chinese Revolution 1800–1985.* New York: Harper & Row, 1986.

Fairbank, John K., and Albert Feuerwerker. *The Cambridge History of China, Republican China 1912–1949,* vol. 12. Cambridge: Cambridge University Press, 1986.

Fairbank, John K., and Kwang-Ching Liu, eds. *The Cambridge History of China: Late Ch'ing 1800–1911,* vol. 10. Cambridge: Cambridge University Press, 1978.

Fairbank, John King, Martha Henderson Coolidge, and Richard J. H. B. Smith. *Morse: Customs Commissioner and Historian of China.* Lexington: University Press of Kentucky, 1995.

Fairbank, John King, and Merle Goldman, eds. *China: A New History,* Cambridge, MA: Harvard University Press, 1998.

Fenby, Jonathan. *Modern China: The Rise and Fall of a Great Power, 1850–2008.* New York: HarperCollins, 2008.

Feuerwerker, Murphey, Rhoads Murphey, and Mary C. Wright, eds. *Approaches to Modern Chinese History.* Berkeley: University of California Press, 1967.

Goldman, Merle, and Leo Ou-fan Lee. *An Intellectual History of Modern China.* Cambridge: Cambridge University Press, 2002.

Hammond, Kenneth J., and Kristin Stapleton, eds. *The Human Tradition in Modern China.* Lanham, MD: Rowman & Littlefield, 2007.

Honig, Emily, Jonathan Lipman, and Gail Hershatter. *Remapping China: Fissures in Historical Terrain.* Berkeley: University of California Press, 1993.

Hsieh, Winston. *Chinese Historiography on the Revolution of 1911: A Critical Survey and a Selected Bibliography.* Stanford, CA: Hoover Institution Press, 1975.

Hsu, Immanuel C. Y., *The Rise of Modern China.* New York: Oxford University Press, 2000.

Lawrance, Alan. *China since 1919: Revolution and Reform: A Sourcebook.* New York: Routledge, 2004.

Mackerras, Colin. *China in Transformation 1900–1949.* White Plains, NY: Longman, 1998.

Peterson, Willard J., ed. *The Cambridge History of China: Part 1. The Ch'ing Empire to 1800.* Cambridge: Cambridge University Press, 2003.

Roberts, J. A. G. *A Concise History of China.* Cambridge, MA: Harvard University Press, 1999.

Roy, Denny. *Taiwan: A Political History.* Ithaca, NY: Cornell University Press, 2003.

Schoppa, R. Keith. *Twentieth Century China: A History in Documents.* New York: Oxford University Press, 2004.

Spence, Jonathan D. *The Search for Modern China,* New York: W. W. Norton & Company, 2001.

Vohra, Ranbir. *China's Path to Modernization: A Historical Review from 1800 to the Present.* Englewood Cliffs, NJ: Prentice Hall, 1999.
Wakeman, Frederic E., Joseph Esherick, Wen-Hsin Yeh, and Madeleine Zelin. *Empire, Nation, and Beyond: Chinese History in Late Imperial and Modern Times.* Berkeley: Institute of East Asian Studies, University of California, 2006.
Wasserstrom, Jeffery, ed. *Twentieth-Century China: New Approaches.* New York: Routledge, 2003.

POLITICS

General

Fu, Zhengyuan. *Autocratic Tradition and Chinese Politics.* New York: Cambridge University Press, 1994.
Jenner, W. J. F. *The Tyranny of History: The Roots of China's Crisis.* New York: Penguin, 1994.
Lee, Ching Kwan, and Guobin Yang, eds. *Re-envisioning the Chinese Revolution: The Political and Poetics of Collective Memory in Reform China.* Stanford, CA: Stanford University Press, 2007.
Lee, James Z. *One Quarter of Humanity: Malthusian Mythology and Chinese Realities, 1700–2000.* Cambridge, MA: Harvard University Press, 1999.
Lieberthal, Kenneth. *Governing China: From Revolution through Reform.* New York: W. W. Norton, 2004.

Manchu Dynasty

Andrade, Tonio. *How Taiwan Became Chinese: Dutch, Spanish and Han Colonization in the Seventeenth Century.* New York: Columbia University Press, 2008.
Anthony, Robert J., and Kate Jane Leonard, eds. *Dragons, Tigers, and Dogs: Qing Crisis Management and the Boundaries of State Power in Late Imperial China.* Ithaca, NY: East Asia Program, Cornell University, 2003.
Banno, Masataka. *China and the West, 1858–1861: The Origins of the Tsungli Yamen.* Cambridge, MA: Harvard University Press, 1964.
Bartlett, Beatrice S. *Monarchs and Ministers: The Grand Council in Mid-Ch'ing China, 1783–1820.* Berkeley: University of California Press, 1994.
Bays, Daniel H. "The Nature of Provincial Political Authority in Late Ch'ing Times: Chang Chih-tung in Canton, 1884–1889." *Modern Asian Studies* (October 1970).
Bello, David Anthony. *Opium and the Limits of Empire: Drug Prohibition in the Chinese Interior, 1729–1850.* Cambridge, MA: Asia Center, Harvard University, 2005.

Benedict, Carol. *Bubonic Plague in 19th Century China*. Stanford, CA: Stanford University Press, 1996.

Bickley, Gillian, ed. *A Magistrate's Court in Nineteenth Century Hong Kong: Court in Time*. Hong Kong: Chinese University Press: 2005.

Chang, Hsin-pao. *Commissioner Lin and the Opium War*. Cambridge, MA: Harvard University, 1964.

Chu, T'ung-tsu. *Local Government in China under the Ch'ing*. Cambridge, MA: Council on East Asian Studies, Harvard University, 1962.

Crossley, Pamela Kyle. *Orphan Warriors: Three Manchu Generations and the End of the Qing World*. Princeton, NJ: Princeton University Press, 1990.

Dunnell, Ruth W. *New Qing Imperial History: The Making of Inner Asian Empire at Qing Chengde*. New York: Routledge Curzon, 2004.

Elliott, Mark C. *The Manchu Way: The Eight Banners and Ethnic Identity in Late Imperial China*. Stanford, CA: Stanford University Press, 2001.

Fay, Peter W. *The Opium War: Barbarians in the Celestial Empire in the Early Part of the Nineteenth Century and the War by Which They Forced Her Gates Ajar*. Chapel Hill: University of North Carolina Press, 1998.

Hansson, Anders. *Chinese Outcasts: Discrimination and Emancipation in Late Imperial China*. Leiden: Brill, 1996.

Hickey, Paul Christopher. *Bureaucratic Centralization and Public Finance in Late Qing China, 1900–1911*. Cambridge, MA: Harvard University Press, 1990.

Huang Pei. *Autocracy at Work, a Study of the Yung-cheng Period, 1723–1735*. Bloomington: Indiana University Press, 1974.

Isett, Christopher M. *State, Peasant, and Merchant in Qing Manchuria, 1644–1862*. Stanford, CA: Stanford University Press, 2006.

Jones, William C., trans. *The Great Qing Code: A New Translation*. New York: Oxford University Press, 1994.

Kuhn, Philip. *Rebellion and Its Enemies in Late Imperial China: Militarization and Social Structure, 1796–1864*. Cambridge, MA: Harvard University Press, 1970.

Kuhn, Philip, and Timothy Brook, eds. *National Polity and Local Power: The Transformation of Late Imperial China*. Cambridge, MA: Council on East Asian Studies, Harvard University, 1989.

Lee, Dominic S. F. *The American Missionaries, the Mandarins and the Opium War: Canton, China (circa 1839)*. Anchorage: Little Susitna Press, 2000.

Liu, Kwang-ching. "The Limits of Regional Power in the Late Ch'ing Period: A Reappraisal." *Tsing Hua Journal of Chinese Studies* (July 1974).

Min Tu-ki. *National Polity and Local Power: The Transformation of Late Imperial China*. Cambridge, MA: Harvard University Press, 1989.

Peers, Chris, and Christa Hook. *Late Imperial Chinese Armies 1520–1840*. London: Reed International Books, 1997.

Perdue, Peter C. *China Marches West: The Qing Conquest of Central Eurasia*. Cambridge, MA: Harvard University Press, 2005.

Polachek, James M. *The Inner Opium War.* Cambridge, MA: Council on East Asian Studies, Harvard University, 1992.

Pong, David. *Shen Pao-chen and China's Modernization in the Nineteenth Century.* New York: Cambridge University Press, 1994.

Reardon-Anderson, James. *Reluctant Pioneers: China's Expansion Northward, 1644–1937.* Stanford, CA: Stanford University Press, 2005.

Reed, Bradly. *Talons and Teeth: County Clerks and Runners in the Qing Dynasty.* Stanford, CA: Stanford University Press, 2000.

Strassberg, Richard E., contr. and trans. *Inscribed Landscapes: Travel Writing from Imperial China.* Berkeley: University of California Press, 1994.

Struve, Lynn A., ed. and trans. *Voices from The Ming-Qing Cataclysm: China in Tiger's Jaw.* New Haven, CT: Yale University Press, 1993.

Vollmer, John. *Ruling from the Dragon Throne: Costume of the Qing Dynasty, 1644–1911.* Berkeley: Ten Speed Press, 2003.

Wakeman, Frederic E., Joseph Esherick, Wen-Hsin Yeh, and Madeleine Zelin. *Empire, Nation, and Beyond: Chinese History in Late Imperial and Modern Times.* Berkeley: Institute of East Asian Studies, University of California, 2006.

Wakeman, Frederic E., and Carolyn Grant, eds. *Conflict and Control in Late Imperial China.* Berkeley: University of California Press, 1975.

Waley, Arthur. *The Opium War through Chinese Eyes.* Stanford, CA: Stanford University Press, 1968.

Wong, J. Y. *Deadly Dreams: Opium and the Arrow War (1856–1860) in China.* New York: Cambridge University Press, 1998.

Wright, Mary C., ed. *China in Revolution: The First Phase, 1900–1913.* New Haven, CT: Yale University Press, 1968.

Reforms

Bays, Daniel H. *China Enters the Twentieth Century: Chang Chih-Tung and the Issues of a New Age, 1895–1909.* Ann Arbor: University of Michigan Press, 1978.

Cohen, Paul A. *Between Tradition and Modernity: Wang Tao and Reform in Late Ching China.* Cambridge, MA: Council on East Asian Studies, Harvard University, 1987.

Cohen, Paul, and John Schrecker, eds. *Reform in Nineteenth Century China.* Cambridge, MA: Harvard University Press, 1976.

Esherick, Joseph W. *Reform and Revolution in China: The 1911 Revolution in Hunan and Hubei.* Ann Arbor: Center for Chinese Studies, University of Michigan, 1999.

Karl, Rebecca E., and Peter Gue Zarrow, eds. *Rethinking the 1898 Reform Period: Political and Cultural Change in Late Qing China.* Cambridge, MA: Asia Center, Harvard University, 2002.

Kwong, Luke S. K. *A Mosaic of the Hundred Days: Personalities, Politics, and Ideas of 1898.* Cambridge, MA: Harvard University Press, 1984.

———. *T'an Ssu-t'ung, 1865–1898: Life and Thought of a Reformer.* Leiden: Brill, 1996.

Reynolds, Douglas R., ed. and trans. *China, 1895–1912: State Sponsored Reforms and China's Late-Qing Revolution: Selected Essays from Zhongguo Jindai Shi.* Armonk, NY: M. E. Sharpe, 1995.

———. *China, 1898–1912: The Xinzheng Revolution and Japan.* Cambridge, MA: Council on East Asian Studies, Harvard University, 1993.

Wright, Mary C. *The Last Stand of Chinese Conservatism: The T'ung-chih Restoration, 1863–1874.* Stanford, CA: Stanford University Press, 1969.

Qing Rulers

Aisin-Gioro, Pu Yi. *From Emperor to Citizen: The Autobiography of Aisin-Gioro Pu Yi.* Translated by W. J. F. Jenner. New York: Oxford University Press, 1987.

Bland, J. O. *China under the Empress Dowager.* New York: Krishna Press, 1972.

Chen, Keji, ed. *Imperial Medicaments: Medical Prescriptions Written for Empress Dowager Cixi and Emperor Guangxu with Commentary.* Beijing: Foreign Languages Press, 1996.

Leonard, Jane Kate. *Controlling from Afar: The Daoguang Emperor's Management of the Grand Canal Crisis, 1824–1826.* Ann Arbor: Center for Chinese Studies, University of Michigan, 1996.

Rawski, Evely. *The Last Emperors: A Social History of Qing Imperial Institutions.* Berkeley: University of California Press, 1998.

Seagrave, Sterling. *Dragon Lady: The Life and Legend of the Last Empress of China.* New York: Knopf, 1992.

The Republic

Bedeski, Robert E. *State-Building in Modern China: The Kuomintang in the Prewar Period.* Berkeley: Institute of East Asian Studies, University of California, 1981.

Bergere, Marie-Claire. *The Golden Age of the Chinese Bourgeoisie, 1911–1937.* New York: Cambridge University Press, 1989.

Chen, Leslie H. Dingyam. *Chen Jiongming and the Chinese Federalist Movement: Regional Leadership and Nation Building in Early Republican China.* Ann Arbor: Center for Chinese Studies, University of Michigan, 1999.

Des Forges, Roger. *Hsi-liang and the Chinese National Revolution.* New Haven, CT: Yale University Press, 1973.

Dutton, Michel. *Policing Chinese Politics: A History.* Durham, NC: Duke University Press, 2005.

Eastman, Lloyd. *The Abortive Revolution: China under Nationalist Rule, 1927–1937.* Cambridge, MA: Harvard University Press, 1974.

Eastman, Lloyd., et al. *The Nationalist Era in China, 1927–1949.* Cambridge: Cambridge University Press, 1991.

Eugenia Lean. *Public Passions: The Trial of Shi Jianqiao and the Rise of Popular Sympathy in Republican China.* Berkeley: University of California Press, 2007.

Fewsmith, Joseph. *Party, State and Local Elites in Republican China: Merchant Organizations and Politics in Shanghai, 1890–1930.* Honolulu: University of Hawaii Press, 1984.

Fung, Edmund. *In Search of Chinese Democracy: Civil Opposition in Nationalist China.* Cambridge: Cambridge University Press, 2000.

Geisert, Bradley K. *Radicalism and Its Demise: The Chinese Nationalist Party, Factionalism, and Local Elites in Jiangsu Province, 1924–1931.* Ann Arbor: Center for Chinese Studies, University of Michigan, 2001.

Hamilton, William Stenhouse. *Notes from Old Nanking, 1947–1949: The Great Transition.* Canberra: Australian National University Press, 2004.

Houn, Franklin. *Central Government of China, 1912–1928: An Institutional Study.* Madison: University of Wisconsin Press, 1957.

Huang, Jianli. *The Politics of Depoliticization in Republican China: Guomindang Policy Towards Student Political Activism, 1927–1949.* New York: Peter Lang, 1998.

Huters, Theodore. *Bringing the World Home: Appropriating the West in Late Qing and Early Republican China.* Honolulu: University of Hawai'i Press, 2005.

Jordan, Donald. *The Northern Expedition: China's National Revolution of 1926–1928.* Honolulu: University of Hawai'i Press, 1976.

Levich, Eugene William. *The Kwangsi Way in Kuomintang China, 1931–1939.* Armonk, NY: M. E. Sharpe, 1993.

Mi, Chan-chen, and Zhao Wang. *The Life of General Yang Hucheng.* Hong Kong: Joint Publishing Company, 1981.

Nathan, Andrew. *Peking Politics, 1918–1923: Factionalism and the Failure of Constitutionalism.* Ann Arbor: Center for Chinese Studies, University of Michigan, 1998.

Scalapino, R., and George T. Yu. *The Chinese Anarchist Movement.* Berkeley: University of California Press, 1969.

Sheridan, James E. *China in Disintegration: The Republican Era in Chinese History, 1912–1949.* New York: Free Press, 1970.

Shih, Paul K. T., ed. *The Strenuous Decade: China's Nation-Building Efforts, 1927–1937.* Jamaica, NY: St. John's University Press, 1970.

Strauss, Julia C. *Strong Institutions in Weak Polities: State Building in Republican China, 1927–1940.* Oxford: Clarendon Press, 1998.

Tien, Hon-mao. *Government and Politics in Kuomintang China, 1927–1937.* Stanford, CA: Stanford University Press, 1972.

Wang, Cheng. *The Kuomintang: A Sociological Study of Demoralization. China during the Interregnum, 1911–1949.* New York: Garland, 1982.

Wasserstrom, Jeffrey. *Student Protests in Twentieth-Century China: The View from Shanghai.* Stanford, CA: Stanford University Press, 1991.

Wakeman, Frederic E. *Spymaster: Dai Li and the Chinese Secret Service.* Berkeley: University of California Press, 2003.

———, ed. *Reappraising Republican China.* Oxford: Oxford University Press, 2000.

Wilbur, C. Martin. *The Nationalist Revolution in China, 1923–1928.* Cambridge: Cambridge University Press, 1984.

Woodhouse, Eiko. *The Chinese Hsinhai Revolution: G. E. Morrison and Anglo-Japanese Relations, 1897–1920.* New York: Routledge Curzon, 2004.

Law and Constitution

Bernhardt, Kathryn, and Philip C. Huang. *Civil Law in Qing and Republican China.* Stanford, CA: Stanford University Press, 1994.

Bickley, Gillian, ed. *A Magistrate's Court in Nineteenth Century Hong Kong: Court in Time.* Hong Kong: Chinese University Press, 2005.

Cohen, Jerome, Randle Edwards, and Fu-mei Chang Chen, eds. *Essays on China's Legal Tradition.* Princeton, NJ: Princeton University Press, 1980.

Fairbank, John K. *Chinese Thought and Institutions.* Chicago: University of Chicago Press, 1957.

Huang, Philip C. *Code, Custom and Legal Practice in China: The Qing and the Republic Compared.* Stanford, CA: Stanford University Press, 2001.

———. *Civil Justice in China: Representation and Practice in the Qing.* Stanford, CA: Stanford University Press, 1998.

Jones, William C., trans. *The Great Qing Code: A New Translation.* New York: Oxford University Press, 1994.

Macauley, Melissa A. *Social Power and Legal Culture: Litigation Masters in Late Imperial China.* Stanford, CA: Stanford University Press, 1998.

Pan, Wei-tung, *The Chinese Constitution: A Study of Forty Years of Constitution-Making in China.* Westport, CT: Hyperion Press, 1983.

Sun Yat-sen

Bergere, Marie-Claire. *Sun Yat-sen.* Stanford, CA: Stanford University Press, 1998.

Janse, Maqrrius. *The Japanese and Sun Yat-sen.* Cambridge, MA: Harvard University Press, 1954.

Lum, Yansheng Ma, and Raymond Mun Kong Lum. *Sun Yat-Sen in Hawai'i: Activities and Supporters.* Honolulu: University of Hawai'i Press, 1999.

Lyon, Sharman. *Sun Yat-sen: His Life and Its Meaning; A Critical Biography.* Stanford, CA: Stanford University Press, 1968.

Schiffrin, Harold Z. *Sun Yat-sen and the Origins of the Chinese Revolution.* Berkeley, University of California Press, 1968.

———. *Sun Yat-sen, Reluctant Revolutionary.* Boston: Little, Brown and Co., 1980.

Sun, Yat-sen. *The Triple Demism of Sun Yat-Sen.* Translated by Pasquale d'Elia. New York: AMS Press, 1974.

Widmer, Ellen, and Kang-I Sun Chang. *Sun Yat-sen: Frustrated Patriot.* New York: Columbia University Press, 1976.

Chiang Kai-shek

Chieh-Ju, Chen. *Chiang Kai-Shek's Secret Past: The Memoir of His Second Wife, Chen Chieh-Ju.* Contr. Lloyd E. Eastman. Boulder, CO: Westview, 1994.

Crozier, Brian, and Eric Chou. *The Man Who Lost China: The First Full Biography of Chiang Kai-Shek.* New York: Scribner, 1976.

Fenby, Jonathan. *Chiang Kai-shek: China's Generalissimo and the Nation He Lost.* New York: Carroll & Graf, 2004.

Furuya, Keiji, and Chung-ming Chang. *Chiang Kai-Shek: His Life and Times.* New York: St. John's University Press, 1981.

Loh, Pichon Pei Yung. *The Early Chiang Kai-shek: A Study of His Personality and Politics, 1887–1924.* New York: Columbia University Press, 1971.

Sainsbury, Keith. *The Turning Point: Roosevelt, Stalin, Churchill, and Chiang-Kai-Shek, 1943—The Moscow, Cairo, and Teheran Conferences.* Oxford: Oxford University Press, 1985.

Revolutionary Theory

Apter, David E., and Tony Saich. *Revolutionary Discourse in Mao's Republic.* Cambridge, MA: Harvard University Press, 1994.

Bernal, Martin. *Chinese Socialism to 1907.* Ithaca, NY: Cornell University Press, 1976.

Dirlik, Arif. *Anarchism in the Chinese Revolution.* Berkeley: University of California Press, 1991.

———. *Marxism in the Chinese Revolution.* Lanham, MD: Rowman & Littlefield, 2005.

———. *The Origins of Chinese Communism.* New York: Oxford University Press, 1989.

Karol, K. S. *China: The Other Communism.* New York: Hill and Wang, 1967.

Knight, Nick. *Marxist Philosophy in China: From Qu Qiubai to Mao Zedong, 1923–1945.* New York: Springer, 2005.

Meisner, Maurice. *Marxism, Maoism, and Utopianism*. Madison: University of Wisconsin Press, 1982.

Mohanty, Manoranjan, ed. *Chinese Revolution: Comparative Perspectives on Transformation of Non-Western Societies*. Delhi: Ajanta, 1992.

Schram, Stuart R. *The Thought of Mao Tse-tung*. Cambridge: Cambridge University Press, 1989.

Schurman, Franz. *Ideology and Organization in Communist China*. Berkeley: University of California Press, 1969.

Womack, Brantly. *The Foundations of Mao Zedong's Political Thought, 1917–1935*. Honolulu: University of Hawai'i Press. 1982.

Zarrow, Peter G. *Anarchism and Chinese Political Culture*. New York: Columbia University Press, 1990.

Nationalism

Croizier, Ralph. *Koxinga and Chinese Nationalism: History, Myth and the Hero*. Cambridge, MA: East Asian Research Center, Harvard University, 1997.

Johnson, Chalmers. *Peasant Nationalism and Communist Power: The Emergence of Revolutionary China, 1937–1945*. Stanford, CA: Stanford University Press, 1962.

Karl, Rebecca E. *Staging the World: Chinese Nationalism at the Turn of the Twentieth Century*. Durham, NC: Duke University Press, 2002.

Laitinen, Kauko. *Chinese Nationalism in the Late Qing Dynasty: Zhang Binglin as an Anti-Manchu Propagandist*. London: Curzon Press, 1990.

Reinhold, Christiane I. *Studying the Enemy: Japan Hands in Republican China and Their Quest for National Identity*. New York: Routledge, 2001.

Schneider, Lawrence A. *Ku Chieh-kang and China's New History: Nationalism and the Quest for Alternative Traditions*. Berkeley: University of California Press, 1971.

Schram, Stuart R. *Imperialism and Chinese Nationalism: Germany in Shantung*. Cambridge, MA: Harvard University Press, 1971.

Smith, S. A. *Like Cattle and Horses: Nationalism and Labor in Shanghai, 1895–1927*. Durham, NC: Duke University Press, 2002.

Tsu, Jing. *Failure, Nationalism, and Literature: The Making of Modern Chinese Identity, 1895–1937*. Stanford, CA: Stanford University Press, 2005.

Ven, Hans van de. *War and Nationalism in China*. London: Routledge, 2003.

Waldron, Arthur N. *From War to Nationalism: China's Turning Point, 1924–1925*. New York: Cambridge University Press, 1995.

Communist Movement

Barnett, Doak. *China on the Eve of Communist Takeover*. New York: Praeger, 1963.

Benton, Gregor. *Mountain Fires: The Red Army's 3 Year War in South China, 1934–1938.* Berkeley: University of California Press, 1994.

———. *New Fourth Army: Communist Resistance along the Yangtze and the Huai.* Berkeley: University of California Press, 1992.

Bianco, Lucien. *Origins of the Chinese Revolution, 1915–1949.* Translated by Muriel Bell. Stanford, CA: Stanford University Press, 1971.

Busky, Donald F. *Communism in History and Theory.* New York: Praeger/ Greenwood, 2002.

Chang, Kuo-fao. *The Rise of the Chinese Communist Party: The Autobiography of Chang Kuo-tao.* Lawrence: University of Kansas Press, 1972.

Chen, Yung-fa. *Making Revolution: The Communist Movement in Eastern and Central China, 1937–1945.* Berkeley: University of California Press, 1986.

Compton, Boyd, trans. *Mao's China: Party Reform Documents, 1942–1944.* Seattle: University of Washington Press, 1966.

Davis-Friedman, Deborah. *Long Lives: Chinese Elderly and the Communist Revolution.* Cambridge, MA: Harvard University Press, 1983.

Dirlik, Arif, and Maurice Meisner, eds. *Marxism and the Chinese Experience.* Armonk, NY: M. E. Sharpe, 1989.

Eudin, Xenia, and Robert North. *M. N. Roy's Mission to China: The Communist Kuomintang Split of 1927.* Berkeley: University of California Press, 1963.

Gao, James Z. *The Communist Takeover of Hangzhou: The Transformation of City and Cadre, 1949–1954.* Honolulu: University of Hawai'i Press, 2004.

Hinton, William. *Fan Shen: A Documentary of a Revolution in a Chinese Village.* New York: Vintage Books, 1966.

Hofheinz, Roy. *The Broken Wave: The Chinese Communist Peasant Movement, 1922–28.* Cambridge, MA: Harvard University Press, 1977.

Ip, Hung-yok. *Intellectuals in Revolutionary China, 1921–1949: Leaders, Heroes and Sophisticates.* New York: Routledge Curzon, 2005.

Jacobs, Dan. *Borodin: Stalin's Man in China.* Cambridge, MA: Harvard University Press, 1981.

Kataoka, Tetsuya. *Resistance and Revolution in China: The Communists and the Second United Front.* Berkeley: University of California Press, 1986.

Keating, Pauline B. *Two Revolutions: Village Reconstruction and the Cooperation Movement in Northern Shaanxi, 1934–1945.* Stanford, CA: Stanford University Press, 1997.

Kim, Ilpyong J. *The Politics of Chinese Communism: Kiangsi under the Soviet.* Berkeley: University of California Press, 1974.

Leutner, Mechthild. *The Chinese Revolution in the 1920s: Between Triumph and Disaster.* New York: Routledge Curzon, 2002.

McDonald, Angus. *The Urban Origins of Rural Revolution: Elites and the Masses in Hunan Province, China, 1911–1927.* Berkeley: University of California Press, 1978.

Meisner, Maurice. *Mao's China and After: A History of the People's Republic.*

New York: Free Press, 1999.

Saich, Anthony J. *The Origins of the First United Front in China: The Role of Sneevliet.* Leiden: Brill, 1991.

———. *The Rise to Power of the Chinese Communist Party.* New York: M. E. Sharpe, 1996.

Saich, Anthony J., and Hans van de Ven. *New Perspectives on the Chinese Communist Revolution.* New York: M. E. Sharpe, 1995.

Schrecker, John E. *The Chinese Revolution in Historical Perspective.* New York: Praeger, 2004.

Sheel, Kamal. *Peasant Society and Marxist Intellectuals in China: Fang Zhimin and the Origin of a Revolutionary Movement in the Xinjiang Region.* Princeton, NJ: Princeton University Press, 1989.

Shum, Kui-kwong. *The Chinese Communists' Road to Power: The Anti-Japanese National United Front, 1935–1945.* Oxford: Oxford University Press, 1988.

Soloman, Richard H. *Mao's Revolution and the Chinese Political Culture.* Berkeley: University of California Press, 1971.

Stranahan, Patricia. *Underground: The Shanghai Communist Party and the Politics of Survival, 1927–1937.* Lanham, MD: Rowman & Littlefield, 1998.

Thaxton, Ralph. *Salt of the Earth: The Political Origins of Peasant Protest and Communist Revolution in China.* Berkeley: University of California Press, 1997.

Thomas, S. Bernard. *Labor and the Chinese Revolution: Class Strategies and Contradictions of Chinese Communism, 1928–1948.* Ann Arbor: Center for Chinese Studies, University of Michigan, 1983.

Thornton, Richard. *The Comintern and the Chinese Communists.* Seattle: University of Washington Press, 1969.

Uhalley, Stephen. *A History of the Chinese Communist Party.* Stanford, CA: Stanford University Press, 1988.

Van Slyke, Lyman P. *Enemies and Friends: The United Front in Chinese Communist History.* Stanford, CA: Stanford University Press, 1967.

Ven, Hans van de. *From Friend to Comrade: The Founding of the Chinese Communist Party, 1920–1927.* Berkeley: University of California Press, 1991.

Wou, Odoric. *Mobilizing the Masses: Building Revolution in Henan.* Stanford, CA: Stanford University Press, 1994.

Yeh, Wen-hsin. *Provincial Passages: Culture, Space, and the Origins of Chinese Communism.* Berkeley: University of California Press, 1996.

Yick, Joseph K. S. *Making Urban Revolution in China: The CCP-GMD Struggle for Beiping-Tianjin, 1945–1949.* Armonk, NY: M. E. Sharpe, 1995.

Yan'an

Beechert, Edward D., and Alice M. Beechert, eds. *From Kona to Yenan: The Political Memoirs of Koji Ariyoshi.* Honolulu: University of Hawai'i Press, 2000.

Carter, Carolle J. *Mission to Yenan: American Liaison with the Chinese Communists 1944–1947.* Lexington: University Press of Kentucky, 1997.

Colling, John. *The Spirit of Yenan: A Wartime Chapter of Sino-American Friendship.* Hong Kong: API Press, 1991.

Head, William P. *Yenan: Colonel Wilbur Peterkin and the American Military Mission to the Chinese Communists, 1944–1945.* Chapel Hill, NC: Documentary Publications, 1987.

Peterkin, Colonel W. J. *Inside China 1943–1945: An Eyewitness Account of America's Mission in Yenan.* Baltimore: Gateway Press, 1992.

———. *China in Revolution: The Yenan Way Revisited.* Armonk, NY: M. E. Sharpe, 1995.

Selden, Mark. *The Yenan Way in Revolutionary China.* Cambridge, MA: Harvard University Press, 1971.

Snow, Edgar. *Red Star over China.* New York: Modern Library, 1944.

Vladimirov, Peter. *The Vladimirov Diaries: Yenan, China: 1942–1945.* New York: Doubleday & Co., 1975.

Mao Zedong

Bloodworth, Dennis. *The Messiah and the Mandarins: Mao Tse-tung and the Ironies of Power.* New York: Atheneum, 1982.

Cheek, Timothy. *Mao Zedong and China's Revolution: A Brief History with Documents.* Hampshire, UK: Palgrave Macmillan, 2002.

Ch'en, Jerome. *Mao and the Chinese Revolution.* London: Oxford University Press, 1965.

Chevrier, Yves. *Mao and the Chinese Revolution.* Translated by David Stryker. Northampton, MA: Interlink Books, 2004.

Kampen, Thomas. *Mao Zedong, Zhou Enlai and the Evolution of the Chinese Communist Leadership.* Copenhagen: Nordic Institute of Asian Studies, 2000.

Meisner, Maurice. *Mao Zedong: A Political and Intellectual Portrait.* Cambridge: Polity, 2007.

Schram, Stuart R, ed. *Mao's Road to Power: Revolutionary Writings, 1912–1949: The Rise and Fall of the Chinese Soviet Republic, 1931–1934.* Vol. 4. Armonk, NY: M. E. Sharpe, 1997.

Schwartz, Benjamin I. *Chinese Communism and the Rise of Mao.* Cambridge, MA: Harvard University Press, 1961.

Spence, Jonathan D. *Mao Zedong.* New York: Viking Penguin, 1999.

Stefoff, Rebecca. *Mao Zedong: Founder of the People's Republic of China.* Brookfield, CT: Millbrook Press, 1996.

Wilson, Dick, ed. *Mao Tse-tung in the Scales of History: A Preliminary Assessment.* Cambridge, MA: Harvard University Press, 1977.

Other Political Leaders

Bonavia, David. *Deng*. Hong Kong: Longman, 1989.

Byron, John, and Robert Pack. *Claws of the Dragon: Kang Sheng—the Evil Genius Behind Mao—and His Legacy of Terror in People's China*. New York: Simon and Schuster, 1992.

Chen, Jerome. *Yuan Shih-kai*. Stanford, CA: Stanford University Press, 1972.

Chen, Tu-hsiu. *Chen Duxiu's Last Articles and Letters, 1937–1942*. Translated by Gregor Benton. Honolulu: University of Hawai'i Press, 1998.

Dittmer, Lowell. *Liu Shao-ch'i and the Chinese Cultural Revolution: The Politics of Mass Criticism*. Cambridge, MA: Harvard University Press, 1974.

Hsüeh, Chün-tu. *Huang Hsing and the Chinese Revolution*. Stanford, CA: Stanford University Press, 1961.

Lee, Feigon. *Chen Duxiu, Founder of the Chinese Communist Party*. Princeton, NJ: Princeton University Press, 1983.

Lescot, Patrick, and Steven Rendall. *Before Mao: The Untold Story of Li Lisan and the Creation of Communist China*. New York: Ecco, 2004.

Li, Laura Tyson. *Madame Chiang Kai-shek and Her China*. Norwalk, CT: EastBridge, 2004.

MacKinnon, Stephen R. *Power and Politics in Late Imperial China: Yuan Shikai in Beijing and Tianjin, 1901–1908*. Berkeley: University of California Press, 1981.

Meisner, Maurice. *Li Ta-chao and the Origins of Chinese Marxism*. Cambridge, MA: Harvard University Press, 1967.

Pickowicz, Paul G. *Marxist Literary Thought in China: The Influence of Ch'u Ch'iu-pai*. Berkeley: University of California Press, 1981.

Terrill, Ross. *Madame Mao: The White-Boned Demon*. Stanford, CA: Stanford University Press, 2000.

Young, Ernest P. *The Presidency of Yuan Shih-k'ai: Liberalism and Dictatorship in Early Republican China*. Ann Arbor: University of Michigan Press, 1977.

ECONOMY

General

Balazs, Étienne. "The Birth of Capitalism in China." In *Chinese Civilization and Bureaucracy: Variations on a Theme*. New Haven, CT: Yale University Press, 1964.

Ch'en, Jerome. *State Economic Policies of the Ching Government, 1840–1895*. New York: Garland, 1980.

Dunstan, Helen. *Conflicting Counsels to Confuse the Age: A Documentary Study of Political Economy in Qing China, 1644–1840*. Ann Arbor: Center for Chinese Studies, University of Michigan, 1996.

Feuerwerker, Albert. *The Chinese Economy, 1870–1949*. Ann Arbor: Center for Chinese Studies, University of Michigan, 1995.

Hao Yen-p'ing. *The Comprador in 19th Century China: Bridge between East and West*. Cambridge, MA: Harvard University Press, 1970.

Lu, Aiguo. *China and the Global Economy since 1840*. New York: St. Martin's, 1999.

Myers, Ramon H. *Did the Chinese Economy Develop in the 19th and 20th Centuries?* Stanford, CA: Hoover Institution, Stanford University, 1990.

Pomeranz, Kenneth. *The Great Divergence: China, Europe and the Making of the Modern World Economy*. Princeton, NJ: Princeton University Press, 2000.

Rawski, Evelyn, G. Tomas, and Lillian Li, eds. *Chinese History in Economic Perspective*. Berkeley: University of California Press, 1992.

Richardson, Philip. *Economic Change in China, 1800–1950*. New York: Cambridge University Press, 1999.

Slack, Edward R. *Opium, State and Society: China's Marco-Economy and the Guomindang, 1924–1937*. Honolulu: University of Hawai'i Press, 2001.

Struve, Lynn A. *To Achieve Security and Wealth: The Qing Imperial State and the Economy, 1644–1911*. Ithaca, NY: Cornell University Press, 1992.

Wright, Tim. *The Chinese Economy in the Early Twentieth Century: Recent Chinese Studies*. New York: St. Martin's, 1992.

Agriculture

Anderson, E. N. *The Food of China*. New Haven, CT: Yale University Press, 1988.

Bell, Lynda. *One Industry, Two Chinas: Silk Filatures and Peasant-Family Production in Wuxi County, 1865–1937*. Stanford, CA: Stanford University Press, 1999.

Brandt, Loren. *Commercialization and Agricultural Development: Central and Eastern China, 1870–1937*. New York: Cambridge University Press, 2005.

Huang, Philip C. *The Peasant Economy and Social Change in North China*. Stanford, CA: Stanford University Press, 1985.

———. *The Peasant Family and Rural Development in the Yangzi Delta, 1350–1988*. Stanford, CA: Stanford University Press, 1990.

Lin, A. *The Rural Economy of Guangdong, 1870–1937: Studies on the Chinese Economy*. New York: St. Martin's, 1997.

Marks, Robert B. *Tigers, Rice, Silk, and Silt: Environment and Economy in Late Imperial South China*. New York: Cambridge University Press, 1998.

Purdue, Peter C. *Exhausting the Earth: State and Peasant in Hunan, 1500–1850.* Cambridge, MA: Harvard University Press, 1958.
Rawski, Evelyn Sakkida. *Agricultural Change and the Peasant Economy of South China.* Cambridge, MA: Harvard University Press, 1972.
Wang, Yeh-chien. *Land Taxation in Imperial China, 1750–1911.* Berkeley: University of California Press, 1971.

Industry

Casalis, Laura, and Gianni Guadalupi, eds. *Cotton and Silk Making in Manchu China.* New York: Rizzoli International, 1980.
Farnie, Douglas A., and David J. Jeremy, eds. *The Fibre that Changed the World: The Cotton Industry in International Perspective, 1600–1990s.* Oxford: Oxford University Press, 2004.
———. *Studies in the Economic History of Late Imperial China: Handicraft, Modern Industry, and the State.* Ann Arbor: Center for Chinese Studies, University of Michigan, 1995.
Feuerwerker, Albert. *China's Early Industrialization: Sheng Hsuan-Huai (1844–1916) and Mandarin Enterprise.* Cambridge, MA: Harvard University Press, 1970.
———. "Handicraft and Manufactured Cotton Textiles in China, 1871–1910." *Journal of Economic History* (June 1970).
Jacobsen, Robert D. *Imperial Silks: Ch'ing Dynasty Textiles in the Minneapolis Institute of Arts.* Chicago: Art Media Resources, Limited, 2000.
Kennedy, Thomas. *The Arms of Kiangnan: Modernization in the Chinese Ordnance Industry, 1860–1895.* Boulder, CO: Westview, 1978.
Kerr, Rose. *Chinese Ceramics: Porcelain of the Qing Dynasty 1644–1911.* London: V & A Enterprises, 1998.

Finance

Beal, Edwin George. *The Origin of Likin, 1853–1864.* Cambridge, MA: Harvard University Press, 1958.
Deng, Gang. *The Premodern Chinese Economy: Structural Equilibrium and Capitalist Sterility.* London: Routledge, 1999.
Cheng, Linsun, et al. *Banking in Modern China: Entrepreneurs, Professional Managers, and the Development of Chinese Banks, 1897–1937.* New York: Cambridge University Press, 2007.
Hao, Yen-p'ing. *Money and Monetary Policy in China 1845–1895.* Cambridge, MA: Harvard University Press, 1965.
King, Frank H. H. *Money and Monetary Policy in China, 1845–1895.* Cambridge, MA: Harvard University Press, 1965.
Zelin, Madelin. *The Magistrate's Tael: Rationalizing Fiscal Reform in Eighteenth Century Ch'ing China.* Berkeley: University of California Press, 1985.

Trade and Market

Ch'uan, Han-shang, and Richard A. Kraus. *Mid-Ch'ing Rice Markets and Trade: An Essay in Price History.* Cambridge, MA: Harvard University Press, 1975.
Gao, James Z. "Myth, Memory, and Rice History of Shanghai, 1949–1950." *Chinese Historical Review* 11, no. 1 (Spring 2004).
Buoye, Thomas M. *Manslaughter, Markets and Moral Economy: Violent Disputes over Property Rights in 18th-Century China.* New York: Cambridge University Press, 2000.
Li, Lilian M. *China's Silk Trade: Traditional Industry in the Modern World, 1842–1937.* Cambridge, MA: Harvard University Press, 1981.
Nadler, Daniel. *China to Order: Focusing on the 19th Century and Surveying Polychrome Export Porcelain Produced during the Qing Dynasty 1644–1908.* Paris: Vilo International, 2001.
Rozman, Gilbert. *Population and Marketing Settlements in Ch'ing China.* New York: Cambridge University Press, 1982.
Skinner, G. William. *Marketing and Social Structure in Rural China.* Ann Arbor, MI: Association for Asian Studies, 2001.
Wade, Robert. *Governing the Market: Economic Theory and the Role of Government in East Asian Industrialization.* Princeton, NJ: Princeton University Press, 1990.

Foreign Investment

Hou, Chi-ming. *Foreign Investment and Economic Development in China, 1840–1937.* Cambridge, MA: Harvard University Press, 1965.
Kinney, Henry W. *Modern Manchuria and the South Manchurian Railway Company.* Tokyo: Japan Advertiser Press, 1928.
Le Fevour, Edward. *Western Enterprise in Late Ch'ing China: A Selective Survey of Jardine, Matheson and Company's Operations, 1842–1895.* Cambridge, MA: Harvard University Press, 1970.
Liu, Kwang-ching. *Anglo-American Steamship Rivalry in China, 1862–1874.* Cambridge, MA: Harvard University Press, 1962.
Overlach, T. W. *Foreign Financial Control in China.* New York: Macmillan, 1919.
Thomas, Stephen C. *Foreign Intervention and China's Industrial Development, 1870–1911.* Boulder, CO: Westview, 1984.
Willoughby, Westel W. *Foreign Rights and Interests in China.* Baltimore: Johns Hopkins University Press, 1972.

Regional Economy

Chao, Kang. *The Economic Development of Manchuria: The Rise of a Frontier Economy.* Ann Arbor: Center for Chinese Studies, University of Michigan, 1983.

Godley, Michael R. *The Mandarin-Capitalists from Nanyang: Overseas Chinese Enterprise in the Modernization of China, 1893–1911*. New York: Cambridge University Press, 1981.

Li, Bozhong. *Agricultural Development in Jiangnan, 1620–1850*. New York: St. Martin's, 1998.

Pietz, David Allen. *Engineering the State: The Huai River and Reconstruction in Nationalist China, 1927–1937*. New York: Routledge, 2002.

Pomeranz, Kenneth. *The Making of a Hinterland: State Society and Economy in Inland North China, 1853–1937*. Berkeley: University of California Press, 1993.

Vermeer, E. B., ed. *Development and Decline of Fukien Province in the 17th and 18th Centuries*. Leiden: Brill, 1990.

Urban Development

Bernett, Robert. *Lhasa: Streets with Memories*. New York: Columbia University Press, 2006.

Buck, David D., ed. *Urban Chance in China: Politics and Development in Tsinan, Shantung, 1890–1949*. Madison: University of Wisconsin Press, 1978.

Cochran, Sherman, and David Strand, eds. *Cities in Motion: Interior, Coast, and Diaspora in Transnational China*. China Research Monographs, edited by Wen-hsin Yeh, 62. Berkeley: Institute of East Asian Studies, University of California, 2007.

Carroll, John M. *Edge of Empires: Chinese Elites and British Colonials in Hong Kong*. Cambridge, MA: Harvard University Press, 2005.

Carter, James Hugh. *Creating a Chinese Harbin: Nationalism in an International City, 1916–1932*. Ithaca, NY: Cornell University Press, 2002.

Dong, Madeleine Yue. *Republican Beijing: The City and Its Histories*. Berkeley: University of California Press, 2003.

Dunnell, Ruth W. *New Qing Imperial History: The Making of Inner Asian Empire at Qing Chengde*. New York: Routledge Curzon, 2004.

Elvin, Mark, ed. *The Chinese City between Two Worlds*. With G. William Skinner. Stanford, CA: Stanford University Press, 1974.

Esherick, Joseph W., ed. *Remaking the Chinese City: Modernity and National Identity, 1900–1950*. Honolulu: University of Hawai'i Press, 2000.

Finnane, Antonia. *Speaking of Yangzhou: A Chinese City, 1550–1850*. Cambridge, MA: Harvard University Press, 2004.

Gaubatz, Piper Rae. *Beyond the Great Wall: Urban Form and Transformation on the Chinese Frontiers*. Stanford, CA: Stanford University Press, 1996.

Goodman, Bryna. *Native Place, City and Nation: Regional Networks and Identities in Shanghai, 1853–1937*. Berkeley: University of California Press, 1995.

Huang, Shijian, ed. *Customs and Conditions of Chinese City Streets in the 19th Century: 360 Professions in China*. Shanghai: Shanghai Classics Publishing House, 1999.

Jackowiak, William R. *Sex, Death, and Hierarchy in a Chinese City: An Anthropological Perspective.* New York: Columbia University Press, 1993.

Murphey, Rhoads. *The Treaty Ports and China's Modernization: What Went Wrong?* Ann Arbor: Center for Chinese Studies, University of Michigan, 1970.

Naquin, Susan. *Peking: Temples and City Life, 1400–1900.* Berkeley: University of California Press, 2000.

Rowe, William T. *Hankow: Commerce and Society in a Chinese City, 1796–1889.* Stanford, CA: Stanford University Press, 1984.

———. *Hankow: Conflict and Community in a Chinese City, 1796–1895.* Stanford, CA: Stanford University Press, 1989.

Skinner, G. William, ed. *The City in Late Imperial China.* Stanford, CA: Stanford University Press, 1977.

Skinner, G. William, and Mark Elvin, eds. *The Chinese City between Two Worlds.* Stanford, CA: Stanford University Press, 1974.

Stapleton, Kristin E. *Civilizing Chengdu: Chinese Urban Reform, 1895–1937.* Cambridge, MA: Asia Center, Harvard University, 2000.

Shanghai

Barber, Noel. *The Fall of Shanghai.* London: Macmillan, 1979.

Chen, J. T. *The May Fourth Movement in Shanghai: The Making of a Social Movement in Modern China.* Leiden: Brill, 1971.

Coble, Parks M. *The Shanghai Capitalists and the Nationalist Government, 1927–1937.* Cambridge, MA: Harvard University Press, 1986.

Henriot, Christian. *Shanghai, 1927–1937: Municipal Power, Locality, and Modernization.* Berkeley: University of California Press, 1993.

Hershatter, Gail. *Dangerous Pleasures: Prostitution and Modernity in Twentieth-Century Shanghai.* Berkeley: University of California Press, 1997.

King, Frank H. H. *The History of the Hong Kong and Shanghai Banking Corporation.* 3 vols. Cambridge: Cambridge University Press, 1987–88.

Lu, Hanchao. *Beyond the Neon Lights: Everyday Shanghai in the Early 20th Century.* Berkeley: University of California Press, 1999.

Macpherson, Kerrie L. *A Wilderness of Marshes: The Origins of Public Health in Shanghai, 1843–1893.* New York: Oxford University Press, 1987.

Motono, Eiichi. *Conflict and Cooperation in Sino-British Business, 1860–1911: The Impact of Pro-British Commercial Network in Shanghai.* New York: St. Martin's, 1999.

Murphey, Rhoads. *Shanghai, Key to Modern China.* Cambridge, MA: Harvard University Press, 1953.

Reed, Christopher A. *Gutenberg in Shanghai: Chinese Print Capitalism, 1876–1937.* Honolulu: University of Hawai'i Press, 2004.

Wakeman, Frederic E. *Policing Shanghai 1927–1937.* Berkeley: University of California Press, 1996.

Wakeman, Frederic E. *The Shanghai Badlands: Wartime Terrorism and Urban Crime, 1937–1941*. Cambridge: Cambridge University Press, 1996.

Wakeman, Frederic E., and Wen-hsin Yeh. *Shanghai Sojourners*. Berkeley: Institute of East Asian Studies, University of California, 1992.

Yeh, Wen-hsin. *Shanghai Splendor: Economic Sentiments and the Making of Modern China, 1843–1949*. Berkeley: University of California Press, 2007.

Yue, Meng. *Shanghai and the Edges of Empires*. Minneapolis: University of Minnesota Press, 2006.

Hong Kong and Macao

Banham, Tony. *Not the Slightest Chance: The Defence of Hong Kong, 1941*. Vancouver: University of British Columbia Press, 2003.

Buckley, Roger. *Hong Kong: The Road to 1997*. Cambridge: Cambridge University Press, 1997.

Berlie, J. A. *Macao 2000*. New York: Oxford University Press, 1999.

Courtauld, Caroline, May Holdsworth, and Simon Vickers. *The Hong Kong Story*. Hong Kong: Hong Kong University Press, 1997.

Herbert S. Yee. *Macau in Transition: From Colony to Autonomous Region*. Hampshire, UK: Palgrave Macmillan, 2001.

King, Frank H., Catherine E. King, and David J. King, eds. *The Hong Kong Bank in Late Imperial China, 1864–1902: On an Even Keel*. New York: Cambridge University Press, 1988.

Le Pichon, Alain. *China Trade and Empire: Jardine, Matheson and Co. and the Origins of British Rule in Hong Kong, 1827–1843*. Oxford: Oxford University Press, 2006.

Lee, Leo Ou-fan. *City between Worlds: My Hong Kong*. Cambridge, MA: Harvard University Press, 2008.

Pittis, Donald, and Susan J. Henders, eds. *Macao: Mysterious Decay and Romance*. Oxford: Oxford University Press, 1998.

Pui-Tak, Lee. *Colonial Hong Kong and Modern China: Interaction and Reintegration*. Hong Kong: Hong Kong University Press, 2006.

Snow, Philip. *The Fall of Hong Kong: Britain, China, and the Japanese Occupation*. New Haven, CT: Yale University Press, 2003.

Tsai, Jung-fang. *Hong Kong in Chinese History: Community and Social Unrest in the British Colony, 1842–1913*. New York: Columbia University Press, 1993.

Wordie, Jason. *Streets: Exploring Hong Kong Island*. Hong Kong: Hong Kong University Press, 2002.

International Economy

Cowan, C. D. *The Economic Development of China and Japan*. London: Routledge, 2006.

Eng, Robert Y. *Economic Imperialism in China: Silk Production and Exports, 1861–1932.* Berkeley: University of California Press, 1986.

Fairbank, John King, Martha Henderson Coolidge, and Richard J. Smith. *Customs Commissioner and Historian of China.* Lexington: University Press of Kentucky, 1995.

Hao, Yen-p'ing. *The Commercial Revolution in Nineteenth Century China: The Rise of Sino-Western Mercantile Capitalism.* Berkeley: University of California Press, 1986.

Shiroyama, Tomoko. *China during the Great Depression: Market, State, and the World Economy, 1929–1937.* Cambridge, MA: Harvard University Press, 2008.

Sugihara, Kaoru ed. *Japan, China, and the Growth of the Asian International Economy, 1850–1949.* Oxford: Oxford University Press, 2005.

Trescott, Paul B. *Jingji Xue: History of the Introduction of Western Economic Ideas into China, 1850–1950.* New York: Columbia University Press, 2006.

Van Dyke, Paul A. *The Canton Trade: Life and Enterprise on the China Coast, 1700–1845.* Hong Kong: Hong Kong University Press, 2005.

Self-Strengthening Movement

Chan, Wellington K. K. *Merchants, Mandarins, and Modern Enterprise in Late Ch'ing China.* Cambridge, MA: Harvard University Press, 1977.

Cheng, Ying-wan. *Postal Communication in China and its Modernization, 1860–1896.* Cambridge, MA: Harvard University Press, 1970.

Leibo, Steven A. *Transferring Technology to China: Prosper Giquel and the Self-Strengthening Movement.* Berkeley: Institute of East Asian Studies, University of California, 1985.

Kim, Kwan Ho. *Japanese Perspectives on China's Early Modernization: The Self-Strengthening Movement, 1860–1895: A Bibliographical Survey.* Ann Arbor: Center for Chinese Studies, University of Michigan, 1974.

Zelin, Madeleine. "Capital Accumulation and Investment Strategies in Early Modern China: The Case of the Furong Salt Yard." *Late Imperial China* (June 1988).

———. *The Merchants of Zigong: Industrial Entrepreneurship in Early Modern China.* New York: Columbia University Press, 2005.

MILITARY

General

Aijmer, Goran, and Jon Abbink, eds. *Meaning of Violence: A Cross Cultural Perspective.* New York: New York University Press, 2000.

Antony, Robert J. *Like Froth Floating on the Sea: The World of Pirates and Seafarers in Late Imperial South China*. Berkeley: Institute of East Asian Studies, University of California, 2003.

Boretz, Avron. "Martial Gods and Magic Swords: Identity, Myth, and Violence in Chinese Popular Religion" *Journal of Popular Culture* 29, no. 1 (1995).

Dreyer, Edward L. *China at War, 1901–1949*. White Plains, NY: Longman, 1996.

Elleman, Bruce A. *Modern Chinese Warfare, 1795–1989*. London: Routledge, 2001.

Fung, Edmund. *The Military Dimension of the Chinese Revolution: The New Army and Its Role in the Revolution of 1911*. Vancouver: University of British Columbia Press, 1980.

Giquel, Prosper. *A Journal of the Chinese Civil War 1864*. Translated by Debbie Weston. Honolulu: University of Hawai'i Press, 1985.

Graham, Gerald S. *The China Station: War and Diplomacy 1830–1860*. New York: Oxford University Press, 1979.

Lary, Diana, and Stephen R. MacKinnon, eds. *The Scars of War: The Impact of Warfare on Modern China*. Vancouver: University of British Columbia Press, 2001.

Lipman, Jonathan N., and Steven Harrell. *Violence in China: Essays in Culture and Counterculture*. Albany: State University of New York Press, 1990.

Liu, F. F. *A Military History of Modern China: 1924–1949*. Princeton, NJ: Princeton University Press, 1956.

Murray, Williamson, MacGregor Knox, and Alvin Bernstein, eds. *The Making of Strategy: Rulers, States, and War*. New York: Cambridge University Press, 1994.

O'Brien, Anita M. "Military Academies in China, 1885–1915." In *Perspectives on a Changing China: Essays in Honor of Professor C. Martin Wilbur on the Occasion of His Retirement*, edited by Joshua A. Fogel and William T. Rowe. Boulder, CO: Westview, 1979.

Rawlinson, John L. *China's Struggle for Naval Development, 1839–1895*. Cambridge, MA: Harvard University Press, 1967.

Rowe, William T. *Crimson Rain: Seven Centuries of Violence in a Chinese County*. Stanford, CA: Stanford University Press, 2007.

Rummel, R. J. *China's Bloody Century: Genocide and Mass Murder since 1900*. New Brunswick, NJ: Transaction, 1991.

Tohmatsu, Haruo, and H. P. Willmott. *A Gathering Darkness: The Coming of War to the Far East and the Pacific, 1921–1942*. Lanham, MD: SR Books, 2004.

Van de Ven, Hans, ed. *Warfare in Chinese History*. Leiden: Brill, 2000.

Waldron, Arthur N. "The Warlord: Twentieth-Century Chinese Understandings of Violence, Militarism, and Imperialism." *American Historical Review* 96, no. 4 (October 1991).

Wright, Richard N. J. *The Chinese Steam Navy 1862–1945*. Annapolis, MD: Naval Institute Press, 2001.

Xu, Guangqiu. *War Wings: The United States and Chinese Military Aviation, 1929–1949*. Westport, CT: Greenwood, 2001.

Xu, Guoqi. *China and the Great War: China's Pursuit of a New National Identity and Internationalization*. New York: Cambridge University Press, 2005.

Wang, David Der-wei. *Clouds over Tianshan: Essays on Social Disturbance in Xinjiang in the 1940s*. Leifsgade, Denmark: Nordic Institute of Asian Studies Press, 1998.

Zarrow, Peter G. *China in War and Revolution 1895–1949*. London: Routledge, 2005.

Rebellions

Anderson, Flavia. *The Rebel Emperor*. London: Gollancz, 1958.

Billingsley, Philip. *Bandits in Republican China*. Stanford, CA: Stanford University Press, 1988.

Buck, David D., ed. *Recent Studies of the Boxer Movement*. Armonk, NY: M. E. Sharpe, 1987.

Cheng, James Chester. *Chinese Sources for the Taiping Rebellion, 1850–1864*. New York: Oxford University Press, 1963.

Chesneaux, Jean. *Peasant Revolts in China 1840–1949*. London: Thames & Hudson, 1973.

Chu, Wen-chang. *The Moslem Rebellion in Northwest China, 1862–1878: A Study of Government Minority Policy*. The Hague: Mouton, 1966.

Clarke, Prescott, and J. S. Gregory. *Western Reports on the Taiping: A Selection of Documents*. Canberra: Australian National University, 1982.

Cohen, Paul A. *History in Three Keys: The Boxers as Event, Experience, and Myth*. New York: Columbia University Press, 1997.

Cole, James H. *The People versus the Taipings: Bao Lisheng's "Righteous Army of Dongan."* Berkeley: Institute of East Asian Studies, University of California, 1981.

Dorrill, William F. "The Fukien Rebellion and the CCP: A Case of Maoist Revisionism." *China Quarterly* 37. (January–March, 1969).

Elliott, Jane E. *Some Did It for Civilization, Some Did It for Country: A Revised View of the Boxer War*. Hong Kong: Chinese University Press, 2002.

Esherick, Joseph W. *The Origins of the Boxer Uprising*. Berkeley: University of California Press, 1987.

Forster, Keith. *Rebellion and Factionalism in a Chinese Province: Zhejiang, 1966–1976*. Armonk, NY: M. E. Sharpe, 1990.

Gray, Jack. *Rebellions and Revolutions: China from the 1800s to 2000*. New York: Oxford University Press, 2002.

Gregory, J. S. *Great Britain and the Taipings*. New York: Praeger, 1969.

Harrington, Peter. *Peking 1900: The Boxer Rebellion.* Oxford: Osprey, 2001.

Heath, Ian, and Michael Perry, *The Taiping Rebellion 1851–1866.* London: Reed, 1994.

Jen Yu-wen. *The Taiping Revolutionary Movement.* New Haven, CT: Yale University Press, 1973.

Jenks, Robert Darrah. *Insurgency and Social Disorder in Guizhou: The "Miao" Rebellion, 1854–1873.* Honolulu: University of Hawai'i Press, 1994.

Keown-Boyd, Henry. *The Fists of Righteous Harmo NY: A History of the Boxer Uprising in China.* London: Leo Cooper, 1991.

Kim, Ho-dong. *Holy War in China: The Muslim Rebellion and State in Chinese Central Asia, 1864–1877.* Stanford, CA: Stanford University Press, 2004.

Michael, Franz. "Military Organization and the Power Structure of China during the Taiping Rebellion." *Pacific Historical Review* (1949).

Michael, Franz, and Chang Chung-li. *The Taiping Rebellion: History and Documents.* 3 vols. Seattle: University of Washington Press, 1966.

Naquin, Susan. *Millenarian Rebellion in China: The Eight Trigrams Uprising of 1813.* New Haven, CT: Yale University Press, 1976.

Nicholls, Bob. *Bluejackets and Boxers: Australia's Naval Expedition to the Boxer Uprising.* Sydney: Allen & Urwin, 1986.

Perry, Elizabeth. *Chinese Perspectives on the Nien Rebellion.* Armonk, NY: M. E. Sharpe, 1981.

———. *Rebels and Revolutionaries in North China, 1845–1945.* Stanford, CA: Stanford University Press, 1980.

Pollock, John Charles. *Gordon: The Man behind the Legend.* London: Constable, 1993.

Preston, Diane. *The Boxer Rebellion: The Dramatic Story of China's War on Foreigners that Shook the World in the Summer of 1900.* New York: Berkley Publishing Group, 2001.

Purcell, Victor. *The Boxer Uprising: A Background Study.* New York: Cambridge University Press. 1963.

Reilly, Thomas H. *The Taiping Heavenly Kingdom: Rebellion and the Blasphemy of Empire.* Seattle: University of Washington Press, 2004.

Sharf, Frederic Alan. *China, 1900: The Eyewitnesses Speak: The Experience of Westerners in China during the Boxer Rebellion, as Described by Participants in Letters, Diaries and Photographs.* London: Greenhill Books, 2000.

Shih, Vincent C. Y. *The Taiping Ideology: Its Sources, Interpretations and Influences.* Seattle: University of Washington Press, 1967.

Smith, Richard J. *Mercenaries and Mandarins: The Ever-Victorious Army in Nineteenth Century China.* Millwood, NY: KTO Press, 1978.

Spence, Jonathan D. *God's Chinese Son: The Taiping Heavenly Kingdom of Hong Xiuquan.* New York: W. W. Norton, 1996.

———. *The Taiping Vision of a Christian China, 1836–1864.* Waco, TX: Baylor University Press, 1998.

Teng, Ssu-yu. *New Light on the History of the Taiping Rebellion.* New York: Russell & Russell, 1966.

———. *The Nien Army and Their Guerilla Warfare, 1851–1868.* Paris: Mouton & Co., 1961.

Teng, Yuan-chung. *Americans and the Taiping Rebellion: A Study of American-Chinese Relationship, 1847–1864.* Taipei: China Academy, 1982.

Tiedemann, R. G. "Boxers, Christians and the Culture of Violence in North China." *Journal of Peasant Studies* 25, no. 4 (1998).

Wagner, Rudolf G. *Reenacting the Heavenly Vision: The Role of Religion in the Taiping Rebellion.* Berkeley: Institute of East Asian Studies, University of California, 1982.

Wakeman, Frederic E. *Strangers at the Gate: Social Disorder in South China, 1839–1861.* Berkeley: University of California Press, 1966.

Wilson, Andrew R. *The Ever-Victorious Army: A History of the Chinese Campaign under Lt. Col. C. G. Gordon, C.B.R.E. and of the Suppression of the Tai-ping Rebellion.* San Francisco: Chinese Materials Center, 1977.

Wong, R. Bin. "Food Riots in the Qing Dynasty." *Journal of Asian Studies* (August 1982).

The Opium War

Basu, Dilip K. "The Opium War and the Opening of China: A Historiographical Note." *Ch'ing-shih wen-t'i* (December 1977).

Beeching, Jack. *The Chinese Opium Wars.* London: Hutchinson, 1975.

Bello, David Anthony. *Opium and the Limits of Empire: Drug Prohibition in the Chinese Interior, 1729–1850.* Cambridge, MA: Asia Center, Harvard University, 2005.

Chang, Hsin-pao. *Commissioner Lin and the Opium War.* Cambridge, MA: Harvard University Press, 1964.

Fay, Peter W. *The Opium War: Barbarians in the Celestial Empire in the Early Part of the Nineteenth Century and the War by Which They Forced Her Gates Ajar.* Chapel Hill: University of North Carolina Press, 1998.

Polachek, James M. *The Inner Opium War.* Cambridge, MA: Council on East Asian Studies, Harvard University, 1992.

Wong, J. Y. *Deadly Dreams: Opium and the Arrow War (1856–1860) in China.* New York: Cambridge University Press, 1998.

Warlordism

Chan, Anthony B. *Arming the Chinese: The Western Armaments Trade in Warlord China, 1920–1928.* Seattle: University of Washington Press, 1985.

Ch'en, Jerome. *The Military-Gentry Coalition: China under the Warlords.* Toronto: University of Toronto Press, 1979.

Ch'i, Hsi-sheng. *Warlord Politics in China, 1916–1928.* Stanford, CA: Stanford University Press, 1976.

Gillin, Donald. *Warlord: Yen His-shan in Shansi Province, 1911–1949.* Princeton, NJ: Princeton University Press, 1967.

Lary, Diana. *Region and Nation: The Kwangsi Clique, 1925–37.* New York: Cambridge University Press, 1974.

————. *Warlord Soldiers: Chinese Common Soldiers, 1911–1937.* New York: Cambridge University Press, 1985.

Lin, Alfred H. Warlord, "Social Welfare and Philanthropy: The Case of Guangzhou under Jitang, 1929–1936." *Modern China* 30, no. 2 (2004).

McCord, Edward A. *The Power of the Gun: The Emergence of Modern Chinese Warlordism.* Berkeley: University of California Press, 1993.

McCormack, Gavan. *Chang Tso-lin in Northeast China, 1911–1928: China, Japan and the Manchurian Idea.* Stanford, CA: Stanford University Press, 1977.

Kapp, Robert. *Szechwan and the Chinese Republic: Provincial Militarism and Central Power, 1911–1938.* New Haven, CT: Yale University Press, 1973.

Pye, Lucian. *Warlord Politics: Conflict and Coalition in the Modernization of Republican China.* New York: Praeger, 1971.

Sheridan, James E. *Chinese Warlord: The Career of Feng Yu-Hsiang.* Stanford, CA: Stanford University Press, 1966.

Suleski, Ronald Stanley. *Civil Government in Warlord China: Tradition, Modernization and Manchuria.* New York: Peter Lang, 2002.

Sutton, Donald S. *Provincial Militarism and the Chinese Republic: The Yunnan Army, 1905–25.* Ann Arbor: University of Michigan Press, 1980.

Van de Ven, Hans. "Public Finance and the Rise of Warlordism." *Modern Asian Studies* 30, no. 4, (1996).

Wou, Odoric. *Militarism in Modern China: The Career of Wu Peifu, 1916–1939.* Canberra: Australian National University Press, 1978.

Sino-Japanese Wars

Barrett, David D. *Dixie Mission: The United States Army Observer Group in Yenan, 1944.* Berkeley: Center for Chinese Studies, University of California, 1970.

Barrett, David P., and Lawrence N. Shyu. *Chinese Collaboration with Japan, 1932–1945: The Limits of Accommodation.* Stanford, CA: Stanford University Press, 2001.

Belden, Jack. *Retreat with Stilwell.* New York: Knopf, 1943.

Boyle, John Hunter. *China and Japan at War: The Politics of Collaboration, 1937–1945.* Stanford, CA: Stanford University Press, 1972.

Brook, Timothy. *Collaboration: Japanese Agents and Local Elites in Wartime China.* Cambridge, MA: Harvard University Press, 2005.

Bunker, Gerald. *The Peace Conspiracy: Wang Ching-wei and the China War, 1937–1941.* Cambridge, MA: Harvard University Press, 1972.

Chang, Iris. *The Rape of Nanking: The Forgotten Holocaust of World War II.* New York: Penguin, 1998.

Chennault, Claire, and Robert B. Hotz. *Way of a Fighter: The Memoirs of Claire Lee Chennault.* New York: G. P. Putnam's Sons, 1949.

Ch'i Hsi-sheng. *Nationalist China at War: Military Defeats and Political Collapse, 1937–1945.* Ann Arbor: University of Michigan Press, 1998.

Cornelius, Wanda, and Thayne Short. *Ding Hao: America's Air War in China, 1937–1945.* Gretna, LA: Pelican, 2005.

De Fremery, Colonel. *A Dutch Spy in China: Reports on the First Phase of the Sino-Japanese War (1937–1939).* Leiden: Brill, 1999.

Eastman, Lloyd. *Seeds of the Destruction: Nationalist China in War and Revolution, 1937–1949.* Stanford, CA: Stanford University Press, 1984.

Eldridge, Fred. *Wrath in Burma: The Uncensored Story of Gen. Stilwell.* Garden City, NY: Doubleday, 1946.

Ford, Daniel. *Flying Tigers: Claire Chennault and His American Volunteers, 1941–1942.* Washington, DC: Smithsonian Institution Press, 1991.

Goodman, David S. G. *Social and Political Change in Revolutionary China: The Taihang Base Area in the War of Resistance to Japan, 1937–1945.* Lanham, MD: Rowman & Littlefield, 2000.

Kushner, Barak. *The Thought War: Japanese Imperial Propaganda.* Honolulu: University of Hawai'i Press, 2006.

Li, Fei Fei, Robert Sabella, and David Liu, eds. *Nanking 1937: Memory and Healing.* Armonk, NY: M. E. Sharpe, 2002.

Li, Lincoln. *The Japanese Army in North China, 1937–1941: Problems of Political and Economic Control.* New York: Oxford University Press, 1978.

MacKinnon, Stephen R. *Wuhan, 1938: War, Refugees, and the Making of Modern China.* Berkeley: University of California Press, 2008.

Paine, S. C. M. *The Sino-Japanese War of 1894–1895: Perceptions, Power, and Primacy.* New York: Cambridge University Press, 2003.

Shin'ichi, Yamamuro. *Manchuria under Japanese Dominion.* Translated by Joshua A. Fogel. Philadelphia: University of Pennsylvania Press, 2005.

Smith, Felix. *China Pilot: Flying for Chiang and Chennault.* Washington, DC: Brassey's, 1995.

Sun, Youli. *China and the Origins of the Pacific War, 1931–1941.* Hampshire, UK: Palgrave, 1993.

Thorne, Christopher. *Allies of a Kind: The United Sates, Britain, and the War against Japan, 1941–1945.* New York: Oxford University Press, 1978.

Totani, Yuma. *The Tokyo War Crimes Trial: The Pursuit of Justice in the Wake of World War II.* Cambridge, MA: Harvard University Press, 2008.

Wilson, Sandra. *The Manchurian Crisis and Japanese Society, 1931–33.* London: Routledge, 2002.

Yeh, Wen-hsin. *In the Shadow of the Rising Sun: Shanghai under Japanese Occupation.* New York: Columbia University Press, 2004.

Yin, James. *The Rape of Nanking: An Undeniable History in Photographs.* Chicago: Triumph Books, 1997.

Yoshida, Takashi. *The Making of "The Rape of Nanking": The History and Memory of the Nanjing Massacre in Japan, China, and the United States.* New York: Oxford University Press, 2006.

The Long March

Fritz, Jean. *China's Long March: 6,000 Miles of Danger.* New York: Putnam, 1988.

Jocelyn, Ed, and Andrew McEwen. *The Long March.* London: Constable and Robinson, 2006.

Salisbury, Charlotte Y. *Long March Diary: China Epic.* New York: Walker, 1986.

Salisbury, Harrison Evans. *The Long March: The Untold Story.* New York: Harper & Row, 1985.

Wilson, Dick. *The Long March of 1935: The Epic of Chinese Communism's Survival.* New York: Viking Press, 1971.

Yang, Benjamin. *From Revolution to Politics: Chinese Communists on the Long March.* Boulder, CO: Westview, 1990.

Young, Helen Praeger. *Choosing Revolution: Chinese Women Soldiers on the Long March.* Urbana: University of Illinois Press, 2001.

The Civil War

Donovan, Pester. *The Red Army in Kiangsi, 1931–1934.* Ithaca, NY: Cornell University Press, 1976.

Hooton, E. R. *The Greatest Tumult: The Chinese Civil War, 1936–49.* New York: Macmillan, 1991.

Leary, William. *Perilous Mission: Civil Air Transport and CIA Covert Operations in Asia.* Tuscaloosa: University of Alabama Press, 1984.

Levine, Steven I. *Anvil of Victory: The Communist Revolution in Manchuria, 1945–1949.* New York: Columbia University Press, 1987.

Melby, John. *The Mandate of Heaven, Record of a Civil War: China 1945–1949.* Toronto: University of Toronto Press, 1968.

Pepper, Suzanne. *Civil War in China: The Political Struggle, 1945–1949.* Berkeley: University of California Press, 1978.

Shaw, Chonghal Petey. *The Role of the United States in Chinese Civil Conflicts, 1944–1949.* Salt Lake City: C. Schlacks, Jr., 1991.

Waldron, Arthur N. *The Chinese Civil Wars 1911–1949.* New York: Oxford University Press, 2002.

Wedemeyer, Albert C. *Wedemeyer on War and Peace.* Stanford, CA: Hoover Institute Press, 1987.

Westad, Odd Arne. *Cold War and Revolution: Soviet-American Rivalry and the Origins of the Chinese Civil War, 1944–1946*. New York: Columbia University Press, 1993.

FOREIGN RELATIONS

General

Fraser, George MacDonald. *Flashman and the Dragon*. New York: Knopf, 1986.

Liao, Kuang-Sheng. *Anti-Foreignism and Modernization in China, 1860–1980: Linkage between Domestic Politics and Foreign Policy*. Hong Kong: Chinese University Press, 1990.

Mayer, Arno J. *Political Origins of the New Diplomacy, 1917–1918*. Cleveland, OH: World, 1964.

Mungello, David E. *The Great Encounter of China and the West, 1500–1800*. Lanham, MD: Rowman & Littlefield, 2005.

Murphey, Rhoads. *The Outsiders: The Western Experience in India and China*. Ann Arbor: University of Michigan Press, 1977.

Murray, Dian. *Pirates of the South China Coast, 1790–1810*. Stanford, CA: Stanford University Press, 1987.

Perdue, Peter C. *China Marches West: The Qing Conquest of Central Eurasia*. Cambridge, MA: Harvard University Press, 2005.

Thomson, H. C. *China and the Powers: A Narrative of the Outbreak of 1900*. Westport, CT: Hyperion Press, 1981.

Wang, Gungwu, and Chin-keong Ng, eds. *Maritime China in Transition 1750–1850*. Wiesbaden: Harrassowitz, 2004.

Cultural Encounter

Ch'en, Jerome. *China and the West: Society and Culture, 1815–1937*. Bloomington: Indiana University Press, 1979.

Haddad, John Rogers. *The Romance of China: Excursions to China in U.S. Culture, 1778–1876*. New York: Columbia University Press, 2008.

Hevia, James L. *Cherishing Men from Afar: Qing Guest Ritual and the Macartney*. Durham, NC: Duke University Press. 1995.

Howland, D. R. *Borders of Chinese Civilization: Geography and History at Empire's End*. Durham, NC: Duke University Press, 1996.

Joao, De Pina-Cabral. *Between China and Europe: Person, Culture and Emotion in Macao*. Oxford: Berg, 2002.

Spence, Jonathan D. *The Chan's Great Continent: China in Western Minds*. New York: W. W. Norton, 1998.

Wang, Dong. *Managing God's Higher Learning: US-China Cultural Encounter and Canton Christian College (Lingnan University), 1888–1952*. Lanham, MD: Rowman & Littlefield, 2007.

Unequal Treaties

Carnegie Endowment for International Peace, ed. *Treaties and Agreements with and Concerning China, 1919–1929*. Buffalo, NY: William S. Hein & Company, 1999.

Fairbank, John K. *Trade and Diplomacy on the China Coast: The Opening of the Treaty Ports, 1842–1854*. Cambridge, MA: Harvard University Press, 1964.

Frank, V. S. "The Territorial Terms of the Sino-Russian Treaty of Nerchinsk, 1689." *Pacific Historical Review* (August 1947).

Grosse-Aschhoff, Angelus Francis J. *The Negotiations between Ch'i-Ying and Lagrené, 1844–1846*. St. Bonaventure, NY: Franciscan Institute, 1950.

Hertslet, Edward, ed. *Treaties, &C., between Great Britain and China; and between China and Foreign Powers; Orders in Council, Rules, Regulations, Acts of Parliament, Decrees, and Notifications Affecting British Interests in China, in Force on the 1st January, 1896*. 2 vols. London: Homson, 1896.

Johnstone, William C. "International Relations: The Status of Foreign Concessions and Settlements in the Treaty Port of China." *American Political Science Review* 31.5 (October 1937).

Kuo, Ping Chia. "Caleb Cushing and the Treaty of Wanghia, 1844." *Journal of Modern History* 5, no. 1 (1933).

Sebes, Joseph, and Thomas Pereira. *The Jesuits and the Sino-Russian Treaty of Nerchinsk (1689): The Diary of Thomas Pereira*. Rome: Institutum Historicum S. I., 1962.

Teng, Ssu-yu. *Chang Hsi and the Treaty of Nanking, 1842*. Chicago: University of Chicago Press, 1944.

Wang, Dong. *China's Unequal Treaties: Narrating National History*. Lanham, MD: Lexington Books, 2005.

Wang, Shên-tsu. *The Margary Affair and the Chefoo Agreement*. London: Oxford University Press, 1940.

Multinational Relations

Akami, Tomoko. *Internationalizing the Pacific: The United States, Japan, and the Institute of Pacific Relations in War and Peace, 1919–45*. London: Routledge, 2001.

Broadbent, James, Suzanne Rickard, and Margaret Steven. *India, China, Australia: Trade and Society, 1788–1850*. Glebe, UK: Historic Houses Trust of New South Wales, 2003.

Brook, Timothy, and Bob T. Wakabayashi, eds. *Opium Regimes: China, Britain and Japan, 1839–1952.* Berkeley: University of California Press, 2000.

Cochran, Sherman. *Encountering Chinese Networks: Western, Japanese, and Chinese Corporations in China, 1880–1937.* Berkeley: University of California Press, 2000.

Davies, John Paton. *Dragon by the Tail: American, British, Japanese, and Russian Encounters with China and One Another.* New York: W. W. Norton, 1972.

Fairbank, John K. *China's Response to the West: A Documentary Survey 1839–1923.* Cambridge, MA: Harvard University Press, 1954.

Field, Andrew. *Royal Navy Strategy in the Far East, 1919–1939.* London: Frank Cass, 2004.

Goldstein, Erik. *The Washington Conference, 1921–22: Naval Rivalry, East Asian Stability and the Road to Pearl Harbor.* Portland, OR: Frank Cass, 1994.

O'Brien, Phillips Payson. *British and American Naval Power: Politics and Policy, 1900–1936.* Westport, CT: Praeger, 1998.

China and Great Britain

Brunero, Donna. *Britain's Imperial Cornerstone in China: The Chinese Maritime Customs Service, 1854–1949.* New York: Routledge Curzon, 2005.

Coates, P. D. *The China Consuls: British Consular Officers, 1843–1943.* London: Oxford University Press, 1988.

Fan, Fa-ti. *British Naturalists in Qing China: Science, Empire, and Cultural Encounter.* Cambridge, MA: Harvard University Press, 2004.

Gerson, Jack J. *Horatio Nelson Lay and Sino-British Relations, 1854–1864.* Cambridge, MA: Harvard University Press, 1972.

Greenberg, Michael. *British Trade and the Opening of China 1800–1842.* New York: Hyperion, 1997.

Hoare, J. E. *Embassies in the East: The Story of the British and Their Embassies in China, Japan and Korea from 1859 to the Present.* Richmond, VA: Curzon, 1999.

Lau, Kit-ching. *Anglo-Chinese Diplomacy in the Careers of Sir John Jordan and Yüän Shih-kai.* Hong Kong: Hong Kong University Press, 1978.

Melancon, Genn. *Britain's China Policy and the Opium Crisis: Balancing Drugs, Violence and National Honour, 1833–1840.* Burlington, VT: Ashgate, 2003.

Tuck, Patrick J. N. *Britain and the China Trade 1635–1842.* London: Routledge, 1999.

Wang, Gungwu. *Anglo-Chinese Encounters since 1800: War, Trade, Science and Governance.* Singapore: National University of Singapore, 2003.

Wong, R. Bin. *China Transformed: Historical Change and the Limits of European Experience.* Ithaca, NY: Cornell University Press 2000.

China and the United States

Borg, Dorothy, and Waldo H. Heinrichs. *Uncertain Years: Chinese-American Relations, 1947–1950.* New York: Columbia University Press, 1980.

Carr, Caleb. *The Devil Soldier: The American Soldier of Fortune Who Became a God in China.* New York: Random House, 1992.

Cohen, Warren I. *American Response to China: A History of Sino-American Relations.* New York: Columbia University Press, 1990.

Elleman, Bruce A. *Wilson and China: A Revised History of the Shandong Question.* Armonk, NY: M. E. Sharpe, 2002.

Etzold, Thomas H. *Aspects of Sino-American Relations since 1784.* New York: New Viewpoints, 1978.

Fairbank, John K. *The United States and China.* 4th ed. Cambridge, MA: Harvard University Press, 1983.

Hunt, Michael H. *The Making of a Special Relationship: The United States and China to 1914.* New York: Columbia University Press, 1983.

Iriye, Akira. *Across the Pacific: An Inner History of American-East Asian Relations.* New York: Harcourt, 1967.

Israel, Jerry. *Progressivism and the Open Door: America and China, 1905–1921.* Pittsburgh, PA: University of Pittsburgh Press, 1971.

Neils, Patricia. *China Images in the Life and Times of Henry Luce.* Lanham, MD: Rowman & Littlefield, 1990.

Service, John S. *The Amerasia Papers: Some Problems in the History of US-China Relations.* Berkeley: Center for Chinese Studies, University of California, 1971.

———. *Lost Chance in China: The World War II Despatches of John S. Service.* New York: Random House, 1974.

Swisher, Earl, ed. *China's Management of the American Barbarians, A Study of Sino-American Relations, 1841–1861, with Documents.* New Haven, CT: Yale University Press, 1953.

———. *Early Sino-American Relations, 1841–1912: The Collected Articles of Earl Swisher.* Boulder, CO: Westview, 1977.

Stueck, William. *The Wedemeyer Mission: American Politics and Foreign Policy during the Cold War.* Atlanta: University of Georgia Press, 1984.

Tomimas, Shutaro. *The Open-Door Policy and the Territorial Integrity of China.* Arlington, VA: University Publications of America, 1976.

Tsou, Tang. *America's Failure in China, 1941–50.* Chicago: University of Chicago Press, 1963.

Valone, Stephen J. *A Policy Calculated to Benefit China: The United States and the China Arms Embargo, 1919–1929.* Westport, CT: Greenwood Press, 1991.

Varg, Paul A. *The Closing of the Door: Sino-American Relations, 1936–1946.* East Lansing: Michigan State University Press, 1973.

Wong, Sin Kiong. *China's Anti-American Boycott Movement in 1905: A Study in Urban Protest.* New York: Peter Lang, 2002.

China and Japan

Duus, Peter, ed. *The Japanese Informal Empire in China, 1895–1937*. Princeton, NJ: Princeton University Press, 1989.

Emmerson, John. *The Japanese Thread: A Life in the U.S. Foreign Service*. New York: Holt, Rinehart & Winston, 1978.

Fogel, Joshua. *A Nakae Ushikichi in China: The Mourning of the Spirit*. Cambridge, MA: Harvard University Press, 1989.

———, ed. *The Role of Japan in Liang Qichao's Introduction of Modern Western Civilization to China*. Berkeley: Institute of East Asian Studies, University of California, 2004.

Iriye, Akira. *After Imperialism: The Search for a New Order in the Far East, 1921–1931*. Cambridge, MA: Harvard University Press, 1965.

———, ed. *The Chinese and the Japanese: Essays in Political and Cultural Interactions*. Princeton, NJ: Princeton University Press, 1979.

Kim, Key-Hiuk. *The Last Phase of the East Asian World Order: Korea, Japan, and the Chinese Empire, 1860–1882*. Berkeley: University of California Press, 1979.

Lu, Yan. *Re-understanding Japan: Chinese Perspectives, 1895–1945*. Honolulu: University of Hawai'i Press, 2004.

Morley, James William. *Japan's Foreign Policy, 1868–1941: A Research Guide*. New York, Columbia University Press, 1974.

Moulder, F. V. *Japan, China and the Modern World Economy*. New York: Cambridge University Press, 1979.

Reinhold, Christiane I. *Studying the Enemy: Japan Hands in Republican China and Their Quest for National Identity*. London: Routledge, 2001.

China and Other Countries

Andrews, E. M. *Australia and China: The Ambiguous Relationship*. Carlton, Victoria: Melbourne University Press, 1985.

Bickers, Robert, and Christian Henriot. *New Frontiers: Imperialism's New Communities in East Asia, 1842–1953*. Manchester, UK: Manchester University Press, 2000.

Cady, John Frank. *The Roots of French Imperialism in Eastern Asia*. Ithaca, NY: Cornell University Press, 1967.

Evans, John L. *Russian Expansion on the Amur 1848–1860: The Push to the Pacific*. Lewiston, NY: Edwin Mellen, 1999.

Franke, Wolfgang. *Sino-Malaysiana: Selected Papers on Ming and Qing History and on the Overseas Chinese in Southeast Asia, 1942–1988*. Singapore: South Seas Society, 1989.

Hsu, Immanuel C. Y. *China's Entrance into the Family of Nations: The Diplomatic Phase, 1858–1880*. Cambridge, MA: Harvard University Press, 1960.

Larsen, Kirk W. *Tradition, Treaties, and Trade: Qing Imperialism and Choson Korea, 1850–1910.* Cambridge, MA: Asia Center, Harvard University, 2008.

Newby, L. J. *The Empire and the Khanate: A Political History of Qing Relations with Khoqand, 1760–1860.* Leiden: Brill, 2005.

Paine, S. C. M. *Imperial Rivals: China, Russia, and Their Disputed Frontier, 1858–1924.* Armonk, NY: M. E. Sharpe, 1996.

Wang, Gungwu. *Nanhai Trade: The Early History of Chinese Trade in the South China Sea.* Singapore: Times Academic Press, 1998.

Wolff, David. *To the Harbin Station: The Liberal Alternative in Russian Manchuria, 1898–1914.* Stanford, CA: Stanford University Press, 1999.

Diplomats and Institutions

Anderson, David L. *Imperialism and Idealism: American Diplomats in China, 1861–1898.* Bloomington: Indiana University Press, 1986.

Banno, Masataka. *China and the West: 1858–1861: The Origins of the Tsungli Yamen.* Cambridge, MA: Harvard University, 1964.

Bickley, Gillian. *The Golden Needle: The Biography of Frederick Stewart (1836–1889).* Hong Kong: Hong Kong Baptist University, 1997.

Buhite, Russell D. *Patrick J. Hurley and American Foreign Policy.* Ithaca, NY: Cornell University Press, 1973.

Chong, Key Ray. *Americans and Chinese Reform and Revolution, 1898–1922: The Role of Private Citizens in Diplomacy.* Lanham, MD: University Press of America, 1984.

Cooley, James C., Jr. *T. F. Wade in China: Pioneer in Global Diplomacy 1842–1882.* Leiden: Brill, 1981.

Craft, Stephen G. *V. K. Wellington Koo and the Emergence of Modern China.* Lexington: University Press of Kentucky, 2003.

Esherick, Joseph W. *Last Chance in China: The World War II Despatches of John S. Service.* New York: Random House, 1974.

Kahn, E. J., Jr. *The China Hands: American Foreign Service Officers and What Befell Them.* New York: Viking, 1975.

Meng, Ssu-ming. *The Tsungli Yamen: Its Organization and Functions.* Cambridge, MA: Harvard University Press, 1962.

Moser, Michael J., and Yeone Wei-chih Moser, *Foreigners within the Gates: The Legations at Peking.* New York: Oxford University Press, 1993.

Shaw, Yu-ming. *An American Missionary in China: John Leighton Stuart and Chinese-American Relations.* Cambridge, MA: Council on East Asian Studies, Harvard University, 1992.

Stuart, John Leighton. *Fifty Years in China: The Memoirs of John Leighton Stuart, Missionary and Ambassador.* New York: Random House, 1954.

———. *The Forgotten Ambassador: The Reports of John Leighton Stuart, 1946–1949.* Boulder, CO: Westview, 1981.

Foreigners in China

Bruner, Katherine G., John K. Fairbank, and Richard Smithe, eds. *Entering China's Service: Robert Hart's Journals, 1854–1863*. Cambridge, MA: Harvard University Press, 1986.

O'Brien, Neil L. *An American Editor in Early Revolutionary China: John William Powell and the China Weekly/Monthly Review*. New York: Routledge, 2003.

Spence, Jonathan D. *To Change China: Western Advisers in China, 1620–1960*. New York: Penguin Books, 1980.

Stanley, Margaret, Daniel H. Bays, and Helen Foster Snow. *Foreigners in Areas of China under Communist Jurisdiction before 1949: Biographical Notes and a Comprehensive Bibliography of the Yenan Hui*. Lawrence: Center for East Asian Studies, University of Kansas, 1987.

Strong, Tracy B., and Helene Keyssar. *Right in Her Soul: The Life of Anna Louise Strong*. New York: Random House, 1983.

Stross, Randall E. *The Stubborn Earth: American Agriculturalists on Chinese Soil, 1898–1937*. Berkeley: University of California Press, 1986.

Thomson, James Claude. *While China Faced West: American Reformers in Nationalist China, 1928–1937*. Cambridge, MA: Harvard University Press, 1969.

Thomson, John. *Thomson's China: Travels and Adventures of a Nineteenth-Century Photographer*. New York: Oxford University Press, 1994.

Tuchman, Barbara Wertheim. *Stilwell and the American Experience in China, 1911–1945*. New York: Grove, 2001.

Wright, S. F. *Hart and the Chinese Customs*. Belfast: Win. Mullan and Son, 1950.

SOCIETY

General

Allee, Mark A. *Law and Local Society in Late Imperial China: Northern Taiwan in the Nineteenth Century*. Stanford, CA: Stanford University Press, 1994.

Chiang, Yung-chen, et al. *Social Engineering and the Social Sciences in China, 1919–1949*. New York: Cambridge University Press, 2006.

Chung, Stephanie P. Y. *Chinese Business Groups in Hong Kong and Political Change in South China, 1900–1920s*. New York: St. Martin's, 1998.

Feng, Chongyi, and David S. G. Goodman. *North China at War: The Social Ecology of Revolution, 1937–1945*. Lanham, MD: Rowman & Littlefield, 2000.

Freedman, Maurice. *The Study of Chinese Society*. Stanford, CA: Stanford University Press, 1979.

Ho Ping-ti. *The Ladder of Success in Imperial China: Aspects of Social Mobility, 1368–1911.* New York: Columbia University Press, 1962.

———. "The Paradigmatic Crisis in Chinese Studies: Paradoxes in Social and Economic History," *Modern China* 17, no. 3 (1991).

———. *Studies on the Population of China, 1368–1953.* Cambridge, MA: Harvard University Press, 1959.

Kleinman, Arthur. *Social Origins of Distress and Disease: Depression, Neurasthenia, and Pain in Modern China.* New Haven, CT: Yale University Press, 1986.

Mazumdar, Sucheta. *Sugar and Society in China.* Cambridge, MA: Harvard University Press, 1998.

Naquin, Susan. *Chinese Society in the Eighteenth Century.* New Haven, CT: Yale University Press, 1987.

Platt, Stephen R. *Provincial Patriots: The Hunanese and Modern China.* Cambridge, MA: Harvard University Press, 2007.

Ropp, Paul S. *Dissent in Early Modern China: Ju-Lin Wai-Shih and Ch'ing Social Criticism.* Ann Arbor: University of Michigan Press, 1981.

Sakakida-Rawski, Evelyn. *The Last Emperors: A Social History of Qing Imperial Institutions.* Berkeley: University of California Press, 1998.

Sheehan, Brett. *Trust in Troubled Times: Money, Banks, and State-Society Relations in Republican Tianjin.* Cambridge, MA: Harvard University Press, 2003.

Wolf, Arthur, ed. *Studies in Chinese Society.* Stanford, CA: Stanford University Press, 1978.

Zelin, Madeleine, Jonathan K. Ocko, and Robert Gardella. *Contract and Property in Early Modern China.* Stanford, CA: Stanford University Press, 2004.

Social Changes

Brokaw, Cynthia. *The Ledgers of Merit and Demerit: Social Change and Moral Order in Late Imperial China.* Princeton, NJ: Princeton University Press, 1991.

Eastman, Lloyd. *Family, Fields, and Ancestors: Constancy and Change in China's Social and Economic History, 1550–1949.* New York: Oxford University Press, 1988.

Leung, Yuen-Sang. *The Shanghai Taotai: Linkage Man in a Changing Society, 1843–1890.* Honolulu: University of Hawai'i Press, 1991.

Pong, David, and Edmund S. K. Fung. *Ideal and Reality: Social and Political Change in Modern China 1860–1949.* Lanham, MD: University Press of America, 1985.

Schmalzer, Sigrid. "Breeding a Better China: Pigs, Practice, and Place in a Chinese County, 1929–1937." *Geographical Review* 92, no. 1 (2002).

Zheng, Zhenman. *Family Lineage Organization and Social Change in Ming and Qing Fujian.* Honolulu: University of Hawai'i Press, 2001.

Gender

Ayscough, Florence. *Chinese Women: Yesterday & To-day.* Boston: Houghton Mifflin Company, 1937.

Bernhardt, Kathryn. *Women and Property in China, 960–1949.* Stanford, CA: Stanford University Press, 1999.

Brownell, Susan, and Jeffery Wasserstrom. *Chinese Femininities and Chinese Masculinities.* Berkeley: University of California Press, 2002.

Byron, John. *Portrait of a Chinese Paradise: Erotica and Sexual Customs of the Late Qing Period.* London: Quartet Books, 1987.

Cass, Victoria. *Dangerous Women, Warriors, Grannies and Geishas of the Ming.* Lanham, MD: Rowman & Littlefield, 1999.

Chang, Kang-I Sun, and Haun Saussy, eds. *Women Writers of Traditional China: An Anthology of Poetry and Criticism.* Stanford, CA: Stanford University Press, 1999.

Dooling, Amy D. *Women's Literary Feminism in Twentieth Century China.* Hampshire, UK: Palgrave Macmillan, 2005.

Fong, Grace S. *Herself and Author: Gender, Agency, and Writing in Late Imperial China.* Honolulu: University of Hawai'i Press, 2008.

Fong, Grace S., Nanxiu Qian, and Harriet T. Zurndorfer, eds. *Beyond Tradition & Modernity: Gender, Genre, and Cosmopolitanism in Late Qing China.* Boston: Brill, 2004.

Furth, Charlotte, Susan Mann, and Vivien W. Ng. "Women in Qing Period China—a Symposium." *Journal of Asian Studies* (February 1987).

Gilmartin, Christina K., et al, eds. *Engendering China: Women, Culture, and the State.* Cambridge, MA: Harvard University Press, 2005.

———. *Engendering the Chinese Revolution: Radical Women, Communist Politics, and Mass Movements in the 1920s.* Berkeley: University of California Press, 1995.

Goodman, Bryna, and Wendy Warson, eds. *Gender in Motion: Divisions of Labor and Cultural Change in Late Imperial and Modern China.* Lanham, MD: Rowman & Littlefield, 2005.

Henriot, Christian. *Prostitution and Sexuality in Shanghai: A Social History, 1849–1949.* Cambridge: Cambridge University Press, 2001.

Hershatter, Gail. *Dangerous Pleasures: Prostitution and Modernity in Twentieth-Century Shanghai.* Berkeley: University of California Press, 1997.

———. *Women in China's Long Twentieth Century.* Berkeley: University of California Press, 2007.

Hinsch, Bret. *Passions of the Cut Sleeve: The Male Homosexual Tradition in China.* Honolulu: University of Hawai'i Press, 1990.

Holdsworth, May. *Adorning the Empress.* Hong Kong: Form Asia, 2002.

Honig, Emily. *Sisters and Strangers: Women in the Shanghai Cotton Mills, 1919–1949.* Stanford, CA: Stanford University Press, 1986.

Huang, Martin W. *Negotiating Masculinities in Late Imperial China.* Honolulu: University of Hawai'i Press, 2006.

Kazuko Ono. *Chinese Women in a Century of Revolution, 1850–1950.* Stanford, CA: Stanford University Press, 1989.

Ko, Dorothy. *Cinderella's Sisters: A Revisionist History of Footbinding.* Berkeley: University of California Press, 2005.

———. *Teachers of the Inner Chamber: Women and Culture in 17th Century China.* Stanford, CA: Stanford University Press, 1994.

Lee, Lily, and Xiao Hong, eds. *Biographical Dictionary of Chinese Women: The Qing Period, 1644–1911.* Vol. 1. Armonk, NY: M. E. Sharpe, 1998.

Leung, Angela Ki Che. *Medicine for Women in Imperial China.* Boston: Brill, 2006.

Mann, Susan. *The Talented Women of the Zhang Family.* Berkeley: University of California Press, 2007.

Mann, Susan, and Yu-Yin Cheng. *Under Confucian Eyes: Writings on Gender in Chinese History.* Berkeley: University of California Press, 2001.

Mungello, D. E. *Drowing Girls in China: Female Infanticide in China since 1650.* Lanham, MD: Rowman & Littlefield, 2008.

Ng, Vivien W. "Ideology and Sexuality: Rape Laws in Qing China." *Journal of Asian Studies* (February 1987).

Ropp, Paul, Paola Zamperini, and Harriet T. Zurndorfer, eds. *Passionate Women: Female Suicide in Late Imperial China.* Leiden: Brill, 2002.

Siu, Bobby. *Women of China: Imperialism and Women's Resistance, 1900–1949.* Atlantic Highlands, NJ: Humanities, 1981.

Sommer, Matthew H. *Sex, Law and Society in Late Imperial China.* Stanford, CA: Stanford University Press, 2000.

Spence, Jonathan D. *The Death of Woman Wang.* New York: Viking, 1978.

Stockard, Janice. *Daughters of the Canton Delta: Marriage Patterns and Economic Strategies in South China, 1860–1930.* Stanford, CA: Stanford University Press, 1989.

Stranahan, Patricia. *Yan'an Women and the Communist Party.* Berkeley: Institute of East Asian Studies, University of California, 1984.

Tseng, Chi-fen. *Testimony of a Confucian Woman: The Autobiography of Mrs. Nie Zeng Jifen, 1852–1942.* Edited and translated by Thomas L. Kennedy. Athens: University of Georgia Press, 1993.

Wang, Zheng. *Women in the Chinese Enlightenment.* Berkeley: University of California Press, 1999.

Widmer, Ellen, and Kang-I Sun Chang. *Writing Women in Late Imperial China.* Stanford, CA: Stanford University Press, 1997.

Wolf, Margery, and Roxanne Witke, eds. *Women in Chinese Society.* Stanford, CA: Stanford University Press, 1975.

Wu, Cuncun. *Homoerotic Sensibilities in Late Imperial China.* New York: Routledge Curzon, 2004.

Yeh, Catherine Vance. *Shanghai Love: Courtesans, Intellectuals, and Entertainment Culture, 1850–1910*. Seattle: University of Washington Press, 2006.

Ying, Hu. *Tales of Translation: Composing the New Woman in China, 1898–1918*. Stanford, CA: Stanford University Press, 2000.

Young, Helen Praeger. *Choosing Revolution: Chinese Women Soldiers on the Long March*. Urbana: University of Illinois Press, 2001.

Ethnicity

Atwill, David G. *The Chinese Sultanate: Islam, Ethnicity, and the Panthay Rebellion in Southwest China, 1856–1873*. Stanford, CA: Stanford University Press, 2005.

Benite, Zvi Ben-Dor. *The Dao of Muhammad: A Cultural History of Muslims in Late Imperial China*. Cambridge, MA: Harvard University Press, 2005.

Crossley, Pamela Kyle. *The Manchus: The Peoples of Asia*. Cambridge, MA: Blackwell, 1997.

Dikötter, Frank. "*Racial Identities in China: Context and Meaning*." *China Quarterly* 138 (June 1994).

Hostetler, Laura. *Qing Colonial Enterprise: Ethnography and Cartography in Early Modern China*. Chicago: University of Chicago Press, 2005.

Leong, Sow-Theng, Tim Wright, and William G, Skinner. *Migration and Ethnicity in Chinese History: Hakkas, Pengmin, and Their Neighbors*. Stanford, CA: Stanford University Press, 1997.

Lo, Ming-cheng Miriam. *Doctors within Borders: Profession, Ethnicity, and Modernity in Colonial Taiwan*. Berkeley: University of California Press, 2002.

Rhoads, Edward. *Manchus and Han: Ethnic Relations and Political Power in Late Qing and Early Republican China, 1861–1928*. Seattle: University of Washington Press, 2000.

Tamanoi, Mariko Asano, ed. *Crossed Histories: Manchuria in the Age of Empire*. Honolulu: University of Hawai'i Press, 2005.

Tuttle, Gray. *Tibetan Buddhists in the Making of Modern China*. New York: Columbia University Press, 2007.

Frontiers

Andrade, Tonio. *How Taiwan Became Chinese: Dutch, Spanish and Han Colonization in the Seventeenth Century*. New York: Columbia University Press, 2008.

Anthony, Robert J., and Kate Jane Leonard, eds. *Dragons, Tigers, and Dogs: Qing Crisis Management and the Boundaries of State Power in Late Imperial China*. Ithaca, NY: East Asia Program, Cornell University, 2003.

Chew, Daniel. *Chinese Pioneers on the Sarawak Frontier, 1841–1941.* New York: Oxford University Press, 1990.

Cooke, Nola, and Tana Li, eds. *Water Frontier: Commerce and the Chinese in the Lower Mekong Region, 1750–1880.* Lanham, MD: Rowman & Littlefield, 2004.

Forbes, Andrew D. W. *Warlords and Muslims in Chinese Central Asia: A Political History of Republican Sinkiang, 1911–1949.* Cambridge: Cambridge University Press, 1986.

French, Patrick. *Tibet, a Personal History of a Lost Land.* New York: Knopf, 2003.

Goldstein, Melvyn C. *A History of Modern Tibet, 1913–1951: The Demise of the Lamaist State.* Berkeley: University of California Press, 1991.

Lee, James Z. *Political Economy of a Frontier: Southwest China, 1250–1850.* Cambridge, MA: Harvard University Press, 2000.

Leibold, James. *Reconfiguring Chinese Nationalism: How the Qing Frontier and Its Indigenes Became Chinese.* New York: Palgrave Macmillan, 2007.

Liu, Xiaoyuan. *Frontier Passages: Ethnopolitics and the Rise of Chinese Communism, 1921–1945.* Stanford, CA: Stanford University Press, 2004.

Millward, James A. *Beyond the Pass: Economy, Ethnicity, and Empire in Qing Central Asia, 1759–1864.* Stanford, CA: Stanford University Press, 1998.

Roy, Denny. *Taiwan: A Political History.* Ithaca, NY: Cornell University Press, 2003.

Waley-Cohen, Joanna. *Exile in Mid-Qing China: Banishment to Xinjiang, 1758–1820.* New Haven, CT: Yale University Press, 1991.

Labor

Cochran, Sheman, Andrew C. K. Hsieh, and Janis Cochran, eds. *One Day in China: May 21, 1936.* New Haven, CT: Yale University Press, 1983.

Hershatter, Gail. *The Workers of Tianjin, 1900–1949.* Stanford, CA: Stanford University Press, 1986.

Howard, Joshua H. *Workers at War: Labor in China's Arsenals, 1937–1953.* Stanford, CA: Stanford University Press, 2004.

Northrup, David. *Indentured Labor in the Age of Imperialism, 1834–1922.* New York: Cambridge University Press, 1995.

Perry, Elizabeth. *Shanghai on Strike: The Politics of Chinese Labor.* Stanford, CA: Stanford University Press, 1993.

Smith, S. A. *Like Cattle and Horses: Nationalism and Labor in Shanghai, 1895–1927.* Durham, NC: Duke University Press, 2002.

Strand, David. *Rickshaw Beijing: City People and Politics in the 1920s.* Berkeley: University of California Press, 1989.

Tawney, R. H. *Land and Labor in China.* New York: Harcourt Brace & Company, 1932.

Peasants and Rural Life

Duara, Prasenjit. *Culture, Power, and the State: Rural North China, 1900–1942.* Stanford, CA: Stanford University Press, 1988.

Edgerton-Tarpley, Kathryn. *Tears from Iron: Cultural Responses to Famine in Nineteenth-Century China.* Berkeley: University of California Press, 2008.

Faure, David, and Tao Tao Liu, eds. *Town and Country in China: Identity and Perception.* Hampshire, UK: Palgrave, 2001.

Fei, Xiaotong. *From the Soil: The Foundations of Chinese Society.* First published 1947. Translated by Gary Hamilton and Zheng Wang. Berkeley: University of California Press, 1992.

———. *Peasant Life in China: A Field Study of Country Life in the Yangtze Village.* London: Routledge, 1939.

Han, Xiaorong. *Chinese Discourses on the Peasant, 1900–1949.* Albany: State University of New York Press, 2005.

Harrison, Henrietta. *The Man Awakened from Dreams: One Man's Life in a North China Village, 1857–1942.* Stanford, CA: Stanford University Press, 2005.

Hartford, Kathleen, and Steven Goldstein, eds. *Single Sparks: China's Rural Revolutions.* Armonk, NY: M. E. Sharpe, 1989.

Hayford, Charles W. *To the People: James Yen and Village China.* New York: Columbia University Press, 1990.

Howard, Joshua H. *Rural China: Imperial Control in the 19th Century.* Seattle: University of Washington Press, 1960.

Jones, Stephen. *Plucking the Winds: Lives of Village Musicians in Old and New China.* Leiden: CHIME Foundation, 2004.

Isett, Christopher M. *State, Peasant, and Merchant in Qing Manchuria, 1644–1862.* Stanford, CA: Stanford University Press, 2006.

Lee, James, and Cameron Campbell. *Fate and Fortune in Rural China: Social Stratification and Population Behavior in Liaoning 1774–1873.* New York: Cambridge University Press, 1997.

Li, Huaiyin. *Village Governance in North China, 1875–1936.* Stanford, CA: Stanford University Press, 2005.

Little, Daniel. *Understanding Peasant China.* New Haven, CT: Yale University Press, 1989.

Neils, Patricia. *China Images in the Life and Times of Henry Luce.* Lanham, MD: Rowman & Littlefield, 1990.

Prazniak, Roxann. *Of Camel Kings and Other Things: Rural Rebels against Modernity in Late Imperial China.* Lanham, MD: Rowman & Littlefield, 1999.

Ruf, Gregory A. *Cadres and Kin: Making a Socialist Village in West China, 1921–1991.* Stanford, CA: Stanford University Press, 1999.

Siu, Helen F. *Agents and Victims in South China: Accomplices in Rural Revolution.* New Haven, CT: Yale University Press, 1989.

Gentry and Merchants

Chan, Wellington K. K. *Merchants, Mandarins, and Modern Enterprise in Late Ch'ing China.* Cambridge, MA: East Asian Research Council, Harvard University, 1977.

Chang, Peng-yuan. "Political Participation and Political Elites in Early Republican China: The Parliament of 1913–1914." Translated by Andrew J. Nathan. *Journal of Asian Studies* 37, no. 2 (1978).

Enatsu, Yoshiki. *Banner Legacy: The Rise of the Fengtian Local Elite at the End of the Qing.* Ann Arbor: Center for Chinese Studies, University of Michigan, 2004.

Esherick, Joseph W., and Mary B. Rankin, eds. *Chinese Local Elites and Patterns of Dominance.* Berkeley: University of California Press, 1990.

Fewsmith, Joseph. *Party, State and Local Elites in Republican China: Merchant Organizations and Politics in Shanghai, 1890–1930.* Honolulu: University of Hawai'i Press, 1985.

Garrett, Valery M. *Heaven is High and the Emperor Far Away: Mandarins and Merchants in Old Canton.* New York: Oxford University Press, 2002.

Lufrano, Richard J. *Honorable Merchants: Commerce and Self-Cultivation in Late Imperial China.* Honolulu: University of Hawai'i Press, 1997.

Mann, Susan. *Local Merchants and the Chinese Bureaucracy, 1750–1950.* Stanford, CA: Stanford University Press, 1987.

Schoppa, R. Keith. *Chinese Elites and Political Change: Zhejiang Province in the Early Twentieth Century.* Cambridge, MA: Harvard University Press, 1982.

Zhang, Xin, et al. *Social Transformation in Modern China: The State and Local Elites in Henan, 1900–1937.* New York: Cambridge University Press, 2006.

Intellectuals

Chang, Hao. *Chinese Intellectuals in Crisis: Search for Order and Meaning, 1890–1911.* Berkeley: University of California Press, 1987.

Chang, Hao. *Liang Ch'i-ch'ao and Intellectual Transition in China.* Cambridge, MA: Harvard University Press, 1971.

Fogel, Joshua A., and Peter G. Zarrow, eds. *Imagining the People: Chinese Intellectuals and the Concept of Citizenship, 1890–1920.* Armonk, NY: M. E. Sharpe, 1997.

Gasster, Michael. *Chinese Intellectuals and the Revolution of 1911: The Birth of Modern Chinese Radicalism.* Seattle: University of Washington Press, 1969.

Grieder, Jerome B. *Hu Shih and the Chinese Renaissance: Liberalism in the Chinese Revolution, 1917–1937.* Somerville: Replica Books, 2000.

Huang, Philip C. *Liang Ch'i-ch'ao and Modern Chinese Liberalism.* Seattle: University of Washington Press, 1972.

Hummel, Arthur William, ed. *Eminent Chinese of the Ch'ing Period (1644–1912)*. Washington, DC: U.S. Government Printing Office, 1943.

Levenson, Joseph. *Liang Ch'i-ch'ao and the Mind of Modern China*. Cambridge, MA: Harvard University Press, 1953.

Lin, Xiaoqing Diana. *Peking University: Chinese Scholarship and Intellectuals, 1898–1937*. Albany: State University of New York Press, 2005.

Rankin, Mary B. *Early Chinese Revolutionaries: Radical Intellectuals in Shanghai and Chekiang, 1902–1911*. Berkeley: University of California Press, 1971.

———. "Public Opinion and Political Power: *Qingyi* in Late Nineteenth Century China." *Journal of Asian Studies* (May 1982).

Reardon-Anderson, James. *Elite Activism and Political Transformation in China: Zhejiang Province, 1865–1911*. Stanford, CA: Stanford University Press, 1986.

Schwarcz, Vera. *The Chinese Enlightenment: Intellectuals and the Legacy of the May Fourth Movement of 1919*. Berkeley: University of California Press, 1986.

———. *Time for Telling Truth Is Running Out: Conversations with Zhang Shenfu*. New Haven, CT: Yale University Press, 1992.

Schwartz, Benjamin I. *In Search of Wealth and Power: Yen Fu and the West*. Cambridge, MA: Harvard University Press, 1964.

Weston, Timothy B. *The Power of Position: Beijing University, Intellectuals, and Chinese Political Culture, 1898–1929*. Berkeley: University of California Press, 2004.

Yeh, Wen-hsin. *Provincial Passages: Culture, Space, and the Origins of Chinese Communism*. Berkeley: University of California Press, 2007.

Missionaries

Bays, Daniel H., ed. *Christianity in China from the Eighteenth Century to the Present*. Stanford, CA: Stanford University Press, 1996.

Brandt, Nat. *Massacre in Shansi*. Syracuse, NY: Syracuse University Press, 1994.

Cohen, Paul A. *China and Christianity: The Missionary Movement and the Growth of Chinese Anti-Foreignism, 1860–1870*. Cambridge, MA: Harvard University Press, 1963.

Covell, Ralph R. *W. A. P. Martin, Pioneer of Progress in China*. Washington, DC: Christian University Press, 1978.

Fairbank, John K., ed. *The Missionary Enterprise in China and America*. Cambridge, MA: Harvard University Press, 1974.

Hunter, Jane. *The Gospel of Gentility: American Women Missionaries in Turn-of-the-Century China*. New Haven, CT: Yale University Press, 1984.

Hyatt, Irwin. *Our Ordered Lives Confess: Three Nineteenth Century American Missionaries in East Shantung*. Cambridge, MA: Harvard University Press, 1976.

Lee, Dominic S. F. *The American Missionaries, the Mandarins and the Opium War: Canton, China (circa 1839)*. Anchorage: Little Susitna Press, 2000.

Lee, Joseph Tse-Hei. *The Bible and the Gun: Christianity in South China, 1860–1900*. London: Routledge, 2003.

Liu, Kwang-ching. *American Missionaries in China*. Cambridge, MA: Harvard University Press, 1970.

Lodwick, Kathleen L. *Crusaders against Opium: Protestant Missionaries in China, 1874–1917*. Lexington: University Press of Kentucky, 1996.

Mungello, David. *Curious Land: Jesuit Accommodation and the Origins of Sinology*. Stuttgart: Franz Steiner, 1985.

Sweeten, Alan R. *Christianity in Rural China: Conflict and Accommodation in Jiangxi Province, 1860–1900*. Ann Arbor: University of Michigan Press, 2001.

Wilbur, C. Martin, and Julie H. Lien-ying. *Missionaries of Revolution: Soviet Advisers and Nationalist China, 1920–1927*. Cambridge, MA: Harvard University Press, 1989.

Diaspora

Chin, Ung Ho. *The Chinese of South East Asia*. London: Minority Rights Group, 2000.

Forte, Madeleine. *Dreaming of Gold, Dreaming of Home: Transnationalism and Migration between the United States and South China, 1882–1943*. Stanford, CA: Stanford University Press, 2001.

Khun, Philip A. *Chinese among Others: Emigration in Modern Times*. Lanham, MD: Rowman & Littlefield, 2008.

López-Calvo, Ignacio. *Imaging the Chinese in Cuban Literature and Culture*. Gainesville: University Press of Florida, 2008.

Pan, Lynn. *Sons of the Yellow Emperor: A History of the Chinese Diaspora*. New York: Little, Brown & Company, 1990.

Reid, Anthony, and Kristine Alilunas-Rodgers. *Sojourners and Settlers: Histories of Southeast Asia and the Chinese*. Honolulu: University of Hawai'i Press, 2001.

Schwarcz, Vera. *Bridge across Broken Time: Chinese and Jewish Cultural Memory*. New Haven, CT: Yale University Press, 1998.

Wang, Gungwu. *The Chinese Overseas: From Earthbound China to the Quest for Autonomy*. Cambridge, MA: Harvard University Press, 2000.

Wilson, Andrew R. *Ambition and Identity: Chinese Merchant Elites in Colonial Manila, 1880–1916*. Honolulu: University of Hawai'i Press, 2004.

Inequality and Discrimination

Bhalla, A. S., and Shufang Qiu. *Poverty and Inequality among Chinese Minorities*. London: Routledge, 2006.

Cole, James H. "Social Discrimination in Traditional China: The To-Min of Shaohsing." *Journal of the Economic and Social History of the Orient* 25, no. 1 (1982).

Han, Bangqing. *The Sing Song Girls of Shanghai.* Translated by Eillen Chang. New York: Weatherhead East Asian Institute, Columbia University, 2005.

Hansson, Anders. *Chinese Outcasts: Discrimination and Emancipation in Late Imperial China.* Leiden: Brill, 1996.

Honig, Emily. *Creating Chinese Ethnicity: Subei People in Shanghai, 1850–1980,* New Haven, CT: Yale University Press, 1992.

Lu, Hanchao. *Street Criers: A Cultural History of Chinese Beggars.* Stanford, CA: Stanford University Press, 2005.

Watson, Rubie S., and Patricia Ebrey. *Inequality among Brothers: Class and Kinship in South China.* New York: Cambridge University Press, 1985.

———. *Marriage and Inequality in Chinese Society.* Berkeley: University of California Press, 1991.

Social Organization

Cushman, Jennifer, ed. *Family and State: The Formation of a Sino-Thai Tin-Mining Dynasty 1797–1932.* New York: Oxford University Press, 1992.

Ebrey, Patricia, and James Watson. *Kinship Organization in Late Imperial China, 1000–1940.* Berkeley: University of California Press, 1986.

Faure, David. "The Lineage as a Cultural Invention: The Case of the Pearl River Delta." *Modern China* (January 1989).

Mann, Susan. "Widows in the Kinship, Class, and Community Structures of Qing Dynasty China." *Journal of Asian Studies* (February 1987).

Stacey, Judith. *Patriarchy and Socialist Revolution in China.* Berkeley: University of California Press, 1983.

Szonyi, Michael. *Practicing Kinship: Lineage and Descent in Late Imperial China.* Stanford, CA: Stanford University Press, 2003.

Waltner, Ann. *Getting an Heir: Adoption and the Construction of Kinship in Late Imperial China.* Honolulu: University of Hawai'i Press, 1990.

Watt, John. *The District Magistrate in Late Imperial China.* New York: Columbia University Press, 1972.

Xu, Xiaoqun. *Chinese Professionals and the Republican State: The Rise of Professional Associations in Shanghai, 1912–1937.* Cambridge: Cambridge University Press, 2001.

Public Sphere and Civil Society

Brook, Timothy, and Michael B. Frolic. *Civil Society in China.* Armonk, NY: M. E. Sharpe, 1997.

Kwan, Man Bun. *The Salt Merchants of Tianjin: State-Making and Civil Soci-*

ety in Late Imperial China. Honolulu: University of Hawai'i Press, 2001.

Pagden, Anthony. "Western Concept of Civil Society in the Context of Chinese History." In *Civil Society: History and Possibilities*, edited by Sudipta Kaviraj and Sunil Khilnani. New York: Cambridge University Press, 2001.

Wakeman, Frederic E., et al. Symposium: "'Public Sphere'/'Civil Society' in China? Paradigmatic Issues in Chinese Studies, III." *Modern China* (April 1993).

Wang, Di. *Street Culture in Chengdu: Public Space, Urban Commoners, and Local Politics, 1870–1930*. Stanford, CA: Stanford University Press, 2003.

———. *The Teahouse: Small Business, Everyday Culture, and Public Politics in Chengdu, 1900–1950*. Stanford, CA: Stanford University Press, 2008.

Secret Society

Cai Shaoqing. "On the Origin of the *Gelaohui*," *Modern China* (October 1984).

Chang, Maria H. *The Chinese Blue Shirt Society: Fascism and Development Nationalism*. Cambridge, MA: Harvard University Press, 1985.

Chesneaux, Jean, ed. *Popular Movements and Secret Societies in China, 1840–1950*. Stanford, CA: Stanford University Press, 1972.

———. *Secret Societies in China in the 19th and 20th Centuries*. London: Heinemann, 1971.

Davis, Fei-ling. *Primitive Revolutionaries of China: A Study of Secret Societies of the Late Nineteenth Century*. Honolulu: University of Hawai'i Press, 1977.

Mah, Adeline Yen. *Chinese Cinderella and the Secret Dragon Society*. New York: HarperCollins, 2005.

Martin, Brian G. *The Shanghai Green Gang: Politics and Organized Crime, 1919–1937*. Berkeley: University of California Press, 1996.

Murray, Dian H., and Baoqi Qin, eds. *The Origins of the Tiandihui: The Chinese Triads in Legend and History*. Stanford, CA: Stanford University Press, 1995.

Ownby, David. *Brotherhoods and Secret Societies in Early and Mid-Qing China: The Formation of a Tradition*. Stanford, CA: Stanford University Press, 1996.

Ownby, David, and Mary F. Somers Heidhues, *"Secret Societies" Reconsidered: Perspectives on the Social History of Modern South China and Southeast Asia*. Armonk, NY: M. E. Sharpe, 1993.

CULTURE

General

Elman, Benjamin A. *A Cultural History of Civil Examinations in Late Imperial China*. Berkeley: University of California Press, 1999.

―――. *From Philosophy to Philology: Intellectual and Social Aspects of Change in Late Imperial China*. Cambridge, MA: Council on East Asian Studies, Harvard University, 1984.

Goldman, Merle, and Lee Leo Ou-fan. *An Intellectual History of Modern China*. New York: Cambridge University Press, 2001.

Haar, Barend J. ter. *Telling Stories: Witchcraft and Scapegoating in Chinese History*. Leiden: Brill, 2006.

Kleinman, Arthur, and Lin Tsung-yi, eds. *Normal and Abnormal Behavior in Chinese Culture*. Dordrecht, the Netherlands: Reidel, 1981.

Perry, Elizabeth, and Jeffrey N. Wasserstrom. *Popular Protest and Political Culture in Modern China*. Boulder, CO: Westview, 1992.

Smith, Richard J. *China's Cultural Heritage: The Qing Dynasty, 1644–1912*. Boulder, CO: Westview, 1994.

Thigersen, Stig. *A County of Culture: Twentieth-Century China Seen from the Village Schools of Zouping, Shandong*. Ann Arbor: University of Michigan Press, 2002.

Wile, Douglas. *Lost T'ai-chi Classics from the Late Ch'ing Dynasty*. Albany: State University of New York Press, 1996.

Yeh, Wen-hsin. *The Alienated Academy: Culture and Politics in Republican China, 1919–1937*. Cambridge, MA: Council on East Asian Studies, Harvard University, 1990.

Young, Louise. *Japan's Total Empire: Manchuria and the Culture of Wartime Imperialism*. Berkeley: University of California Press, 1998.

Confucianism and Philosophy

Bary, Theodore de, and Tu Weiming. *Confucianism and Human Rights*. New York: Columbia University Press, 1998.

Chow, Kai-wing. *The Rise of Confucian Ritualism in Late Imperial China: Ethics, Classics, and Lineage Discourse*. Stanford, CA: Stanford University Press, 1994.

Crossley, Pamela Kyle. *A Translucent Mirror: History and Identity in Qing Imperial Ideology*. Berkeley: University of California Press, 1999.

Elman, Benjamin A. *Classicism, Politics, and Kinship: The Ch'ang-Chou School of New Text Confucianism in Late Imperial China*. Berkeley: University of California Press, 1990.

Henderson, John B. *Scripture, Canon and Commentary: A Comparison of Confucian and Western Exegesis*. Princeton, NJ: Princeton University Press, 1991.

Lin, Yu-sheng. *The Crisis of Chinese Consciousness: Radical Antitraditionalism in the May Fourth Era*. Madison: University of Wisconsin Press, 1979.

Liu, Kwang-ching, ed. *Orthodoxy in Late Imperial China*. Berkeley: University of California Press, 1990.

Madsen, Richard. *Morality and Power in a Chinese Village*. Berkeley: University of California Press, 1984.

Ng, On Cho, and Qingjia Wang. *Mirroring the Past: The Writing and Use of History in Imperial China*. Honolulu: University of Hawai'i Press, 2005.

Thompson, P. M. *The Shen Tzu Fragments*. New York: Oxford University Press, 1979.

Tien, Ju-kang. *Male Anxiety and Female Chastity: A Comparative Study of Chinese Ethical Values in Ming-Ching Times*. Leiden: Brill, 1988.

Tu, Weiming. *Confucian Traditions in East Asian Modernity: Moral Education and Economic Culture in Japan and the Four Mini-Dragons*. Cambridge, MA: Harvard University Press, 1996.

Intellectual Currents

Anderson, Marston. *The Limits of Realism: Chinese Fiction in the Revolutionary Period*. Berkeley: University of California Press, 1989.

Ewell, John, trans. *Re-inventing the Way: Dai Zhen's "Evidential Commentary on the Meanings of Terms in Mencius."* Ann Arbor: University of Michigan Press, 1990.

Fitzgerald, John. *Awakening China: Politics, Culture and Class in the Nationalist Revolution*. Stanford, CA: Stanford University Press, 1996.

Lee, Leo Ou-fan. *Shanghai Modern: The Flowering of a New Urban Culture in China, 1930–1945*. Cambridge, MA: Harvard University Press, 1999.

Lin, Lydia H. *Translingual Practice: Literature, National Culture, and Translated Modernity: China, 1900–1937*. Stanford, CA: Stanford University Press, 1995.

Ng, Vivien W. *Madness in Late Imperial China: From Illness to Deviance*. Norman: University of Oklahoma Press, 1990.

Yeh, Wen-hsin. *Becoming Chinese: Passages to Modernity and Beyond*. Berkeley: University of California Press, 2000.

Modernity

Alitto, Guy. *The Last Confucian: Liang Shu-ming and the Chinese Dilemma of Modernity*. Berkeley: University of California Press, 1986.

Chu, Samuel C., and K. C. Liu, eds. *Li Hung-Chang and China's Early Modernization*. Armonk, NY: M. E. Sharpe, 1994.

Dittmer, Lowell, with Samuel Kim. *China's Quest for National Identity*. Ithaca, NY: Cornell University Press, 1993.

Grasso, June M., Jay Corrin, and Michael Kort. *Modernization and Revolution in China: From the Opium Wars to World Power*. Armonk, NY: M. E. Sharpe, 2004.

Hsiao Kung-ch'uan. *A Modern China and New World: K'ang Yu-wei, Reformer and Utopian, 1858–1927*. Seattle: University of Washington Press, 1975.

Pong, David. *Shen Pao-Chen and China's Modernization in the Nineteenth Century.* New York: Cambridge University Press, 1994.

Rogaski, Ruth. *Hygienic Modernity: Meanings of Health and Disease in Treaty-Port China.* Berkeley: University of California Press, 2004.

Wakeman, Frederic E., and Wang Xi. *China's Quest for Modernization: A Historical Perspective.* Berkeley: Institute of East Asian Studies, University of California, 1997.

The May Fourth Movement

Chow, Kai-wing. *Beyond the May Fourth Paradigm: In Search of Chinese Modernity.* Lanham, MD: Lexington Books, 2008.

Chow, Tse-tsung. *The May Fourth Movement: Intellectual Revolution in Modern China.* Cambridge, MA: Harvard University Press, 1974.

Dolezelová-Velingerová, Milena, and Oldrich Král. *The Appropriation of Cultural Capital: China's May Fourth Project.* Cambridge, MA: Asia Center, Harvard University, 2001.

Hayford, Charles Wishart. *To the People: James Yen and Village China.* New York: Columbia University Press, 1990.

Hu, Sheng. *From the Opium War to the May Fourth Movement.* Beijing: Foreign Languages Press, 1991.

Lieberthal, Kenneth. *Perspectives on Modern China: Four Anniversaries.* Armonk, NY: M. E. Sharpe, 1991.

Lin, Yusheng. *The Crisis of Chinese Consciousness: Iconoclasm in the May Fourth Era.* Chicago: University of Chicago Press, 1970.

Rosen, Richard Barry. *The National Heritage Opposition to the New Culture and Literary Movements of China in the 1900's.* Berkeley: University of California Press, 1969.

Schwarcz, Vera. *Chinese Enlightenment: Intellectuals and the Legacy of the May Fourth Movement of 1919.* Berkeley: University of California Press, 1986.

Schwartz, Benjamin Isadore, and Charlotte Furth. *Reflections on the May Fourth Movement: A Symposium.* Cambridge, MA: East Asian Research Center, Harvard University, 1972.

Shih, Chung-wen. *Return from Silence: China's Writers of the May Fourth Tradition.* Washington, DC: George Washington University Press, 1983.

Zhou, Cezong. *The May Fourth Movement: Intellectual Revolution in Modern China.* Stanford, CA: Stanford University Press, 1967.

Popular Culture

Brokaw, Cynthia. *Commerce in Culture: The Sibao Book Trade in the Qing and Republican Periods.* Cambridge, MA: Asia Center, Harvard University, 2007.

Chang, K. C, ed. *Food in Chinese Culture: Anthropological and Historical Perspectives.* New Haven, CT: Yale University Press, 1977.

Cochran, Sherman, ed. *Inventing Nanjing Road: Commercial Culture in Shanghai, 1900–1945.* Ithaca, NY: Cornell University Press. 1999.

Guo, Qitao. *Ritual Opera and Mercantile Lineage: The Confucian Transformation of Popular Culture in Late Imperial Huizhou.* Stanford, CA: Stanford University Press, 2005.

Ho, Virgil. *Understanding Canton: Rethinking Popular Culture in the Republican Period.* New York: Oxford University Press, 2006.

Hung, Chang-tai. *Going to the People: Chinese Intellectuals and Folk Literature, 1918–1937.* Cambridge, MA: Harvard University Press, 1985.

———. *War and Popular Culture, Resistance in Modern China, 1937–1945.* Berkeley: University of California Press. 1994.

Johnson, David, Andrew Nathan, and Evelyn S. Rawski, eds. *Popular Culture in Late Imperial China.* Berkeley: University of California Press, 1985.

Xu, Guoqi. *Olympic Dreams: China and Sports, 1895–2008.* Cambridge, MA: Harvard University Press, 2008.

Material Culture

Berliner, Nancy. *Yin Yu Tang: The Architecture and Daily Life of a Chinese House.* Cambridge, MA: Harvard University Press, 2004.

Dickinson, Gary, and Linda Wrigglesworth, *Imperial Wardrobe.* New York: Ten Speed Press, 2000.

Garrett, Valery M. *Traditional Chinese Clothing in Hong Kong and South China, 1840–1980.* New York: Oxford University Press, 1988.

Hong Kong Art Museum. *Tributes from Guangdong to the Qing Court.* Hong Kong: Chinese University Press, 1987.

Hong Kong Art Museum. *Qing Imperial Porcelain of the Kangxi, Yongzheng and Qianlong Reigns.* Hong Kong: Chinese University Press, 1995.

National Palace Museum, Taipei. *Monochrome Porcelain of the Ch'ing Dynasty.* Torrance, CA: Heian International Publishing, 1994.

Literature

Anderson, Marston. *The Limits of Realism: Chinese Fiction in the Revolutionary Period.* Berkeley: University of California Press, 2005.

Brokaw, Cynthia, and Kai-wing Chow, eds. *Printing and Book Culture in Late Imperial China.* Berkeley: University of California Press, 2005.

Chow, Kai-wing. *Publishing, Culture and Power in Early Modern China.* Stanford, CA: Stanford University Press, 2004.

Hockx, Michel. *Literary Society of Republican China.* Lanham, MD: Rowman & Littlefield, 2008.

Huang, Martin W. *Literati and Self-Re/Presentation: Autobiographical Sensibility in the Eighteenth-Century Chinese Novel.* Stanford, CA: Stanford University Press, 1995.

Hung, Eva. *Paradoxes of Traditional Chinese Literature: An Analysis of Literary Works from the Tang Dynasty to the Late Qing.* Hong Kong: Chinese University Press, 1997.

Kowallis, Jon Eugene von. *The Subtle Revolution: Poets of the "Old Schools" during Late Qing and Early Republican China.* Berkeley: Institute of East Asian Studies, University of California, 2005.

Langhli, Charles A. *The Literature of Leisure and Chinese Modernity.* Honolulu: University of Hawai'i Press, 2008.

Lee, Leo Ou-Fan. *Voices from the Iron House: A Study of Lu Xun.* Bloomington: Indiana University Press, 1987.

Leong, Karen J. *The China Mystique: Pearl S. Buck, Anna May Wong, Mayling Soong, and the Transformation of American Orientalism.* Berkeley: University of California Press, 2005.

Link, Perry. *Mandarin Ducks and Butterflies: Popular Fiction in Early Twentury-Century Chinese Cities.* Berkeley: University of California Press, 2005.

Liu, Jianmei. *Revolution plus Love.* Honolulu: University of Hawai'i Press, 2004.

Pollard, David E. ed. *Translation and Creation: Readings of Western Literature in Early Modern China, 1840–1918.* Erdenheim, PA: John Benjamins, 1998.

Schmidt, J. D. *Within the Human Realm: The Poetry of Huang Zunxian, 1848–1905.* New York: Cambridge University Press, 1994.

Schneider, Joseph, and Laihua Wang. *Giving Care, Writing Self: A "New" Ethnography.* New York: Peter Lang, 2000.

Shang, Wei. *Rulin Waishi and Cultural Transformation in Late Imperial China.* Cambridge, MA: Asia Center, Harvard University, 2003.

Wang, Te-Wei. *Fin-de-Siècle Splendor: Repressed Modernities of Late Qing Fiction, 1849–1911.* Stanford, CA: Stanford University Press, 1997.

Film and Arts

Bao, Yuheng, Lin Mu, and Letitia Lane. *Art and Artists of Chinese Modern Painting, 1890–1949.* Lewiston, NY: Edwin Mellen, 2005.

Cahill, James. *The Painter's Practice: How Artists Lived and Worked in Traditional China.* New York: Columbia University Press, 1995.

Chou, Ju-hsi. *Art at the Close of China's Empire.* Chicago: Art Media Resources, 1999.

Chung, Anita. *Drawing Boundaries: Architectural Images in Qing China.* Honolulu: University of Hawai'i Press, 2005.

Hu, Jubin. *Projecting a Nation: Chinese National Cinema before 1949.* Hong Kong: Hong Kong University Press, 2003.

Kikychi, Yuko. *Refracted Modernity: Visual Culture and Identity in Colonial Taiwan.* Honolulu: University of Hawai'i Press, 2007.

Mackerras, Colin, ed. *The Chinese Theater from Its Origins to the Present Day.* Honolulu: University of Hawai'i Press, 1983.

Pang, Laikwan. *Building a New China in Cinema: The Chinese Left-Wing Cinema Movement, 1932–1937.* Lanham, MD: Rowman & Littlefield, 2002.

———. *The Distorting Mirror: Visual Modernity in China.* Honolulu: University of Hawai'i Press, 2008.

Till, Barry. *The Manchu Era (1644–1912): Arts of China's Last Imperial Dynasty.* Victoria, Canada, Art Gallery of Greater Victoria, 2004.

Zhang, Yijin, *Cinema and Urban Culture in Shanghai, 1922–1943.* Stanford, CA: Stanford University Press, 1999.

Journalism

Britton, Roswell S. *The Chinese Periodical Press, 1800–1912.* Taipei: Ch'engwen Publishing, 1966.

Liu, Yutang. *A History of the Press and Public Opinion in China.* New York: Greenwood Press, 1968.

Matter, A. H. *New Term for New Ideals: A Study of the Chinese Newspaper.* Shanghai: Presbyterian Mission Press, 1922.

Mittler, Barbara. *A Newspaper for China? Power, Identity, and Change in Shanghai's News Media, 1872–1912.* Cambridge, MA: Asia Center, Harvard University, 2004.

Judge, Joan. *Print and Politics: "Shibao" and the Culture of Reform in Late Qing China.* Stanford, CA: Stanford University Press, 1996.

Polumbaum, Judy. *China Ink: The Changing Face of Chinese Journalism.* Lanham, MD: Rowman & Littlefield, 2008.

Ting, Lee-hsia Hsu. *Government Control of the Press in Modern China, 1900–1949.* Cambridge, MA: Harvard University Press, 1974.

Religion

Ben-Dor Benite, Zvi. *The Dao of Muhammad: A Cultural History of Muslims in Late Imperial China.* Cambridge, MA: Asia Center, Harvard University, 2005.

Berger, Patricia Ann. *Empire of Emptiness: Buddhist Art and Political Authority in Qing China.* Honolulu: University of Hawai'i Press, 2003.

Chan, Sin-wai. *Buddhism in Late Ch'ing Political Thought.* Boulder, CO: Westview, 1985.

Chang, Chun-Shu, and Shelley H. Chang. *Redefining History: Ghosts, Spirits, and Human Society in P'u Sung-ling's World, 1640–1715*. Ann Arbor: University of Michigan Press, 1998.

Dott, Brian R. *Identity Reflections: Pilgrimages to Mount Tai in Late Imperial China*. Cambridge, MA: Harvard University Press, 2005.

Fairbank, John K., ed. *The Missionary Enterprise in China and America*. Cambridge, MA: Harvard University Press, 1974.

Goossaeft, Vincent. *The Taoists of Peking, 1800–1949: A Social History of Urban Clerics*. Cambridge, MA: Harvard University Press, 2007.

Herken, Gregg. *Brotherhood of the Bomb: The Tangled Lives and Loyalties of Robert Oppenheimer, Ernest Lawrence, and Edward Teller*. New York: Henry Holt, 2002.

Kohn, Livia, ed. *The Taoist Experience: An Anthology*. Albany: State University of New York Press, 1993.

Kutcher, Norman. *Mourning in Late Imperial China, Filial Piety and the State*. New York: Cambridge University Press, 1999.

Lee, Dominic S. F. *The American Missionaries, the Mandarins and the Opium War: Canton, China (circa 1839)*. Anchorage: Little Susitna Press, 2000.

Liu, Kwang-ching, and Richard Shek, eds. *Heterodoxy in Late Imperial China*. Honolulu: University of Hawai'i Press, 2004.

Mungello, David. *Curious Land: Jesuit Accommodation and the Origins of Sinology*. Stuttgart: Franz Steiner, 1985.

Naquin, Susan, and Chun-fang Yu, eds. *Pilgrims and Sacred Sites in China*. Berkeley: University of California Press, 1994.

Overmeyer, Daniel. *Folk Buddhist Religion: Dissenting Sects in Late Traditional China*. Cambridge, MA: Harvard University Press, 1976.

———. *Religions of China: The World as a Living System*. San Francisco: Harper & Row, 1986.

Rawski, Evelyn, and James L. Watson, eds. *Death Ritual in Late Imperial and Modern China*. Berkeley: University of California Press, 1988.

Tarocco, Francesca. *The Cultural Practices of Modern Chinese Buddhism: Attuning the Dharma*. New York: Routledge, 2007.

Williams, Frederick Wells. *The Life and Letters of Samuel Wells Williams, LL.D., Missionary, Diplomatist, Sinologue*. Wilmington, DE: Scholarly Resources, 1972.

Education

Ayers, William. *Chang Chih-tung and Educational Reform in China*. Cambridge, MA: Harvard University Press, 1984.

Bai, Limin. *Shaping the Ideal Child: Children and Their Primers in Late Imperial China*. Hong Kong: Chinese University Press, 2005.

Bailey, Paul. *Reform the People: Changing Attitudes towards Popular Education in Early Twentieth-Century China*. Vancouver: University of British Columbia Press, 1990.

Bastid, Marriame. *Educational Reform in Early Twentieth Century China*. Translated by Paul Beile. Ann Arbor: University of Michigan Press, 1988.

Curran, Thomas D. *Educational Reform in Republican China: The Failure of Educators to Create a Modern Nation*. New York: Edwin Mellen, 2005.

Elman, Benjamin A., and Alexander B. Woodside, eds. *Education and Society in Late Imperial China, 1600–1900*. Berkeley: University of California Press, 1994.

Hsiung, Ping-chen. *A Tender Voyage: Children and Childhood in Late Imperial China*. Stanford, CA: Stanford University Press, 2005.

Keenan, Barry C. *The Dewey Experiment in China: Educational Reform and Political Power in the Early Republic*. Cambridge, MA: Harvard University Press, 1977.

Lutz, Jessie. *China and the Christian Colleges, 1850–1950*. Ithaca, NY: Cornell University Press, 1971.

Ng, Peter Tze Ming. *Changing Paradigms of Christian Higher Education in China, 1888–1950*. Lewiston, NY: Edwin Mellen, 2002.

Ni, Ting. *The Cultural Experiences of Chinese Students Who Studied in the United States during the 1930s–1940s*. Lewiston, NY: Edwin Mellen, 2002.

West, Philip. *Yenching University and Sino-Western Relations, 1916–1952*. Cambridge, MA: Harvard University Press, 1976.

Ye, Weili. *Seeking Modernity in China's Name: Chinese Students in the United States, 1900–1927*. Stanford, CA: Stanford University Press, 2001.

Science

Bodde, Derk. *Chinese Thought, Society and Science: The Intellectual and Social Background of Science and Technology in Pre-modern China*. Honolulu: University of Hawai'i Press, 1991.

Bray, Francesca. *Technology and Gender: Fabrics of Power in Late Imperial China*. Berkeley: University of California Press, 1997.

Dodgen, Randall A. *Controlling the Dragon: Confucian Engineers and the Yellow River in Late Imperial China*. Honolulu: University of Hawai'i Press, 2001.

Gao, James Z. *Meeting Technology's Advance: Social Changes in China and Zimbabwe at the Railway Age*. Westport, CT: Greenwood, 1997.

Hostetler, Laura. *Qing Colonial Enterprise: Ethnography and Cartography in Early Modern China*. Chicago: University of Chicago Press, 2005.

Hu, Danian. *China and Albert Einstein: The Reception of the Physicist and His Theory in China 1917–1979*. Cambridge, MA: Harvard University Press, 2005.

Kwok. D. W. *Scientism in Chinese Thought, 1900–1950.* New Haven, CT: Yale University Press, 1965.

Orleans, Leo. *Sciences in Contemporary China.* Stanford, CA: Stanford University Press, 1980.

Waley-Cohen, Joanna. "China and Western Technology in the Late Eighteenth Century." *American Historical Review* (December 1993).

Medicine and Health

Barnes, Linda L. *Needles, Herbs, Gods, and Ghosts: China, Healing, and the West to 1848.* Cambridge, MA: Harvard University Press, 2005.

Bowers, John Z. *Western Medicine in a Chinese Palace: Peking Union College, 1917–1951.* Philadelphia: Josiah Macy, Jr., Foundation, 1972.

Cochran, Sherman. *Chinese Medicine Men and Consumer Culture in China, 1880–1956.* Cambridge, MA: Harvard University Press, 2006.

Crozier, Ralph. *Traditional Medicine in Modern China: Science, Nationalism, and the Tensions of Cultural Change.* Cambridge, MA: Harvard University Press, 1968.

Dikotter, Frank. *Sex, Culture, and Modernity in China: Medical Science and the Construction of Sexual Identities in the Early Republican Period.* Honolulu: University of Hawai'i Press, 1995.

Earquhar, Judith. *Knowing Practice: The Clinical Encounter of Chinese Medicine.* Boulder, CO: Westview, 1994.

Unschild, Paul U. *Medicine in China: A History of Ideas.* Berkeley: University of California Press, 1985.

About the Author

James Zheng Gao is an associate professor of history at the University of Maryland at College Park. Born and raised in China, he obtained an MA in political science from Peking University and served as an assistant professor at the university. Gao came to the United States in 1985 and began to study at the University of California, Berkeley, later transferring to Yale. He received his MA and PhD in history from Yale University in 1994. He has previously been an assistant professor at Newport News University and a research associate at the Institute of East Asian Studies at the University of California, Berkeley. He has written the books *Meeting Technology's Advance: Social Changes in China and Zimbabwe in the Railway Age* (1997) and *The Communist Takeover of Hangzhou: The Transformation of City and Cadre, 1949–1954* (2004). He has also written numerous articles, including "From Rural Revolution to Urban Revolutionization: A Case Study of Luzhongnan," "War Culture, Nationalism, and Political Campaigns, 1950–53," "The Status of Women in 17th Century China," "Myth, Memory, and Rice History in Shanghai," and "The Call of the Oases: The 'Peaceful Liberation' of Xinjiang, 1949–1953." He received the Robert D. Gries Prize from Yale University in 1994, a Summer Grant of the National Endowment for the Humanities in 1995, and the Hopkins Fellowship in 2006. He is currently working on a book-length project titled "Shanghai Market: Rice Consumers, Merchants, and the State, 1866–1955."